INDIA'S FIRST DICTATORSHIP

CHRISTOPHE JAFFRELOT

PRATINAV ANIL

India's First Dictatorship

The Emergency, 1975–1977

HURST & COMPANY, LONDON

First published in the United Kingdom in 2020 by
C. Hurst & Co. (Publishers) Ltd.,
41 Great Russell Street, London, WC1B 3PL
This paperback edition first published in 2025 by
C. Hurst & Co. (Publishers) Ltd.,
New Wing, Somerset House,
Strand, London WC2R 1LA

A Cataloguing-in-Publication data record for this book
is available from the British Library.

ISBN: 9781805263210

This book is printed using paper from registered sustainable
and managed sources.

www.hurstpublishers.com

For Tara and Sara

CONTENTS

CONTENTS

PART II

CAUSES AND BEYOND: WHAT MADE THE EMERGENCY
"NECESSARY" AND POSSIBLE?

LIST OF TABLES

ABBREVIATIONS

ABVP	Akhil Bharatiya Vidyarthi Parishad
ADM	Additional District Magistrate
AFL-CIO	American Federation of Labor and Congress of Industrial Organisations
AFP	Agence France-Presse
AIADMK	All-India Anna Dravida Munnetra Kazhagam
AICC	All-India Congress Committee
AIR	All India Radio
AIRF	All-India Railwaymen's Federation
AITUC	All-India Trade Union Congress
BARC	Bhabha Atomic Research Centre
BBC	British Broadcasting Corporation
BCSS	Bihar Chhatra Sangharsh Samiti
BJP	Bharatiya Janata Party
BKD	Bharatiya Kranti Dal
BLD	Bharatiya Lok Dal
BSF	Border Security Force
CBI	Central Bureau of Investigation
CEC	Central Election Committee
CEO	Chief Executive Officer
CFSA	Congress Forum for Socialist Action
CIA	Central Intelligence Agency
CID	Criminal Investigation Department
CISF	Central Industrial Security Force
CITU	Centre of Indian Trade Unions
COAS	Chief of Army Staff

ABBREVIATIONS

COFEPOSA	Conservation of Foreign Exchange and Prevention of Smuggling Activities Act
CPB	Congress Parliamentary Board
CPI	Communist Party of India
CPI(M)/CPM	Communist Party of India (Marxist)
CPP	Congress Parliamentary Party
CPSU	Communist Party of the Soviet Union
CRPF	Central Reserve Police Force
CWC	Congress Working Committee
DAP	Delhi Armed Police
DAVP	Directorate of Advertising and Visual Publicity
DC	Democrazia Cristiana
DCC	District Congress Committee
DDA	Delhi Development Authority
DIR	Defence of India Rules
DISIR	Defence and Internal Security of India Rules
DM	Deutsche Mark
DMK	Dravida Munnetra Kazhagam
DSPE	Delhi Special Police Establishment
DTC	Delhi Transport Corporation
DUTA	Delhi University Teachers Association
EPW	*Economic and Political Weekly*
FCO	Foreign and Commonwealth Office
FICCI	Federation of Indian Chambers of Commerce and Industry
FIR	First Information Report
FISI	Friends of India Society International
FRG	Federal Republic of Germany
GDP	Gross Domestic Product
GNP	Gross National Product
GU	Gujarat University
GVA	Gross Value Added
HAL	Hindustan Aeronautics Limited
HMS	Hind Mazdoor Sabha
HMV	His Master's Voice
HSS	Hindu Swayamsevak Sangh
I&B	Information and Broadcasting
IAS	Indian Administrative Service
IB	Intelligence Bureau
IBM	International Business Machines Corporation

ABBREVIATIONS

ICSSR	Indian Council of Social Science Research
IDPL	Indian Drugs and Pharmaceuticals Limited
ILO	International Labour Organization
IMF	International Monetary Fund
INTUC	Indian National Trade Union Congress
ITBP	Indo-Tibetan Border Police
IUD	Intra-Uterine Device
IUML	Indian Union Muslim League
JI	Jama'at-i-Islami
JNU	Jawaharlal Nehru University
JP	Jayaprakash Narayan
JUH	Jamiat-ul-Ulema-i-Hind
KC	Kerala Congress
KGB	Komitet Gosudarstvennoy Bezopasnost
KMLP	Kisan Mazdoor Lok Paksha
LDP	Liberal Democratic Party of Japan
LG	Lieutenant Governor
LSE	London School of Economics
LSS	Lok Sangharsh Samiti
MCD	Municipal Corporation of Delhi
MEA	Ministry of External Affairs
MGR	Maruthur Gopala Ramachandran
MHA	Ministry of Home Affairs
MHAP	Ministry of Home Affairs Papers
MISA	Maintenance of Internal Security Act
MLA	Member of Legislative Assembly
MLP	Madhu Limaye Papers
MNC	Multinational Corporation
MNF	Mizo National Front
MP	Member of Parliament
MRTPA	Monopolies and Restricted Trade Practices Act
NBC	National Broadcasting Company
NC	National Conference
NDMC	New Delhi Municipal Corporation
NDP	National Domestic Product
NFIR	National Federation of Indian Railwaymen
NMML	Nehru Memorial Museum and Library
NRI	Non-Resident Indian
NYT	*New York Times*

ABBREVIATIONS

OPEC	Organization of Petroleum Exporting Countries
PA	Public Address
PCC	Pradesh Congress Committee
PIO	Principal Information Officer
PMO	Prime Minister's Office
PMS	Prime Minister's Secretariat
PMSP	Prime Minister's Secretariat Papers
PNB	Punjab National Bank
PTI	Press Trust of India
RAW	Research and Analysis Wing
RBI	Reserve Bank of India
RPI	Republican Party of India
RSEB	Rajasthan State Electricity Board
RSS	Rashtriya Swayamsevak Sangh
SBI	State Bank of India
SCIF	Shah Commission of Inquiry Files
SCP	Shah Commission Papers
SCR	*Shah Commission Report*
SEC	Securities and Exchange Commission
SSP	Samyukta Socialist Party
SSWIG	*Selected Speeches and Writings of Indira Gandhi*
STD	Sexually Transmitted Disease
SVD	Samyukta Vidhayak Dal
SW	*Statesman Weekly*
TIT	Technological Institute of Textiles
TOI	*Times of India*
UGC	University Grants Commission
UK	United Kingdom
UN	United Nations
UNFPA	United Nations Fund for Population Activities
UNI	United News of India
UP	Uttar Pradesh
US	United States of America
USSR	Union of Soviet Socialist Republics
WASP	White Anglo-Saxon Protestant
YC	Youth Congress

GLOSSARY

acharya	Hindu preceptor
adivasi	tribesman
andolan	protest
anibani	commotion
anushasan parva	an era of discipline
auqaf	Muslim endowments
babu	bureaucrat
bandh	general strike
bandobasti	the art of settling matters
bandwala	bandsman
bewas	widows
bhangi	Dalit cleaners from the human waste-collecting caste
bhangra	a popular dance form in North India
bigha	a traditional unit of land measurement
chhokri	slip of a girl
chor bazaar	flea market
chowki	police station
crore	ten million
dalal	middleman
danda	stick
dharma yuddha	religious war
dharna	peaceful demonstration
ganja	cannabis
Garibi Hatao	Get Rid of Poverty
gherao	a protest in which workers prevent managers from leaving a place of work

GLOSSARY

goonda	gangster
gram sevak	extension worker
gumties	kiosks
guru–shishya parampara	a traditional relationship between the master and his disciples, usually marked by deference
hartal	strike
hukumshahi	authoritarianism
imam	Muslim cleric
Inquilab Zindabad	Long Live the Revolution
jawan	soldier
janata sarkars	people's governments
jhuggi	slum
khadi	Indian homespun cotton cloth
khassi	castration
khokha	unauthorised shop
kisan sabhas	peasants' associations
lalach	greed
lakh	hundred thousand
lathi	stick
lokshahi	democracy
mataji	dear mother
matka	a kind of numbers racket
mofussil	originally, the regions of India outside the three East India Company capitals of Bombay, Calcutta, and Madras; more generally, the countryside
morcha	march
muneem	accountant
muth	temple
padayatras	marches on foot
panchayats	local governments
patels	local bosses commanding police power
patwaris	bookkeepers
phansi kothi	the death row cell
pracharak	organiser
prant pracharak	provincial organiser
qaum	the Muslim community
quintal	a unit of weight equal to 100 kg
rabi	the grain crop sown in September and reaped in the spring

GLOSSARY

rickshawala	rickshaw puller
sadvipras	the spiritually enlightened
sambhaag pracharak	regional organiser
sangathan	mobilisation
sanghchalak	organiser
sanyasi	Hindu religious mendicant
sarkari sant	the state's saint
sar-karyavaha	general secretary
sarsanghchalak	RSS chief
satyagraha	passive political resistance
savarna	the upper castes
shakha	chapter; literally, a branch
swayamsevak	the RSS' foot soldiers
tahsildar	revenue official
taluka	an administrative district for taxation purposes, typically comprising a number of villages
tantric	relating to the sexual doctrines of the Hindu or Buddhist tantras, in particular the use of meditation, yoga, and ritual
tehsil	an administrative area in parts of India
thali	metal plate
thelawala	costermonger
vibhag pracharak	portfolio organiser
yuvak kendra	youth centre
zabardasti	force
zamindari	a system of land tenure prevalent in pre- and colonial India
zamindars	the gentry that acted as middlemen between peasants and rulers
zila	an administrative district in India

PREFACE

This book has a long history. In the late 1990s one of us—Christophe Jaffrelot—signed a contract to write a book on the Emergency with Hurst and Co., his main publisher since 1996. The project was derailed for two reasons: first, other books took priority; and second, the interviews on which this book was supposed to be built appeared unreliable. Some of the participants who had played a role in the Emergency did not properly recall events, and many had disappeared in the course of time.

This project was revived when Sunil Khilnani gave Jaffrelot access to Granville Austin's papers at the Johns Hopkins University, where both jointly taught a course in 2009–10. Among the most precious documents in this collection were transcripts of the hearings of the Shah Commission in 1977–8. These primary sources, it seemed to us, were not available any-where else.[1]

---

[1] We have digitised and made these papers available online (https://exhibits.stanford.edu/conflict-sasia/feature/shah-commission-papers) as part of the Archive on Legacies of Conflict in South Asia, a collaboration between UC Berkeley's Initiative on Political Conflict, Gender and People's Rights and the Stanford Libraries. This has been made possible thanks to Angana Chatterji, research anthropologist and co-chair of the Initiative on Political Conflict, Gender and People's Rights, Center for Race and Gender, University of California, Berkeley, who has imagined this Archive and led the process of its creation. For more, see https://exhibits.stanford.edu/conflict-sasia/about/timeline-and-announcement-40aaab79-b85f-47c8–84b4–8e2606b2448e. Hard copies of the papers have been deposited by Sunil Khilnani at Ashoka University (Sonipat, India) as part of its Archives of Contemporary India, a project initiated by Mahesh Rangarajan. We are grateful to all of them and to Deepa Bhatnagar, director of the Ashoka

The project, then, was revived a second time a few years later, when Jaffrelot met his former Sciences Po student Pratinav Anil in London, where Jaffrelot was teaching (at King's College) and Anil was studying (at the LSE). It had the support of Michael Dwyer, the publisher at Hurst, who agreed to sign a new contract for the old project.

When the original plans were made in the 1990s, there were very few books on the Emergency. Most of the existing literature consisted of journalistic accounts which, while empirically thorough, were not interested in analysing this phase of Indian history in a comparative or theoretical perspective.[2] Over the last twenty years, many new books have seen the light of day, but, again, much of this writing has been journalistic or autobiographical.[3] Few social scientists, to whom we try to do justice and whose theses we discuss below, however, have attempted to *interpret* the Emergency, a task that is even more necessary in today's India, as we show in our concluding chapter.[4]

For opening doors, literal and metaphorical, we thank Granville Austin—whom Jaffrelot met a few months before he passed away in Washington, DC—Supriya Ambwani, Abhimanyu Chandra, Uday Chandra, Abhishek Choudhary, Kai Friese, Polly O'Hanlon, Archita Jha, Sopan Joshi, Lal Chand Lala, Srinath Raghavan, Thomas Owen-Smith, and Taylor Sherman. The staff at the British Library of Political and Economic Science, National Archives of India, Nehru Memorial Museum and Library, King's India Institute, British Library, and the Bodleian Library in no small way facilitated this research, making it a pleasant experience even. So much more than a copy-editor, Rukun Advani did a great job with the editing, as one would expect from him. Thanks are also due to Daisy Leitch for proofreading and shepherding this book through publication. Michael Dwyer supplied the wonderfully apposite title. Our greatest debt is to Sara and Tara, our better halves, for their patience and generosity, both supplied incom-

---

Archives of Contemporary India. A digital version of the Shah Commission papers is also available on the Ashoka website: www.ashoka.edu.in>academics>ashoka archives>catalogues>shah commission papers

[2] See, among others, Nayar, *The Judgement*; Bose and Dayal, *For Reasons of State*; Dayal and Bose, *The Shah Commission Begins*; and Jayakar, *Indira Gandhi*.

[3] See for instance Kapoor, *The Emergency*; Dhar, *Indira Gandhi, the "Emergency"*.

[4] See, in chronological order, Zins, *Strains on Indian Democracy*; Chandra, *In the Name of Democracy*; Hewitt, *Political Mobilisation and Democracy in India*; Rao, Jr., *The Emergency*; and Prakash, *Emergency Chronicles*.

mensurately and with scant regard for what might be understood as reasonable demands of one's partner. As is now conventional, though, we take full responsibility for the errors contained in these pages.

INTRODUCTION

Late on the evening of 25 June 1975, Prime Minister Indira Gandhi and Siddhartha Shankar Ray, her trusted *consigliere*, drove to Rashtrapati Bhavan, the presidential palace atop Raisina Hill in New Delhi. For over three-quarters of an hour, Ray explained to Fakhruddin Ali Ahmed, once a lawyer and now president of the republic, their plan to impose an "Emergency".[1]

Triggered by Article 352 of the Indian constitution, the Emergency was the "panic button" *ne plus ultra*.[2] Once pressed, all troubles posed by the media, the opposition parties, the judiciary, and even factions within the incumbent Congress party could be eliminated in one fell swoop. Moreover, under the provisions of such an Emergency, the fundamental rights guaranteed under Article 19—which included, *inter alia*, the right of free speech and expression, and the right to "assemble peacefully and without arms", form unions, and move the courts to enforce civil rights—would be suspended; government officials in the states made answerable to the union government, overriding the principles of federalism; prior restraint of the media and the mass incarceration of politicians and journalists rendered legal.

Ahmed had precious little to ask before giving his imprimatur to what would, quite literally, extinguish Indian democracy overnight. He had certainly thought about the possibility of such a move: Mrs Gandhi had been

---

[1] For a blow-by-blow account, see Austin, *Working a Democratic Constitution*, p. 295ff.

[2] A phrase of one of her closest advisers, P.N. Dhar. See his account of Mrs Gandhi during the Emergency: *Indira Gandhi, the "Emergency", and Indian Democracy*, p. 262.

contemplating action that stretched the frontiers of constitutional acceptability for a while, and news of it had travelled from R.K. Dhawan, additional private secretary to the prime minister, to his brother, K.L. Dhawan, who served as the president's assistant.[3] At 11.45 p.m., Ahmed shirked confrontation and signed the declaration Ray and Mrs Gandhi had put before him.[4]

Soon after, at around 2 a.m., the electricity supply to the newspaper offices on Bahadur Shah Zafar Marg, New Delhi's Fleet Street, was cut off.[5] This was swiftly followed by the arrests of leading figures in the opposition: Jayaprakash Narayan, the spearhead of an extra-parliamentary movement aimed at overthrowing the prime minister; Morarji Desai, Indira Gandhi's long-standing nemesis, once within the Congress, now without;[6] Lal Krishna Advani, president of the Hindu nationalist Jana Sangh; Jyotirmoy Basu, deputy leader of the Communist Party of India (Marxist); Raj Narain, the prime minister's opponent in her Rae Bareilly parliamentary constituency in the 1971 election;[7] Piloo Mody, one of the founders of the now defunct Swatantra party that had represented big business and the rural aristocracy;[8] and Chandra Shekhar and Mohan Dharia, both less-than-pliant Congress MPs. The middle and upper echelons of the six major opposition parties—Desai's Congress (O), the Jana Sangh, BLD, SSP, CPI(M), and DMK—found themselves behind bars as well.[9]

[3] Nayar, *The Judgement*, p. 39.

[4] Ahmed's own version of that night, which he recorded in a diary, will never be known. Badar Durrez, his son, discovered it in 1977 but chose against publication because he was certain it would "ruin the careers of many current politicians": *India Today*, 15 December 1977. The matter has not surfaced since.

[5] Orders to this effect were sent by the lieutenant governor of Delhi to the Delhi Electric Supply Undertaking around 10 p.m. See the *Shah Commission Report* [hereafter *SCR*], *Interim Report 1*, p. 23. The *Statesman* and the *Hindustan Times* managed to print their 26 June editions because, unlike the other papers which were covered by the New Delhi Municipal Corporation, the offices of these two were supplied power by the Municipal Corporation of Delhi. The former is the governing body of a few small and affluent neighbourhoods in central Delhi, while the rest of the city is governed by the latter.

[6] The 1969 split in the country's grand old party produced the incumbent Congress (Requisitionist) headed by Indira Gandhi, and the Desai-led Congress (Organisation) in the opposition.

[7] At the time of his arrest, he was a Rajya Sabha MP of the Bharatiya Lok Dal, the party of the gentry.

[8] The Swatantra was dissolved in August 1974, its MPs joining the BLD *en masse*.

Five hours later—7 a.m. on 26 June—cabinet ministers arrived for a meeting at 1 Safdarjung Road, Mrs Gandhi's residence, where they were informed that a state of emergency had been proclaimed the previous night, and that 676 politicians were in custody.[10] Only one figure, Defence Minister Swaran Singh, questioned the necessity of the action. Mrs Gandhi offered no reply and Singh clammed up. The other cabinet ministers instinctively recognised this as a context where discretion might be the better part of valour: her silences meant disapproval. Many of them owed their positions to her and had in recent years witnessed the transfusion of competencies from their ministries to the Prime Minister's Secretariat. The meeting was over in less than thirty minutes.[11]

By 11 a.m. a regime of prior restraint had been imposed. News now had to be cleared by the Press Information Bureau in Shastri Bhavan before it could be printed.[12] The incarcerated could not be named, nor could their pictures be released. Prior restraint in offices was complemented by censorship in the street. The *Hindustan Times*, which had already been printed that day, was taken out of circulation and its hawkers threatened with legal action. The mouthpieces of the Hindu nationalist Rashtriya Swayamsevak Sangh—the weekly *Organiser* and the daily *Motherland*—and their vernacular equivalents, the Marathi daily *Tarun Bharat* and the Hindi monthly *Rashtra Dharma*, met the same fate and, soon after, their offices were sealed. The Hindi paper's publisher, Rashtra Dharma Prakashan, tried in

---

[9] The SSP denoted the Samyukta Socialist Party; the DMK, the Dravida Munnetra Kazhagam, a regional party advancing Tamil interests; and the CPI(M), the Communist Party of India (Marxist), encountered before. For all the acronyms by which the major political parties of the time were known, see the abbreviations list.

[10] Declaring a state of emergency typically entails cabinet ratification. This was circumvented by referring to Rule 12 of the Government of India (Transaction of Business) Rules, 1961, which allowed for the proclamation to precede matters of protocol: Mrs Gandhi to Ahmed, 25 June 1975, Ministry of Home Affairs Papers, File VI/11034/56/80(29)/ISDVI. Among those who learnt of the Emergency only that morning were P.N. Dhar, secretary to the prime minister; B.D. Pande, cabinet secretary; and Atma Jayaram, director of the Intelligence Bureau: *SCR*, vol. 1, p. 25.

[11] The next day saw a repeat when Mrs Gandhi spoke to thirty of the country's top bureaucrats.

[12] Ajoy Bose, 20 April 2018, interviewed by Farah Yameen, Oral Histories in the Long Emergency Collection.

vain to find legal advisers in its native Lucknow to challenge the lockdown. The few lawyers who decided to take on the case were quickly incarcerated under the Defence of India Rules. Other political outlets were not spared either: Piloo Mody's conservative *March of India*, trade unionist George Fernandes' *Pratipaksha*, and Jayaprakash Narayan's *Everyman* were all forced to go into administration.[13] Such moves broadly reflected the aspirations of Indira Gandhi, who believed that the national press had to be "committed" to Delhi's political masters or else suffer the consequences of being at odds with them. "In a battle, the enemy's supply line is cut off," the prime minister would later say of the press.[14]

There were other enemies, too. As a white paper justifying the Emergency had it, "in the 1967 elections, power came to be distributed among a large number of heterogeneous parties and groups, and this led to instability."[15] During the Emergency, S.S. Ray reiterated this logic: "if Congress disintegrated, India would be disintegrated [*sic*]."[16] The party president Dev Kant Barooah held similar ideas: "The opposition were neither in the Constituent Assembly [*sic*] nor are they here [now] ... They are irrelevant to the history of India," he said to the Rajya Sabha.[17] Such thinking betrayed an unease with electoral competition, the plurality of interests, and representative politics—the very stuff of democracy—within the Congress.[18]

If the grand old party could brook no criticism from opposition parties and the media, it suffered extra-parliamentary action even less. The eighteen months preceding the Emergency had witnessed a burgeoning movement under the aegis of Jayaprakash "JP" Narayan, calling for Mrs Gandhi's ouster. After being confined to two states in east and west India—Bihar and Gujarat—in March 1975 the movement shifted its focus to the capital. On the afternoon of 25 June, just a few hours before Mrs Gandhi and Ray paid Ahmed a visit, Narayan headed a major rally at the Ramlila Grounds, less than four miles north-east of the presidential palace. Despite the large crowds, however, it appeared that the protests were losing steam with every passing month. A bold move seemed in order. Later that evening, the leading figures of five major opposition parties met at the Uttar Pradesh

---

[13] Henderson, *Experiment with Untruth*, pp. 79–94.

[14] *Indian Express*, 8 January 1976, cited in Hart, "Introduction", p. 20.

[15] *Why Emergency?*, p. 1.

[16] Zaidi (ed.), *The Annual Register of Indian Political Parties, vol. 23*, p. 332.

[17] *Rajya Sabha Debates*, vol. 98, no. 8 (12 November 1976), col. 33.

[18] For more on this theme, see Embree, "The Emergency as a Signpost to India's Future", pp. 59–67.

Niwas, where Charan Singh, leader of the Bharatiya Lok Dal, was lodged, and consolidated their parties into a new formation, the Lok Sangharsh Samiti—literally the People's Struggle Front.[19] Morarji Desai was to serve as its chairman, Nana Deshmukh of the Jana Sangh became secretary, and Asoka Mehta of Desai's Congress (O) treasurer. The LSS' first order of business was to announce a nationwide agitation that would commence on 29 June, its aim being to bring down the government.[20]

This was a critical juncture. As a fresh force on the political scene, Narayan's movement spoke to the disenchanted at a time of economic stagnation and pervasive corruption. Moreover, his rallying cry—"total revolution"—was ambiguous enough to accommodate a mosaic of concerns. The JP Movement, as it came to be known, thus became the point of identification for a variety of social groups both on the Left and Right, representing the growing resentment on the streets and in parliament.

The protests around and preceding Narayan's movement appeared to many observers at the time to be the birth pangs of a new catch-all party.[21] That an insurrection against the political order now seemed to entail joining the order itself was seen as the maturing of Indian political life as it transitioned from the "Congress system". Within this system, opposition parties served as "parties of pressure", influencing policy only indirectly by changing the balance of opinion within the Congress. Whereas now a two-party system was taking shape in which genuine electoral competition and the possibility of quinquennial alternation would result in the strengthening of the democratic process.[22]

This was not to be. As time wore on, it became increasingly clear that neither Jayaprakash Narayan nor Indira Gandhi were keen to fight by the Queensberry rules. And events came to a head in the second week of June 1975.

---

[19] The parties were the Congress (O), Jana Sangh, Socialist Party, BLD, and Akali Dal. They had the CPM's and the DMK's sympathies, too: B.K. Goswami, Deputy Commissioner, Delhi, to P.R. Rajgopal, Secretary of the Shah Commission, 8 November 1977, Ministry of Home Affairs Papers, File VI/11034/56/80(29)/ISDVI.

[20] Ibid. Part of the programme was a "Lok Shikshak Week", a grassroots campaign aimed at securing the prime minister's resignation.

[21] See, for example, Manor, "Indira and After", pp. 315–24; Joshi and Desai, "Towards a More Competitive Party System in India", pp. 1091–116.

[22] Kothari, "The Congress 'System'", p. 1162.

INDIA'S FIRST DICTATORSHIP

The Consequences of Ahmedabad and Allahabad

On 12 June 1975 the Congress was routed in the Gujarat state election by the Congress (O)-led coalition, the Janata Morcha. Winning only 75 of the 182 seats—down from 140—the grand old party had lost power in the state for the first time. Mrs Gandhi had run a strident campaign, staying in the state for eleven days and addressing 119 meetings.[23] It was rare for a prime minister to take such keen interest in state politics, but the odd circumstances had demanded it: a massive wave of protest in Ahmedabad and other Gujarati cities had prompted the resignation of incumbents and the calling of fresh elections, offering the Congress the one chance it had to demonstrate its popular support and discredit the extra-parliamentary movement. And yet personal defeat at the hands of old foes—the conveners of the Janata Morcha included Desai, Advani, and Raj Narain—was not even the worst piece of news to reach the ears of Mrs Gandhi on that day.[24]

Also on that fateful day, the Allahabad High Court found against her in an election case. The hearing had taken four years, and finally Justice Jag Mohan Lal Sinha had written up a 258-page judgment.[25] The stakes were at once small and large: small because of the nature of the offence, and large because of its implications. The charge raised against her was that she had made use of the services of Yashpal Kapoor, the Congress gofer and her most important aide in the Prime Minister's Secretariat, to "further her election prospects", breaking an electoral rule that forbade the use of state employees for private gain.[26] It was more a technical error, a "peccadillo" as the papers put it, for Kapoor had begun working on Mrs Gandhi's campaign on 7 January 1971 but had left his government position only six days later, remaining a state employee in the official records until 25 January.[27]

---

[23] Shah, "The 1975 Gujarat Assembly Election in India", p. 274.

[24] *Times of India*, 17 and 18 June 1975, both p. 1.

[25] *Statesman Weekly*, 14 June 1975, p. 1.

[26] Indian law declared this a "corrupt practice". A 1971 parliamentary committee had sought to reclassify a number of offences from "corrupt" to "illegal", which was a downgrade in the hierarchy of electoral sins. Unfortunately for the prime minister, the use of government officers was not one of them. If it was, the counterfactual arises: would Mrs Gandhi still have imposed the Emergency? Kapoor was known for shady dealings. Holed up in a Lucknow hotel called Capoor's in 1970, he had allegedly brought about the fall of the Congress (O) government by purchasing legislators "for Rs 40,000–100,000 each": Brass, *An Indian Political Life*, p. 82.

[27] *Economist*, 21 June 1975, p. 1. "It is as though a head of government should go to the block for a parking ticket": *Guardian*, 16 June 1975, p. 9.

There was a second trespass: Mrs Gandhi had also used state employees, this time Uttar Pradesh officials, to build the rostrums for her rallies.[28] The practice was the norm in India, Kapoor would later argue; and besides, neither of these offences could have altered the outcome, for her rival, the Socialist candidate Raj Narain, had lost by a margin of over 100,000 votes.[29]

Still, the two misdemeanours held the possibility of unseating Mrs Gandhi. She was disqualified by the Allahabad judgment from contesting elections for six years, whereas being a member of parliament was one of the requirements of being prime minister.[30] Working against her was also a precedent of her own making: in 1968 she had inveigled Chenna Reddy, a cabinet minister, into resigning when he was found guilty of corrupt electoral practices under the People's Representation Act. At the time, a new piece of legislation had been considered to retrospectively absolve Reddy—and in a similar but unconnected incident another political colleague, D.P. Mishra—from wrongdoing. But no such legislative step had in fact been taken.[31]

In the run-up to Allahabad, Mrs Gandhi had resorted to all conceivable means in order to achieve a favourable judgment. An Uttar Pradesh MP reportedly offered Rs 500,000 to Justice Sinha, while retired Chief Justice D.S. Mathur led him to believe he would be made a Supreme Court judge in exchange for a favourable ruling. The chief minister of Andhra Pradesh spread a false rumour, suggesting that Sinha had revealed his decision to Jayaprakash Narayan.[32] The Intelligence Bureau dispatched an "experienced" sleuth to try and "find out which way the wind was blowing"—and probably steer it as well.[33] The judgment had been repeatedly delayed, the

[28] Mrs Gandhi was absolved from a third transgression when Justice Sinha rejected Narain's challenge to the constitutional validity of the Representation of the People (Amendment) Act, 1974—a hasty piece of legislation she had rammed through parliament to discount a number of expenses from total campaign expenditures. This retroactively reduced the cost of her campaign, making Narain's petition redundant.

[29] This paragraph draws on Bhushan, *The Case That Shook India, passim.* Subsequent to his defeat, Narain was elected to the Rajya Sabha on a BLD ticket.

[30] The relevant extracts of the ruling are reproduced in SCP, Subject File 1, p. 1.

[31] Nayar, *The Judgement,* p. 15.

[32] The chief minister, J. Vengal Rao, apologised to the High Court for this in 1996: Austin, *Working a Democratic Constitution,* p. 316.

[33] Rajeswar, *India,* p. 75.

last time to prevent the verdict from influencing the Gujarat elections that were held on 8 June.

The road forward was unclear. A stay on the judgment for twenty days meant there was enough time to appeal to the Supreme Court. Resignation, on the other hand, could carry political mileage, even the prospect, much needed in the present climate, of Mrs Gandhi adorning "the mantle of self-less morality".[34] She could have returned later, enlisting the support of either parliament or the people—that is, either retroactively expunged the offence by a constitutional amendment, or called a snap election. The parliamentary route would have entailed convening the Lok Sabha within the twenty days stipulated by Sinha. Rustling up a qualified majority on such short notice would, of course, have been arduous.[35] While her party had the numbers in the lower house, the growing number of dissidents threatened to upset the balance. Indeed, Mrs Gandhi had received confidential reports from the Intelligence Bureau on 18 June saying she enjoyed the unconditional support of only 191 Lok Sabha and 81 Rajya Sabha MPs.[36] The popular option was the better one: she could have enlisted the help of the chief election commissioner, T. Swaminathan, who had thrown her a lifeline—his statutory authority allowed him to remove any disqualifications that could prevent her contesting the 1976 elections.[37]

Ray and party president D.K. Barooah, Mrs Gandhi's confidants, had no advice to proffer when she suggested she resign.[38] But her sons, Sanjay and Rajiv, did: they were firm in their opposition to plans involving even a temporary relinquishing of office.[39] "Mummy, we must fight it out. Don't

---

[34] Hart, "Introduction", p. 4.

[35] Amendments required a majority in both houses of their total membership, a two-thirds majority of all present and voting, and a majority in at least half the state assemblies.

[36] This was 36.5 and 33.3 per cent of the total strength of the Lok Sabha and Rajya Sabha, respectively—far short of the two-thirds majority needed for constitutional amendments. For the IB report, see Jayaram to Dhar, 18 June 1975, SCP, Subject File 1, pp. 25–6. According to the IB director, it was "normal or usual practice" for him to pass on such intelligence to the prime minister: Jayaram to Justice J.C. Shah, no date, SCP, Subject File 1, p. 96.

[37] Swaminathan had previously served as cabinet secretary, the civil servant at the top of the pecking order: *Times of India*, 18 June 1975, p. 7.

[38] Ray later suggested she bide her time until the Supreme Court's judgment. See the statement of Krishan Chand, November 1977, SCP, Subject File 1, p. 38.

[39] *Times of India*, 13 June 1975, p. 9. Following convention, this book will refer to Indira Gandhi as "Mrs Gandhi" and to her son as "Sanjay".

resign. I shall stand by you," Sanjay told her.[40] By the time the Supreme Court exonerated her, they reasoned, seasoned party leaders might well have grown powerful enough to block the return of a maligned prime minister. And what if the Supreme Court ruled against her? And what if the 1976 elections went the way of the Gujarat poll?

Over the next fortnight, the constituencies that came out in her favour were legion. Among them were the Communist Party of India, then allied to the Congress in parliament; the National Students Union of India—the grand old party's student union—which generally sided with the prime minister against her enemies within the party; the heavy industry majors and the five main chambers of commerce; as well as government employees and unions affiliated with INTUC and AITUC, the Congress' and the CPI's union networks, respectively.[41] After some hesitation, Congress state leaders also threw their weight behind her.[42] On Delhi's streets, Sanjay and Dhawan staged rallies and marches to protest the high court ruling.[43]

"A wave had to be created" to tide over Mrs Gandhi's troubles, Delhi Lieutenant Governor Krishan Chand noted at the time.[44] To this end, he placed the municipal corporation, transportation system, and local bureaucracy at her disposal. In those heady days, a total of 1761 buses belonging to the Delhi Transport Corporation (DTC) were requisitioned—at a cost of Rs 400,000, paid for by the taxpayer—by Chand, who doubled as its chairman, to ferry people from the conurbations and rural peripheries to 1 Safdarjung Road, where slogans of fealty were voiced. Buses conveyed votaries from small-town Haryana, Rajasthan, and Uttar Pradesh to Delhi, and trains freighted them in from the larger and distant metropolises of Varanasi, Lucknow, and Kanpur.[45]

---

[40] Kaul, *My Years Through Raj to Swaraj*, p. 146.

[41] "Daily summary of information of CID (Special Branch), Delhi", 12–25 June 1975, Ministry of Home Affairs Papers, File VI/11034/56/80(29)/ISDVI.

[42] Chapter 7 chronicles, *inter alia*, the initial resistance mounted by some Congressmen against the prime minister.

[43] *SCR*, vol. 1, p. 17.

[44] Deposition of Navin Chawla, secretary to the lieutenant governor, no date, SCP, Subject File 1, p. 119.

[45] For his efforts, U.S. Shrivastuv, director of transport and Krishan Chand's man, was made chairman of the DTC in 1976, despite his lack of qualifications: *SCR*, vol. 1, pp. 68–70. See also ibid., pp. 17, 20; statements of J.R. Anand, DTC traffic manager, SCP, Subject File 1, p. 43; Jaswant Singh, depot manager of Okhla-II, DTC, 27 November 1977, ibid., pp. 44–7. However, if a government official involved in the process is to be believed, the mobilisation of public transport for

At the centre of this massive propaganda effort in the capital to prove Mrs Gandhi's indispensability were Chand and the man to whom he owed his office, Navin Chawla, on paper his secretary. Chawla, who in turn owed his standing to his friendship with Sanjay, called the shots in the state administration, doing the dirty work for the prime minister's son whenever the occasion demanded.[46] From 12 June onward, Chand and Chawla withdrew buses from their scheduled routes, and bribed government employees with "milk, bread, and other eatables" as well as the prospect of shirking their work to attend sloganeering events that were, by all accounts, festive. People danced the bhangra while a "band of Mohan Meakins Company" played on. Effigies of Justice Sinha were burnt and placards asking "Is Mr Sinha a CIA Agent?" brandished. *"Desh ki neta—Indira Gandhi/ Court ka faisla—Nahi manenge"* (Indira Gandhi—the country's leader/ The Court's decision—we won't accept) chanted the crowds.[47] Chawla's hirelings targeted in particular the notoriously ill-paid "Class IV employees"—blue-collar state personnel—roughing up those who refused to be bused to the staged rallies and threatening them with disciplinary action and arrest. Sanction for such coercion, of course, came from on high, with Mrs Gandhi closely monitoring the counter-protests from her residence, where the capital's administrative elite—Chand, Chawla, Deputy Inspector General P.S. Bhinder, NDMC President P. Behl, and Delhi Municipal Commissioner B.R. Tamta—would periodically turn up to receive the latest set of instructions. Further down the chain of command, the police provided logistical

---

party propaganda was merely a "convention": deposition of N.K. Garg, deputy commissioner of Rohtak, 12 November 1977, ibid., pp. 198, 200. Garg recalls buses being requisitioned for political purposes in 1971 as well. Anand maintained that "we have never followed the normal rules". For Delhi's lieutenant governor, a breakdown in public transport was but a minor inconvenience—citizens could well have used "private buses", "scooters and so on". See his deposition, no date, ibid., pp. 101, 153.

[46] During the Emergency, for instance, this included creating prison cells with asbestos roofs to "bake" political prisoners inside. Sanjay allegedly had Krishan Chand bumped off two years later. The press consensus at the time, however, was that he committed suicide soon after the publication of the Shah Commission reports. See Frank, *Indira*, pp. 423, 531; *SCR*, vol. 2, pp. 39, 44, 46.

[47] Statements of S.P. Goyal, assistant engineer at NDMC, 28 November 1977, SCP, Subject File 1, p. 55; K.P. Saxena, Rajghat Power House controller, 2 December 1977, ibid., p. 83; J.C. Wadhwa, senior clerk at NDMC, 29 November 1977, ibid., p. 64

support, ensuring "discipline"—soon to become a watchword for the Emergency regime—in the city.[48] State governments were drawn into the effort as well: Rajasthan Chief Minister Hari Deo Joshi pledged to send around "five to seven thousand persons" to the rallies, for which fifty-eight trucks were dispatched; his Haryana counterpart Bansi Lal called upon nearby district magistrates to muster Congress workers from their regions and transport them to the capital.[49]

Meanwhile, Sanjay and his group were busy preparing an "arrest list" to rub out the opposition. The press fell into this category as well, an early indication of the kind of authoritarian impulses that were to come over the republic's rulers during the Emergency. A rough draft was ready by 15 June and, over the next week, a number of people saw and contributed names to it. Major inputs came from the Research and Analysis Wing (RAW), India's recently constituted and cryptically named premier intelligence agency, whose ostensible mandate was foreign operations. Because it reported directly to the prime minister, the RAW became a convenient tool for domestic intelligence gathering: dossiers were prepared on political opponents, pressmen, and even Mrs Gandhi's critics within the Congress.[50] More names were added by Minister of State for Home Affairs Om Mehta, a trusted lieutenant of Sanjay's whose *raison d'être* was to allow him to bypass Home Minister K. Brahmananda Reddy; Chief Minister Bansi Lal of Haryana; Home Secretary S.L. Khurana, who took office just three days before the Emergency (replacing Nirmal Mukherjee, who, in Sanjay's words was "too legalistic");[51] and Dhawan, who had only recently succeeded his younger cousin Yashpal Kapoor as Mrs Gandhi's personal assistant—the latter being the "gazetted officer" at the centre of the Allahabad imbroglio.[52] By the morning of 25 June the chief ministers of Andhra

---

[48] *SCR*, vol. 1, p. 20; statements of Ramesh Nandan Bhatnagar, junior clerk at NDMC, 26 November 1977, SCP, Subject File 1, p. 51; Jagdish Lal, station house officer at Police Station Hathin, Gurgaon, 28 November 1977, ibid., p. 72; Tamta, 5 August 1977, SCP, Subject File 2, p. 155.

[49] Supplementary Statement of M.K. Miglani, Gurgaon district magistrate, 30 November 1977, SCP, Subject File 1, pp. 79–80; Kapur, *What Price Perjury?*, p. 39.

[50] Raman, *The Kaoboys of R&AW*, pp. 49–53.

[51] Nayar, *The Judgement*, p. 31.

[52] There was an extemporaneous element to the list-making. Names were added at whim—such as Congressman Ram Dhan's—and removed with equal impulsiveness, as with Petroleum and Chemicals Minister K.D. Malaviya and *Hindustan*

Pradesh, Karnataka, Madhya Pradesh, Rajasthan, Bihar, Haryana, Punjab, and West Bengal had been apprised of the impending arrests.[53] As key figures of the Indian establishment, they constituted the main channel between 1 Safdarjung Road and the rest of the country, creating, as it were, a system of information dependence—in part, of Mrs Gandhi's own making—that cut the prime minister and her son off from dissenting voices.[54]

At first, the awesome powers of the Emergency did not quite sink in. When the arrest lists were distributed among the higher echelons of the Delhi police, instructions were also issued to the rank and file to arrest, under Section 107 of the Indian Penal Code—usually applied to vagrants—some of the major figures of the opposition. To this end, model First Information Reports (FIRs) began circulating in Uttar Pradesh police stations. But it was not long before Delhi's rulers and policemen got on top of the new situation: FIRs and Section 107 were unnecessary when the Maintenance of Internal Security Act (MISA)—hitherto invoked primarily against smugglers—was at their disposal, for it allowed arrests without charge.[55] After some mild protests the police contingent, led by Delhi's deputy commissioner Sushil Kumar, caved in to the demands of their political masters—Dhawan did much of the arm-twisting in these meetings—and began signing blank warrants. "Dependable" officers, such as Haryana's P.S. Bhinder, were brought into the Special Intelligence Branch to ease the process of arrests.[56] To facilitate the production of MISA warrants on an

---

Times editor George Verghese. Mrs Gandhi signed off on all lists: *SCR*, vol. 2, p. 33.

[53] J. Vengal Rao, Devaraj Urs, P.C. Sethi, Harideo Joshi, Jagannath Mishra, Bansi Lal, Zail Singh, and Siddhartha Shankar Ray, respectively: *SCR*, vol. 1, pp. 22–3.

[54] Indeed, counsellors tried in vain to persuade Sanjay against arresting Narayan. A lesson drawn from decades spent struggling for independence was that there existed a causal link between a political leader's entry into prison as victim and his exit as martyr. Krishan Chand, for one, warned that "Shri Jai Prakash [*sic*] Narayan's arrest would make it more difficult to preserve public peace than if he was not arrested": Krishan Chand, November 1977, SCP, Subject File 1, p. 38.

[55] Despite this, police officers mention the scramble to issue warrants under MISA as late as the night of 25 June: statement of Bhawanimal, inspector general of police, Delhi, no date, SCP, Subject File 1, pp. 35–6. Later that night, around 2.30 a.m., they realised that under MISA, arrests could be "made forthwith": statement of S.H. Mohan, senior superintendent of police, Rohtak, 14 November 1977, ibid., pp. 77–8.

[56] Nayar, *The Judgement*, p. 38; *SCR*, vol. 2, p. 32.

industrial scale, the Delhi administration increased the number of issuing authorities from two to seven.[57] A similar process was at work at the state level, where chief ministers drew up lists and warrants of their own in collaboration with inspectors general of police, chief secretaries, and district magistrates.[58]

Thereafter, events moved swiftly. On 18 June the Congress Parliamentary Party passed a resolution—450 votes in favour, 44 against—proclaiming Mrs Gandhi "indispensable to the nation".[59] Two days later, she addressed a largely rented crowd of 50,000 at the Boat Club in Delhi.[60] Flanked by her family, she vowed to serve the people "till her last breath"; her opponents, she declared, "are not only after my chair, they want to murder me and my family."[61] On 22 June frantic efforts were made by the government to prevent Narayan from leading a major rally at the Ramlila Grounds in the capital, first by progressively delaying his flight from Patna and finally by cancelling it altogether.[62]

Battles on the streets were fought in parallel with the one in the courts. To take up her appeal in the Supreme Court, Mrs Gandhi sought out Nani Palkhivala, Bombay lawyer and senior director in the Tata industrial empire, who had famously challenged and defeated her administration in the courts not long before.[63] Ideological differences, if any, were cast aside now that Mrs Gandhi was in need of some skilful lawyering. Her

[57] Before the Emergency, only the offices of the lieutenant governor and district magistrate were granted such powers. In the first week of the altered regime, competencies were extended to the five additional district magistrates as well: *SCR*, vol. 2, p. 33. Still, the demand for MISA warrants outpaced their authorisation, necessitating the use of Sections 108 and 151 of the Criminal Procedure Code to secure arrests. The prisoners were detained under MISA once the paperwork came through: ibid., p. 35.

[58] *SCR*, vol. 3, pp. 16, 65–6, 68, 101.

[59] *Statesman Weekly*, 21 June 1975, p. 9.

[60] Frank, *Indira*, p. 372. Another account puts the attendance at one million: Mehta, *The Sanjay Story*, p. 100.

[61] Mehta, *The Sanjay Story*, p. 100. Barooah, who was known for his drollery, composed a hagiographic Urdu couplet for the occasion: *"Indira tere subah ki jai, tere sham ki jai/ tere kaam ki jai, tere naam ki jai"* (Indira, great at morn, great by evening/ Hallowed is your work, and hallowed be thy name).

[62] The rally nevertheless proceeded without him: *SCR*, vol. 1, p. 20.

[63] She had been forced to abandon, briefly, the nationalisation of fourteen banks and the abolition of privy purses of former princes once the apex court had struck them down as unconstitutional.

chances looked bright. Since the court was on vacation, the appeal for a stay against the Allahabad judgment was to be made before the single judge on duty, Justice V.R. Krishna Iyer, who, it transpired, was "ideologically on her side". Indeed, his appointment in 1972 had been resisted by Chief Justice S.M. Sikri, who was not keen on a former communist minister on his benches.[64]

After hearing both sides for two days—23 and 24 June—Iyer concluded that Mrs Gandhi's was not one of the "graver electoral vices".[65] She could continue as prime minister, even take part in parliamentary debates, but not vote in the Lok Sabha or draw her salary as an MP until a larger bench, once justices returned from furlough, ruled on her appeal.[66] The Lok Sabha was not in session, nor was Mrs Gandhi strapped for cash. The judgment, then, was little more than a rap on the knuckles. Still, this was enough for the opposition parties to double down on extra-parliamentary action. Barring the communists, they were now united on the question of unseating Mrs Gandhi.[67] The next day, 25 June, Narayan addressed a mammoth crowd at the Ramlila Grounds: it was time for state employees to tender their resignations *en masse*, he thundered, enjoining the armed forces to make common cause with his movement.[68] Mrs Gandhi promised to respond in kind.

Contingency plans for some kind of authoritarian measures had been in the works since at least 8 January 1975. That day, Ray had written to the prime minister describing in detail an ordinance that he had conceived: once promulgated, it would authorise the police, ready with arrest lists, to "swing into action", incarcerating politicians, journalists, and other enemies

---

[64] Iyer had served as minister of law, home, and irrigation from 1957 to 1959 in the Communist Party of India-run government in Kerala. Mrs Gandhi's team had also received a heads-up: a CBI employee who happened to know Iyer's brother had had a conversation with Devendra Sen, his boss, about the kind of evidence the judge would have preferred to see in court. See Tandon, *PMO Diary*, p. 406.

[65] In his judgment, Iyer was sympathetic. The "draconian law" could be done away with by "a wakeful and quick-acting legislature", he recommended: Austin, *Working a Democratic Constitution*, p. 318.

[66] This, in legal jargon, was a "conditional stay", the best—given the constraints of precedents—Iyer could muster for Mrs Gandhi, who would have preferred an "absolute stay", the temporary lifting of all disqualifications: *SCR*, vol. 1, p. 21.

[67] The CPI(M) did not join the other parties on the streets, but affirmed that Mrs Gandhi must resign; the CPI, on the other hand, continued to support her decision, remaining faithful to the coalition.

[68] *Why Emergency?*, passim.

of the state all in the span of "twenty-four hours".[69] In principle, this authoritarian alloy, combining the use of constitutional provisions with brute police power, was to be employed to decimate the Anand Marg—a Hindu militant group—as well as the RSS. This, in essence, was the West Bengal strategy writ large. As chief minister of the eastern state, Ray had presided over a period of massive state violence against communists, years during which the Youth Congress had taken over cities, universities, and the countryside, putting paid to the Left across the state. In the event, Ray's letter served as the blueprint for the Emergency. Other members of the administration were on the same wavelength. D.P. Dhar, for his part, had on at least two occasions between January and June suggested that the president "suspend the Constitution and set it aside".[70] On various occasions, Mrs Gandhi too had shown her preference for "drastic, emergent [*sic*] action", or some form of "shock treatment".[71]

On 24 June, Ray, working from the prime minister's residence, ordered a copy of the constitution from the Parliament Library and spent the evening perusing it with hermeneutical rigour. The founding fathers had placed in this document untrammelled reserve powers at the disposal of the state. These were listed between Articles 352 and 360, provisions that were kept dormant but ready for deployment when thought necessary. Many of the constitutional measures used by the colonial government to provide legal ballast for preventive detention and the suspension of human rights had been retained *in toto* by the successor state. This in part reflected the times it was written in: the new nation was reeling from the effects of Partition, ridden with social cleavages, and at war with enemies both within and without.[72] While Nehru, the first premier, had resorted to many of these provisions to deal with the Congress' foes in the republic's peripheries—notably in Kerala and the North East—a nationwide state of emergency to suppress internal dissent had never been in the offing. Emergencies had been declared on two previous occasions: during the 1962 and 1971 wars

---

[69] The letter is reproduced in Smita Gupta, "Ghost Writers of 1975", *Outlook*, 2 November 2009.

[70] Austin, *Working a Democratic Constitution*, p. 304.

[71] Frank, *Indira*, p. 374; *Times of India*, 12 July 1975, p. 1.

[72] The state was engaged in attempts to secure Kashmir, Hyderabad, and other princely states; suppress communists in Telangana; and drive underground the RSS, which was banned after the murder of M.K. Gandhi. For a masterly account of this period and the constitutional dilemmas it threw up, see Austin, *The Indian Constitution*.

with China and Pakistan, respectively—the former was lifted in 1968, and the latter was still in place at the time Ray was skimming through the constitution (it was only lifted in 1977). These, however, had been in response to external threats.

In fact, it took a vivid imagination to conceive of an "internal Emergency"—as Ray suggested—for it never appeared as a distinct category in Article 352.[73] Indeed, the article simply stated that an emergency could be imposed as a response to a threat posed to the country by "war or external aggression or internal disturbance", whereas Ray interpreted it to mean that *two* emergencies—one internal and the other external—could run concurrently.[74] Hedging the language of Article 352, he argued that the Emergency in place since 3 December 1971 was an "external" one,[75] making possible the imposition of a second, albeit "internal", Emergency.[76] Such a pretzelled interpretation of the law would prove hard even for loyalists to digest: "But we already have an emergency," was Brahmananda Reddy's

[73] *SCR,* vol. 1, p. 30.

[74] Ibid.

[75] Arbitrary power was exercised under the external Emergency as well: apropos of fundamental rights, the right to appeal to the courts was suspended in November 1974, nearly three years after the war had ended. Criticism of this Emergency was common. For instance, a March 1975 seminar protesting the state of emergency had among its speakers Narayan, Advani, Madhu Limaye, J.B. Kripalani of the Socialist Party, former Attorney General C.K. Daphtary, and former Supreme Court justices K.S. Hegde and A.N. Grover: Advani, *My Country, My Life*, p. 199. "Several hundred thousand people" marched alongside Narayan on 6 March in New Delhi to present a charter of demands to parliamentarians, one of which was to call off the state of emergency: Chandra, *In the Name of Democracy*, p. 62.

[76] Such a reading was made impossible after the Emergency of 1975–7, when a 1978 amendment struck out the "internal disturbance" clause in Article 352. At the cabinet meeting of 26 June 1975, no minister wondered how "the Emergency" could be imposed when one was already in session. While opposition parties had routinely protested against the 1971 Emergency and the "danger posed by the increasing use of MISA and DIR"—both preventive detention laws—and had, in addition to the meeting mentioned in the footnote above, organised a conference that brought together a number of opposition leaders for this purpose on 15 and 16 February 1975, the cabinet had completely forgotten about its expanded powers, an indication of how cut off the ruling establishment had become: interview with Karan Singh in New Delhi on 11 April 2018; "Summary of Discussions with Party Leaders", 16 February 1975, Jayaprakash Narayan Papers, Instalment III, Subject File 333.

knee-jerk reaction the next day.[77] The specific use of Article 352, however, was vital. For, when triggered, it automatically set in motion a nested series of other articles: the next eight listed after it. Under their provisions, parliament could extend its term one year at a time; the union legislate on matters traditionally the preserve of the states; and the executive prevent citizens from appealing to the courts to enforce fundamental rights.[78] In essence, for Ray and the rest of the rulers of the republic, an "internal Emergency" was the perfect legal cover for plans already at hand: mass arrests, press censorship, and authoritarian fiat.

Making Sense of the Emergency

When one speaks of the Emergency, large numbers are in order: over its brief duration, eleven million Indians were sterilised and 110,000 locked up.[79] In Delhi alone, of the city's five million citizens, 700,000 were displaced by the gentrification drive and 161,000 sterilised in programmes masterminded by Sanjay.[80] The sheer institutional violence made possible by a declaration that remained—on the face of it—within the confines of constitutional and democratic practice poses the question: what kind of regime was this?

In constitutional terms, the regime incontrovertibly enjoyed *carte blanche* to recast institutions, and even society. Certainly, despite their reservations over vesting Article 352 with near-imperial powers, the founding fathers of the republic had placed scarcely any restraints that could check its usage. One of them—that emergency powers need parliamentary ratification within two months—was easily overcome by Mrs Gandhi in the first few weeks of the Emergency. In fact, the parliamentary session of July and August 1975 was a charade. A fifth of opposition MPs had been incarcerated and the rest drowned out, first by a media that was not allowed to report dissenting speeches, and second by Congress parliamentarians of the Lower House who passed law after law sanctioning and widening the scope of emergency powers. Judicial independence was similarly compro-

---

[77] Frank, *Indira*, p. 378.

[78] This paragraph draws on Hewitt, *Political Mobilisation and Democracy in India*, pp. 59–60, and Austin, *Working a Democratic Constitution*, p. 295ff.

[79] *SCR*, vol. 3, pp. 134, 207.

[80] It was reported that 150,105 "structures" in the capital were razed to the ground: *Blitz*, 24 December 1977, p. 21.

mised, tampered from within by preferential appointments and from without by the transfer of competencies to the executive.

Even so, the Emergency cannot be characterised as a uniformly authoritarian regime. For its policies and implementation varied in the course of time, were not imposed in the same manner in every state, and left the institutional pillars of democracy—the judiciary, parliament, and the media—with some room for manoeuvre.

The first part of the book deals with the political, economic, institutional, personal, and regional aspects of the Emergency. Chapters 1 through 3 present the balance sheet, as it were, of the regime in order to define its brand of authoritarianism. The first chapter looks at state repression and the discourse that served as its justification. The next one focuses on the political economy of the Emergency, the divergence between the promissory "socialist" rhetoric of Mrs Gandhi's Twenty-Point Programme and *dirigiste* corporatism in practice. The third analyses the manner in which institutions—in particular the Lok Sabha, which gave India a façade of parliamentarism while lawmakers wasted away in jail, and the judiciary, which on paper bespoke law and order at a time when judges had lost much of their independence at the hands of the executive—were subverted even as the regime continued to maintain the fiction of legality. The next two, Chapters 4 and 5, examine the temporal and spatial variations that characterised the regime, respectively. *Circa* December 1975, an informal dynastic transition occurred at 1 Safdarjung Road, the result of which was the change in accent of the Emergency's programmes. Prime Minister Indira Gandhi's powers waned, as did interest in her Twenty-Point Programme, while the extra-constitutional powers of Sanjay Gandhi waxed, with deferential state leaders competing with one another to implement his Five-Point Programme. It was as a part of Sanjay's twin obsessions—family planning and urban gentrification—that some of the worst instances of state violence took place in the framework of a "sultanist" variant of authoritarianism. But the spatial reach of these policies was not uniform: the arbitrary powers of the Emergency were a stronger presence in the Hindi belt than in the South, and in the states ruled by the Congress than in the holdouts.

The second part of the book asks a different question: Why the Emergency? Chapter 6 revisits the immediate causes—the JP Movement and the Allahabad High Court verdict—by relocating them in the larger perspective of India's socio-economic crisis and the tensions between the executive and the judiciary. Beyond these, we shift our attention in Chapter 7 to the factors that enabled authoritarianism in the longer run, singling out two key developments: first, the personalisation and centralisation of power within both the Congress and the government; and, following from that, the second, the deinstitutionalisation of the grand old party in particular and the state in general, a process that gained momentum in the late 1960s. Chapter 8 discusses the heteroclite nature of the coalition backing the Emergency: among its most vocal supporters were the CPI and the private industrial empires, both of which organised large rallies in support of Mrs Gandhi. Less emphatic, but of greater numerical significance, was the approval of the middle classes and the bureaucracy: both had the means to challenge authoritarian rule but preferred not to so long as their sectional interests were being served.

All the same, the Emergency was lifted after eighteen months. The third part of the book attempts to account for this puzzle. Why did Mrs Gandhi announce a snap election in 1977? Certainly, opposition to the regime played no role in the decision. For, as we show in Chapter 9, the media and the judiciary were an inadequate counterbalance to the Emergency, their dissidence effortlessly thwarted by Mrs Gandhi's censors and wardens. The largely dismal performance of the fourth estate, in particular, was a truth captured well by Advani's wry taunt: "When you were merely asked to bend, you chose to crawl."[81] But the opposition fared no better: most of its components, including the Sangh Parivar, oscillated between resistance and capitulation, proving utterly incapable of sustained and effective mobilisation. Indeed, in stark contrast to the received narratives of daring acts of courage and literary heroism, popular in Hindu nationalist as in liberal lore, the picture that emerges in these pages is one of chaos and confusion, of distrustful leaders gunning for one another and ever ready to cut a deal with Delhi's rulers. As for more concerted efforts to resist the regime—few and far between as they were—such as those attempted by socialists like George Fernandes, or by the Akali Dal, they were subjected to repression.

Chapter 10 grapples with the different hypotheses that account for the lifting of the Emergency: foreign pressure, directly and indirectly applied; Mrs Gandhi's *mea culpa*, induced by the realisation that Sanjay had gone too far and become too violent in implementing the Emergency's programmes; and, more importantly perhaps, her self-assurance, her certainty that no one could defeat her at the polls.

[81] *New York Times,* 11 May 1977, p. 3.

The Conclusion locates the Emergency in the history of postcolonial India: was it a parenthesis, a turning point, or was the difference between it and the periods that bookended it more a matter of degree than nature? How exceptional was this episode for the average Indian? Comparing the Emergency to the quarter-century of democracy that preceded it and to the decades following it suggests—especially when seen from certain regions (such as India's peripheries) and from the eyes of certain classes (the country's working poor in particular)—*not very much.*

India's first dictatorship, then, was neither a parenthesis, nor so much a turning point, but a concentrate of a style of rule, an élan alive today, if in attenuated form, as it was in the late 1960s. Indeed, it is the continuities, not the contrasts, between the three periods that stand out: a preference for corporatist governance and a lack of ideological coherence; the liberal recourse to emergency powers, many of them pilfered from colonial statute books; a simultaneous evocation of rule in the name of the masses and their denigration; and a dialectical relationship between populism and authoritarianism wherein the people are presented, in the rhetoric of Delhi's rulers, as a classless, undistinguished whole even as actually existing policies continue to work, in keeping with a hierarchical conception of society that has for long been supported by social sanction in the Indian setting, to the benefit of the few. All of these aspects of Indian political life, though, appear in less pronounced form on either side of the Emergency, which, as we will see in the chapters that follow, brought them into sharper relief. In the event, to revisit the Emergency is to revaluate characterisations of India as the "world's largest democracy".

PART I

THE VARIETIES OF AUTHORITARIANISM

WHAT KIND OF REGIME WAS THE EMERGENCY?

As a regime, the Emergency tends to escape categorisation. But it can be better understood using Juan Linz's typology, which provides a multitude of variants on authoritarianism and totalitarianism on the basis of three criteria: the degree of pluralism, the extent of mobilisation in society, and the role of ideology.[1]

The Emergency was certainly not a totalitarian system, as Granville Austin points out: "The Emergency had its limits. Considerable individual and political freedom existed within it, ideological purity was not demanded, opponents were not shot."[2] The Congress lacked the ideological zeal, as it were, required for such undertakings. It neither exercised power in the name of an ideology nor made any attempt at encouraging popular participation. On the contrary the regime encouraged the depoliticisation of society—of universities, factories, and the countryside.[3] The Youth Congress, the shock troops of the party headed by the prime minister's son, was probably the only exception to this, its membership growing from

---

[1] Linz, *Totalitarian and Authoritarian Regimes*.

[2] Austin, *Working a Democratic Constitution*, p. 389, n2.

[3] *SW*, 16 August 1975, p. 3; *SW*, 4 October 1975, pp. 3, 9. This trend was recognised by Rajni Kothari during the Emergency itself: see his "Restoring the Political Process", p. 19.

700,000 to six million over the twenty-one months of Emergency rule. In the absence of party cadres, the Congress leadership lacked the ability of totalitarian regimes to diffuse ideas and implement policies. More significantly, a totalitarian system would not have stopped short of carrying out mass purges of the ruling elite; Mrs Gandhi, however, did: just a handful of Congress MPs and MLAs were incarcerated and only 0.19 per cent of the country's bureaucrats were dismissed.[4] Nor was there a systematic use of terror, a defining feature of totalitarianism.[5] The death toll was probably less than a couple of thousand, paltry when placed beside figures for other autocracies.[6] Moreover, censorship did not systematically prevent some newspapers from publishing news the regime found unpalatable, and the judiciary retained a certain limited autonomy—that it sometimes chose not to use, as we shall see.

Instead, the Emergency is best characterised as an authoritarian regime which encouraged the depoliticisation of society, tolerated opposition so long as it operated in a highly circumscribed space, and faced dissident elements within the establishment itself.

But there are many different types of authoritarianism. Given the odium attached to class struggle by Delhi's rulers, and their willingness to accommodate industrialists and crush labour militancy, it could be said that the Emergency has clear affinities with the corporatist variant that Linz identifies as "organic statism". But in late 1975 and early 1976, when Sanjay began asserting himself, the Emergency started to exhibit key features of another category of authoritarian regime that Linz, after Max Weber, theorises as "sultanism".

[4] *SCR*, vol. 3, pp. 34–6.

[5] See Arendt, *The Origins of Totalitarianism*, p. 460ff. Linz, however, argues that terror is "neither a necessary nor sufficient characteristic of totalitarian systems": Linz, *Totalitarian and Authoritarian Regimes*, p. 74.

[6] While 1774 died on the sterilisation tables, about a hundred met the same fate in prison, and possibly a couple of thousand were killed in police shootings, torture chambers, and the demolition programmes across the country. It is hard to put an exact number because many of these figures are undoubtedly under-reported. As for the death tolls in individual episodes, the divergence between official and unofficial figures only compounds the problem. In relation to the Turkman Gate deaths, for instance, the figures vary between 6 and 1200.

1

A CONSTITUTIONAL DICTATORSHIP

For the citizens of Emergency India, the very first day of the new regime, 26 June 1975, started with doublespeak. Inaugurating the new dispensation over All India Radio, Prime Minister Indira Gandhi was keen in her broadcast to emphasise its legality. That it remained well within the perimeter of the constitution, and that the proclamation of a state of emergency was, in fact, a response to an extra-constitutional threat, was a theme she would rehearse time and again. As she put it in her first address:

> I am sure you are all conscious of the deep and widespread conspiracy which had been brewing ever since I began to introduce certain progressive measures of benefit to the common man and woman of India. In the name of democracy, it has been sought to negate the very functioning of democracy. Duly elected governments have not been allowed to function, and in some cases, force has been used to compel members to resign in order to dissolve lawfully elected assemblies.[1]

On 27 June, in another radio address, Mrs Gandhi argued that "the kind of programme envisaged by some of the opposition groups is not compatible with democracy, is anti-national by any test and could not be allowed."[2] This kind of casuistry—saving democracy by negating it—was to become one of the defining characteristics of the regime. It involved the daily benumbing of people's senses through radio, television, and print by pro-

---

[1] For the full broadcast, see Gandhi, *Era of Discipline*, p. 14ff.
[2] Ibid., p. 16.

paganda reminiscent of *Nineteen Eighty-Four.* "An extraconstitutional challenge ... was constitutionally met", Mrs Gandhi proclaimed on one occasion.[3] "Some personal rights have to be kept in abeyance for the human rights of the nation [*sic*]", she said on another.[4] Such pronouncements have often been used by authoritarian rulers, notably in Latin America.[5] Closer to home, Indians in 1975 would have remembered the use of similar sophistry by the Pakistani generals who seized power in 1958, and by Bangladesh's Prime Minister Mujibur Rahman, who consolidated his rule in December 1974 by suspending civil liberties and declaring a state of emergency.[6] Mrs Gandhi and her party, which largely chorused her view, shared this peculiar conception of democracy. Her foreign minister, Y.B. Chavan, indicated his preference for "a democratic system, but one not confined to elections", for such a democracy, with polls "enacted after every five years through general elections", was "a farce".[7] Similarly, a prominent figure of the Congress Left, Shashi Bhushan, had little trouble reconciling the Emergency with democracy: he had long been in favour of such a "limited dictatorship".[8] Mrs Gandhi's Communist allies were not to be outdone: "the Anglo-Saxon concept of democracy [is] an anachronism in these days of people's awareness", noted the secretary of the West Bengal CPI.[9]

Disciplining Democracy

In her speech to the Lok Sabha on 22 July, Mrs Gandhi laid out a fuller statement of her understanding of democracy:

> Any narrow definition of democracy which tries to ignore realities can only mean the growth of political ideas which are anti-democratic ... The great national task we face makes it necessary for us to evolve a political system in which the right balance is struck, in which the essence of freedom is maintained while conditions are created for a higher level of social discipline and economic progress.[10]

---

[3] Austin, *Working a Democratic Constitution*, pp. 307–8.

[4] *Times* (London), 7 November 1978, p. 14.

[5] Linz, *Totalitarian and Authoritarian Regimes*, p. 26.

[6] Jaffrelot, *The Pakistan Paradox*, pp. 303–8; Bari, *States of Emergency and the Law*, pp. 173–7.

[7] Y.B. Chavan, cited in Selbourne, *An Eye to India*, p. 104.

[8] Shashi Bhushan, cited in *TOI*, 10 August 1973, p. 1.

[9] Gopal Banerjee, cited in Lockwood, *The Communist Party of India and the Indian Emergency*, p. 124.

[10] Ibid., p. 27.

Dissent, then, was anti-national; and democracy dependent on discipline. The third pillar of this version of democracy was an ecumenical indigenism. For Mrs Gandhi there was a contemporary Western version of such a polity, and then there was hers. Two months before declaring the Emergency she suggested that:

> [The] words "Freedom" and "Democracy" have not had the same meaning through the ages. When the Greeks spoke of "demos", they did not mean all the people but only a sixth or eighth of the adult population. Women and slaves were excluded. Even today, when some party [*sic*] speak of "the people", they exclude many classes and groups. What we in India are doing is to ensure that the people mean all the people.[11]

Over the duration of the Emergency she continued tinkering with this notion, exploring—and stretching—its conceptual boundaries. On 8 January 1976 she argued that "the Emergency, obviously, means some curbs on democracy", but it was justifiable because "democracy is not an end. Democracy is a tool, a means of achieving something."[12] In this utilitarian perspective, democracy served only to keep India "united": "only a democratic form will hold a country of our diversity of language, religion and customs together, because only democracy enables all the people to participate."[13] In other words, even by her own admission, the concentration of power, by virtue of its centripetal logic, had the potential to destabilise the republic. But then again, this view was entirely dispensable. "The unity of India depends on a strong central government", she said to the Rajya Sabha in November 1976.[14]

While such statements illustrate her Orwellian repertoire, they also serve as reflections of her ideal type of democracy. Here, references to liberal principles—the rule of law and individual freedom—are omitted, and emphasis placed solely on the demotic aspects of democracy: the people and their socio-economic well-being. Thus, the national good trumps political pluralism, and popular participation the need for electoral legitimacy.

Of equal import to this strained notion of democracy was "discipline", a word Mrs Gandhi repeated *ad nauseam* through the months of authoritarian rule. On 22 February 1976 a symposium on the theme "Disciplined Democracy" was convened in Bombay. In her inaugural address the prime

---

[11] *SSWIG*, vol. 3, p. 522.
[12] Ibid., p. 244.
[13] Ibid., p. 262.
[14] Ibid., p. 297.

minister noted *en passant* that she would have preferred a different title—
"Discipline in Democracy"—because the noun, unlike the adjective, did not
suggest coercion; nonetheless, she endorsed the approach of the organisers,
for Indians had become "too lax, too self-centred, too permissive, too indis-
ciplined [*sic*]."[15] Others in the grand old party were not far behind. As the
party president D.K. Barooah put it, "a man is a performing flea, he can be
trained."[16] For N.K.P. Salve, a Congress MP from Madhya Pradesh, "*danda
democracy*"—that is, a democracy that wielded the disciplining stick—vastly
improved the older, softer version.[17] Vinoba Bhave, leader of the Sarvodaya
movement, whose fellow traveller Jayaprakash Narayan had campaigned to
oust the prime minister, dubbed the Emergency an "*anushasan parva*"—an
era of discipline. Less than a week into it, and again a couple of months
later, he blessed Mrs Gandhi at his *ashram* in Paunar, Maharashtra.[18]

But what exactly did "discipline" mean to these leaders? In an interview
with the *Observer*, Mrs Gandhi offered some ideas by way of clarification:
"The foundations of our democracy have been well laid and we cherish its
values. It is a way of life which demands broadmindedness on the part of
government and a sense of discipline and responsibility from every citizen
and more particularly from those in the opposition."[19] Here, "the opposition" referred not only to the other political parties but also to the media.

In line with her 1971 campaign slogan "Garibi Hatao" (get rid of poverty), Mrs Gandhi's claim was that a state of emergency was necessary to
improve the lives of the poor. In one of her interviews she noted that
while "the economic programme was not the reason for the Emergency",
it had "created the right climate for its implementation."[20] A democratic
dispensation, her argument went, was ill-suited to achieve socio-economic change, for the judiciary, at the time a bastion of conservatism,
would have opposed it:

> Over the last two centuries we have adopted the Anglo-Saxon juridical sys-
> tem, which often equates liberty with property, and which has not made

---

[15] Ibid., p. 257.

[16] Selbourne, *An Eye to India*, p. 255.

[17] Mavalankar, *"No, Sir"*, p. 72.

[18] Bhave had been Narayan's mentor but proved to be a turncoat during the
Emergency. For this he earned the sobriquet "*sarkari sant*" (the state's saint):
TOI, 1 July 1975, p. 1; *TOI*, 25 February 1976, p. 1.

[19] *Observer*, 13 July 1975, p. 6.

[20] Gandhi, *Era of Discipline*, p. 141.

adequate provision for the needs of the poor and weak ... When we wanted to abolish traditional landlordism, when we wanted to nationalise banks in order to break the monopoly of a few business houses, when we wanted to do away with the feudal princely order, the law said it could not be done, and the law had to be changed.[21]

But even with the new regime, this old enemy persisted in blocking meaningful reform. In December 1975 she laid into the judiciary for her failure to secure justice for the poor.[22] Four months later, laying the foundation stone of an annexe of the Supreme Court in New Delhi, she took her critique a step further:

[I]n early times, law was a device for the defence of the rights of the few. Today's effort is to make it into an instrument for safeguarding the interests of the many. As I have said previously, law must become a tool for social change. Similarly, the Constitution cannot be a sealed book. It must be a living document, serving a growing and evolving society.[23]

She made clear that the battles which had raged between the executive and the judiciary since 1967 were far from over. "Democracy means the rule of the people", she declared, defining it in contradistinction to the rule of law: the former was the domain of parliament, the latter the judiciary.[24]

That parliamentary supremacy was to ensure the ability of the legislature to reform the constitution was stressed in her defence of the Forty-second Amendment Bill before the Lok Sabha in October 1976: "We have always maintained that Parliament has an unfettered, unqualified and unabridgeable right to amend the Constitution. We do not accept the dogma of the basic structure."[25] She was referring to the "basic structure doctrine" of the Supreme Court, which held that there was an unamendable substratum of the constitution that parliament could not touch—an important point to which we will return in Chapters 3 and 6.

Even in her responses to the NBC, Mrs Gandhi—who was usually more diplomatic with the foreign press—insisted that "the essence of parliamentary democracy does make Parliament supreme so far as all executive action is concerned."[26] Because of her vice-like hold over Congress lawmak-

---

[21] Ibid., pp. 133–4.

[22] *SSWIG*, vol. 3, p. 238.

[23] Ibid., p. 587.

[24] Gandhi, *Era of Discipline*, p. 82.

[25] *SSWIG*, vol. 3, p. 288.

[26] "Gandhi, *Era of Discipline*, p. 161.

ers, what this meant in effect was that *her* rule was supreme; and this came at the expense of the rule of law. As a consequence, debates in parliament counted for less than the will of the prime minister, who asserted her authority by communicating directly with the public.

Her speech announcing the Emergency's Twenty-Point Programme on 1 July 1975 exemplified this affective connection. "I am going to speak to you today", she began reassuringly, before reeling off a list of promises.[27] This style was not abandoned even during the last days of authoritarian rule. "I have come to you not as prime minister, but as your sister, as one of you", she told crowds in March 1977.[28] Establishing a personal rapport with the people entailed repeated occurrences on radio and television, as well as a special broadcast, "Prime Minister Speaks to the People", on both media. In one episode, recorded shortly after the Supreme Court invalidated the verdict of the Allahabad High Court on 10 November 1975—in effect acquitting her of electoral malpractice—she referred to the crowds that came to see her:

> My countrymen, brothers and sisters, I am not delivering any address today. I have come to meet you and to have a heart-to-heart talk with you. The last few years and months have been full of troubles and tribulations. We have in a way all passed through hard tests. Some people came to see me. Whatever happens—good or bad—thousands and *lakhs* of people came to my place here, and we see the same phenomenon now. All types of people are coming here— farmers, workers, *rickshawalas*, *thelawalas*, men, and women. This morning about a thousand *bandwalas* came here.[29]

References to crowds at her doorstep were a regular feature in Mrs Gandhi's speeches. In them she saw validation of her rule which, in the absence of elections, otherwise appeared tenuous. But her refusal to acknowledge dissent did not mean that it had been vanquished. Indeed, its end would require more than the monopolisation of discourse.

A Decimated Opposition: Imprisonment and Torture

In the effort to create a "disciplined democracy", two laws were put to use that allowed for indiscriminate incarceration of political opponents and dissidents: the Maintenance of Internal Security Act (MISA) and the

---

[27] Zaidi, *Full Circle*, p. 17.
[28] Scott, "Emerging from the Emergency", p. 82.
[29] Gandhi, *Era of Discipline*, p. 60.

Defence of India Rules (DIR). In 1978 the Shah Commission disclosed that 110,806 citizens had been arrested under the DIR and MISA during the twenty-one months of authoritarian rule, adding that political prisoners, as opposed to common criminals, accounted for at least half that figure.[30] However, in the moral economy that governed Emergency India, no difference was made between the two categories: the detention of both political dissidents and what were called "anti-social elements" was justified on the grounds that they were, collectively, a "small minority group ... holding the rest of the community to ransom and creating an atmosphere of helplessness and demoralisation within the country."[31] Sitting Congress MLAs, who should logically have fallen into the former category, were incarcerated as "anti-social elements" and "economic offenders", while illegal gamblers, ordinarily classed with criminals, were plucked from the streets and locked up "for holding secret meetings against the Emergency."[32] Some of the categories for detention were vacuous enough to baffle all efforts at classification: citizens were locked up for "moral turpitude", "spreading disaffection", and being "hardcore teachers [*sic*]".[33]

Neither of the two laws that sanctioned preventive detention were new, indicating continuities between the "democratic" and "authoritarian" regimes. MISA was passed in May 1971, hot on the heels of the Congress' electoral triumph.[34] Its authoritarian potential, even at the time, was not

---

[30] *SCR*, vol. 3, p. 134. The Shah Commission, which had as its chairman retired chief justice J.C. Shah, was appointed on 28 May 1977 by the Janata government that came to power in the Emergency's aftermath. The inquiry into the regime and its improprieties published its findings in three volumes in March, April, and August 1978. This rough parity between political and criminal prisoners is confirmed in individual states as well. For instance, 2794 of Maharashtra's 5473 MISA detainees were arrested for "anti-social" reasons; the rest, for political ones: "Arrests in Maharashtra", no date, SCIF, File 41011/10/MHR/77-T-4.

[31] *The Emergency: Its Impact*, p. 10.

[32] *SCR*, vol. 3, pp. 57, 113, 90.

[33] Ibid., p. 111. In most cases, no reasons were given at all. See, for instance, the "prisoner data questionnaires" in "Documentation of Emergency Period in India", MLP, microfilm copy, reel 10.

[34] A contemporary parallel is to be found in the Unlawful Activities (Prevention) Amendment of 2019 passed not long after the BJP's victory at the polls: see the cover story in *Frontline*, 25 October 2019 (https://frontline.thehindu.com/cover-story/article29618049.ece), accessed on 30 October 2019. A number of accounts incorrectly suggest that MISA was introduced during or after the December 1971 war: Kapoor, *The Emergency*, p. 172; Hart, "Introduction", p. 18; Thomas, *Indian*

lost on the opposition. Indeed, the condemnation was cross-partisan: the Jana Sangh's Atal Bihari Vajpayee wondered if "these powers" could one day be used "against political opponents"; the CPM's Jyotirmoy Basu speculated that its sanction could allow the prime minister to "keep herself and her party perpetually in power"; and Congress-nominated Anglo-Indian MP Frank Anthony worried about due process because the courts, he believed, had been "completely ousted".[35] Within the year such voices were vindicated. In the span of twelve months, 6000 were arrested under the new provisions.[36] The act, in theory, allowed law-enforcement agencies to detain persons threatening the defence of India, the security of the state, or the maintenance of public order; in practice it was used to quash all forms of dissent. Incarceration could continue for twelve months or "until the expiry of the Defence and Internal Security of India Act, 1971"—an unlikely scenario since the lawmakers who passed the act were also the only people who could retract the measure. Those taken into custody under it could not benefit from legal help. The terms of detention were to be decided case by case by a three-person advisory board which included at least one active or retired high court judge who was also to be the board's chair. But in truth, on account of the collusion between magistracy and police, the "advisory board was practically an [*sic*] eye-wash".[37] State governments had to "review" the cases as well. This too proved a damp squib during the Emergency. For instance, in a total of 6956 arrests, the Uttar Pradesh government found not even one where the detaining authorities were out of line. Similarly, the Tamil Nadu government confirmed all but

---

Security Policy, p. 101. The upshot of this error is to see the act as being guided by *raison d'état*, when in fact the Congress rulers evidently had domestic concerns in mind: opponents of the party and its programmes. Naturally, the scapegoats were foreign. In Parliament, Congressmen defended the legislation by suggesting that migrants from East Pakistan posed a "threat to the security of India". Its real reasons were not lost on the media. The *Hindustan Times* worried that Mrs Gandhi's government was "addicted" to repressive legislation, hence its use for "wholly unintended and miscellaneous purposes": Mussells, "Democracy and Emergency Rule in India", pp. 80, 82.

[35] The quotations are from the speeches the MPs gave in parliament on 16 and 17 June 1971, reproduced in *SCR*, vol. 3, p. 39.

[36] Nayar, *India After Nehru*, p. 203.

[37] Baldev, *India from Indira to Morarji*, pp. 19–20. For the full text of MISA and the amendments it saw during the Emergency, see ibid., pp. i–xvi.

one of the 1027 cases put before it; West Bengal 1 out of 311; and Haryana 5 out of 200.[38] Indeed, as an insider later revealed, the review process had been gamed to ensure "secrecy and expedition".[39]

The Emergency gave MISA new impetus. On 29 June an ordinance saw to it that courts were prevented from applying the concept of "natural justice" to detentions under it. Moreover, the grounds for detention could now be withheld from detainees for up to four months.[40] On 15 July, a second ordinance provided for the sequestration of property of those who had "absconded" as well as the arrest of foreign citizens.[41] Two further amendments to MISA enacted by ordinance on 17 October and 16 November made the disclosure of the grounds for arrest at first unnecessary and then confidential.[42] In effect, in less than five months, reason and review were done away with. The next year, in June 1976, MISA was amended yet again to extend the maximum period a detainee could be held from twelve to twenty-four months.[43]

The DIR had an even older history. Collectively, it was a set of 156 rules promulgated via ordinance during the 1962 war to legalise preventive detention and preclude judicial review. In this sense the DIR was essentially a refurbished version of the wartime Defence of India Acts of 1915 and 1939 that could disallow those detained under it the right to legal representation and habeas corpus relief, and ban the publication of documents it deemed "objectionable". In 1969 the rules expired and the Congress, lacking the numbers in parliament, was unable to renew it. But with a fresh

---

[38] *SCR*, vol. 3, p. 41.

[39] Statement of Jagmohan, Deputy Secretary to the Lieutenant Governor, Delhi, no date, SCP, Subject File 12, p. 246.

[40] Previously, Article 22 dictated that grounds for detention be disclosed within three months. Its suspension on 27 June allowed for the amendment. But, in practice, no one was ever released even then. In the words of Delhi District Magistrate Sushil Kumar, it was always a "mechanical exercise": *SCR*, vol. 2, p. 37.

[41] *SW*, 19 July 1975, p. 1.

[42] The ordinances were incorporated into the Maintenance of Internal Security (Amendment) Act on 25 January 1976. They could be applied retroactively from 29 June 1975: *SCR*, vol. 3, p. 40. The November amendment also allowed for the re-arrest of citizens when older detention orders had lapsed. This was done at the instance of Haryana government officials, who had complained to Attorney General Niren De that its High Court was preventing arrests citing a MISA clause that forbade re-arrests: ibid., pp. 66–7.

[43] *SCR*, vol. 1, p. 5.

mandate from the people in 1971, it had them quickly reinstated.[44] On 30 June 1975, five days into the Emergency, the rules were given an expanded mandate and renamed the Defence and Internal Security of India Rules.[45] In one sense, this was more potent than MISA: during the 1977 elections, while those locked up under the DIR were not entitled to postal ballot papers, MISA detainees were. Yet in another, it was MISA that was the more lethal, because under it securing bail was next to impossible; here the DIR was more accommodating.[46]

During the Emergency two novelties rendered the DIR and MISA more redoubtable than before. Prior to June 1975 the two acts had only been used in the country's peripheries and were subject to the scrutiny of moderately independent review panels. But in the new regime even the Hindi belt was not spared and the review process was eliminated.[47]

In principle, all carceral powers came to be vested in the hands of the state governments, whose higher echelons comprised the only officials who could release detainees.[48] However, the chain of command was never clear: when orders challenging state or local bureaucracies came from the Prime Minister's Secretariat, the Home Ministry, or the Central Bureau of Investigation, at times the latter set prevailed over the former; at others, the proximity of the regional *satraps* to Mrs Gandhi and Sanjay meant that they could stave off the centre's influence.[49] For instance, when Delhi's local administrators were accused by the Home Ministry of "misusing" emergency powers, they stood their ground largely because they had the

[44] Mussells, "Democracy and Emergency Rule in India", p. 42.

[45] As the press did at the time, this book will refer to the rules not as DISIR, but by the old acronym, DIR.

[46] See the wireless message from the Deputy Chief Electoral Officer, Rajasthan, to all collectors, Inspector General for Prisons, and the Home Commissioner, 2 March 1977, MHAP, File VI/11034/80/56(299)/ISDVI.

[47] Similarly, district magistrates were stripped of the discretionary role they could play in freeing detainees: *SCR*, vol. 2, pp. 36–8.

[48] For instance, at least eleven figures in Delhi were released on orders from the lieutenant governor or his secretary: ibid., pp. 36, 44.

[49] See, for instance, the bureaucratic tussle between the Ministry of Home Affairs and the Delhi administration to release MISA detainees: ibid., pp. 43, 45. There were also cases where the career bureaucrats of ministries and their politician bosses gave conflicting orders. Here, the latter prevailed, as was the case when Om Mehta, the minister of state for home affairs, and those lower down in the MHA, made inconsistent requests of the Delhi administration: ibid., p. 41.

lieutenant governor's—and metonymically the prime minister's—backing.[50] In another case it appeared that the Home Ministry was calling the shots on arrests, sending out a list of figures it wanted jailed to the Rajasthan government, which unquestioningly did its bidding.[51]

Another law that came in handy was the Conservation of Foreign Exchange and Prevention of Smuggling Activities Act. Enacted in December 1974, it made possible the arrest of hoarders and smugglers before detention orders could be issued. During the Emergency, politicians too were incarcerated under its provisions. Like its counterparts, COFEPOSA was beefed up through the liberal use of parliamentary amendments. In August 1975 detentions under it became harder to challenge.[52] In June the following year it was decided that detainees could be held for up to two years without having to reveal the grounds for arrest,[53] and for a year before they had to be paraded before an advisory board.

So, the government had armed itself with all the legal armour it needed to detain anyone it wished and, as we will see at greater length in Chapter 6, it had begun to do so *before* June 1975. Who, then, were its targets? Among those who went to jail, the most prominent personalities were the leaders of the opposition and the JP Movement: Narayan himself; the CPI(M)'s V.S. Achuthanandan and Jyotirmoy Basu; Jana Sanghis L.K. Advani and Bhairon Singh Shekhawat; Socialists Madhu Dandavate, Madhu Limaye, Sharad Yadav, and Raj Narain; the BLD's Biju Patnaik and Piloo Mody; the Congress (O)'s Morarji Desai; and the Congress' very own Young Turks Ram Dhan, Mohan Dharia, and Chandra Shekhar.[54] Other Congressmen were not spared either: six sitting MLAs in Tripura were locked up for "hobnobbing" with their CPI(M) counterparts.[55] Another Congressman, Bhim Sen Sachar, eighty-two, former chief minister of Punjab, was arrested on 26 July for protesting against the restrictions

---

[50] Statement of Shailja Chandra, Special Secretary, Home Ministry, 17 February 1978, SCP, Subject File 24, pp. 50–8.

[51] *SCR*, vol. 1, p. 88.

[52] Hence a COFEPOSA detention could not be voided even if the grounds for it were "vague", "non-existent", "not relevant", or "invalid for any other reason whatsoever": Austin, *Working a Democratic Constitution*, p. 310.

[53] Previously, it was one year: ibid.

[54] The Young Turks were suspended along with three other Congress MPs—Krishan Kant, Shambhu Nath Mishra, and T. Lakshmikanthamma—on 26 June 1975 for "anti-party activities": *Congress Marches Ahead—XI*, p. 13.

[55] *SCR*, vol. 3, p. 111.

placed on the media. Along with seven others, he had written an open letter, fairly conservative in tone, to the prime minister just two days earlier: "we have no political axe to grind ... we do not challenge your right to arm yourself with additional powers ... the common people of Delhi now talk in hushed tones as they do in communist societies ... we propose to advocate openly the right of public speech and public association and freedom of the press." But R.K. Dhawan, additional private secretary to the prime minister, found even this measured critique seditious: he telephoned Sushil Kumar, Delhi's district magistrate, and had all eight of them arrested under MISA.[56] Two days later, Sachar's son-in-law, the journalist Kuldip Nayar, was incarcerated as well. In similar fashion, Congress party workers in West Bengal opposed to the dominant S.S. Ray-led faction were jailed in June 1976.

Locking up members of the ruling party served Mrs Gandhi's purpose of nipping other potential doubters in the bud. There were many in the middle and higher echelons of the party who contemplated taking a principled stand against the Emergency—for instance, K.C. Pant, the junior home minister, and Karan Singh, the health and family planning minister, both of whom went on a "long drive" together to try and get their heads around the regime in its early days. In the end both chose to step back from the precipice.[57]

The opposition parties were not banned, but their top echelons were imprisoned. Political panjandrums were sent mostly to four jails. A few parliamentarians, including the Jana Sangh's Advani and Vajpayee, and the Socialist party's Madhu Dandavate and Samar Guha, were arrested in Bangalore where they were, as members of a parliamentary delegation, discussing an anti-defection bill.[58] The rest were regrouped in Delhi's Tihar Jail, and in two prisons—at Rohtak and Ambala—in nearby Haryana.[59] In

[56] For the entire letter, see MLP, reel 13.

[57] Interview with Karan Singh in New Delhi on 11 April 2018. "Ultimately, for better or for worse, we decided to support her": Karan Singh, *Autobiography*, p. xvii. Pant had been an unflagging defender of MISA in parliament since 1971. It is unclear what kind of a principled stand he could have taken: *SCR*, vol. 3, pp. 39, 41.

[58] A few days later, Advani and Dandavate were shipped to Rohtak's prison, and, because a habeas corpus petition had been requested in Bangalore, they were transported back for a court hearing. Vajpayee, who had just been operated upon, remained in Bangalore.

[59] At the time, Rohtak's carceral population was nearly twice what it could hold. Ambala was running at full capacity: *SCR*, vol. 3, p. 139.

Tihar, MISA detainees were clustered in three wards and prevented from writing to their families, who were formally informed of the arrests only on 31 August 1975. Soon after, they were allowed visitors once a month, and from October once a week.[60] Few detainees had access to newspapers, the rest not even to the propaganda-filled airwaves. Each prisoner was entitled to a daily allowance of Rs 2.50. This was doled out not in cash but as coupons, the legal tender of the carceral world.

The effects of the absence of due process could be discerned in the nature of punishment for older crimes, which became more severe during the Emergency. For instance, in Secunderabad in December 1975, after spending three years in prison for the murder of a landlord "widely hated for his extortions, atrocities, and violence", two peasants were hanged—despite appeals for clemency from 130 Supreme Court lawyers, six former high court judges, and three former chief justices.[61] Negotiating the prison system, however, was still possible, especially if one belonged to the elite. In March 1976, for instance, Advani, despite being a detainee, was allowed to travel to Gandhinagar on parole to scrutinise and file his nomination papers to the Rajya Sabha.[62] Similarly, *Financial Express* reporter Virendra Kapoor was paroled after his wife appealed to the lieutenant governor's secretary and the paper's editor lobbied the Home Ministry.[63] Others were less lucky: the Jana Sangh's Hans Raj Gupta and Congressman Ram Dhan both tried unsuccessfully to secure parole.[64]

Certainly, one's carceral experience in Emergency India was to an extent a function of one's place in society. In the main, a "caste system" of detainees was maintained across the country. Class A prisoners—MPs, MLAs, and "prominent political leaders"—were typically entitled to fans, radios, cigarettes, "special diets", clothing, bedding, furniture, "60 grams of washing soap", "25 grams of coconut oil", and *en suite* lavatories; Class B cells held political prisoners of a lower stature; and Class C "economic offenders" and

---

[60] Sinha, *Operation Emergency*, p. 82.

[61] Selbourne, *An Eye to India*, p. 334.

[62] He was elected to the Rajya Sabha the next month but remained incarcerated until January 1977: Advani, *A Prisoner's Scrap-Book*, pp. 128–30.

[63] His "crime", admittedly, was trifling: he had tried to prevent one of Sanjay's lieutenants from "thrashing" a "socialist youth": Kapoor, *The Emergency*, p. 101.

[64] The former had fallen sick in prison, and the latter had to visit his family after his "brother suddenly expired": "Arrests and Detentions in Delhi During Emergency", SCP, Subject File 8, pp. 167–70.

"ordinary prisoners".[65] Class A and B convicts were allowed visitors more frequently than their Class C peers; they could enjoy the services of jail libraries and even receive expurgated books and periodicals from friends and family. In Gujarat, all prisoners who paid more than Rs 5000 in taxes—broadly, those in the professions—were bumped up to Class A. Similarly, in the Andaman and Nicobar Islands, class mobility in prisons depended on "social status" and "education". And in Uttar Pradesh, district magistrates were entrusted with a screening process to "prevent anti-social elements and criminals from securing superior class facilities."[66] As in the caste system, those within each category were then subdivided along a branch hierarchy. Within the class of very important prisoners were those such as Morarji Desai and Jayaprakash Narayan, housed outside the prison system in relatively comfortable houses.[67] The Socialists and Sanghis, on the other hand—figures such as Jyotirmoy Basu, Raj Narain, and K.R. Malkani—were kept in solitary confinement. The only exception was Kerala, where all detainees were housed in classless prisons.[68] Division by religion existed too. For instance, in Bangalore, all Muslims, whether political prisoners or not, were clustered together; the same went for Hindus—pickpockets, Anand Margis, and Jana Sanghis shared cells.[69]

Sanitary conditions in the prisons were abysmal. Sewage overflowed and water was only available for a few hours each day. In some prisons, like the Reis Magos Jail in Goa, an inadequate water supply necessitated taking prisoners to nearby lakes where they would replenish their buckets for the day, carrying back as much they could to their cells.[70] At Tihar, ninety-six inmates shared three dry latrines. The chapatis were "half-baked" and the *daal* came with "flies floating on the surface".[71] Inevitably, there was contagion.

The Indian carceral system was already notorious for its congestion, operating at a 20 per cent over-capacity even before the Emergency.[72] It

---

[65] Ibid., pp. 136, 146, 148; "Facilities to MISA Prisoners—Maharashtra", 9 September 1976, in MLP, reel 7.

[66] *SCR*, vol. 3, pp. 138, 147, 145, 139, 150, 149.

[67] Narayan put up at the guest house of the Postgraduate Institute of Medical Education and Research, Chandigarh; Desai, the Haryana State Tourist Centre: ibid., p. 150.

[68] Ibid., pp. 139, 142.

[69] Advani, *My Country, My Life*, pp. 212–13.

[70] *SCR*, vol. 2, p. 39; *SCR*, vol. 3, p. 151.

[71] Nayar, *In Jail*, pp. 22, 29.

[72] Against a capacity of 183,369, Indian jails accommodated 220,146 citizens on

was estimated at the time that the jails would need an additional outlay of Rs 190 crores to get them in good shape.[73] The new regime made even this huge figure appear paltry by comparison. But this could be explained away. For Mrs Gandhi had a disarmingly simple method for measuring her country's carceral population: "It's a small number of people", she said to the *New York Times*, "very small, relative to India's whole population."[74]

Tihar, built to accommodate 1273, housed 4250 inmates.[75] Similar overcrowding obtained elsewhere: in the east, the prison at Jamshedpur built for 137 prisoners housed 1200; in the west, in Maharashtra, four major prisons held twice as many inmates as it was meant to, leading to the expeditious construction of thirty-nine "additional barracks" and a new prison at Kalyan, which became operational in March 1976.[76] In the country's centre, Madhya Pradesh's carceral population was a third as large again as its maximum capacity; thirteen died in the state, either while being detained or within a month of being paroled.[77] Carceral centres in other states piled up bodies as well: 30 in Uttar Pradesh, 16 in Maharashtra, 11 in West Bengal, 8 in Gujarat, 3 in Haryana, and 1 in Bihar.[78] Prisoners were often shuffled from one jail to another in attempts to manage the enlarged penal population.

The quantitative jolt to the prison system was matched with one that could be described as qualitative: unlike the largely youthful and lumpen inmates that it housed before 1975, its new lot were older and frailer, leaving the prison staff entirely unequipped to handle their alimentary and medical needs. Maharashtra's prisons were a case in point: during their incarceration, more than a sixth of the inmates were either hospitalised or

---

1 January 1975: *SCR*, vol. 3, p. 135. For the continuities in the carceral conditions before and during the Emergency—overcrowding, the use of torture, and the resort to expansive and repressive legislation—see Mary Tyler's interview in *Prisoners of Conscience*, dir. Anand Patwardhan (1978), and her memoir, *My Years in an Indian Prison.*

[73] *SCR*, vol. 3, p. 136.

[74] *NYT*, 27 April 1976, p. 11.

[75] *SCR*, vol. 2, p. 39.

[76] Nayar, *The Judgement*, p. 133; *SCR*, vol. 3, pp. 143–4.

[77] "Note on the reply to questionnaire on Treatment in Jails sent by the Government of Madhya Pradesh", 9 January 1978, SCIF, File 41011/9/MP/77-T-4.

[78] *SCR*, vol. 3, pp. 59, 139–40, 144, 149–50.

made to undergo medical treatment. In Mizoram, prisoners frequently contracted diarrhoea and dysentery.[79]

The stress to the prison system is borne out by a number of examples. In the absence of psychiatric hospitals, some states began locking up political prisoners alongside "lunatics".[80] In others, doctors were instructed not to prescribe expensive drugs. Budgetary constraints meant that prisoners sometimes had to be denied spectacles and cervical collars. The jailers were equal victims of the Emergency: in its course, "all leave for jail staff was cancelled, and the warders and matrons were on call twenty-four hours a day seven days a week."[81] When it came to the coercive sterilisation programme in Uttar Pradesh, the state made no distinction between jailer and jailed: it demanded that 1500 citizens on each side of the prison bars be sterilised.[82] The attendant social costs were borne by those outside as well. Detainees complained of how, with fewer hands on the farm, crops were left to rot; bank interest accrued for shopkeepers no longer around to run their enterprises; a Jama'at-i-Islami detainee's brother and mother died from the shock of his arrest; others complained of the stigma of prison, the "loss of respectability" for their families.[83]

Carceral conditions were such that revolts multiplied. In Ambala, female detainees who were routinely beaten up by wardens went on a collective hunger strike, demanding an end to the brutality.[84] Another hunger strike at Hazari Bagh Jail in Bihar resulted in a violent clash with the jail staff, who thrashed the prisoners, throwing two of them into a well and severely injuring a third—an octogenarian who later died in a local hospital. Reading between the lines of the Shah Commission reports is a difficult task, but one thing is certain: its authors used meiosis to conceal what were incontrovertibly graver acts of state violence. In Gujarat, for instance, a scuffle between guards and prisoners ended with a "mild *lathi* charge". In Maharashtra, eighty-nine detainees sustained injuries in a "scuffle" with the wardens. In a Karnataka jail riot, three detainees and four police officers were injured; in another, in Orissa, twenty-seven detainees and wardens were. Five riots occurred in the jails of Madhya Pradesh. Hunger

---

[79] Ibid., pp. 135, 144, 152.

[80] Ibid., p. 144.

[81] Lewis, *Reason Wounded,* p. 166.

[82] *SCR*, vol. 3, p. 194.

[83] All from letters to the Shah Commission, written in English and Marathi, MLP, reel 11.

[84] Lewis, *Reason Wounded,* pp. 144–5.

strikers in Uttar Pradesh were put in fetters and thrown into solitary confinement. Jailbreaks occurred in Calcutta's Presidency Jail, Delhi's Tihar, and Bihar's Bhagalpur. In the first of these, fifty inmates blew their way out of the heavily guarded prison and escaped while some were shot dead by Central Reserve Police officers who had been tipped off.[85]

Torture was routine in prisons and police stations. Early on in the Emergency, thanks to prior restraint, Mrs Gandhi's administration managed to keep its widespread use under wraps, but by around August 1976 it had become common knowledge. By then, independent-minded papers such as the *Indian Express* could with some degree of accuracy mention in their editorials that at least twenty-two citizens had died under duress in prison.[86] After the Emergency, *Blitz*, a popular Bombay weekly, noted how "sadistic maniacs in the police force perpetrated various crimes against victims in their custody during the Emergency. The crimes vary from sexual perversions and molestations, to robbery and murder, putting even the notorious Marquis de Sade to shame."[87] Not even the country's elites were spared: among those subjected to the horrors of the Indian carceral system were C.L. Lakhanpal, president of the Punjab and Haryana High Court; Bhairav Bharati, former Madhya Pradesh MLA and trade unionist who died in prison; Mrinal Gore, Socialist MLA from Bombay, who was locked up in the Akola district prison with a "violent lunatic" and made to share a latrine with a "female criminal leper"; and Sulochana, an actress in her teens who was "molested and stripped every day for thirty days."[88]

The ex-royal and conservative MP Gayatri Devi and her stepson Bhawani Singh—a retired lieutenant colonel who was the eldest son of the former Jaipur maharaja—were arrested under COFEPOSA.[89] The charges against them were trumped up: while the Reserve Bank of India was aware of Gayatri Devi's demesnes in the republic, as well as of her property and trusts in the United Kingdom, the United States, and the Bahamas (not to

[85] *SCR*, vol. 3, pp. 138–9, 142–6, 149.

[86] Sahgal, *Indira Gandhi*, p. 168.

[87] *Blitz*, 28 May 1977, p. 7, cited in Baldev, *India from Indira to Morarji*, p. 62.

[88] Transcript of interview with Madhu Dandavate, Acc. No. 778, NMML Oral History Project, p. 117; Henderson, *Experiment with Untruth*, pp. 36–7. Sometime during the Emergency, Navin Chawla, the lieutenant governor's secretary, suggested that "troublesome *detenues*" be locked up "with the lunatics": *SCR*, vol. 1, p. 39.

[89] The Swatantra MP from Jaipur starting from 1962, she was Maharani of Jaipur until 1971, when royal privileges and titles were abolished.

mention a safe deposit box in an Italian bank), all this information was "lost" on its way to the Enforcement Directorate, which pressed charges against her for concealing foreign income.[90] Kept in a C Class cell at Tihar, she was locked up with fellow ex-royal and MP Vijaya Raje Scindia, once the Rajmata of Gwalior.[91] Scindia had given up the idea of fleeing to Nepal and had, along with her right-hand man Sambhajirao Angre, wound up—for want of space—at Tihar's *phansi kothi* (death row cell).[92] Scindia and Devi were incarcerated with "prostitutes and female criminals" who, according to the latter, "were all over the place; it was like living in a *bazaar* with squabbling women." Four and a half months into her imprisonment she capitulated, writing to Mrs Gandhi to say she had "decided to give up politics ... [I] will not take any further interest in politics as the Swatantra Party has already defunct [*sic*] and I have decided not to join any political party."[93] She secured parole a month later.

The elite may have had it bad, but far worse treatment was meted out to the rest of the population, as the Shah Commission testimonies, memoirs, and Amnesty International reports bear witness.[94] For instance, Rajan, a university student in Calicut, was arrested on 1 March 1976 and taken to Kakkayam, one of the five torture chambers in Kerala, where, after being subjected to the "roller treatment"—whereby a steel roller is weighed down by a couple of police officers and rolled over the victim's legs—he was killed. Another common practice in Emergency India was to put detainees on the "aeroplane": their arms were tied behind them and they were left dangling for long hours by a rope attached to a pulley. The detainees were also stamped on with ammunition boots, beaten "on the spine", made to sit in stress positions, deprived of sleep, made to "lie on slabs of ice", burnt

---

[90] *SCR*, vol. 1, pp. 78–9.

[91] Interviews with Vijaya Raje Scindia and Sambhajirao Angre in Shivpuri and Delhi on 1 September 1987 and 20 November 1989, respectively. As a Jana Sangh MP, Scindia represented Guna, Madhya Pradesh. She had crossed the floor many times, being elected as a Congress MP in 1957 and 1962, before winning on a Swatantra ticket in 1967 and then a Jana Sangh one in 1971.

[92] *Telegraph* (Calcutta), 15 March 2008; Scindia, *Princess*. Other former princes, such as Narendra Singh Judeo, ex-maharaja of Panna, were detained during the Emergency as well: Jaffrelot, *The Hindu Nationalist Movement and Indian Politics*, p. 293.

[93] *SCR*, vol. 1, p. 81.

[94] See, for instance, Lewis, *Reason Wounded*; Varier, *Memories of a Father*; *Amnesty International Report*, p. 131.

with cigarettes, had "electrical live wires inserted" into "the crevices" of their bodies, chilli powder "smeared into [their] nose and rectum", policemen "urinate in their mouths", and made to sodomise and fellate one other. There were occasions when the republic's political masters tried to curb the gratuitous use of torture, such as when the home minister called upon the chief secretaries of the states to desist from "torture and third-degree methods". The request, in this instance as in others, was simply ignored by those lower down the hierarchy.[95]

Torture also served ends that went beyond the quashing of dissent, one of which was to embroil Mrs Gandhi's rivals within the Congress in criminal cases. Jagjivan Ram, agriculture and irrigation minister, was her first target. During the tense weeks of June 1975, Mrs Gandhi had seen him as a potential usurper. Even after the Emergency was declared, suspicions lingered. On 26 June, a rattled Ram told journalist Kuldip Nayar that his phone was being tapped and that "he was expecting arrest."[96] He was not put behind bars, but the police tried to force his lieutenants to discredit him. One of these, P.N. Singh, a member of the Delhi Metropolitan Council who was close to both the Young Turks—Chandra Shekhar in particular—and Ram, and had supported the latter's informal prime ministerial bid, was arrested and taken to a torture chamber at the Red Fort. There he was asked to read aloud the following declaration: "I am asked by Jagjivan Ram, the [sic] union minister of India, to plot assassination against [sic] Mrs Indira Gandhi, Sanjay Gandhi and Barooah."[97] Despite being tortured, Singh refused. Shortly after, the police arrested Kulwant Kumar Gupta, an associate of Ram's private secretary Triveni Sahai. Gupta was taken to Tihar and asked by a CID officer to inveigle Sahai into acknowledging that he had, acting on Ram's instructions, given Gupta Rs 2000 to hire a hitman to bump off Mrs Gandhi, Sanjay, and Barooah. In the end, Sahai was taken to Tihar, but he too said nothing that could incriminate Ram. As for Ram himself, he waited out the rest of the Emergency before turning coat and floating his own party, the Congress for Democracy.

Torture was also used to gather information on the whereabouts of political fugitives. According to Kuldip Nayar, "in Delhi's Red Fort, a very

<hr>

95 *Torture of Political Prisoners in India*, pp. 13–14; Selbourne, *An Eye to India*, p. 322; "Torture of Political Prisoners in India", March 1976, in MLP, reel 2; Morris-Jones, "Whose Emergency—India's or Indira's?", p. 460.
96 Nayar, *The Judgement*, p. 44. His paranoia was not unfounded: *SCR*, vol. 1, p. 31.
97 Baldev, *India from Indira to Morarji*, pp. 283–4.

sophisticated room filled with the latest gadgets from abroad was used to extort confessions. Floodlights were focused on a *detenu* for hours with sound effect in the background, to break him down. Intelligence officers would interrogate him for long and record all his movements and remarks through audio-visual tapes."[98]

Among those tortured were the two brothers of George Fernandes, the socialist trade-union leader who was probably the most active member of the underground—the Delhi Police had even placed a Rs 5000 price on his head.[99] One of them, Michael Fernandes, a trade-union leader at the Indian Telephone Industries in Bangalore, was imprisoned in the city under MISA on 23 December 1975, where he languished for five months. Lawrence Fernandes, the other brother, filed a habeas corpus petition in February 1976, hoping to have Michael released, but instead wound up in prison himself three months later.[100] On the evening of 1 May, the Corps of Detectives, Karnataka's specialised investigation agency, dragged Lawrence from his house and took him to a torture chamber where "he was received with a slap so stunning" that he fainted.[101] Upon coming around he found himself naked, receiving a shower of *lathi* blows from ten constables. They demanded George Fernandes' whereabouts, certain that Lawrence, who accompanied his brother's wife and son from Bangalore to Madras in September 1975, was withholding information. Upon reviving, he found he had been "put on the aeroplane".[102]

He was left dangling until 3 a.m., after which he passed out a second time. He was deprived of food and a police officer threatened to urinate in his mouth when he asked for water. The next morning he was in such bad shape that the officers feared producing him in court. He was shunted to and fro by the Corps of Detectives between their torture chamber, the lock-up in Bangalore's Vyalikaval Police Station, and Davangere Jail in north Karnataka, where he was finally thrown in a cell "full of cockroaches, bugs, and mosquitoes". When he complained of chest pains, the police took him

---

[98] Nayar, *The Judgement*, p. 85.

[99] "Alleged Wrongful Confinement and Torture of Shri Lawrence Fernandes by the Police and Maltreatment in Jail", SCP, Subject File 10, p. 4.

[100] See the letter their mother, Alice Fernandes, wrote to the president of India—copies were sent to the prime minister and other members of the central and Kerala governments as well. They are reproduced in Nayantara Sahgal's biography of her cousin: *Indira Gandhi*, pp. 166–7.

[101] Rawla and Mudgal, *All the Prime Minister's Men*, p. 99.

[102] Deposition of Lawrence Fernandes, 3 February 1978, SCP, Subject File 10, p. 33.

to a hospital in Bangalore where they denied him the recommended, but possibly incriminating, X-ray. It was later discovered that the *lathi* blows had fractured a metatarsal bone. By this time they had doctored documents and framed him for blowing up railway lines in the state—in truth, his brother George was responsible for some of these incidents, and Lawrence had nothing to do with them. "Being a bloody Christian", he could not have been telling the truth, the cops surmised, taking away his rosary.[103]

On the morning of 10 May he was told he would be produced before a magistrate, whom he had to convince that he had, in fact, been arrested the same day at a bus stop. They threatened to torture the rest of his family if he said anything amiss. Drugged and dizzy, Lawrence was then schlepped barefoot to the court room, the swellings on his legs bruising and ballooning. He burst into tears before the magistracy but said nothing, fearing reprisal. After the hearing he was heavily drugged again. This resulted in a burst of dysentery that lasted three days. He was later locked up in a reeking cell in the state capital's central prison. The two brothers were now in the same jail but were prevented from seeing each other. Lawrence went on a two-day hunger strike—in which he was joined by other prisoners, including Madhu Dandavate, general secretary of the Socialist party—demanding better accommodation and an end to solitary confinement.[104] At the end of his incarceration Lawrence was but a "bag of bones, for he had lost twenty kilograms."[105]

Another Bangalore family to suffer the worst of the police state were the Reddys. In order to locate George Fernandes, the police arrested Pattabhi and Snehalata Reddy in Bangalore in May 1976. The husband was a Telugu poet and film producer, the wife a theatre actress who had appeared in a few films. Pattabhi's 1970 movie *Samskara*—adapted from U.R. Ananthamurthy's eponymous novel, a trenchant disquisition on Brahmanical rule in the countryside—in which Snehalata played the lead, had made the duo the face of the Kannada New Wave, the temporary ban on the film to appease livid Brahmins burnishing their radical credentials.[106] The Reddys were Socialists

---

[103] Ibid., pp. 40, 37, 29; "Alleged Wrongful Confinement and Torture of Shri Lawrence Fernandes by the Police and Maltreatment in Jail", SCP, Subject File 10, p. 10.

[104] Statement of Lawrence Fernandes, 5 May 1978, SCP, Subject File 10, p. 109.

[105] He was released on 7 March 1977: Rawla and Mudgal, *All the Prime Minister's Men*, p. 100.

[106] *Indian Express*, 3 January 1970, p. 10.

who had in the early months of the Emergency helped George Fernandes establish his underground network in the South—especially after S. Venkatram, who headed the Socialist party's Central Parliamentary Board, was arrested—and sabotage railway lines, in the process eliciting the suspicions of the local police.[107] First, the police carted away the Reddys' children, Konarak and Nandana, and questioned them about George Fernandes' whereabouts. Later, Snehalata's octogenarian father was interrogated all night. Finally, they arrested Snehalata under MISA and put her in a C Class detention cell infested with bandicoots, "without air or even a window", and a hole in the floor that passed for a lavatory.[108] Eight months of incarceration broke her completely, after which she was released. She died a month later, leaving behind a diary cataloguing the perversions of the jail superintendent.[109]

Next to political opponents and their sympathisers, members of banned organisations formed the largest contingent amongst the incarcerated. On 4 July, twenty-six outfits were declared illegal.[110] They belonged to five groups: the Naxalites, Anand Marg, Jama'at-i-Islami, RSS, and separatists such as the Mizo National Front.[111] Within a month, "2300 RSS men, 700 Jama'at members, and 400 Naxalites" were sent to jail.[112] Many of them were tortured.

The Naxalites were a peasant army that, from its beginnings in three villages in West Bengal in 1967, had mushroomed across a quarter of Indian territory.[113] Already whittled down by the state's counterinsurgency operations between 1969 and 1972—the leader of the movement, Charu Mazumdar, died in police custody in 1972—the Naxalites were decimated further by the 25,000 arrests made during the Emergency.[114] Students were

---

[107] Reddy, *Baroda Dynamite Conspiracy Case*, p. 85; Rawla and Mudgal, *All the Prime Minister's Men*, p. 107. See also the autobiography of T.V. Rajeswar, whose role in arresting George Fernandes earned him the president's police medal: *India*, pp. 80–5.

[108] Reddy, *A Prison Diary*, p. 10.

[109] Ibid. She was released on parole on 13 December 1976 and died on 20 January.

[110] The ban was invoked using the DIR. The list can be found in *The Emergency: Its Impact*, p. 8.

[111] The latter was banned a month later on 6 August: *SW*, 9 August 1975, p. 1.

[112] Limaye, *Janata Party Experiment*, vol. 1, p. 133.

[113] By the early 1970s, Naxalite cadres were to be found in West Bengal, Bihar, Uttar Pradesh, the Punjab, Jammu and Kashmir, Andhra Pradesh, and Kerala: Dasgupta, *The Naxalite Movement*, pp. 28–30.

[114] Kohli, *Democracy and Discontent's*, pp. 149, 277–84.

frequent targets. Jampal Chandra Sekhar Prasad, one of the leaders of the Progressive Democratic Students Union of Hyderabad's Osmania University, and Neelam Rama Chandraiah, a member of the Andhra Pradesh Committee of the CPI (Marxist-Leninist), were both tortured by the police. They remained silent. Failing to extract information about the movement, the police hauled them to a nearby forest where they were tortured again and shot dead.[115] A similar fate met the Progressive Organisation for Women, many of whose members were Naxalites. Most of its top leadership was behind bars by early 1976, as was its president, who was tortured for eighteen days.[116]

The Anand Marg was a Hindu revivalist outfit established in 1955 by a railway accountant and sometime swami, Prabhat Ranjan Sarkar, the mind behind the Progressive Utilisation Theory—"Proutism" for short—a system of thought whose spiritual thrust was "destined to eliminate the economic doctrines of communism and capitalism for ever."[117] Despite its esotericism, the Marg was no small cult: it counted 250,000 members, including "60,000 overseas", whose ultimate aim was to establish a dictatorship of the "*sadvipras*", the spiritually enlightened.[118] Violence, however, was not incompatible with such spirituality: its founder ordered a hit on seven disillusioned Margis in 1970—only one escaped alive. Anand Margis also unsuccessfully attempted to bump off the chief justice of India in 1975. The same year, in what was perhaps the biggest political assassination since M.K. Gandhi's in 1948, they blew up a stage, killing L.N. Mishra, a cabinet minister who was also the Congress' chief fundraiser.[119] With such attacks on government figures, Sarkar hoped the state, fearing more reprisals, would desist from

---

[115] Rawla and Mudgal, *All the Prime Minister's Men*, p. 109.

[116] Scott, "Emerging from the Emergency", pp. 28–9.

[117] Kishore, *Anand Marg*, pp. 3–16; Drieberg and Mohan, *Emergency in India*, pp. 68–9.

[118] Mussells, "Democracy and Emergency Rule in India", pp. 153–4.

[119] Kishore, *Soiling the Saffron Robe*, pp. 28–32; *TOI*, 24 June 1975, p. 5. As of 2014, the Marg boasts two million adherents across 180 countries. They continue to sporadically make international news: in 1976 they knifed an Indian High Commission official in London; in 1978 bombed the Hilton Hotel in Sydney; and in 1995 airdropped an arms cache that included "hundreds of AK-47s" via a Danish gunrunner: Sabyasachi Bandopadhyay, "Explained: Ananda Magra [*sic*], a controversial road", *Indian Express*, 11 December 2014 (https://indian-express.com/article/cities/kolkata/explained-ananda-magra-a-controversial-road/), accessed on 1 September 2018.

"hounding" him for the 1970 murders.[120] As was to be expected, his plan backfired. When the Emergency was declared, the Ministry of Information and Broadcasting went on a war footing with a campaign of calumny that played on contemporary homophobia: its propaganda carried quotes from Sarkar's wife insinuating she left him because of his "filthy acts", which included "convincing" boys that they were girls in a previous incarnation and then sleeping with them. Sarkar himself had been in prison since 1971 and, along with eight henchmen, was convicted in a much-publicised trial in 1976. Acephalous, defamed, and forced underground, this cult posed virtually no threat to Emergency India. Nevertheless, in the eyes of the regime it paid to exaggerate its potential. So, just as the Naxalite threat was inflated to attack strikers and protesters of all stripes, the categorising of state employees as Anand Margis served to rid government of possible critics.[121]

The Jama'at-i-Islami, a Muslim revivalist body established in 1941, was by far the most anodyne organisation banned during the Emergency. While initially committed to the creation of an Islamic state, three decades of powerlessness had mellowed its once-firebrand leadership which, by the mid-1970s, was lending support to Congress candidates and even undertaking social work with the Arya Samaj, its Hindu equivalent.[122] In 1970, the JI resolved to work within the confines of "secularism" and "democracy". It concentrated its efforts on bettering the condition of Muslims: improving literacy, encouraging charity, defending the autonomy of Muslim personal laws, and the like.[123] That it was banned—ostensibly for "fanning communal frenzy among Muslims"—revealed less about the organisation than it did the lineaments of Indian secularism, which for the state meant a commit-

---

[120] Chand Joshi, "Ananda Marg: The bloody face of religion", *India Today*, 17 April 2015 (https://www.indiatoday.in/magazine/indiascope/story/19761231-ananda-marg-the-bloody-face-of-religion-819538-2015-04-17), accessed on 1 September 2018.

[121] See, for instance, the case of S.N. Sharma, a Jaipur-based advocate detained under MISA, and his wife, a lecturer at the Maharani College fired from her job: Dayal and Bose, *The Shah Commission Begins*, pp. 97–100.

[122] *TOI*, 10 November 1974, p. 4.

[123] Ahmad, *Islamism and Democracy in India*; Hasan, "Indian Muslims since Independence", p. 821. The JI's interests in electoral politics were restricted to a handful of districts in Jammu and Kashmir, where it contested elections, occasionally sending a few legislators to the state assembly: Wright, "Muslims and the 1977 Indian Elections", p. 1212.

ment to a kind of "even-handedness" that impelled it to ban Muslim organisations alongside Hindu ones, often with scarce regard for any sense of proportionality: compared to the RSS, the JI boasted tiny cadres, a marginal presence in but a few enclaves, and a shifty ideology that had little purchase in the currents of Indian intellectual life.[124] During the Emergency, a Jama'at youth leader was arrested for "planning to dynamite" a power station.[125] Several JI figures raising money for the organisation found themselves incarcerated for spreading "propaganda".[126]

The objectives of the Mizo National Front, an insurgent group founded in 1961 and operating in the Mizo hills of Assam, oscillated between demanding secession and greater regional autonomy, depending on conditions of the day. When it was banned in 1975, the MNF's main grievance was the violent rule of the armed forces that had "governed" the area for well over a decade, crippling the tribal economy and causing a man-made famine—the military administrators drew inspiration from Operation Starvation, Britain's infamous counterinsurgency in Malaysia in 1951—that decimated the Mizos.[127] As with the ban on the Marg, the decision to supress the MNF was part of a larger propaganda campaign. Indeed, the Emergency regime took credit for "pacifying" the North East, where local tribesmen had waged a low-intensity insurgency against the Indian state, whose sparse redistributive and bureaucratic—but abundant paramilitary—presence had alienated citizens and failed to supplant tribal loyalties with national ones. During the Emergency, Mrs Gandhi's regime, after claiming that it had "succeeded" in convincing the Naga and Mizo underground movements of the "futality [sic] of pursuing the path of violence", signed accords with the two groups in November 1975 and July 1976, respectively.[128] In the event, not many Nagas and Mizos wound up behind bars: 99 and 206, respectively.[129] All the same, the peace borne out of the brief escalation of para-

---

124 *TOI*, 5 July 1975, p. 1. Indeed, while the RSS could count some two to three million members among its ranks, the corresponding figure for the JI was 2831: *Economist*, 24 January 1976, p. 32; Agwani, "God's Government", p. 266.

125 *TOI*, 17 October 1975, p. 6.

126 *SCR*, vol. 3, p. 121; *TOI*, 13 July 1975, p. 7.

127 In March 1966, less than six weeks after she took office, Mrs Gandhi had the air force carpet-bomb Aijal—as Aizawl was then known—the capital of Mizo Hills district: Rangasami, "Mizoram", pp. 655, 661.

128 See the note by P.P. Shrivastav, Director (NE), Ministry of Home Affairs, 7 January 1977, MHAP, File 5/22/76-RP.

129 *SCR*, vol. 3, p. 134.

military violence that was followed by sweeteners to the rebel leadership turned out to be short-lived. Radical elements of the Naga and Mizo militants dissociated themselves from the groups that signed the accords, leading to a renewed bout of confrontation and leaving unaddressed the structural problems at the heart of both north-eastern societies: the bloated presence of the armed forces and the wall of silence around them; a traditionalist and moribund economy; and the dreary existence of the majority, marked by surveillance and starvation.[130]

The largest of the banned organisations was the Rashtriya Swayamsevak Sangh. Banning the RSS had been on the cards for a while. As early as 8 January—six months before the Emergency—S.S. Ray had written to Mrs Gandhi asking her to arrest Jayaprakash Narayan and ban the RSS. When Kuldip Nayar got wind of this, he immediately alerted the *Indian Express* as well as *Motherland*, the Jana Sangh daily, which carried a story on 30 January suggesting that the ban would take effect in four days. Suppression was contemplated on many other occasions too, the saffron brigade having long been a thorn in the flesh of the prime minister, who correctly identified it as the linchpin of Narayan's movement.[131] When the Jana Sangh, the RSS' political wing, organised a demonstration in Delhi in March 1974 she had personally handed the inspector general of police "a list of leaders she wanted arrested".[132] When this was met with some resistance she had, with Dhawan and Sanjay's collaboration—in one of the first instances of the latter wielding informal power in the capital—some of the city's administrators transferred. As early into the Emergency as 26 June 1975, she laid into the RSS, contrasting her democratic convictions to its totalitarian tendencies:

> The forces at work for the destruction of our democracy were similar to Nazism. Nazism functioned through small groups which infiltrated various sections of national life creating misunderstanding and confusion. Sometimes it made scapegoat of a minority in the country like Germany where the Nazis made scapegoat of the Jews and exterminated them in millions [*sic*]. This was the method of the RSS which was an important wing of the Jan Sangh [*sic*].[133]

---

[130] *TOI*, 5 September 1975, p. 1; *TOI*, 20 November 1975, p. 1; Rangasami, "Mizoram", pp. 653–62; Srikhanth and Thomas, "Naga Resistance Movement and the Peace Process in Northeast India", p. 68 *et passim*.

[131] See Chapter 6.

[132] Nayar, *The Judgement*, pp. 26–7.

[133] Ibid., p. 38.

On 22 July, in her speech before the Lok Sabha, she played on the totalitarian metaphor, defending its aptness on two grounds. First, she deplored "the type of training that they give to younger people in their *shakhas* [local branches of the RSS], the violence they preach." And second, she described them as fascists because "fascism is the use of falsehood. Over and above everything, it is the propagation of the big lie. It is the use of whispering campaigns, the search for scapegoats. This has been the major weapon of the Jan Sangh and the RSS."[134] In all, 2794 RSS people were incarcerated during the Emergency.[135]

Besides the opposition and the banned organisations, Mrs Gandhi trained her eye on university campuses. "Noble institutions of learning", she would later suggest, had "turned into hot-beds of political intrigue."[136] In Emergency India, quick work was made of academic freedom. On 25 and 26 July the police conducted a massive operation at Delhi University, arresting 175 students and twenty-five lecturers. In particular, efforts were made to cripple the Delhi University Teachers Association, which at the time was dominated by the RSS' student union, the Akhil Bharatiya Vidyarthi Parishad—teachers too could be members of this student body. To this end ABVP leader and Delhi University Students' Union president Arun Jaitley, and DUTA as well as ABVP president Om Prakash Kohli were arrested, the latter even tortured.[137] In Ludhiana, a leader of the Students' Federation of India was shot dead, and in Bhopal, university students were forced to attend Youth Congress rallies. To monitor student activity, police inspectors went undercover, enrolling themselves as students and spying on dissenters. But universities, Barooah clarified, had no reason to fear such activity, for "a policeman is like a doctor, preventing as well as curing violence."[138] By January 1976 a number of politics departments across the country were operating "at half strength", their numbers whittled down by arrests and intimidation.[139]

---

[134] *Lok Sabha Debates*, vol. 53, no. 2 (22 July 1975), col. 46.

[135] Jaffrelot, *The Hindu Nationalist Movement in India*, p. 276.

[136] Indira Gandhi to Justice J.C. Shah, 21 November 1977, MHAP, File VI/11034/80/56(328)/ISDVI.

[137] On Jaitley's experience of the Emergency, see Kapoor, *The Emergency*, p. 34ff. Kohli, who was lame in one leg, was forced to stand in jail for twenty-four hours at a stretch: Mankekar and Mankekar, *Decline and Fall of Indira Gandhi*, p. 49.

[138] Selbourne, *An Eye to India*, p. 165.

[139] Ibid., p. 164.

In addition to those arrested for dissent, real or imagined, others were detained under MISA for failing to grease the wheels of illegal endeavours. The detention of twelve inspectors of the Textile Committee is a case in point. In April 1976 a consignment of textiles meant for export by a company called Indira International wound up at the committee's Delhi office. During their routine check on the quality of the goods, the customs officers discovered that the power-loom cloth samples had been "misdeclared" as mill-made—the two were subject to different taxes—enabling Indira International to falsely claim a higher duty drawback.[140] Soon, a representative of the company arrived and threatened the customs officers, suggesting that the company belonged to Amteshwar Anand, Sanjay's mother-in-law, and that they would have "to pay the price" for "harassment".[141] And sure enough they did. On 1 June, two customs inspectors were arrested. The Central Bureau of Investigation and the Delhi Police—both competing "to take the laurels for these unjustified detentions"—were asked to frame the arrested men for "corrupt practices", "plotting to overthrow the government", and "bringing [sic] bad name to the country" by allowing "sub-standard" textiles to find their way into foreign markets.[142] Detention orders under MISA were served to all twelve officers, who were then packed off to Tihar. Such occurrences, it might be noted in passing, are common to all authoritarian regimes, which, once established, devour not only their enemies but even their agents.

In another episode, IAS officer Mangal Behari, who had been appointed chairman of the Rajasthan State Electricity Board in September 1974 for a three-year tenure, was on 30 June 1975 transferred to the Revenue Board at Ajmer by the chief minister. The reason was, he told the Shah Commission, that he had refused a demand from the Prime Minister's Secretariat a few weeks prior to the transfer. Behari was to send a hundred trucks and 10,000 workers of the RSEB gratis to rally in support of Mrs Gandhi on 20 June. In his testimony to the Shah Commission, the state's chief minister, Harideo Joshi, admitted that he was behind the transfer, but went on defend his decision: "Behari should consider himself

---

[140] The so-called "duty drawback" is a tariff rebate to make manufactures more competitive.

[141] In truth, the company's proprietor was Indira Doddy, but Anand had "considerable financial interest in the firm": *SCR*, vol. 1, p. 67; Dayal and Bose, *The Shah Commission Begins*, p. 40.

[142] *SCR*, vol. 1, pp. 65–6.

lucky that he had not been arrested under MISA."[143] He added that he had in fact done Behari a favour for which he had had to bend over backwards—and "because of this, I was accused of being soft to [*sic*] Anand Marg and RSS people."[144]

The objective of the regime, in short, was to create an atmosphere of fear where MISA, or the threat of it, had become, in Bose and Dayal's words, "a way of everyday administration".[145] What was once an emergency provision designed for exceptional circumstances had effectively become the new norm. In some cases the act was used quite straightforwardly as a tool for extortion. For instance, an accountant and three of his associates from Bahadurgarh in Haryana were jailed on Bansi Lal's orders because they refused to "donate" money to him.[146] Old scores, too, were settled with MISA. Primila Lewis, a social worker who had campaigned for a minimum wage for labourers on farms owned by Mrs Gandhi and B.K. Nehru in Mehrauli, was locked up and even deprived parole to see her ailing father.[147] Foreign nationals were not spared either. India's jails housed at least 377 Pakistanis, 49 Bangladeshis, 83 Iranians, and 7 "foreigners" from unnamed countries who had overstayed their visas.[148]The logic of arresting based on "lists" produced curious results: there were cases of mistaken identity that were never corrected—the people wrongly detained were not released.[149] In other cases "detention orders were issued against persons who had already died."[150] In some instances the detaining authorities behaved as though they were the thought police: H.R. Khan, the editor of an Uttar Pradesh weekly *Operation Kanauj*, was arrested because he only "profess[ed] outward support" to the Emergency when in fact he "had no

---

[143] To Joshi's credit, he was probably speaking the truth. Mrs Gandhi only reluctantly agreed to reinstate him in December 1976: "Yes, but an eye should be kept on him from time to time"," she noted at the time: *SCR*, vol. 1, p. 89.

[144] Dayal and Bose, *The Shah Commission Begins*, p. 112.

[145] Ibid., p. 38.

[146] "Detentions Under MISA during the Emergency in Haryana and the Treatment of the *Detenus* in Jail", no date, SCIF, File A-41011/40/77-T4.

[147] *SCR*, vol. 2, p. 44.

[148] All were detained during the Emergency under MISA: *SCR*, vol. 3, pp. 60, 94, 100, 127; *Prisoners of Conscience*, dir. Anand Patwardhan (1978). In Rajasthan, another fifty-three were detained "on account of alleged suspicious association with Pakistanis": *SCR*, vol. 3, p. 106.

[149] See the case of Prabir Purkayastha, a JNU student, in Prakash, *Emergency Chronicles*, p. 28ff.

[150] *SCR*, vol. 3, pp. 88-9.

faith in it"—it was contended that he "inwardly opposed the policies of the Congress".[151] The profile of those arrested suggested a lack of method in the madness: *anybody* could be incarcerated under MISA without charge. Burglars, "ordinary criminals", black marketeers, juvenile delinquents, hawkers, trespassers, "eve-teasers",[152] bootleggers, dacoits, "*matka* gamblers",[153] "smugglers of foodgrains", blue-collar workers, shopkeepers who failed to display marked down prices for their wares in line with the new policy to roll back inflation, ganja dealers, opium smugglers, moneylenders, "receivers of stolen properties", militants, former royals, functionaries, pamphleteers, party workers, teenagers, trade unionists, farmers, lawyers, doctors, teachers, businessmen, "prostitutes and pimps"—all were part of the silent 110,000 locked up in Mrs Gandhi's prisons.[154]

The Media: Prior Restraint and Propaganda

If political opponents of all kinds wound up in prison, the free press fared no better. It was in the early 1970s that Mrs Gandhi developed her aversion to the media. At the time, she had felt, perhaps not unjustifiably, that the press had collectively waged a campaign against her, opposing the nationalisations of 1969, railing against the ascendancy of the Congress Left, and siding with the judiciary and the JP Movement. Confirming her suspicion that the private media wanted her head on a platter was the press reaction to the 24 June judgment. The editorial headlines said it all: "A Time to Go", declared the *Hindustan Times*; resignation was "The Only Way" for the *Statesman*, "The Only Course" for the *Indian Express*.[155]

Why such animus? Much of the Anglophone press was owned at the time by India's largest industrial houses, legislative efforts since 1971 to diffuse ownership having foundered.[156] In 1974 the government had tried again to

---

[151] Ibid., p. 117.

[152] A South Asian euphemism for men who harass women in public that caught on in the 1950s: Misri, "Eve-Teasing", pp. 305–7.

[153] A kind of numbers racket. For a cinematic portrayal, see *Dharmatma*, a 1975 Bollywood remake of *The Godfather* whose protagonist is a *matka* baron.

[154] Collectively, they were dubbed "anti-social elements": *SCR*, vol. 2, pp. 59–62; *SCR*, vol. 3, pp. 43, 49, 64, 124; "A Report on the Scrutiny of MISA Detention Files of Andhra Pradesh State", SCIF, File 41011/10/77/AP-T-4; *SW*, 5 July 1975; MLP, reel 10.

[155] These editorials are reproduced *in extenso* in Sinha, *Operation Emergency*, pp. 33–5.

[156] Verghese, "Press Censorship Under Indira Gandhi", p. 221.

limit the power of the press by directing newspapers to publish no more than ten pages daily on account of a newsprint shortage.[157] This directive, though, had been struck down by the Supreme Court. But given the minuscule readership in India—just about 1.5 per cent of the country's citizens were newspaper subscribers, and only a quarter of these read the Anglophone dailies—Mrs Gandhi's obsession with blaming the media for the republic's ills and her own unpopularity was a clear indication of authoritarian leanings.[158] "Freedom of the press has come to mean the freedom to attack Indira Gandhi and to dub as toadies anyone who supports her," she said to the Indian Federation of Working Journalists two weeks into the Emergency, referring to herself, as one does, in the third person.[159] "Doctors bury their mistakes. Lawyers hang them. But journalists put theirs on the front page," she said on another occasion.[160]

In an interview with Agence France-Presse in early 1976, by which time the prior restraint regime was well in place, she justified censorship by suggesting that the fourth estate was built on a conservative superstructure: "most of the press belongs to the big business. It is not an independent press."[161] Speaking to the Rajya Sabha, she took this argument to its logical conclusion: "Once there were no newspapers, there was no agitation. The agitation was in the pages of the newspapers. If you ask why there is censorship of the press, this is reason why."[162] Her litany of complaints against the press included the charge that newspapermen "are so western-oriented that today they take all their ideas from there [*sic*]." Worse, the press was given to criticism. "If you have a press that is against everything that is being done and is constantly saying that nothing is being done and it is of no importance, then it breaks the country's spirit."[163]

---

[157] Baldev, *India from Indira to Morarji*, p. 261.

[158] As early as 1968, Mrs Gandhi was castigating the press for not realising that "freedom cannot exist without responsibility ... let it not undermine the confidence and spirit of the people by speaking only of the failures and not of the victories of the people." At the time of the Emergency, the aggregate daily circulation of all newspapers in the country was 9.4 million; of all papers in English 2.3 million: Pendakur, "Mass Media during the 1975 National Emergency in India", pp. 36, 39.

[159] Austin, *Working a Democratic Constitution*, p. 311.

[160] Mehta, *The New India*, p. 65.

[161] *SSWIG*, vol. 3, p. 752.

[162] Gandhi, *Era of Discipline*, p. 37.

[163] *SSWIG*, vol. 3, p. 752.

It followed, as already noted, that one of the first actions of the new regime was to cut the power supply to the printing presses of the capital's leading papers. By the next evening, 26 June, the government had the censorship apparatus up and running. The catalyst for the speedy process was one of Sanjay's relatives, Kuldip Narang, a "fledgling businessman" who supplied a copy of the censorship rules and bureaucratic norms that had evolved around the Marcos regime in the Philippines.[164] This document, which was handed to him by friends in Delhi's American embassy and then in turn to Sanjay, served as the blueprint for the Emergency's prior restraint regime.

Soon, reshuffles moved with dispatch. The principal information officer (PIO), Dr A.R. Baji, was appointed chief censor. Within weeks he in turn was replaced by the even more compliant Harry J. D'Penha, until then Baji's PIO. A joint secretary of the Prime Minister Secretariat, P.N. Behl, was given the reins of the All India Radio's news services division. On the second day of the Emergency, Vidya Charan Shukla, replacing Inder Kumar Gujral as information and broadcasting (I&B) minister, was in effect anointed the cynosure of the censorship architecture. Shukla brought with him to the new job his right-hand man K.N. Prasad, an IB and CBI alumnus who had served under him as joint secretary when he headed the Ministry of Defence Production.[165]

Changes to personnel paved the way for more structural reform. Bureaucratic and legal sanction for the new press regime moved quickly: a Home Ministry order approved it on 26 June, and a presidential order legitimised it the next day. As early as 30 June, Shukla directed that censor officers "be stationed at newspaper offices in each major centre of publication, beginning with Delhi."[166] A few days later the newly minted blue pencillers were supplied handbooks which detailed every possible press transgression that they were to detect and expunge.[167] The commandments

---

[164] Kuldip Narang, whose wife was a cousin of Mrs Gandhi's, was probably aware of the high regard in which Filipino authoritarianism was held by Sanjay. "One of the few books" that adorned his bookshelf was Ferdinand Marcos' *The Democratic Revolution in the Philippines*, a copy which the dictator had gifted his mother: Thakur, *All the Prime Minister's Men*, p. 150; Nayar, *The Judgement*, p. 25; Dhar, *Indira Gandhi, the "Emergency", and Indian Democracy*, p. 329.

[165] Dayal and Bose, *Shah Commission Begins*, p. 191.

[166] Kapur, *What Price Perjury?*, p. 202.

[167] Guidelines were issued on 3 July 1975 and revised with added strictures on 4 and 13 July. Shukla was aided by K.N. Prasad, Harry J. D'Penha, and A.J. Kidwai, secretary of the information and broadcasting ministry: *SCR*, vol. 1, p. 34.

could only be implemented, not divulged, and measures were taken to prevent the handbooks from being leaked.[168] When the leak happened nonetheless, newspapermen learnt that they were encouraged to partake in "suppressing news themselves" and do "nothing to promote feelings of enmity" between classes.[169] Censorship was imposed under Rule 48 of the Defence of India Rules and defined in the most expansive terms possible: the publication of "any matter relating to [any] subject" could be suppressed.[170] Added to this were prior restraint or "pre-censorship"—as the contemporary media called it—injunctions.

Thus, all news relating to arrests, detentions, or the nature of the Emergency had to be cleared by the I&B apparatus before it could be printed. One of the first orders the censors sent out was to prohibit the papers from reporting the ongoing Supreme Court proceedings against Mrs Gandhi and the upcoming parliamentary session. At various instances, censors proscribed the publication of court judgments and parliamentary proceedings; reports of strikes, protests, and factionalism in the Youth Congress and the parent party; arms deals with the United States; news of inflation; stories on the north-eastern insurgencies; opinion pieces that criticised turncoats who after years of opposition had joined the Congress, made analogies between British and postcolonial carceral policies, or suggested the need for mediation between Delhi's rulers and opposition parties.[171] By the end of July, a thriving media that was once the "freest between the Rhine and the Japan Sea" was reduced to a collection of party organs.[172]

The momentum had been built. On 5 August the censors rehearsed plans that would allow them to disconnect the telex machines of potentially dissenting citizens by using a cocktail of repressive legislation, both DISIR,

---

[168] Transcript of *New York Times* reporter Anthony Lukas' interview with George Verghese, editor of the *Hindustan Times*, "Press Censorship in India", p. 4, in MLP, reel 2.

[169] The guidelines are reproduced in Selbourne, *An Eye to India*, pp. 374–5. See rules 1 and 11.

[170] Powers conferred to the state under Rule 48 of the DIR were wrested from the Home Ministry and placed in the hands of the I&B ministry: *SCR*, vol. 1, p. 36.

[171] *SCR*, vol. 1, pp. 35–7; Notes from Home Secretary, Gandhinagar, to Home Secretary, New Delhi, 6, 19, and 30 September 1975, MHAP, File II-14011/35/75-S&P(D-IV) KW 4; Hiro, *Inside India Today*, pp. 266–7; Sorabjee, *The Emergency*, pp. 26–38.

[172] Lukas, "India is as Indira Does", p. 89.

1975 and the Indian Telegraph Act, 1885.[173] Over the next few months people and presses to have their telephones and teleprinters disconnected included the United Press International, Reuters, R. Ramanujan of *Newsweek*, William Borders of the *New York Times*, Jacques R. Leslie Jr. of the *Los Angeles Times*, Werner Adam of the *Frankfurter Allgemeine*, and Carlos Widmann of *Süddeutsche Zeitung*.[174] The problem lay not just with the foreign press. For those "anti-national" Indian journalists that hung about the Press Club of India, said Yunus, Mrs Gandhi's press attaché,

> earn more money writing for English or American papers than they do from their own. They act as stringers for foreign papers even when they hold prestigious positions as editors, assistant editors, and special correspondents in leading dailies in their own country. Pride in their position does not still the greed for money or the passion for recognition in the West.[175]

There were also other ways to make the press dance attendance on Delhi's rulers: withholding advertisements was a tried and tested method. Before the Emergency, Bansi Lal had "tamed" the Chandigarh *Tribune* by denying it government advertisements and having the police fine vehicles that transported the paper to Haryana or even passed through the state. After 25 June 1975 this policy assumed a more industrial and clinical character. The Directorate of Advertising and Visual Publicity (DAVP), the agency in charge of placing advertisements to promote ministries and public-sector undertakings, was tasked with gauging the pliability of newspaper editors. In a complementary effort, Baji was asked on 29 June to prepare a list of the leading journals in the country, categorising them as either "friendly", "neutral", or "hostile".[176] "Friendly" papers included the *Amrita Bazar Patrika*—the "whole-hoggers", in Baji's words—*Hindu*, *Hindustan Times*, and *Times of India*; the *Statesman*, *Tribune*, *Indian Express*, and even the pro-CPI *Patriot* were "hostile"; and the *Deccan Chronicle*, *Pioneer*, and *Financial Express* "neutral". In October, Shukla decided to "stop advertisements and press facilities, if any, in regard to hostile newspapers", and "feed publicity materials to friendly and neutral newspapers only."[177]

---

[173] "Summary Records of Discussions Held in the Room of Shri C.V. Narasimhan, Joint Secretary, Ministry of Home Affairs", 5 August 1975, MHAP, File II-14011/8/75-S&P(D-IV).

[174] See MHAP, File II-14011/9/75-S&P(D-IV), *passim*.

[175] Yunus, *Persons, Passions, and Politics*, p. 237.

[176] *SCR*, vol. 1, pp. 39–41.

[177] Dayal and Bose, *Shah Commission Begins*, p. 266. Hence the *Amrita Bazar Patrika*

By contrast turncoats such as the Urdu *Dastan-e-Watan*, once a "pro-Jana Sangh" journal "now supporting the Congress", were rewarded with advertisements and related privileges.[178]

Meanwhile, between 1974–5 and 1976–7 the DAVP's advertisement budget doubled to Rs 28 million. While eighty-nine journals were denied advertisements "mostly on political grounds", money was lavished on the Congress house organs: disbursements to the *Socialist India* were bumped up from Rs 18,647 in 1975–6 to Rs 111,740 the next year; the *Socialist Bharat*, Rs 14,918 to Rs 105,236; the *Sab Saath*, Rs 6555 to Rs 52,623. Funds for CPI, CPI(M), Socialist, and Jana Sangh papers were slashed.[179]

The journals that crossed the red line by criticising the Emergency—such as Rajmohan Gandhi's weekly *Himmat*; *Tughlak*, a Tamil fortnightly edited by Cho Ramaswamy; and *Mainstream*, edited by Nikhil Chakravartty (one of the country's most famous investigative journalists)—were subjected to more thoroughgoing pre-publication censorship.[180] In December 1976, when Delhi's censors threatened to have *Mainstream* sealed under MISA, it ceased publication. Others folded earlier: the *Opinion*, a four-page weekly edited by retired civil servant A.D. Gorwala; *Seminar*, a left-wing monthly whose issues were typically symposia on specific themes; and *Sadhana*, a Marathi weekly run by Pune socialist Yadunath Thatte—all published their last issues in July.[181] The CIA-funded *Quest* followed in August.[182] The Gujarati weekly *Nireekshak* shut in September. Most of them, it appears, were taken by surprise when pre-censorship orders arrived in the post: "We sat down to face the fact that 2500 copies of our staid and sober jour-

---

had its revenues from DAVP advertisement more than doubled to Rs 1,010,696; the *National Herald* more than tripled to Rs 870,555: *SCR*, vol. 1, p. 41.

[178] *SCR*, vol. 1, p. 40.

[179] Ibid., pp. 41–2.

[180] Ibid., p. 37. Nikhil Chakravartty was once an admirer of Mrs Gandhi's. Just a week before the Emergency, he suggested that she be made immune from the Allahabad Court decision, parliament dissolved, and a new constituent assembly convened: Atma Jayaram to P.N. Dhar, 18 June 1975, SCP, Subject File 1, p. 28.

[181] International Press Institute, "Press Squeeze in India: Smaller Periodicals Are Also Feeling the Pinch", *IPI Report*, October 1976, Jayaprakash Narayan Papers, Instalment III, Subject File 320; *NYT*, 26 July 1976, p. 3; Dayal and Bose, *Shah Commission Begins*, p. 205; *Lok Sangharsh Samiti*, 15 December 1976, p. 1, in MLP, reel 13.

[182] *NYT*, 26 December 1977, p. 1.

nal, with a limited, specialised interest, was a threat to 600 million people", observed Raj Thapar, co-founder of *Seminar*.[183]

On 8 December 1975, the first of three ordinances banned the publication of "objectionable matter" and allowed the government to extract securities from the organisations violating it.[184] Superseding it, an act passed on 28 January deemed as "objectionable matter" all books, pamphlets, leaflets, sheets of music, maps, charts, paintings, drawings, photographs, and "other visible representation" that showed the government in a poor light.[185]

The second repealed the Parliamentary Proceedings (Protection of Publication) Act, 1956, popularly known as the Feroze Gandhi Act, because its main architect had been Mrs Gandhi's husband, a parliamentarian who had died in 1960. This piece of legislation had allowed the press to publish extracts from parliamentary debates and shielded its personnel from prosecution.[186] The Lok Sabha subsequently replaced the ordinance with an act on 11 February, the representatives of the people having agreed on the principle that all that happened in parliament was to stay in parliament.[187] Preceding this, on 8 January the right to move the court to enforce free speech had been suspended.

The third abolished the Press Council of India, an informal body set up in 1966 to hear complaints by and against the press as well as protect press freedom. Here, Emergency apologist K.K. Birla's hand was at work. The head of a dynastic conglomerate and family friend of the Gandhis, Birla was the subject of a complaint filed before the council. It was alleged that he had fired George Verghese, editor of the daily he owned, the *Hindustan Times*, because the paper was growing critical of the Emergency, even if only mildly so. When the tycoon got word that the council would dress him down for violating press freedom, it became apparent that it was the coun-

---

[183] Thapar, *All These Years*, p. 430.

[184] This included materials that "bring into hatred or contempt or excite disaffection towards the Government" or made defamatory remarks about the prime minister, president, vice president, speaker of the Lok Sabha, members of the council of ministers, and state governors. A transgression could result in a year of imprisonment and the closure of the printing press. The act is reproduced in Sorabjee, *The Emergency*, pp. 41–61.

[185] Nehru had passed a similar act in 1951, repealing it six years later.

[186] Falk, *Feroze*, p. 199.

[187] One of the last instances where extracts were reproduced *in toto* was in *Seminar*, vol. 197, no. 1 (January 1976), pp. 33–42.

cil itself that would have to go. It was officially abolished on 31 December 1975 and replaced with an impotent government committee.

Institutional reordering was supplemented with the throttling of individuals. Many journalists had their accreditation withdrawn, and some were imprisoned. In the first year of the Emergency a total of 9876 journalists were arrested and 2974 court cases "registered for publication and distribution of clandestine literature."[188] Kuldip Nayar, editor of the *Indian Express*, was one of those who found himself behind bars. In mid-July 1975, a few days after writing a letter to Indira Gandhi in which he criticised censorship and challenged her assertion that all newsmen were supporting the opposition, he received a threatening note from H.Y. Sharada Prasad, the prime minister's information adviser.[189] Ignoring it, Nayar convened a meeting at the Press Club where he asked his colleagues to sign a resolution condemning the Emergency. Shukla got wind of this and immediately wrote to him demanding that he hand over the list of signatories to the I&B ministry. Nayar refused to comply. Having been twice warned by the watchful eyes of the censorship regime, he was arrested under MISA on 26 July.[190] He was released two months later, after his wife filed a petition in the Delhi High Court.

Other newspapermen were less lucky. K.R. Malkani, RSS ideologue and editor of the *Motherland*, and Lala Jagat Narain, owner of Jullundur's *Hind Samachar*, for instance, spent the whole period of the Emergency in prison.[191] Even for those outside there was no real security—they were acutely aware of having managed to escape the government's radar only momentarily. This was the case with Gourkishore Ghosh and Barun Sengupta—both journalists of the *Anand Bazar Patrika* who had written stories critical of West Bengal's chief minister, S.S. Ray—who heard through the grapevine that they were to be arrested under MISA. While Ghosh was caught, Sengupta escaped and sought Sanjay's protection in Delhi. The arrangement seemed to work at first because Ray and Sanjay did not enjoy the best rapport, but, not long after, Sengupta was arrested as well.[192]

---

[188] Note by Naresh Chandra, Under Secretary, Ministry of Home Affairs—Desk IV, 14 September 1976, MHAP, File II-14011/35/75-S&P(D-IV) Part II.

[189] Nayar, *In Jail*, p. 5.

[190] See his statement before the Shah Commission, reproduced in ibid., pp. 127–40.

[191] Malkani, *The Midnight Knock*, p. 89; *TOI*, 4 January 1977, p. 1.

[192] Nayar, *The Judgement*, p. 47.

Foreign correspondents, only nominally freer than the domestic press, had to submit to the censorship regime or risk losing their press accreditation. On 29 June 1975, fifty of them were gathered at the I&B ministry headquarters at Shastri Bhavan where Shukla instructed them to follow the same set of guidelines as the domestic press. If they did not, they would face "very stern and stiff action", he warned, hinting at expulsion.[193] In July, Mrs Gandhi was more categorical. She ordered that "foreign correspondents refusing to furnish undertakings and submit writings for pre-censorship should be deported."[194] In February 1976 the government reconstituted the Central Press Accreditation Committee, adding a third government nominee to the team of eleven.[195] By the end of the Emergency, twenty-nine foreign correspondents had been denied entry visas and fifty-one had had their accreditation revoked.[196]

One of the expelled pressmen was Lewis M. Simons of the *Washington Post*, who had alleged in a piece that Sanjay slapped Mrs Gandhi across the face six times at a dinner party—neither retaliation nor reprimand had followed, wrote Simons, because "she is scared to death of him".[197] Another was the BBC's Mark Tully. Reading his dispatches Mohammad Yunus, a family friend of the prime minister's, had asked Gujral during his last days at the I&B ministry to "send for Mark Tully, pull down his trousers, give him a few lashes and send him to jail."[198] Luckily for Tully, this never came to pass, but the BBC's operations were shut down and he was barred from entering India for two years. Others expelled for unflattering reportage included Peter Hazelhurst of the *Times*, Kevin Rafferty of the *Financial Times*, *Newsweek*'s Loren Jenkins, Jacques R. Leslie Jr. of the *Los Angeles Times*, the *Guardian*'s Martin Woollacott, and Peter Gill of the *Daily Telegraph*.[199] The foreign correspondents who remained had to sign "a bond agreeing to abide by the pre-censorship laws."[200] In September 1976 it was announced that the foreign press would no longer have to submit to censorship, but in practice the government continued to place obstacles before correspondents, delaying visas and subjecting them to surveillance.

---

[193] Thakur, *All the Prime Minister's Men*, p. 59.
[194] Dayal and Bose, *Shah Commission Begins*, p. 231.
[195] *SCR*, vol. 1, p. 43.
[196] *White Paper on Misuse of Mass Media*, pp. 37–8, 61–2.
[197] *Guardian*, 14 July 1975, p. 11.
[198] Tully and Masani, *From Raj to Rajiv*, p. 119.
[199] Lifschultz, "The Backlash of Emergency", pp. 26–7.
[200] *SCR*, vol. 1, p. 44.

The film industry was another target. Shukla made many trips to Bombay, extending his censorship empire to include Bollywood. A film by Gulzar, *Aandhi*, which presented a female politician who resembled Indira Gandhi—right down to the single white streak girdled by a shock of black hair—and chronicled her fractious relationship with her husband, was banned. The same fate met *Kissa Kursi Ka*, a mordant commentary on the republic's first family, which included the line "Sir, give this young man the license to manufacture small cars because he learnt it in his mother's womb," said of a Sanjay stand-in; *Andolan*, a Gandhi biopic set in 1942, which the censors thought was too allegorical; and *All the President's Men*, because it was believed that Indian audiences might see Nixon as Mrs Gandhi.[201] The popular singer Kishore Kumar, whose songs topped the 1970s charts, had all his songs pulled off the airwaves for his refusal to croon at Geeton Bhari Shaam, a "musical extravaganza" organised by the Youth Congress to collect funds for Sanjay's notoriously coercive sterilisation programme.[202]

Newswires were yet other targets for emasculation. As early as 26 July 1975 a meeting chaired by Mrs Gandhi had concluded that "the organisation of news agencies needs restructuring."[203] Soon the idea of centralising all four of the major ones was floated by Yunus, who joined the board of directors of the merged organisation when it came into existence.[204] Merging the Press Trust of India, the United News of India, Hindustan Samachar, and Samachar Bharati was not an easy task. The PTI was forced to consider this option in December 1975 when it was reminded that it owed the government Rs 7 million. The UNI had opposed the idea of a merger in November that year, but it too was put under duress: its tele-

---

[201] Ahmed, "1978—Kissa Kursi Ka". *Kissa Kursi Ka* was India's "first political film", Raj Thapar declares, "a horror film", also a "state of the nation" film: Thapar, *All These Years*, p. 394. It was directed by Amrit Nahata, a Congress MP.

[202] He also refused to collaborate with other Bollywood figures—G.P. Sippy, B.R. Chopra, Shree Ram Bohra, and Subodh Mukherjee—in the production of propaganda material for AIR and Doordarshan. Soon HMV decided to stop recording with the singer on its "own initiative". Kumar capitulated a month later, writing a letter of apology to C.B. Jain, joint secretary of the I&B ministry, who immediately had the ban on his work lifted: "Ban on Using Songs of Kishore Kumar", no date, SCP, Subject File 26, pp. 3–6; *Satya Samachar*, 12 June 1976, p. 8, in MLP, reel 1.

[203] Dayal and Bose, *Shah Commission Begins*, p. 233.

[204] Yunus, *Persons, Passions, and Politics*, p. 227.

printer connections to government offices were discontinued; the All India Radio's dues to it withheld; G.G. Mirchandani, the UNI editor and general manager, forced into retirement; and on 15 January 1976 Shukla announced that AIR would, in two weeks, discontinue its services altogether. A month later, after pressuring P.C. Gupta and Ram Tarneja, chairmen respectively of the PTI and UNI boards, Shukla succeeded in merging the two agencies.[205] On 1 February, Samachar was created as the republic's only news agency by combining the PTI and UNI amalgam with Hindustan Samachar and Samachar Bharati, making it the sixth-largest news agency in the world. This behemoth was placed in the pliant hands of G. Kasturi, editor of the *Hindu*, who regularly consulted with K.N. Prasad, Shukla's Man Friday. The new general manager of the Samachar, Wilfred Lazarus, was equally biddable—he would send the government lists of his own personnel to vet. The editorial staff of the agency now made decisions about coverage at the government's behest. Most of the staff of the former agencies who had opposed the merger were, quite predictably, made to resign or consider early retirement.

The centralisation of information made it easier for the Congress to reign over the media, expanding the airwaves monopoly it already enjoyed through AIR. To guarantee pliability, other steps were taken. It might be recalled here that in 1966 Mrs Gandhi, then the I&B minister, had pushed for the setting up of the Chanda Committee to make AIR more autonomous from government.[206] A few months later, however, by which time she had become prime minister, she refused to follow through on its recommendations—a portent of things to come. In April 1976 the bar on recruiting members of political parties to AIR was removed. Mrs Gandhi had freed herself to pack with her own nominees the vacant 140 new positions that had opened up in March that year. Shortly after the change in recruitment policy, three Congress party workers were appointed as part-time correspondents.[207] In his testimony to the Shah Commission, S.C. Bhatt, director of the AIR's news service, gave the lowdown on the politicisation of radio during the Emergency:

> Distortion of news in AIR began immediately after the proclamation of the Emergency. In December 1976, 2207 lines were devoted in the news bulletins

---

[205] The merger took place on 24 January 1976: *SCR*, vol. 1, pp. 42–3.

[206] Transcript of interview with I.K. Gujral, Acc. No. 797, NMML Oral History Project, p. 99.

[207] "Formation of Samachar", no date, SCP, Subject File 15, pp. 144–61.

to pronouncements of spokesmen of the ruling party as against only 34 lines to the opposition parties. In December 1974, the figure was 571 for the ruling party and 522 lines for the opposition. The situation changed dramatically and drastically on 26 June 1975 when rigid constraints were imposed on AIR with instructions, written as well as unwritten, given by the Ministry of I&B, at times the minister himself and also direct from the PM's Secretariat.[208]

AIR and its television counterpart Doordarshan were, to put it in a nutshell, the *fons et origo* of a new personality cult. Initially, Mrs Gandhi was the main beneficiary of this propaganda. Over the twenty-one months of Emergency rule her pronouncements were carried on 171 occasions on newsreels and on Samachar Darshan, the televised weekly news programme in Hindi. But gradually, building a cult of personality around Sanjay took priority: between 1 January 1976 and 18 January 1977 he was the subject of 192 news bulletins on radio. Television did not lag behind: over the same period the prime minister's son appeared on 265 of Doordarshan's national telecasts in coverage that cost the republic's taxpayers Rs 833,055.[209] The shift in focus from Gandhi *mère* to Gandhi *fils*, it appears, occurred around the time of the Congress session of December 1975.[210] Shortly after, Shukla asked the PTI to delegate Chaman Lal Bhardwaj, one of its "special correspondents", to cover Sanjay.[211] The agency initially resisted—it was against their policy to assign beat reporters to specific individuals, even if it were the prime minister. But when the PTI was replaced by Samachar, Shukla prevailed in having journalists follow Sanjay and write puff pieces detailing the minutiae of his daily life.

It was almost as if only two leaders existed in the country, Mother and Son. Shukla was instrumental in bringing this about. As early as 29 June 1975, noting the "over-emphasis" on Congress figures other than the prime minister, he ordered AIR and Doordarshan to avoid "undue stress on ministers in the news coverage." Muscling in on the private media as well, he directed Baji "to contact editors of various newspapers in Delhi to ensure that they accord prominent publicity" to Mrs Gandhi, "both news-wise and

---

[208] Dayal and Bose, *Shah Commission Begins*, p. 298.

[209] *SCR*, vol. 1, pp. 44–6.

[210] This is Vinod Mehta's assessment, which checks out with our own, based on a perusal of two privately owned dailies, the *Statesman* and the *Indian Express*. See Mehta, *The Sanjay Story*, p. 182.

[211] Dayal and Bose, *Shah Commission Begins*, p. 259.

photo publicity-wise".[212] Of course, the negligible reach of the private press meant that the regime's interference with the state-owned media was, as noted above, far more significant.[213]

December 1975 saw the publication of *The Spirit of India*, a four-volume hagiography of the prime minister, spanning 2500 pages with 800 photographs.[214] In 1976 two multi-media campaigns celebrated, respectively, "A Decade of Achievement"—Mrs Gandhi took office in 1966—and "A Year of Fulfilment", commemorating one year of Emergency rule.[215] The main takeaways from both were the same: that Mrs Gandhi, a leader of the people, had made sacrifices, including in her personal life, to better the lot of the masses. The Films Division, whose weekly newsreels were shown before film screenings to an audience of the 80 million or so who visited the 10,000 cinemas across the country every week, harped on the same theme: while shooting *A Day with the Prime Minister* its local units were told to cover Mrs Gandhi's tour of the country by focusing "on the attention shown by the people ... Their spontaneous joy, feelings, and enthusiasm should be captured through the camera eye."[216] Another film, *A New India Begins*, compared Jayaprakash Narayan to Hitler and Mussolini, condemning the "nefarious plan of the opponents of democracy in India."[217] Vastly expensive propaganda films were either purchased—such as *Indus Valley to Indira Gandhi*, for Rs 1,190,000—or produced, as was the unironically titled *Thunder of Freedom*, for which Doordarshan coughed up Rs 117,000.[218] AIR played its part too, collating 200 quotations from the prime minister's speeches for everyday airing.[219]

---

[212] Ibid., pp. 188–9. See Chapter 9 for the press' response to the Emergency regime's exhortations and restrictions.

[213] Because of the high levels of illiteracy in the country, radio and television reached far more citizens than did print. In 1976, the AIR reached 17.5 million "licensed radio receivers", and Doordarshan, 5.1 million viewers. By comparison, the largest English dailies, the *Indian Express* and the *Times of India*, sold only 404,000 and 347,000 copies, respectively: Pendakur, "Mass Media during the 1975 National Emergency in India", pp. 36–7.

[214] *SW*, 27 December 1975, p. 5.

[215] Its general tenor: Mrs Gandhi prevailed over the "recrudescence of divisive forces causing conflicts and violence" and vanquished "extremist political groups" that were "clearly subversive of our constitution": from a chapter titled "The Domestic Scene" in "A Decade of Achievement" in MHAP, File 10/4/75-RP.

[216] Dayal and Bose, *Shah Commission Begins*, p. 228.

[217] Pendakur, "Mass Media during the 1975 National Emergency in India", p. 38.

[218] *Statesman*, 10 August 1977.

[219] *SCR*, vol. 1, p. 46.

A CONSTITUTIONAL DICTATORSHIP

Negative coverage of the ruling party was, of course, forbidden. Shukla admitted before the Shah Commission that factionalism within the Congress in particular and divisions in society at large were not reported because "we did not want instability in the country ... We wanted to highlight only those sets of facts which related to the process of development of the country. Other sets which caused demoralization were not to be highlighted."[220] Corporatism, in short, had trickled into the superstructure of society.

* * *

On account of its "limited pluralism", the Emergency fulfils the first criterion of authoritarian regimes in Juan Linz's formulation. For political parties had not been banned, even if many of their leaders were behind bars and some of them tortured. Parliament remained functional, despite many MPs wasting away in jail. Elections too proceeded without interruption, albeit only at the local level—general elections were repeatedly postponed. The media continued to play a role in society, though dissenting pressmen found themselves routinely censored.

Moreover, the ambivalent character of this regime was also reflected in the constitutional dimension of the new dispensation. For, by using one of its provisions to bring the Emergency into existence, Mrs Gandhi had made certain not to step outside the boundaries of the constitution. Here, in essence, was a regime of the type that Linz describes as a paradox: a "constitutional dictatorship".[221] Certainly, constitutional amendments reduced the independence of the judiciary and strengthened the executive; all the same, *formally* this process followed legal procedures that for the better part were validated by the Supreme Court. The law was used to, as it were, undermine the law. Nevertheless, this fixation on the legal cloaked processes that were much the obverse: for it was coercion and brute power that aided Delhi's rulers in bringing the country to heel during the Emergency. Old institutions remained, but they did so under novel pressures.

Furthermore, the Emergency also shares some characteristics with other kinds of authoritarian regimes in Linz's typology. As a postcolonial state led by a single party in which the shibboleths of an earlier generation were rapidly becoming a wasting asset, and whose leaders, in the face of adversity and anomie, pushed the country into an increasingly authoritarian

---

[220] Dayal and Bose, *Shah Commission Begins*, pp. 302–3.
[221] Linz, *Totalitarian and Authoritarian Regimes*, p. 61.

direction, Emergency India had much in common with a number of African "postindependence mobilisational authoritarian regimes".

Indeed, it would be inexact to see the Emergency as a world-historical anomaly. In the mid-1970s democracies were indisputably not the norm. Only about 27 per cent of the world's nations could be called democracies, many of them merely in a formal sense.[222] In the mid-1970s, three of India's neighbours turned to presidentialism—Burma in 1974, Bangladesh in 1975, and Sri Lanka in 1978—and a fourth, Pakistan, adopted a new constitution in 1973 with a highly presidentialised prime ministership.[223] In a sense, these subcontinental similarities can be accounted for by the analogous reactions of elites to popular furies unleashed by a common set of malaises: high unemployment; foreign dependence; growing rural–urban, regional, and class divisions; and an incomplete demographic transition.[224] Mrs Gandhi's *autogolpe* was also a repeat of Park Chung Hee's and Ferdinand Marcos'. Both were elected as democratic leaders of their countries—the South Korean president in 1963 and the Filipino in 1965—but ruled as dictators from 1972 onwards.[225]

Most of these regimes, it appears, had another feature in common: a certain rejection of ideology, and therefore an element of depoliticisation, which represents a second distinctive trait of authoritarianism for Linz, and which found expression primarily in a specific political–economic setting.

[222] Diamond, *Developing Democracy*, p. 25.

[223] Ayesha Jalal discerns a common trajectory in India, Pakistan, and Bangladesh in the 1970s: all witnessed—in quick succession—economic stagnation, a turn towards populism, inadequate reform in an effort to preserve the status of the ruling classes, and, finally, autocratic clampdown: see Jalal, *Democracy and Authoritarianism in South Asia*, pp. 136–50.

[224] Morrison, "Asian Drama, Act II", p. 24 *et passim*.

[225] For the parallels, see Gupta, "A Season of Caesars", pp. 315–49.

2

THE POLITICAL ECONOMY OF THE EMERGENCY

LOOKING FOR IDEOLOGY

Authoritarian regimes, Juan Linz suggests, have no ideology.[1] Instead, they rely on a "mentality" that derives from the personality of their leaders and in the first instance makes for rather banal rhetoric.[2] But this "mentality" also serves a clear purpose by promoting depoliticisation and satisfying the heterogenous support base that, on a quotidian level, makes the regime possible in the first place, as we will see in Chapter 8. Depoliticisation—for Linz one of the main defining characteristics of authoritarianism—is not only a *consequence* of the lack of ideology, that is, an absence of utopias and mobilisation, but also an *objective*, for such regimes prefer not to see angry masses in the streets. After all, authoritarian states, unlike totalitarian ones, are more or less inept when it comes to channelling and controlling demonstrations. Far better, then, to ensure that people's activities be limited in the public sphere.

The only legitimate mobilisations, in effect, are those in support of the leader. Hence the complementarity of authoritarianism and populism. For populism has no ideology either. Mudde and Kaltwasser define it as a "thin-

---

[1] *Totalitarian and Authoritarian Regimes*, p. 164.

[2] Drawing on Theodor Geiger, Linz defines mentalities as "ways of thinking and feeling, more emotional than rational, that provide noncodified ways of reacting to different situations." Ibid., p. 162.

centered ideology that considers society to be ultimately separated into two homogenous and antagonistic camps, 'the pure people' versus 'the corrupt elite'."[3] But while the word "ideology" is used here, even if in a qualified manner, Mudde himself wonders if it is apposite since no specific public policies emerge from populist discourse.[4] Other theorists of populism are even more hesitant to attribute an ideological dimension to populism. Kurt Weyland, for one, sees it simply as "a political strategy through which a personalistic leader seeks or exercises government power through direct, unmediated, uninstitutionalized support from large numbers of followers."[5] Here, demagoguery and opportunist acts trump ideas. If there is no ideology, then what is left is a political style relying on emotions, promises, and the direct relation between a leader and "his" or "her" people; for this reason, the leader claims to embody the political will. Pierre Ostiguy puts it pithily: the popularity of a populist leader derives from an ability to be "both *like me ... and* an *ego-ideal*."[6]

Populism, then, is a political style that mobilises people by liberally borrowing ideas from both the Left and Right, and by channelling fear and anger to creative ends. In the case of populisms of the Left, a receptive audience is convinced it can dislodge the ruling elite.[7] In the case of populisms of the Right (or *national* populisms), the people targeted by the leader comprise sons of the soil who are defined against an Other that supposedly poses a threat to them.[8] Promises of instant change and the ejection of a corrupt elite are common to both. In the event, the affinities between populism and authoritarianism are plain to see. For authoritarian leaders, like populist ones, prefer to emulate the ruling ideologies of their time to give their discourse ballast.[9] Moreover, and more importantly, the pretensions of populists to popular embodiment accords them, in their own view and in the eyes of their followers, greater legitimacy than any institution, be it the judiciary, the armed forces, parliament, or political parties. Already in the 1950s, Edward Shils was arguing that "populism identifies the will of the people with justice and morality", making irrelevant constitutional

---

[3] Mudde and Kaltwasser, *Populism*, p. 6.

[4] Mudde, "Populism", pp. 29–47.

[5] Weyland, "Clarifying a Contested Concept", p. 14.

[6] Emphasis in the original. Ostiguy, "Populism", p. 74.

[7] On populists of the Left, see Laclau, *On Populist Reason*.

[8] Germani, *Authoritarianism, Fascism and National Populism*.

[9] Linz, *Totalitarian and Authoritarian Regimes*, p. 165.

checks and balances.[10] To the populist leader, in short, *le peuple c'est moi.* What need, then, for pluralism?[11]

Mrs Gandhi's regime certainly exhibited many of the characteristics of populist authoritarianism. Her Twenty-Point Programme, for one, was nebulous enough to be described as ideologically schizophrenic, drawing preponderantly on the Left but also on the Right, even as her nepotistic and corporatist policies suggested, in practice, an inverse relation with both ends of the spectrum. While the politics of fear and rage was missing from her rhetoric—there was too much paternalism for that—there was certainly a semblance of anti-elitism, a contempt for institutions and a desire for depoliticisation in Mrs Gandhi's élan.

The Twenty-Point Programme and its Contradictions

"Some people talk of revolution. Our government has already begun one", Mrs Gandhi announced swaggeringly a day into the Emergency.[12] But what were her aims? The Twenty-Point Programme—or the twenty-one-point programme, for the policies announced over radio on 1 July were not enumerated—culled from over 150 suggestions received from the ministries, was supposed to be an answer.[13] Lacking in originality, and at times even substance, the points, in sum, were an ideological miscellany that had, over the decades, come to define Congress policy. They spanned a spectrum which at one end contemplated actually existing socialism for the benefit of the many, and on the other stridently defended the corporatist interests of the few. Previously, there had been the equally muddled Ten-Point Programme of 1967 and the Thirteen-Point Programme of 1974.[14] The Emergency months would produce more enumerated but equally incoherent wish lists: a Seven-Point Action Programme to eliminate varieties of violence, an Eight-Point Action Programme for altering "socioeconomic

---

[10] Shils, *The Torment of Secrecy*, p. 98.

[11] On the rejection of pluralism by authoritarian leaders, see Müller, *What is Populism?*

[12] *The Hindu*, 26 June 1975, cited in Hart, "Introduction", p. 28.

[13] It was soon whittled down to twenty to make a round number: Nayar, *The Judgement*, p. 57.

[14] The first was in response to the poor showing at the polls, and the second, which was also known as the Narora programme, was to reinvigorate the party with cadre politics: *Congress Marches Ahead—X*, pp. 300–1.

attitudes", a Five-Point Programme aimed at urban renewal, and a Four-Point Plan of Action for "removing regional imbalances".[15]

In any case the Twenty-Point Programme only served to provide some *post hoc* economic ballast to the Emergency whose development certainly preceded, and remained independent of, programmatic cohesion. Besides, it had obvious propaganda value: a Delhi police band rendered the programme into a "musical score", while the Ministry of Information and Broadcasting, with some artistic license, made a Tamil ballet version of it.[16] That its contents were only of secondary importance was underscored by the contradictions to be found within it. Some of the points simply reiterated policies that ambitious ministers had already commenced—the first word of the first point, "continuance", set the tone of the document—such as Minister for Heavy Industries T.A. Pai's attempts to forge "peaceful" industrial relations through a "disciplined" workforce, or Minister of State for Finance K.R. Ganesh's war on smugglers.[17]

Fifteen of the points aimed to further the social revolution that had been the central promise of Congress mass politics: reducing the prices of essential commodities; implementing land ceilings and making progress on redistribution; housing the landless and other "weaker sections" of society; forgoing the arrears of the rural and indigent millions through a moratorium on debt repayment; declaring debt bondage illegal; bringing five million more hectares under irrigation and improving the connectivity of underground water networks; "reviewing" minimum wage legislation; increasing power production; developing the handloom sector; imposing a ceiling on urban landholdings; cracking down on tax evasion; confiscating the properties of smugglers; offering students essential commodities at controlled prices; subsidising books and stationery; and piloting a new programme aimed at job creation and training. The remaining five points broadly belonged to Mrs Gandhi's corporatist agenda, to which we will return below.

What Land Reform?

An appraisal of Emergency India's economic record can start with the question of land reform, which figured prominently in the Twenty-Point

---

[15] *The Emergency: Its Impact*, pp. 21–3.

[16] Selbourne, *An Eye to India*, p. 196.

[17] The programme is reproduced *in toto* in Zaidi, *Full Circle*, pp. 125–6. See also *TOI*, 30 March 1975, p. 1; *TOI*, 19 August 1974, pp. 1, 3.

Programme. In essence, Mrs Gandhi's decade in power, not unlike her father's seventeen years at the helm, were marked by inertia in the countryside. Both reigns saw the passage of laws in Delhi and the state capitals aimed at imposing ceilings and extending ownership to a majority of the rural poor being fought tooth and nail by the former *zamindars*—tax collectors who acted as middlemen between the cultivators and the colonial state before *zamindari* was abolished in the early 1950s. This class managed to derail land redistribution by "employing" the old tenants as farmhands, showing that the latter were in effect no longer being "taxed" by them; hiring lawyers to challenge expropriation and dragging out court cases *ad infinitum*; and parcelling out chunks of land to friends and family to make it seem that their estates were in compliance with ceiling legislation, thereby keeping potential expropriators at arm's length. The virtual absence of the state at the village level, too, helped quash land reform. With the help of *patels* and *patwaris*—local bosses commanding police power and bookkeepers, respectively—the gentry had all the means to kill redistributive measures.[18]

During the Emergency the possibility of effective land reform was very real. The judiciary, long a stumbling block on this front, had been weakened, and authoritarianism had freed Mrs Gandhi from electoral obligations—and therefore from the need to please the gentry that was the backbone of the Congress elite.[19] Still, Mrs Gandhi and her technocrats remained averse to consequential land reform, for it would reduce the agricultural surplus to the detriment of the rural rich, whereas the last five-year plan had committed India to rapid industrialisation, capital for which was to come from the countryside. Simply put, Mrs Gandhi's planners were arguing that the poor terms of trade between agriculture and industry made it a state imperative to turn a blind eye to rural inequality. They also warned her that land reform could lead to a growing demand for goods and services in the countryside—as the rural citizenry would be better off—which could drive up costs in cities, and thus convince the middle classes to take to the streets.[20] In the face of higher prices, it was likely that the urban working classes would demand more wages, possibly turning their employers, the Indian capitalist elite, against her. Indeed, holding

---

[18] The best accounts of the land reforms are Frankel, *Political Economy*; Warriner, *Land Reform in Principle and Practice*, pp. 136–217; Herring, *Land to the Tiller*.

[19] See Jaffrelot, *India's Silent Revolution*, Chapter 4.

[20] Vicziany, "Coercion in a Soft State", p. 382.

down the prices of essential commodities had been the touchstone of Congress economic policy since at least September 1972.[21]

Conservatism in the states, too, played its part in obstructing land reform. Kerala makes for as good an example as any in delineating the imbrication of gentry and Congress interests. While the Twenty-Point Programme was heralded in the state with plaudits, plans quickly went sour in November 1975 when the state Congress struck a deal with the Kerala Congress, the party of the landowning Syrian Christians and upper castes.[22] The Finance Ministry in the state had previously been in the hands of the Congress' K.G. Adiyodi, a votary of tax reform and expropriation. Both, predictably, had the potential of becoming a thorn in the flesh of the landed elite.[23] Citing "harassment", the farming lobby had Adiyodi replaced with the KC's K.M. Mani. Soon after taking office, Mani gave his ministry a dressing down, railing against his predecessor's "over-assessments".[24] The reformist budget was dropped and in its place came one which benefited small-scale merchants and bullock capitalists. As it turned out, the 1975 drive saw just 570,000 acres made available for redistribution, much of it uncultivable forest land. By the end of the year, half this figure remained undistributed. The remainder was handed out to 350,000 families, leaving each of them with less than an acre on average. Moreover, in keeping with precedent, the expropriations were geared towards dispossessing Namboodiri Brahmin families, in what was essentially an effort to hit at the CPI(M)'s support base.[25] The rest of the gentry

---

[21] *Congress Marches Ahead—VI*, p. 32. "The holding of the prices of the essential commodities" finds mention in the opening paragraphs of the finance minister's 1976 budget speech and in separate speeches by Pranab Mukherjee and T.A. Pai after the budget, underscoring its status as a shibboleth: *Ministry of Finance, Budget for 1976–77*, p. 1; *SW*, 27 March 1976, p. 3.

[22] As is conventional, whenever the Congress is prefixed with a state in this book— for example "Maharashtra Congress"—it refers to the state-level organisation of Mrs Gandhi's Indian National Congress. The only exception is Kerala, where the Kerala Congress refers to the party of that name, while the INC in the state is simply called the "state Congress".

[23] *TOI*, 19 August 1975, p. 7.

[24] Nossiter, "State-Level Politics in India", p. 45.

[25] Namboodiri Brahmins first developed an affinity for Marxism in the 1930s: see Deleury, *India*, p. 181. This, however, did not undermine the commitment to Brahmanical projects. Well into the 1960s, CPI(M) founder E.M.S. Namboodiripad continued to justify the caste system as a "scientific division of labour": Jaffrelot, *India's Silent Revolution*, p. 255.

benefited from the long delay between the announcement of the policy and the actual requisitioning of land, an interval in which only "the stupid or senile" failed to divide their large holdings into smaller parcels and hand them over to members of their extended families.[26] The happenings in Kerala were pretty much representative of events in the rest of the country.

During the Emergency, a total of sixteen of India's twenty-two states enacted fresh land ceiling laws or substantially amended old ones to facilitate redistribution.[27] There was much at stake. For between 1961–2 and 1970–1, surplus landholdings had risen from 24 to 31 per cent of the total agricultural land in the country.[28] Simply to reverse this—let alone embark upon newer and more audacious land reform—would have meant redistributing at least 25 million acres.[29]

Mrs Gandhi filled the airwaves with anticipation: ceiling laws were to be fully implemented by 30 June 1976. The government had set itself the rather modest target of redistributing only 4.4 million acres.[30] This, in its view, was the total "surplus" land, that is, land held in excess of the ceiling. The correct figure was certainly higher, given that this acreage represented only about 1 per cent of the total landholdings—400 million acres—in the country.[31]

In the event, only 1.7 million acres were expropriated, of which less than two-thirds—about 1.1 million—were redistributed. To put it into historical perspective, this was a better feat than the pitiful 62,000 acres redistributed between 1972 and 1975, but paltry compared to the 14 million figure for

[26] Nossiter, "State-Level Politics in India", p. 49.

[27] "Land Reforms—Paper Prepared for Home Minister", 7 January 1976, MHAP, File 5/26/75–RP.

[28] Hart, "Introduction", p. 25. The number of the landless rose from 17.3 to 31.3 million in the same period. The land consolidation between 1961 and 1971 in Punjab was most remarkable. The number of precarious households owning less than five acres grew from 17 to 56 per cent in this period: Frankel, "Compulsion and Social Change", p. 220.

[29] Hart, "Introduction", p. 25.

[30] Sau, "Indian Political Economy", p. 618.

[31] Data showed that the top 4 per cent of households owned around 31 per cent— itself a conservative estimate since it could not possibly account for fictitious land transfers—of the national holdings, that is, around 124 million of the republic's 400 million acres. Ergo, the excess figure was incontrovertibly more than the 1 per cent the government was targeting. One estimate puts the surplus landholdings at 42 million acres: Blair, "Mrs Gandhi's Emergency", p. 256; Ladejinsky, "Land Ceilings and Land Reform", p. 404.

Nehru's early years in power.[32] While authoritarian fiat certainly helped Mrs Gandhi achieve more than she had under a democratic dispensation—in which local notables were needed to fight elections—Frankel's damning assessment—that the government failed "to use such absolute powers" conferred by the Emergency to bring "about social change"—still holds.[33] For, as she points out, the "Political Implementation Committees" in charge of seeing through land reform were, in reality, only a marginal force in the Indian countryside. As before, then, it was local-level Congress party men—MPs, MLAs, *panchayat* leaders, and Youth Congress cadres—and bureaucrats that wielded real power, the same conservative forces that had time and again buried land reform.

All the same, the Emergency achieved more than the regime that preceded it. As a result, by February 1976 reports emerged of increased violence against Dalit recipients of redistributed land.[34] Expropriated landlords prevented the newly entitled from cultivating their plots. Aiding the sticks were the suits. By late 1975, 800,000 court cases were pending, challenging the transfer of a total of 653,000 acres earmarked for redistribution.[35] To obviate the judicial challenge, in all but five states ceiling laws were placed in the Ninth Schedule, the part of the constitution exempt from judicial review.[36]

However, Mrs Gandhi had little interest in using her parliamentary supremacy to make land reform unchallengeable in the courts. When the Swaran Singh Committee began recommending constitutional changes in February and March 1976, she instructed it not to propose removing the right to property from among the fundamental rights of the constitution. As a consequence, the Congress Left's proposal to replace the right to property with the right to work was shot down. "Public opinion was not ready [for it]", the prime minister felt.[37] In the meanwhile, she preoccupied herself with more consequential matters that public opinion could digest, such as appending the word "socialist" to the description of the republic in the

---

[32] Frankel, *India's Political Economy*, pp. 507, 552; Rudolph and Rudolph, *In Pursuit of Lakshmi*, p. 315.

[33] Frankel, *India's Political Economy*, p. 552. See also Jaffrelot, *India's Silent Revolution*, pp. 136–43.

[34] Selbourne, *An Eye to India*, pp. 213–14.

[35] *Economic Times*, 26 December 1975, cited in Hart, "Introduction", p. 26.

[36] "Land Reforms—Paper Prepared for Home Minister", 7 January 1976, MHAP, File 5/26/75–RP.

[37] Austin, *Working a Democratic Constitution*, p. 361.

constitution's preamble. So it was that the only fundamental right left standing after the flurry of amendments in Emergency India was the right to property. After all, as the deputy minister of labour put it, "capital formation" and "the savings habit" could not be jeopardised.[38] C. Subramaniam reiterated the logic: "Of course, we cannot expect everybody to own land. It is not necessary also ... If we reduce all the farmers into small farmers without the capacity to invest, that will also become counter-productive."[39]

Mrs Gandhi worried about savings, too. She demanded that banks "make spirited and imaginative efforts to increase their contributions to national savings", and set savings targets to this end.[40] Certainly, India's rates of capital formation lagged behind the rest of the world's. In the late 1960s and early 1970s, the country registered capital formation rates of 12 to 15 per cent of NDP, while global averages hovered between 22 and 25 per cent. But the low figures were the result of the nature of the Indian economy, dominated as it was by farmers who, in the main, were untaxed and reluctant to channel rural surpluses into banks. In the trade-off between capital formation and land reform, it was clear where the Congress' heart lay. For while Mrs Gandhi's regime foundered on land reform, it still succeeded in bringing the rate of capital formation in the private sector up from 15.5 to 17.7 per cent between 1974–5 and 1975–6.[41]

In the Name of the Poor

As with land reform, so with other policies aimed at bettering the lives of the poor, such as the abolition of bonded labour.[42] This had, on 24 October 1975, been officially done away with for the second time, the Constituent Assembly having already banned it in 1950.[43] As was the case after the previous pronouncement, legal precepts and social realities remained worlds apart. In the absence of an efficient rural credit system, re-abolition

---

[38] Selbourne, *An Eye to India*, p. 148.

[39] Zaidi, *The Annual Register of Indian Political Parties, vol. 24*, pp. 408–9.

[40] "Prime Minister's Minutes on the need for continued and greater financial discipline", 26 March 1976, MHAP, File 10/5/76–RP.

[41] *India 1977–78*, p. 163; *Seminar*, vol. 193, no. 1 (September 1975), p. 22.

[42] This is the Indian term for debt bondage, wherein a person "sells" himself in order to repay debts owed to landowners or loan sharks. In most cases, the value of the person's labour proves to be inadequate, which results in debt bondage being carried forward from one generation to the next.

[43] *Seminar*, vol. 198, no. 1 (February 1976), p. 18.

achieved little: the poor and the landless continued to rely on moneylenders who would beguile them into bondage. A year into the Emergency, the government claimed that it had "freed" 51,223 citizens from enthralment. Nevertheless, as "a conservative estimate" suggested, at least 600,000 to 700,000 remained in debt bondage.[44] A 1978 survey put forward the even higher figure of 2.62 million.[45]

If the state failed to dent the hold of moneylenders in the countryside, it was not for want of denouncing them. Indeed, an early executive decision made during the Emergency, which came close on the heels of the moratorium on debt repayment, was the establishment of "regional rural banks". Soon after the ordinance that created them on 26 September 1975—the bill, piloted by Pranab Mukherjee in the Lok Sabha, was passed a week later on 2 October—it was also legislated by twelve states. But lawmaking was one thing, implementation another. Indeed, the first meeting between Pranab Mukherjee—the minister of state in charge of the department of revenue and banking—and the chief executives of the rural banks only took place in February 1976.[46] By the end of the Emergency, a mere eighteen rural banks had come into existence. Moreover, their dependence on the Reserve Bank of India's issued share capital, meagre as it was, further hampered their ability to lend. Co-operative and nationalised banks suffered from the same financial malaise.[47] Given the virtual absence of state lending agencies, then, moneylenders continued as monopolistic creditors in the *mofussil*. Mrs Gandhi's government did little to hide what it really felt about the country's indebted peasants. Here there was no paternalism but just contempt. The "real" reason why "people get indebted", Finance Minister C. Subramaniam said to the Lok Sabha in August 1975, is that "they want to imitate the rich ... it is the educated elite, the richer section of the people, who spoil the poorer sections by their own wasteful expenditure."[48]

All the same, assessing the impact of the regime's rural policies is a tough ask. Indeed, we have two rather contrasting accounts from Maharashtra. On the one hand, Lee I. Schlesinger suggests that while debt was written

---

[44] Note on bonded labour, 21 June 1976, PMSP, File 37/633/1976 PMS.

[45] Srivastava, "Bonded Labor in India", p. 4.

[46] Mukherjee, *The Dramatic Decade*, p. 103, n40.

[47] Frankel, *India's Political Economy*, p. 554.

[48] *Lok Sabha Debates*, vol. 54, no. 11 (4 August 1975), cols 157–8. It must be remembered that, although Subramaniam was part of the Congress Left, his belief in "healthy industrial relations" also led him to suggest in 1972 that supporting "all strikes was deplorable": *Congress Marches Ahead—VI*, p. 89.

off by Delhi's rulers, the lack of an alternative credit system in villages ensured that the status quo was maintained.[49] On the other, Suryakant Waghmore points out that in Beed district:

> Dalits activists have made the most out of the Emergency period of government under Indira Gandhi in 1975–7 (referred to as *aanibani* locally) by spreading the word that the law had changed drastically and all the loans (mostly grains) that were given to Dalits by the *savarnas* [upper castes] were waived. They also asked the Marathas to return cattle and other belongings of Dalits that had been taken possession of as security for loans given to them.[50]

What of the "review" of the minimum wage? A number of states raised it by 15 per cent on average: men in most states were now to be paid around Rs 4.5 a day, women and children slightly less—the state legislations structurally embedded gender and age pay gaps by prescribing lower pay for the latter.[51] This, it was hoped, would make up for the inflationary erosion of real wages, which had led to much unrest in the early 1970s. But, as press accounts made clear, employers did little to respect statutory requirements.[52] With unions in a shambles, even the organised sector had little bargaining power to ensure its enforcement.

The implementation of the Urban Land Ceiling Act of 1976 was similarly mired in a "protective thicket of collusion, evasion, and corruption."[53] Already in December 1975, a good three months before its passage, the cabinet secretary had resigned himself to failure on this front, calling on states to water down ceilings. Instead of doubling down on "outright acquisition", Mrs Gandhi's regime suggested that states place equal emphasis on "selective acquisition" with adequate compensation.[54] They were also asked to consider "the idea of lease-hold", which would allow landlords to retain permanent and absolute tenure of land, while the state would hold by lease

---

[49] Schlesinger, "The Emergency in an Indian Village", p. 628.

[50] Waghmore, *Civility against Caste*, pp. 65–6.

[51] *SW*, 14 February 1976, p. 7.

[52] Selbourne, *An Eye to India*, pp. 207–15.

[53] Ibid., p. 211.

[54] In this tiered system, the compensation was a per cent value of the market price. For urban land worth under Rs 25,000, the figure was 100 per cent; for the most expensive properties, whose whole value exceeded Rs 125,000, 33.33 per cent: "Comments of Planning Commission on the Urban Land (Ceiling & Regulation) Bill 1975–Section 10 thereof", no date, P.N. Haksar Papers, Instalments I and II, Subject File 86.

the property for a fixed period.[55] While reports in the press reassured readers of the speed at which ceilings were being implemented, in practice the workings of government were marked by dubiety. In February 1976, for instance, the prime minister was asked in parliament if anything could be done about "Shri Buty and his two or three brothers" who owned 551 houses in the posh neighbourhood of Sitabaldi in Nagpur that collectively fetched an annual rent of Rs 650,205.[56] Five months later Mrs Gandhi's private secretary noted that "there does not appear to be any law under which holding of such property by members of a family can be prohibited."[57] Moreover, a number of loopholes in the original legislation allowed landowners to dodge ceilings. For example, if a building had already been constructed on a tract of land, the ceiling did not allow for expropriation so long as the owners did not sell, lease, gift, or transfer "such built-up property". "Four bamboo sticks with a tin or covering on top" could well fit this description. Similarly, land held by religious trusts, *auqaf*, banks, and charities was exempted from this piece of legislation, paving the way for the creation of spurious entities that met such criteria.[58] In the final analysis, only 2 per cent of the 410,595 acres identified as "surplus" urban land was expropriated, and only 0.37 per cent of that acreage was used by state governments to build affordable housing.[59]

Relatedly, another important policy of the Emergency regime was the provision of public housing. As with so much else in the Twenty-Point Programme, this drew on promises of old. Indeed, it was in 1972 that the state had pledged to provide by 1979 four million plots of land to rural labourers. During the Emergency, however, the imperative of meeting targets all but eclipsed the reason for them: the housing of India's working poor.

[55] Cabinet Secretariat to H.R. Gokhale, Minister of Law, Justice, and Company Affairs, 5 December 1975, P.N. Haksar Papers, Instalments I and II, Subject File 86. Leaseholds are common in England and Hong Kong, where land is leased to "buyers" for 999 and 70 years, respectively. On the other hand, freehold property rights are common in the United States.

[56] N.S. Sreeraman, Private Secretary to the Prime Minister, 16 February 1976, PMSP, File 17/1532/1973 PMS.

[57] Note by N.S. Sreeraman, 3 July 1976, PMSP, File 17/1532/1973 PMS.

[58] "Comments on the Revised Urban Land Ceiling Bill, 1975", no date, P.N. Haksar Papers, Instalments I and II, Subject File 86. *Auqaf* (sing. *waqf*) are Muslim charitable endowments; they also serve the useful function of protecting family wealth from taxation and expropriation, allowing for the smooth transfer of capital from one generation to the next.

[59] Srinivas, "Land and Politics in India", p. 2483.

Emblematic of this was the creation of Potemkin villages, such as the one that came up like lightning in the district of Satara in Maharashtra: in the name of productivity, forty-six houses appeared virtually overnight, miles from any jobs or amenities. To the locals the settlement quickly came to be known as a "*begharwadi*—hamlet of the homeless".[60] It owed its construction to one simple reason: the state of Maharashtra needed to meet its target of housing a million families in 100,000 projects by the end of March 1976.[61] This, in turn, was part of the national target of 6.53 million houses; by mid-1976, 246,000 had been built. But even this figure needs to be qualified, for two states, Gujarat and Uttar Pradesh, accounted for the bulk of them.[62]

As far as job creation was concerned, Mrs Gandhi made clear early on that the intention was to employ the few, not the many: measures were to be taken "to increase employment opportunities for *educated young people*."[63] The illiterates—71 per cent of the population according to the 1971 census—were of little interest to policy-makers, it seemed. Nor were the 5.6 million citizens who had registered themselves unemployed.[64] In practical terms, emphasis was placed on "apprenticeship training", which was meted out to 133,981 youths by June 1976. While the objective was to place them in both the public and the private sector, the programme only succeeded in relation to the latter, in which 90 per cent of the jobs were secured. The states by contrast, which were tasked with generating apprenticeships to government departments and the public sector, managed to fill only half their vacancies.[65] The Orissa government simply decided to disburse land to the "educated jobless", hoping that they would start their own "small trades and businesses"—a handout to the lettered bourgeoisie, if to anybody.[66]

The points aimed at pacifying the restive student population—subsidised provision of essential commodities, books, and stationery—showed uneven

---

[60] Schlesinger, "The Emergency in an Indian Village", p. 635.

[61] The Maharashtra state government's reply to the "Questionnaire on Misuse and Abuse of Powers", 9 January 1978, SCIF, File SCI/35/MHAR/77AA/T3.

[62] No end date was mentioned. At this rate, it would take until 2002 to build all the houses: Zaidi, *The Annual Register of Indian Political Parties*, vol. 24, p. 79. However, see also Frankel, who cites an Emergency-era pamphlet announcing that three million houses had been built in the first year of authoritarian rule: Frankel, *India's Political Economy*, p. 550.

[63] Emphasis added: Zaidi, *Full Circle*, p. 20.

[64] *India 1977–78*, p. 377.

[65] Note on apprenticeship training, 5 July 1976, PMSP, File 37/633/1976 PMS.

[66] *SW*, 9 August 1975, p. 4.

progress. Of the 500,000 students surveyed in university hostels, about 229,000 had access to subsidised commodities. The private–public partnership, inevitably, prevented the "benefits of reduced bills from being passed on to the students", conceded the government. The report card for the provision of books and stationery, however, was more satisfactory: 104,000 "book banks" were created across the republic. Still, a mere five states—Kerala, Madhya Pradesh, Haryana, Punjab, and Rajasthan—accounted for 89 per cent of them.[67]

To Delhi's rulers all these limitations were more than compensated for by Mrs Gandhi's phenomenal success in reducing prices. This was advertised by her spin doctors on all platforms, and soon even the regime's harshest critics came to concede reluctantly that some good had come out of the Emergency. Indeed, dulled by repetition, this "achievement" has, even in histories, come to acquire the weight of consensus.[68]

Certainly, for a time the going was so good that an opposition figure expressed a worry: "if she keeps this up we might have a dictatorship by popular will."[69] But most of the "gains" were born out of the tight monetary policy put in place months before the authoritarian turn. Disinflation, then, owed more to the Reserve Bank of India's 6 per cent ceiling on annual money supply growth than shuffling policemen and the deferral of elections; in practice, money in circulation grew by 6.2 per cent in 1974–5, and 5.4 per cent in the first half of 1975–6.[70] This is not to discount the importance of authoritarianism, which helped lower demand: workers' bonuses were slashed, unions rendered powerless, and a portion of citizens' wages held as compulsory deposits. On the supply side, however, the "gains" had even less to do with the new dispensation. Foodgrain prices had peaked in September 1974 and descended over the nine months preceding the Emergency.[71]

---

[67] Note on supply of essential commodities, books, and stationery to students at controlled prices, 6 July 1976, PMSP, File 37/633/1976 PMS.

[68] See, for instance, the following histories, memoirs, and biographies: Chandra, *In the Name of Democracy*, p. 185; Nayar, *The Judgement*, p. 43; Dhar, *Indira Gandhi, the "Emergency", and Indian Democracy*, p. 265; Jayakar, *Indira Gandhi*, p. 235; Moraes, *Mrs Gandhi*, p. 223.

[69] *Times* (London), 17 July 1975, p. 4.

[70] See the Planning Commission's note on "The Current Industrial Situation—Some Suggestions for Corrective Action", 6 November 1975, P.N. Haksar Papers, Instalment III, Subject File 354.

[71] *Economic Survey, 1976–1977*, p. 1.

But prices remained stable only as long as the monsoons permitted good wheat and rice harvests. The monsoon of 1975 saw the "best distributed rainfall" since 1940, the Ministry of Finance enthused.[72] Therefore the year saw national records being broken, with 118 million tons of foodgrain produced—the average of the preceding three years was 100.9 million tons. The import of 7.4 million tons—as against 4.9 and 3.6 million in 1974 and 1973, respectively—further strengthened the Emergency regime's hands, allowing it to create a buffer stock large enough to absorb price fluctuations in the short run. Here, global forces were at work: imports had risen primarily because the surge in commodity prices had come to an end during the last months of 1974. In brief, there appeared to be a problem of plenty. To reduce the burden on overflowing silos, the government even began "urging households to hoard foodgrains".[73] But the locust years were far from over. Foodgrain production in 1976 was to decline by 7.9 per cent from the previous year.[74] Indeed, from March onward, prices began climbing again. In the next six months the price index rose 10 per cent.[75]

As for the fiscal policies pursued by Mrs Gandhi, they only betrayed the regime's conservatism. Tax breaks were offered to the tiny segment of the upper-middle class that earned between Rs 6000 and Rs 15,000, money for which was freed up by increasing indirect taxation on goods and services. This continued the trend of making taxes more regressive: the ratio of indirect to direct taxes during Mrs Gandhi's decade in power grew from 2.93 in 1966 to 5.31 in 1976, placing a bigger burden on the poor.[76] But this alone proved inadequate. How, then, were the tax breaks—"the loss of revenue will be of the order of Rs 40 crores"—to be financed?[77] "Education and social welfare are the fields where it is easiest to make financial cuts", Mrs Gandhi proclaimed with surprising candour.[78] Education, in her opinion, had long been conflated with institutions such as schools and colleges. Instead, she contended, it would be better to recognise that "education is a

---

[72] Frankel, *India's Political Economy*, p. 554.

[73] Toye, "Economic Trends and Policies in India during the Emergency", p. 305.

[74] *Economic Survey, 1977–1978*, p. 4.

[75] Toye, "Economic Trends and Policies in India during the Emergency", p. 307.

[76] These are my calculations based on percentage figures in Selbourne, *An Eye to India*, p. 428.

[77] See the note of the Planning Commission (Economic Division) on "raising of the exemption limit for income tax", 18 July 1975, P.N. Haksar Papers, Instalment III, Subject File 354.

[78] Selbourne, *An Eye to India*, p. 61.

lifelong process". As a consequence, "non-formal education" led by a "large number of voluntary organisations" would have to share in the burden. This would be a "move toward the learning society" in which the state would no longer need to do the heavy lifting when it came to "imaginative programmes and schemes".[79]

In other words, Mrs Gandhi was calling for the state to shirk, if not abdicate, its pedagogic responsibilities in a nation where over seven in ten were illiterate. These were necessary sacrifices to ensure that the 730,000 taxpayers (0.12 per cent of the national population) who earned between Rs 6000 and Rs 8000 (per capita income being around Rs 366) were exempted from taxation; and those earning between Rs 8000 and Rs 15,000 received tax breaks in the range of Rs 45 and Rs 264.[80] Given that there were only 3.8 million taxpayers in the country, such tax breaks were, in effect, only for the country's 1 per centers.[81] Moreover, there were further tax breaks, this time specifically extended to the well-heeled. Wealth taxes were slashed from a maximum of 8 to 2.5 per cent, and the tax rate for incomes above Rs 100,000 brought down from 77 to 66 per cent.[82] This, it was expected, would lower the republic's tax revenues from Rs 3.25 to Rs 3.08 billion.[83]

Among the regime's priorities, fighting corruption in order to help the poor—allegedly its first victims—was on a par with the Twenty-Point Programme. Indeed, for Mrs Gandhi it was one of the *raisons d'être* of the regime: for to clean up corruption the country needed a strong government, hence authoritarianism—an argument familiar to Pakistanis who had heard it *ad nauseam* after every coup. Pranab Mukherjee, the minister of state for finance, too, retrospectively looked at the Emergency as a means of "putting the house in order" by fighting financial crime. To this end, in his memoirs he points to the amending of the Conservation of Foreign Exchange and Prevention of Smuggling Activities Act and the passage of the Smugglers and Foreign Exchange Manipulators (Forfeiture of Property) Act.[84]

---

[79] Discussion paper of the Central Advisory Board of Education Committee on Non-Formal Education, 16 July 1976, Planning Commission Papers, File Q–16027/9/76-Edn. Non-formal education was a hybrid of state funds and voluntarism. For its provisions, see the *Main Schemes of Non-Formal Education in the Fifth Five Year Plan*, p. 8 *et passim*.

[80] *20–Point Economic Programme*, p. 26.

[81] *India 1977–78*, p. 174.

[82] *Economic Survey, 1976–1977*, p. 26.

[83] *Ministry of Finance, Budget for 1976–77*, p. 23.

[84] Mukherjee, *The Dramatic Decade*, p. 87.

The scourge of smuggling had been on the minds of administrators for quite some time. Certainly, curbing this menace made sense, but not just from a moral perspective. For less gold and a lighter footprint of Western consumer society would also translate into a citizenry of greater fiscal rectitude, or so it had long been thought by the country's planners. But the extent to which this was a policy priority was never clear. In September 1974, for instance, Mrs Gandhi had K.R. Ganesh, her minister in charge of cracking down on smuggling, removed from the cabinet, apparently for being too zealous, and V.V. Badami, the director of investigations at the income tax department who was liaising closely with him, demoted and sent packing to Madras for discovering that the Jindals, a family conglomerate with close ties to Bansi Lal, were involved in smuggling.[85] All smugglers, then, were not a nuisance to Mrs Gandhi; only a small subsection of them were. In fact, the crackdown during the Emergency was in the main geared to curbing the election funding of the Congress' electoral opponents. For instance, in Kerala the targets were primarily the Moplahs, the Kerala Muslims who supported the Muslim League.[86] In other instances the anti-smuggling drive was just the noble façade behind which ordinary political forces were at work: unofficial contracts between politicians and businessmen would often rely on the hidden threat of the latter being booked for smuggling if the arrangements went awry.[87] While a few high-profile cases commanded much press attention—such as the arrests of reputed racketeers Haji Mastan and Yusuf Patel—in their shadow were cases where influential "economic offenders" were released on parole, the officials responsible for their arrest transferred and replaced with bent personnel.[88]

But the regime scarcely needed to lift a finger in its war against contraband to achieve results. In September 1975 the decision to float the rupee—hitherto it had been pegged to the pound—ensured that remittances from

---

[85] Tandon, *PMO Diary*, p. 377.

[86] Nossiter, "State-Level Politics in India", p. 43.

[87] This had precedents. Capitalists were routinely pressed into disgorging a part of their incomes to pay for the Congress' electoral campaigns—tax raids and false charges were the usual threats that ensured the party had its way: Kochanek, "Briefcase Politics in India", p. 1291.

[88] The *Shah Commission Interim Reports* point out that three economic offenders— Bali Ram Sharma, Ramesh Kumar Rakheja, Brij Mohan Lamba—were released on parole: *SCR*, vol. 2, p. 42. The same was the practice in Gujarat: *TOI*, 10 January 1976, p. 9.

Indians abroad were now more likely to pass through official channels, the depreciated rupee being more lucrative than smuggled gold.[89] Luck helped too: the IMF's decision to auction its gold holdings sent prices crashing, turning remitters away from the metal. The result of these developments, in short, was that remittances shot up from Rs 800 million to Rs 2 billion within a year, putting many a smuggler out of business.[90]

Overall, however, the anti-smuggling drive proved a damp squib. Mrs Gandhi backed down from plans to see off "economic offenders" in "summary trials". In fact, in Emergency India smugglers and tax evaders were treated as a privileged class and given preferential treatment: as part of the Voluntary Disclosure Scheme, with the final eleven weeks of 1975 declared a "grace period" during which purloined riches could be disclosed without criminal charges being pressed. In addition to immunity, a "concessionary rate of taxation" was granted to the malefactors, despite the protestations of the CPI and DMK in parliament. The government even promised to "deal with compassion" and keep the tax records of tax dodgers secret from other government departments.[91] By the end of November, then, smugglers and tax evaders had immunity from prosecution, did not have to disclose the source of their income, and could spread their tax liabilities among their family members.[92] Indeed, Mrs Gandhi looked the other way even as many of these artful dodgers refused to co-operate with the authorities: some of these, on returning from work in the city, checked straight into St George's Hospital in Bombay, where their "heart ailments" were supposedly being treated.[93] The regime also abandoned a countrywide property survey that was to ascertain ill-gotten gains. "We want to avoid a witch-hunt", said

---

[89] Smuggling is mostly done in gold. By the mid-1970s, 250 tons of gold was being smuggled into India every year: Hiro, *Inside India*, p. 33. This arrangement was, strictly speaking, a loosely fixed exchange-rate system in which the rupee was pegged to an "undisclosed basket of currencies" and allowed to float within 2.25 per cent of what the RBI found acceptable. Still, what followed was a gradual but "sizeable depreciation" between 1975 and 1992: EPW Research Foundation, "Effective Exchange Rate for the Rupee", p. 128.

[90] Toye, "Economic Trends and Policies in India during the Emergency", p. 309.

[91] *SW*, 24 January 1976, p. 13.

[92] The Planning Commission's reservations—"it would not be logically correct to suggest that the remedy lies not in the improvement of procedures or administration but in a scheme or confession"—were ignored: "Extracts from Planning Commission letter No. 25/75–Econ. of September 15, 1975 to Ministry of Finance", 15 September 1975, P.N. Haksar Papers, Instalment III, Subject File 354.

[93] Selbourne, *An Eye to India*, p. 201.

Pranab Mukherjee, initially minister of state for finance and then revenue minister, who was in charge of the fight against corruption.[94]

Mukherjee owed his ascent in part to the fact that he was both very well networked and loyal: an associate of Sanjay, he had helped the young man settle scores with an old nemesis who happened to be his boss, Finance Minister C. Subramaniam. In December 1975 the latter's long-held scepticism towards Sanjay's Maruti enterprise was to cost him dearly: the flagship anti-smuggling drive as well as tax competencies were taken from his ministry and handed over to Mukherjee, now revenue minister with a new department of his own.[95] In this role Mukherjee went after Sanjay's enemies, old and new. Among those targeted was Mantosh Sondhi, an engineer employed by the Ministry of Industry at the Bokaro Steel Plant, who was responsible for collecting information on Maruti as part of a parliamentary investigation.

On the other hand, Mukherjee was more than willing to forgive friends of the grand old party. For instance, during a tax raid on Baroda Rayon Corporation in April 1976, when it transpired that V.K. Shah, the managing director, was a major donor to the Congress, Mukherjee had the officers of the income tax department hand him the evidence from the "search and seizure" operation. Soon after, when the investigating officers asked to see the material to check for tax anomalies, they were told there was nothing to look for. The files vanished; their contents to this day "remain a mystery".[96] Quite unsurprisingly, then, the war on "economic offenders" resulted in far fewer cadavers than its generals had expected. At the end of the grace period, undeclared income worth only $1.6 billion was reported, for which the tax receipts were just about $270 million.[97] According to the Planning Commission, in 1975 "rolling black money" was worth at least $25.3 billion.[98] In sum, just around 6 per cent of this highly undervalued figure for black money in the country was declared, of which the smugglers and tax evaders paid less than 17 per cent of their laundered fortunes

---

[94] *SW*, 6 December 1975, p. 1. Between 1982 and 2017, he would go on to serve, *inter alia*, as defence, finance, and foreign minister, leader of the Lok Sabha and Rajya Sabha, and president of the republic.

[95] After the tax competencies were stripped from his department, C. Subramaniam suffered a heart attack.

[96] *SCR*, vol. 2, p. 14.

[97] Hart, "Introduction", p. 25.

[98] Selbourne, *An Eye to India*, p. 202.

as taxes.[99] In comparison, the highest tax band into which the country's law-abiding citizens fell was 77 per cent.[100]

The abuse of power was, of course, not restricted to Mukherjee's ministry. Undoubtedly, it was endemic to the Emergency. Even the trivial stipulation that shopkeepers display prices of all goods and discount them at state-sanctioned percentages was used to assail the regime's enemies.[101] For instance, Sanjay used this policy to attack P.N. Haksar, former principal secretary to the prime minister, who had in the past counselled Mrs Gandhi to curb her youngest son's influence in the administration. Thus, Haksar's octogenarian uncle, who owned a fabric shop called Pandit Brothers in Connaught Place, New Delhi, fell victim to a tax raid that was to unearth wholesale tax evasion—but all it threw up were minor infractions. This was followed by a "price tag raid" on the Chandni Chowk shop owned by the Haksars, also in the capital.[102] While a thorough search yielded not a "single" item "without a tag", Haksar's uncle was nevertheless charged for violating the Delhi Essential Articles (Display of Price) Order, 1975.[103]

[99] This was even more dismal than the efforts of three previous attempts at "voluntary disclosure" undertaken by Finance Ministers C.D. Deshmukh, T.T. Krishnamachari, and Morarji Desai. In sum, the tax yield from the three efforts was 23.4 per cent of the amount disclosed. My calculations, based on Mukherjee, *The Dramatic Decade*, p. 95.

[100] In effect, smugglers were being taxed at the basic rate of 17 per cent. The rates paid for incomes between Rs 8001–15,000; Rs 15,001–20,000; Rs 20,001–25,000; Rs 25,001–30,000; Rs 30,001–50,000; Rs 50,001–70,000; Rs 70,001–100,000; and incomes above that were 17, 20, 30, 40, 50, 60, 70, and 77 per cent, respectively. Using the data in Frankel, *India's Political Economy*, p. 555, one arrives at the figure of Rs 64,000 for the amount of money declared by smuggler per capita—a figure far higher than the lowest tax band. What this amounted to was an incentive to dodge taxes that year and then declare it under this scheme. See *SW*, 20 March 1976, p. 9. Given that the focus was on high-profile smugglers who owned property across the country and were "absconding throughout the country", it is safe to assume that most of them were rich enough to be taxed in the higher brackets: Mukherjee, *The Dramatic Decade*, pp. 86–7.

[101] While the enforced markdowns were 10 per cent on paper, authorities on the streets typically insisted on discounts in the range of 15 to 20 per cent: deposition of Kundan Lal Jaggi, Bata employee, 17 February 1978, SCP, Subject File 8, p. 84.

[102] Ramesh, *Intertwined Lives*, pp. 359–61.

[103] "Sales Tax and Price Tax Raids on the Shops of M/s Pandit Brothers", no date, SCP, Subject File 18, p. 5. He was released three days later, but only after CPI leader Aruna Asaf Ali brought the matter up with the prime minister.

The Twenty-Point Programme, in short, achieved little economically and devolved into a set of vendettas against the regime's adversaries past and present. But there remains another important aspect of it which needs to be considered. For if most of the programme seen so far represented the "progressive" face of the Emergency, the rest of it manifested its corporatist dimensions.

Dirigiste Corporatism

In their construal of society as a single whole—as a *dirigiste* polity where the free and pluralist representation of class interests was impermissible—Delhi's rulers during the Emergency betrayed a political vision that was corporatist to the hilt. Indeed, Philip Schmitter—a major theoretician of this "ism"—could have well been speaking in the language of the Twenty-Point Programme when he defined corporatism as:

> [A] system of interest representation in which the constituent units are organized into a limited number of singular, compulsory, non-competitive, hierarchically ordered and functionally differentiated categories, recognised or licensed (if not created) by the state and granted a deliberate representational monopoly within their respective categories in exchange for observing certain controls on their selection of leaders and articulation of demands and supports.[104]

Seen from a world-historical perspective, such a coupling of corporatism and authoritarianism is not unusual, for it forms one of Juan Linz's ideal types of the latter: the "organic state", where the institutionalisation and regulation of sectional interests are taken to their extreme.[105]

As we have seen, then, the Twenty-Point Programme was Janus-like. Alongside the fifteen points that promoted—on paper at least—the interests of the majority were the remaining five, which worked mostly to the benefit of industrialists and the middle class: liberalising investment procedures; introducing "new schemes for workers' associations in industry", a euphemism for crushing labour in the name of class collaboration; implementing a "national permit scheme for road transport", in practice extending unfettered access to state markets across the country to private sector monopolies;[106] giving the middle class major tax breaks by exempting those

---

[104] Schmitter, "Still the Century of Corporatism", pp. 93–4.
[105] Linz, *Totalitarian and Authoritarian Regimes*, p. 214.
[106] *TOI*, 21 August 1975, p. 7.

earning under Rs 8000 from all tax obligations; and imposing an austerity programme to reduce public spending.

Scarcely a month had elapsed since the declaration of the Emergency when Krishan Kant, a Young Turk, stood up in parliament and asked, perhaps only half in jest, "if this is really a swing to the left or whether it is not, in fact, a swing to the right?"[107] Certainly, for this MP of the Congress Left, the chasm between rhetoric and reality at the time smacked of betrayal. But truth be told, his reaction was disingenuous. The Congress Left had never been a strong force in the republic in the first place: land reform had foundered, working-class wages could scarcely support a dignified life, and the welfare state had, since its inception, one foot in the grave. This was the legacy of a kind of political grammar that evolved in the late colonial and early postcolonial period, whose watchword, one of Gandhian vintage, was "trusteeship"—the preference for class collaboration and the attendant allergy to class struggle. Corporatism, in a word. All the same, authoritarianism, with its expanded vocabulary of discipline, productivity, efficiency, and nationalism, allowed for the deepening of this logic.

Among the most significant changes the new regime introduced was a crackdown on trade unionism. On 15 November 1975, in her inaugural speech at the general council of the Indian National Trade Union Congress, the grand old party's union, Mrs Gandhi regretted "the multiplicity of unions" and the number of man-days lost to strikes. That figure had fallen from 33.6 million in 1974 to 16.7 million the following year, but this was still "a great deal", she complained: "we need the co-operation of the working classes to make a better India, to provide the goods that are needed for our defence, for our agriculture, and for our daily lives."[108] Barooah echoed her: trade unions were "trying to mislead the working class and sabotage production."[109]

To this end, strikes were banned and 2000 unionists locked up.[110] The largest unions in the republic, the Congress' INTUC and the CPI's AITUC, were "disciplined" from within, and the HMS, the union of the Socialists, from without, while the biggest union without state sponsorship and the only one to oppose the new dispensation, the CPI(M)'s Centre of Indian Trade Unions, was severely weakened by the incarceration of twenty of its leaders.[111] New

---

[107] *Rajya Sabha Debates*, vol. 93, no. 2 (22 July 1975), col. 62.

[108] *SSWIG*, vol. 3, pp. 367, 362.

[109] *SW*, 5 July 1975, p. 1.

[110] Selbourne, *An Eye to India*, p. 181.

[111] Rudolph and Rudolph, "To the Brink and Back", p. 388.

committees in the name of better industrial relations were foisted on the unions. Ostensibly, this was done to promote "workers' participation", which, as Mrs Gandhi put it, was "essential to create in the worker a genuine interest in the growth and well-being of the industry in which he is employed."[112]

Here the prime minister already had a head start: in the 1950s Nehru had established institutions in which capitalists, trade unionists, and representatives of the state were supposed to work together. But Mrs Gandhi wanted to go further and establish a National Apex Body where workers and management of both the private and public sectors would "sit together and try to find ways of solving problems."[113] By January 1976 state labour advisory boards and apex bodies had mushroomed across the country. Below them, "shop councils" were formed at the factory level, each of which consisted of an equal number of representatives of workers and managers. The latter, of course, had the upper hand: "the chairman of the council will be nominated by the management and the workers will elect a vice-chairman from amongst themselves", read the charter. What of its remit? "The charge of the councils will be: increase of production, productivity and overall efficiency of the shop, including the elimination of wastage of resources—men, material and financial."[114]

While these organisations officially let on that employees were on a par with employers, the former certainly lost out to the latter, being subjected during the Emergency to a wage freeze, a ban on strikes, and a reduction of the annual wage bonus. It must be remembered that "bonus" is a misnomer in India: it refers not to an extra payment as a reward for good performance but a mandatory "deferred wage entitlement".[115] Here, especially, the effects of creeping authoritarianism were plain to see: in 1971, when India was still a democracy, Mrs Gandhi had introduced the mandatory payment of an 8.33 per cent bonus to workers, as against 4 per cent earlier. In June 1974, autocratic impulses already manifest, the Wage Freeze Act was rammed through parliament: half of every citizen's dearness allowance— annual wage adjustments to take into account inflation—was to be withheld

---

[112] *SSWIG*, vol. 3, p. 370.

[113] Ibid., p. 369.

[114] Gandhi, *Era of Discipline*, p. 322.

[115] Selbourne, *An Eye to India*, p. 216. This was a logic widely accepted in political discourse: see the transcript of interview with Madhu Dandavate, Acc. No. 778, NMML Oral History Project, p. 71.

from them as a "compulsory deposit". By June 1976 Rs 10 billion in wages had wound up with the government through such sequestrations.[116]

And finally, on 25 September 1975, the new dispensation having made electoral considerations entirely unnecessary, the bonus was slashed back to 4 per cent by ordinance. As Mrs Gandhi saw it, "what was the worth of [sic] bonus or salary or any other rights of the workers if the economy could not be protected, if there was serious inflation and the value of the rupee fell?"[117] Moreover, the new edict added that only companies making profits for four consecutive years would need to pay this bonus. Given the large scope of earnings manipulation—including the "sole selling agency" system—at the disposal of firms and their accountants,[118] this gave employers enough room for manoeuvre to do away with the "illogical" bonuses altogether.[119] Over the next few months, wages plummeted too. Docking workers' pay "was not a pleasant decision", Finance Minister Subramaniam noted, but it had to be done, "even if it hurt the workers".[120] Blue-collar employees were already, at the time, victims of a regime that allowed for arbitrary wage deductions. Ostensibly the sum was meant to aid workers in time of disease and distress—the Indian state had never taken up such social security commitments—but workers were often cheated out of them. In January 1976 the labour minister admitted that the state was Rs 280 million in arrears on payments due to workers.[121]

The case of the Indian Telephone Industries, a state-owned enterprise in Bangalore, illustrates how industrial relations worked in Emergency India:

[116] See the note by S. Habeebullah, Under Secretary to the Government of India, Department of Personnel and Administrative Reforms, 7 November 1974, MHAP, File 22/1/74–AIS–II.

[117] *SW*, 22 November 1975, p. 1.

[118] This allowed manufacturers to assign exclusive marketing rights to a single company, which may well have been a subsidiary. As a palliative measure, the sole selling agency system was banned for five years in the sugar and vegetable-oil industries. But enough loopholes remained on offer to accountants: Erdman, "The Industrialists", p. 145.

[119] As Mrs Gandhi put it to World Bank president Robert McNamara: *TOI*, 11 November 1976, p. 1. "There is no major policy difference between the Bank and India", McNamara exclaimed on the same trip. He also discerned "a willingness to find practical solutions to economic problems rather than an attitude of falling back on 'socialist ideologies and didactic debate'": Kapur, Lewis, and Webb, *The World Bank*, pp. 293, 478.

[120] *SW*, 4 October 1975, p. 10.

[121] *TOI*, 24 January 1976, p. 13.

promised a 20 per cent bonus in line with the company's profits before the authoritarian turn, the in-house union now faced an emboldened management that reneged on its commitment—8 per cent was all the workers would get. When the 8000 workers resorted to a "peaceful sit-in" in front of the chairman's office, the foremen summoned the police who "brutally *lathi*-charged" them, taking a hundred under custody. Frustrated, the workers drew inspiration from the Luddites, causing "much damage" to the machinery in their battle with the police.[122] When a similar demand was made at the Hindustan Machine Tools factory in Andhra Pradesh, the president of the union was thrown in jail. In Maharashtra, striking employees of the Bombay Port Trust were hauled off to prison after they were falsely accused of "having association with the banned organisations [*sic*]."[123] In Bombay, tax raids were conducted on the premises of trade-union leaders of the All-India Bank Employees Union to harass them for their opposition to the bonus ordinance. No evidence was found to support the wild allegations emanating from the CBI—"extorting money for donations", "receiving various other pecuniary benefits", and "having a standard of living much above that warranted by his known sources of income."[124] When the AITUC organised a one-day strike to protest the slashing of the bonus in January 1976, the government responded by having "30,000 to 40,000" workers arrested.[125]Squeezing the working class further was the government's decision to jack up rents. For instance, the Maharashtra Housing Board raised "service charges" across Greater Bombay "by 55 to 100 per cent" in January 1976. Congressmen too became victims of the regime. Former Bombay mayor and incumbent president of the Bombay Port Trust Union Shanti Patel, for instance, was arrested under MISA for allowing a strike to proceed.[126] In the face of such violence, unions preferred capitulation to resistance. In the steel industry, for example, the INTUC, AITUC, HMS, and CITU collectively made an agreement with the state: in exchange for higher wages, the unions promised not to raise a dispute for the next four years.[127]

The working classes having now been "disciplined", Mrs Gandhi exclaimed in parliament that "industrial relations had improved almost

---

[122] *Satya Samachar*, 10 November 1976, pp. 4–5, in MLP, reel 1.

[123] *SCR*, vol. 3, pp. 48, 90.

[124] "Harassment of Trade Union Leaders", no date, SCP, Subject File 14, pp. 4–5.

[125] *Guardian*, 10 January 1976, p. 2.

[126] *TOI*, 12 January 1976, p. 5.

[127] Selbourne, *An Eye to India*, p. 217.

beyond imagination."[128] Wadud Khan, former director of a Tata enterprise who was now director of a public-sector steel company, was exuberant at the prospect of increased profitability: low wages and high productivity meant more exports, more foreign exchange, and reduced trade deficits, he reasoned.[129] Indeed, in 1976–7 India registered a trade surplus—the only year it did in the 1970s—on the back of cheapened labour facilitated by authoritarian rule, but also because of the stabilisation of oil prices, increased aid, higher remittances, and the rise in domestic oil production spurred by discoveries at Bombay High, an offshore oilfield on the western continental shelf.[130]

But, despite the new dispensation, growth in the private industrial sector remained moribund in comparison to the public sector. To offset this, the shareholding class was given, as it were, a "bonus": restrictions on scrip issues and cash dividends were eased.[131] Moreover, the future prospects of Indian businesses appeared bright: production had grown in leaps and bounds.[132] These levels of growth, the captains of industry could be certain, were to be sustained in coming years. After all, their biggest champion now resided in government. Inaugurating the National Convention on Productivity on 10 November 1976, Mrs Gandhi urged workers to produce more: "Efficiency means making people give of their best and this will be possible if they have a sense of partnership", she said breathlessly.[133] Through the months of authoritarian rule, efficiency was increased by "compell[ing] workers to work on holidays" and by "heavily increas[ing] their workload".[134] Indeed, it was in the name of efficiency that 275,000 workers were made redundant in the first year of the Emergency alone.[135]

Mrs Gandhi, then, had set the stage for the worst mining disaster in Indian history. Certainly, miners in the country were already in the most

[128] *Lok Sabha Debates*, vol. 53, no. 1 (21 July 1975), col. 72.

[129] *SW*, 9 August 1975, p. 1. At a time of ballooning trade deficits—which had risen from Rs 251 crores in 1972–3 to Rs 977 crores in 1974–5—this was a major concern.

[130] Nayyar, "India's Balance of Payments", p. 649.

[131] *Economic Survey, 1975–1976*, p. 1.

[132] In 1975–76, coal production had risen to 98 million tons from the previous year's 88 million; steel, 6 million tons from 5.5; cement, 17 from 14.5; fertilisers, 1.8 from 1.5.

[133] *SSWIG*, vol. 3, p. 394.

[134] Chaudhuri, "Disturbed Industrial Situation", p. 656.

[135] *Observer*, 27 June 1976, p. 8.

precarious of circumstances: by the government's own admission, "periodical unemployment" and the need for extensive "medical care" had pushed nearly "40 to 50 per cent" of them into debt, "fattening the pockets of the moneylenders" who "perpetrated atrocities" on the colliery workers.[136] But the disaster that transpired in Bihar at the close of 1975 could only have been the *dénouement* of a state-of-the-union novel, capturing in a single episode the spirit of Emergency India.

On 27 December 1975, at the Chasnala colliery in Dhanbad, more than 370 miners were killed when over 100 million gallons of water gushed into the mine.[137] Managed by the state and declared a safety hazard on many occasions—emphasis had even been laid on the "danger of inundation"—the mine symbolised the monumental failure of Mrs Gandhi's industrial relations policy.[138] Only a few months earlier, Dhanbad miners protesting abysmal conditions and irregular pay had been shot at by the police. Despite this, and similar instances across the republic, on 1 November the government had unveiled its Twelve-Point Programme for coal mines: collieries would now run seven days a week; but—small mercies—"with staggered holidays for workers" each of them would have "to put in only six days of work".[139] And just a month before the accident, the CITU had complained to the ILO about the frequent arrest of miners as well as raised wage and safety concerns. The night before the accident, the miners had been on strike, again because of the "dangerous conditions" in the shafts. But the bosses—reflecting the cult of productivity that had percolated from the political to the managerial classes—remained steadfast that daily production be raised by 50 per cent.

The result was the most fatal coal mining disaster in the history of the country. It was also the two hundred and twenty-second accident of the year, all the preceding ones together having already claimed 288 lives, more than double the death toll of 1974.[140] When it occurred, there were no pumps at the colliery to dry the mines. These had to be imported post-haste from Poland and the Soviet Union. By the time they arrived, the bodies of

---

[136] See IAS officer K.B. Saxena's report, "Problem of Indebtedness Among Industrial Labour: A Case Study of Dhanbad Coalfield" that was circulated in the MHA in July 1975, five months before the disaster in the town: MHAP, File 8/5/75–RP.

[137] The government figure of 372 was certainly an underestimate. By March 1976 the toll had risen to 431. Bodies continued to be unearthed through the year.

[138] *SW*, 2 August 1975, p. 14; Selbourne, *An Eye to India*, p. 251.

[139] *SW*, 8 November 1975, p. 4.

[140] *SW*, 10 January 1975, p. 10.

the miners had been completely obliterated—the death toll was estimated by counting belts and battery lamps. None of this induced remorse, let alone reform, in Delhi's rulers. Just three days after the disaster, Mrs Gandhi was already telling the "poorer and weaker sections" of society to do "not what can be asked for, but what can be given for greater production."[141] Two weeks after the disaster, the calls for more coal production were resumed, this time after striking a trade deal to export "about 350,000 tonnes of coal" to Bangladesh by the end of February. To this end, production targets were raised by an additional 10 per cent for the new year.[142] And it was only after Communist parliamentarians pointed out that the Workmen's Compensation Act was preventing the victims' families at Chasnala from being paid compensation (they were disqualified because their annual incomes were above the Rs 500 threshold) that the Labour Ministry agreed to make an exception and authorise a payout.[143] When the CPI(M) tried to organise a "silent procession in memory" of the dead colliers, Delhi refused permission.[144]

Making the unions impotent certainly was a godsend to industrialists: only 2.3 million man-days were lost between July and December 1975, compared to the four times greater figure for the corresponding period of the previous year. Public-sector output grew by 15 per cent and stock markets rose by almost 10 per cent in the interim, highlighting a peculiarity of the Emergency regime, and indeed of all business-friendly autocracies: even the political upheavals generated by authoritarian governance were not enough to dislodge investors' faith in the ability of the state to safeguard their interests. As B.K. Nehru, Mrs Gandhi's cousin and high commissioner to London, put it, this was the great advantage that dictatorships had over liberal regimes: "A rise in their [the peoples'] standard of living is not permitted till such time as the rulers think that a sufficient rate of saving—and of growth—can be maintained."[145] That the regime cared less for workers than for their employers was evident from its approach to child labour, too. For when it was suggested that the ten million Indians workers aged fourteen and under be removed from labour markets, the Ministry of Education counselled that it was "not only not

---

141 Selbourne, *An Eye to India*, p. 250.
142 *SW*, 17 January 1976, p. 1; *SW*, 6 March, p. 4.
143 *SW*, 24 January 1976, p. 10.
144 Chatterjee, *Keeping the Faith*, pp. 267–8.
145 Mehta, *The New India*, p. 79.

feasible but also *not desirable* at the present state of the country's economic level."[146]

* * *

When the balance sheet is drawn, it becomes apparent that while Mrs Gandhi met with considerable success in pursuing her corporatist policies, her redistributionist ambitions produced mixed results.[147] This is in keeping with the nature of authoritarianism and populism, the two "isms" that Delhi's rulers welded together during the Emergency. For this blend fits with the kind of depoliticisation that Linz witnesses in such societies. The reason is that neither of these "isms" are ideologies as such. It is not surprising, then, that the kind of mobilisation that took place during the Emergency displayed no attachment to ideas but only to the country's rulers. That corporatism trumped welfarism also conforms to the behaviour of what Linz calls "organic states". The suppression of rival institutions and the resistance—the subjects of Chapters 3 and 9, respectively—during the Emergency, too, was par for the course.

Furthermore, the ambivalences of the Twenty-Point Programme are consistent with the hybrid nature of populism. For, on the one hand, populists are not socialists, even if they identify with the Left, as Mrs Gandhi did; yet, on the other, they cannot ignore the people in whose name they rule. Populism, in essence, is as much the product of inequality as it is a tactical response to its contestation. The upshot is twofold. First, that elites, as in the Emergency, strengthen their hold over power and resources by enlisting the support of the people, and uniting them over and above class differences in order to better preserve the social status quo. Second, that in diffusing social tensions, elites invariably offer a few sops to the poor. During the Emergency, for instance, land reform was marginally more thorough than it was before,

---

[146] Selbourne, *An Eye to India*, p. 64. Emphasis added. The statement is from 25 May 1976. This was in reference to the ILO's Minimum Age Convention, 1973. India ratified it only in 2017.

[147] A growing trend in the academy is to look for the harbingers to the 1991 neo-liberal turn in earlier premierships. Corbridge and Harriss see it in Rajiv Gandhi's tenure (1984–9), Maiorano in Indira Gandhi's final term (1980–4). Here we discern traces of it during the Emergency. Of course, such ideas had currency in the early postcolonial years as well, as Frankel's analysis of the Nehruvian political economy reveals. See Corbridge and Harriss, *Reinventing India*, pp. 102–4; Maiorano, *Autumn of the Matriarch's*, pp. 86–95; Frankel, *India's Political Economy*, pp. 201–45.

wages slightly higher, and commodity prices moderately lower. But, as we have seen, the open class war the state waged against the poor offset whatever little progressivism Mrs Gandhi's government represented.

Unable to articulate any consistent ideology, Mrs Gandhi fell back on personality cult and nationalism, both in tandem because she saw herself as embodying the nation and protecting it from its enemies. Defending the country from foreign threats became the official line. Here was a "politics of fear" well in tune with Mrs Gandhi's deep sense of insecurity.[148] While such rhetoric rarely percolated into popular discourse, it is clear that virtually the entire top leadership of the Congress was willing to partake in the hysteria over "big powers" and "external interference".[149] In the new dispensation, Mrs Gandhi, *primus inter pares*, played a key role in threat inflation: few speeches justifying the imposition of authoritarian rule were complete without references to the "foreign hand"—more often than not the CIA—at work in India. D.K. Barooah concurred: "the dark forces of neo-imperialism and eastern racial arrogance"—that is, the United States and China—were trying "to snuff out the light of democracy in this part of the world ... a nuclear base [is] being developed in Diego Garcia."[150] Other ministers pointed fingers at nemeses closer home: Pakistan was "arming itself feverishly", Bansi Lal contended; the "anti-India trend" in Bangladesh was growing, suggested Chavan.[151] The curbs on foreign contributions to Indian NGOs—which, in the words of Deputy Home Minister F.H. Mohsin, who shepherded the bill in parliament in March 1976, were "polluting the body politic"—was of a piece with this worldview.[152] In a word, India's rulers during the Emergency exchanged ideology for fear and nationalism.

[148] This strategy, which has gained momentum after 9/11, has been theorised only recently but is relevant to analyse Mrs Gandhi's politics in the 1970s. See Gore, "The Politics of Fear", pp. 779–98. More on this in Chapter 7.

[149] See, *inter alia*, *SW*, 3 January 1976, p. 9; *SW*, 10 January, p. 1; *SW*, 17 January, p. 5; *SW*, 28 February, p. 1.

[150] *SW*, 6 December 1975, p. 1.

[151] *SW*, 6 March 1976, p. 14.

[152] *TOI*, 30 March 1976, p. 1. In his bid to neutralise NGOs, Modi followed in Mohsin's footsteps in 2014 after the Intelligence Bureau blamed "foreign-funded non-governmental organisations" for "negatively impacting economic development" to the tune of "2–3 per cent" of Indian GDP "per annum": *Indian Express*, 7 June 2014 (https://indianexpress.com/article/india/india-others/foreign-aided-ngos-are-actively-stalling-development-ib-tells-pmo-in-a-report/), accessed on 1 September 2018. In 2018, some 20,000 NGOs receiving foreign funds found their licenses revoked.

3

SUBVERTING INSTITUTIONS

REMNANTS OF DEMOCRACY

The most peculiar aspect of Mrs Gandhi's authoritarian regime, incontrovertibly, was that, while imposing its will over society in an increasingly despotic manner, it left the judiciary and parliament intact, at least formally so. For there was considerable concern on the part of Delhi's rulers over maintaining some semblance of legality: all political activity had to appear constitutionally permissible. To both international and domestic audiences, then, the retention of legislative and judicial checks and balances could be sold as evidence of democratic continuity—"the very summoning of parliament is proof that democracy is functioning in India", Mrs Gandhi declared in July 1975.[1]

But both parliament—many of whose members were in jail—and the judiciary were under attack. Immediately after declaring the Emergency, Mrs Gandhi issued an ordinance that, among other repressive measures, subjected parliamentary proceedings to censorship and suspended the question hour. Constitutional amendments placed the election of the president, vice president, prime minister, and speaker of the Lok Sabha beyond the scrutiny of the courts. It was now stipulated that ordinances could no longer be challenged in any court of law, and a provision was added to MISA prohibiting release on bail, both measures making the

---

[1] *SSWIG*, vol. 3, p. 187.

judiciary even more redundant. Electoral laws, along with a number of property laws, MISA, and COFEPOSA were placed in the Ninth Schedule, the part of the constitution beyond the reach of judicial review. Judges had even fewer prerogatives left for defending individual liberties, because a presidential order suspended for the duration of the Emergency the right of citizens to move the courts to enforce fundamental rights. The Forty-second Amendment went even further: the Supreme Court was forbidden from adjudicating the constitutionality of state laws, high courts were prohibited from issuing stays, and fundamental rights could no longer be invoked to challenge arrest.

Despite being considerably weakened, both parliament and the judiciary continued to play, albeit marginally, a role in holding the executive to account. Some parliamentarians criticised the regime in the Lok and the Rajya Sabhas, and some judges resisted the Emergency's legal transgressions.

The Façade of Parliamentarism

After 25 June 1975 the Congress was keen to provide the regime with some democratic ballast. The Emergency had after all been imposed constitutionally, and came to be endorsed constitutionally by parliament too. As Article 352 necessitated the approval of both houses of parliament within two months of its declaration, the president of the republic, going through the motions, summoned the monsoon session on 9 July. The session, which in the event commenced on the 21st—more pressing matters had to be taken care of in the interim, such as the ordinance that subjected parliamentary proceedings to censorship—was a circumscribed affair. Suspended were the question hour, motions by private members, and parliamentary privilege.

The session did not, however, transpire without debate. While fifty-nine Lok Sabha and Rajya Sabha parliamentarians were behind bars, the rest remained free to attend.[2] The first resolution, which called for the suspension of the question hour, for instance, met stiff resistance. The DMK's Era Sezhiyan railed against it; P.K. Deo of the BLD used his time at the lectern to describe the Emergency as "the swan song of democracy"; and Young Turk Mohan Dharia, who had been ejected from the Congress in March 1975 for giving Jayaprakash Narayan an audience, denounced what he saw as the "virtual surrender of the sovereign parliament to the executive."[3] But

---

[2] *Amnesty International Report*, p. 131.

[3] *Lok Sabha Debates*, vol. 53, no. 1 (21 July 1975), cols 26–7, 31, 36, 44.

these voices were in a minority. The Lok Sabha approved the suspension of the question hour 301 to 76; the Rajya Sabha 147 to 32.

Then came the main resolution concerning the approval of the Emergency, moved by Jagjivan Ram.[4] Mrs Gandhi had cleverly asked him to play this part. Ram had been a doubter, a possible contender for her job, even; but now he had little choice but to appear as her lieutenant. Only six hours of debate were slotted for this major issue. The spectrum of responses ranged from resistance to resignation. Not that resistance counted for much in the world of prior restraint: no parliamentary speech could ever have made it to the press. Nevertheless, CPI(M) parliamentarians fearlessly laid into the regime: A.K. Gopalan, who had just returned from a spell in prison, recalled the "inhuman treatment" inflicted on him and worried about the fate of the "2000 or 3000" comrades still behind bars.[5] He also accused the Congress of having quite conveniently patronised the RSS and Anand Marg in the past. Even Indrajit Gupta, CPI leader and Emergency apologist, took umbrage at the "stupid and unintelligent censorship".[6] The follow-up act was the Jana Sangh's Jagannathrao Joshi, who defended his party and the RSS. The DMK's Era Sezhiyan, the next speaker, appealed to Mrs Gandhi's better instincts:

> Oftentimes we may not have agreed with you but we all did agree on the functioning of democracy in this country and in this House. What has happened to this atmosphere? Why are we arraigned against each other, facing each other, to make you call us traitors, and equate us with those who are anti-national?[7]

The next day an independent MP, P.G. Mavalankar, presented the Emergency as a "constitutional dictatorship", borrowing a term from political science that Juan Linz would later use, but one that this parliamentarian, an accomplished scholar in his own right, had probably learnt from an older academic, Clinton Rossiter.[8] Another unaffiliated parliamentarian, Srinagar MP Shamim Ahmed Shamim, declared that "Mrs Gandhi is not a dictator, but she has begun to walk the road to dictatorship."[9] The best

---

[4] Ibid., col. 73 ff.

[5] Ibid., cols 87–8.

[6] Ibid., col. 128. However, he defended censorship on principle, suggesting it be imposed "for the purpose of weakening rightist forces": ibid., col. 104.

[7] Ibid., col. 168.

[8] *Lok Sabha Debates*, vol. 53, no. 2 (22 July 1975), col. 226; Rossiter, *Constitutional Dictatorship*.

[9] Nayar, *The Judgement*, p. 76. His translation from the Hindi.

defence that the prime minister could muster in response was that the "parliamentary system", in fact, stood unaltered. But the two sides were playing different games for different stakes. For the opposition MPs—their lives on the line—were trying to win the argument, while Mrs Gandhi, self-assured, could well dispense with argument altogether. The Congress, naturally, coasted to victory. The Lok Sabha approved the declaration of Emergency 336 to 59 on 23 July; the Rajya Sabha 136 to 33 the day before.[10] Nevertheless, in quick succession, the legislative successes were followed by defeats of a different order. Here the casualty was legitimacy. First, in the Rajya Sabha, Socialist leader N.G. Goray read out a statement on behalf of the opposition benches announcing a boycott of the remainder of the session.[11] Then the Lok Sabha followed suit, where non-Congress parliamentarians staged a walkout in unison.[12] For the rest of the session, both houses passed all resolutions *sans* opposition.[13]

Congressmen gleefully welcomed these developments and the possibilities of constitutional change they opened up. For Karan Singh the Emergency was an opportunity to consider "the deeper question of evolving a constitutional structure better suited to the requirements and genius of the nation."[14] In this session Mrs Gandhi hoped not only to legalise the new dispensation but also considerably amend the constitution. To this end the Thirty-ninth Amendment stipulated that ordinances could no longer be challenged in any court of law, and the MISA Amendment Act clarified that informing detainees of the grounds for their arrest was no longer obligatory. Both bills passed in parliament with scant dissent, the opposition protesting *in absentia* and Congressmen expressing not so much as a single thought that could offend their ruler's sensibilities—an attitude that partly explained why Mrs Gandhi could continue to play the parliamentary game (to which we will return in Part II).

The first parliamentary session of the Emergency was also an opportunity for Finance Minister C. Subramaniam to present the Twenty-Point

---

[10] *Lok Sabha Debates*, vol. 53, no. 2 (22 July 1975), cols 56ff, 42.

[11] Nayar, *The Judgement*, pp. 77–8.

[12] Mavalankar, *"No, Sir"*, p. 19.

[13] Save one lone opponent in the Lok Sabha, Shamim Ahmed Shamim, the independent who occasionally voted to express dissent: see, *inter alia, Lok Sabha Debates*, vol. 53, no. 3 (23 July 1975), col. 158; *Lok Sabha Debates*, vol. 53, no. 5 (25 July 1975), col. 171.

[14] Singh to Gandhi, 28 June 1975: "Some Aspects of Recent Affairs", in Alam, *Kashmir and Beyond*, p. 280.

Programme at greater length—and for seventy-five Congress and CPI MPs to take to the dais and panegyrise it.[15] In the context of the programme, Pranab Mukherjee, then minister of state for finance, moved an amendment to the Conservation of Foreign Exchange and Prevention of Smuggling Activities Act. "In the present Emergency", he noted, "the disclosure of grounds of detention to such persons and compliance with the usual procedures of reference to the advisory boards would not be in the larger interests of the nation."[16] Thus, reasons of state invoked, the imperative to supply a reason for arrest was done away with. Curtailing civil liberties was justified in the name of social justice. Indeed, even decades later, in his autobiography Mukherjee defends the amendment in these terms, observing that it was only two months before the Emergency that two smugglers arrested under COFEPOSA were let out of prison, apparently because "just one of the many grounds" was found invalid. It was high time, then, that "this loophole and other shortcomings of the Act were plugged."[17] In the same session, Home Minister K. Brahmananda Reddy moved another amendment to MISA, this time to make incarceration under it unbailable. As he tautologically argued, "we have had a few instances of persons securing their release on bail. It has, therefore, become necessary to include a specific provision in MISA prohibiting release on bail."[18]

Towards the end of the session, Indira Gandhi had parliament turn to more personal matters. Moved by Law Minister H.R. Gokhale, a new bill sought to reverse Justice Sinha's judgment that had invalidated her election. Under it, assistance to a candidate by a public servant was no longer a corrupt practice. Two more points were laid on with a trowel. First: what of the dates of appointment and termination of service of government employees? These would be the same as those published in the official gazette. The amendment was retroactive and so made Yashpal Kapoor's transgression redundant. And second: what of election expenses? Only money spent from the date of the candidate's nomination was to be taken into account. This made irrelevant the charge that Mrs Gandhi had spent more than Rs 35,000—the limit—on the campaign trail. It also allowed

---

[15] See the *Lok Sabha Debates*, vols 53 and 54, nos 9, 10, and 11 (31 July and 1–2 August 1975), indices *et passim*.

[16] *Lok Sabha Debates*, vol. 53, no. 3 (23 July 1975), col. 189.

[17] Mukherjee, *The Dramatic Decade*, p. 85.

[18] *Lok Sabha Debates*, vol. 53, no. 5 (25 July 1975), col. 83. In any case, those granted bail were often quickly rearrested: *SCR*, vol. 2, p. 36.

elected representatives who had been disqualified because of corrupt practices to petition the president for a remission.[19]

Parallel to this effort was an attempt to prevent the courts from passing judgment on matters relating to the office of prime minister. On 5 August a Congress backbencher suggested that Mrs Gandhi be made immune from judicial scrutiny.[20] To this end, two days later—the last day of the session—the Thirty-ninth Amendment was tabled in the Lok Sabha for all of 150 minutes. Why the rush? On 11 August a bench of five judges headed by the chief justice was to hear Mrs Gandhi's appeal regarding her disqualification. This bill—the handiwork of Ray, Chavan, Gokhale, and Rajni Patel—had long been in the making. As Chavan had put it in the wake of the Allahabad judgement, "what happens to Indira today happens to India tomorrow."[21] Approved post-haste, it empowered parliament to create an authority singly for the purpose of monitoring the election of the prime minister, president, vice president, and speaker of the lower house.[22] Courts were barred from challenging this authority, for "to protect this great democracy", as the law minister argued, it was essential to insulate higher office from "outside authority".[23] Moreover, all ongoing proceedings against these four figures were terminated.[24] After opposition MPs walked out, the Thirty-ninth Amendment passed 336 to 0.[25] Defence Minister Swaran Singh was among the few Congressmen, along with Subramaniam and Ram, who felt that the amendment had "gone too far", but all three nevertheless went along with it.[26] With its passage, it was now time to take

[19] *Lok Sabha Debates*, vol. 54, no. 12 (5 August 1975), cols 2, 7.

[20] Hiro, *Inside India*, p. 265.

[21] Austin, *Working a Democratic Constitution*, p. 321.

[22] These provisions were contained in Article 329A, created for this purpose.

[23] Mussells, "Democracy and Emergency Rule in India", p. 147. The election laws were the Representation of the People Acts of 1951 and 1974 and the Election Laws Amendment Act of 1975.

[24] The Fortieth Amendment, which was introduced on 21 May 1976, added sixty-three laws to the Ninth Schedule. This included the Prevention of Publication of Objectionable Matter Act, 1976, fifty-eight property laws, and four non-property ones. It was passed unanimously. By the end of 1976, 178 articles were insulated from judicial review, nearly twice the 1974 figure. Austin, *Working a Democratic Constitution*, p. 320; Hewitt, *Political Mobilisation and Democracy in India*, p. 135.

[25] *Lok Sabha Debates*, vol. 55, no. 14 (7 August 1975), col. 115. In the index, this appears as the "Fortieth Amendment", but as the amendment of clauses makes clear, it was the Thirty-ninth: ibid., col. 82.

[26] Austin, *Working a Democratic Constitution*, p. 322.

"a fresh look at the whole fundamental structure of the Constitution itself", Gokhale said.[27]

But that would have to wait, at least momentarily, for to put Mrs Gandhi in the clear a few holes still needed plugging. The Rajya Sabha approved the Thirty-ninth Amendment on 8 August; seventeen state assemblies ratified it the next day—a Saturday—in special sessions; and on 10 August—a day before the hearings—the president signed off on it. In the interim, on 9 August, the Rajya Sabha passed the Forty-first Amendment, which exempted the president, vice president, and prime minister from criminal proceedings, even for crimes they may have committed before they took office.[28] Mrs Gandhi, then, was about to grant herself lifetime immunity from judicial and criminal prosecution. However, Congressmen felt that this was an overkill and could lead to international disapproval, which might then hurt the government's plans to court more aid and investment from abroad. C. Subramaniam, leading the charge, convinced Mrs Gandhi of the bill's futility. In the event, the bill was pulled from the Lok Sabha. Later, however, it was passed in January 1976 and allowed to lapse in early 1977 when parliament was dissolved.[29]

The first parliamentary session under the Emergency, then, was marked by both the legitimation of Mrs Gandhi authoritarian rule and the resilience of parliamentarism. Procedurally, there was little change in the business of law-making before and after 25 June 1975. Parliamentarians from the opposition benches found this particularly unsettling. Muddling along from one strategy to another, they charted a course between Scylla and Charybdis, boycotting debate some days and taking part in it on others.

The winter session, usually held in the last two months of every calendar year, was cancelled, and instead on 5 January 1976 a "special" joint session of both houses was convened. Protocol remained unaffected by the exceptional circumstances and attempts were made to project an air of normalcy: the president gave an address and the prime minister introduced the new faces of her cabinet. The elephant in the room was, of course, the virtual absence of the opposition which, in a rare moment of unity, had agreed to a collective boycott. Lone efforts by the few opposition MPs who attended the session, including Mavalankar and Sezhiyan, to weaken government

---

[27] *Lok Sabha Debates*, vol. 55, no. 14 (7 August 1975), col. 59.

[28] The president was already exempted from criminal proceedings by Article 361. Clearly, the focus was on the office of prime minister.

[29] Austin, *Working a Democratic Constitution*, p. 323.

bills were quickly shot down by the Congress' brute majority.[30] Indeed, during this session law upon law was passed: on 22 January MISA was given a boost, allowing for the immediate re-arrest of those whose detention orders had expired or been revoked. The bill, which took a battering from the CPI(M), Mrs Gandhi's Communist allies, and even Gokhale, who was in favour of judicial review, nevertheless passed 181 to 27.[31] The weight of the law minister's conscience, it transpired, was not as heavy as he let on: he assented to the majoritarian position after being assured at a cabinet meeting that a "reviewing board" would act as *de facto* judicial review.[32] On 28 January parliament passed three bills curtailing press freedoms based on ordinances from the previous year. Attempts by the CPI and the CPI(M), led by Indrajit Gupta and Dinendranath Bhattacharya, respectively, to introduce amendments to weaken them were shot down 152 to 35, 154 to 32, and 141 to 36. In desperation, Bhattacharya shouted out to the deputy speaker, ironically: "with the ayes, you kindly add the number of MPs who are in jail."[33]

On 4 February the next order of business was to put before Parliament the party decision to extend the life of the Emergency by a year—as "permitted" by Article 83 of the constitution—and shirk the election due in March.[34] This had been resolved at the Congress' Seventy-fifth Plenary Session—its first in three years—in Chandigarh on 31 December 1975, where Sanjay and his clique had demonstrated their ascendancy.[35] The extension passed 165 to 20.[36] On the face of it, delaying the election made little sense. The media and the opposition were at their nadir, and economic signs predicted a secular decline from here on: inflation was going to be on the rise, demand on the decline, and the chance of another good harvest slim.[37] Resentment could only grow. That the Congress decided to hold off

---

[30] Ibid., pp. 41–2.

[31] See the contretemps between Brahmanand Reddy defending the bill and Indrajit Gupta and Dinendranath Bhattacharya opposing it: *Lok Sabha Debates*, vol. 56, no. 12 (22 January 1976), cols 182–226.

[32] Nayar, *The Judgement*, p. 121.

[33] Mavalankar, *"No, Sir"*, p. 79.

[34] *Lok Sabha Debates*, vol. 56, no. 20 (4 February 1976), col. 103. For more on the Plenary, see Chapter 4.

[35] Zaidi, *The Annual Register of Indian Political Parties—vol. 23*, p. 330.

[36] *Lok Sabha Debates*, vol. 56, no. 20 (4 February 1976), col. 195.

[37] By May 1976 the new FICCI president could declare that India was in the midst of a long-term recession.

elections notwithstanding suggests that, rhetoric apart, its commitment to the polls was suspect.

This was not lost on the other parties, whose leaders soon organised a conference chaired by Socialist leader N.G. Goray in Gandhinagar, the capital of Gujarat, a state still governed by the opposition. During it Mavalankar's suggestion, that all opposition MPs resign *en bloc* on the last day of their term, 18 March 1976, found no takers. In the event, only two lawmakers—Socialists Madhu Limaye and Sharad Yadav, both in prison—resigned.[38]

But when the new session, another "special" one—this time convened to push through the monumental Forty-second Amendment—commenced on 25 October 1976, the four largest opposition parties chose to steer clear of it.[39] Only 370 of the 545 MPs were sighted in parliament—Congressmen and Communists virtually to a man—leaving Mrs Gandhi foaming at the mouth: the boycotters were "escaping responsibility" in their "abuse of democracy", she thundered.[40]

Mrs Gandhi certainly put a premium on formal parliamentarianism. But what has been described so far does not adequately show her predilection for its antipode: presidentialism. This should come as no surprise, given the rise in the number of ordinances—a symptom of her allergy to parliamentarianism—her regime issued: from 4 in 1973, to 14 in 1974, and 34 in the three sessions of the Lok Sabha in the year following June 1975.[41]

Leading the call for constitutional change was B.K. Nehru, the prime minister's cousin and extravagant high commissioner in London,[42] who suggested a "French-type constitution" with Mrs Gandhi at the helm of a Gaullist presidency.[43] Indeed, the use of France as a reference point had

---

[38] See Chapter 9.

[39] Mavalankar, *"No, Sir"*, pp. 105, 223. For more on this amendment, see the next section.

[40] Austin, *Working a Democratic Constitution*, pp. 381–2.

[41] Hewitt, *Political Mobilisation and Democracy in India*, pp. 100, 125.

[42] "My foreign allowance had been raised ... but the money was so short that we could not afford to go to a theatre let alone the opera or the ballet, or to dine ... at the Traveller's Club ... It was ironic that while as a student I could afford regularly to dine at restaurants and go to the theatre": Nehru, *Nice Guys Finish Second*, p. 553.

[43] Ambassador Nehru wrote irate letters to the *Times*, whose scribes, he contended, failed to understand the importance of a strong executive: "I have great respect for Mr Levin's views on Wagner; I have much less for his views on the Indian Constitution ... I do not write on Wagner; I wish he did not write on the Indian Constitution": see his letter of 12 January 1977, B.K. Nehru Papers, Subject File

become something of an *idée fixe* in the family. Mrs Gandhi liked to compare the "chaotic state of affairs" in 1975 India to "France when de Gaulle came to power in 1958."[44]

But the currency of these ideas was not restricted to the thought-world of the Gandhis. A resolution at the December 1975 Plenary Session of the Congress, for instance, sought to make the constitution "more responsive to the current needs of the people."[45] Bansi Lal was blunter: "Get rid of all this election nonsense. If you ask me, just make our sister president for life."[46] Also doing the rounds among the party's top brass was an "anonymous paper" calling for the adoption of a presidential system.[47] The pamphlet extolled the French and American models which, in its rather quaint view, guaranteed "the unobstructed working of the executive". Interestingly, it ended with an appendix of extracts from world constitutions seen as worthy of emulation: France, with strengthened executive powers since the coming of the Fifth Republic in 1958; Italy, all of whose prime ministers since 1946 belonged to the same party; and Japan, where the LDP—which like the DC in Italy was hegemonic—had held power continuously since 1955.[48] Congress rule, after all, belonged to the same genus.

But the hostile reactions from the legal community and the press that followed the "leak" of this disquisition convinced Mrs Gandhi that the republic was not yet prepared to swallow such far-reaching constitutional change. She dissociated herself from the document in February 1976, calling it a fake aimed at creating a "scare".[49] In fact, she turned the

---

41. He spent the Emergency giving lectures at embassies and universities on both sides of the Atlantic railing against the Westminster model, under which India had become a "functioning anarchy": see his speech of 17 September 1975, B.K. Nehru Papers, Subject File 16.

[44] *SCR*, vol. 1, p. 27.

[45] *Congress Marches Ahead—XIII*, p. 10.

[46] Nehru, *Nice Guys Finish Second*, p. 559.

[47] A.R. Antulay, a Maharashtra MLA until 1976 and Rajya Sabha MP thereafter, claimed authorship of this document: see Antulay, *Democracy, Parliamentary or Presidential*, p. 132. Supposedly a secret, Antulay's article was leaked by Barooah, who was testing the waters: Austin, *Working a Democratic Constitution*, p. 352. The document itself is reproduced in Noorani, *The Presidential System*, pp. 105–21.

[48] But Mrs Gandhi personally found the comparison with the United States distasteful. "Since our president [will] be elected directly by the people, he should enjoy more authority and powers even than the American president", she asserted: *Economist*, 3 January 1976, p. 9.

[49] Austin, *Working a Democratic Constitution*, pp. 352–3.

stick in the reverse direction when French Prime Minister Jacques Chirac visited Delhi that month: "power should not be concentrated but be with the people", she told the AFP, dismissing as rumours any plan for the adoption of presidentialism.[50]

What Rule of Law? The Decline of the Judiciary and the Making of a Police State

"That Montesquieu theory is getting outdated", Lok Sabha Speaker Gurdial Singh Dhillon announced a month into the Emergency, declaring open season on the judiciary.[51] This was the latest instalment in the battle waged by parliament—and metonymically the executive—against the courts since independence. It was also the most conclusive of them, authoritarian fiat enabling parliament to reduce the judiciary to a shadow of its former self.

Indeed, in Emergency India the scope of the *Rechtsstaat* had shrunk radically. On 27 June 1975, for instance, a presidential order invoked Article 359 to suspend for the duration of the Emergency the right of any citizen, Indian or foreign, to move the courts to enforce the fundamental rights found in Articles 14, 21, and 22. These articles guaranteed "equality before the law"; the right to a lawyer; and that no person be "deprived of his life or personal liberty" or "be detained in custody without being informed, as soon as may be, of the grounds for such arrest."[52] Not long after, the Criminal Procedure Code was instrumentalised to ban meetings involving five or more citizens. Moreover, Mrs Gandhi saw to the passage of the Thirty-eighth Amendment on 23 July, which made the declaration of the Emergency and proclamations and ordinances promulgated under it immune from judicial review.[53] This pulled the rug from under the argument of Canarese lawyers who, in attempting to free their clients from prison, were suggesting at the High Court in Bangalore that the Emergency was unconstitutional, the president having signed off on it before the cabinet was consulted.[54] With the better part of fundamental rights and insti-

---

[50] Ibid., p. 357.

[51] *Lok Sabha Debates*, vol. 54, no. 12 (5 August 1975), col. 17.

[52] The next provision of Article 22 was also made redundant: "Every person who is arrested and detained in custody shall be produced before the nearest magistrate within a period of twenty-four hours": *TOI*, 28 June 1975, p. 1.

[53] It was passed 342 to 1. Shamim was the defiant one: *Lok Sabha Debates*, vol. 53, no. 3 (23 July 1975), col. 139.

[54] This line of reasoning had initially yielded results for lawyers, who succeeded

tutional checks and balances no longer enforceable, all that was left of the judiciary was a complex of kangaroo courts stamping executive decisions *sans* interference. Three episodes showed the near-complete capitulation of the judges: the November 1975 judgment on the legality of Mrs Gandhi's election to the Lok Sabha, the habeas corpus case of April 1976, and the Forty-second Amendment of November that year. There were, of course, qualitative differences: the courts were complicit in their own relegation in the former two set pieces, which were fought on its turf, and entirely absent in the third one, which played out in parliament.

Let us look first at Mrs Gandhi's controversial election. On 11 August, when her case finally reached the apex court, it was met with a new stumbling block that had also been a problem of old: the "basic structure" of the constitution. When Asoke Sen, former law minister and Mrs Gandhi's present lawyer, requested the court to reverse Justice Sinha's Allahabad judgment in light of the Thirty-ninth Amendment, he was challenged by the plaintiff's lawyer, Shanti Bhushan, who argued that the court had to attest to its constitutional validity first.[55] In his opinion the amendment, along with the Election Laws Amendment Act, violated the "basic structure" of the constitution, harking back to debates over the limits of parliamentary power that the executive and judiciary had jousted over since the late 1960s.[56] In the event, Chief Justice A.N. Ray, an Indira Gandhi appointee—more on him in Chapter 6—postponed hearings by two weeks, enough time to get enough judges on board. Upholding unanimously the provisions of the Thirty-ninth Amendment, the Supreme Court reversed the Allahabad verdict on 7 November 1975. But the apex court also showed that it retained some independence when, by a 4 to 1 vote—Ray, surprisingly, was part of the majority—it quashed the clause in the amendment that divested the

---

in getting some detainees released on 17 July. However, the government was already a step ahead: just minutes after detainees were released, they would promptly be rearrested by policemen, who this time cited the MISA amendment of 29 June that allowed for detention without the need to disclose grounds: Austin, *Working a Democratic Constitution*, p. 335.

[55] Asoke Sen had replaced Nani Palkhivala, who had quit the job in protest once the Emergency got under way. On the judgment, see the Introduction; for the amendment, the section above.

[56] The terms of this debate can be defined as follows: to the government, amendments could well overhaul the "basic" architecture of the constitution; to the judges, its malleability was circumscribed by the intent of the founding fathers.

courts of the power to adjudicate on the election of the prime minister.[57] Such a provision, the quartet argued, went against the grain of the basic structure doctrine. This was a Pyrrhic victory, for the judges had demonstrated that they had no interest in locking horns with Mrs Gandhi, even as they remained steadfast in defence of their jobs.

But the fighting season was not over. At the time, hundreds of writ petitions were pending in high courts. Now, it transpired, each of them had a new argument at their disposal: the state's policies went against the basic structure. But which rights were basic and which were not? The new judgment had spurred demands for explication. Mrs Gandhi, too, felt she could benefit from clarity. The attorney general, Niren De, along with the Tamil Nadu advocate general, now made an application on her behalf to the Supreme Court, asking it to "review"—in other words revoke—the basic structure doctrine. Ray, in response, constituted a bench to hear the matter on 10 November. On that day, De and Palkhivala faced off on the question, the former in favour of the review, the latter against. But on the third day of the hearings Ray dissolved the thirteen-judge bench. Despite having upheld the "basic structure" in the election case, Ray made it clear that he was still a creature of the government. It appears that in an assembly of judges at the chambers that morning—12 November—Ray had realised that his colleagues were against the review. This was a major blow for Mrs Gandhi.[58] It was at about this time that the "anonymous paper" seen above began floating around in Congress circles, calling, *inter alia*, for a constitutional amendment that would make the cabinet responsible for the appointment of all judges of the republic.[59]

In the second round of jousting, the Supreme Court showed itself more pliable.[60] The opening salvo came from the high courts, who had ingeniously commenced upon the use of writs to subvert authoritarian impulse. During the first wave of arrests in June 1975, MISA detainees had challenged their detention in several high courts on the basis of a preliminary objection: they were "asking for release by the issuance of a writ of habeas corpus."[61] The line of reasoning was simple. The roots of habeas corpus lay

---

[57] This was fourth clause of Article 329A. Justices Ray, Khanna, Chandrachud, and Mathew were in the majority; Beg dissented: *TOI*, 8 November 1975, pp. 1, 6–7.

[58] Nayar, *The Judgement*, p. 94.

[59] Noorani, *The Presidential System*, p. 105.

[60] A précis of the case can be found in Seervai, *The Emergency, Future Safeguards*, pp. 8–59.

[61] *ADM Jabalpur v. S. S. Shukla*, SCR (1976), p. 175. A number of activist lawyers—

in common law—that it was *prior* to fundamental rights—and as a result courts could enforce it, amendments notwithstanding. But on 29 June an ordinance amending MISA had put an end to this, disallowing courts from resorting to any law prior to the constitution.[62] But newer strategies evolved. The Madhya Pradesh High Court, for instance, which ruled on 1 September, held that neither emergency powers nor the Thirty-eighth Amendment abridged the power of courts to issue writs of habeas corpus. Similarly, its Delhi counterpart declared illegal on the same grounds the incarceration of journalist Kuldip Nayar and ordered his release on 13 September. By December, seven high courts had allowed habeas corpus petitions: forty-three detainees, four of them MPs, were freed from prison.

Mrs Gandhi decided to take matters up with the Supreme Court. The hearings began on 15 December. The government's lawyer, Niren De, argued that "there is no personal rights law for the time being": MISA amendments, presidential orders, and the Emergency had made it unnecessary.[63] Shanti Bhushan and Soli Sorabjee, on the other hand, contended *à la* the high courts that the right to habeas corpus was prior to the constitution. On 28 April 1976 the Court ruled 4–1 in favour of the government's position.[64]

The most pointed attack on the judiciary, however, came with the Forty-second Amendment in what to this day remains the most ambitious attempt at recasting the founding document of the republic. The groundwork was laid by the Swaran Singh Committee, which was appointed on 26 February 1976 to propose far-reaching constitutional changes. The success of piecemeal amendments through 1975 had emboldened Mrs Gandhi to, as she put it, "plug the loopholes in the Constitution".[65] Her party was her chorus. The Punjab assembly had, without any prodding from the cen-

---

among them Shanti Bhushan in Bangalore, and V. M. Tarkunde and Soli Sorabjee in Bombay—had taken up the cause of the detainees: *Seminar*, vol. 196, no. 1 (December 1975), pp. 12–15.

[62] *SW*, 19 July 1975, p. 1.

[63] Nayar, *The Judgement*, p. 123. Based on an interview with Justice Khanna, Austin speculates that De argued listlessly and hoped to lose the case, because he secretly "abhorred the Emergency's harshness". See Austin, *Working a Democratic Constitution*, p. 339.

[64] We will return to the remarks of these judges in Chapter 9, for they deserve to be examined from another angle: as a clear instance of judicial betrayal.

[65] *SW*, 13 March 1976, p. 3.

tre, voted in favour of a new constituent assembly. Similar decisions were made by the Pradesh Congress Committees of Bihar, Haryana, and Uttar Pradesh.[66] With the passing of time, such voices only grew shriller.

On 27 March an opportunity presented itself when the results of the biennial elections to the Rajya Sabha came in: the Congress now enjoyed the necessary two-thirds majority in the upper house that it needed to make changes to the constitution. No longer would it have to rely on its Communist allies or on independents.[67] Swaran Singh, the head of the committee, was enthusiastic: "Let us not forget there is a well-known saying that 'appetite grows with egg [sic]'. People have tasted the fruits of our vast socio-economic programmes of a vital character [sic]. They desire to have more and more of such programmes. To realise that objective ... the Constitution itself ... should be [made] responsive to the needs of the changing society."[68] The twelve-member committee, of which ten were parliamentarians and seven one-time lawyers, submitted its report to the party president on 3 April. Parliamentarism was best left untouched, it recommended. This, however, needs qualification: three of its members, Antulay, Sathe, and C.M. Stephen, felt otherwise. As for the others, a commitment to parliamentarism did not mean an endorsement of checks and balances: centralisation and *raison d'état* would trump federalism and the *Rechtsstaat*.[69]

To this end, judicial review had to be weakened. Courts, the committee recommended, should appoint at least seven judges to every panel and should require at least a two-thirds majority to upturn amendments—this was a dig at both the one-man bench Allahabad judgment and the 6–5 majority that ruled against the government in *Golak Nath v. State of Punjab*. Moreover, the scope of Article 31C should be expanded to ensure that no "directive principle" can be questioned in court on the basis that it violates "fundamental rights".[70] Furthermore, questions relating to revenue—land reform and ceilings, nationalisation, procurement, distribution—should be dealt with not in courts but in separate tribunals; the option of selectively declaring states of emergency in specific regions of the republic, rather

[66] Austin, *Working a Democratic Constitution*, p. 377.

[67] *SW*, 3 April 1976, p. 14.

[68] *Congress Marches Ahead—XIII*, p. 40.

[69] Sathe later wrote a volume in praise of presidentialism. In the absence of a "switch over", strengthening the hands of the executive would suffice: see Sathe, *Two Swords in One Scabbard*, p. 88ff.

[70] For *Golak Nath* and the reasons why Delhi's rulers saw fit to privilege fundamental rights over directive principles, see Chapter 6.

than having one for all of it, worked into the constitution; and a separate nine-member body created to deal with procedures concerning the disqualification of the president, vice president, and MPs. After the committee submitted its final report on 14 August, parliament was ready to act on its recommendations. The Forty-second Amendment Bill was introduced in the Lok Sabha on 1 September.

In many ways the amendment went further than the committee. Certainly, the former's basic contours were adapted from the latter—the amendment of Article 31C; separate tribunals; the need for a two-thirds majority to rule on the constitutionality of laws—but new clauses were tacked on as well: on matters of "public utility", high courts were prohibited from issuing stays; the Supreme Court forbidden from adjudicating the constitutionality of state laws;[71] fundamental rights rendered ineffective to challenge any arrest under the new Article 31D, which prohibited "anti-national activities";[72] the president and governors freed from having to comply with the advice of the election commission in cases relating to the disqualification of MPs and MLAs;[73] emergency powers expanded to allow legislation to breach fundamental rights even in states not under emergency; a state of emergency exempted from the need for annual parliamentary approval; the duration for which a state could remain under President's Rule without parliamentary approval was extended from six months to a year;[74] parliament's term from five to six years; the words "secular" and "socialist" added to the constitution's preamble as modifiers to describe the republic; quorum requirements for

[71] They were to be allowed to adjudicate only on central laws. State laws, then, were to become the turf of high courts. Inversely, the latter were prohibited from adjudicating on central laws.

[72] "Anti-national activity" was a supple notion that included a range of activities from secession to "the disruption of public services": Kogekar, "Constitution Amendment Bill", p. 1660.

[73] In any case, the president acted only on the advice of the council of ministers. This meant that Mrs Gandhi could, as it were, pardon herself. For good measure, the Forty-second Amendment also removed the ambiguity in Article 74: no longer was the president just advised by the council of ministers—the head of state was now bound to "act in accordance with such advises [sic]." On this point see Sathe, "Forty-fourth Constitutional Amendment", p. 1707.

[74] President's Rule allows the Union to exercise control over states by suspending the executive powers of the state government if it feels the latter is unable to discharge its constitutional duties. Until 1994, no justification was needed to impose President's Rule, making its use almost always capricious.

amendments done away with; and Article 368 amended to make all amendments—even those involving fundamental rights—unchallengeable "in any court on any ground".[75]

The sprawling ambition in part reflected the haphazard conditions it was written in: all of Mrs Gandhi's legal experts—especially Gokhale, operating from the Law Ministry; Ray, lodging at the prime minister's house; and Rajni Patel, stationed in a suite at the Ashoka Hotel—were out to prove their loyalty, adding clause after clause to strengthen executive powers and protect her person. Moreover, the prime minister and her allies had fostered a climate in which not only hostility but direct threats to judges were permissible. During the parliamentary debates, for instance, C.M. Stephen, who was on the Swaran Singh Committee, declared that if the courts ever had the "temerity to defy" parliament again, "it will be a bad day for the judiciary ... we have got our methods."[76] After both houses ratified the bill in early November, it became clear that it was the very nature of the Indian polity that had been transformed.[77] In sum, the authoritarian regime had consolidated its rule.

If consolidation entailed centralising power in the hands of the executive, it also meant turning the republic into a police state. Fortunately for Mrs Gandhi, a plausible justification for strengthening the security establishment was not hard to come by. For, in a sense, the groundwork had already been laid before the Emergency. In the months leading up to it, the ruling party in Delhi made much of the possibility of a military threat to the regime. This it did by culling statements from Jayaprakash Narayan's speeches and painting him and his people as a bunch of "desperadoes belonging to criminal organisations" like the Anand Marg, "wedded to violence" and eager for military intervention.[78] For instance, Narayan had said in an interview that he was ready to "ask the army and the police to rise in revolt if necessary at the appropriate time."[79] Conveniently, such pronouncements lent credence to the government's narrative.

All the same, for the better part of the previous three decades, civil-military relations had been more or less free from controversy, and Mrs Gandhi was least worried about the prospect of a generals' revolt. A few days

---

[75] For relevant extracts, see Mirchandani, *Subverting the Constitution in India,* pp. 82–97.

[76] *Lok Sabha Debates,* vol. 65, no. 8 (2 November 1976), col. 149.

[77] The Lok Sabha passed it 366 to 4; the Rajya Sabha, 190 to 0.

[78] *Why Emergency?,* pp. 24, 27, 29.

[79] Ibid., p. 29.

before the Emergency was declared, the prime minister recalled the chief of army staff, Tapishwar Raina, who was on tour, an indication of her strong rapport with the generals. When he was with the press, Raina tended to sidestep questions of war, peace, and domestic instability: "this belongs to the realm of politicians", he would say plainly.[80]

The real risk, then, was not the opposition using the army, but Mrs Gandhi making use of men in uniform to establish a militarised dictatorship. Over her decade in power she had showed no hesitation using paramilitaries—*inter alia*, the Border Security Force (BSF), Central Reserve Police Force (CRPF), Indo-Tibetan Border Police (ITBP), Central Industrial Security Force (CISF), and the Home Guards—for police functions. In dealing with the "law and order situation" in the aftermath of the Allahabad judgment, for instance, at least seven BSF and CRPF battalions were dispatched to the capital.[81]

By the time the Emergency was declared, Mrs Gandhi commanded from the centre around 600,000 policemen and paramilitaries. The police in the states accounted for another 750,000. To this military-state complex the armed forces added yet another 1,050,000, a tenth of whom had been newly recruited in the most recent expansion of 1974–5.[82] Similarly, the Research and Analysis Wing (RAW), a newly constituted intelligence agency, saw its budget rise from Rs 50 million to Rs 1 billion between 1968 and 1975. The military budget, too, grew, albeit in less dramatic fashion, in the run up to and during the Emergency, from $2.05 billion in 1974 to $2.57 billion two years later.[83]

Fully co-opted into the Emergency regime, the military was assigned a policing role: the passage of armoured regiments was a common sight in the capital during the early days of the new dispensation.[84] "The central park of Connaught Place was a vision of khaki, with rifles and shields and Sten guns", a journalist later recalled.[85] Soldiers were

---

[80] *SW*, 14 June 1975, p. 13.

[81] J.C. Pandey, Joint Secretary, Ministry of Home Affairs to J.N. Roy, Deputy Inspector General, Shah Commission of Inquiry, 14 November 1977, MHAP, File VI/11034/56/80(29)ISDVI.

[82] Weiner, "India's New Political Institutions", pp. 898–9; International Institute for Strategic Studies, *The Military Balance*, p. 55.

[83] Blair, "Mrs Gandhi's Emergency", p. 250; Maxwell, "Woman on a White Horse", p. 361 *et passim*; Nayar, *India After Nehru*, p. 94.

[84] *Guardian*, 10 July 1975, p. 3.

[85] Thapar, "Just to Remember", p. 32.

also tasked with the crackdown on smugglers in the peripheries of the republic.[86]

The complicity of the intelligence agencies was even greater. Before 25 June 1975, the RAW "made a significant contribution" in helping the Congress prepare a list of politicians that it wanted arrested.[87] Afterwards, its chief, R.N. Kao, oversaw the surveillance of "judges, academics, political opponents, journalists, state and central ministers, top civil servants", and even members of the armed forces and other intelligence agencies.[88] Up until the end of the Emergency the RAW continued working "outside its charter", even channelling "secret funds" to the prime minister. Mrs Gandhi also saw the new regime as an opportunity to pack the PMS and ministries with intelligence officers, their intimidation skills being a valuable asset to silence dissent.[89] For instance, all day-to-day meetings with the directors of AIR and Doordarshan were conducted by renowned spook K.N. Prasad at the I&B ministry. The prime minister enjoyed a good rapport with the Intelligence Bureau as well, having used its services in the past to "ascertain the political views and sympathies of candidates for the post of judges."[90] Its partisanship never in doubt, the IB also undertook a survey of public attitudes to the Emergency in the spring of 1976, concluding that "it would be good to take" the opposition "by surprise by announcing elections in September or October after releasing the prisoners on the first anniversary of the Emergency."[91] The same went for the CBI. In the two weeks of plotting and instability that preceded the Emergency, when her position seemed most precarious, Mrs Gandhi's strategy was to try and "win over" as many Congressmen as possible; for the rest, the "recalcitrant" ones, she had the bureau "set on them".[92]

No force within the security establishment—the armed forces, police, and intelligence agencies—then, challenged the Congress rulers. With their sectional interests of jobs and funds met, the men in uniform readily became an arm of the grand old party in Emergency India.

---

[86] *SW*, 6 December 1975, p. 10.
[87] Nayar, *The Judgement*, p. 37.
[88] Hiro, *Inside India*, p. 267.
[89] Ibid.; Nireekshak, "Willing to be Corrupted", p. 684; Tandon, *PMO Diary*, p. 400.
[90] Tandon, *PMO Diary*, p. 376.
[91] Rajeswar, *India*, p. 90.
[92] Tandon, *PMO Diary*, p. 394.

Nepotism, Arbitrariness, and State Capture

The judiciary, parliament, and the security establishment were not the only institutions weakened during the Emergency. The same fate befell others, and indeed some of these were quite literally captured by Delhi's rulers. Sitting at the centre of this growing web of nepotism and graft in public office were none other than Mrs Gandhi and Sanjay. We could begin our survey of authoritarian arbitrariness with the Reserve Bank of India before turning to airlines, banks, corporations, and dealerships.

Just a month after the Emergency was declared, Finance Minister C. Subramaniam was informed that N.C. Sen Gupta, the interim Reserve Bank of India governor, was set to retire in August 1975. While perusing the curricula vitae of economists in his search for an incumbent, he was made aware of K.R. Puri's existence by the prime minister. However, Puri, chairman of the Life Insurance Corporation of India, was not to Subramaniam's liking: he lacked "an adequate academic background" and had "a very limited area of specialisation, unconnected with banking and finance."[93] But, under pressure from the prime minister, he quickly cast aside his reservations. The third member (alongside Mrs Gandhi and Subramaniam) of the appointments committee, the home minister, was not even consulted in the decision-making process. K.R. Puri was sworn in as RBI governor in August 1975. His first order of business, *sans* consultation with his colleagues, was to raise the credit limit for Maruti, the automobile company owned by the prime minister's son.[94]

Public-sector banks, too, received the RBI treatment. This time the heavy lifting was done by Revenue and Banking Minister Pranab Mukherjee. In June 1976 it was decided that the chairman of the State Bank of India, R.K. Talwar, should retire before the expiry of his term in February 1977. Mukherjee proposed that T.R. Varadachary, SBI managing director, take his place. In parliament the SBI Act was amended to allow for the termination of Talwar's services.[95] In the meantime, Mukherjee inveigled Talwar into dropping "certain matters indicative of improprieties on the part of

---

[93] *SCR*, vol. 1, p. 53.

[94] The credit limit for private-sector borrowers was doubled to Rs 20 million because Maruti, which had borrowed Rs 9.5 million, wanted an additional Rs 2.5 million from the CBI. Shifting the goalposts on borrowing limits helped the bank secure RBI approval. See *Reserve Bank of India: Volume 3*, p. 129.

[95] This came to be known as the "Talwar amendment", which allowed for the eponymous figure's dismissal without justification: Vaghul, *R.K. Talwar*, p. 22.

Varadachary" that were to be brought up at an SBI board meeting.[96] Having set the stage, Mrs Gandhi sprang into action. In July 1976 she approved Mukherjee's proposal and later that month appointed Varadachary chairman of the SBI, flouting the rules of the appointments committee by refusing to consult with the RBI.[97] It later emerged that Sanjay Gandhi was behind Mukherjee's machinations. Talwar, it transpired, had refused to restructure a loan to a failing cement company without first being given the CEO's head on a platter.[98] The latter was a friend of Sanjay's, and the two connived to have Talwar replaced with Varadachary, who proved more amenable. Even before his appointment, he was readily receiving instructions from Sanjay on "staff matters" and the governing of the SBI.[99]

The Punjab National Bank witnessed similar interference. In July 1975 its chairman, P.L. Tandon, was to retire and be replaced by its deputy general manager, O.P. Gupta. In what was to be a mere formality, the succession was put before the appointments committee. All its members except the prime minister signed off on it.[100] Mrs Gandhi instead suggested that T.R. Tuli, the chairman of a tiny private sector bank, be given reins to the public-sector giant. She prevailed over the others, and Tuli was made chairman of the PNB in August 1975. He proved his worth in March 1976 when he was complicit in letting Associated Journals—which published the *National Herald*, a house journal of the Congress—run up an overdraft of Rs 830,000. The company, which had opened an account with the PNB only days before withdrawing the gargantuan sum, had terrible business practices: much of the overdrawn amount was meant to defray the demurrage charges for imported machinery that had remained uncollected for over five months in Bombay. Also, in a clearly illegal move, they were using one of their properties, Herald House, as security not just for the PNB overdraft but also a second mortgage. The company had, besides, been making losses to the tune of Rs 1 million a year. Well into 1978, Associated Journals had repaid only Rs 20,000, barely covering the interest accrued on the overdraft. The real reason for Tuli's actions was crystal clear. He owed his position to the prime

---

[96] *SCR*, vol. 1, p. 55.

[97] Ibid. Mukherjee maintains that the RBI was consulted, but only orally. Talwar was given thirteen months' leave—effectively a dismissal: Vaghul, *R.K. Talwar*, p. 26.

[98] Vaghul, *R.K. Talwar*, p. 22.

[99] *SCR*, vol. 1, p. 56.

[100] The others included Establishment Officer U.C. Aggarwal, Finance Minister Subramaniam, and Home Minister Reddy.

minister, who, through the interlocution of Minister for Chemicals and Fertilisers P.C. Sethi, had compelled him to return the favour.[101]

In another case Pranab Mukherjee sent a proxy from his ministry to talk Tuli into issuing KRSMA Chemicals three letters of credit worth Rs 930,000 for the import of chemicals. Tuli was forced to oblige, for the company's proprietor was S.P. Mehta, the father-in-law of a brother of Om Mehta of the Home Ministry. Later, however, it emerged that the cash-strapped company could not afford to buy most of the imported chemicals, leaving the PNB holding the product, having already spent Rs 915,000 on it. The bank had been duped: an assessment showed that at prevailing market prices the chemicals were expected to fetch only half that amount. Once again, the PNB had been used to enrich Delhi's rulers and their distant relatives.[102]

In a third case, Tuli ingratiated himself with Sanjay in October 1976 by waiving interest penalties accrued by Maruti and lowering the interest rate on its loans.[103] It was also alleged, but never proven, that Tuli—when he was head of the New Bank of India—had arranged a Rs 7,000,000 loan to Maruti.[104] With money flowing in from all sides, Maruti had become by the end of the Emergency a conglomerate not unlike some of India's largest business houses, involved in everything from banking to licensing to importing to serving as middleman for American manufacturing giants.

Similarly, Mrs Gandhi, through Dhawan at the PMS, found an opportunity to pack the boards of Air India and Indian Airlines with allies in February 1976, when the terms of both boards approached expiry. Dhawan ensured that the names of Mrs Gandhi's acolytes made it to the new board, while others, who were due for promotion, were dropped. Decrying interference, P.C. Lal, the chairman and managing director of Indian Airlines, resigned. But meddling in the affairs of the company did not end there. In October that year Mrs Gandhi had P.N. Dhar, who headed the PMS, coax Raj Bahadur, the tourism and civil aviation minister, into considering Boeing 737s over F-27s and BAC-111s in the airline's plans for

---

[101] "Clean Overdraft by PNB to Associated Journals Limited", no date, SCP, Subject File 21, pp. 10–19.

[102] "Facility Provided by PNB to KRSMA Chemicals Private Limited", no date, SCP, Subject File 21, pp. 177–81.

[103] By lowering the interest rate on its loans by 1.5 per cent, Tuli saved Maruti Rs 70,347.65: PNB manager to M.K. Jain, Under Secretary, Shah Commission of Inquiry, 29 October 1977, SCIF, File 1(e)/DLI/5–11/77.

[104] R.K. Bhole, Bombay Stock Exchange to the Secretary of the Shah Commission, 3 October 1977, SCIF, File 1(e)/DLI/5–11/77.

expansion.[105] Thus, before any route testing could be carried out, the Interline Committee's report finalised, or a system study conducted, the decision had already been taken. Rajiv Gandhi, Mrs Gandhi's elder son, was brought into the decision-making process. An Indian Airlines pilot, he now passed verdict on financial projections, concluding that the 737 was best suited to the republic's needs.[106] In December, Bahadur was replaced by K. Raghuramaiah, who was pressured by Dhawan to deliver. The new minister overruled his staff, who were of the opinion that more study could lead to a better purchase. On 17 January 1977 a report in the *Wall Street Journal* revealed that Venezuelan bureaucrats had accepted kickbacks from Boeing for the sale of a 737. An SEC investigation would later find that the American corporation had greased the palms of officials in at least seven countries.[107] Mrs Gandhi asked Raghuramaiah to keep the contract on hold until the controversy blew over. On 9 February—by which time the news cycle had moved on—the ministry inked the Rs 30.55 crore deal to purchase three 737s.[108]

Aside from Sanjay, the other major figure in Mrs Gandhi's web of nepotism was her yoga instructor Dhirendra Brahmachari, who, even before the Emergency, had used his proximity to the prime minister to acquire a gun factory in Jammu, a "lavishly furnished" ashram in Kashmir, and several "luxurious buildings".[109] Mrs Gandhi had also tasked him with more than a few cabinet appointments and dismissals in the early 1970s. In the new dispensation, graft continued unabated. Brahmachari purchased an aircraft from an American firm and tried to smuggle it into his ashram without paying a customs charge. When he was caught red-handed, he insisted it was a "present". But when "Shri Bedford D. Maule of Maule Aircraft Corporation" denied ever gifting the yogi a plane, it transpired that Brahmachari had paid for it in cash—using "illegally acquired foreign money" while visiting New York, no less. Nevertheless, no action was taken, in part because the officer in charge of the investigation, a deputy director of the Enforcement Directorate, A.M. Sinha, was "overawed by the personality of Brahmachari", saintly and six feet tall. Sinha was not alone.

---

[105] The former two were American airliners; the latter British.

[106] *SCR*, vol. 1, pp. 76, 78.

[107] Adams, *The Politics of Defense Contracting*, p. 252.

[108] *SCR*, vol. 1, pp. 74–8.

[109] Transcript of interview with I.K. Gujral, Acc. No. 797, NMML Oral History Project, p. 143.

Pranab Mukherjee wrote to customs ordering them to clear the plane post-haste without charging duty—the plane, after all, belonged to an ashram, a "charitable institution" whose "main aim was to provide higher training in yoga to the [*sic*] students." Descriptions of it, however, suggest that a non-profit it most definitely was not. Indeed, the ashram was a study in 1970s opulence, boasting a cave-like building "built like a tree with the floors cantilevered" from a staircase; bathrooms chequered with "coloured glazed tiles"; verandahs and kitchens with "marble floors"; and rooms fitted with "luxury items": Japanese crockery, folding beds, electric kettles, hair driers, and, for some reason, vibrators. That guests paid upward of Rs 10,000 for five nights suggests the place was more posh hotel than ashram.[110] A couple of months later, Brahmachari had his application to construct an airstrip at the ashram rejected because of its proximity to a military airbase. This time, the "flying swami", as he was by then known, had Defence Minister Bansi Lal reverse the decision. Over the next couple of months, the yogi's aircraft was regularly spotted between Delhi and Jammu, often with either of Mrs Gandhi's sons in the cockpit.[111] His ashram also invested Rs 300,000 in Maruti.[112]

As with the centre, so with the states. That local *satraps* mimicked the leaders of the republic in their unholy trinity of venality, nepotism, and authoritarianism can be discerned by casting an eye over Bansi Lal's Haryana. Early on in the Emergency, Lal decided to help two of his courtiers: Ram Chander, "a milk vendor who happened to be very close to him", and R.C. Mehtani, a "lower division clerk" whose "meteoric rise" had propelled him in the span of a few years to the post of officer on special duty to the chief minister.[113] Chander, who was related to Mehtani's brother-in-law's wife, it transpired, coveted the Khodays dealership in the state; as it happened, the brewery's sole proprietor was Commander Pritam Dutta, navy veteran and liquor magnate. In August 1975, Lal, who wanted to oblige his subordinate, tried having Dutta arrested under MISA but failed because of the deputy commissioner's protestations. The functionary was then summarily transferred and the task of maligning Dutta fell to the

---

[110] *SCR*, vol. 2, pp. 25, 26, 29–30.

[111] In the 213 flights accounted for in the log book, Sanjay was present in 73 of them, and Rajiv 19: ibid., p. 29.

[112] Birla, *Brushes with History*, pp. 148–9.

[113] Officers on special duty are ranked between secretary and under-secretary; *SCR*, vol. 3, p. 21.

excise and taxation commissioner. Soon, a raid was conducted, "minor irregularities" found, the dealership licence cancelled, and the baron sent off to jail.[114] Not long after, it was discovered that the dealership was now in the hands of "M.M. & Co., Faridabad", owned by the son of a mutual relative of Chander's and Mehtani's.[115]

This was far from being a solitary instance of nepotistic arbitrariness. Another case, the "Riwasa episode" of 1974, involved Surender Singh, the son of Bansi Lal. Taking a dislike to Bhanwar Singh, a student union leader at Bhiwani College, Surender, escorted by a posse of policemen, stormed into his house in Riwasa, Haryana and dragged Bhanwar, his sister, and their grandmother to the police station, where the siblings were "stripped naked" and "made to lie on the same cot" while the octogenarian woman was "kicked to death".[116] For his efforts the deputy superintendent who helped execute the caper was promoted. The journalist who broke the story, Makhan Lal Kak of the *Tribune*, was framed on false charges and locked up on the very first day of the Emergency.[117] In the months that followed, the chief minister's son began developing his own patronage networks. As a fixer, he ensured jobs for his clients, typically young men who frequented employment exchanges. When in November 1975 Ishwar Lal Choudhary, a district employment officer in Bhiwani, reluctantly "expressed his inability" to help some of them find a job—they "did not possess the requisite qualifications"—Surender Singh responded by having the local deputy superintendent of police invite Choudhary to meet Bansi Lal at his Bhiwani residence where several other district functionaries were to be present as well.[118] It was a trap. As soon as he got there, he was whisked away by the police, served with MISA charges, and locked up in the Hissar district jail.

It would not be the last time Surender Singh got away with graft. The next target was Pitambar Lal Goyal, whose family rivalry with the Bansi Lals was the stuff of Haryana lore. The feud, apparently, had begun when

[114] Deposition of J.K. Duggal, Excise and Taxation Commissioner, Haryana, 2 June 1978, SCP, Subject File 11, p. 208.

[115] "Detention of Cdr (Retd) Pritam Dutta of Rohtak", no date, SCP, Subject File 11, p. 133.

[116] *TOI*, 5 May 1977, p. 5; Chib, *Nineteen Fateful Months*, pp. 52–8. Chib was Professor of Geography at Punjab University.

[117] Deposition of M.L. Kak, no date, SCP, Subject File 7, p. 194.

[118] "Detention under MISA of Shri Ishwar Lal Choudhary", no date, SCP, Subject File 8, p. 97.

Goyal's parents backed Devi Lal, an independent, against Bansi Lal in the 1962 Vidhan Sabha elections, and had continued intermittently ever since. The next generation had carried it forward. In the early 1970s, Goyal had blocked Surender's candidature to the local bar council. The Emergency, then, was a time for revenge. Surender had his father contact the medical examiners who were overseeing the Haryana civil service examination that Goyal had just taken, and had them declare the youth medically unfit to be a mandarin. The original answer to the question, "is there any evidence of disease of the genital organs?", had been "no": this was changed to "chronic epididymitis", a testicular infection caused by an STD. Joining the civil service also required a "verification report" from the police station. Bansi Lal had this document altered as well: it now read that Goyal had a "Naxalite bent of mind".[119] He was, in short, declared both physically and mentally unfit. Finally, Bansi Lal and his son issued orders to have Goyal locked up. Tipped off before the police could arrive, Goyal escaped, only to find that his grandfather, father, and uncle had been incarcerated as bargaining chips. They were kept in custody for two weeks, after which Goyal surrendered to secure their release. Now, with his bureaucratic career nipped in the bud, he went on to do time as a MISA detainee. His father joined him in jail shortly after. In late January 1976, when Goyal applied to take the examination again, this time from prison, Lal had the Haryana Detenus (Conditions of Detention) Second Amendment Order, 1976 steamrollered through the state assembly in less than two weeks, preventing all detainees from taking any "academic or competition examinations during the period of detention."[120]

In brief, the effortless temporal, spatial, and consanguineous segues between Mrs Gandhi and Sanjay, Bansi Lal and Surender Singh, public service and private enterprise, the poverty of the state and the venality of its elite, "democracy" before 1975 and "dictatorship" after, were all signs of the times, of political centralisation, of arbitrariness, of immunity from prosecution—at first *de facto* and then *de jure*—and of a complete disregard for the citizens of the republic.

* * *

The apparently ambivalent character of the Emergency regime stemmed not only from its effort to seek social legitimation for itself—evident from

---

[119] *SCR*, vol. 3, pp. 24–5.
[120] Ibid., p. 26.

the general tenor of the Twenty-Point Programme—but also from the fact that Mrs Gandhi sought to remain within the framework of legality. The regime, then, was not a new one as such: the constitution was retained and the plan to adopt a presidential system abandoned. But the institutions that were the pillars on which Indian democracy rested were under attack. With the arrest of nearly five dozen MPs, parliament was under siege, and on account of the several constitutional amendments the independence of the judiciary was severely diminished.

Even so, had Congress MPs put up a stand against her, Mrs Gandhi would have been forced to attenuate her programmes; pressure emanating from some quarters, in the main from friends and ministers, was already checking some of her authoritarian impulses. The Supreme Court, too, could have compelled her to mend her ways had its judges ruled differently on habeas corpus and cases relating to individual freedom and fundamental rights. These counterfactuals are important because they show that establishment politicians and lawyers played an important role in greasing the wheels of the authoritarian regime. As we will see in Chapters 8 and 9, most Congress MPs and judges remained pliable to the very end. Suffice it to say for the moment that the Emergency was more of an authoritarian than a totalitarian regime: there remained room for manoeuvre which the institutions of "the world's largest democracy" could have exploited.

State institutions such as the RBI, and public-sector undertakings, especially in the banking sector, had considerably less elbow room. Bureaucrats were threatened with transfer and arrest and brought to heel. The recalcitrant were replaced either by Mother or Son. This aspect of the Emergency—nepotism, arbitrariness, the pursuit of vendettas—is in keeping with the nature of authoritarian regimes, and more specifically in the typology of Linz, a particular category of it: "sultanism", a style of rule which, as the next chapter explores, was strongly associated with Sanjay's élan.

4

AN ERA OF SULTANS

SANJAY'S EMERGENCY

Demarcating the Emergency into periods proves a difficult task because no self-evident milestones mark either shifts in power or the transition from one sequence of events to another. All the same, one can periodise, for the events of 1976 stood in contrast to those of 1975. While the earlier months of the authoritarian regime are associated with the primacy of Indira Gandhi, the later ones are with the ascent of her 29-year-old son Sanjay, and rightly so.[1] As time went by, his influence waxed and hers waned. But the absence of any matricidal strife made the transition seamless, making it harder to identify any single watershed. There is, then, only one Emergency, not two, for the difference between the institutional changes wrought by Mother and Son was only a matter of degree.

Undoubtedly, Sanjay was omnipresent right from the beginning. He stood by his mother—both figuratively and physically on the rostrums— when the going got rough for the prime minister. On the day the Emergency was declared, it was he who personally called the Congress chief ministers and orchestrated the crackdown on the opposition. But Caesarism took hold only sometime during the winter of 1975. By the early months of the following year he had concentrated enough power in his hands to initiate his own programmes, adding dramatic and tragic layers to the history of state violence in Emergency India.

---

[1] See, *inter alia*, Chandra, *In the Name of Democracy*, pp. 156–245.

125

For her part Mrs Gandhi played a key role in facilitating her son's rise to power. The reason for this was not solely familial. As Uma Vasudev speculates, propping up a right-wing Sanjay was crucial in broadening support for the Emergency regime.[2] With her Twenty Points aimed at placating the poles of society, and his bourgeois Five Points everyone in between, the ruling clique hoped that through this triangulation it would dominate the entire spectrum, leaving no room for other parties to carve out political niches of their own.

An admixture of dynastic and artful politics there may have been in Mrs Gandhi's promotion of Sanjay, but there was never any confusion over which side of the scale was heavier. On a number of occasions during the Emergency she made it known to friend and foe alike that "an attack on Sanjay is an attack on me."[3] It was only a matter of time before the clique around her apportioned some of its sycophancy to her son. Cabinet ministers, who basically saw themselves less as members of a collegiate body than as viziers in a sultanate, were quick to adapt to the new situation. Congress president D.K. Barooah, for example, compared the ascendancy of Sanjay to what in his view were the enlightened despotisms of Akbar and Ranjit Singh, both of whom had kingdoms bequeathed to them when they were "merely in their teens".[4] Mrs Gandhi was keen to encourage such manifestations of deference, even demanding that her chief ministers "be in touch with Sanjay" at all times.[5] Those who showed signs of reluctance in this regard risked disgrace. For instance, Swaran Singh and Inder Kumar Gujral, the defence minister and the information and broadcasting minister, respectively, lost their jobs for being less than amenable.

Sanjay, however, was not content with the support of only those who swore by Mrs Gandhi's leadership. In building a parallel power structure, he patronised a group of supporters who owed their allegiance to him and him alone. As was to be expected, the thought-world of the younger clique reflected his thinking, not unlike the way that his mother's circle did hers. The major difference was a matter of degree. The right-hand men of Gandhi *mère* were willing to push the country into a more authoritarian direction but needed time to convince themselves and others of their moral and legal

---

[2] She dubbed this Mrs Gandhi's "theory of parallel politics": Vasudev, *Two Faces of Indira Gandhi*, p. 50.

[3] Ibid., p. 180.

[4] Ibid., pp. 182–3.

[5] Nayar, *The Judgement*, p. 108.

rectitude. Such encumbrances eluded the Sanjay camarilla. This became clear on 25 June 1975, when the two worlds collided. That night, when S.S Ray, the legal mastermind behind the Emergency, found out about the plan to cut off electricity to the printing presses, he was furious. "This is not what we discussed. This is not on", he said to R.K. Dhawan at the secretariat. Mrs Gandhi too feigned anger when Ray confronted her and reassured him: "there will be electricity and no courts will be closed."[6] But when news reached Bansi Lal—"the boorish gauleiter of Haryana", in the words of the journalist Janardan Thakur—that Ray was thwarting their plans, he said to Sanjay: "Throw him out, he is spoiling the game. He thinks too much of himself as a lawyer although he knows next to nothing."[7] With Mrs Gandhi's approval, Sanjay and his cabal had their way, shuttering the presses and sidelining her in-crowd.

In essence, the kind of rule Sanjay inaugurated in Delhi, the Hindi belt, and beyond was typical of what Weber calls "sultanism", a regime marked by "the extreme development of the ruler's discretion."[8] In his elaboration of this Weberian notion, Linz describes it as a form of "personal rulership" where "loyalty to the ruler is motivated by a mixture of fear and rewards to his collaborators. The ruler exercises his power without restraint at his own discretion and above all unencumbered by rules or by any commitment to an ideology or value system."[9] Among his "collaborators" are "members of his family, friends, cronies, business associates, and men directly involved in the use of violence to sustain the regime."[10]

Such regimes are in effect bereft of ideology, demonstrate indifference when it comes to mobilisation, and blur the boundaries between "public treasury and private wealth"—all evident from the nepotistic dimensions of the Emergency we have already noted.[11] The first and third of these characteristics were especially true of the Sanjay regime; the second, not so much. For even if popular mobilisation was only secondary to Sanjay's putschist manoeuvres in party and government, the lumpen warriors of the Youth Congress nevertheless tried to mobilise popular support, and even came close to capturing both the state and the grand old party.

[6] Frank, *Indira*, p. 378.

[7] Ibid., p. 378; Thakur, *All the Prime Minister's Men*, p. 45.

[8] Weber, *Economy and Society*, p. 232.

[9] Linz, *Totalitarian and Authoritarian Regimes*, p. 151.

[10] Ibid., p. 152.

[11] Ibid.

The Making of a Parallel Power Structure

It was not just because of his proximity to power, but also his élan and allies, that Sanjay was most suited to the task of deepening the authoritarianism of the Emergency.

Firstly, the élan. Sanjay's thinking was characterised by a "preference—indeed, a need—for sharp, simple solutions to problems of truly byzantine complexity."[12] This was a reflection of his personality and the circumstances surrounding his intellectual formation. His teachers and classmates at the posh Doon School would later remember him as a "desperately sad" teenager, remarking upon his "uncommunicative nature" and his "inability to make friends".[13] Since he was fond of automobiles, having spent his late teen years carjacking and accumulating speeding tickets, a family friend in 1964 set him up for an apprenticeship at the Rolls-Royce plant in Crewe. But the unruly young man failed to find peace during his stay in England: he drove without a licence, caused road accidents, possibly stole a car, and failed to complete his internship.[14] Summing up his youth, his biographer Vinod Mehta writes: "Despite having access to the best of opportunities, his entire career till 25 June 1975 was one short, sad list of defeats. He had failed as a student, he had failed as an apprentice, he had failed with women."

But this was to change. When the Emergency was declared, Mehta continues, "Sanjay realized that he had a unique opportunity to correct his past. Now he was going to prove himself to all those who had ridiculed him as a failure. With one spectacular, speedy success—the salvation of India—he would wipe out his previous record."[15] But Sanjay was entirely lacking in ideas. To an enthusiastic Khushwant Singh's series of questions, all he could do was offer platitudes or betray his ignorance. Was he close to Jawaharlal Nehru? "As close as other people are to their grandfathers." Feroze Gandhi? "Yes—like any son is to his father." Indira, Rajiv? "Yes, my relationship is no different than that of anyone else with his brother or mother." Influences? "I cannot recall any." Books that inspire? "I cannot think of any." "Poetry? Fiction? History? Biography?" "None of those." "Do you read the *Weekly*?" "Only the jokes and comics." God? "I am not particu-

---

[12] This was James Manor's assessment after speaking to a number of Congress politicians in 1977: see Manor, "Indira and After", p. 319.

[13] Mehta, *The Sanjay Story*, p. 42.

[14] Ibid., pp. 65–6.

[15] Ibid., pp. 230–1.

larly religious. But I am not anti-religious either." Politics? "I consider politics very boring." Urban planning in Delhi certainly inspired him, but he could not elaborate on the subject.[16] His Five-Point Programme would reflect this lack of imagination and his missionary zeal to prove himself.

Secondly, the allies. In this regard, Gandhi *fils* was not unlike Gandhi *mère*. He demanded fierce loyalty from his supporters who, in return, were allowed to run their own fiefdoms and programmes. But there was a crucial difference. Indira Gandhi's loyalists were typically career politicians; Sanjay's, friends he had made as an automobile entrepreneur. An early associate was Arjun Das, a mechanic he befriended when he returned to India. His brother Rajiv, who had met Das on a road when the latter had helped him repair a burst tyre, had introduced them in 1967. "Das was a gold mine of rare and secret information", Mehta writes.[17] He knew Delhi's junkyards, workshops, and *chor bazaars* (flea markets) inside out. Together, in their spare time, the duo would plunder scrap markets for spare parts, piecing together cars at a shed they hired in Gulabi Bagh. Such were the humble beginnings of Maruti, India's own people's car.

The Indian government had had a "small car" project in the pipeline since the late 1950s. After a decade of indecision, it was decided to hand over the project of producing 50,000 cars annually to the private sector. Fourteen firms, including Renault, Citroën, Morris, Mazda, Toyota, and Volkswagen, sent in bids. Sanjay's newly floated company, Maruti, named after the wind god, was one of them.[18] The prime minister's son at twenty-three had no experience in the business. But the forces of supply, demand, and right connections were stacked in his favour. Maruti put in the cheapest tender and won. "Soon little Marutis should be seen on the roads of Haryana and Delhi, and a month or two later they will be running between Kalimpong and Kanyakumari", a journalist noted at the time.[19] Not everyone was elated, however. In fact, parliament and the press were united in their disapproval, the highlight of which was the walkout staged by all opposition MPs in March 1973.

At first Mrs Gandhi was on the defensive. "My son is a delicate young man", she said, "and with whatever money and energy he has, he has mod-

---

[16] An August 1976 interview, cited in Singh, *Indira Gandhi Returns*, pp. 78–9.

[17] Mehta, *The Sanjay Story*, p. 67.

[18] Ibid., p. 71.

[19] Khushwant Singh in the pages of *Illustrated Weekly of India*, cited in Guha, *An Anthropologist Among the Marxists*, p. 199.

elled a car, not a posh one, but one fairly comfortable and suitable to Indian conditions ... my son has shown enterprise and I could not say no to him."[20] But then she waxed vehement, cloaking the nepotism in terms of the national good: surely she was not being asked to deny him the opportunity "just because he is my son. Then how am I going to justify my policy to encourage the young men in the country?"[21]

The next step for Sanjay was to look for land on which to build the factory. The chief minister of Haryana, Bansi Lal, who was to become one of his closest associates during the Emergency, made him an offer.

Bansi Lal represented a new type of politician, who broke into the ranks of the Congress' patrician polity by assiduously cultivating its powerful figures but without internalising what this class considered *comme il faut*. A peasant's son, he had worked as a *muneem* (accountant) in a grain shop and run a bus service before obtaining his bachelor's degree and becoming a "briefless lawyer".[22] He then joined the Congress, getting elected to the Rajya Sabha because of an embarrassing gaffe on the part of the party's selection committee: seeing too many Jats on the list, they picked out Lal, a Jat whose name suggested he was a Bania.[23] Their candidate spent the next six years in Delhi, ingratiating himself with Gulzarilal Nanda, a senior Congressman who had twice served as interim prime minister. At the end of his term, this "*dalal* of Nanda"—to use his rival Devi Lal's words—was sent to Chandigarh in 1968 to head the Haryana government, making him the youngest chief minister in the country. He was forty-one. Ensconced in the state capital, Lal fashioned himself after the former Punjab chief minister Pratap Singh Kairon, "the Al Capone of Indian politics" who was killed in 1965, "gangster-style in a hail of bullets on a darkened road."[24] During his tenure, Lal turned Haryana into a police state. Six years into his job he had already locked up more than 143,000 citizens.[25] The press suffered under him as well. In 1974 he had gangsters demolish the building that housed the offices of *Chetna*, a Bhiwani newspaper, after claiming it was illegal.[26] Even before the Emergency, he made no bones about his ways. "You are too democratic and soft", he would chide Mrs Gandhi, or

---

[20] Indira Gandhi, 24 September 1970, cited in Mehta, *The Sanjay Story*, p. 72.
[21] *New York Times*, 18 May 1973, p. 6.
[22] Nayar, *The Judgement*, p. 7.
[23] Thakur, *All the Prime Minister's Men*, p. 37.
[24] Lukas, "India is as Indira Does", p. 88.
[25] Thakur, *All the Prime Minister's Men*, p. 44.
[26] Ibid., p. 46.

behenji, sister, as he called her. "I would have put all of them behind bars", he once said of Haryana's opposition.[27]

In Sanjay's rise Lal saw a new Nanda. When it came to his notice that the prime minister's son was shopping for land for Maruti, the Haryana chief minister promptly offered some in the district of Gurgaon, conveniently located on the edges of South Delhi.[28] On 10 July 1971, 1500 peasants of the villages Mahaluda, Dhundera, and Khetpur were notified that the 445 acres they collectively owned would be requisitioned by the Haryana government for less than a third of the market value.[29] Lal even arranged for a government loan to cover Maruti's costs for this purchase. With these two moves, he had cemented his rapport with the first family. Or, as he put it, "I have taken possession of the calf and naturally the cow is always at my beck and call."[30]

Now, with farmers evicted and capital secured, Sanjay could get down to the business of making cars. In November 1972 he unveiled a prototype amidst much fanfare, but improvements, and more crucially mass production, required more capital. To this end two public banks, the Central Bank of India and Punjab National Bank, were asked to cough up considerable sums. Private investors put in money as well, and in exchange had their tax arrears forgiven and prison sentences commuted.[31] Among these investors were eight family members of L.N. Mishra, the Congress fundraiser-in-chief and sometime minister who was assassinated in 1975.[32] Curiously, however, the more the funds grew, the harder it became for Sanjay to deliver his vehicle. The cost of the project was rapidly revised upwards, from Rs 46.5 million in August 1970 to Rs 170 million in December 1972.[33] Concurrently the market price of the car moved from upper-middle-class affordability—Rs 6000 in 1970—to the prohibitive sum of Rs 25,000 in 1975.[34]

Sanjay was losing hope. "By the end of 1974 he had virtually written off his cherished car project."[35] Its only use now was to extract as much money

[27] Nayar, *The Judgement*, p. 24.

[28] On the making of Gurgaon and the development of Maruti's factories and townships, see Oldenburg, *Gurgaon*.

[29] Rawla and Mudgal, *All the Prime Minister's Men*, p. 89.

[30] Thakur, *All the Prime Minister's Men*, p. 48.

[31] Selbourne, *An Eye to India*, p. 114.

[32] Mehta, *The Sanjay Story*, pp. 76–7.

[33] Selbourne, *An Eye to India*, p. 114.

[34] Rajni Patel, President of the Bombay PCC, to Indira Gandhi, 15 December 1975, PMSP, File 17/407/1975 PMS.

[35] Mehta, *The Sanjay Story*, p. 84

for his family as possible. To this end he created a consultancy firm, Maruti Technical Services, which milked Rs 1 million from the parent firm, ostensibly for "services" rendered to Maruti, in effect siphoning public money for personal gain through this shell company.[36]

The resort to criminality in part stemmed from the self-assurance that only a leading figure of the national elite could have. He was certain that any attempts to uncover the murky dealings of Maruti would be shot down—which of course they were. Thus, in April 1975 four CBI officers investigating Maruti's import of machinery—in response to a parliamentary inquiry at the instance of the CPI(M)'s Jyotirmoy Basu—were told by R.K. Dhawan of the PMS to "desist from collecting information". Dhawan then pressured CBI director Devendra Sen to discipline his staff. Soon after, the four officers were smeared as corrupt and their houses raided. As was to be expected, evidence of "assets disproportionate to their known sources of income" was found wanting.[37] Nevertheless, they were either suspended, transferred, or forced to go on leave with half-pay.[38]

It came as a stroke of luck for Sanjay that just when he saw his road to automobile success approaching a *cul-de-sac*, a new career path opened up. Politics. For this novel venture he cultivated another ally, R.K. Dhawan. The first cousin of his mother's former secretary Yashpal Kapoor, Dhawan too had served as Mrs Gandhi's staffer. From being her assistant in 1962 when she was chairman of the New York World Fair's advisory committee, he became one of her "several stenographers" when she became prime minister.[39] In 1971 he inherited his cousin's job. Not long after, he began currying favour with the figure most likely to inherit his boss' job, Sanjay.

In June 1975 Sanjay, Lal, and Dhawan sprang into action. When Mrs Gandhi contemplated resigning, this troika prevailed over everyone else in convincing her otherwise. But, even during that fateful fortnight, Sanjay's caucus was not central to the decision-making process: Mrs Gandhi had her own set of advisers, figures like Ray, Satpathy, and Barooah, and her own power centres, the Prime Minister's Secretariat and the "kitchen cabinet"—people and institutions Sanjay did not appreciate because of their apparent

---

[36] Ibid., pp. 67–70.

[37] *SCR*, vol. 1, p. 60.

[38] Ibid., p. 61. In another case, in July 1975, an investigation into "two ladies" fronting for anonymous Maruti shareholders was shut down: *SCR*, vol. 2, pp. 17–19.

[39] Thakur, *All the Prime Minister's Men*, p. 102.

leftism.[40] To undermine them he would need his own set of people, institutions, and ideas.

In the wake of the Allahabad High Court verdict, Sanjay decided to make himself useful by mobilising support and managing the press. He was after all, in his mother's words, "a doer, not a thinker".[41] On 20 June he organised a mammoth rally at Delhi's Boat Club. Five days later, when his mother and Ray were poring over constitutional volumes in search of a veneer to cloak the power grab, Sanjay was the one calling chief ministers and preparing them for the crackdown.

He also kept one eye on the media. Noticing that the Congress had less than complete control of the airwaves, he took umbrage at I.K. Gujral's handling of the Ministry of Information and Broadcasting. Gujral, a loyalist who stood by Mrs Gandhi against Desai and filled the state-run airwaves with propaganda—even shutting down programmes and suppressing reportage at her instance—had on the eve of the Emergency made a slip-up in the coverage of the Boat Club rally.[42]

To Mrs Gandhi, no bigger evidence was needed of her indispensability than the attendance of some 50,000 supporters at this rally. "It was the biggest in the world", she later exclaimed.[43] But the spectacle was not televised and Gujral became the whipping boy.[44] Sanjay alerted his mother of the I&B minister's inability to get his journalist friends to do his bidding.[45] Mrs Gandhi then called him in. "You are very soft", she said bluntly to him, "we want someone who can deal with the media with a stern hand. Vidya [Charan Shukla] would be the right man in the new situation."[46] On 28 June,

---

[40] In reality, figures like Barooah were hardly socialists. As he himself admitted, "we have no ideology, we have a culture!" Cited in an interview with Bechtoldt, "Indira's India", p. 299.

[41] Vasudev, *Two Faces of Indira Gandhi*, p. 136.

[42] By his own admission: transcript of interview with I.K. Gujral, Acc. No. 797, NMML Oral History Project, pp. 129–31.

[43] Nayar, *The Judgement*, p. 32.

[44] Another of Mrs Gandhi's rallies was described as "gigantic" in an AIR broadcast. She angrily phoned Gujral to say it should have said "very large" instead. Such instances only multiplied that summer. On other occasions, she had the scripts of entire broadcasts vetted before airing: transcript of interview with I.K. Gujral, Acc. No. 797, NMML Oral History Project, p. 134.

[45] Mehta, *The Sanjay Story*, p. 100.

[46] Thakur, *All the Prime Minister's Men*, p. 56; transcript of interview with I.K. Gujral, Acc. No. 797, NMML Oral History Project, p. 151.

Shukla was handed the job and Gujral shunted to the Planning Commission.[47] Shukla, scion of a powerful family in Madhya Pradesh—his father and elder brother were both former chief ministers—was more pliable than that "communist", Sanjay reasoned. Moreover, he "was good at *bandobasti*", the art of settling matters.[48]

Now that he was ready to step up, Mrs Gandhi asked Sanjay to concentrate his energies on Delhi. He set to work, building his team. In addition to Arjun Das—who had left his garage and got himself elected to the Delhi Metropolitan Council in 1971—he took under his wing a number of bureaucrats, policemen, politicians, and toughs. Some of them, of course, had been inducted into positions of power before the Emergency, during Sanjay's Maruti years.

Navin Chawla was one such figure. An IAS officer, he had met Sanjay in England when still a student and Sanjay a Rolls-Royce intern. As additional district magistrate of South Delhi, "he was the officer who had 'sealed' the marriage of Sanjay and Maneka" in September 1974.[49] By then, Chawla had Sanjay's ear, which he put to good use. Insinuating that Delhi's lieutenant governor, Baleshwar Prasad, supported Narayan—"he is a Kayastha from Bihar, a JP man"—he convinced the first family to have him replaced in October that year with Krishan Chand, a retired ICS officer whom Chawla had "interviewed" over dinner. The *ci-devant* functionary would remain eternally grateful to Sanjay's confidant, appointing the thirty-year-old as his secretary. After the Emergency, Chand would tell Charan Singh, "I was not involved in anything. My secretary was my boss"—an oversimplification, but like all heuristics, one with an element of truth.[50]

Another key figure of the Delhi caucus appointed before the Emergency was Pritam Singh Bhinder, a police officer from the Haryana cadre. As senior superintendent of Gurgaon, Bhinder had been entrusted by Bansi Lal to ensure that the construction of the Maruti plant proceeded apace without interference from farmers and workers. Evidently he was good at his job. Bhinder and Sanjay had built a strong enough rapport with one another for the prime minister's son to have this policeman appointed deputy inspector general of police for Delhi in January 1975 despite his ineligibility for the job: in theory it was open only to officers of the union

---

[47] "A political cow shed", as Haksar would put it: Gujral, *Matters of Discretion*, p. 52.
[48] Mehta, *The Sanjay Story*, p. 100.
[49] Thakur, *All the Prime Minister's Men*, p. 131.
[50] Ibid., p. 132.

territory.[51] The Shah Commission would describe Bhinder as a "hatchet-man" tasked with purging the police and the CBI.[52] B.R. Tamta was another member of Sanjay's sleeper cell, already in a position of power at the time the Emergency was declared. In 1973 he was a deputy commissioner in charge of water supply in the Municipal Corporation of Delhi (MCD). Pulling the right strings—Arjun Das was an associate of his—Tamta secured a meeting with Sanjay. In weeks he was sworn in as commissioner of the MCD.[53]

More important than this troika was a man Sanjay had no role in promoting: Jagmohan. Here it was synergy that counted, not clientelism. Jagmohan headed what was an especially important institution for Sanjay, the Delhi Development Authority (DDA). A young IAS officer, Jagmohan had resigned from the elite service to join the DDA in 1967 under a state government scheme. For many this was folly, but for him it was a calling. As is clear from his multi-volume oeuvre, urban planning was a passion for this bureaucrat. He quickly rose through the ranks and in 1971 Lieutenant Governor A.N. Jha appointed him vice chairman.[54]

During the Emergency Old Delhi was to become the playground of Sanjay's twin obsessions: gentrification and family planning by way of bulldozing and forced sterilisation. While Jagmohan was his key ally for the former, for the latter it was Begum Rukhsana Sultana. *Née* Meenu Bimbet, Sultana was raised Hindu, taking on the faith of her father, air force officer Paddy Bimbet, before converting to Islam to have a better shot at inheriting her maternal grandfather's fortunes. The elder sister of a Bombay actress, Sultana had "quit college half way because it had nothing to teach her", and moved to Goa, selling jewellery before returning to Delhi to become a social worker.[55] But she found more lucrative activities during the Emergency when she graduated from Sanjay's "ice-cream buddy", as she would proudly tell anyone who cared to listen, to being a key figure of his network.[56] The

---

[51] Dayal and Bose, *For Reasons of State*, p. 176. Bose was a Naxalite turned reporter for the *Patriot*, Dayal a human rights activist. Both in their twenties, Dayal and Bose authored this volume in nineteen days, piecing together what was perhaps the first book-length journalistic account of the Emergency.

[52] *SCR*, vol. 1, p. 67.

[53] Thakur, *All the Prime Minister's Men*, p. 141; Statement of Tamta, 5 August 1977, SCP, Subject File 2, p. 155.

[54] The *ex officio* chairman of the DDA was the lieutenant governor himself.

[55] Thakur, *All the Prime Minister's Men*, pp. 115–18.

[56] Kidwai, *24 Akbar Road*, p. 61.

sultan of Delhi was quick to realise the utility of making Sultana, a Muslim, his poster-girl for the sterilisation programme—for the leaders of the *qaum* had by resorting to Quranic interpretation made it known they were going to oppose sterilisation tooth and nail. This did not deter Sultana from establishing a family-planning centre at Dujana House in the Jama Masjid area, the heart of Muslim Delhi. Through the middle months of the Emergency the "queen of the walled city" became a regular in Old Delhi's streets, instantly recognisable in her "sunglasses and chiffon saris",[57] where she would cast about for Muslim women to inveigle into sending their husbands to her basement clinic. When that did not work, she would resort to extortion. Aided by "the most notorious lumpens of the area",[58] men like Razoo and his gang, who were known to run protection rackets, Sultana would drag men off the streets and into her camp. Standing orders from on high ensured that no criminal case could be registered against them at the Jama Masjid police station. On 13 February 1976, Krishan Chand appointed her "the only non-official member of the Motivational Committee on Family Planning."[59] By the end of the Emergency she had made Rs 84,210 by "motivating" 8407 citizens to get sterilised, two of whom were Muslim *imams*, a fact the government did much to highlight.[60]

Such were the *dramatis personae* of the parallel power structure. What of the shifting balance of power itself? Here, the later months of 1975 proved crucial.[61] N.K. Seshan, Mrs Gandhi's private secretary, discerned a gradual and silent transition: "It became more and more clear that the files I was submitting to the prime minister were being seen by someone else ... Certain files would not come back at all. Slowly I changed the habit of submitting files directly and started routing them through the other centre of power."[62] Across Delhi Sanjay instituted a system of "secrophones" which allowed him to contact ministers and top officials directly, without having to go through the usual channel of secretaries. By December Sanjay was to

[57] Frank, *Indira*, p. 405.

[58] Dayal and Bose, *For Reasons of State*, p. 39.

[59] Mussells, "Democracy and Emergency Rule in India", p. 164.

[60] Wright, Jr., "Muslims and the 1977 Indian Elections", p. 1220.

[61] The *Times of India*, the newspaper of record, throws up 6 hits for "Sanjay" in July 1975. For the next four months, the figures are 5, 11, 18, and 17. From December 1975 the figures go up sharply, peaking in January 1977: 28, 41, 42, 31, 32, 35, 30, 27, 50, 55, 47, 80, 85, and 100. Qualitatively, too, changes are discerned. The thrust on Sanjay's pronouncements in the early days of the regime is replaced with an accent on his actions in the later months.

[62] Seshan, *With Three Prime Ministers*, p. 123.

be found firing ministers and chief ministers of the old order, replacing them with cronies of his own. Bansi Lal became defence minister that month, taking over from the Congress veteran Swaran Singh, whose sin was looking askance at Sanjay's growing influence, although he had never made this explicit.[63] Singh's was a not-uncommon attitude among senior Congressmen, and Sanjay was aware of it—one of the reasons why he was ready to fire even on suspicion rather than threat. This was about the time when he had confessed to a West German paper that he had a penchant for dictatorships—though "not of the Hitler type", he quickly added.[64] In fact, as mentioned, his role model was Marcos.

In trying to consolidate power, the prime minister's son quickly realised that Mrs Gandhi's faithful would continue to be a stumbling block for his programme. Some of these figures even refused to speak with Sanjay. His solution was to circumvent them and rely on those lower down the pecking order. To cut out cabinet ministers, he cultivated ministers of state. Om Mehta, minister of state for home affairs, was one of those who gradually made redundant his boss K. Brahmananda Reddy. Another junior minister of state, Pranab Mukherjee, played an analogous role in the Finance Ministry, sidelining C. Subramaniam, who loathed Sanjay. Also in the penultimate rung of the ministerial hierarchy, but *de facto* in the driving seat, were S.K. Misra in Defence, N.K. Singh in Commerce, and V.S. Tripathi in Information and Broadcasting. In Delhi, too, the tail wagged the dog: it was Chawla, not Chand, who called the shots.

The Ministry of Health and Family Planning, however, was an exception to this style of rule. While Sanjay ignored Karan Singh, the minister—the two made not even a single public appearance together despite the emphasis on family planning during the Emergency—he never felt the need to have a loyal understrapper in the ministry.[65] Pressure was applied directly on state governments to fulfil and revise sterilisation targets. This was enabled in part by the decision of Singh's ministry to "not interfere with the freedom of action of the state governments." In the course of the Emergency it received over 300 complaints but chose to sit on them: "no action need be taken by us ... The state [government] is competent to do so."[66]

---

[63] Replacing Bansi Lal as chief minister of Haryana was Banarsi Das Gupta, a cipher.

[64] Nayar, *The Judgement*, p. 24.

[65] Interview with Karan Singh in New Delhi on 11 April 2018.

[66] "Implementation of the Family Planning Programme During the Emergency", SCP, Subject File 5, pp. 65–6.

At first, Sanjay's experiments with public policy took place primarily in his laboratory, Delhi. By the early days of the Emergency a ritual had evolved. The regulars would come to 1 Akbar Road early in the morning, wait in the anteroom until Sanjay freed himself from his Youth Congress duties, and then huddle in his office. The clique that attended these events was a mix of politicians, friends, and bureaucrats—figures such as Lal, Mehta, Shukla, Dhawan, Jagmohan, Tamta, S.L. Khurana, V.S. Ailawadi, and Mohammad Yunus.[67] Here, cabinet rearrangements were hammered out, ministerial positions discussed, and factionalism played out. Typically, the "debate" commenced when Dhawan and Mehta contradicted one another. In this turf war the prime minister's secretary usually had the backing of Chand and Bhinder, while the minister of state had Khurana's. Sanjay, of course, was the arbiter.[68] After the meeting he would retire to his office, call them one by one and listen to them snipe at one another, the natural consequence of the siege mentality he had fostered. This was all in the spirit of competition; it helped in decision-making, Sanjay felt.

While the capital was Sanjay's cynosure, he did not shy from flexing his muscles beyond the union territory. This he did in two ways: at the top was the tried and tested method previously seen with the ministries, involving the replacement of state satraps and party bosses with useful ciphers; and at the bottom was the transformation of the Youth Congress into a loyal army. On Sanjay's advice AICC treasurer and union minister Uma Shankar Dikshit, who had managed the war chest in the 1971 elections, was dropped.[69] A new bagman was sought as replacement. To this end P.C. Sethi, chief minister of Madhya Pradesh, was brought in as union minister for fertilisers and chemicals. After criticising Gurdial Singh Dhillon, the speaker of the Lok Sabha, for poorly managing the house, Sanjay had him replaced with Bali Ram Bhagat. Changes were introduced in state administrations as well. In November 1975 the Uttar Pradesh chief minister, H.N. Bahuguna, who had refused to support K.K. Birla's candidature to the Rajya Sabha, was replaced by Sanjay's creature N.D. Tiwari. When Sanjay visited Lucknow in early 1976, Tiwari waxed lyrical to an audience about

---

[67] Khurana was the home secretary; Ailawadi, secretary of the New Delhi Municipal Committee; Yunus managed the *National Herald,* a Congress paper, and served as special envoy to the prime minister. See his memoir: Yunus, *Persons, Passions, and Politics,* pp. 221–3.

[68] Dayal and Bose, *For Reasons of State,* p. 73.

[69] He was made governor of Karnataka—in effect, promoted into irrelevance.

how his patron was "gifted with the same divine vision" as the Pandavas in Kurukshetra.[70] In similar card shuffles Sanjay had S.C. Shukla restored as chief minister of Madhya Pradesh and Nandini Satpathy removed as chief minister of Orissa.[71]

The only state boss of "the Left" that Sanjay failed to dislodge was Bengal's S.S. Ray. He did succeed in clipping the chief minister's wings, though. He deputed an old Doon School friend, Kamal Nath, to Calcutta, assigning to him the broad remit of general troublemaker. In this regard Sanjay could vouch for him: a "voluble, loud lad" who liked "to throw his money around" and was known to have "failed two years in a row" at school, Nath knew how to raise hell.[72] As the son of a Calcutta business-man, Nath was also on home turf. Arriving in the eastern state capital, he had V.C. Shukla—who until then was thought to be an ally of Ray's—cancel state-sponsored advertisements to all Calcutta newspapers, weakening the chief minister's rapport with the local press.[73] A second blow landed when Ray, falling out of favour with local elites because of Nath's machinations, was divested of his home portfolio.[74]

Simultaneously, Sanjay took control of the Youth Congress, a perfect vessel for the making of a praetorian guard. At the time, the YC was largely the work of Nurul Hasan, education minister from 1972 to 1977, who had set up a number of *yuvak kendras* (youth centres or branches) with the intention of "absorbing the lumpen youth of village and town and turning them into partially criminalised cadres for the ruling party."[75] Its tensions with the parent party pre-dated Sanjay as well. As early as 28 June 1975, just three days into the Emergency, Karan Singh was writing wearily to the prime minister, carping about the "perennial conflict between the Youth Congress and the main party."[76]

Despite its formidable reputation, in 1975 the YC was but a paper organisation outside West Bengal. In that state the leadership of

---

[70] Thakur, *All the Prime Minister's Men*, p. 128.

[71] Soon after, AIR began broadcasts railing against Satpathy. Orissa was placed under President's Rule: *SCR*, vol. 1, p. 45.

[72] Mehta, *The Sanjay Story*, p. 45.

[73] Thakur, *All the Prime Minister's Men*, p. 151.

[74] Ibid. On the marginalisation of S.S. Ray, see *Satya Samachar*, 26 September 1976, p. 11, in "Documentation of Emergency Period in India", MLP, microfilm copy, reel 1.

[75] Thapar, *All These Years*, p. 382.

[76] Singh, "Some Aspects of Recent Affairs", in Alam, *Kashmir and Beyond*, p. 280.

Priyaranjan Das Munshi, who in 1971 became its first elected president, proved vital. Transforming it into an organisation structured around full-time cadres, Munshi made sure that the parent party was forced to acknowledge its strength. In the 1972 state elections 75 of the 239 Congress candidates were YC men.[77] But wherever it was active, it came to be known for its criminal activities, "from breaking up meetings to murder."[78] And its programme consisted of little "beyond a vague nationalism and a strong anti-communism."[79]

In rebooting the YC, Sanjay accentuated both its lumpen nature and its rudderlessness. He put one of his associates, Ambika Soni, in charge of a membership drive. Fired by the 1969 Congress split, Soni, the daughter of a former chief secretary of Punjab and wife of an IFS officer, had left her job as a receptionist in Delhi's Air France office to join Indira Gandhi's party. Moving up the ranks of the Women's Front of the AICC, she then built a rapport with Chandrajit Yadav, one of its general secretaries. On 13 June 1975 she attracted media attention when she slapped one of the demonstrators demanding Mrs Gandhi's resignation. Vinod Mehta observes that this was "probably Mrs Soni's finest hour", one which earned her her future job in a flash.[80]

Together, Sanjay and Soni also saw to it that a number of affluent but inexperienced young men were put in organising roles. As it happened, their career trajectories were not unlike Sanjay's: a passage from "India's most expensive prep schools" to wasted years at either the best universities or nowhere in particular; from there directly on to leadership positions. As for the burgeoning cadres, they were "inexperienced youths of a different kind". The numerical strength of the YC jumped from 700,000 to 6 million between late 1975 and early 1977.[81] The RSS made a not-insignificant contribution: after the organisation was banned, its members joined the YC in droves.[82] Neophytes, even those above thirty-five, the mandated age limit, were welcomed into leadership roles in the YC as well—these were typically men commanding muscle power.[83]

---

[77] Narain and Sharma, "The Fifth State Assembly Elections in India", p. 326.

[78] Mehta, *The Sanjay Story*, p. 95.

[79] Mendelsohn, "The Collapse of the Indian National Congress", p. 56.

[80] Mehta, *The Sanjay Story*, p. 97. On her role in the imprisonment of Virender Kapoor, see Kapoor, *The Emergency*, p. 103ff.

[81] Manor, "Party Decay and Political Crisis in India", pp. 28–9.

[82] Lockwood, *The Communist Party of India*, p. 145.

[83] Mehta, *The Sanjay Story*, p. 109.

It was in September 1975 that Sanjay expressed interest in the YC for the first time, summoning its state presidents to the capital and lecturing them on their mission.[84] In early November he decided that Munshi had become a liability. He had Dhawan contact his point man in Calcutta, Debi Prasad Chattopadhya, in order to get Munshi to resign. When Munshi made desperate attempts to meet Mrs Gandhi and make his case in person, the replies from her office were consistent: she simply had "no time". In the end he decided to meet Sanjay himself. "You are against me and my mother. You will have to quit", Sanjay said in his usual prosaic, telegraphic style.[85] And that was that.

Instead of taking over from him, Sanjay had Soni sworn in as YC president on 13 November. *De facto* executive decision of course resided with him, but this way he could maintain plausible deniability. Indeed, Sanjay never took on a leadership position in the organisation; he was content to have himself unanimously elected on 9 December as one of the many members of its national committee.

In these early months it was unclear what Sanjay wanted from the YC. At first it appeared that he envisioned a cultural role for it. To this end he found himself coveting the International Youth Centre. Housed in the fashionable quarters of Chanakyapuri, the centre had been built in the late Nehru years to foster cultural exchanges, giving young people inexpensive recreational and hostel facilities. But in Emergency India the "undesirable activities of foreigners in this building"—and their "connections" with the Jana Sangh, RSS, and the CIA, no less—were no longer welcome; so the building was sequestrated under the DIR.[86] Ambika Soni was inducted into the centre's reconstituted board of trustees, whose older members were threatened into retirement. However, not long after, the sultan realised that shepherding a cultural scene was not his calling. Given to pendular swings in humour, Sanjay veered off into new fixations, handing over the centre to the Delhi State Industrial Development Corporation in November 1975.[87]

---

[84] Ibid., p. 106.

[85] Thakur, *All the Prime Minister's Men*, p. 136. In Mehta's version, Mrs Gandhi asked Munshi to resign at a meeting on 8 November: Mehta, *The Sanjay Story*, p. 106.

[86] *SCR*, vol. 2, pp. 63, 66.

[87] It remained in YC hands between 30 August and 29 November that year. In September 1976, the Centre changed hands yet again, this time coming into the possession of the National Institute of Social Studies and Research, an organisation that offered training to members of the AICC. Mrs Gandhi inaugurated the

A clearer vision for the YC emerged subsequently. In Delhi, under the aegis of Jagdish Tytler, its state president, the rank and file became experts in extortion. Marauding bands of Youth Congressmen patrolled the capital, demanding that passers-by either produce a sterilisation certificate or "cough up Rs 300".[88] It was the petite bourgeoisie, in particular, that bore the brunt. Either they had "not properly displayed the mandatory price tags" or perhaps not marked down prices enough: "'Donate Rs 100 or we'll call the police' was the customary threat."[89] In this period the YC branched out into organised crime as well, with Sanjay ordering hits on local underworld figures.[90] Racketeering in Muzaffarnagar, Uttar Pradesh, turned out to be particularly lucrative for the YC, which managed to extract Rs 1 million from textile merchants, *rickshawalas*, gas-station owners, factory bosses, and the transport mafia.[91]

Within the Youth Congress a separate body, the Nehru Brigade, was created as a proper militia.[92] In Delhi its leader was Ramesh Dutta, who was to become the city's deputy mayor in 2004. But real power lay with Arjun Das, whose protection rackets pre-dated the Emergency by a year.[93] Das, however, was not content with simply enriching the YC's coffers. He had begun lining his own pockets too. When, as part of Sanjay's gentrification drive, demolitions commenced in Arjun Nagar, Arjun Das, who owned a flat in the neighbourhood, was handed thirteen apartments "in the choicest DDA colonies" of the city as part of the rehabilitation.[94] The DDA official responsible for the allocation made his apprehensions of the time known to the Shah Commission in no uncertain terms: Das was a "powerful man", a "professional *goonda*" and it would have been "difficult to say no to him" even had he demanded a "hundred flats".[95]

---

first of these courses that month: "The Vishwa Yuvak Kendra", SCP, Subject File 23, pp. 3–17.

88 *Lok Sangharsh Samiti*, 23 November 1976, p. 3, in MLP, reel 1.

89 Mehta, *The Sanjay Story*, p. 115.

90 Frank, *Indira*, p. 397.

91 *Lok Sangharsh Samiti*, 23 November 1976, p. 3, in MLP, reel 1.

92 This Nehru Brigade should not be mistaken for the Nehru Brigade or 4th Guerrilla Regiment that was a unit of the Indian National Army during the Second World War.

93 Thakur, *All the Prime Minister's Men*, p. 141.

94 *SCR*, vol. 2, p. 113.

95 Statement of Ranbir Singh, Executive Officer, DDA, 6 February 1978, SCP, Subject File 4, pp. 206–8.

But criminality and graft were not ends in themselves. To make a successful bid for power, Sanjay needed to acquire the reputation of a good administrator. So on 22 February 1976 he announced his Five-Point Programme, shorter and more succinctly put than his mother's Twenty Points: family planning, slum clearance, planting trees, eradicating illiteracy, abolishing caste and dowry.[96]

The new year also witnessed Sanjay's transformation into a mainstream politician. No longer would he operate behind closed doors. His face was to be plastered on walls, voice heard on radio and television, presence felt at rallies. In January 1976 his commitments included meeting a Yugoslav "youth delegation" and addressing Dalits in the capital. The following month he began his peregrinations, visiting Calcutta, Patna, and Bhopal. In March he covered Bikaner, Hyderabad, and Lucknow. In April, Ferozepur, Amritsar, and Baraut. In May, Agra, Lucknow, Sitapur, Lakhimpur. And from June until the end of the Emergency he spent at least five to seven days every month in towns across the country, chief ministers in tow, addressing audiences at Congress and YC meetings and sending out instructions to local bureaucrats and politicians.[97]

By November 1976 his hold on power was plain to see. In a reflection of its self-assurance, the YC held its "first annual convention" at the same time, 21 and 22 November, and at the same place, Jawahar Nagar in Guwahati, as its parent organisation. Sanjay was the star attraction: he "was taken in a procession flanked by horse riders and motorcycle outriders. He stood throughout the route, waving at thousands of men, women, and children who cheered him and greeted him with claps."[98] One poster read: "Sanjay Gandhi, you are the helmsman of our new India, the country's last resort." "Welcome future light of India" read another. In his address Sanjay contrasted the Congress unfavourably with its youth wing: "A year ago the Congress held its session in Chandigarh while the Youth Congress held a cell meeting. This year the Youth Congress is holding its session while the Congress will hold a small cell meeting", he concluded triumphantly.[99] Indeed, while Mrs Gandhi had been the linchpin of the

[96] *TOI*, 22 February 1976, p. 9. In different versions, it is "Sanjay's Programme" or the "Four-Point Programme". Abolishing illiteracy is sometimes rendered as "each one, teach one", and slum clearance as "beautification".

[97] *White Paper on Misuse of Mass Media*, pp. 78–9.

[98] Mehta, *The Sanjay Story*, p. 126.

[99] Ibid., p. 128.

Chandigarh Congress in December 1975—"a row of glamour girls sang a chorus, '*Indira Hindustan Ban Gaee*' [Indira has become India]"—in Guwahati the mantle had fallen upon her son.[100] Ambika Soni seconded the claim, helpfully adding that "Congressmen obstruct the work of the Youth Congress. They fear that the Youth Congress may take the lead in their areas by hard work. We are not hungry for power, but we will fight back if you people [*sic*] continue to obstruct us."[101] As the room thundered with applause, party president Barooah remained seated on his perch in the front row, staring at his shoes. The reaction of his boss, however, could not have been more different. In her valedictory address Mrs Gandhi panegyrised the youths in attendance: "You have stolen our thunder, and it should be that way. I have firm faith in the youth of India. If they can look after this country then India's future is safe."[102]

The Guwahati session was just one of many episodes during the Emergency in which Gandhi *mère* seemed ready to buttress Gandhi *fils* and the YC at the parent party's expense. In another instance, when Chandrajit Yadav mentioned *en passant* to Mrs Gandhi that Sanjay's popularity was just a function of his ability to hire crowds, she replied incredulously that "some people are jealous because Sanjay is really popular."[103] When the sultan demanded that a quarter of the union government's 54-member council of ministers be replaced by YC men, she readily acquiesced. Not long after, he and Dhawan began "interviewing" the ministers at 1 Safdarjung Road, dropping figures they disliked on the spur of the moment. Lower down the chain, at the sub-district level, the same process was at work: YC personnel were quickly supplanting Congressmen in party and government.[104]

Mrs Gandhi's willingness to shore up Sanjay despite his gaffes and despotic bent seems, at first blush, mystifying. Part of the answer to this puzzle resides in her own disenchantment with the Congress in 1976. After the 1969 split and the botched attempt at transforming it into a party built on cadres in 1974, she had come to realise that this electoral machine of the gentry was impervious to change. But this, as P.N. Dhar notes, had been at best a tepid attempt; she really had "no interest in reforming and rejuvenat-

---

[100] Thapar, "Just to Remember", p. 34.

[101] Mehta, *The Sanjay Story*, p. 127.

[102] Ibid., p. 129.

[103] Nayar, *The Judgement*, p. 107.

[104] Lockwood, *The Communist Party of India*, p. 145.

ing her party."[105] It was one of the reasons why she had come to rely so heavily on bureaucrats.

But by around the middle months of 1976 she had lost confidence in the bureaucracy as well. It was "unfortunate", she noted, that "when a programme is left entirely to the bureaucracy or to the administration, it does not always go along the lines or in the spirit in which it was envisaged."[106] The next-best alternative available in the marketplace of administrators appeared to be the Youth Congress. That her son headed it, which could pave the way for a smoother transition of power than the one between her father and her, was an added attraction.

Yet in letting Sanjay run amok Mrs Gandhi had taken a major risk. With all the power at his disposal—the Delhi caucus, loyal cabinet and chief ministers, the Youth Congress and Nehru Brigade, and allies at the Prime Minister's Secretariat and residence—he had the potential to scuttle her programme and implement in its place one of his own liking. And this is precisely what he did. As time went on, the Twenty Points receded from view and, in the hard sell of Sanjay's Five Points that followed, the accent further narrowed to just two: family planning and urban renewal.

Family Planning and Gentrification; or, Sterilisations and Deportations

From Family Planning to Man-Hunt

In its recourse to coercive sterilisation, the Emergency regime did not introduce anything new to the Indian family-planning landscape. Indeed, the Indian state had been trying to reduce population growth, specifically by rooting out "undesirables", for well over a quarter of a century before India's authoritarian turn. The novelty of Sanjay's drive lay rather in the sheer scale on which the programme was carried out; in the use of myriad government departments to diffuse the policy; and in offloading the duties of the state onto citizens.

The Congress had expressed demographic concerns as early as the 1930s. And these were not limited to simple Malthusian worries over too little produce as against too many mouths. There was already an element of eugenics in these ideas, the result of internalising the race science that the British had popularised in the subcontinent. In 1947 the Indian National

---

[105] Dhar, *Indira Gandhi, the "Emergency", and Indian Democracy*, p. 266.
[106] *SSWIG*, vol. 3, p. 278.

Congress Subcommittee on Population expressed its fears over the growing "mispopulation": the minorities and lower castes were breeding too fast, causing a "deterioration" in the "racial make-up" of the country.[107] In the postcolony, such concerns were never to be voiced so brazenly again; however, the targeting of Muslims, Dalits, and the poor was to remain.

In the 1950s attitudes towards the population explosion had been lax, in part because the magnitude of the problem had yet to be gauged. For Nehru it was inevitable that with economic growth would come lower fertility rates.[108] The 1961 census, however, caught the government unawares: its estimate of 1.2 per cent population growth widely underestimated progenitive activity in the republic. The real figure was closer to 2.3 per cent.[109] Alarmed at the news, and armed with an impressive array of Malthusian statistics, family planners set to work on what they saw "as a supply problem".[110] Surely, all that was needed was to increase the availability of clinics and contraceptives. Despite much research, the administrators never once suspected that it might be a problem of demand: that high infant mortality rates, for instance, could be the reason why people tended to have more children. Perhaps not everyone was convinced of the merits of small families after all. As a result, massive investments in family planning ensued: in 1961 the Third Five-Year Plan allotted 7.9 per cent of the health budget to it, sextupling the previous plan's percentage. The leaps made during the two plans that followed were equally dramatic: the corresponding figure rose to 16.2 per cent in 1969 and 39.3 per cent in 1974.[111]

Over time, however, research grew more sophisticated. Now it was seen as both a demand and supply problem. Family planners became convinced that the answer lay in both reducing levels of inequality—by land

---

[107] Vicziany, "Coercion in a Soft State—Part 2", p. 562, n9.

[108] Williams, "Storming the Citadels of Poverty", p. 480.

[109] Frankel, *India's Political Economy*, pp. 150, 185.

[110] The best account of the thought-world of the family planners is a two-part piece by Marika Vicziany. See her "Coercion in a Soft State—Part 1", pp. 373–402; and idem, "Coercion in a Soft State—Part 2", pp. 557–92.

[111] The three-year hiatus (1966–9) was dubbed the "plan holiday", hence the Fourth Five-Year Plan begins only in 1969. The total family-planning outlays in absolute figures tell the story of an even more spectacular rise: the Second Five-Year Plan (1956) allotted Rs 3 crores to it, while the next three plans—1961, 1969, 1974—gave 27, 95, and 516 crores, respectively, to family planning. A substantial chunk of these budgets went into building infrastructure for, and incentivising, sterilisations. See Vicziany, "Coercion in a Soft State—Part 1", p. 379.

redistribution, for example—and increasing the number of medical facili-ties.[112] Even so, Congress conservatism on land reform made the former impossible, while the latter, dubbed the "extension education approach", for it aimed to diffuse knowledge through Primary Health Centres and campaigning workers, could not produce the rapid results the administra-tion wanted.

When the old idea of diffusion was discarded, the new policy adopted in its place—the "target oriented and time bound approach"—was again geared towards providing and popularising family planning. As before, then, the focus was on the supply side. Tackling the real sources of the population explosion—inequality, infant mortality—was not on the cards. This was the prologue to the Emergency's sterilisation drive: incentives were handed out to those who underwent vasectomies and tubectomies or had an intra-uterine device fitted. The union government footed the bills and the states implemented the policies in conjunction with the family-planning department.

The government's own assessment was that the programme was a phe-nomenal success. Over 95 per cent of all birth control users in 1973 had begun using such technology since 1965, when the policy shift took place. In the eight-year period nearly 67 per cent of couples using birth-control measures had undergone sterilisation—the rest either wore condoms, fitted IUDs, or ingested the pill.[113] The big surge was witnessed in 1970, when a new programme was piloted in Ernakulam, Kerala, where the first major vasectomy camp was set up.[114] This was also the first instance where emphasis was placed on "motivators": spirited citizens who were given Rs 10—quintupling the previous amount—for every person they brought to the sterilisation tables.[115] In top-down fashion, district authorities handed out quotas to government departments and *panchayats*. The latter hunted within their catchment areas and beyond for recruits, who were trans-

---

[112] A number of researchers in the 1970s had arrived at these conclusions. On the correlation between inequality and fertility, see Bhattacharyya, "Income Inequality and Fertility", pp. 5–19; for the effect of land reform on fertility, see Ratcliffe, "Social Justice and the Demographic Transition", pp. 123–44; for the causal link between access to medical facilities at the time of parturition and falling birth rates, see Nair, "Decline in Birth Rate in Kerala", pp. 325, 335.

[113] Vicziany, "Coercion in a Soft State—Part 1", p. 384.

[114] Ibid., p. 388.

[115] This sum paid to motivators would hold until the end of the Emergency. See Table 3 in Vicziany, "Coercion in a Soft State—Part 2", p. 566.

ported to the Cochin Town Hall, where the scalpels were at work. The cornucopia of cash incentives led to an unprecedented number of people being sterilised, and within a few weeks similar camps began mushrooming in other states as well.[116]

Why did the state resort to this most extreme form of contraception? The logic that made sterilisations sought after was simple: it assured permanence and efficiency. In contrast, condoms fared worse on the former metric, and IUDs on the latter. Studies had shown that the blood loss caused by fitted devices could harm undernourished women, a sizeable portion of India's poor.[117] The accent on sterilisation also grew out of the divergence in family-planning implementation between urban and rural areas. And the government had done little to reverse this bias: for instance, in January 1970, out of the 3.54 million condoms sold—the state had tied up with the private sector to sell subsidised condoms in a bid to increase availability—only 118,000 of them wound up in the *mofussil*.[118] As for the few programmes that the state had created to disburse condoms for free, they failed too, with gratis Nirodh condoms falling in the hands of unscrupulous dealers and quickly finding their way into the open market.[119] The government's conclusion that outreach and persuasion were not working, then, was in line with its urban bias. The general denigration of the rural masses by urban government workers made it easier for family planners to treat villagers as a subhuman lot. "Since many of the farmers are illiterate, it is sometimes necessary to compel them to take up schemes", an officer noted.[120] And doctors made it known that they too shared in the functionaries' contempt when they described to the political scientist Marika Vicziany "the Hamlet effect": speed and evasive action were needed to ensure that clients did not—like the eponymous Shakespearean character who, in taking revenge, had temporised—hesitate and withdraw their consent.

Compounding the problem of lack of access to contraception was the abortion law, unchanged since Victorian times, which regarded the termination of pregnancy as a punishable crime. Abortion was legalised

---

[116] Three camps organised by the district collector over the span of a month produced 63,000 sterilisations in Ernakulam: Dandekar, "Family Planning Programme", p. 2152.

[117] Dandekar and Nikam, "What Did Fail?", p. 2394.

[118] Vicziany, "Coercion in a Soft State—Part 1", p. 385, n43.

[119] Banerji, "Will Forcible Sterilisation Be Effective?", p. 667.

[120] Heginbotham, *Cultures in Conflict*, p. 107.

only in 1971, a move partially aided by a growing lobby that saw it as a strategy to curb the demographic explosion.[121] But this policy shift was not the dramatic solution to tame population growth that the family planners were after.

That most doctors rarely visited rural areas only increased the imperative for hasty and permanent solutions.[122] A sterilisation surgery lasted just five minutes, required no hospitalisation, and necessitated only a rudimentary set of tools. The person under the scalpel was placed under local anaesthesia, and, in the case of men, the *vas deferens* was simply cut. Doctors were typically paid Rs 5 per sterilisation and saw it in their interest to deploy the quickest method. Coupled with this was the doctors' "Malthusian cast of mind", a proclivity for "curative rather than preventive medicine", a worldview that "resemble[d] those of shop-keepers". The general tendency among them was also to acquiesce to whatever the bureaucrats told them, in part because it was the state that handed down "drugs, equipment, and potential patients" to doctors, even those working in their private capacity.[123] And even if doctors overcame all this, their room for manoeuvre was small. Poor pay, interference from ministries that monitored prescription costs and kept doctors in tight hierarchies to prevent autonomous functioning, and the stiff competition they faced from ascendant indigenous medicine men—"ayurvedic graduates", "semi-literate herbalists", "spiritual and religious healers"—tended to ensure docility.[124] It was the kind of climate that in some senses made the doctors equal victims of the sterilisation regime once it got under way. Most of them were subjected to twelve-hour shifts and prevented from taking leave even on Sundays and holidays.[125]

Moreover, sterilisations were popular because they belonged to the general dispensation of the era. Annually, 100,000 to 150,000 Americans, mostly black and poor, were coercively sterilised, often under the threat that their

[121] Hirve, "Abortion Law, Policy and Services in India", p. 114.

[122] Recanalisations—the reversal of sterilisations—were possible but complex. Even if the funds and required expertise were available, there was only a "60 to 80 per cent" chance of recanalising the *vas deferens* successfully; for fallopian tubes, this figure fell to "20 to 40 per cent": Pai, "Sterilisation as a Technique of Fertilisation Control", p. 173.

[123] This was Vicziany's assessment after interviewing a number of doctors in 1978: see her "Coercion in a Soft State—Part 2", pp. 581–3.

[124] Jeffery, "Allopathic Medicine in India", pp. 101–13.

[125] *SCR*, vol. 3, p. 178.

benefits would be withdrawn.[126] Across the Atlantic, England was in the throes of "vasectomania" as well, with the *Sunday Times* asking men to do the "patriotic operation".[127]

In India the massive productivity drive had led to over a million sterilisations every year since 1967–8, peaking at 3.1 million in 1972–3 before falling to just under a million the next year. This was the result of severe budgetary constraints at the centre. As state incentives fell, so did sterilisations, demonstrating that it was poverty and desperation that led people to exchange their fertility for some cash, not a "voluntarist" belief in family planning, as the government narrative had it.

In March 1974 the minister for health and family planning, Karan Singh, abolished cash inducements for sterilisation. His department alone could not carry the entire burden, he suggested. "Schools, hospitals, and *crèches*" had to do their bit, too.[128] But frustration did not mean defeat. Privately, Singh congregated a group of scientists and expressed his desire for a "crash programme on fertility reduction ... a breakthrough equivalent to the explosion of the nuclear device."[129]

In July the breakthrough came in the form of a $40 million grant from the United Nations Fund for Population Activities. This was the single largest grant the organisation had ever made to any country. And the sum appeared to come from nowhere. Indeed, since 1969 India had received only $2.5 million from the UNFPA, an average of half a million dollars each year. Finally, the sterilisation programme could continue. Despite the rhetoric of the Indian officials at the 1974 Bucharest Conference on Population, where Karan Singh had famously declared that "development is the best contraceptive", policy in praxis worked towards cash-induced sterilisation rather than structural change.[130] Indeed, during the Emergency liberal cash incen-

---

[126] The sterilisation scandal broke in 1973, but was quickly overshadowed by Watergate. See Dowbiggin, *The Sterilisation Movement*, pp. 177–80. Even as late as the early 2000s, sterilisation was the preferred method of contraception for 23 per cent of Americans: Mosher and Jones, *Use of Contraception in the United States*, p. 8.

[127] Unlike in India, however, in both countries the main targets were women. The English programme was of a lower magnitude, generating half the number of hysterectomies as the United States, proportionally speaking. Dowbiggin, *The Sterilisation Movement*, pp. 168, 174.

[128] Vieziany, "Coercion in a Soft State—Part 1", p. 396.

[129] Ibid., p. 397.

[130] Whitney, "Population Planning in Asia in the 1970s", p. 345.

tives were revitalised. Money was not to become a problem again—World Bank aid for this endeavour kept the programme afloat, as did occasional grants, such as the £3 million the British handed the republic's family planners in March 1976. The advice of dissenters went unheeded. "We are not Malthusians, but the westerners have Mrs Gandhi's ears", one of the prime minister's advisers complained at the time.[131] Flush with cash, the old "cafeteria approach"—in which a "wide spectrum of temporary and permanent contraceptive methods" were placed on the counter—was quickly dispensed with.[132] In its place came a simpler policy: "chop them up".[133]

This was not apparent at first. On 1 August 1975, when Karan Singh declared in parliament the government's intention "to reduce the birth rate by one point per thousand per year over the next ten years"—that is, from 35 to 25 per thousand, in effect collapsing population growth rates from 2.4 to 1.4 per cent—he had in mind very different ideas.[134] Interestingly, when Mohan Dharia, by then one of the Emergency's most trenchant critics, responded by proposing "compulsory sterilisation" for families with "more than three children", it was Karan Singh, the government voice, who rejected it. He suggested that at present "other methods", such as raising the marriageable age and freezing the statewise distribution of seats in parliament until 2001, would suffice.[135] How quickly the tables would turn.

It was in December 1975 that the contours of what became a pillar of Sanjay's programme became clear. Under his direction the first major campaign of forced sterilisation was launched in Delhi that month. In the new year some effort was made to look beyond the scalpel, such as when parliament raised the minimum marriage age from 15 to 18 for women and from 18 to 21 for men.[136] But the focus on sterilisation, in its alloy of statist coercion and incentivisation, was never in question. Of the former, eugen-

---

[131] The adviser was not named: *TOI*, 4 July 1977, p. 8.

[132] *SCR*, vol. 3, p. 154; Kumari, "Permanent Sterilisation to Long-Acting Reversible Contraception", p. 150.

[133] Thapar, *All These Years*, p. 419.

[134] *Lok Sabha Debates*, vol. 53, no. 10 (1 August 1975), col. 30. Singh misquoted the figures slightly: in reality, the Family Planning Programme sought a targeted reduction from 39 per thousand in the Third Five-Year Plan to 32 in the Fourth, and 25 in the Fifth. In 1974, the objective of meeting this final target—25 per thousand—was given more time: it had to be achieved by end of the Sixth Plan in 1984: "Implementation of the Family Planning Programme during the Emergency", no date, SCIF, File 41011/7/77–T–4 vol. VI.

[135] *Lok Sabha Debates*, vol. 53, no. 10 (1 August 1975), cols 67, 32; *SCR*, vol. 3, p. 205.

[136] *SW*, 24 April 1976, p. 4.

ics was implicit in the targeting of Muslims and, more generally, the poor. The latter was structured around a tiered system in which couples that signed up for sterilisation with two children or less were given Rs 150; with three offspring, Rs 100; with more, Rs 70.[137] All the same, in the early phase of the Emergency it was clear that sterilisations were not a priority. In fact, more citizens were sterilised in 1972–3 (3.1 million) than in 1975–6 (2.6 million). The next year, however, witnessed a massive increase: 8.1 million vasectomies and tubectomies.

As time wore on, attitudes hardened. This was due in part to other contraceptive methods receding from view: for instance, the number of IUD insertions in the first half of the financial year 1975–6 fell by a sixth in the corresponding period of 1976–7.[138] In 1975–6 "about 33.33" per cent of all citizens who used some form of family planning were sterilised; condoms, IUDs, and the pill accounted for the rest; in 1976–7, 42.4 per cent.[139] But there was, more importantly, a change in thinking. Health Minister Karan Singh's changing views over the course of the regime serve as an index of the growing obduracy. What began as whimpering apologia quickly turned into strident defence. In October 1975 Karan Singh appeared to be hedging his bets:

> While I am not at this stage advocating compulsion, it is essential that our policy should exhibit the determination of the government to bring home the realisation of the importance of the containment of population to individual families. This can be done by *enforcing a judicious and carefully selected mixture of incentives and disincentives.*[140]

By January the passage of time had blunted some of this nuance: "it was necessary to introduce some sort of compulsion", he suggested.[141] In April

[137] Karan Singh, Minister of Health and Family Planning, "National Population Policy", 16 April 1976, SCIF, Subject File 118. A Home Ministry document put the figures even lower: Rs 100, 50, and 25, respectively: see their memo on the "Implementation of Family Planning Programme", 7 September 1976, SCIF, Subject File 104. In practice, the sums doled out by the government and in the black market for sterilisations ranged from Rs 50 to Rs 1200.

[138] From 316,900 to 262,700: "Implementation of the Family Planning Programme during the Emergency", SCIF, File 41011/7/77–T–4 vol. VI.

[139] "Statement Giving the Gist of the Replies of the Ministry of Health and Family Welfare to the Questionnaire on Family Planning and Comments Thereon", SCIF, File 41011/7/77–T–4 vol. II.

[140] Emphasis added. Singh to Indira Gandhi, 10 October 1975, cited in *SCR*, vol. 3, p. 153.

[141] Minutes from the Consultative Committee of MPs, 20 January 1976, cited in ibid., p. 154.

he was ready to leave the door more ajar than before: if "a state legislature decides that it is necessary to pass legislation for compulsory sterilisation, it may do so."[142] Still, as his National Population Policy document showed, he had some reservations about the use of force: an equal emphasis ought to be laid on other contraceptive measures, he had noted then.[143] In December he began showing signs of passive aggression: "You see, sterilisations are the most dramatic and the most easily quantifiable of the various methods of population control. And therefore, obviously the emphasis is upon them."[144] And by the end of the Emergency he spoke with the feverish passion of a sterilisation zealot: "you cannot make an omelette without breaking eggs."[145]

In 1976 sterilisation targets were given to states and Sanjay took charge of the effort to see them followed through. For instance, in Maharashtra family-planning officials had to complete the 500,000[th] sterilisation of the year before he visited the state in October 1976.[146] In Bihar the state leadership worried that, in exceeding the assigned target by 60 per cent, its figures were too "low compared to the achievements of Uttar Pradesh and Madhya Pradesh."[147] More "gentle pressure" was needed, they concluded.[148] As for Madhya Pradesh itself, where the 1975–6 figures went up ninefold the next year, the chief secretary worried in November 1976—when "only" 55,000 sterilisations took place—that the "state was in danger of lagging behind other states."[149] Orissa's overstrung minister of state for health and family planning had similar fears, despite having won the Karve Award for "outstanding performance in family planning" twice.[150] For its part the union government did its best to keep state leaders on edge. According to the new rules of the 1976–7 budget the Planning Commission could withhold 8 per cent of the central assistance funds

---

[142] Ibid., p. 171.

[143] Karan Singh, "National Population Policy", 16 April 1976, SCIF, Subject File 118, pp. 168–71.

[144] Extract from an interview titled "How We Did It", published in the December 1976 issue of *Central Calling*: "Implementation of the Family Planning Programme during the Emergency", SCIF, File 41011/7/77–T–4 vol. VI.

[145] Nehru, *Nice Guys Finish Second*, p. 565.

[146] *SCR*, vol. 3, p. 184.

[147] Ibid., p. 173.

[148] Ibid.

[149] Ibid., p. 183.

[150] In 1969–70 and 1970–71, respectively: ibid., p. 187.

that it allotted to the states if it deemed their family-planning performance unsatisfactory.[151]

The target mania encouraged states to get bolder in their prognoses. For instance, the Uttar Pradesh government, eager to prove its usefulness to the centre, raised the target from 400,000 in 1975 to 1.5 million the next year. The Maharashtra government, recognising that demands from above necessitated that "control measures ... be adopted on a war footing", wanted to cross the seven-figure threshold as well—the new target moved from the previous year's 568,000 to 1.2 million.[152] Bihar exceeded twofold the target of 300,000 sterilisations set for it, leading Bindeshwari Dubey, the state's health minister, to revise targets to 1 million by the end of the financial year 1976–7. In Himachal Pradesh each time the target was met it was thought inadequate: in the period between March and August 1976 alone, targets were raised four times.[153]

The fixation with numbers led the programme to grow more coercive over time. And even when the political leadership tried to show its disapproval of violent methods, the language used was deliberately obscure: "force" should be abjured, but citizens should be "intensively motivated".[154] As for Mrs Gandhi's own ambivalence on this question, it was in reality more of a *carte blanche*: "the question of compulsion will be left to the states", she said, "they will decide whether they want it."[155] As it turned out, most of them did. Evidence from the Shah Commission shows how gratuitous some of operations were: among the citizens coercively sterilised was a "mentally retarded" single man of twenty picked up by the police in the capital and only released after he "consented"; an unemployed youth from Gurdaspur who had decided to strike out on his own in Delhi (the trauma of sterilisation eventually drove him to suicide); and a seventy-

---

[151] A. Chandra Sekhar, Special Secretary, Ministry of Health and Family Planning to R.S. Mathur, Desk Officer in the same ministry, 15 June 1976, SCIF, File 41011/7/77–T–4 vol. III.

[152] Maharashtra failed in this endeavour. With 833,000 sterilisations in 1976, the state fell short of its target, despite the frantic traffic of letters moving to and fro between despairing officials in various echelons of the public health department: Madhav S. Palnitkar, Secretary, Public Health to the Urban Development and Public Health Department, 10 January 1976, SCIF, File 41011/7/77–T–4 vol. III; *SCR*, vol. 3, p. 207.

[153] *SCR*, vol. 3, p. 178.

[154] Ibid., p. 199.

[155] *Indian Express*, 6 April 1976, p. 5.

year-old villager in Haryana caught in a police raid and sterilised in a camp despite the doctors' protestations to the police.[156]

For their efforts the sterilisation Stakhanovites were handsomely rewarded. For instance, the municipality of 100,000–500,000 people with the "highest cumulative performance calculated in terms of sterilisation and IUD insertions" was given Rs 75,000 in prize money. Analogously, a smaller municipality received Rs 50,000 for pulling off a similar feat.[157] The Kerala government instituted a number of awards, "cash prizes", "shields", and other memorabilia for the individuals and institutions—health workers and medical officers, urban centres and voluntary organisations—with the most industrious knives.[158] In Bihar and Uttar Pradesh, officials who achieved 200 per cent of their targets had their wages bumped up.[159] In Delhi, Krishan Chand announced that doctors, nurses, and teachers would receive a Rs 100 honorarium if they could "motivate fifty cases".[160]

But as the enthusiasm grew, so did the fatalities. Reports surfaced of citizens dying after contracting "post-operative tetanus/infection complications" and "generalised peritonitis".[161] Much of this can be attributed to the carelessness that stemmed from working in the high-octane environment. Poorly administered local anaesthesia led citizens to complain about excruciating pain during operations. Septic wounds multiplied as surgeons grew sloppy in sterilising their tools. Two journalists who visited the indisposed languishing in hospitals after mishaps in the sterilisation camps described vivid scenes: "Sick women carpeting the floor of the ward", "stitches broken", "puss oozing out", "the smell of antiseptic lotion, blood, and sweat."[162] A number of

---

[156] "Purchase of Sterilisation Cases" and "Complaint of Shri Shangara Masih", no dates, SCP, Subject File 6, pp. 139, 195; *SCR*, vol. 3, p. 32.

[157] "Family Planning Programme Scheme of Group Incentive Awards by Government of India to Corporations and Municipalities for the Year 1976–77", 28 January 1977, SCIF, Subject File 1120.

[158] "Gist of Instructions Issued by the Government of Kerala in the Course of Implementation of the Family Planning Programme During the Period of Emergency", SCIF, File 41011/8/77–T4.

[159] *SCR*, vol. 3, pp. 172, 194.

[160] Dayal and Bose, *For Reasons of State*, p. 135.

[161] Serla Grewal to all medical officers, state family-planning officers, and regional directors, 29 March 1975 and 22 July 1976, SCIF, File 41011/7/77–T–4 vol. III; M.D. Saigal to all state family-planning officers, regional directors, and officers of the family-planning department, 13 February 1976, SCIF, File 41011/7/77–T–4 vol. III.

[162] Dayal and Bose, *For Reasons of State*, pp. 14–15.

dispatches—most of which went unheeded—by the health secretary, additional secretary, and deputy commissioner of the department of family planning highlighted the consequences of target fixation and negligence.[163]

The sterilisation drive relied on the bureaucracy. At the top of the chain of command was Serla Grewal, additional secretary in the Health Ministry, who toured the country to see that all went as planned. While visiting Bihar she was scathing: "if adjoining state like UP can perform 1.2 *lakhs* of sterilisations in one month, why can't Bihar come up to it? [*sic*]".[164] To meet her demands, an elaborate bureaucratic pyramid had been established. In the main, state targets were distributed across districts based on their "eligible populations".[165] Similarly, district collectors did the maths before handing out quotas to *tahsildars* (revenue officials), who in turn enlisted *panchayats* in the countryside. At this level, schoolteachers, *gram sevaks* (extension workers), and *patwaris* (accountants) were recruited to canvass eligible men and women and ship them to family-planning centres, each of which serviced a cluster of fifteen to twenty villages.[166] Additionally, specific targets were allotted to government ministries, departments, and hospitals. For instance, as part of the "post-partum programme" of 1976, it was decided that at least 75 per cent of women with "three or more living children" who admitted themselves into the maternity wards of the 449 participating institutions would be sterilised.[167]

Some states followed their own idiosyncratic policies. For example, in Haryana every cabinet minister was allotted a district, their political careers made contingent on the number of sterilisations they could extract. In Uttar Pradesh the 1.5 million quota was divided equally between the health, education, and remaining ministries.[168] To ensure implementation,

---

[163] Gian Prakash, Serla Grewal, and M.D. Saigal, respectively: SCIF, File 41011/7/77–T–4 vol. III, *passim*; *SCR*, vol. 3, p. 155.

[164] Ibid.

[165] In some cases, they followed an even more arbitrary formula: in Maharashtra, the target was fixed at "17.62 per 1000 population": Chief Executive Officer, Dhule Zilla Parishad to the Block Development Officer, 23 June 1976, SCIF, Subject File 1117.

[166] This is an inductive generalisation inferred from a file that covers the districts of Jalgaon, Nanded, Sangli, Satara, Nashik, Parbhani, Kolaba, Beed, and Buldana, all in Maharashtra: SCIF, Subject File 1120, *passim*.

[167] Kum Suma Subbanna, Under Secretary to the Government of India, Ministry of Health and Family Planning to "All State Governments/Union Territories", 25 August 1976, SCIF, File 41011/7/77–T–4 vol. VI.

[168] *SCR*, vol. 3, pp. 176, 193–4.

all states adopted some system of retribution. For instance, in Bihar employees of the family-planning department were censured if they failed to reach 100 per cent of their targets; their wages were frozen if they fell below 75 per cent; and they were fired if they fell below the 50 per cent mark.[169] In 1976, 1500 family-planning staff fell in the latter category—all were dismissed. The same fate met 266 officials in a single *zila* (administrative district) in Maharashtra, while another 1704 were fined across the state for not meeting their targets.[170]

But nowhere was the family-planning drive implemented with more zeal and co-ordination than in Delhi, Ground Zero of Sanjay's modernist project, where it officially commenced in November 1975. In a sign of what was to come, in August a sterilisation camp had already been set up at Kasturba Gandhi Hospital in the Jama Masjid area, a Muslim neighbourhood singled out by authorities because it had become something of a holdout. On 15 August, Independence Day, the city's leading cleric had famously battled the prime minister in an informal war of words. Perched on the Red Fort for her annual address, Mrs Gandhi had made a speech that boomed across Old Delhi with the aid of countless loudspeakers, but not without competition: Syed Abdullah Bukhari, the imam atop the Jama Masjid, was busy rivalling her with a harangue of his own against sterilisations.[171] He made it known that the faithful would be denied their last rites were they to co-operate in any way with the family-planning programme. At the hospital, doctors set to work furiously, performing 425 tubectomies in fifteen days. But that was not enough. A special camp was organised again in December, by which time Sanjay had thrown himself into the programme.

Not long after, family-planning centres began mushrooming everywhere in the capital. Here, under Sanjay's direction, the implementation committee of the Five-Point Programme coined for the family-planning department a new slogan, *Hum Do Hamare Do* (Us Two, Our Two), replacing the previous one, *Do Ya Teen Bas* (Two or Three, Not More).[172] But more important than persuasion were the harder edges of policy reform. In this new dispensation, parents with two or more children were given access to free medical aid only if one of them could produce a sterilisation certificate.

---

[169] *Times* (London), 8 November 1978, p. 18.

[170] *SCR*, vol. 3, pp. 172, 185–6.

[171] Nayar, *The Judgement*, p. 88. See also Ahmed, *Muslim Political Discourse in Postcolonial India*, p. 141ff.

[172] Dayal and Bose, *For Reasons of State*, p. 123.

This was piloted with the bureaucracy, and in it the health department was naturally the first to be touched. But the sterilisation contagion spread quickly. Other government institutions soon became fair game: on orders from above, the MCD was soon demanding all its employees with three or more children to submit to the scalpel. With the DDA, this applied to employees with two children, too. Employees who resisted the scheme found their salaries withheld, services terminated, and ration cards invalidated.[173] Teachers at MCD schools had to "motivate" at least five people to get sterilised in order to receive their salary.[174] Krishan Chand decreed that migrant workers from other states were to be given jobs only if they had less than two children or a sterilisation certificate. Class IV employees of the education directorate were denied access to free education and asked to vacate state accommodation if they failed to send five volunteers to the camps *every day*.[175]

Not even this was enough. Sanjay launched an intensive drive to have 7100 citizens in the capital sterilised between 14 and 30 April. To this end state departments and local authorities were asked to meet quotas from their own ranks: thus, the health department had to motivate 1300 sterilisations; Delhi Electric Supply Undertaking 1000; Water Supply Undertaking 1000; garden department 500; urban community development department 300; City Terminal Tax Office 100; property department 100; and so on.[176] That summer, targets were revised yet again. This time even the Delhi police—spared thus far, in part because their co-operation was essential for the smooth running of the regime—was made to contribute: 2000 policemen, including three superintendents, were vasectomised. At least three constables died as a result of the operation, prompting a police revolt that had in any case been long brewing.[177]

By mid-1976 sterilisations had become the order of the day, in particular in the political circles depending upon Sanjay's good will: the YC, Congress units in Delhi and the Hindi belt, and the ministries. In the Delhi Pradesh Congress Committee "it became a race to power", recounted one of its workers: "Sanjay Gandhi was judging men on the number of vasectomies they had got performed."[178] In Uttar Pradesh the

[173] *SCR*, vol. 3, pp. 166–7.
[174] Ibid., p. 201.
[175] Ibid, pp. 134, 153.
[176] Ibid., pp. 138–9.
[177] Ibid., p. 140.
[178] Ibid., p. 142.

number of operations rose from an average of 331 a day in June to 1578 in July and 5644 in August, when the YC took charge of special camps in the state.[179] In Karnataka, schools were temporarily converted into sterilisation centres, and in Haryana the camps moved like circus troupes from one *zila* to the next every month, traversing the length and breadth of the *mofussil*.[180] In Bihar a pushy district magistrate prevented the state's transport department from collecting road taxes until its officials agreed to get themselves sterilised.[181]

Virtually all states turned to their bureaucracies in their desperate quest to fulfil targets. In February 1976 the Punjab government forbade employees pregnant with their third child from taking maternity leave and accessing food loans, and made it possible to fine and imprison families with more than two children.[182] Some states, such as Karnataka, Bihar, Madhya Pradesh, Rajasthan, and Gujarat, tried to have all their employees with three or more children sterilised; others, including Andhra Pradesh, Haryana, Punjab, Uttar Pradesh, and Himachal Pradesh, set the threshold at two children. A few governments provided for an upper age limit of fifty-five, but in practice they had no qualms about operating on sexagenarians and septuagenarians.[183] In November 1976 the union announced an ambitious policy that was to be implemented nationally. "Every government servant" had to "ensure that he does not have more than three children after 30 September 1977", its ultimatum read. And if the functionary already did, "he should ensure that this number is not exceeded after that date."[184] State employees who violated the diktat would no longer be entitled to maternity leave, children's education allowances and scholarships, travel concessions, food rations, firearm licences, canal water supply, tax exemptions, medical treatment, state accommodation, and advances for

---

[179] Nayar, *The Judgement*, p. 134.

[180] *SCR*, vol. 3, pp. 176, 181.

[181] The brinkmanship did not work, however, and the district magistrate was forced by the state's chief secretary to rescind his order: ibid., p. 174.

[182] Selbourne, *An Eye to India*, p. 275. There was one exception to this rule. If any of the children were handicapped, or if both belonged to the same sex, the civil servants were permitted a third offspring: "Gist of Instructions Issued by the Government of Punjab in the Course of Implementation of the Family Planning Programme During the Period of Emergency", SCIF, File 41011/8/77–T4.

[183] *SCR*, vol. 3, pp. 159, 175, 180, 190, 195.

[184] See the memorandum on the "National Population Policy", 17 November 1976, Ministry of Home Affairs Papers, File 28016/3/78–Estt(A).

costly purchases. Their restoration was made contingent on sterilisation. This, of course, never came to pass because the Emergency was called off a couple of months later.

While in 1975–6 only two states—Haryana and Maharashtra—had revised targets upwards; twenty of the country's thirty-one states and union territories did the same in 1976–7. Not only were targets revised, they were also exceeded. In 1974–5 only five states and seven union territories achieved this feat; the next year, ten and four did; in 1976–7, eighteen and five.[185] But the numbers were never enough. Inescapably, the private sector became the next frontier. Employers were asked to "motivate" their workforce in order to secure licences and escape police harassment. Bosses did as asked, putting pressure on their employees: only if they returned with sterilisation certificates could they hold on to their jobs.

But the business of getting citizens to "motivate" one another was an ill-conceived policy from the word go. And in tethering the policy to a set of housing inducements, it rapidly and inevitably devolved into a market economy whereby sterilisation certificates became the currency to purchase subsistence dwelling.[186] For instance, in Welcome, a Delhi neighbourhood studied by Emma Tarlo that offered such habitation, 28 per cent of all plots were allotted to those in possession of sterilisation certificates, which could be procured either by undergoing the operation oneself or by "motivating" someone else. In this process, the motivated traded in their fertility for cash, which the motivator paid in exchange for a sterilisation certificate that served as currency to procure a plot of land in a resettlement colony. And in the same manner that the sterilisation programme had become imbricated with housing policy in cities, so did it with the business of land reforms in the countryside. When redistributing land in Goa, Daman, and Diu, for instance, priority was given to landless peasants who possessed sterilisation certificates.[187]

Typically, the motivator was a figure better off than the motivated; after all, "motivation" required liquidity. And most of the motivators entered this market knowing well the arbitrage opportunities on offer, because motivating cost far less than what the sale of a plot could fetch.[188] In some instances,

---

[185] "Statement Giving the Gist of the Replies of the Ministry of Health and Family Welfare to the Questionnaire on Family Planning and Comments Thereon", SCIF, File 41011/7/77–T–4 vol. II.

[186] Tarlo, *Unsettling Memories.*

[187] *SCR*, vol. 3, p. 203.

[188] Tarlo, *Unsettling Memories*, pp. 198–201.

the "motivated" was a parent, and the "motivator" his child. This had multiple advantages: the offspring could set up a nuclear family as a home owner whilst also retaining fertility. In some cases, religion prompted becoming a motivator rather than undergoing the surgery. Muslims preferred this. In May 1976, Darul Uloom Deoband, India's premier Muslim seminary, issued a *fatwa* declaring sterilisation contrary to Islamic injunction.[189]

However, a handful of Muslim leaders, such as Maulana Zaid Abul Hasan Farooqi, lent support to the programme.[190] Mohammad Yunus, Sanjay's friend, was pressed into acting as a poster boy for the "good Muslim" as well: "I am a classic example of the success of family planning", he said, "I am the forty-second child of my father, and I have only one child—a son."[191] Farooqi went further, publishing in 1976 a slender volume, *Islam and Family Planning*, in which he called on members of his community to embrace the sterilisation programme; printing and distribution costs were borne by the DAVP. When it came to the Information and Broadcasting Ministry's attention that Muslim Meos of the villages of Gurgaon in Haryana were showing "some amount of resistance" to the programme, 10,000 copies of Farooqi's book were quickly dispatched to the district.[192] A number of Urdu journals—*Ajkal, Shama,* and *Din Duniya*—agreed to the ministry's request to publish articles in praise of sterilisation.[193] However, the Muslim locals had little use for such propaganda: as the ministry's secretary later acknowledged, a majority of the Meos were illiterate.[194] Until October 1976 they successfully resisted the sterilisation drive, "not allowing even a single government official to enter the village" they had clustered in.[195] But then on the twelfth of that month, the local officials cut off their electricity supply for twenty-five days. And on 6 November 700 policemen armed with rifles and tear-gas equipment thundered into the village. As a deputy inspector general of police put it, it was better to "go into action erring on the side of having extra strength rather than being under strength." His men browbeat 180 villagers into trucks and ferried them to a nearby town

---

[189] *Satya Samachar,* 12 June 1976, p. 6, in MLP, reel 1.

[190] S.M.H. Burney, Secretary, I&B ministry, "Publicity in Favour of Family Planning Particularly in Urdu Language", 30 April 1976, SCIF, Subject File 118.

[191] Mehta, *The New India,* p. 121.

[192] Burney, Note on the Meos, 7 October 1976, SCIF, Subject File 118.

[193] Idem, "Publicity in Favour of Family Planning Particularly in Urdu Language", 30 April 1976, SCIF, Subject File 118, pp. 75–6.

[194] Idem, Note on the Meos, 7 October 1976, SCIF, Subject File 118, p. 60.

[195] *SCR,* vol. 3, p. 29.

where they were forcibly sterilised.[196] Minorities were targeted in Madhya Pradesh, too. A 21-year-old "bachelor Mohamedan [*sic*]" was whisked away to the sterilisation table, as were thirteen *adivasis* (tribesmen), two of whom died after developing sepsis.[197] The eugenical instinct extended to sterilising the infirm as well: lepers were singled out in Maharashtra, continuing a long tradition of institutionalised discrimination against them.[198]

Emma Tarlo finds that it was common in Delhi for Muslims to have motivated two or three citizens to secure homes for themselves, indicating that they were probably pressured more than their Hindu counterparts because the authorities knew they were more averse to sterilisation and, as a result, more likely to cough up large sums. In other instances this economistic logic gave way to an openly confessional one: authorities insisted that Muslims motivate only their fellow believers.[199]

But one did not have to be a member of a minority community to suffer the worst of the "motivation" regime: one simply needed to be poor. Those living in slums were regularly threatened with eviction by the DDA authorities who claimed that their houses were illegal and had to be demolished. The only way to "regularise"—make legal—their existing homes was to get hold of a sterilisation certificate. Faced with this dilemma, many resorted to—as the term of art went—"voluntary sterilisation" in order to safeguard their homes. In a few cases, where houses had already been destroyed a sterilisation certificate allowed citizens to reconstruct them, albeit at their own cost, on the same spot.[200]

As targets kept rising, volunteers grew scarcer. A serious mismatch developed in the market for sterilisation certificates, sending prices skyrocketing in this non-pecuniary economy. Regularising tiny strips of land sometimes required not one but two—or, in the case of better housing, even four—sterilisation certificates.[201] Because the sterilisation regime had become inex-

---

[196] Ibid., pp. 28, 30. Khurshid Ahmed, former general secretary of the Haryana PCC, tried stopping the raid, only to be told off by Banarsi Das Gupta, the chief minister, "this is a matter of pride for the Haryana government. The raid *will* take place": ibid., p. 31. My translation from the Hindi.

[197] *SCR*, vol. 3, p. 183.

[198] Ibid., p. 185. See, for instance, the 1888 legislation that called for the strict segregation of male and female lepers to prevent reproduction: Buckingham, *Leprosy in Colonial South India*, pp. 151–2.

[199] Tarlo, *Unsettling Memories*, p. 192.

[200] Ibid., p. 169; *SCR*, vol. 3, p. 98.

[201] Tarlo, *Unsettling Memories*, pp. 165–6.

tricably linked to the housing sector, these changes came to be reflected in the motivation market. So, while the government would pay motivators Rs 10 as commission, and the motivated around Rs 50 for surrendering their fertility, the real value of the transaction lay hidden in the black market, where motivators were paying anything between Rs 100 to Rs 1200 to procure certificates.[202] A thriving trade in forged certificates developed as well, with counterfeiters making a switch from the usual business of university certificates to the more lucrative one of sterilisation documentation.[203]

Indeed, market opportunities were manifold. *Dalals* (middlemen) would purchase certificates in poor neighbourhoods and sell them in upmarket ones for a profit. Sometimes, shopkeepers acted both as police informants and bail bondsmen, the bail being contingent on sterilisation. They would first inform the police of the whereabouts of people sleeping rough. Then, policemen on the beat would "chance upon" them and have them locked up. Next, the shopkeepers would approach them, offering to pay bail if they agreed to get themselves sterilised. Finally, the spoils were distributed: three-quarters of the certificates would be kept by the shopkeepers who would sell them for a profit, and the remainder by police officers who would use them to meet their targets.[204]

Tarlo has read agency into these actions, even seeing an "entrepreneurial approach" in the "thousands of men and women who competed for plots in the resettlement colonies of Delhi"—in other words, not just in the unscrupulous middlemen but in the urban poor more generally.[205] In a conversation with a DDA clerk, who indicated that "many people" were sterilised not "by force" (*zabardasti se*) but "out of [their own] greed" (*lalach se*), Tarlo sees the conventional "image of innocent victims" reversed.[206] What follows is a quick rundown of such "victims turned agents": tenants wresting properties from their landlords on the back of sterilisation; residents

---

[202] See, *inter alia*, "Statement showing motivation money due to Smt Kaushalya Raman paid to staff of Red Cross Society by ESI Dispensary Okhla" and "ESI Dispensary Shahdara", no dates, SCP, Subject File 6, pp. 100, 118–19. For market prices, see Tarlo, *Unsettling Memories*, pp. 189–91.

[203] Fake university degrees typically sold at Rs 300–400, while the new sterilisation certificates cost Rs 50. That forgers shifted from the former to the latter is indicative of the large volumes the newer market commanded: Vicziany, "Coercion in a Soft State—Part 1", p. 373, n4.

[204] Tarlo, *Unsettling Memories*, p. 187.

[205] Idem, "From Victim to Agent", pp. 2921, 2926.

[206] Idem, *Unsettling Memories*, pp. 92–3.

refusing to be at the receiving end of this policy, deciding instead to turn the stick in the opposite direction by becoming middlemen; cheats hoodwinking unsuspecting buyers into purchasing plots of land with disputed ownership; and industrial workers undergoing the operation for an additional cash award of Rs 50 from the state.[207]

"Pragmatic opportunists" they certainly were, but by emphasising the "entrepreneurialism" of the poor Tarlo risks tilting the balance between agency and structure in the former's favour—an inaccurate representation, as she herself recognises *passim*. Gaming a system geared against them had its obvious limits. As Tarlo notes, when the Emergency ended, sterilisation certificates quickly lost their status as passports to resettlement housing, leaving many hopefuls homeless. In the period between 1977 and 1982 the DDA first lost control over slums and then wrested them back from the MCD. Both changes came with new regulation in which many were "left dangling by the authorities", especially those "still awaiting plots". This was, after all, for the precariat only "the normal state of affairs in resettlement colonies."[208]

During the Emergency Mrs Gandhi was quite frank in discussing the family-planning programme as if it were some kind of class war:

> In India ... in the expanse of indigence there are large islands of indulgence, so that the diseases of malnutrition coexist with those of affluence ... We cannot proceed on the assumption that general progress will automatically improve the condition of the poorest and weakest. Such percolation effect would take far too long. A frontal attack is needed. Public health strategy while forging ahead in areas of promise (such as Maharashtra, Kerala, and Punjab), must pay special attention to the more backward regions such as Bihar and east UP as well as tribal belts ... Increasingly, the doctor's mediation is required not only to postpone death but to prevent birth.[209]

In other words, poverty was not a reflection of poor state policy but of the proclivities of the poor, who begat more poor; the solution therefore was to prevent the poor from spawning poverty by sterilising them. The press welcomed Mrs Gandhi's classist eugenicism. When access to free medical care was made contingent on the ability to produce a sterilisation certificate, *The Hindu* was of the opinion that it was "time to instil in the

---

[207] Ibid., pp. 103–20.

[208] Ibid., pp. 99–100.

[209] Mrs Gandhi's Address to the Association of Physicians of India, 22 January 1976, SCIF, File 41011/7/77–T–4 vol. III.

minds of the poorer sections that they have a responsibility to society."
Birth control measures should be made "a condition for eligibility to public
largesse", it added.[210]

Bulldozing the Poor

The gentrification of Delhi was Sanjay's other priority. During the
Emergency around 700,000 were displaced from inner-city Delhi to mostly
Muslim and Dalit ghettoes in the peripheral conurbations. This was done
in order to bring the city up to the standards of modern gentrification, or,
as Sanjay put it, "beautification". In this endeavour he found a ready ally in
Jagmohan, who, as we will see below, had already set himself the same task.

Here, unlike in the family-planning programme, the bureaucrat was not
one step behind the politician. Jagmohan was already a powerful figure.
Despite the DDA being run by the lieutenant governor, by the early 1970s
Jagmohan had, by packing its thirteen-member governing board with his
wingmen, "succeeded in dominating" the authority "so completely" that it
was his writ that ran in the Delhi housing world, not the LG's.[211] And as
the Shah Commission later observed, with the change in dispensation
Jagmohan "became a law unto himself".[212]

The DDA chief was known to make no bones about his elitism. As he saw
it, he was not just battling Delhi's inner-city slums but "slum culture" itself.
In a book aimed at extenuating his role in the Emergency, Jagmohan writes
that "the real problem of slums is not taking people out of slums, but slums
out of people." And the solution? Cart off "a sizeable portion of the poor"
to the peripheries of cities. While getting a job in one of the "resettlement
colonies" might prove difficult—Jagmohan refers to this only *en passant*—
the poor would come to love them nonetheless, for they provide "fresh air,
light, pure water, and greenery", "balance ... our needs and resources", and
"narrow ... the gap between urban and rural living."[213]

This call for a gentrified utopia was not in itself a radical departure from
conventional opinion. The demolition of the homes of Delhi's precariat
dated back to the Jhuggi Jhompri Removal Scheme of 1958, which sped the
process by which squatters' settlements could be flattened and the lands

---

[210] *Hindu*, 12 January 1976, cited in Selbourne, *An Eye to India*, p. 275.
[211] Dayal and Bose, *For Reasons of State*, p. 91.
[212] *SCR*, vol. 2, p. 118.
[213] Jagmohan, *Island of Truth*, pp. 14, 15, 72.

they inhabited sold to real estate developers. The squatters themselves were leased MCD or DDA dwellings, which often consisted of incomplete structures with poor amenities. But the occupants rarely had the luxury to build new lives in these new homes. Floods and the insatiable desires of gentrifiers—who were always on the lookout for newer neighbourhoods to spruce up—forced them to migrate from one resettlement colony to another, often under police threat. And not all squatters were this lucky: a 1960 census had distinguished between "eligible" and "ineligible squatters"; the former were those who had been in Delhi since July 1960 or earlier and could be resettled, the latter those who had migrated to the capital after that date and were made to leave the city altogether, serving as an example to aspiring migrants of the hostile world awaiting them.[214]

The difference in Jagmohan's approach lay in the segregationist tone of his urban policies. Moreover, he was ready to follow through on this, as the resettlement colony of Welcome in East Delhi showed: the better part of its residents were Muslims from inner-city ghettoes that witnessed the worst of the DDA demolitions. Another novelty lay in the scale of his ambition.[215] Its Olympian quality owed to the kind of figures Jagmohan measured himself against. His role model was Baron Haussmann, whose mid-nineteenth-century gentrification had famously pushed the Parisian working classes out into the peripheral *banlieues rouges*. As Jagmohan saw it, had Haussmann "not cleared the slums of Place du Carrousel, ill de la city [*sic*] and area around Norte [*sic*] Dame, and not built the great highways, the boulevard St. German [*sic*], St. Michal [*sic*], Malesherbes, Magenta ... Paris would have been today an ugly and despicable town ... a sick and soulless city."[216]

As he saw it, the *parisien* tragedy of the 1840s was writ large in the Purani Dilli (Old Delhi) of the 1970s:

> Swamped by the flow of migrants after 1947 and mauled badly by the ruthless violation of the municipal bye-laws, Shahjahanabad stands before us today as a battered, sick, and over-burdened city. It seems to have lost its centre, its soul. It appears even insensitive to pain. Most of the residents are not even

---

[214] Tarlo, *Unsettling Memories*, p. 72, n6.

[215] Yet another was his kitsch poetry. For the general tenor of his corpus, see the poem "This Battered Child of Shahjahan": "I know/ I am no genius/ No Haussmann reborn/ No Lutyens with a chance/ Or Corbusier with Nehru's arms .../ For a while/ I thought/ In my papers/ In my voiceless sketches/ Warmly drawn/ Lay the hope of a silken dawn/ For this battered child of Shahjahan": Jagmohan, *Island of Truth*, pp. 10–11.

[216] Ibid., pp. 9–10.

conscious of the filth and odour around them ... Such is their tragedy. Such is the culture of poverty, degradation and indifference that breeds in Shahjahanabad today.[217]

In a romantic and nostalgic vein Jagmohan describes the walled city as a living organism and justifies doing away with the lesser mortals that inhabit it. They could simply be sent *Yamuna paar* (beyond the river Yamuna), the line that delineated Delhi's eastern border in Jagmohan's imagination.

Before the Emergency, as it happened, Sanjay had little in common with the DDA urbanist. In 1971, while still a debutant on the Indian political scene, the prime minister's son had made a name for himself by *opposing* demolitions.[218] Interestingly, at the time it was the ostensibly left-wing press that supported gentrification, with the *EPW's* Romesh Thapar decrying the "invasion of squatters" and championing the work of the NDMC president Shrichand Chhabra and "his outstanding contribution to the cleaning up and beautification of the capital."[219] During and after the Emergency, however, both Thapar and Sanjay went through the looking glass.

Under the new dispensation, Jagmohan's first forays into urban engineering took shape in November 1975. The first target was the area around the Jama Masjid, more specifically the bazaar jutting out from the giant steps of the mosque complex.[220] For the DDA chief this part of town was "virtually a hell hole, a cemetery of living men, with diseases and disability hovering around."[221] All of it would have to go before it could be rebuilt from scratch. The next step was building a gentrified shopping centre in place of the Paiwalan Complex that surrounded the Jama Masjid peninsularly—a cluster of 150 shops that sold everything from leather

[217] Jagmohan, *Rebuilding Shahjahanabad,* pp. 32–3. This slim volume was published just weeks before the Emergency was declared.

[218] He tried in vain to prevent the demolition of some *jhuggies* in the capital. For disobeying Sanjay's orders, the NDMC president was removed from office by Mrs Gandhi three months before his term expired: Thapar, "A "Routine" Transfer", p. 895.

[219] Ibid.

[220] In the cack-handed job masterminded by MCD Commissioner B.R. Tamta, Kala Mahal, briefly the residence of seventeenth-century monarch Shah Jahan, was accidentally flattened along with the shops, leaving behind only "traces of old stucco and some idea of the ancient." See the report by Salman Haidar, Director (Spl), PMS, 3 September 1975, PMSP, File 7/383/1975 PMS.

[221] Statement of Jagmohan, SCP, Subject File 3, p. 12.

goods and woollen clothes to birds, goats, sheep, second-hand motor parts, local delicacies, and peepal leaves.[222] But this time Sanjay and Jagmohan did not immediately have their way.

On behalf of the Delhi Wakf Board's tenants, some of whom owned shops in and about the complex, Syed Ahmed Hashmi, MP and general secretary of the Jamiat-ul-Ulema-i-Hind, sent a telegram to the prime minister asking her to reconsider the demolition proposal.[223] The Anjuman-e-Tajran Union of the local petite bourgeoisie seconded the JUH's plea, as did the PMS' Salman Haidar who wrote to Jagmohan on behalf of the Delhi Urban Art Commission.[224] Forced to reconsider his plans, the DDA chief "issued instructions not to demolish the Paiwalan building."[225]

But in November the bulldozers came rolling in, chaperoned by shuffling CRPF soldiers. Crowds were dispersed with tear gas and two-thirds of the *khokhas* ("unauthorised" shops) were demolished along with two municipal schools. When the bulldozers were done, trucks made "well over" a thousand trips to clear the rubble. But the ordeal was worth it; the desired result had been achieved. "If one now stood at Esplanade Road", one had the mosque, three hundred metres south of the high street, in one's line of sight. "Jama Masjid was now clean."[226] MCD chairman Mir Mushtaq Ahmad "heartily congratulated" Mrs Gandhi for restoring "the original views of the historic Jama Masjid." "I am sure, in the long run", he added, "the entire Muslim community ... will appreciate and admire your determination and courage in getting the plan implemented."[227] The president of the republic, Fakhruddin Ali Ahmed, echoed both the sentiment and the language, telling Jagmohan how much he "appreciated" the plans.[228] Praise also flowed from Rajya Sabha MP Khurshed Alam Khan, novelist Mulk Raj Anand, and surprisingly, Mahmood Qamar, secretary of the Delhi Wakf

---

[222] Mohan, *The World of Walled Cities*, pp. 20–1.

[223] Telegram from Hashmi to Indira Gandhi, 18 September 1975, PMSP, File 7/383/1975 PMS. Ashok Pradhan, additional district magistrate (central), opposed the demolitions too, stating that the "illegal" constructions in fact existed even in 1892 and that the razing could weaken the foundations of the Jama Masjid: *SCR*, vol. 2, p. 83.

[224] Anjuman-e-Tajran Union to Indira Gandhi, 3 September 1975, PMSP, File 7/383/1975 PMS.

[225] Jagmohan to Haidar, 3 October 1975, PMSP, File 7/383/1975 PMS.

[226] Dayal and Bose, *For Reasons of State*, p. 82.

[227] 26 November 1975, PMSP, File 7/383/1975 PMS.

[228] *SCR*, vol. 2, p. 84.

Board, who had opposed the Paiwalan plans. None were particularly interested in how or where citizens were resettled so long as they disappeared from sight.[229]

The Paiwalan shopping centre, however, never saw the light of day. That, after all, would have only created a new Muslim ghetto. No compensation was paid either, leaving citizens sleeping rough and students studying in tents. This was part of the plan. As Mohammad Yunus put it, the premise of the MCD–DDA "joint operation" at Jama Masjid was to have "all these Muslims who are supporting the Imam dragged and thrown out of the city."[230] Jagmohan was equally unwilling to indemnify the displaced. Citing land-registry documents from 1938, he argued that *every* building demolished under his supervision was illegally built on public land.[231] "The squatters", he stated plainly, "were not actually entitled to anything"; those who were given some land in some corner of the city should have been thankful for the small mercies of the DDA.[232]

If the Paiwalan episode is largely forgotten today, it is the events that transpired at Turkman Gate on 19 April 1976 remain fixed in Indian collective memory as the *ne plus ultra* of authoritarian excess—and for good reason. First, the gate's location gave the event a certain immediacy: it lay in the heart of the republic's capital. Second, the incident involved minorities in one of the poorest neighbourhoods of the country—adjusted for purchasing power—on the receiving end, and the rich and powerful, most notably the prime minister's son, on the other. In essence, it was the stark chasms that separated the two sides—class, wealth, power—that invested the event's violent outcome with a sense of tragedy that made it so narratable. This is perhaps why scarcely a year passes without the publication of countless opinion pieces and essays commemorating the event. Third, and closely linked to the second, the few hours over which the episode unfolded highlighted with remarkable compression the resolution with which citizens were prepared to resist the regime, its police and paramilitary brutality. And remarkably, their *démarche* owed not to some pre-existing solidarities, such as those forged by common membership of a party or union, but simply by the experience of common suffering under a tyranny.

---

[229] Jagmohan, *Island of Truth*, pp. 51–2.
[230] *SCR*, vol. 2, pp. 82–3.
[231] Statement of Jagmohan, no date, SCP, Subject File 3, p. 40.
[232] Statement of Jagmohan, 17 December 1977, SCP, Subject File 4, p. 419.

Early in the morning of 13 April, bulldozers flanked by two police platoons congregated outside the tombs of Shah Turkman—a thirteenth century Sufi saint—and his followers. About a hundred citizens, mostly YC workers, were sufficiently alarmed by the sight to go and see MCD councillor Arjun Das and make sense of what they had just seen.[233] He looked surprised and turned to the man seated next to him, V.C. Shukla, who rang Jagmohan, asking him to call off the demolition squad: the better half of the residents of this Old Delhi neighbourhood had not only secured NDMC approval a long time ago, they also regularly paid into council coffers.[234] As for the rest—just over two-fifths of the houses did not have proper documentation—their "illegality" stemmed from a peculiar policy the postcolonial state had adopted in the early 1950s. In the main, these were properties whose original owners had moved to Pakistan in 1947, leaving their kin to take them over and negotiate the Evacuee Property Act. Under it, all lands belonging to those who had emigrated to the Muslim homeland could be impounded as enemy property. These remaining residents, then, had worked out arrangements with local authorities that were often only quasi-official.[235]

Reassurances flowed in the opposite direction, from Jagmohan to Shukla to Das to the delegation, which returned to Old Delhi only to find that the bulldozers had already flattened fifty buildings. They turned to Das again, who, two days later, took them to Rukhsana Sultana: she had taken charge of the sterilisation camp at Dujana House, midway between Jama Masjid and Turkman Gate, on the same day. She offered conditional help. She would take the matter up with Sanjay only if the locals agreed to set up a family-planning camp at Turkman Gate and "supply at least 300 cases within this week." Desperate, the residents suggested they were ready to negotiate the figure provided suitable alternative accommodation was forthcoming: the DDA planned to "relocate" them to the poorly connected and sparsely inhabited eastern settlements of Trilokpuri and Nandnagri, whereas they preferred the transit camps of nearby Mata Sundari Road or Minto Road. "You can go to hell", came the reply from Razoo, Sultana's gangster associate.[236]

Tensions continued to rise. The next day, 16 April, "a woman constable was dragged into a house by some miscreants" before being rescued by a

---

[233] Dayal and Bose, *For Reasons of State*, p. 37

[234] *SCR*, vol. 2, p. 97.

[235] Ibid., p. 99.

[236] Dayal and Bose, *For Reasons of State*, p. 41.

CRPF officer who was injured in the altercation.[237] A group of Youth Congress activists met Sanjay the day after and presented him with a petition signed by more than a thousand people calling for the end of demolitions at Turkman Gate. Sanjay allegedly "nodded once", indicating that the meeting was over; when they left he "tore up the memorandum into neat little shreds."[238]

The demolitions proceeded apace that day, raising fears among the Muslim community that the Jama Masjid was to be flattened as well. On Sunday the 18th, a day of rest for the bulldozers, a delegation met Jagmohan, reiterating their demands to be deported *en bloc* and not too far off. Betraying that gentrification was as much a confessional project as a classist one, the DDA chief replied: "Do you think we are mad to destroy one Pakistan to create another Pakistan? We will give you plots in Trilokpuri and Khichripur, and you will have to go like the five *lakh* other persons we plan to resettle."[239]

The only important political figure who helped the protesters was Subhadra Joshi, Congress MP for Chandni Chowk, who initiated a *dharna* (peaceful demonstration) outside the NDMC office and tried in vain to approach the other power centre, Indira Gandhi. "Either you do not have time or you do not want to know what is happening. Strange!", she wrote to the prime minister.[240] Piqued, Mrs Gandhi had her removed from the chairmanship of the Minorities Department of the AICC. She had been "inciting the minorities", Joshi was told on her dismissal.[241] That became the official government line: that the Muslims of Turkman Gate were apparently eager to have their houses demolished but for the meddling agitation of activists and reactionary outfits such as the Jama'at-i-Islami and the Indian Union Muslim League.[242]

---

[237] *SCR*, vol. 2, p. 120.

[238] Dayal and Bose, *For Reasons of State*, p. 43.

[239] Ibid., p. 45.

[240] Thakur, *All the Prime Minister's Men*, p. 146. Her attempts to prevent other demolitions in her constituency were similarly given the cold shoulder by B.R. Tamta, Krishan Chand, and Om Mehta. She complained about this to Mrs Gandhi in another letter: Of late, "people in high places have taken to 'high hearing'", she wrote in Hindi using the latter phrase *"ooncha sunna"*, which figuratively meant "hard of hearing": *SCR*, vol. 2, pp. 79–82.

[241] Ibid., p. 81.

[242] Krishan Chand, Navin Chawla, and Mir Mushtaq Ahmad authored a statement to this effect: ibid., p. 134. Jagmohan blames the JI and IUML too: see Jagmohan, *Island of Truth*, pp. 144–5.

Meanwhile, according to Bose and Dayal, whose account of the Turkman Gate episode is perhaps the most accurate one, the sterilisation operations intensified. A family-planning van flanked by two cars would go out every morning carrying Razoo, his gang, and some constables. They would pick up "ragged men" from their streets, get them to sign their consent to sterilisation at the Jama Masjid police *chowki*, and then haul them into the Dujana House camp. In the basement was a "sterilisation operation theatre where a group of doctors and nurses" conducted "rapid-fire operations on their screaming victims."[243]

On 19 April, a group of local women decided to confront the scalpels at work in Dujana House. Early in the morning, one of them, clad in burqa, lay down in front of Rukhsana Sultana's van, which was making off with her husband. While the constables busied themselves dragging her out of the way, her man, along with others in the van, escaped. Infuriated, the police arrested a "venerable" resident of the area, Mirza, who was trying to interpose. In response the whole neighbourhood broke out in cries of *hartal* ("Strike!"), demanding a total shutdown of shops. By 11:30 a.m. all of them around the Jama Masjid were shuttered. Sensing victory, the group of women went to Dujana House demanding that Rukhsana close the camp for good. A fracas ensued in which the "queen of the walled city" narrowly made her escape.[244]

These parallel developments explain why massive police reinforcements were called upon. The Syed Faiz-e-Elahi *dargah* (saint's tomb), just across Asaf Ali Road from Turkman Gate, was teeming with police trucks bringing in battalions of the CRPF, DAP, and BSF. The Nehru Brigade had mingled with their ranks, blurring the line between party and state, private militia and military. Armed constables encircled the neighbourhood, confronting 500 women and 250 children on *dharna* who remained "unintimidated by the guns and bayonets", refusing to let the bulldozers flatten their homes. The standoff lasted a couple of hours in the April sun. At 1:30 p.m. a policeman was seen hitting a woman with a *lathi*. Soon after, Ramesh Dutta, chief of the Nehru Brigade, who, in a bid to thwart the protest had already ensured that the crowd's drinking-water supply was taken away from them, threw a stone in their direction.[245]

[243] Dayal and Bose, *For Reasons of State*, p. 49.

[244] This incident convinced Jagmohan that all that followed was "entirely" due to the camp at Dujana House, and not the demolitions: see his statement, SCP, Subject File 3, p. 7.

[245] Dayal and Bose, *For Reasons of State*, pp. 53, 55.

Within minutes a shower of stones and Molotov cocktails began raining upon the Brigade and the protesters, retaliation leading to counter-retaliation. Around the same time a large section of the crowd that had been waiting for Subhadra Joshi to return with H.K.L. Bhagat—minister for works and housing, who was to call off the demolitions—decided to leave, quite sure that the long delay meant they had been stood up. Sensing "movement in the crowd", the police panicked, resorting to tear gas and then firing shots in the air. Many in the crowd found refuge in the Fazal-e-Ilahi Mosque—almost 2000 of them were huddled inside at the time of the afternoon prayer—but this did not deter the Nehru Brigade or the policemen. With a go-ahead from Deputy Inspector General P.S. Bhinder, they went in and asked the imam where the fugitives were. When he refused to speak, they threatened to beat him up along with his little son. In their account of events they later insisted that this was because the imam and Kamayuddin, a local leader, were "provoking" the crowd with inflammatory speeches in the mosque.[246] They did not pressure the cleric for long; it was probably easier to smoke the protesters out from the nooks and crannies they were hiding in, they reasoned. Over the next half an hour the mosque "became an abattoir" in which protesters were found and killed, blood splaying out "in pools" on the mosque floor.[247] Others escaped and hid behind the Kali Masjid, where they engaged in a low-intensity battle with the police, using sticks and stones.

A column of 500 men—it was unclear who had organised them—came to the rescue of those still battling the police at the site of the *dharna*, ambushing them from Delite Cinema on Asaf Ali Road and capturing a police station. The pincer movement was a masterstroke for another reason too: because of the wind direction, attempts to disperse the protesters with tear gas proved ineffective. The sub-divisional magistrate then ordered a *lathi* charge, and the superintendent of police sent for paramilitary reinforcements.[248] Within the hour, eight companies of the DAP, one of the BSF, six of the CRPF, and three other platoons came marching in.[249] "Two blank firing orders" were handed to them.[250]

---

[246] *SCR*, vol. 2, p. 121.

[247] Dayal and Bose, *For Reasons of State*, p. 58.

[248] A.K. Paitandy and R.K. Ohri, respectively.

[249] *SCR*, vol. 2, p. 122.

[250] They were signed by Ohri and R.K. Sharma, Sub-Divisional Police Officer: ibid., p. 132.

Constables opened fire at 2:30 p.m. while the DAP and CRPF chased protesters into the narrow bylanes of Shahjahanabad. With their new orders the constables fired to kill and not to disperse; the paramilitaries moved in, attempting to "flush out" protesters from the houses in which they were hiding.[251] The chase continued on rooftops, in houses, and through alleys. By 4 p.m. the police had outflanked the protesters and recaptured the police station, rescued stabbed constables at the mosque, and after splitting into five parties regained control over the parts of Turkman Gate from which protesters had been pelting stones. "Moving from rooftop to rooftop", the paramilitaries secured the perimeter of Shahjahanabad.[252]

At 4:30 p.m. police vans with fitted PA systems began cruising the streets, announcing that a curfew had been declared and arresting anyone who seemed not to care. But the violence was not over. This was followed by "a systematic wave of looting and raping" in the neighbourhood.[253] The police "entered houses, beating up the men and even women and children mercilessly", "took away jewellery", smashed glass and crockery, and molested "the local girls", one of whom jumped out of a balcony. In one instance a policeman used his rifle butt to thrash a citizen on his leg, which had already "been wounded by a bullet".[254]

It is hard to arrive at the total number of casualties at Turkman Gate. For one, we have a very small paper trail on account of the government's decision to censor all news relating to the "incident". That the police chose to drag bodies to the police station and not the mortuary—which, in fact, was closer—makes the received figures even more suspect. Jagmohan puts the death toll at six, as does the Shah Commission and a functionary who oversaw the excavation of bodies after the demolitions. Other accounts give wildly different figures: the historian Bipan Chandra suggests 20 were killed; the journalist Kuldip Nayar says 150; Delhi University academic Aditi Gupta puts it at 400; Emma Tarlo and the journalist Tavleen Singh have both come across the figure of 1200; Mohammad Yunus of 1611.[255]

---

[251] Ibid., p. 123.

[252] Ibid., pp. 124, 130.

[253] Dayal and Bose, *For Reasons of State*, p. 63.

[254] *SCR*, vol. 2, pp. 129–30.

[255] Ibid., pp. 134, 137, 131, 141. Jagmohan, *Island of Truth*, p. 121; Chandra, *In the Name of Democracy*, p. 210; Nayar, *The Judgement*, p. 139; Tarlo, *Unsettling Memories*, p. 38; Singh, *Durbar*, p. 40; Yunus, *Persons, Passions, and Politics*, p. 251; interview with A (anonymous) in New Delhi on 9 April 2018. While there was no love lost between this bureaucrat (A) and his Congress masters

What is clearer is what followed. In the aftermath of the state's victory over its citizenry the former doubled down while the latter, out of resignation and under pressure, became passive.

With the rebellion quelled and curfew imposed, the DDA men returned the same evening with state-of-the-art floodlights, six bulldozers, and a motor grader to expedite work at night. With the neighbourhood placed under an indefinite curfew, they finished the "clearance operations" on 27 April. Within a fortnight a total of 841 buildings had been razed to the ground.[256]

The survivors who were not behind bars were given fifteen days' notice to take all their possessions from Old Delhi—whatever they could recover from the rubble—and leave for the resettlement colonies. On paper these were the embodiment of planning: 32 per cent of the land was earmarked for residential complexes, 16 per cent for parks, 13 per cent for "metalled roads", and the rest for footpaths, shops, and "community facilities". "Ambitious projects" in the vicinity, such as the Mother Dairy Factory and a number of "fish and meat processing plants", were to provide employment.[257] But when the prospective residents arrived at what they thought would be the leafy suburban paradise of Mangolpuri, they found, in the words of Bose and Dayal who visited the place, that "the brick hutments that crisscrossed one another in geometrical pattern were mostly half built. Some had no roofs, others had only two walls."[258] The colony's eighteen latrines were roofless and doorless. People had to queue for hours to use them. Families were typically allotted only twenty-five square yards of land—"even an animal can't be kept" in that space, Justice Shah would later remark to Jagmohan.[259]

The DDA refused to sponsor the building of houses, leaving the families to spend hundreds of rupees to purchase sand, cement, and other construction material. The few food-processing plants were hardly enough to absorb the surplus workforce, many of whom had no experience in dealing with milk, meat, or fish. As a result, large sections of the gig economy that serviced Delhi's middle classes—masons, milkmen, watchmen, hawkers, sweepers, carpenters, tailors, painters, servants, chiromancers, priests, and

---

during the Emergency—hence no reason to underplay the figures—he dismisses the four-digit figure as the product of journalistic fantasies.

[256] *SCR*, vol. 2, pp. 99–100.

[257] Statement of Jagmohan, SCP, Subject File 3, pp. 34, 36.

[258] Dayal and Bose, *For Reasons of State*, p. 100.

[259] Brass, *An Indian Political Life*, p. 187.

the like—had to continue working in Old Delhi, the added hours of commute compounding their precarity.[260] The nearest medical facility and ration shop, too, were miles away. Malnourished and immiserated, the citizens of the camp were left to fend for themselves.[261]

The only senior politician who took up their cause was Sheikh Abdullah, chief minister of Jammu and Kashmir, who visited Turkman Gate and the colonies. When he returned to Srinagar, he wrote Indira Gandhi a long letter describing the poor living conditions *Yamuna paar* and condemning the attacks on "secularism" that her "beloved son" was spearheading "right under her nose". But the reprimand from the Muslim leader only made Delhi's first family dig in its heels. Mrs Gandhi made it known that she "did not approve of the letter".[262] When a largely Muslim delegation from Trilokpuri, one of the worst resettlement colonies that Abdullah had seen on his Delhi trip, came to Sanjay with some complaints, he replied: "first go and get a certificate from Sheikh Abdullah praising the DDA. Then we will give you facilities ... Give me a signed list of 800 persons who can be arrested under MISA for having attacked the police that day [19 April] ... You are all liars ... You have made false complaints to Sheikh Abdullah. You must suffer for it now."[263]

A figure who knew him well speculated that Sanjay's animosity towards Muslims was tied to his dislike for Syed Abdullah Bukhari, the imam of the Jama Masjid and a prominent anti-Congress voice. The immediate trigger had been a rally on 2 February 1975 that Bukhari had organised to protest the decision of the Delhi Wakf Board to derecognise him as the Jama Masjid imam.[264] That day, Sanjay had Bukhari arrested under MISA and "beaten thoroughly" in prison.[265] What followed was a confrontation

---

[260] "Occupational Patterns of the Families", SCP, Subject File 3, p. 94.

[261] Jagmohan denies this: "had the conditions been so bad ... and the resettlers so bitter ... would they have voted so enthusiastically for Sajjan Kumar, Congress candidate, particularly when he had wholeheartedly supported the clearance-cum-resettlement drive?" See Jagmohan, *Triumphs and Tragedies of Ninth Delhi*, p. 248. Indeed, Kumar, who stood from Nangloi, was one of the few Congressmen to be elected to the MCD in 1977. However, the *Times of India* suggests that Kumar owed his popularity for the obverse reason, that he could lobby for the "regularisation" of "unauthorised colonies": *TOI*, 31 December 1993, p. 9.

[262] Thakur, *All the Prime Minister's Men*, p. 147.

[263] Ibid.

[264] *TOI*, 3 February 1975, p. 1.

[265] Interview with A (anonymous) in New Delhi on 9 April 2018.

between Muslim protesters and the police that left six dead and a hundred injured.[266] This further hardened Sanjay's Islamophobic views.[267]

If the spirited but failed resistance of Old Delhi's residents marked the high point of opposition to the authoritarian regime, the rest of the demolitions underscored how ordinary the business of bulldozing was elsewhere. This owed, in the main, to the blitzkrieg·fashion in which they were conducted: more often than not the bulldozers would appear at the sites without forewarning, leaving residents with no time to co-ordinate collective action, appeal to local political fixers, or take matters to the courts. The accompaniment of paramilitaries and the looming threat of arrest achieved the same ends.[268] Both these developments, of course, were enabled by the Emergency, the legitimacy it bestowed on Delhi's urbanists to use force, work quickly, and indulge in their "modernist" plans. By Jagmohan's own admission this was, in Delhi's 1200-year history, only the ninth attempt at forging a new capital city on the ruins of old, and could only be accomplished because of the removal of legal and administrative oversight.[269]

No longer did "clearance operations" require the lieutenant governor's or the "prime minister's personal permission".[270] Officials who carped about "legal procedures" were either sidelined or put on leave. For its part the DDA began dispatching its demolition squads to neighbourhoods where it had no jurisdiction.[271] At times when MCD officials appeared diffident, suggesting that they could only bring down "unauthorised" buildings, Jagmohan helpfully offered to fill in: "the DDA would demolish the rest."[272]

Many accounts bear witness to the speed at which the demolitions took place. A woman in Sultanpur Majra in north-west Delhi came back from a night out at the movies—ironically, she had been to see *Roti, Kapda, aur*

---

[266] *TOI*, 3 February 1975, p. 1.

[267] Interview with A (anonymous) in New Delhi on 9 April 2018.

[268] Accounts of the demolitions usually mention the presence of a "large posse of police": *SCR*, vol. 2, pp. 85, 91, 112.

[269] There have been eight "Delhis" in medieval and modern history, we are told in Jagmohan's part-history, part-manifesto, *Island of Truth*, pp. 172–5: Lalkot, Siri, Tughlaqabad, Jahanpanah, Firozabad, Purana Qila, Shahjahanabad, and Lutyens' New Delhi. Jagmohan's imprint was to define the ninth.

[270] This was how B.S. Dass, Commissioner of the MCD, saw it: *SCR*, vol. 2, pp. 77, 81.

[271] In many parts of the city, the MCD and NDMC, as local bodies, were the "competent authorities", and not the DDA, which was a creature of the union government

[272] Ibid., pp. 91, 101, 104.

Makaan (Food, Clothing, and Shelter)—to find her house flattened.[273] In the villages of Sarai Peepal Thala and Bhalswa Jahangir Pur, land set aside for redevelopment in 1966 and 1967, respectively, had nearly fallen off the DDA radar because "illegal" constructions and inadequate paperwork had resulted in a decade of stalling. But with the new regime, in the summer of 1976 demolitions commenced posthaste.[274] In another incident, to get around the need for the lieutenant governor's approval, without which places of worship could not be bulldozed, Jagmohan summarily declared that the Arya Samaj Temple at Green Park was a "fake temple" and had it levelled, former MP Ram Gopal Shalwale's protestations notwithstanding.[275]

"Bulldozers were instruments of development, and not of demolitions", Jagmohan would later proclaim.[276] But during the Emergency, eyewitnesses recalled, the machines were spotted bearing a more menacing legend: "I am deaf, I am blind, I am dumb."[277] In other words, it was pointless to get in their way. Indeed, in such a climate resistance was short-lived and futile.[278] Citizens that went up to the political classes to appeal for clemency or tried to move the courts were arrested under MISA, while the demolitions continued unabated.[279]

Jagmohan and Sanjay continued to clear "slums" and evict the poor until the end of the Emergency. Homes that flanked the All India Radio transmitting station, constructions off the Delhi University campus, buildings in the neighbourhoods of Andheria Mor, Arjun Nagar, Bhagat Singh Market, Jhandewalan, and Karol Bagh—none were spared.[280] No amount of government permits, electricity and water bills, and tax records could change the fate of a property that fell within the targeted sites. The Shah Commission

---

[273] Ibid., p. 91.

[274] "*De novo* acquisition proceedings were initiated" only on 23 March 1977: ibid., p. 92.

[275] Statement of Jagmohan, 17 December 1977, SCP, Subject File 2, p. 241.

[276] Jagmohan, *Island of Truth*, p. 71.

[277] Statement of Jagmohan, 17 December 1977, SCP, Subject File 4, p. 407.

[278] For instance, when DDA officials visited an army veteran's house to inform him that his house was to be demolished, they were shooed away by the old man who threatened to open fire. But when the bulldozers arrived he was helpless, and his house succumbed to the deft blows of the ripper shanks: *SCR*, vol. 2, pp. 106–7.

[279] See, *inter alia*, statement of C.R. Sharma, Arjun Nagar resident, 6 February 1978, SCP, Subject File 4, p. 102.

[280] *SCR*, vol. 2, pp. 86–9, 108–13,

remarked upon the "punitive and almost vindictive attitude exhibited by the authorities": telephone and electricity lines were disconnected for extended periods; curfews similarly prolonged; furniture tossed about; and citizens trying to move the courts—"cantankerous" men, as livid NDMC officials put it—imprisoned until they dropped their petitions, accepting that they themselves had demolished their own homes.[281]

When a UN agency commissioned Jagmohan to author a report on Delhi's gentrification, he wrote unabashedly that "we have removed all *jhuggies* from the city. We have demolished 1.2 *lakh* housing units in the slums. That is 7 *lakh* people."[282] Jagmohan was given a Padma Bhushan for his efforts in 1977. He later joined the BJP, serving three terms as a member of parliament and briefly becoming urban development minister in Atal Bihari Vajpayee's cabinet.[283] In both capacities he continued his war against "the huge net-work [*sic*] of illegal squatters", shipping minorities to the city's peripheries, and in the process anchoring the Delhi of "our future" to the "glorious strands of our past".[284]

It would be remiss to suggest that the gentrification drive was uniquely a plot hatched by a handful of protagonists in a handful of neighbourhoods of the capital. For the ideas of Jagmohan and Sanjay were common currency in the country.[285] Indeed, slums were demolished in Karnal, Rohtak, Bhiwani, Gurgaon, Lucknow, and beyond.

In Bombay, for instance, the Janata Colony that housed 70,000 was flattened by the planners of the Bombay Municipal Corporation to make way for the construction of 700 flats for the employees of the department of atomic energy.[286] Ironically, this demolished housing complex in a periph-

---

[281] Ibid., pp. 86–8, 138.

[282] Dayal and Bose, *For Reasons of State*, p. 96.

[283] That Jagmohan moved from one party to another is not particularly surprising, considering he equated politics of any kind with anomie. His oeuvre is basically a series of put-downs of "inefficient" politicians and bureaucrats. See, *inter alia*, Jagmohan, *Soul and Structure of Governance*, pp. 59–175.

[284] Ibid., pp. 466–7.

[285] The focus on Delhi in this chapter, in essence, reflects the Delhi-centric narrative of the Emergency. For instance, in the three reports of the Shah Commission, demolitions in the capital are described over sixty-three pages. For the rest of country, the same subject matter is summarised in ten. Journalistic accounts and memoirs set during the Emergency have the same bias. However, as the three tables cataloguing the spread of complaints, sterilisations, and detentions in the next chapter demonstrate, the reach of the Emergency was nationwide.

[286] Clibbens, "The Destiny of this City", pp. 52–4.

eral neighbourhood of Bombay was not a slum, as advertised, but a state-sanctioned resettlement colony.[287] But this was just semantics. It was only natural for the resettled to be asked to resettle elsewhere if the powers that be demanded it. Since the early 1960s the nearby Department of Atomic Energy had been clamouring for its removal. As Homi Sethna, the architect of the country's atomic bomb programme, put it in a letter to Mrs Gandhi in February 1975, the colony was "a definite threat to security in BARC [Bhabha Atomic Research Centre]", India's nuclear nerve centre.[288] The prime minister concurred and wrote to the chief minister, V.P. Naik, asking him to "see the matter through to its logical conclusion."[289]

Six years had passed since the colony's residents were first issued eviction notices, but materially nothing had changed. However, with the *carte blanche* of authoritarianism, Naik saw through the passage of the Maharashtra Vacant Land (Prohibition of Unauthorised Occupation and Summary Eviction) Act, which barred civil courts from adjudicating on demolitions.[290] In May 1976 Janata Colony was razed to the ground and its inhabitants shifted to Mankhurd in the east. Like the colonies Sheikh Abdullah saw in Delhi, this one offered neither *pucca* housing nor any amenities. The citizens also had the misfortune of arriving at just about the time the monsoon had begun, the attendant diseases and floods decimating the population of this settlement in the months that followed.

Along the lines that BARC turfed out citizens in Chembur, the Indian Railways and the Indian Armed Forces did so in the neighbourhoods of Ghatkopar and Malad, respectively. And these were not isolated cases. What transpired in such colonies was part of a larger city-wide project: on 4 January 1976 the Maharashtra government had tasked 7000 functionaries to enumerate all the illegal "huts" in 850 colonies scattered across the state capital. Through the Emergency, 12,000 of the city's 260,000 "huts" were demolished. This was repeated in the smaller towns of Pune, Kolhapur, Aurangabad, and Beed.[291]

In West Bengal small retailers were given twelve hours to destroy their own houses and shops or have demolition squads do it for them at a cost of

---

[287] Deshpande, "Resettling a Squatter Resettlement", p. 521.

[288] Clibbens, "The Destiny of this City", pp. 52–4. The Bhabha Atomic Research Centre (BARC) is in Trombay, a coastal neighbourhood just south of Chembur.

[289] Ibid., p. 55.

[290] Ibid. It was passed on 11 November 1975: *SCR*, vol. 3, pp. 208, 214.

[291] *SCR*, vol. 3, pp. 214–15.

sixty rupees an hour.[292] Bihar's "anti-encroachment policy"—strengthened in scope and proofed against the courts over three ordinances in December 1975 and January 1976—led to 66,141 "offending structures" covering over 22,000 acres of city and countryside being "disposed of" during the Emergency. While there was only "one reported case of police firing" in the state, the Shah Commission noted that "the presence of force at the time of demolitions was almost a precondition." In Madhya Pradesh, new legislation made it possible to imprison "encroachers". The appellation had the intended dehumanising effect. Demolition squads in the state went about flattening hovels, shops, and *gumties* (kiosks) even during the monsoons, fully aware that there were no alternative housing or jobs available for their inhabitants. In Uttar Pradesh, Lucknow's streets were widened by demolishing houses "without payment of a single penny of compensation."[293]

While the razing and making of buildings is at the heart of all gentrification projects, it must be remembered that these are essentially *social* enterprises, not merely architectural ones. Ideas of hygiene, productivity, and order are integral to them. Thus, it was no accident that, in remaking Delhi, Sanjay and Jagmohan masterminded a canicide that took the lives of 20,000 dogs, drove out cows and buffaloes kept by milkmen in the city, and rounded up beggars and street vendors across the city.[294]

This, again, was a nationwide phenomenon. The drive to "clean Bombay" involved "removing garbage, catching stray dogs and animals ... removing unauthorised hawkers, rag-pickers ... [all] to make the city cleaner and beautiful." The "menace" that the state capital's 75,000 beggars posed, too, was dealt with.[295] It was decided to treat them as free labour; opinion pieces in the leading dailies chorused government demands that "unproductive" beggars be set to work to clean the city gratis.[296] Moreover, ordinances were passed to allow for the arrest and sterilisation of beggars, as

---

[292] Selbourne, *An Eye to India*, p. 271.

[293] Bihar's "Answer to Questionnaire on Demolition", SCIF, File 5/BHR/77/78–D; *SCR*, vol. 3, pp. 210, 213–14; Brass, *An Indian Political Life*, p. 180.

[294] Dayal and Bose, *For Reasons of State*, p. 85. Interestingly, there is a Parisian parallel here that Jagmohan might appreciate. The modernisation of the French capital in the mid-nineteenth century too was accompanied by the wholesale killing of strays, the "radical biopolitical reordering of human–canine geographies" being a not unnatural aspect of projects of urban renewal: Pearson, "Stray Dogs and the Making of Modern Paris", p. 138.

[295] *TOI*, 29 September 1976, cited in Clibbens, "The Destiny of this City", p. 57.

[296] Clibbens, "The Destiny of this City", p. 59.

well as the transportation of "able-bodied" ones to the city's peripheries, where they were made to work unpaid on construction projects in Kukadi and Jayakwadi.[297] The only beggars exempted from this draconian ordinance were "*sadhus* and saffron-clad *sanyasis*".[298] In Punjab a policy of state-sanctioned begging was put into place: "only deserving applicants" were given "permission" to "solicit money, food, or other gifts". And in Karnataka the Prevention of Beggary Act, 1975 was hastily passed to allow the police to round up beggars and forcibly sterilise them in district hospitals.[299] Hawkers were not spared either, many of whom were picked up on the pretext that they were selling magazines of the underground press, "prejudicial material" that undermined national security.[300]

* * *

Sanjay's brief hold on power was, in short, both a continuation and exaggeration of Mrs Gandhi's rulership. By early 1976 the parallel power structure that had evolved around him was both competing with the state and contemplating its eventual takeover. In this enterprise the insurgents had a strong leader in Sanjay; a ruling class that consisted of his friends, bureaucrats in Delhi's ministries, and chief ministers; a core constituency in the rapidly multiplying ranks of the Youth Congress, the body that also acted as its parent party's shock troops; and a programme whose focus came to be narrowed down to two policies aimed at urban renewal: the sterilisation of millions and the eviction of the inner-city poor to "resettlement colonies" in the peripheries of cities.

While these two "achievements" are remembered as representative of the atrocities perpetrated by the Emergency regime, they were in fact only more extreme versions of past practices. Still, it must be noted that mass sterilisation and deportation targeted the very poor in whose name Mrs Gandhi claimed to speak from the very beginning of the Emergency.

Certainly, Sanjay's attempts to capture the state by dominating the bureaucracy, the party, and his parallel power structure, as well as his

---

[297] Ibid. In Maharashtra alone, 2457 beggars had been sent to construction sites by May 1976. However, many of them managed to escape the forced labour.

[298] Selbourne, *An Eye to India*, p. 267.

[299] EPW Research Foundation, "Clippings", p. 166.

[300] See, for instance, the case of Mam Chand, an "almost illiterate" hawker arrested for the entire duration of the Emergency for displaying on his cart a single copy of *March of the Nation: SCR*, vol. 2, p. 48.

nepotistic efforts to control the commanding heights of the economy show that he was pushing the Emergency into a different direction, giving authoritarianism the shape of sultanism—as theorised by Max Weber and applied to contemporary political formations by Juan Linz. Such a regime, as the latter has it, is characterised by:

> the personalistic and particularistic use of power for essentially private ends of the ruler and his collaborators ... Support is based not on a coincidence of interest between pre-existing privileged social groups and the ruler but on the interests created by his rule, the rewards he offers for loyalty, and the fear of his vengeance. The boundaries between the public treasury and the private wealth of the ruler become blurred ... It is this fusion between the public and the private and the lack of commitment to impersonal purposes that distinguishes essentially such regimes from totalitarianism.[301]

The sultan's, then, was a peculiar style of rule. For, on the one hand, Sanjay's Emergency represented a kind of authoritarianism that had many features in common with the regime Mrs Gandhi had established in 1975. But, on the other, he was even more ruthless and more of a centraliser than his mother, and proved even readier than her to exercise hegemony over opposition parties and the lower classes. Yet, the limits of his power became obvious over time. Temporally, his stint at the top was too short-lived to develop into the Marcos-like regime that was his ideal. Spatially, too, it was fettered: Delhi was the epicentre, and the further one got away from the capital, the more his power dissipated. It is to this uneven geography of tyranny that we now turn.

[301] Linz, *Totalitarian and Authoritarian Regimes*, p. 151.

5

THE UNEVEN GEOGRAPHY OF TYRANNY

Within the Indian union competition between the states, instigated in no small measure by Mrs Gandhi and Sanjay, was one of the most striking aspects of Emergency rule. The inter-state rivalries began in fact on the very first day, when various states vied with one another to arrest as many citizens as possible. On 26 June, for instance, the Delhi Police's "small arrest list" was criticised from above because, apparently, "neighbouring states" had produced "much larger" ones.[1] The force immediately set about making additions.

But federalism also played a moderating role. For even if the federal setting could not inoculate India's states against authoritarianism, in some cases it nevertheless helped them resist the authoritarian impulses of the centre.

Which is why Mrs Gandhi and Sanjay tried to deprive the states of their power in key domains. Fiscally, at least, centralisation did not prove difficult. Just a month into the Emergency, Finance Minister C. Subramaniam saw through the amendment of four tax laws to facilitate the government's battle against black money and tax evasion.[2] The bill empowered commissioners of the Income Tax Department to supersede state tax authorities and conduct search and seizure operations in areas once out-

---

[1] *SCR*, vol. 2, p. 33.

[2] The Wealth Tax Act of 1957, Income Tax Act of 1961, Gift Tax Act of 1958, and Companies (Profits) Surtax Act of 1964: Rao, Jr., *The Emergency*, p. 60.

185

side its jurisdiction. Similarly, the newly rediscovered Delhi Special Police Establishment Act of 1946 now allowed for a wide expansion of the centre's powers. In October 1975 the titular police agency was dispatched to Meghalaya to investigate, over the heads of local law enforcement officials, violations of the Gift and Wealth Tax Acts.[3] Such moves served two purposes. First, they demonstrated the vigilance of the central leadership, which was ready to shake states out of their torpor and generate useful propaganda in the process. Second, by showing the states that certain competencies were above their station the union government was priming the nation for more centralisation, and perhaps even a move towards a unitary state.

But this was one half of a two-pronged strategy whose mutual exclusivity was to come to the fore sooner than later. So, while on the one hand, Mrs Gandhi and her son busied themselves with beefing up the powers of the centre and blunting the authority of state governments, on the other, "little replicas of Sanjay"—to use Ajoy Bose's phrase—were propped up across the republic to promote the Emergency's programmes.[4] So it was that Delhi's rulers promoted loyalist state leaders such as the criminally minded Bansi Lal, who was favoured by Sanjay, and the heavy-handed S.S. Ray, who was championed by Mrs Gandhi. Delhi's rulers, in essence, were consolidating power by undermining federalism as well as by depending on it, both at once.

The freshly installed *satraps*, however, were often incapable of deepening the reach of the Emergency because they had to deal with local bosses and power structures that put up stiff resistance. In any case such a strategy could work only in Congress-ruled states. In Tamil Nadu and Gujarat, opposition parties were in control. In Kerala, the Congress was in power in a coalition and its partners acted as the *de facto* opposition to authoritarian impulse.

In some states controlled by the Congress the chief ministers were so well entrenched that Mrs Gandhi and Sanjay could not easily dictate terms.

---

[3] V. Ramakrishnan, Secretary to the Government of Meghalaya, Home Department, to the Deputy Secretary, Department of Personnel and Administrative Reforms, Cabinet Secretariat, 4 October 1975, MHAP, File 228/3/75-AVD-II. Similar letters of "consent" transferring state competencies to the DSPE were sent by officials in, *inter alia*, Karnataka, Uttar Pradesh, Assam, Himachal Pradesh, Kerala, and Bihar to the Home Ministry: see the MHAP, File 228/3/75-AVD-II, *passim*.

[4] Ajoy Bose, 20 April 2018, interviewed by Farah Yameen, Oral Histories in the Long Emergency Collection.

Karnataka was a case in point, where the chief minister, Devaraj Urs, convinced the centre he was doing its bidding while furtively blunting the Emergency's more draconian measures in a bid to consolidate his own power. Poor communications and the bovine rate of diffusion, too, ensured an uneven spread of tyranny. For people in cities had it harder than their peers in the countryside, in the North than in the South.

Eventually, as P.N. Dhar suggests, the worst of the Emergency's transgressions were to be found where Sanjay and his clique ruled supreme, which was in the triangle of Delhi–Haryana–West UP, spanning less than 5 per cent of the country's land mass.[5] Certainly, this view is overstated in the majority of narratives of the Emergency, not least because of the solipsism of its chroniclers who have, in the main, been historians teaching in the capital and contemporary politicians and journalists *au courant* with Delhi's corridors of power. All the same, a case for the poor diffusion of authoritarianism can be made using data from the Shah Commission reports, the results of the 1977 election, and by reconstructing the political dilemmas of state leaderships *vis-à-vis* their national counterparts, local rivals, and industrial lobbies.

Without detracting from its nationwide impact, it is possible to suggest that the effects of the Emergency were more strongly registered in Dhar's triangle and the Hindi belt as a whole than in the two opposition-ruled states of Gujarat in the west and Tamil Nadu in the south. The remaining southern states—Kerala, Karnataka, and Andhra Pradesh—and the state that shares a border with the latter two, Maharashtra, were also spared the worst of the regime: the further from Delhi the state, then, the lighter the footprint of the Emergency within it.

Another North–South Divide

No measure captures the North–South divide—a contrast usually presented in cultural terms—of the Emergency quite as well as the snap election of March 1977 does. The returns from the Hindi heartland were a rude shock for the Congress. It won just 2 seats out of 226. Its position in the four southern states, however, remained intact, where it swept 92 of the 129 seats. The fortunes of the grand old party's biggest rival, the Janata party, were diametrically opposed to it: the anti-Emergency coalition netted 116

---

[5] Dhar, *Indira Gandhi, the "Emergency", and Indian Democracy*, p. 267.

seats in the Hindi belt and a paltry 3 in the South. An opinion poll conducted shortly before the election, too, highlights this divide. While a third of the respondents in both halves of the republic disagreed that functionaries had used emergency powers to "harass the common people", twice as many in the North agreed with the statement as in the South.[6] Culling statistics from the Shah Commission leads to the same conclusion.

As Tables 5.1–5.4 show, there was a concentration of bureaucratic transgressions—"instances of abuse of authority" in the language of the commission—detentions, demolitions, and sterilisations in the North. But some caveats are in order.

Table 5.1: State-wise Abuses of Authority*

State	Instances of abuse of authority	Instances of abuse of authority per million population
Southern States	*1605*	*10.70*
Andhra Pradesh	479	9.87
Karnataka	609	18.33
Kerala	250	10.68
Tamil Nadu	267	5.96
Other States	*8413*	*18.39*
Bihar	669	10.60
Uttar Pradesh	1874	18.81
Haryana	708	61.68
Rajasthan	651	21.69
Punjab	460	30.32
Himachal Pradesh	137	35.40
Gujarat	234	7.70
Madhya Pradesh	1387	29.56
West Bengal	399	8.07
Maharashtra	940	16.61
Orissa	624	25.83
Assam	229	14.02
Sikkim	6	22.81
Tripura	43	23.83
Manipur	13	10.43
Meghalaya	7	5.96
Nagaland	4	6.20
Jammu and Kashmir	28	5.28

---

[6] IIPO opinion poll, cited in Schlesinger, "The Emergency in an Indian Village", p. 58.

Union Territories	*1881*	*228.06*
Delhi	1797	349.41
Lakshadweep	0	0
Pondicherry	5	9.29
Dadra and Nagar Haveli	4	44.94
Chandigarh	27	76.16
Andaman and Nicobar Islands	16	105.26
Goa, Daman, and Diu	13	13.37
Arunachal Pradesh	18	32.73
Mizoram	1	2.42
Ministries and Departments of the Central Government	*4091*	–
Total	15,990	25.97

Source: *Shah Commission of Inquiry: Third and Final Report* (New Delhi: Government of India Press, 6 August 1978), pp. 218–19. The population during the Emergency was arrived at by averaging the 1971 and 1981 census figures, which were taken from the *Economic Survey, 2014–15*, p. A134.

* This figure excludes detentions, demolitions, and coercive instances of family planning, all of which have been dealt with by the commission—and in this book—in different tables. In the main, this "very wide-ranging and omnibus term of reference", as the Shah Commission put it, refers to interference with the bureaucracy, "matters including premature retirements, dismissals", and the supersession of officials. The figures were culled from the complaints received by the Shah Commission. They are undoubtedly an underestimate, since in a number of "instances of abuse" the victims would not have complained if they were illiterate, tardy in their response, or fearful of retribution: *SCR*, vol. 3, p. 34.

For one, the bias of the commission was all too evident from its Delhi-centric methodology. In relation to the capital, it referred to a number of government documents, called in and questioned hundreds of witnesses, and dispatched investigation teams to corroborate facts before pronouncing its conclusions. For the rest of the country this assiduity gave way to reliance on a set of "questionnaires" that were sent out to the states and union territories, all of which replied in accordance with their own whims. For instance, the Jammu and Kashmir, Tamil Nadu, Sikkim, Nagaland, Arunachal Pradesh, Mizoram, Andaman and Nicobar Islands, Dadra and Nagar Haveli, and Lakshadweep governments stated that no demolitions were carried out within their borders during the Emergency.[7] The proposi-

---

[7] *SCR*, vol. 3, p. 208. Thus the figures in Table 5.3 for these states only include complaints made directly to the commission.

tion was coolly accepted by the commission. Because the Assam and West Bengal governments did not reply to the questionnaire in time, no mention of demolitions in the two states was made in the reports, which otherwise carried brief remarks and some statistics about the gentrification drives in all of them.[8]

For another, there was considerable under-reporting. And this was true for the whole country, even Delhi: of the 700,000 displaced and 161,000 sterilised in the capital, only 1248 and 1254, respectively, filed complaints with the commission.[9] The odds that a citizen would report an Emergency transgression were even lower in the rest of the country, which had not merited the inquiry's undivided attention. This was especially true of the southern states, where it was harder for citizens to speak up against the incumbent Congress rulers: the party continued to control the South, barring Tamil Nadu, even after the March 1977 general election upset; in the North, in contrast, the Janata and its allies swept away the grand old party in the state elections of June. Varying literacy rates, too, could have contributed to under-reporting: while 65.08 per cent of Delhi was literate, only 34.45 per cent of the whole country was. This could explain the divergence in the popular response to the Shah Commission's advertising campaign in search of plaintiffs.[10]

But because the dearth of data holds true equally for all parts of the country barring the capital, there is no reason to completely distrust the commission's complaint figures. For want of a better alternative, a case can still be made that the further one went from the capital the lower the density of Emergency excesses. For instance, Haryana and Orissa both fell into Janata hands in June 1977—yet the former, with less than half the latter's population, registered complaints a quarter as large again, and also over twice as many detentions per capita.[11] As for the differential rates of literacy, they did not prevent illiterates, rural or urban, from appearing before the commission and testifying against the regime.[12] Moreover, there is no

---

[8] See the numerous letters between 13 September 1977 and 11 April 1978 exhorting the West Bengal state government to reply to the questionnaire on demolitions and abuses of authority—all to no avail. The West Bengal government *did* send in its reply in the end, but by that time the commission's third and final report had already been published: Shah Commission of Inquiry Files, File SCI/16(WB)/77/T.III.

[9] *SCR*, vol. 3, pp. 210, 220.

[10] Clibbens, "The Destiny of this City", pp. 53, 63.

[11] The population of Haryana in 1971 was 10 million; of Orissa 21.9 million.

[12] See, *inter alia*, statement of Mam Chand, an "almost illiterate" Delhi hawker:

reason to believe that the biases of the commission were not shared by Delhi's rulers during the Emergency. Much has been made of Sanjay's obsession with Delhi and the Hindi belt, and for good reason.

Table 5.2: State-wise Detentions

State	Detentions under MISA	Detentions under DISIR	Total detentions	Detentions per million population
Southern States	*3439*	*13,244*	*16,683*	*111.26*
Andhra Pradesh	1135	451	1586	32.68
Karnataka	487	4015	4502	135.53
Kerala	790	7134	7924	338.63
Tamil Nadu	1027	1644	2671	59.62
Other States	*30,232*	*59,358*	*89,590*	*195.80*
Bihar	2360	7747	10,107	160.09
Uttar Pradesh	6956	24,781	31,737	318.64
Haryana	200	1079	1279	111.42
Rajasthan	542	1352	1894	63.10
Punjab	440	2423	2863	188.73
Himachal Pradesh	34	654	688	177.75
Gujarat	1762	2643	4405	144.94
Madhya Pradesh	5620	2521	8141	173.52
West Bengal	4992	2547	7539	152.47
Maharashtra	5473	9799	15,272	269.84
Orissa	408	762	1170	48.43
Assam	533	2388	2921	178.84
Sikkim	4	0	4	15.21
Tripura	77	99	176	97.53
Manipur	231	228	459	368.08
Meghalaya	39	20	59	50.26
Nagaland	95	4	99	153.37
Jammu and Kashmir	466	311	777	146.55
Union Territories	*1317*	*3216*	*4533*	*549.59*
Delhi	1012	2851	3863	751.12
Lakshadweep	0	0	0	0
Pondicherry	54	63	117	217.47

no date, SCP, Subject File 11, pp. 253–5; testimonies of Safed Khan and Mauja, agriculturists who had their statements written by others, no dates, SCP, Subject File 5, pp. 119, 218.

Dadra and Nagar Haveli	0	3	3	33.71
Chandigarh	27	74	101	284.91
Andaman and Nicobar Islands	41	88	129	848.68
Goa, Daman, and Diu	113	0	113	116.20
Arunachal Pradesh	0	1	1	1.82
Mizoram	70	136	206	498.79
Total	34,988	75,818	110,806	179.95

Source: SCR, vol. 3, p. 134.

Note: "Detention" here refers to both arrest and detention, because the Shah Commission did not distinguish between the two. The former refers to incarceration in prison, the latter to confinement under supervision. Hence, this data cannot gauge the qualitative difference between the treatment meted out to, say, Morarji Desai on the one hand, and Lawrence Fernandes on the other. Desai was held in the Haryana State Tourist Centre—a stone's throw from the hot springs resort town of Sohna. Meanwhile, Fernandes, languishing in Karnataka's prisons, was tortured.

Table 5.3: State-wise Demolitions

State	*Demolitions*	*Demolitions per million population*
Southern States	*279*	*1.86*
Andhra Pradesh	75	1.55
Karnataka	126	3.79
Kerala	63	2.69
Tamil Nadu	15	0.33
Other States	*2476*	*5.41*
Bihar	226	3.58
Uttar Pradesh	425	4.27
Haryana	300	26.13
Rajasthan	193	6.43
Punjab	66	4.35
Himachal Pradesh	18	4.65
Gujarat	18	0.59
Madhya Pradesh	628	13.39
West Bengal	204	4.13
Maharashtra	89	1.57
Orissa	251	10.39
Assam	35	2.14
Sikkim	0	0
Tripura	4	2.22
Manipur	18	14.43
Meghalaya	0	0

Nagaland	0	0
Jammu and Kashmir	1	0.19
Union Territories	*1256*	*152.28*
Delhi	1248	242.66
Lakshadweep	0	0
Pondicherry	1	1.86
Dadra and Nagar Haveli	0	0
Chandigarh	4	11.28
Andaman and Nicobar Islands	0	0
Goa, Daman, and Diu	3	3.08
Arunachal Pradesh	0	0
Mizoram	0	0
Ministries and Departments of the Central Government	*28*	–
Total	4039	6.56

Source: SCR, vol. 3, pp. 209–10.

Table 5.4: State-wise Sterilisations, 1975–6 and 1976–7

State	Sterilisations				
	1975–6	*1976–7*	*Total*	*Sterilisations per thousand population*	*Increase in 1976–7 over 1975–6 (%)*
Southern States	*713,147*	*2,006,930*	*2,720,077*	*18.14*	*181*
Andhra Pradesh	165,163	741,713	906,876	18.69	349
Karnataka	120,671	488,861	609,532	18.35	305
Kerala	156,622	206,600	363,222	15.52	32
Tamil Nadu	270,691	569,756	840,447	18.76	110
Other States	*1,878,981*	*5,967,404*	*7,846,385*	*17.15*	*218*
Bihar	165,531	680,000	845,531	13.39	311
Uttar Pradesh	128,000	837,000	965,000	9.69	554
Haryana	57,942	222,000	279,942	24.39	283
Rajasthan	86,000	364,760	450,760	15.02	324
Punjab	53,083	139,905	192,988	12.72	164
Himachal Pradesh	16,830	100,740	117,570	30.38	499
Gujarat	153,000	317,000	470,000	15.46	107
Madhya Pradesh	112,000	1,001,000	1,113,000	23.72	794
West Bengal	206,421	880,000	1,086,421	21.97	326
Maharashtra	611,000	833,000	1,444,000	25.51	36

Orissa	125,040	322,984	448,024	18.55	158
Assam	147,545	226,205	373,750	22.88	53
Sikkim	0	262	262	1.00	–
Tripura	4140	12,600	16,740	9.28	204
Manipur	847	6286	7133	5.72	642
Meghalaya	2100	7513	9613	8.19	258
Nagaland	0	355	355	0.55	–
Jammu and Kashmir	9502	15,794	25,296	4.77	66
Union Territories	*32,627*	*157,875*	*190,502*	*23.10*	*384*
Delhi	22,510	138,517	161,027	31.31	515
Lakshadweep	56	149	205	5.69	166
Pondicherry	4688	8030	12,718	23.64	71
Dadra and Nagar Haveli	241	695	936	10.52	188
Chandigarh	1163	2590	3753	10.59	123
Andaman and Nicobar Islands	242	1376	1618	10.64	469
Goa, Daman, and Diu	2800	5571	8371	8.61	99
Arunachal Pradesh	22	268	290	0.53	1118
Mizoram	905	679	1584	3.84	−25
Total	2,624,755	8,132,209	10,756,964	17.47	210

Source: SCR, vol. 3, p. 207.

In sum, a clear picture emerges of an uneven geography of tyranny. As Table 5.1 shows, even if Delhi and the union territories are excluded, the number of "instances of abuses of authority" in per capita terms that the North registered was over two-thirds as much again as that in the South. Similarly, as Table 5.2 illustrates, the northern citizen was three-quarters as likely again to be arrested in Emergency India as his southern counterpart.

The ratio of "political" to "non-political" detentions also indicates the totalising nature of the Emergency in the North. As the Shah Commission noted, the former exceeded the latter in the four southern states, as well as in Rajasthan, West Bengal, Himachal Pradesh, Haryana, and Orissa.[13] The reverse was true of the Hindi heartland—Bihar, Uttar Pradesh, and Delhi— but also of Gujarat and Goa. In other words, in the Hindi belt's densest regions not just opposition figures but also ordinary citizens were far more likely to earn the wrath of local authorities and find themselves arbitrarily incarcerated.[14] In part, this carceral geography reflected the weakness of

[13] *SCR*, vol. 3, p. 42.
[14] Ibid.

local leaders who felt the need to prove their worth to the central leadership. It is no accident that S.C. Shukla and N.D. Tiwari, chief ministers of Madhya Pradesh and Uttar Pradesh—states that recorded the steepest detention figures—were in precarious positions. Both were parachuted in as chief ministers six months into the Emergency and had to fend off attacks from the loyalists of their immediate predecessors—P.C. Sethi and H.N. Bahuguna, respectively—which they did by presenting dizzyingly long lists of detainees to Delhi's rulers. This sent a clear message: surely, if they could bang up thousands, they could also do Delhi's bidding on every other count.

Little could be done to curb the enthusiasm of the state leaderships once they had internalised the logic that the higher the number of arrests the greater their job security. Attempts were made by the centre to rein in the Shuklas and Tiwaris when it became increasingly obvious that the DIR and MISA were being used "indiscriminately".[15] For her part Mrs Gandhi cautioned chief ministers to use the repressive legislations "sparingly and with the greatest care."[16] But the efforts were too little too late. In any case most of these eleventh-hour deliberations were upended by a new hare-brained scheme. On 3 January 1976 the Home Ministry issued instructions to the state governments that they were hereon "to obtain the advice of the central government before releasing a MISA *detenu.*"[17] This was not a "legal requirement", it hastened to add, but nevertheless necessary "in the overall context of the Emergency."[18] Predictably, the Home Ministry was unable to cope with the deluge of telegrams, letters, and cyclostyled or stereotyped copies of parole requests flooding its desks. Many a time states with overcrowded jails were eager to see the back of some detainees that were languishing unjustly in prison, awaiting the centre's approval to come through. Often, it never did.[19] In effect, the states and the union were both responsible for massive arrests in the North: the latter for propping up ciphers in states who needed to demonstrate their power through carceral numbers and by sitting on parole requests, the former for unhesitatingly ordering the arrest of innocent citizens in the first place.

---

[15] See the letter the Home Ministry sent out to the state governments on 10 September 1975, reproduced in ibid., p. 44.

[16] Mrs Gandhi to the chief ministers, 3 July 1975 and 31 July 1976: ibid., p. 45.

[17] Ibid., p. 46.

[18] Ibid.

[19] Ibid., pp. 46, 67.

The North and the West also loomed large in Mrs Gandhi and her son's imagination because of an important development that both preceded the Emergency and which was to an extent its official *raison d'être*: the JP Movement. Unsurprisingly, the movement's two strongholds, Gujarat and Bihar, were the states where MISA was used most "extensively against students", many of whom had taken part in the protests.[20]

The figures from Sanjay's twin programme of gentrification and family planning bear out the North–South divide as well. As can be seen from Table 5.3, citizens outside the southern quartet of states were three times as likely to see their houses demolished than those in it. While the sterilisation figures in both regions appear roughly the same, as Table 5.4 demonstrates, the difference in the rate of increase makes for a remarkable contrast. The Hindi belt—Delhi, Rajasthan, Himachal Pradesh, Uttar Pradesh, Haryana, Madhya Pradesh, and Bihar—witnessed a 468 per cent increase in the number of operations between the first and second year of the Emergency. The corresponding figure for the four southern states was 181 per cent. It is fair to conjecture that the larger of the two numbers betrays greater coercion. To make better sense of the aggregates and averages, of course, requires an empiricism of a different, more qualitative, kind.

The Hindi Epicentre

If statistical indicators alone suffice, the role of Delhi as Ground Zero of the Emergency emerges with crystal clarity. The number of bureaucratic transgressions per capita in the capital were over thirteen times the national average; demolitions a staggering thirty-seven times; detentions over four times; and sterilisations 80 per cent more. The Congress' electoral losses of 1977, the upshot of this barbarity, confirm this hypothesis: a 34.3 per cent decline in vote share from 1971. The nosedive was steeper in only three other states—Haryana, Himachal Pradesh, and Jammu and Kashmir.

Within the capital, the nerve centre of the authoritarian regime was not the union government but the union territory administration. This was because Sanjay, as Delhi Lieutenant Governor Krishan Chand put it, had been "handed over the running of Delhi" by his mother.[21] The difference

---

[20] Ibid., pp. 44, 58, 63. A lot of students who had participated in the JP Movement were picked up in Uttar Pradesh as well: ibid, p. 116.
[21] *SCR*, vol. 2, p. 45.

between the union and Delhi administrations is borne out by a curious feature of the sterilisation regime. While central government employees in the capital adhered to a laxer version of the family-planning programme— penalties kicked in only if one of the parents was not sterilised within ten months after the birth of the third child—those in the employ of the union territory were subject to a much harsher regime: here there was no time lag, with sanctions coming into force after the birth of a second child.[22] As Davidson Gwatkin notes, the logic of sterilisation targets originated in the Delhi ministries under Sanjay's control, and from there steadily radiated outwards following the contours of his power—and by extension his mother's, his party's, and the state's. Their hold was "extraordinarily strong in the Hindi heartland" but progressively weaker "as it proceeded further into" the west, north-east, and south.[23]

That Delhi affairs loomed so large in Sanjay's universe was clear from the factotums he chose to regularly interact with. Reconstructing a typical day in "late 1975", Bose and Dayal's account of the Emergency lists the figures who would swing by the sultan's house on 1 Safdarjung Road every morning: Jagmohan, the Delhi Development Authority vice chairman; V.S. Ailawadi, secretary of the New Delhi Municipal Committee; H.K.L. Bhagat, president of the Delhi Pradesh Congress Committee; Navin Chawla, secretary to the lieutenant governor of Delhi; P.S. Bhinder, Delhi deputy inspector general; and B.R. Tamta, commissioner of the Municipal Corporation of Delhi.[24] As Tamta noted, the princeling essentially behaved like the "*de facto* ruler of the [Delhi] Municipal Corporation."[25] The same could be said about his management of the NDMC, Delhi PCC, DDA, and the Delhi police.

It was not by accident, then, that some of the earliest demolitions in the capital took place along the Delhi–Gurgaon road that was part of the prime minister's son's commute. Houses in Samalkha, the village Sanjay passed *en route* to his Maruti factory, were destroyed and its residents evicted on New Year's Eve 1975 to widen the highway.[26] Similarly Kapas Hera, another village that added precious minutes to Sanjay's commute—in his words "a village of scoundrels" and "an eyesore"—was flattened in September 1975.[27]

---

[22] *SCR*, vol. 3, p. 159.

[23] Gwatkin, "Political Will and Family Planning", p. 42.

[24] Dayal and Bose, *For Reasons of State*, p. 33.

[25] In the words of Tamta: *SCR*, vol. 2, p. 79.

[26] "Demolition in Samalkha Village", no date, SCP, Subject File 2, pp. 67–8.

[27] *SCR*, vol. 2, pp. 103, 107.

Business interests were also involved in these depredations. The village lands bordering the Maruti complex had attracted a number of factories while Sanjay's own estates remained for the most part deserted. To get the industrial units to relocate, he had their MCD licences revoked and plans for demolition announced. The graft was sold to the press as environmentalism: industrial units in Kapas Hera "polluted the atmosphere", Jagmohan proclaimed to the *Hindustan Times*; they were better off in Sanjay's complex.[28] When the factory owners obtained a stay order from the courts, they were told the document was "not worth the paper it's printed on."[29]

Andheria Mor, too, fell within Sanjay's line of vision. Located on the Mehrauli–Chattarpur road that he often took to get to his mother's farmhouse, this village was for him nothing more than a roadblock. Demolition squads were dispatched and when the residents came up to the prime minister's son with documents proving their tenancy, he dismissed them as forgeries.[30] The bulldozers began their work there in October 1975. Similarly, the decision to demolish shops in Karol Bagh owed more to events in Sanjay's mind than to the world outside. Taking it into his head that the shopkeepers of the neighbourhood were "pro-Jana Sangh", he felt they should pay the price for their wrong-headed loyalty. Their protests fell on deaf ears: when they came to see him with documents to prove the legality of their shops, he "flung them aside contemptuously."[31] Upon occasion Sanjay's attention lit upon nearby states as well. In the winter of 1975, for instance, he masterminded demolitions in Agra and Varanasi in an effort to clean up the towns before the "tourist season".[32] But for the most part it was only Delhi that mattered to him.

The Emergency's excesses may have remained a Delhi-centric phenomenon had it not been for the number of chief ministers and senior bureaucrats on board the Sanjay bandwagon. So it was that in 1976, the accent shifted from Mrs Gandhi's negatively defined Emergency—an end to the opposition, a quietus to unionisation, the depoliticisation of society—to the heir apparent's positively understood programme of urban renewal and family planning.

---

[28] Ibid., p. 104.

[29] Ibid.

[30] Statement of Gobardhan Das, Shopkeeper, 7 February 1978, SCP, Subject File 2, p. 36.

[31] *SCR*, vol. 2, p. 114.

[32] *SCR*, vol. 3, p. 209.

To Sanjay the northern chief ministers exhibited the exaggerated deference of courtiers as he travelled from state to state in Indian Air Force planes chartered by Om Mehta, R.K. Dhawan, and T.N. Seshan—he could not requisition them himself because he held no official position in the cabinet. To welcome him in Jaipur the Rajasthan chief minister, Harideo Joshi, had 501 arches erected in the state capital. His counterpart in Punjab, Giani Zail Singh, deferred even to Dhawan, suffixing the respectful "ji" to his name in salutations; in one notorious instance, Singh rushed to pick up one of Sanjay's fallen sandals as the latter boarded a plane. Andhra Pradesh's *satraps* welcomed the sultan with "gigantic cardboard" Sanjays lining the roads he traversed.[33] Similar genuflections were made to the prime minister's son by Hitendra Desai and Shyama Charan Shukla, president of the Gujarat PCC and chief minister of Madhya Pradesh, respectively. The reception that Sanjay and his wife Maneka received in Lucknow was, in Janardan Thakur's words, worthy of medieval royalty:

> The state government deployed about 600 trucks and buses to carry the mercenary crowds (their rate: Rs 5 per head and a packet of *puris*) to the Amausi airport where the entire cabinet, the governor, and the assembly speaker stood at attention for the prince's arrival. The plane had not even come to a halt when the crowds rushed on to the runway and all security arrangements went haywire. In the *mêlée*, [Chief Minister] Narayan Dutt Tiwari was seen running towards the plane with a big garland in his outstretched hands. He was so excited he didn't see the thin rope that the security men had tied across the runway to cordon off the crowd. He ran into it and fell flat on his paunch, the garland crushed under him. But he immediately got up and ran, panting to the stairway.[34]

Such sycophancy was not the preserve of the political classes; since many of the states' leading bureaucrats owed their positions to the central leadership, they too were eager to please. For they knew that the surest road to job security lay in increased detentions, sterilisations, and demonstrations of police power. For instance, the Madhya Pradesh government's chief secretary poured scorn on "some district magistrates" who had gone "rather soft in ordering arrests and detentions."[35] The state's inspector general of police was not far behind: "speed up preventive arrests", he radioed the district police authorities.[36]

---

[33] Thapar, *All These Years*, p. 421.
[34] Thakur, *All the Prime Minister's Men*, p. 128.
[35] *SCR*, vol. 3, p. 84.
[36] Ibid.

A survey of the states of the North bears out the uneven diffusion thesis. The brutal suppression of the Akalis in Punjab and the Haryana press and opposition, for instance, demonstrated the strength of the authoritarian regime closest to its home turf.[37] The very night the Emergency was declared, the Punjab police lost no time shuttering the press and destroying all copies of the Chandigarh *Tribune*. Because the town was a union territory, special permits were needed to allow the state police to cross into its borders. These the union, by way of Dhawan, readily provided, the speedy dispatch reflecting the state's importance to Delhi. Soon after, quick work was made of the Akali Dal's "Save Democracy" *morcha* of 9 July 1975.[38] At a major conference in Amritsar the following week, the party resolved to "carry on the struggle till the lifting of Emergency."[39] But by September 1976 seventeen of its twenty MLAs were in prison; its top leadership—Prakash Singh Badal, Gurcharan Singh Tohra, and Jathedar Mohan Singh Tur—detained under MISA; and over 45,000 Sikhs belonging to the party and allied organisations—*inter alia*, the All India Sikh Students' Federation, Punjab Mazdoor Dal, and Bir Khalsa Dal—behind bars, even if only briefly.[40]

The further one got from Delhi's grip, the more blunted the ferocity of the authoritarian regime. In Srinagar, nearly a thousand kilometres to the capital's north, the Jammu and Kashmir chief minister, Sheikh Abdullah, only tacitly acknowledged the Emergency, stating with resignation that it only existed *de jure* in his realms because the state happened to be a part of India, the upshot of which lay in paying lip service to Delhi's promulgations. Nevertheless, as his letters to Mrs Gandhi and visit to the capital's worst-affected Muslim ghettoes showed, he remained extremely critical of the autocratic enterprise. While he acquiesced in the centre's demands by detaining leaders of the opposition, he made sure he let them out on parole "after some time". Moreover, in defiance of Delhi's diktat, he refused to condemn Narayan and the JP Movement.[41]

---

[37] For more on Haryana, see references to Bansi Lal in Chapters 1 and 2.

[38] Grewal, *The New Cambridge History of India, vol. II.3*, pp. 213–14.

[39] *Lok Sangharsh Samiti*, 26 September 1976, p. 5 in "Documentation of Emergency Period in India", MLP, microfilm copy, reel 1.

[40] Ibid.; Nayar, *The Judgement*, p. 64. Because only 2936 were detained under MISA, COFEPOSA, and DISIR in the entire state through the Emergency—let alone just Akali Sikhs in the span of a few months in 1976—it appears that the majority of the 45,000 were just briefly held and then let out without being charged under any of the three acts: *SCR*, vol. 3, p. 100.

[41] Nayar, *The Judgement*, p. 62.

The country's north-eastern periphery was similarly spared. This was reflected in the 1977 electoral showing, in which support for the Congress remained more or less intact. In Assam the party retained its vote share of over 50 per cent, while in Nagaland, Manipur, and Tripura, it actually bettered its 1971 figures. In the majority of the states and union territories in the region—Arunachal Pradesh, Manipur, Meghalaya, and Nagaland—the tri-annual review process in which detainees were released from prisons was "carried out very systematically".[42] Many of the Naga, Mizo, and Manipuri "hostiles" arrested across the region were released once the centre struck peace deals with them.[43] This was the case after the Naga guerrillas and the union reached the Shillong Accord of November 1975 and the July 1976 agreement signed by Mrs Gandhi and the MNF's Laldenga.[44] As part of the same strategy, attempts were made to bring "moderate" opinion that had long been on the other side of the fence into the Congress fold. To this end the Naga National Organisation and the Manipur Hill Union—a 20,000-strong group of "opposition tribals"—were both merged into the local Congresses.[45] Excluding Assam, the sterilisation programme barely registered in the rest of the North East. And unlike the Hindi belt the states and union territories of this region mostly spared citizens above fifty-five from the sterilisation tables, on which only a few north-easterners died.[46]

The eastern states of Orissa and West Bengal, too, confirm the distance thesis. As Table 5.2 shows, the former had among the lowest carceral rates in the country, which was evidenced in the strong performance of the Congress in 1977—the party's vote share, 38 per cent, was the same as in 1971. The chief reason for this was the chief ministership of Nandini Satpathy who, through the Emergency, held her own and refused to cave in to Sanjay's demands, even suggesting that the incorporation of a set of "disincentives" into the sterilisation programme "would only promote sorrow and resentment."[47] For her temerity she was removed from office on

---

[42] The remaining three states and union territories—Assam, Tripura, and Mizoram— had a poorer review process: *SCR*, vol. 3, pp. 53, 92, 94–5, 96, 113, 124, 130.

[43] "Hostiles" is a term the Indian state reserves for rebels of the peripheries, namely, Jammu and Kashmir, the North East, and the island chains.

[44] Ibid., p. 92.

[45] *1977 Yearbook*, p. 176.

[46] In the seven states and union territories, ninety-eight died because of sterilisation, ninety-five of whom were in Assam. All seven citizens above fifty-five sterilised in the region were from Assam: *SCR*, vol. 3, pp. 172, 186–7, 193, 199, 204.

[47] Ibid., p. 189.

16 December 1976, a month before Mrs Gandhi announced elections. In West Bengal, 94 per cent of MISA arrests were made using the unamended version of the act.[48] It was the only state in the country to use this variant. The result was a more thorough scrutiny of detention orders—nearly a sixth of the detainees were released after it was discovered that the grounds for arrest were insufficient.[49] West Bengal was also among the earliest states to dissociate the police from the family-planning programme. It did so in August 1976, while most of the North caught up only in October and November, by which the time the Emergency had nearly run its course.[50]

Like Jammu and Kashmir and the states of the East and North East, the South and the states ruled by opposition parties vitiated some of the Emergency's totalising features. The complexities of regional dynamics, however, necessitate a more thorough treatment.

Gujarat and Tamil Nadu: The Holdout States

In 1975, the only states in which opposition parties held power were what Mrs Gandhi called the "two islands" of Gujarat and Tamil Nadu, both active centres of resistance to the Emergency.[51] Their twenty-one months under authoritarianism did not, however, pass entirely free of union interference. Indeed, by the time Mrs Gandhi announced fresh elections, both states were firmly ensconced in Congress rule. In Gujarat this happened first by the union toppling the Janata Morcha government, followed by nine months of indirect control of the state via President's Rule, and finally by direct rule once Congress had secured the numbers in the assembly. In Tamil Nadu it happened by engineering the downfall of the DMK and, as in Gujarat, imposing rule from Delhi under Article 356. Nevertheless, the challenge mounted by Mrs Gandhi's opponents, the electoral pragmatism of the local Congress elites, and their endemic factionalism—which distracted attention from, and to an extent contained, the tumult, preventing it spilling outside

---

[48] Ibid., p. 120.

[49] Ibid.

[50] Ibid., p. 197.

[51] *SW*, 10 January 1976, p. 1. Jammu and Kashmir was the third, but it mattered less to Delhi's rulers, especially since the Kashmir Accords of February 1975, which had taken the bite out of the National Conference's (NC) politics. Its leader, Sheikh Abdullah, broken after two decades of imprisonment, was made chief minister on condition that the NC give up its plans for eventual self-determination. Since then the state had disappeared from Mrs Gandhi's horizon.

the assembly halls—ensured that authoritarian impulse was more restrained here than in the Hindi belt even after the Congress took charge.

Arguably, in Gujarat the Emergency did not take place at all. For the first ten months the Janata did all it could to resist the centre, harbouring opposition fugitives and defending the free press. In these months, public demonstrations, especially silent marches, student processions, and *bandhs*, were common occurrences in the state.

The centre naturally tried to straitjacket the state government. Chief Minister Babubhai Patel was prevented from making a speech about the Emergency on the radio and encouraged to arrest some local political leaders. He capitulated to the latter demand but managed to get his own way as well, arresting people under the bailable DIR and not MISA—under the latter, incarceration followed stricter rules. And when the union tried to foist prior restraint and the abridging of press freedoms upon the state leader, the results again were mixed. As the centre's voice in the states, the Press Information Bureau chief of Gujarat successfully suppressed most reports critical of the Emergency, allowing into print only local news items that put the Janata incumbents in a bad light. Nevertheless, a few clandestine publications critical of the authoritarian regime, such as the *Janata Chhapu* and *Janata Samachar*, managed to escape censorship and circulate in the state as long as the Janata was in power.[52]

Given the reliance of states on union funds, budgeting remained a challenge for the Janata. Babubhai Patel tried to shore up his coffers by imposing a tax on rural landlords in order to "assist the poorer and weaker sections" of society. However, the Congress—which at the centre was busy recommending that the word "socialist" be added as an adjective to describe the Indian republic in the preamble of the Constitution that very month—led in the state by Hitendra Desai, a creature of the farm lobby, succeeded in shooting down the bill.[53] Simultaneously, Desai engineered defections from the Janata which, as a coalition, was already having trouble holding its own: in the six months to December 1975 the grand old party's strength in the assembly of 182 grew from 74 to 105.[54]

The Gujarat government remained a holdout until early 1976, when it finally collapsed not long after Desai argued that it was no longer able to

---

[52] Note by S.N. Shukla, Deputy Director, Intelligence Bureau, 5 January 1976, Ministry of Home Affairs Papers, File II-13012/80/75-S&P(D-IV).

[53] Selbourne, *An Eye to India*, p. 206.

[54] Limaye, *Janata Party Experiment*, vol. 1, p. 124.

control law and order. Responding to his aspersion, in mid-January the centre dispatched the Home Ministry's K. Rustom to survey the allegedly dysfunctional state. Over the next few days newspapers described in meticulous detail the work of arsonists and rioters in Baroda and beyond, insinuating that Gujarat had indeed lost the plot. On 7 February a Gujarat PCC "inquiry"—in what was one of many instances of the blurring of boundaries between party and state in Emergency India—found that the opposition was responsible for "about 411 cases of physical assault, 3643 cases of threats of violence, and 62 of mob violence."[55] On the 11th, Chimanbhai Patel's KMLP, which had been propping up the Janata with its twelve seats in the assembly, withdrew support and dissolved itself.[56] On 9 March what came to be known as the Baroda Dynamite Conspiracy was uncovered: it transpired that Socialist leader George Fernandes and his friends had been planning to blow up railway lines in the state. In a country already hypersensitive to questions of national security, this had alarm bells ringing. Three days later the Janata discovered in a vote on food grants that it had lost its majority in the assembly.[57] The chief minister resigned and, the next day, President's Rule in the state was proclaimed.

Despite Babubhai Patel and the "conspirators" in the Baroda Dynamite case being behind bars by August 1976, the Congress proved ineffectual in its bid to form a government in Gujarat. The nine months of President's Rule were marred by major factional in-fighting within both parties as well as conflicts between them, the wholesale trading of MLAs having turned the assembly into a veritable bazaar.[58] In the long haul the better institutionalised and richer party was to emerge triumphant. But by the time the Congress cobbled together a coalition, it was already December 1976. Less than four weeks after Madhavsinh Solanki was sworn in as chief minister, Mrs Gandhi announced fresh elections.

Stepping back from the convulsions in the assembly, however, produces a different picture of the Emergency in Gujarat. In the main it was a period marked more by continuity than rupture. For one, the Twenty-Point Programme barely registered in the state. If the Congress' performance on land reform was dismal, the Janata's was deplorable beyond belief. For it declared in July 1975 that it did not have a *single* surplus acre in the state

---

[55] *SW*, 7 February 1976, p. 1.
[56] Research and Policy Division, *Genesis of President's Rule*, p. 13.
[57] Ibid.
[58] Interview with Madhavsinh Solanki, Gandhinagar, 21 April, 2019.

that could be redistributed to the landless. Indeed, this is one of the reasons why the party lost "almost two to one" to the Congress in the state's *panchayat* elections in December 1975.[59]

Second, the tumult in the assembly was not mirrored on the streets, rule by the centre having been broadly met with approval. The governor's drive against the oil merchants and their black-marketeering was widely supported. This pushed much of the groundnut lobby into the arms of the Janata, delivering funds to the party but also the wrath of the people, for whom oil merchants were synonymous with inflation.

Third, unlike most states of the union where Mrs Gandhi attempted to replace older *satraps* with newer and more loyal ones, in Gujarat there was no real Congress establishment to speak of—nothing really there to replace. At the time of the split of the party in 1969 the Congress (Organisation) had walked away with the bulk of the local elites; Mrs Gandhi's vassals had had to make do with a non-existent party apparatus and reinvent themselves as representatives of the rural poor. The prime minister's "Garibi Hatao" campaign of 1971 and the bourgeois politics of the Janata only reinforced the class divide. Cementing it was another peculiarity of Gujarat: here, during the Emergency, unlike most of the country, local industrialists did not support the Congress. Their feeling was that Sanjay's comradeship with their class was restricted to the select few families he chose to patronise, not to capitalists in general. Also bucking the national trend were the industrial workers, most of whom did not desert the Congress in Gujarat. This was because of the concentration of Muslims and Dalits in the working class, both communities feeling that, for want of a better alternative, Congress rule better represented their interests. The Janata, of course, dominated by upper and dominant castes in this state as elsewhere, was more openly confessional than even the Gujarat Congress.[60]

And fourth, following closely from the third, the Gujarat governor K.K. Vishwanathan, a Kerala politician past his prime, was not out to carve for himself a space in regional politics; consequently he did little to impress the centre with incarceration, demolition, and sterilisation figures. Certainly, the opposition was targeted for arrest, especially the RSS and constituents of the Janata such as the Jana Sangh, Socialists, and old

---

[59] Hart, "Introduction", p. 26.

[60] Research and Policy Division, *Genesis of President's Rule, passim*; Wright, Jr., "Muslims and the 1977 Indian Elections", pp. 1210–12; Selbourne, *An Eye to India*, p. 177ff.

Congress.[61] And students too were at the receiving end, their radicalism in 1974 having caused the downfall of Chimanbhai Patel's Congress administration. But securing parole was simpler here than in most parts of the republic. While in many other states the death of one's parent, spouse, and child was more often than not deemed a serious enough reason for parole, in Gujarat even the concerns of everyday commerce were thought adequate. For instance, a large landowner was let off when he suggested that the "agricultural operations" on the "40 *bighas* of land" he owned "were being hampered".[62] Similarly, parole was granted to the owner of an engine-oil dealership who complained that in his absence his "business was suffering".[63]

In short, the weakness of the Congress organisation in Gujarat—its reliance on a form of class politics more distilled than elsewhere, and its desire to project itself as a less conservative and less confessional alternative to the Janata—led it to adopt moderate positions during the Emergency that were not available to the leaderships of the North. The party's weaknesses also helped it escape the factional struggles that were an endemic feature of its organisations elsewhere. For the most part the centre was supportive of this unity, even making an exception for the Gujarat PCC in allowing cash to flow from the centre to the state than the other way around—Mrs Gandhi's *modus operandi* for centralising power after the Congress split of 1969.[64] Ample funds were left for the Gujarat Congress to fight the 1977 elections and keep its constituents satisfied in the interim. The returns partly reflected this. For both the Congress and the opposition, their 1977 showing was comparable with 1971.[65]

Tamil Nadu's trajectory during the Emergency was much of a muchness. During the early months of the regime the DMK chief minister,

---

[61] *SCR*, vol. 3, pp. 60–1.

[62] Ibid., p. 65.

[63] Ibid. Quite inexplicably, parole was denied to two citizens who wished to attend the "last rites" of their grandmother and brother, respectively. With more cases, perhaps, it could be possible to make a general claim that mercantile reasons trumped familial ones in Gujarat.

[64] Manor, "Where Congress Survived", p. 790.

[65] In 1977, the Congress won 10 (in 1971: 11) seats with 46.9 (44.9) per cent of the vote to the Janata alliance's 16 (13) with 49.5 (48.6) per cent. Of course, there was no "Janata" alliance in 1971, for the Congress (O), Swatantra party, Jana Sangh, Socialists, and BKD stood as independent parties; the 1971 figures have been placed in brackets adjacent to the 1977 ones only for the sake of comparability.

Karunanidhi, took a firm stand against authoritarianism, the highlight of which was his condemnation of Delhi's rulers at a July 1975 rally in Madras attended by 100,000. Strikes too were tolerated, in defiance of the corporatism that had overrun the rest of the country. On 24 October, for instance, 400,000 industrial workers in the state went on strike to protest the crippling of labour. At times it appeared the centre had resigned itself to the situation. Noting that "criticism against the ruling party" was commonplace, the top bureaucrat in the state suggested it was for the best that "no action" be "taken against them" as it would "disturb the normalcy".[66] If the streets were given some latitude and local functionaries allowed some fatalism, this was more than compensated for by the targeting of larger papers directly from Delhi. Officers were deputed from the capital to block the publication of a number of stories in the *Hindu*, *Indian Express*, *Swarajya*, and myriad Tamil papers that showed the Congress in a poor light.[67] In September 1975 the union placed three Tamil publications under pre-censorship: this was out of a total of nine across the country, indicating how much trouble this southern state had become for the centre.[68]

As in Gujarat, efforts were made to starve Tamil Nadu of central funds which, in the 1970s, accounted for nearly 40 per cent of a state's budget.[69] Already in 1974 the Fifth Five-Year Plan had allocated far more resources to Congress-ruled states than to Tamil Nadu. The states of the North were of course the recipients of greater largesse: for instance, Punjab was lavished with Rs 111 per capita. In the South, Karnataka, Kerala, and Andhra Pradesh—all in the hands of the grand old party—were indulged less, receiving Rs 50, 45, and 41 per capita, respectively. Meanwhile, the Tamil Nadu government had to make do with a paltry Rs 36.[70]

---

[66] P. Sabanayagam, Chief Secretary, Government of Tamil Nadu, to Thiru A.J. Kidwai, Secretary to the Government of India, Ministry of Information and Broadcasting, 5 January 1976, Ministry of Home Affairs Papers, File II-1401 1/3/75-S&P(D-IV).

[67] Note by K.A. Sundaram, Chief Secretary, Government of Tamil Nadu, 9 July 1976, Ministry of Home Affairs Papers, File II-14011/3/75-S&P(D-IV).

[68] *White Paper on Misuse of Mass Media*, p. 29.

[69] Bagchi, "Rethinking Federalism", p. 24. In the main, the union was responsible for collecting income tax and excise duties, leaving states with only a few sources of revenue. Taxing agriculture, a potentially lucrative source of funds, was left to the states, most of which were run by landed elites who were naturally unwilling to tax themselves.

[70] *SW*, 17 January 1976, p. 7.

In the penultimate months of 1975 a scheme was hatched to strengthen Mrs Gandhi's party and prime the state for Congress rule. This first step was vital because, at the time, the party hardly had any kind of presence in the state. Indeed, in the decade that preceded the Emergency, Tamil Nadu had remained immune to Congress hegemony. The DMK had been in power since 1967, on occasion aligning with Mrs Gandhi's party, most notably after the Congress split of 1969, and then in 1971 when the two parties struck a seat-sharing agreement in the state and general elections. Since her crushing victory across the country in those polls, however, Mrs Gandhi had dispensed with the alliance. There was also another reason why the state had virtually disappeared from Delhi's horizon. In 1971 the Congress had captured only nine of the thirty-nine Lok Sabha seats on offer in Tamil Nadu: the losses, an anomaly in the country, were primarily inflicted by K. Kamaraj, former Congressman and local panjandrum, who had split ways with the prime minister in 1969, taking into the Congress (O) all of the party's bequests. When he died on 2 October 1975 Mrs Gandhi sensed an opportunity to mend relations with the old guard. This she did by flying into Madras and inserting herself into funerary discussions about succession and political survival. She insisted that the southern *satrap* had, in a fit of nostalgia in his dying days, expressed a wish to yoke the two Congresses together and recreate the powerful party machinery that had been invincible in the 1950s. The merger went through in early December, with nearly 70 per cent of the Congress (O)'s executive arm joining Mrs Gandhi's party.[71]

The cajoling done, it was time for the authoritarians to get into character. The DMK government was dismissed on 31 January. President's Rule was declared, ostensibly because Karunanidhi had "misused" his powers and proved himself incapable of curbing "the secessionist tendencies of [his party's] motivated politicians."[72] Thus the Congress, with its 15 seats in a 234-seat assembly—the DMK held 160—came to rule the state directly from the centre.

On 15 February, against the backdrop of the colossal Marina Beach in the state capital, Mrs Gandhi addressed in English "a vast sea of faces"—as her home minister put it—while an interpreter extemporised a Tamil translation: she did not want to foist President's Rule on the southern state, she claimed, but the DMK had "forced her hands". Now Tamil Nadu "had to

---

[71] The rest were absorbed by the DMK and other regional parties: *SW*, 6 December 1975, p. 9.

[72] *The Emergency: Its Impact*, p. 17.

make up for lost time."[73] How? A new commission headed by Supreme Court judge R.S. Sarkaria was set up to investigate allegations of secessionism and corruption.[74] Soon after, a wave of terror washed over the state. Armed police were deployed on the streets, 9000 arrested, and curfews imposed, the centre taking full advantage of the enhanced MISA powers that the Lok Sabha had passed on 22 January.

But when, beatings given and confessions extracted, 7000 of those detained were let off, the Congress decided that the brunt of its suppression ought to be borne by its immediate opponents alone and not by Tamil society at large. As a result the Centre of Indian Trade Unions (CITU) was forced to go into hiding and the DMK thrown into disarray. A vehement D.K. Barooah contemplated a DMK-free South: the Congress should "deal with the DMK not as a mere political rival" but "we should fight to eliminate them as a political party."[75] The "majority" of DMK detainees were not even considered political prisoners—to the rulers of Delhi they were "rowdy elements", or commanded "influence among rowdies" at any rate, and were arrested as such.[76] The treatment meted out to them was so harsh that the DMK chief felt compelled to write to the president of the republic, decrying the "terrorising" of his party: our ranks "have been treated bitterly", he wrote, describing at length the barbarity of the carceral officers. Put into solitary confinement, some of his party men had "been locked inside cells ... for ten days" at a stretch.[77]

Apolitical Tamil citizens had far less reason to fear the new regime. As Tables 5.1–5.3 show, the state scores among the lowest on virtually every indicator of authoritarian transgression, registering about a third the number of instances of abuse of authority as its southern neighbours; less than half as many detentions, and just a tenth the number of demolitions. On the family-planning front, where Tamil Nadu appears on a par with the national as well as southern average, two qualitative differences stand out: first, the incentives and disincentives were introduced on 17 September 1976, much later than elsewhere.[78] In effect, while the sterilisation pro-

---

[73] *SW*, 21 February 1976, p. 3.

[74] *SW*, 7 February 1976, p. 1.

[75] Selbourne, *An Eye to India*, p. 176.

[76] *SCR*, vol. 3, p. 108.

[77] Karunanidhi to Ahmad, 27 February 1976, in "Documentation of Emergency Period in India", MLP, microfilm copy, reel 13.

[78] *SCR*, vol. 3, p. 192.

gramme had reached its peak in the North, Tamil Nadu was only getting started. Second, in 1976, while other states were doubling and tripling the targets set by the centre, the administrators of Tamil Nadu raised them only by 20 per cent.[79] Emblematic of the laxer "motivation" norms were the state's centres of learning: while teachers in most states of the North had to motivate between five to twenty citizens, here the quota was set at two.[80] After the pitiless crackdown of January and February 1976, opposition to the Emergency was muted as well, with the DMK split over whether to resist President's Rule. As late as June that year, hardly any bridges had been built with the resistance in the rest of the country.[81] The Congress (O) also kept at arm's length from it, fearing that moving closer to the DMK, historically a rival, would lead to another "stampede" of its members in the direction of Mrs Gandhi's party.[82]

The 1977 polls, not surprisingly, yielded the Congress a rich harvest, with the party stronger after the merger and the opposition weaker because of incarceration. The Congress nearly doubled its vote share from 12 to 22 per cent, picking up fourteen Lok Sabha seats. It had also been helped by factors external to the Emergency. To an extent, some of the stardust of its ally, the AIADMK, had rubbed off on it: led by popular actor-turned-politician M.G. Ramachandran—MGR to the press—who had split from the DMK in 1972 to start his own outfit, this insurgent party, and by extension the Congress, benefited on the campaign trail from the support of MGR's fellow movie stars Sivaji Ganesan and S.S. Rajendran.[83] The party's split, taken with the widely reviled corruption of its years in power, cost the DMK dearly, its seat share falling from 23 to 1, while the AIADMK picked up 18, mostly at its expense.

The Southern Satrapies *Hold Their Own*

Even early in the Emergency it was evident not only in Tamil Nadu but also in the other three southern states that Delhi's writ counted for much less than in the North. The weakness of the Congress in these southern states gave local leaders greater leeway than in the Hindi belt, where the party

---

[79] Ibid., p. 207.

[80] Ibid., p. 192.

[81] Nimbkar, *Trends in Tamil Nadu Politics*, pp. 31, 46–7. Nimbkar, an employee of the Citizens for Democracy, was Jayaprakash Narayan's emissary in Madras.

[82] Ibid., p. 33.

[83] Ali, "The Fall of Congress in India", p. 45.

was more thoroughly institutionalised: there the centre could plant loyal minions as chief ministers and make all kinds of demands on them. For another, as was seen in Gujarat, the inadequate coffers of the southern state Congresses dictated that these PCCs *receive* funds from Delhi, the other way around being the extractive norm in the North. Because the stakes were lower, politics in the South tended to be more conciliatory. The upshot was that the ranks of zealous believers in Mrs Gandhi and her son's programmes tended to become thinner as one journeyed southwards from the capital.

Nevertheless, the North–South divide must not be overstated. To be sure, the Congress indisputably carried the South in the 1977 election. But it is also true that, thanks in no small part to the distorting effects of plurality voting, regional contrasts have been overdrawn in narratives of the Emergency. A rundown of the grand old party's vote shares can quickly correct this misapprehension: while in Kerala and Tamil Nadu the Congress received 29 and 22 per cent of the votes polled, respectively—in both cases the party improved its 1971 figures by just under 10 per cent—in Karnataka its vote share *fell* from 71 to 56 per cent in the intervening period. In Andhra Pradesh it increased marginally from 55.8 to 57.4 per cent. The latter figure, though, includes the share of the Telangana Praja Samiti, which on the back of its demand for a new state had polled 14.4 per cent in 1971 before folding into the Congress four years later.

Moreover, the different results in the North and South owed in part to electoral pacts struck between the various parties in 1977. If the Janata amalgam consolidated the anti-Congress vote across the Hindi belt, in Tamil Nadu and Kerala opposition unity *declined* between 1971 and 1977, bucking the national trend.[84] This was because in Kerala Mrs Gandhi's party became the cynosure of a five-party coalition, while in Tamil Nadu it struck an alliance with the AIADMK.

---

[84] In an excellent study of the election, Malte Pehl contends that excesses better account for the Congress' poor showing in the North than they do for its better performance in the South. The variable that accounts for both phenomena, however, is anti-Congress unity—an important caveat in a simplistic North–South divide thesis. But by focusing solely on quantitative variables, Pehl's account risks turning the stick in the opposite direction: a complete rejection of the southern exception. It should be noted *en passant* that contra the instincts of a preponderance of psephologists working on India, elections are not the sum of alliances, vote banks, and party machinery. The record of governance past and promises present usually tends to complicate the picture. See Pehl, "Democratic Backlash?", pp. 320–3.

Overall, however, a case can be made for a Southern exception. The repeated failures of the centre to rein in the southern states amply demonstrate that despite Mrs Gandhi's best attempts to erode federalism, or at times ride it to her advantage, politics in the states had a life of their own.

The regional peculiarities were most discernible in Kerala. Here the Emergency's sterilisation drive was partially dampened by the success of the family-planning programme in the early 1970s. A rapid rise in income and improving development indicators, including literacy rates, had resulted in a partial demographic transition. As a consequence, the importance of family planning was recognised by the families themselves, reducing the need for state intervention.[85] Moreover, the success of the cash incentives programme piloted in Kerala had given the state a head start. While coercion was not absent in the implementation of the programme—the poor were targeted here as well—there was no drive to sterilise citizens *en masse*. In essence, its past performance allowed Kerala to resist the badgering to which many other states were subjected by the centre. Recorded instances of resistance were few as well. As a result, Kerala boasted one of the smallest increases in the number of operations between 1975–6 and 1976–7: 32 per cent against the national average of 210 per cent. The total figure of those sterilised, too, showed that here the Emergency period was not very different from the years that preceded it. The number of operations had peaked at 151,000 in 1971–2, falling to less than half in the following years, before returning to 156,000 in 1975–6. Similarly, the number of deaths on the operation tables—forty—were far fewer than those recorded even in some of the smaller states of the North. For instance, with a population a sixth that of Kerala's, Himachal Pradesh's toll was half as large again.[86] Kerala "underperformed" on other indicators as well, registering, in per capita terms, two-fifths the number of demolitions as well as instances of abuse of authority as the national mean (see Tables 5.1 and 5.3).

The only anomaly here appears to be the very high number of detentions chalked up by Kerala's rulers: nearly five times the average of the other southern states. To make sense of this requires understanding the make-up of the coalition in power in Trivandrum. Here the Congress was not in the driving seat and had to contend with the Muslim League and the

---

[85] Kerala witnessed a 16 per cent fall in birth rates between 1970 and 1974: Krishnan, "Demographic Transition in Kerala", p. 1205; Ratcliffe, "Social Justice and the Demographic Transition", pp. 141–2.

[86] *SCR*, vol. 3, pp. 180, 182.

Communist Party of India.[87] The latter's Achutha Menon had held the chief ministership since 1969, while the former lent support in exchange for a few ministries and seat adjustments.[88] When the Emergency was declared the CPI leadership, in particular, welcomed it with both hands despite being caught unawares. For long at the receiving end of state power, the CPI looked at the new dispensation as an opportunity to turn the tables.

As the Shah Commission shows, Kerala was the only state where the DIR and MISA were used to further the class struggle. The main targets were usurious lenders, the managerial class, and black marketeers—ration shop-keepers "misappropriating certain quantities of rice", truckers making off with "seven quintals of ration wheat", and the like. Bosses could earn a MISA sentence if they took an "anti-labour stance", which referred, *inter alia*, to the arbitrary dismissal of workers without compensation, an unwillingness to settle disputes with employees, lockouts, and tax evasion.[89] Moreover, the use of influence as a get-out-of-jail card was not an option. In fact the four-monthly reviews were, as in the North, only a formality in Kerala.[90]

Even so, hostility towards urban industrialists and rural malefactors did not extend to the rest of society. As a result, when the balance sheet is drawn it becomes apparent that transgressions were fewer in Kerala than in the North, and citizens more content with the workings of the coalition. This owed primarily to the assumption of the incumbents that an assembly election was imminent. It was due in October 1975 and, for the troika of parties in power, defeat was a foregone conclusion. Menon's six years at the helm had witnessed high inflation, food scarcity, and spiralling corruption. But then the *deus ex machina* that Trivandrum's rulers were waiting for finally occurred: the Emergency was declared. While the poll was postponed three times during the months of authoritarian rule—the last time on 26 August 1976—Kerala's incumbents remained in perpetual election gear. As it happened, in March 1977

---

[87] The League in North India was opposed to the Congress, leading to Mrs Gandhi's awkward "secular" posturing, in which she condemned the League for "spreading communal poison" in Uttar Pradesh, even as she defended her alliance with it in Kerala in the same breath: Minutes of the CWC Meeting, 15 and 16 September 1973 in All-India Congress Committee, *Congress Marches Ahead—IX*, pp. 101–2.

[88] Seat adjustments refer to agreements in which parties agree not to field candidates in the same constituencies.

[89] *SCR*, vol. 3, pp. 80–1.

[90] Ibid., p. 82.

Kerala was the only state in the union where both general and state elections were held concurrently.

The upshot of being in permanent campaign mode was twofold. First, the Congress, the League, and the CPI did everything in the realm of the possible to weaken the opposition, from cajoling them to defect to consigning them to torture camps. Second, the coalition worked to strengthen the economy, distribute sweeteners across the board, and generally earn the goodwill of citizens who, sooner rather than later, would be queuing at the polling booths.

The main opposition to Menon's government came from the CPI(M), which drew support from the urban working class and the poorer peasantry of the Keralite mofussil. By 1975, years into coalition misrule, the CPI(M) was stronger than ever before. In fact the party was so confident that it could go it alone in the elections that it chose not to affiliate itself with the JP Movement, an association that it felt could only be toxic. Jayaprakash Narayan visited Kerala in May 1975 only to return a disappointed man, having found few takers for his "total revolution". A sounder strategy, the CPI(M) concluded, was the one it was already engaged in. Since autumn 1974 the party had been boycotting the assembly to protest the coalition's refusal to investigate allegations of police brutality against some of its MLAs.[91] In this endeavour it was joined by the Congress (O); the Socialist party; the Kerala Congress, a splinter party dominated by Christians and upper-caste Hindus; and dissident elements of the Muslim League. Before the Emergency it appeared that the opposition parties were moving from strength to strength, and by early June 1975 defections had already reduced the incumbents to a minority government.

All this changed on 25 June. The mid- and high-level cadres of opposition parties found themselves incarcerated. E.M.S. Namboodiripad, the leader of the CPI(M), was briefly placed behind bars as well. Broken, he even contemplated the possibility of a merger between the two parties of the Left, a proposition briskly rebuffed by the CPI.[92] In February 1976 the threat to party survival was so great that the CPI(M) decided to end its two-year boycott of the assembly. Paradoxically, its muted parliamentary participation during the rest of the Emergency suited it better than the boycott did—incarceration and suppression virtually ended after this meek accep-

[91] Nossiter, "State-Level Politics in India", p. 41.
[92] *TOI*, 20 February 1976, p. 8.

tance of authoritarianism. By the end of the year it was patently clear that the CPI(M) was no longer a government in waiting.

If the CPI(M)'s acceptance came grudgingly, that of the Kerala Congress and dissident Leaguers did with even less resistance. As the months wore on, members of both flocked to join the ruling coalition. By November 1975 a hybrid of coercion and persuasion resulted in a formal alliance between the Congress and the Kerala Congress. KC leaders were, on the one hand, threatened with detention for spurious "economic offences" if they repudiated the Congress' deal. At the same time the speakership of the assembly, along with the finance and transport ministries, were handed over to the KC, which was also allowed to field twenty-five candidates in the next assembly election with the assurance that the coalition would leave them uncontested.[93]

The second aspect of the incumbents' strategy was to widen their support base before Delhi called for fresh elections. As the "parity index"—the difference between a farmer's earnings and overheads—fell from 109 in 1974 to 95 the next year, the middle classes benefited at the expense of producers, the joy of the former translating into general bourgeois approval of authoritarian rule. However, the benefits of lower food prices did not trickle down to the state's urban and rural poor—most of whom in any case were long-standing CPI(M) supporters—who tended to be ambivalent about market prices because they purchased their rice and tapioca, both Keralite staples, at subsidised rates from ration shops. The state's 3.6 million ration-card holders had to suffice with 80 grams of rice per day because of the state's poor procurement networks, while in fact over 200 grams was available to every citizen if the produce sold in the open market was taken into account. But the middle class had more reason to celebrate than just cheaper grocery bills. Pleasing them also was a decline in industrial action, the result of "disciplining" labour. The active role played by the Labour Ministry in fostering "unfair competition" benefiting Congress unions at the expense of Communist and Revolutionary Socialist ones had created an "industrial peace".[94] The numbers spoke for themselves: in Kerala 321,000 man-days were lost in the first half of 1975 and only 46,000 in the second. Of course, while similar figures were true of the northern states as well, the class dimension of Kerala's politics worked uniquely to the Congress' advantage. In most of the republic, the absence of genuine economic

---

[93] Nossiter, "State-Level Politics in India", p. 45.

[94] Ibid, p. 48.

reforms coupled with the heavy-handedness of the state alienated the poor, whose votes had contributed to the huge victories Mrs Gandhi's party piled up in 1971 and 1972. But in Kerala the poor were never there for the Congress to alienate; they traditionally voted for the CPI(M). In essence, the benefits of the Emergency accrued to the only class that mattered electorally to the Congress in the state: the urban middle class.[95]

Both a first-mover advantage in the sterilisation programme and the electoral exigencies of the coalition, then, were responsible for the weaker implementation of the Emergency's programmes in Kerala. To these, two more reasons can be adduced: the weakness of the Congress and the selective use of political violence. First, the position of the grand old party. Its inability to implement policies during the Emergency owed not only to it being just one player in a coalition of three parties, but to its poor institutionalisation. The Congress had historically been weak in Kerala, having held an absolute majority in the assembly only once, between 1962 and 1964.[96] Its sudden reversal of fortune during the Emergency was no doubt catalysed by newly acquired executive fiat; but in day-to-day governance the influence of the centre on the politics of the state remained minimal. This was because Sanjay's parallel power structure was unable to make inroads into the Kerala PCC or even the local Youth Congress. In particular, the role of the YC chief in the state, A.K. Antony, proved vital: he not only put up a resolute stand against Sanjay, he even prevented him visiting Trivandrum. Indeed, Kerala was unique in that the YC and parent party worked in unison, collaborating on education reform and curbing the CPI(M) in the countryside. This was unlike the arrangement in many northern states, where youth leaders were in perennial conflict with party honchos, demanding that the latter furnish YC men with tickets and ministerial positions.

Second, the limits of violence. In the main, the long arm of the police was felt most palpably by the opposition parties: the worst was reserved for the CPI(M). Society at large was spared. To be sure, there were some districts that had it worse than others. Mass-scale violence played out mostly in the northern district of Cannanore, where a number of CPI(M) activists were consigned to torture chambers and mowed down by police guns.[97] The results of the 1977 assembly election reflected the geography of intimida-

[95] Nossiter, *Communism in Kerala*, pp. 255–9.

[96] The state was formed in 1956 by merging most of Malabar into Travancore–Cochin.

[97] A.K. Gopalan to Indira Gandhi, 17 September 1975, Jayaprakash Narayan Papers, Instalment III, Subject File 322; Rajappa, "Kerala's Concentration Camps", p. 35.

tion: the CPI(M) garnered local sympathies and swept the coastal districts of north Kerala, where the Congress and CPI paid dearly for their savagery.[98] In other parts of the state, where state violence was more subdued, the grand old party did exceedingly well. No doubt locking up the CPI(M) cadres during the campaign and bringing the smaller parties into the Congress-led alliance contributed to the result. On the whole the CPI(M) that emerged from the Emergency was a party of broken men: of the sixty-eight candidates it fielded in 1977, twenty-four had been imprisoned in those ill-fated twenty-one months and eight had spent them in hiding. There were other factors exogenous to political violence as well. Also benefiting the Congress was the stability of the coalition it was in: it was the first to serve a full term since the state's formation in 1956.[99] In essence a vote for the incumbents was a vote for stability. Moreover, the alliance on the other side of the fence was a rather chaotic affair. A preponderance of tickets was handed to the CPI(M)'s allies, incensing Marxist voters and prospective candidates alike. The inability of the opposition to produce a manifesto in time also indicated the lack of consensus in its ranks—another reason why citizens were likely to distrust it.

As for prison conditions in Kerala, in general they were better than in most parts of the country: sports and recreation facilities were provided; superintendents of jails given relative autonomy to make decisions to allow families to see detainees without requests having to go up the bureaucratic chain, a process where delays and rebuffs were inevitable; and youths held in juvenile prisons, not with the rest of the adult carceral population, as was the norm in Emergency India.[100]

All this is not to suggest that Kerala was heaven on earth during the Emergency. Certainly, incidents of state violence were many—and went under-reported in the Shah Commission. This was in part because the Congress–CPI coalition remained in power after the poll and was reluctant to point the finger at its own men. The state's chief secretary admitted as much when he informed the inspector general of police that they would

---

[98] See the results of the first dozen constituencies—all in the north—listed in this ECI report: Election Commission of India, *Statistical Report on General Election, 1977 to the Legislative Assembly of Kerala*, p. 4.

[99] The instability of the previous years was mostly the result of the Congress government at the centre dismissing the state government whenever its rule in the state—whether independent or in coalition—was jeopardised. This happened in 1959, 1964, and 1970.

[100] *SCR*, vol. 3, pp. 142–3.

"not conduct any sort of enquiry ... that might incriminate the state government, as the present government is only a continuation of the coalition" of before.[101]

Violent resistance to the regime bore witness to the discontent in the state. One such episode was the explosion at the Sabarigiri hydroelectric complex in March 1976, soon after which the Kerala Crime Branch hit upon "a cache of 650 kilogrammes of explosives and 2900 sticks of dynamite."[102] This was attributed to the Naxalites, who in any case were a marginal force in the state, their activities having peaked in Kerala between 1968 and 1970. Moreover, Kunnikal Narayan, the local Naxal chief, had been incarcerated before the authoritarian turn, blunting the command structure of the partisans. But the threat inflation served Trivandrum well: it was used to target all its enemies, and even retroactively justify botched killings. An instance of the latter was the torture and execution of Rajan, an engineering student, by the police. News of this "encounter killing" filled the airwaves through 1976 and the election year that followed, generating an inquiry and general outrage, each feeding the other with growing amplitude. Gradually, details began to emerge: the student in question, erroneously described as a Naxalite after the event, was interrogated by a number of higher-ups, including the deputy inspector general, before being dispatched in March 1976 by the Kakkayam police at one of Kerala's five torture chambers.[103] After the Emergency, Chief Minister K. Karunakaran, who had been Kerala's home minister during the months of authoritarianism, admitted that Rajan had died in police custody. The ensuing uproar resulted in his dismissal and replacement by the YC chief A.K. Antony.[104]

In sum, the carrot-and-stick strategy of the ruling coalition reflected in in the 1977 election results: the Congress increased its vote share from 19.8 to 29.1 per cent, winning all 11 seats it contested in the Lok Sabha; in the assembly, it secured 38 of the 54 seats it fielded candidates in.[105] Its allies— the CPI, Muslim League, Revolutionary Socialist Party, and Kerala

---

[101] K.N. Sreenivasan, Inspector General of Police, Kerala, to P.R. Rajgopal, Secretary, Shah Commission of Inquiry, 18 January 1978, Shah Commission of Inquiry Files, File 41011/10/77/KRL/T-4.

[102] Nossiter, "State-Level Politics in India", p. 42.

[103] Rajan was arrested along with another student, Joseph Chaly. See the latter's testimony in Baldev, *India from Indira to Morarji*, pp. 46–7.

[104] *Hindustan Times*, 24 May 1977, p. 1.

[105] Election Commission of India, *Statistical Report on General Election, 1977 to the Sixth Lok Sabha: Volume 1*, p. 90.

Congress—cornered the remaining nine seats in the general election, and in the assembly took home 65 of the 76 seats where their candidates stood. Whittled down by repression and *en masse* defections, the seven-party combination that ran a campaign mostly against the Emergency won only 28 seats in the assembly and none in the Lower House.[106]

In Karnataka, patterns that bear a stronger resemblance with the politics of the North coexist with those of the South. As in much of the Hindi belt, the competition between the old party guard and the new, centrally appointed state leadership was fierce. D. Devaraj Urs, the neophyte politician parachuted into the chief ministership in 1972, spent most of his term in office extracting as much money as he could from the PCC, remitting it all to the Congress at the centre in the hope that it would convince Mrs Gandhi of his usefulness. This it did. In return for his ability to grease the wheels of the party machinery, he was given a free hand in running state affairs.

Urs' foremost priority, no doubt guided by survival instinct, was to present Delhi with an impressive array of statistics: when it came to bureaucratic transgressions and sterilisations, Karnataka was on a par with the average of the North; its detentions were about 20 per cent more than the southern average; its demolitions twice that. Indeed, this was the principal reason why Karnataka's figures tended to be much higher than, say, Kerala's or Tamil Nadu's.[107]

Nevertheless, Urs did try to keep some sort of lid on the sterilisation programme, even going to the extent of taking measures to dampen the enthusiasm of officials in three districts that seemed to have been carried away by the logic of targets. He also ensured that as few figures of the opposition as possible were locked up, thus preventing any political mileage that imprisonments might provide the opposition in a future election.[108] During the first two weeks of the Emergency, at a time when most Congress-ruled states were jailing political enemies wholesale, no "arrest lists" emerged from Urs' state. Only four politicians—Vajpayee, Advani, Dandavate, and the Congress (O)'s S.N. Mishra—were taken into custody before the ban on twenty-six parties took effect on 4 July. Moreover, this was done at the

---

[106] The seven parties were the CPI(M), Bharatiya Lok Dal, Congress Radicals, Muslim League (Opposition), Revolutionary Socialist Party (National), Kerala Socialist Party, and the Kerala Congress (Pillai).

[107] Manor, "Where Congress Survived", pp. 792–4.

[108] For instance, a BLD figure was released after the state's home secretary noted that the party was not "a force to be reckoned with" in Karnataka: *SCR*, vol. 3, p. 72.

union's instance, not the state leadership's.[109] Later, in January 1976, when the centre put in place the policy which redirected all parole requests to the Home Ministry, Bangalore managed to negotiate some wiggle room: when at first Delhi objected to the release of a batch of prisoners, suggesting that they might start a local "agitation", Karnataka's functionaries prevailed in having them released by replying that this was "not likely".[110] For the duration of the Emergency the centre accepted the state's recommendations and released more than half the detainees that Bangalore no longer wanted in its cells.[111] Similarly, in its dealings with labour militancy and censorship the state was an outlier. In three separate incidents, a "Naxalite labour leader", a Chikmagalur radical who had fomented rebellion among the coffee planters in the estates, and the editor of *Pooravani* who published "unfounded allegations against the government"—all people who would elsewhere have matched the profile of the Emergency's most dangerous enemies—were let off by the state administration.[112] Additionally, nearly two-fifths of all MISA detainees were released in the four-monthly review process headed by the state's home secretary.[113]

When it came to the progressive elements of the Twenty-Point Programme, Urs' record proved better than that of most of his peers. A land-reform law was passed giving tribunals the power to swiftly redistribute land to tenants and the landless. Crucially, Urs ensured that within its provisions was inserted a clause preventing appeals against it. This overcame a major stumbling block that had for most of the union resulted in land-reform failure. Karnataka also instituted debt relief and other redistributive measures during the Emergency. Even so, lest it appear that Urs was some kind of champion of the welfare state, it should be noted that he mostly co-opted members of the old guard—Lingayat and Vokkaliga landowners—the better part of whom retained tickets in the 1977 elections.[114]

---

[109] In the early hours of 26 June, the republic's chief secretary had called on his Karnataka counterpart, asking him to have six MPs arrested. While the four figures mentioned above were caught, the other two—Samar Guha and Subramanian Swamy—escaped. Guha was later arrested: ibid., p. 71.

[110] Ibid., pp. 71–2.

[111] Ibid., p. 76.

[112] Ibid., pp. 73–5.

[113] Ibid., p. 77.

[114] Urs himself belonged to neither the Lingayat or Vokkaliga ruling elite; he hailed from the Arasu caste to which the Mysore maharajas belonged: Manor, "Structural Changes in Karnataka Politics", p. 1867. On the ambivalent character

Urs' strategy of placating the centre while undermining authoritarian impulse locally appears to have served him and his masters well. In the 1977 general election the Congress took all but two of the state's twenty-eight Lok Sabha seats, one of which it lost by only 0.25 per cent of the vote. Nevertheless, the party saw its vote share decline by 14.1 per cent. The Janata made some inroads in cities, winning the Bangalore South constituency with trade-union support. In the rest of the state the opposition campaign's focus on democracy rang hollow to the rural majority, they being far removed from the world of the Bangalore Central Jail where many of the Emergency's transgressions took place.

The predicament that Andhra Pradesh's chief minister, J. Vengal Rao, faced was the same as Urs'. Like his Kannada counterpart, Rao had been deputed to his state because he was a novice. When she put him up for the job in 1973, Mrs Gandhi had hoped that this loyal Velama would in good time establish himself by striking at the party's old guard, a Kamma and Reddi fiefdom run by the influential K. Brahmananda Reddy.[115]

Here, as in Gujarat but unlike in Karnataka, money was channelled from the centre to the state, helping Vengal Rao consolidate power. The bureaucracy, firmly in his grip, was used to target the opposition, weaken the all-powerful Reddis, and even fudge sterilisation figures to propitiate Delhi.[116] Rao operated with a sense of duty, locking up Jana Sanghis and Naxalites and immobilising their funding networks; taking Mrs Gandhi's message of "Garibi Hatao" to the masses and threatening the position of the Reddi gentry; and repeatedly publicising inflated sterilisation figures.[117]

The picture that emerges, then, is of a moderately implemented Emergency: bureaucratic transgressions and demolitions below the southern average, sterilisations marginally above it, and among the low-

---

of Urs' land reforms—breaking the Lingayat or Vokkaliga monopoly on power without expropriating them *en masse*; ending tenancies not to the benefit of the Scheduled Castes but only the Other Backward Castes—see idem, "Pragmatic Progressives in Regional Politics", pp. 201–13.

[115] Velamas, Kammas, and Reddis are all major land-owning castes. While none were underdogs, there were fewer Velamas than there were Kammas and Reddis; consequently they were less powerful.

[116] This was James Manor's assessment after meeting a number of political workers and newspaper editors in the state in 1977. See Manor, "Where Congress Survived", p. 795; *SCR*, vol. 3, pp. 46–7.

[117] *SCR*, vol. 3, pp. 46–7.

est detention rates in the country. No detainee died in prison in Andhra Pradesh.[118] Hyderabad was also slower in getting onto the sterilisation bandwagon. Disincentives to compel civil servants with two or more children were only introduced in late September 1976, the better part of which were to come into effect only on 1 September the following year—in effect, they never materialised.[119] And the number of sterilisation tables that turned into coffins was relatively small: at 135 lives lost, the Andhra figure was on a par with Haryana's 132—the latter's population was less than a quarter the former's.[120]

Like Urs, Vengal Rao resorted to an admixture of co-option and welfarism at election time. In a shrewd move he released at once money that had been set apart for the Scheduled Castes and Tribes over the years. This, coupled with Mrs Gandhi's pro-poor rhetoric that Rao mimicked on the campaign trail, ensured the party safe returns. By wooing Kammas at the last minute with seat allocations, he drew on a coalition that included the latter, most of whom belonged to the gentry; his own caste, the Velamas; and the poor, whose backing was, however, only tactical—they voted for the Congress to undercut Reddi hegemony rather than out of any genuine identification with the Vengal Rao regime. In the event, the grand old party defeated the Janata, which likewise derived its support from a broad spectrum of classes and castes: the urban bourgeoisie, the communist working class, Brahmins, Vaishyas, and Reddi peasants.[121] The Congress won all but one of the state's forty-two seats, its solitary loss being to Neelam Sanjiva Reddy, the man who had nearly become president of the republic in 1969 before Mrs Gandhi's candidate snatched the position from under his nose.

To the southern exception could be added a fifth state: Maharashtra. The sequence of events in it was familiar. As part of her deinstitutionalisation campaign since the Congress split, Mrs Gandhi deputed a cipher, S.B. Chavan, to battle the old guard led by Y.B. Chavan who had, in the late 1950s and 1960s, made the Maharashtra Congress a formidable electoral machine.[122]

---

[118] Ibid., p. 137.

[119] Ibid., p. 171.

[120] Ibid., pp. 171, 178.

[121] Manor, "Where Congress Survived", pp. 794–7.

[122] Technically, Chavan—after his terms as chief minister of Bombay and, later, Maharashtra in 1956–62—manoeuvred Maharashtra politics from behind the scenes, serving variously as defence, home, finance, and foreign minister at the centre between 1962 and 1977, while a loyalist, Vasantrao Naik, chief minister from 1963 to 1975, did his bidding.

Dominated by Maratha landowners, the local PCC had developed a strong patronage network which relied on the sugar lobby and gentry to fill party coffers and guarantee electoral success—in return they benefited from easy credit and subsidies that state banks offered them as well as conservatism on land reform—after which the spoils were occasionally distributed to Dalits, Muslims, and the rest of the urban and rural poor. In February 1975 S.B. Chavan was elevated to pole position in the state. His remit included undercutting the power structure that the earlier Chavan had erected by cutting off bank funds and credit lines to the sugar lobby.

During the Emergency the new man made one miscalculation which, in retrospect, did not appear as fatal as it did at the time. Assuming that the Emergency would last forever, or at any rate a very long time, he decided to go easy on the Y.B. Chavan-dominated establishment, instead concentrating his efforts on implementing the Emergency's programmes in Bombay and neglecting the *mofussil.* So, while the state capital bore the brunt of authoritarian transgressions, the rest of the state got off relatively lightly. The grimness of prison life, too, was a reality removed from the hinterland: nearly two-thirds of the state's carceral population of 15,000 was held in three prisons in Greater Bombay.[123]

When elections were announced, S.B. Chavan's ineptitude turned out a blessing in disguise. By leaving much of the Maharashtrian countryside untouched for most of the duration of the Emergency, the Congress' standing in the state remained more or less intact. And by refusing to confront the Y.B. Chavan faction head on, Mrs Gandhi's puppet had spared powerful antagonists who could muscle in on the candidate selection process. As it turned out, both caucuses were able to corner about half the seats on offer. Swearing not to campaign for the other Chavan, both sides went into the election with meagre funds and different programmes: Y.B. Chavan's faction trying to build a reputation for itself as the victim of the Emergency, and S.B. Chavan's as the fresh face of change that could only be meaningful if given a longer run in office.[124]

Despite the odds stacked against them, the old establishment figures performed marginally better than Mrs Gandhi's arrivistes, winning twelve seats to the latter's eight. The remaining twenty-eight went to the Janata, which, on the whole, won with smaller vote margins than the Congress— underscoring the importance of opposition unity. The exception was

---

[123] *SCR*, vol. 3, pp. 143–4.

[124] Manor, "Where Congress Survived", p. 788.

Bombay, which witnessed a landslide in favour of the alliance: the Janata, benefiting from seat adjustments with the Peasants' and Workers' Party and the CPI(M), took all six constituencies in the city with sizeable margins. It also secured the support of industrial workers who ordinarily voted Socialist. The Brahmin and Marwari middle class that formed the Jana Sangh's base, and the Gujaratis of Bombay who typically backed the Congress (O), were the other components of this coalition, making the Janata's base as much of a potpourri of classes and castes as the one led by the two Chavans.[125]

* * *

Geographical variations in the reach of the Emergency indicate that the regime's excesses were not uniformly felt across India. For far too long, the Emergency years have been analysed solely through national categories and Delhi-centric lenses. The view from the states, however, suggests that federalism in the Indian setting allowed for the uneven impact of authoritarianism. The further the populace happened to be located from the Delhi–Haryana–West UP triangle that formed the Emergency's epicentre, the less they were affected by it. All was not of course down to federalism and geographical distance. A more explicitly political criterion mattered too: the Emergency was less severe in states such as Gujarat and Tamil Nadu where opposition parties were in office (and would remain so for as long as they stayed there) and where Congress chief ministers could resist Delhi's rulers—or implement their orders less forcefully at any rate.

The statistics published by the Shah Commission, as our caveats above suggest, need qualifying. Still, they point to a way of disaggregating the Emergency's topography: namely, by looking at the North–South divide, which in a sense is really a divide between centre and periphery. All the same, it is important to recognise that distance from the centre is not the only variable which needs factoring in. This is because local politics continued to inform the terms in which the regime was understood and implemented. Was the Congress, for instance, so weak when far from Delhi that it had to partner with other parties less interested in imposing Mrs Gandhi's will? Was the state Congress leader strong enough to resist her diktat and Sanjay's? Or did he need to show more zeal in implementing the Emergency's programmes to ingratiate himself with the duo? In

---

[125] Ibid.

many ways, politics proceeded as it had earlier; to a considerable extent it was business as usual in states where the influence of Delhi was felt only marginally.

In sum, across the union, a variety of factors came into play: the strengths and weaknesses of local Congresses *vis-à-vis* the opposition and the party at the centre; the strategies of state elites and bureaucracies; electoral considerations; factional competition; lobby influence; and the solipsism of Delhi's rulers. These were all determinants in the spread of the geography of tyranny which, on the whole, resulted in the Emergency being felt more strongly in the capital, its neighbouring states, and the Hindi belt than in states ruled by the opposition, the North East, and South India.

Conclusion to Part I

The five chapters of the first part of this book have shown that the Emergency was, for a number of reasons, an authoritarian moment, even if of a rather atypical kind. In particular, three peculiarities stand out.

First, there was no regime change. The constitution was not abrogated and replaced. India's political system remained as before the Emergency—federal and parliamentarian. Opposition parties were not banned. Newspapers and journals were in the main subject to censorship but some displayed courage by laying into the new dispensation. The country's prisons were packed with political opponents, many of whom were tortured, but most opposition lawmakers remained free and even attended parliamentary sessions. For her part Mrs Gandhi saw to it that the regime acted within the limits of legality: in fact every anti-democratic step was taken with parliamentary approval. Constitutional amendments helped ensure that nothing was conducted outside the framework of the law. Such reforms considerably weakened individual freedoms and clipped the wings of key institutions, including the judiciary. All the same, they were endorsed by the Supreme Court. The Emergency, then, is a fine instance of the type of regime described by political scientists and also, incidentally, by an independent MP in the Lok Sabha in 1975 as "constitutional dictatorship".

Second, the Emergency, like most authoritarian regimes, lacked an ideology. Certainly, it was declared in the name of progressive values, such as secularism and socialism, two words that were incorporated into the preamble of the constitution in 1976. Mrs Gandhi's ostensible secularism found expression in the banning of communal organisations, including the Anand Marg, the RSS, and the JI. As for the socialist dimension of the regime, it was epitomised by the Twenty-Point Programme, which included among other things a commitment to land reform and public housing. But such egalitarian impulses, which resulted in a modicum of success, were more than compensated for by nepotism and the corporatist overtones of the prime minister's policies.

As we have suggested, then, it seems fitting to describe the Emergency as an "organic statist" regime, one of the seven variants of authoritarianism in Linz's typology. During the Emergency, political authoritarianism and social hierarchies appeared to reinforce each other. The fact that Sanjay Gandhi's gentrification and sterilisation drives targeted Dalits and Muslims in particular reflects the extent to which caste and religious prejudice permeated the ranks of the largely upper-caste elite.

Third, and relatedly, the Emergency encouraged depoliticisation. This resulted partly from the absence of ideological consistency on the part of the ruling class, for it becomes considerably more difficult to think and act politically when confronted with a regime that follows no clear doctrine. Moreover, and more generally, depoliticisation is an upshot of the authoritarian rejection of intellectual debates and ideas; these are unwelcome because they foster dissent. Indeed, authoritarian rulers are anti-intellectual by definition, and the Emergency offered many illustrations of this: Delhi's rulers, for instance, regarded as their enemies not only the media but universities too.

Since the regime could not mobilise people on the basis of ideology, it developed a multivocal style that spoke to different segments of society. Mrs Gandhi, then, was fork-tongued, tailoring her speech to suit her audience, using the language of capital formation at business conclaves and emphasising workers' rights with unionists. All the same there were occasions that demanded a meta-national narrative. Here, the premier would swap ideas for emotions, embellishing her authoritarianism with a dash of populism and nationalism. As we have seen, she tried, for instance, to whip up fears about the role of the United States, accusing it of destabilising the Third World. Similarly, the building of a cult of personality around her was an attempt to secure political approval without ideological content. The result was an increasing reliance on what Ernesto Laclau, in his analysis of populism, calls "empty signifiers"— seemingly vacuous phrases that, in their ability to be variously construed, accommodate a mosaic of concerns.[126] The most famous instance of these was

---

[126] See Laclau, *On Populist Reason*, pp. 159–99.

probably Congress president D.K. Barooah's cringeworthy catchphrase, "India is Indira and Indira is India".[127]

Nationalism, then, was the only "idea" behind which Mrs Gandhi sought to mobilise India's masses. Moreover, this idea, which received considerable support from and amplification in the media, was put to use only to shut down political debate. Those who dissented from this consensus lost legitimacy and were dubbed "anti-national". The depoliticisation of society was also made easier on account of the JP Movement and the strikes orchestrated by the trade-union movement, both developments that created a certain fatigue with politics amongst the middle class.

If the Emergency fulfils all the three criteria of authoritarianism that Linz outlines, it nevertheless did not, temporally speaking, cohere into a discrete sequence. Indeed, the regime needs periodising, even if finding exact dates in this continuum that marked transitions of any kind is scarcely possible. Schematically, the first few months were dominated by Mrs Gandhi's agenda, manifest in the Twenty-Point Programme, whereas from early 1976 Sanjay's Five-Point version, with its attendant focus on mass sterilisation and deportation, came to the fore.

It would seem that the twenty-one months of authoritarian rule can be divided into two sequences, each marked by a discrete set of power centres and personalities. When Sanjay asserted himself he promoted a cluster of personalised institutions in a manner that allowed the Emergency to acquire novel features, not least a grassroots movement centred around a personality cult. This development was made easier by the replacement of experienced chief ministers and bureaucrats with panegyrists. The rise of the Youth Congress at the expense of the parent party gave Sanjay an additional tool. The change of guard was responsible for the criminalisation and lumpenisation of the party, and on account of it, of the state as well: the scion had formed a veritable parallel power structure, as evident from the emergence of the Nehru Brigade. Had he taken power formally instead of haphazardly capturing the state and its resources through indiscriminate acts of nepotism, he would probably have established a full-fledged sultanist regime within which arbitrary despotism is vested in a single person.

Yet not only did the Emergency mutate in character over time, it was not the same everywhere in the country. Its geographical variations are evident

---

[127] Barooah may not have known that Rudolf Hess, deputy führer of Germany, had in 1934 made an equivalence between Hitler and Germany using exactly the same syntax. See Derfler, *The Fall and Rise of Political Leaders*, pp. 165, 251.

in the North–South divide, but also in the contrast between the states governed, initially at any rate, by opposition parties as against those ruled by the Congress. In fact the epicentre of the regime remained, throughout, the national capital, where Sanjay held the reins from Day One; and, radiating powerfully out from Delhi to Haryana, where his automobile factory was located and where his right-hand man, Bansi Lal, held sway; and thence to Uttar Pradesh, not long after N.D. Tiwari, another lieutenant of Sanjay's, was made chief minister. Beyond this perimeter, the rest of the Hindi belt came to be afflicted with Emergency fever, the state leaderships competing with one another to appease Sanjay and his clique by zealously implementing his programme in top-down fashion.

But further away the regime diminished into an apparatus that was far from all-pervasive. Beyond the Vindhyas, politics had a cadence of its own, particularly in the few states that the Congress did not govern. There, in states where the party had to form a coalition, or was not in power at all, or needed to contend with strong party bosses, Mrs Gandhi and Sanjay found considerable resistance to their autocratic programmes.

PART II

CAUSES AND BEYOND

WHAT MADE THE EMERGENCY "NECESSARY" AND POSSIBLE?

On the night the Emergency was declared, Morarji Desai was asked by an Italian interviewer, Oriana Fallaci, if the prime minister would take India down the road of dictatorship. The opposition grandee was categorical in his reply: she "will never do it—she'd commit suicide first."[1] If Desai, a veteran of Indian politics, could not imagine Mrs Gandhi imposing a state of emergency, nobody could, and few did. How, then, do we account for such a counterintuitive decision and make sense of it?

The first part of this book attempted to understand the kind of authoritarianism that the Emergency represented. In the second we try to grapple with the reasons why democracy was suspended in June 1975. In moving from the question of "what authoritarianism" to the question of "why authoritarianism", we will look not only at chains of causality but also at *conditions of possibility*. In essence we will identify both the immediate factors that led to the Emergency as well as their deep roots. A nuanced approach seems necessary, alert to Marx's famous dictum that "men make their own history, but not under conditions of their own choosing."[2]

---

[1] Fallaci, "Mrs Gandhi's Opposition", p. 13.

[2] We follow Sartre's reading of Marx's maxim: structures are not cast in stone but

229

Attention to both agency and structure—the actions of the leading personalities as well as the contours of Indian politics and political economy—is needed to explain the coming of the Emergency.

Prima facie, the declaration of the Emergency was Mrs Gandhi's knee-jerk response to two immediate developments: the JP Movement and the Allahabad judgment. In the event, as we will see in Chapter 6, these popular and legal challenges to her rule harked back to larger issues that had gestated a long time. Indeed, the twin crises of 1975 reflected structural tensions, many over a decade old, within Indian society. In Chapter 7 we shift our attention to other chains of causality and conditions of possibility—focusing in particular on Mrs Gandhi's authoritarian personality and the deinstitutionalisation of the Congress party.

But it was not simply the disposition of Delhi's ruler and the circumstances that the party found itself in that made the Emergency possible. For, once India was under authoritarian rule, a number of agencies aided the regime on a quotidian level. The political partners of the Congress—the CPI, RPI, and Shiv Sena—are cases in point. But, as Chapter 8 shows, so were some sections of the media, the business community, the bourgeoisie, and the trade unions.

---

shaped by agents of the past. An analysis of the politics of the 1950s and 1960s, then, is necessary to explain the Emergency in the decade that followed. See Sartre, *Critique of Dialectical Reason*, pp. 35–6.

6

IMMEDIATE CAUSES

THE JP MOVEMENT AND THE
ALLAHABAD JUDGMENT IN PERSPECTIVE

The Emergency is primarily interpreted as a response to the JP Movement and the Allahabad judgment; the two are linked because the opposition parties saw them as such and were eager to exploit them. United behind Jayaprakash Narayan, they were able to mobilise large crowds against Mrs Gandhi with the knowledge that the court case had made her vulnerable. In a word, she no longer appeared invincible, as she had just five years earlier.

But why were the opposition parties able to sustain such a massive movement over such a long period of time, and why was the judiciary equally adamant to see Mrs Gandhi's head on a platter? Neither development is really comprehensible without context. The political history of earlier decades needs to be gauged, as does the magnitude of the socio-economic crisis that Mrs Gandhi had repeatedly promised to solve.

Certainly, in June 1975 inflation had been brought under control.[1] The JP Movement, having reached its peak in the winter of 1974, "unmistakably was losing its way."[2] The Left was divided, with its three chief factions

[1] Between December 1974 and March 1975 the wholesale price index declined by 7.5 per cent and remained steady thereafter: EPW Research Foundation, "Prices in Perspective", p. 677.

[2] Morris-Jones, "Whose Emergency", p. 455.

either backing the Congress (the CPI), growing sullen in opposition (CPI[M]), or languishing in prison (the Naxalites).[3] The young, once the vanguard of "total revolution", were tiring of radicalism. Indeed, just a couple of months before the Emergency a poll of university students revealed the extent of depoliticisation: 52 per cent supported one-party democracy and found any kind of social conflict "undesirable".[4]

But the Allahabad judgment and the persistence of a latent—and in some states overt—social crisis provided new fodder to the opposition, including the Hindu nationalists of the RSS, Mrs Gandhi's *bête noire*, whose contribution to the JP Movement also partly explains its resilience.

The JP Movement: A Symptom of Larger Threats

By early 1975 Indian politics was more polarised than it had ever been. Crucially, this polarisation was not rooted in ideas. If Mrs Gandhi declared off and on that she detested all "isms", Jayaprakash Narayan said once he did "not believe in any ideology".[5] Their fight was more about power and morality.

Over the span of just a few months, Narayan had transformed into a powerful political operator. It certainly helped his cause that he could cash in on the medley of opposition parties which had turned to him in 1974. Moreover, the parties themselves had come around to the efficacy of consolidation. That year Piloo Mody, for instance, was to be seen writing to fellow Swatantra MP Minoo Masani suggesting a coalition of "all non-Marxist parties" to oppose the Congress.[6] In August, along with five other parties, Swatantra merged with the BKD to form the BLD. And while the latter joined all major opposition parties barring the CPI(M) in the cross-party talks of November 1974 and February 1975, the CPI(M) did in fact campaign alongside Narayan and the other parties for Mrs Gandhi's ouster in those months.[7] This was the beginning of a bipolar party system in which a united opposition—after fits and starts in 1967 under the SVD banner and failure in 1971–2—possibly led by Narayan from the mid-1970s

---

[3] For instance, in 1973 between 15,000 and 50,000 Naxalites were incarcerated and 2000 killed in West Bengal alone: Frankel, *India's Political Economy*, p. 458.

[4] Malik and Marquette, "Democracy and Alienation in North India", pp. 43–5.

[5] Shah, *Protest Movements in Two Indian States*, p. 103.

[6] Masani to Mody, 6 June 1974, cited in Ankit, "Janata Party (1947–77)", p. 43.

[7] The CPM's Jyoti Basu and the DMK's M. Karunanidhi were invited to the first conference but chose not to attend. Karunanidhi sent his MPs to represent him.

on, would confront the Congress not just on the streets but at the polls; and not just on the basis of moral arguments against corruption but in the context of a severe economic crisis.[8] Gujarat was to be the laboratory of this experiment, which was taken up by Bihar soon after.

Gujarat: The Crucible of Protest

It was against a backdrop of crisis that the protests began in 1973. The rains had been scant for the second year in a row, throwing up dust and turmoil, whilst foodgrains and government rations remained scarce. Global commodity prices threw another unforeseeable spanner into the works: the OPEC oil embargo, which pushed up prices by 400 per cent, worsened India's balance of payments.[9] In Gujarat, as elsewhere, the price of meat, foodgrains, and edible oil had risen by over 30 per cent. Oil, butter, and kerosene were to be found mainly in the black market. But—and this was unique to the state—while inflation was making quick work of real income, Chief Minister Chimanbhai Patel was busy colluding with the state's leading groundnut oil barons, pushing prices up even higher.

Patel, who had taken office in July that year by replacing Ghanshyam Oza, was a master politician more than a statesman.[10] Once a professor of economics, he had ventured into politics in the late 1960s with some success as a Congress bagman. Already by 1972 his moves had resulted in the ouster of two chief ministers.[11] In February that year, when Mrs Gandhi anointed Oza chief minister in order to keep out the state's leading troika—Ratubhai Adani, Kantilal Ghia, and Patel himself—the arrangement did not last long. Indeed, it took Patel just seventeen months to have Oza brought down amidst accusations that the latter had dipped into a slush fund paid for by Gujarati industrialists to purchase defectors. But once he replaced Oza the groundnut tycoons that had propelled him into the job came to him demanding their pound of flesh: they expected him to secure funding

---

[8] See, *inter alia*, Manor, "Indira and After", pp. 315–24; Joshi and Desai, "Towards a More Competitive Party System in India", pp. 1091–116.

[9] Oil prices rose from $2.90 a barrel to $11.65 between September and December 1973: Yergin, *The Prize*, p. 784.

[10] Shah, *Protest Movements in Two Indian States*, pp. 24–7.

[11] He had played a minor role in toppling Jivraj Mehta's government in 1963, and a major one in 1971 when his defection from the Congress (O) brought an end to Hitendra Desai's chief ministership: Jones and Jones, "Urban Upheaval in India", p. 1014.

from Delhi to dam the Narmada river.[12] Patel then proceeded to grease palms in the capital, offering, in one estimate, Rs 40 million to fund the grand old party's campaign in the upcoming Uttar Pradesh mid-term election in exchange for the dam. This sum Gujarat's groundnut lobby gladly furnished, for the concessions that Patel had managed to extract from the centre—higher groundnut prices in the state, fewer export restrictions—had allowed them to make that sum many times over.[13] Also to Uttar Pradesh's benefit, and Gujarat's detriment, grain was shipped in large quantities from the latter to the former to ensure stable prices and an electoral victory in UP. In the event, the centre's monthly allotment of grain to Gujarat fell from 105,000 tons in June 1973 to 35,000 in November. Patel, in short, had given the stamp of approval to both a massive increase in edible oil prices and a grain shortage. As a result in 1973 Gujarat's people were confronted with a rather incongruous situation: record groundnut production, which had quadrupled in a year, even as they were paying twice what they did only a while earlier for their staple grain and edible oil.[14]

With inflation levels well over 20 per cent, the middle classes in the state took to the streets. In an unrelated development, Gujarat's bullock capitalists began a revolt of their own, forming the Khedut Samaj to pressure the government into jettisoning a ceiling bill and a levy on paddy fields. Meanwhile, at the Gujarat University (GU) academics railed against Patel's meddling, for he had colluded with university managements to purge academic staff from governing bodies and brought back a GU vice chancellor who had only recently been forced to resign. The aggrieved wrote furious columns in vernacular newspapers, denouncing the Congress and its corruption.[15]

But it was only when a students' *morcha* got under way that the protest movement gained momentum. The state's 160,000 university students had begun railing against the precariousness of their lives. Whilst rioting, they swiped grain from groceries, burned down canteens, carried off empty oil tins, and banged on *thalis* (metal plates)—all acts of symbolic significance.

---

[12] The Madhya Pradesh and Gujarat governments had been locked in dispute over the matter for more than a decade. Neither side could agree on the amount of compensation for submerged land and water-sharing arrangements.

[13] The lobby was particularly powerful in the state. Gujarat accounted for a fifth of the national groundnut produce: Research and Policy Division, *Genesis of President's Rule in Gujarat*, p. 1.

[14] Jones and Jones, "Urban Upheaval in India", p. 1017.

[15] Ibid., pp. 1012–33; Shah, *Protest Movements in Two Indian States*, pp. 3–60; Special Correspondent, "Landed and Landless in Surat District", pp. 974–7.

Soon, they were endorsed by an array of organisations: the RSS-affiliated Akhil Bharatiya Vidyarthi Parishad (ABVP), the most powerful students' union in the state; the Shikshak Mandal, a union of Ahmedabad's primary schoolteachers; the Gujarat State Secondary Teachers Federation; and the Gujarat University Area Teachers Association. More or less the entire education sector was up in arms against Patel and his onslaughts on academic freedom, and on the living standards of students and staff alike.[16]

As the number of protesters swelled through the second half of 1973, Patel was running out of options, his efforts at countermobilisation proving ineffective. Two moves in December that year—measures against black marketeers and hoarders, and a ban on food exports—backfired, enraging the very farmers and traders on whose support the chief minister so heavily relied. By now the Congress (O), Jana Sangh, and factions of the Congress (R) opposed to Patel had joined the protests.[17] On 25 January 1974 the demonstrations reached fever pitch when the newly formed Nav Nirman Andolan, an outfit led by teachers, lawyers, and students that wanted Patel's head, declared a state-wide *bandh*. The police "clashed" with protesters in thirty-three towns across the state, killing forty-two of them; teachers fasted and courted arrest; ration shops were pillaged, "animals dressed as ministers" paraded, and mock funerals of Patel and Mrs Gandhi staged.[18] Three days later the armed forces were sent into the state, forging a peace that lasted but a few days.

Delhi then dispatched the union law minister, H.R. Gokhale, to Ahmedabad to assess the situation. In meetings choreographed by Patel, he spoke to teachers and students who assured him that there had scarcely been any violence in the state and that their demands were being met. But when the law minister was heading back to the governor's residence where he had been put up, he encountered, quite by chance, a large crowd of protesters who brought him up to date with the state of affairs. He realised

---

[16] Ibid., pp. 20–2; Jones and Jones, "Urban Upheaval in India", pp. 1022–3.

[17] In the main, it was the Adani faction of the Congress (R) that backed the protests. But after the Gujarat assembly was dissolved in March, both Patel and Adani switched sides: the former lent support to the protests to prevent the latter's ascent. As for the Jana Sangh, they joined in the demonstrations only "to embarrass the Congress", but on 10 January, when Patel—with whom it sympathised—became a target, it withdrew. See Jones and Jones, "Urban Upheaval in India", pp. 1023, 1025; Wood, "Extra-Parliamentary Opposition in India", pp. 317–18; Shah, *Protest Movements in Two Indian States*, pp. 32–60.

[18] Wood, "Extra-Parliamentary Opposition in India", p. 318.

that what he had witnessed was only a staged performance, that grievances were genuine. Gokhale thereupon arranged for the release from prison of a few students in order to assess the situation further. However, no sooner had the students been released than they were re-arrested; in fact the scene turned into a riot right before Gokhale's eyes. *Lathis* rained down upon students, protesters, and even on the state's education minister who tried frantically to restrain the police. On 9 February the emissary returned to Delhi; within hours of his arrival it transpired that Patel had offered his resignation. The assembly was suspended and President's Rule imposed. Peace returned to the state. Or so it was thought.

Just days later, Gujaratis took to the streets once again, this time pressing for the dissolution of the suspended assembly after it emerged that Patel was drumming up support to have one of his lieutenants, Thakorbhai Patel, made chief minister. By then even the Congress high command had grown uncomfortable with his machinations. On 1 March Chimanbhai Patel was expelled from the party. He then launched a new outfit, the Kisan Mazdoor Lok Paksha, and joined the protesters in their demand for dissolution of the assembly, the bent politician now his own traducer.[19] Ten days later it appeared that the ructions were finally coming to an end. Morarji Desai went on a hunger strike, pressuring Mrs Gandhi to dissolve the assembly. By then, all Jana Sangh and Congress (O) MLAs had already resigned, as had ninety-five Congress legislators, often under pressure: some only did so after their families were threatened; others after their houses had been burned down; still other parliamentarians were "publicly beaten, a few were tarred or stripped naked and forced to ride on donkeys."[20] Four days into Desai's fast Mrs Gandhi capitulated, ending a four-month period of intermittent protests and riots that had left 103 dead and 8237 behind bars. The violence subsided as suddenly as it had begun.[21] It would take twelve months before history repeated itself with protests, riots, and another hunger strike by Desai.

[19] The party won only 12 of the state's 182 seats in the June 1975 elections. Patel even lost his own seat.

[20] Jones and Jones, "Urban Upheaval in India", p. 1029; Wood, "Extra-Parliamentary Opposition in India", p. 319.

[21] Students were given two additional concessions to achieve this result: examinations for the year were cancelled and automatic promotions given to all except those in their final year of study: Jones and Jones, "Urban Upheaval in India", p. 1031.

The troubles in Gujarat had ended, but the discomfiture remained. At a public meeting of the Navnirman Yuvak Samiti, the youth organisation that had been at the centre of the protests in Ahmedabad, a speaker channelled some of the pent-up vitriol: "Indira is not *mataji*. She is worse than a witch. In olden days, people did not allow even the shadow of a widow to fall on them as this was considered inauspicious. Today, because of this widow, there is corruption and rising prices." His follow-up advocated guerrilla warfare. But by then the locus of extra-parliamentary opposition had already shifted 1500 kilometres to the east. The new slogan was "Bihar *bhi* Gujarat *banega*" (Bihar, too, will become Gujarat).[22]

Bihar Takes Over: The Rise of JP

In Bihar events took on a familiar look: protests fuelled by inflation and youth unemployment met by an obstinate state leadership bent on delegitimising them; riots and all-round escalation; recourse to paramilitaries and the police; curfews and a precarious peace. Yet of equal note were the differences between the two states. Quite unlike Gujarat, which was one of the richest states in the republic, Bihar had year after year recorded the lowest per capita income in the country. Around 92 per cent of its 56 million citizens lived in villages, cultivating plots averaging less than three acres. Politics here had been tempestuous: eleven governments had ruled in Patna between 1967 and 1974, years in which the state had thrice been placed under President's Rule.

Here, too, the protests were orchestrated by the ABVP, with the Samajwadi Yuvjan Sabha, the Socialist student union, playing a supporting role. Another major asset of the state's demonstrators was the leadership of Jayaprakash Narayan, a native of Bihar, the long-standing veteran of the protest idiom who had come out of retirement to lead the country into "total revolution", no less.[23]

As a young Gandhian, Narayan had honed these skills as a bit-player in the Quit India Movement of 1942, organising underground activities, training guerrillas in Nepal, sabotaging railway lines, and writing pamphlets in praise of Marxism. "I even plodded through some chapters of *Das Kapital*", he later said of his radical past.[24] But like many other nationalists he grew disillu-

---

[22] Shah, *Protest Movements in Two Indian States*, pp. 50, vii.

[23] Tiwari, *Democracy and Dissent*, pp. 162–74.

[24] Singh, "A New Wave from the Old India", p. 52. His master's thesis was essentially a defence of historical materialism: Salter, "Swaraj and Sweepers", p. 107.

sioned in the early postcolonial years with the party that had been his calling, and left it to join the Socialist party. This period, especially 1952–3, had marked the peak of his career, the highlight of which was his talks with Nehru about the possible absorption of his party into the Congress fold. This failed to materialise, removing Narayan from the line of succession to the premiership, but winning him in the process a dedicated support base which, like him, believed that to hold power was inevitably to be corrupted.[25]

JP left politics in 1954, donating half of his fifty-acre farm and dedicating his life to Vinoba Bhave's Gandhi-inspired Sarvodaya Movement. Its flagship programme was Bhoodan, which aimed to convince landlords by moral suasion to distribute their lands to cultivators, who were to collectively run them. As votaries of welfarism and rural autarky, Sarvodayites were wedded to, as it were, a quixotic fusion of socialism and paternalism. In essence, theirs was a socialism premised on the kind of charity that the upper-caste gentry could extend to landless Dalits without jeopardising their class interests. "Nature's planning is never partial. When it gives appetite to the child, it not only provides the mother [the gentry] with the necessary food, but also inspires her to feed the child [peasants]", Bhave reasoned. This resonated with Narayan's own views on society, one in which "organic communities" would eliminate elections, parliamentary democracy, and the unwholesome divisiveness inherent in "Western" polities. Fifteen years into his Sarvodaya endeavours a sense of disenchantment overcame Narayan: it dawned on him that Bhoodan and Sarvodaya were not going to end rural poverty anytime soon.[26]

In fact, Bhoodan was a spectacular failure. In Bihar, Ground Zero of the movement, it had in 1951 set for itself a five-year target: the "redistribution" of 3,200,000 acres of land from landlords to the landless.[27] But, more than a decade after the programme was supposed to have ended, only 311,000 acres had reached peasant hands, most of them either non-arable

---

[25] Transcript of interview with Jayaprakash Narayan, Acc. No. 323, NMML Oral History Project, pp. 121–2; Scarfe and Scarfe, *J.P.*, pp. 171–2. On his allergy to state power, see Carrasco, "Jayaprakash Narayan and *Lok Niti*".

[26] This paragraph draws on Bhattacharjea, *Unfinished Revolution*, pp. 55–8, 97, 165; Shah, "Ideology of Jayaprakash Narayan", pp. 511–14; Morris-Jones, "The Unhappy Utopia", p. 1031.

[27] The scare quotes are warranted. Bhoodan lands were always only temporarily pledged to peasants. The latter never got to own them.

or of dubious ownership.[28] Narayan's native Bihar had even witnessed an inchoate class war in the late 1960s that was quite removed from the placatory politics of Bhoodan: spontaneous "communist-inspired mobs" expropriated landlords, causing "destruction of property worth more than six crores", a perturbed Narayan noted; landowners, in turn, organised *kisan sabhas* (peasants' associations) to suppress protests.[29] Narayan spent much of his time at Musahari, a particularly violent flashpoint in the state, but his Gandhian "trusteeship" dogma fell on deaf ears.[30]

Branching out from agrarian issues in Bihar, he then tried making his voice felt on the national scene by adopting various conservative positions: party politics should be replaced by a "coalition government" of all parties, Hindi imposed on the South, bank nationalisation reversed, and Mrs Gandhi ejected from office for her alliance with communists.[31] But then, in the early 1970s, he found a new bugbear: corruption, "public enemy number one".[32] Laying into every shape and form of it in *Everyman's Weekly*, a journal he founded in July 1973, Narayan urged the corrupt Congress to relinquish power. In his new avatar he now ran afoul of his old Sarvodaya allies, including Vinoba Bhave, who counselled him against his "negative *satyagraha* [which] had no place in independent India."[33] By this point Narayan could not care less what his old mentor thought. He attributed Bhoodan's failure to its fixation with "building from below", whereas he was now advocating "building from all directions".[34] Culling a phrase from Marxist orthodoxy, he argued for a "total revolution" that would lay waste the present political order and replace parliamentary democracy with a "communitarian or partyless democracy".[35] On other occasions he appeared less certain of his goals: "as far as this movement is concerned, partyless

---

[28] Jannuzi, "India's Rural Poor", p. 188.

[29] Bhattacharjea, *Unfinished Revolution*, p. 166ff.

[30] Scarfe and Scarfe, *J.P.*, pp. 209–14. The classist logic of "trusteeship", as captured by its instigator M.K. Gandhi, was that "capitalists are fathers and workers are children": Addy and Azad, "Politics and Culture in Bengal", p. 106.

[31] Scarfe and Scarfe, *J.P.*, p. 182; Prasad, *Jayaprakash Narayan*, p. 53.

[32] Masani, *Is JP the Answer?*, pp. 50–1.

[33] Bhave's argument was essentially one of national security. Protests were weakening the country, he contended, and this was playing into the hands of the United States, Pakistan, and China. See Harris, "Sarvodaya in Crisis", p. 1041; Narayan, *Prison Diary*, p. 7.

[34] Harris, "Sarvodaya in Crisis", p. 1041.

[35] Prasad, *Jayaprakash Narayan*, pp. 126, 136.

democracy has nothing to do with it. This movement is within the party system, within the Constitution."[36] All the same, the idea was important insofar as it achieved for Narayan's movement a following vast enough for it to constitute a threat to Mrs Gandhi's rule.

But what, in real terms, was his "total revolution"? Narayan's pronouncements suggest it was nothing more than a complex of antinomies designed to triangulate on every possible issue. On the one hand it was a "non-partisan" movement, not "anti-Congress as such"; on the other it sought a grand coalition to overthrow the grand old party: "the Right and the Left must realise that their enemy is the same."[37] This revolution was different from the "Marxian" one because it forsook "coercive means"; nevertheless, one of its key features was "the paralysing of the administration".[38] The demand for "direct democracy" came along with calls for enhancing the powers of unelected *sangharsh samitis*—"watchdogs" that could "ask an MLA to resign if he goes wrong."[39] What would the post-revolutionary utopia look like? At times Narayan suggests all production would be "brought under collective ownership and control"; just a few pages later, "collectivisation" and the "redistribution of land" are deemed futile because such ideas "might require 60 to 70 per cent of the population to be repressed [*sic*]."[40] But the inconsistencies mattered little. Narayan was frank that his was a politics without ideological content: "what was wanted was the end of all ideologies", he once said to the *Statesman*.[41] Some aspects of his revolutionary ideology, however, remained consistent through his oeuvre, especially those relating to targets and political élan: the problems facing society (the black market, inflation, corruption, "inefficiency"); contempt for the academy (abolish degrees, flush out students from the universities and send them to toil in the countryside); the reliance on Hindu metaphors ("purifying" and "cleansing" the body politic with personal "sacrifices"); and appeals to the Indian genius (the problem with "present political and administrative institutions" was that they were "foreign transplantations"; the focus on "industrialisation and technology ... in western society" was unsuited to India).[42]

---

[36] Ostergaard, *Nonviolent Revolution in India*, p. 121.

[37] Narayan, *Towards Total Revolution*, vol. 4, pp. 66–7, 143.

[38] Ibid., vol. 1, p. 221; vol. 4, pp. 80–1.

[39] Ibid., vol. 1, pp. 248–52; vol. 4, p. 91.

[40] Ibid., vol. 1, pp. 52, 60.

[41] Chandra, *In the Name of Democracy*, p. 151.

[42] Narayan, *Towards Total Revolution*, vol. 2, pp. 85–6, 117; vol. 1, p. 192.

When protests broke out in Gujarat and Bihar, events were already ahead of Narayan before he expressed an interest in them. Invigorated by Chimanbhai Patel's dismissal, he later wrote in the pages of *Everyman's Weekly*: "for years I was groping to find a way out ... I wasted two years trying to bring about a politics of consensus. It came to nothing ... Then I saw the students in Gujarat bring about a political change with the backing of the people ... and I knew that this was the way out."[43] But the action had taken place much too quickly for him to intercede. In Bihar, his home turf, things would be different.

Here, the student protests of December 1973 had by mid-January 1974 roiled into a complete rejection of Congress rule. By then, all the opposition parties had come together to call for a state-wide *bandh*. And by mid-February the student unions too had formed an amalgam of their own: the Bihar Chhatra Sangharsh Samiti (BCSS). Presided by Lalu Prasad Yadav, a future chief minister, the BCSS brought together Jana Sanghis, Sarvodayites, and Socialists, excluding only the Communists from their ranks. On 18 March, inspired by the dissolution of the assembly in Gujarat three days earlier, the BCSS staged a *gherao*, besieging the governor's residence and the Patna assembly, offering bangles and vermilion to MLAs, and parading goats branded with the names of cabinet ministers.[44] This was followed by riots. Gangs of burglars and arsonists sauntered about Bihar's towns, railway stations were attacked, bombs set off in fire stations, bricks hurled against post offices, "posh hotels" and food warehouses looted, and the army called in and given instructions to shoot at sight.[45]

On 23 March, amidst the chaos, Narayan sought to hijack the movement by demanding Chief Minister Abdul Ghafoor's resignation. As the self-styled conscience of the nation, Narayan could lend the protests the aura of respectability needed to get members of the political classes and the bourgeoisie on board. Many of them soon joined the movement. Early converts included opposition leaders K.B. Sahay of the Congress (O) and the SSP's Karpoori Thakur, both ex-chief ministers. The latter even ventured to call for a "jihad to end Congress misrule".[46] On 5 June Narayan had

---

[43] Narayan in the *Everyman's Weekly*, 3 August 1974, cited in *Why Emergency?*, p. 23.

[44] Tiwari, *Democracy and Dissent*, p. 38.

[45] Ibid., p. 34; Shah, *Protest Movements in Two Indian States*, p. 91; Chandra, *In the Name of Democracy*, p. 40.

[46] Shah, *Protest Movements in Two Indian States*, p. 86.

the student vanguard accede to his peremptory ways: "I won't agree to be a leader only in name. I will take the advice of all ... but the decisions will be mine and you will have to accept them."[47] Over the next months, what became the JP Movement grew from strength to strength, forming *janata sarkars* (parallel "people's governments") across the state, taking over power grids and ration shops; collecting funds; creating local bureaucracies, courts, and even armies; and exhorting citizens to withhold taxes and resign from public-sector jobs.[48]

The uneasy coalition of sectional interests that the JP Movement brought together in Bihar had its high point during the *bandh* of 3–5 October 1974, which succeeded in "paralysing the government", as Narayan had hoped. With the armed forces brought in, curfew imposed, and all communications and railway lines either shut down or derailed, Patna resembled a city under siege. The dialectic of popular protest and police suppression went through at least six peaks and troughs between March and November before petering out, mainly because the movement failed to make inroads in the countryside, garner working-class support, and sustain enthusiasm in the face of a rising death toll. Moreover, unlike Gujarat where the Congress could barely muster any support for its counter-protests, Mrs Gandhi's *morchas* in Bihar were fairly well attended throughout. Largely relying on the CPI's strong base in the state, which accounted for a third of the party's 550,000-strong cadre, the anti-JP demonstrations were not short of numbers, with attendances of 100,000 being common; nor were they wanting in muscle, for the Communist protesters who turned up at rallies were "armed not only with *lathis* but other weapons." They were in fact instrumental in "subdu[ing] JP's movement".[49]

The limitations of the JP Movement were compensated for by its boldness in action. This confidence derived in part from the RSS's manpower—12,000–15,000 activists in Bihar—which came along with endorsements from the Congress (O), the Socialists, the BLD, and the "*ad hoc* collaboration" offered by the Communists. With these resources at his disposal, the Gandhian leader was quick to make his peace with politi-

---

[47] Ostergaard, *Nonviolent Revolution*, p. 381.

[48] Ibid., pp. 203–7; Shah, *Protest Movements in Two Indian States*, pp. 99–134. These "governments" were created in only 20 of the state's 587 "blocks", the largest unit of governance below the district level.

[49] Sen, *A Traveller and the Road*, p. 341. See also Sen Gupta, "Communism Further Divided", p. 156; Tiwari, *Democracy and Dissent*, p. 93; Nargolkar, *JP's Crusade for Revolution*, pp. 137–8.

cal violence, reasoning that the protests were not of his making, that it was impossible to depoliticise such mass-scale movements, and that the Hindu nationalists would eventually "undergo a sea-change" and reform their ways.[50]

The Sangh Parivar: The Subtext of the JP Movement?

There was nevertheless enough convergence between the JP Movement and the Hindu nationalist organisations for Narayan to remark in 1975 that the "Bihar movement and RSS's work are fundamentally the same."[51] Broadly, their worldviews converged: both Narayan and the Sangh championed decentralisation; rejected the socialism and secularism that they saw as the Congress' ideological imports from the West; and claimed they aspired to M.K. Gandhi's vision of an indigenous utopia, including its eulogy to cottage industry and village life.[52]

Certainly, Narayan let on that he was not particularly hung up on the Sangh Parivar. In his overtures to the CPI(M), for instance, he said to Jyoti Basu in 1974, "if you join" the movement "these fellows [i.e. the RSS] will run away"; Narayan suggested that he had taken them on board only on sufferance, for "our party is not there [*sic*], nothing is there, and they have an organisation."[53] It is likely that these were but superficial extenuations that Narayan cared little about so long as they served his purposes: Basu was convinced and the CPI(M) organised major JP rallies in Calcutta where it was not possible to rely simply on the RSS' meagre Bengali cadres. But the CPI(M) was not fooled for long: in November 1974, concluding that the Sangh was at the centre of the movement, it decided that the party best sit the rest of it out.[54]

The Left could be jettisoned with no love lost, but the relationship between the JP Movement and the Hindu nationalists was another matter. Here, the connection was more organic. Narayan's personal rapport with

---

[50] Narayan, *Prison Diary*, p. 58.

[51] Jaffrelot, *The Hindu Nationalist Movement*, p. 255.

[52] Fox, "Gandhian Socialism and Hindu Nationalism", p. 239.

[53] Transcript of interview with Jyoti Basu, Acc. No. 781, NMML Oral History Project, p. 118.

[54] Chandra, *In the Name of Democracy*, pp. 56–7. After the Allahabad ruling, the CPM gave its tacit support to Narayan's calls for Mrs Gandhi's resignation, agreeing in principle but refusing to campaign alongside the other opposition parties.

RSS leaders helped: in 1967 they had laboured shoulder to shoulder, conducting relief work for the victims of the Bihar drought while the state looked the other way. It was whilst working on such endeavours that Narayan struck up a friendship with Nanaji Deshmukh, a Jana Sangh leader from Uttar Pradesh who too had dabbled in Bhoodan during the mid-1950s. Their comradeship would serve as the isthmus connecting the larger organisations behind them.[55]

If Narayan and Deshmukh were natural allies, it did not mean that the entire leadership of the Sangh Parivar had no reservations about the JP Movement. Since at least the mid-1960s Hindu nationalists had been divided on tactics. As one camp saw it, exorcising political "untouchability"—to use the term in which many of its leaders described the legitimacy deficit that had plagued Hindu nationalist organisations since Gandhi's assassination—required developing a popular front strategy, albeit one of the Right. For Balraj Madhok and other Jana Sanghis, it was time to replace the RSS' *sangathanist* strategy—strengthening the grassroots and eschewing high politics until the time was ripe—with top-down "Indianisation", which in their vocabulary meant Hinduisation. And here public discourse could be altered by uniting the Congress (O), Swatantra, and the Jana Sangh behind a common platform.[56] In the other camp were the proponents of a more thoroughgoing populism. As Atal Bihari Vajpayee, Lal Krishna Advani, and kindred Sanghis saw it, the times called for the incorporation of socialist themes into the Parivar's core message of social conservatism. Only by supporting nationalisation and welfare and participating in workers' strikes and social movements could Hindu nationalists reach out to a wider audience. The dismal showing of all the conservative parties at the polls between 1971 and 1974 made their task considerably easier.[57]

The Parivar, then, was in need of a strategy more in tune with the dispensation. In the event, the top leadership of the RSS showed its preference for Vajpayee's populism—which at any rate was more in line with the *sangathanism* it was familiar with—over Madhok's high-political bridge-building. In practice, the line that Vajpayee toed in the early 1970s, supporting land ceilings and declaring a "National War on Poverty", accommodated Madhok's position through tactical arrangements with the Congress (O) at

[55] Jaffrelot, *The Hindu Nationalist Movement*, pp. 230–54.
[56] Interview with Balraj Madhok, 10 November 1990, New Delhi.
[57] Jaffrelot, *The Hindu Nationalist Movement*, pp. 260–77.

election time. However, in 1971 this strategy, which found expression in a Grand Alliance, failed to prevent Mrs Gandhi's re-election. Moreover, in his own speeches, replete with references to his "concern for the underdog" and "insistence on social justice and equity", Vajpayee increasingly sounded like a poor understudy of Mrs Gandhi.[58]

The troubles in Gujarat and Bihar offered a way out of the impasse. By the early months of 1975 Hindu nationalist leaders, including K.N. Govindacharya, were regularly seen sharing podia with socialists and conservatives alike; by then a third of the BCSS' steering committee were ABVP members.[59] And on 25 June 1975 Deshmukh was made secretary of the Lok Sangharsh Samiti, the confederacy of opposition parties that hoped to bring down Mrs Gandhi's government.[60] In short they were untouchables no more. The JP Movement is "a force for the good of the society", the RSS' *sarsanghchalak* (head) Balasaheb Deoras declared in December 1974. The encomium was reciprocated: "if you are a fascist, then I too am a fascist", Narayan told an RSS crowd in March 1975.[61] He was only half joking. What was remarkable was that this new acceptability had involved precious little compromise on the part of the Parivar. There was no sign of moderation, however defined. The RSS weekly, the *Organiser*, continued peddling conspiracy theories in its editorials. In early January 1975, for instance, it suggested that Nehru had had M.K. Gandhi "mysteriously bumped off" in 1948 in a move to consolidate power. Similarly, Mrs Gandhi was blamed for having Sangh president Deendayal Upadhyaya "brutally murdered" in 1968.[62]

In hindsight, the legitimacy that the JP Movement bestowed the Sangh Parivar was, perhaps, its most lasting achievement. In return, the Parivar helped JP to take his movement beyond Gujarat and Bihar.

A National Movement

Indeed, by the closing months of 1974, the JP Movement had acquired a pan-Indian following. In October that year the movement turned its attention to New Delhi and a new demand: Mrs Gandhi's resignation. As the

[58] Ibid., p. 252. See also Puri, "Era of Indira Gandhi", pp. 148–50.
[59] Interview with K.N. Govindacharya, 19 November 1990, New Delhi.
[60] Interview with Nanaji Deshmukh, 25 February 1994, New Delhi.
[61] *Why Emergency?*, pp. 49, 37.
[62] *Organiser*, 4 January 1975, cited in Chandra, *In the Name of Democracy*, p. 323.

protests began to gather momentum, a clash between its head and the ruler of the executive became inevitable. It was around this time that a number of figures, including P.N. Dhar, secretary of the Gandhi Peace Foundation Radhakrishna, and director of the Gandhian Institute of Studies Sugata Dasgupta took it into their heads that they could get Narayan and Mrs Gandhi to find a workable compromise. The face-to-face took place in the capital on 1 November. But even at the outset it was far from clear if it was possible for the two to hammer out any kind of agreement: Mrs Gandhi was working towards parliamentary supremacy while Narayan was putting together an extra-parliamentary coup.

As Sudipta Kaviraj has observed, with rhetoric borrowed from the Left, conservatism on land reform, the claim to Gandhi's legacy, middle-of-the-road oratorical skills, and dependence on populist coalitions, the two had more in common than either could care to admit.[63] There was also the similar background and the long history of family friendship between the Nehrus and the Narayans.[64] But there was one crucial point of divergence: both viewed JP's role in Indian political life rather differently. Having fashioned himself after M.K. Gandhi and having been one of his associates in the 1940s, Narayan had convinced himself, as had the press and the intelligentsia, that on his shoulders lay the burden of the nation's conscience and possible salvation. For his part, Narayan was quick to discern that since her ascent to power, his beloved "Indu" was beginning to find his shtick unwelcome.[65] In 1971, for instance, when Narayan organised a conference to condemn the genocide in East Pakistan, he discovered through the grapevine that Congress party members were warned not to attend.

---

[63] Kaviraj, "Indira Gandhi and Indian Politics", p. 1703.

[64] Narayan was educated at the universities of California (Berkeley), Iowa, and Wisconsin; Mrs Gandhi at Oxford. While both had received an expensive education in the West, there was, however, a qualitative difference: he lived in crummy hostels, first moonlighting by repackaging and selling at inflated prices local hair lotions and facial creams as exotic "Himalayan drugs", and then working in mines, factories, and abattoirs; Indira Gandhi, on the other hand, lodged in the finest hotels and sanatoria of the Continent. In the early 1930s, Narayan's wife, Prabhavati, had kept a correspondence with Mrs Gandhi's mother, Kamala Nehru. See transcript of the interview with Narayan, Acc. No. 323, NMML Oral History Project, p. 55; Masani, *Is JP the Answer?*, p. 7; Frank, *Indira*, pp. 367–8.

[65] Narayan called Indira Gandhi "Indu" as he had known her since her childhood, but this was less a term of endearment than a wish on his part to be seen as the paterfamilias.

Mrs Gandhi was not going to let a doddering arriviste take centre stage during an international crisis. "What does Indira think of herself? Does she think she can ignore me?" Narayan condescended to reply, "I have seen her as a child in frocks."[66]

The November 1974 meeting, then, was not merely a meeting between two politicians from opposite camps but a confrontation between rivals of old, more a face-off than the hoped for face-to-face. She offered to dismiss the Bihar administration if he would give up clamouring for the downfall of other state governments. But the way he saw it, the cards were stacked in his favour. Things could only get better for his insurgent movement. On account of her court case, her son's bungling of Maruti, corruption scandals, inflation, and growing inequality, she was damaged goods. In short, it was too early to call off his movement. Besides, caving in to her demands whilst his constituents awaited a far-reaching "total revolution" was a bad look. So he refused her offer and the talks broke down into mudslinging. She was establishing a "Soviet-backed dictatorship", he said.[67] His movement was in the pay of the CIA, she replied. He left the room threatening to double down and escalate the protests.

No sooner said than done. On 5 November he led a march in Patna to *gherao* the secretariat and the residences of ministers. The CRPF and BSF entered the scene, attacking the protesters with tear gas and *lathis*. During the episode Narayan was on the receiving end of some of the sticks raining down on the crowd. He demanded that people "face *lathis* and bullets, fill up jails" and allow their properties to be seized. "We must return to Gandhi", he announced. Addressing a rally with a huge portrait of his idol behind him, Narayan proclaimed, "I do not go about setting fires all over the country—the fire is already smouldering under the rulers' seats." Frenzied chants of "Inquilab Zindabad!" (Long Live the Revolution: a war-cry of the 1930s) rang out in the air.[68]

In a couple of weeks, however, the movement had died out. State repression and the bodies piling on the streets proved too much for JP's middle-class supporters who, in any case, had found a growing appreciation for Mrs Gandhi's new monetary discipline. Food prices had begun coming down from September 1974. In the last week of November, in a last-ditch effort, Narayan helped launch the National Coordination Committee of

[66] Jayakar, *Indira*, p. 170.
[67] Frank, *Indira*, p. 372.
[68] Singh, "A New Wave from the Old India", p. 50.

Students and Youth under the direction of ABVP leader Arun Jaitley.[69] Even so, students were returning to college in ever greater numbers while Narayan himself had come to rethink some of his positions. He had, for one, given up the idea of creating a "people's assembly". On 18 November he even agreed to meet Mrs Gandhi's "challenge" electorally: "Since the prime minister has dragged the conflict into the election arena, I shall take my position in the battlefield, not as a candidate, but as a leader", he announced, hedging his risks—leading from behind in effect insulated him from the consequences of defeat.[70]

The one stratum that could have lent the JP Movement the radical tenor it needed to sustain support, and perhaps even pushed Narayan and his allies into adopting substantive policies, was the organised working class whose interest he failed to elicit. Indeed, their own demonstrations of solidarity and resentment coeval with the protests in Gujarat and Bihar were instructive, as we will see below.[71]

Still, its weaknesses notwithstanding, the JP Movement soon staged a comeback, the hiatus having lasted just over a hundred days. On 6 March Narayan led a five-mile march through Delhi in what was the city's largest demonstration ever. Reportedly leading a crowd estimated at between 100,000 and 750,000, Narayan ended his rally at Parliament House where he presented the speaker with a "charter of demands". His calls for electoral reform, land redistribution, and Mrs Gandhi's resignation were, of course, unacceptable to the leadership.

The next month's headlines were dominated not so much by Narayan as by Morarji Desai, who was determined to see Gujarat succeed where Bihar had failed. In replacing Chief Minister Ghafoor with Jagannath Mishra on 11 April, Mrs Gandhi had seen to it that the Bihar agitation lost most of its bite. Desai had pre-empted a similar move in Gujarat on 2 April when he commenced a "fast unto death", demanding that the state go to the polls forthwith. The state was under President's Rule and Mrs Gandhi was hoping she could preserve the status quo until after the harvest season, by which time it would make perfect sense to announce a snap election: a contented countryside would allow her to coast to victory, rendering the

---

[69] The committee also had a second convenor, Anand Kumar, "a sort of dummy" whose lack of affiliation served to cloak ABVP hegemony: Chandra, *In the Name of Democracy*, p. 102.

[70] Masani, *Is JP the Answer?*, pp. 91–3.

[71] See below.

JP Movement harmless. Desai, seventy-nine, was an equally astute politician. As he confessed to the journalist Oriana Fallaci, this was "the battle I had been dreaming of ever since 1969", when Mrs Gandhi had split the party, pulling the rug from under his feet.[72] Now, a week into his fast, she gave in. Elections were to be held in early June.

The Political Economy of the JP Movement

The JP Movement did not pose a threat to Mrs Gandhi only because its leader was a personal rival gunning for her. Nor was the movement a threat only because it had received vital support from old nemeses, the RSS and Morarji Desai included. The deeper reason for the movement being a threat to Mrs Gandhi lay in the fact that it was the symptom of a deep socio-economic crisis that she, for all her populist promises, had failed to solve.

The Social Crisis of the 1970s

The JP Movement had sustained itself for so long not only because of the anger caused by the pervasive corruption of the Congress and the force of the organisations supporting it, but also because of social discontent.[73] This largely explains the magnitude of the protest. The popularity of the JP Movement reflected in particular the Congress' alienation of four strata: the smaller gentry, students, peasants, and the working class. While it was principally the first two that furnished the shock troops of the movement, the political participation of the other two—albeit in other less-organised fora—was of equal import in shaping the *zeitgeist* of unrest in the early and mid-1970s.[74]

At first sight the "bullock capitalists"—to use the Rudolphs' formulation for the middle peasantry—were unlikely protesters. Thus far they had successfully shot down the Congress' attempts to enforce ceilings on land ownership and adopt co-operative farming. As for the policies of the grand old party that had seen the light of day, they had benefited this class

---

[72] Fallaci, "Mrs Gandhi's Opposition", p. 17.

[73] The role of the RSS was equally important in the making of the Anna Hazare movement in the early 2010s. See Baloch, "Crisis, Credibility, and Corruption".

[74] For similar distinctions, see Wilson, "China and South Asia in the 1970s", p. 97; Weisskopf, "The Persistence of Poverty in India", p. 33ff.

immensely: with the abolition of *zamindari*, a whole new generation of former tenants had joined the ranks of the bullock capitalists. Lands owned by the old intermediary class were parcelled out and tenancy declined from 60 to 25 per cent.[75] The early decades of postcolonial rule enabled the bullock capitalists to consolidate power and wealth: their ranks filled legislative chambers across the republic; their incomes remain untaxed.[76] Still, by the early 1970s they had reason to be unhappy. Despite the agrarian rhetoric of Mrs Gandhi's Congress, the Fourth Five-Year Plan (which spanned 1969–74) was simply a repeat of the Third (1961–6), allocating just over a fifth of its outlay to agriculture at a time when over four-fifths of the national population lived in the countryside. State trading in foodgrains had depressed procurement prices during the inflationary spiral of 1971–2, giving farmers the impression that industries and the war economy were all that mattered to the country's rulers. Compounding this was the 4 million ton drop in foodgrain production in the financial year 1971–2, the result of poor rain. And, *a fortiori*, the threat posed by the Congress Left had not entirely receded: the steady barrage of pamphlets, books, and parliamentary interventions from Congress radicals indicated that expropriation and collectivisation were not yet things of the past.[77] Their revolt was plain to see: farmers, in the main, chose not to co-operate with procurement agents, hoarding grain or selling it on the black market instead.[78] New agrarian parties mushroomed, the most important of which were the formations headed by Charan Singh, leader of Uttar Pradesh's gentry.[79] Singh's protestations were aimed at remedying the worsening terms of

---

[75] In other words, those cultivating their own land increased from 40 to 75 per cent of the population engaged in agriculture.

[76] We follow the Rudolphs' delineation of bullock capitalists: those typically self-employed and self-funded producers whose landholdings are between 2.5 and 15 acres. Unlike large landowners, their holdings are not big enough to employ capital-intensive technologies or large numbers of wage labourers. See Rudolph and Rudolph, *In Pursuit of Lakshmi*, pp. 315, 340–2. On the non-taxation of farmers, see Maddison, *Class Structure and Economic Growth*, p. 109.

[77] *Congress Marches Ahead—VII*, pp. 108–11; Frankel, *India's Political Economy*, p. 254.

[78] As a consequence, the government's grain procurement fell by a third in 1973, compared with a year earlier: *Seminar*, vol. 189, no. 1 (May 1975), p. 10.

[79] After a brief career in the Congress, Charan Singh had parted ways with the grand old party to form the Bharatiya Kranti Dal in 1967, which, in 1974, swelled into the Bharatiya Lok Dal, a merger of seven conservative and "socialist" parties that represented kulak interests.

trade between agriculture and industry. Certainly, he was onto something: agriculture had grown by only 12.6 per cent between 1960 and 1969, while mining and large-scale manufacturing grew by 55.4 per cent.[80] With the agrarian crisis of the 1970s, his politics only gained purchase.

While the smaller gentry wanted a larger share of the national pie, the rural poor wanted in on it to start with. The latter's, then, were more primal concerns. The benefits of the production surge in the 1960s had on the whole been cornered by the bullock capitalists. They, with their larger landholdings, had been able to afford high-yielding varieties made available by novel dwarfing and hybridisation technologies, chemical fertilisers, better irrigation facilities, and other accoutrements of the green revolution.[81] Meanwhile, the rural population living in poverty—citizens spending less than Rs 15 a month—grew from 38 per cent in 1960–1 to 54 per cent in 1967–8.[82] Furthermore, job losses, real or perceived, associated with technological advances lent credence to the belief of commentators that sooner rather than later the green revolution would turn red.[83] In this narrative the old politics of vertical mobilisation—in which nota-

[80] Singh, *India's Poverty and Its Solution*, pp. xi–xiv *et passim*. While Singh framed his politics as a classless rural one, the tilt towards the middle and upper peasantry was never in question: Byres, "Charan Singh, 1902–87", pp. 139–89.

[81] This reflected in landholdings: bullock capitalists controlled 41.16 per cent of India's cultivated area in 1954–5, 51.74 per cent in 1971–2. See Visaria and Sanyal, "Trends in Rural Unemployment in India", p. 147.

[82] Bardhan, "On the Incidence of Poverty", p. 246. Rs 15 per month at 1960–1 prices was barely enough to eke out a living. At the time, merely to consume 2700 calories a day cost in raw ingredients Rs 9.61 per month. This was the minimum to maintain a "moderately" active lifestyle, an agrarian one of course being more demanding.

[83] Evidence now shows that the green revolution did in fact create jobs, in the main because high-yielding varieties and tractors led to double and triple cropping, which required more peasants to man farms and their ancillary services. But contemporary perceptions and the growing divergence between the lifestyles of the haves and have-nots would have sufficed to fuel discontent. In any case, the green revolution only took place in a handful of pockets in the country— Punjab, Haryana, and western Uttar Pradesh—where the pre-existence of larger landholdings and adequate irrigation facilities made them ideal sites for the installation of minor irrigation works and the testing of high-yielding varieties. See Bardhan, "Rural Employment, Wages, and Labour Markets", pp. 1063–6. On the disputed hue of the green revolution, see Frankel, *India's Green Revolution*, pp. 8–11 *et passim*.

bles made appeals to those lower down the hierarchy based on caste and traditional notions of deference—were to collapse and be superseded by a new horizontal mobilisation. Class solidarities would of course beget class war.[84] Peasant uprisings were brutally put down in Andhra Pradesh in 1969 and West Bengal in 1972.[85] To offset such occurrences, various outlays for drought relief, access to credit, and rural development were put in place by the central government in the early 1970s, but their impact, by all accounts, was "rather meagre".[86] Funds from such projects were sufficient only to cover 3 million farm hands; in practice even fewer were able to access them, for most of the rural poor possessed no land to collateralise loans with.[87] Moreover, population growth consistently outstripped job creation: survey after survey confirmed this. The Ministry of Agriculture, for instance, estimated in 1973 that 34 per cent of wage-seeking labourers were unemployed.[88]

Organised labour had reasons to protest too. While gross national product increased, and with it inflation, wages grew at only half the rate of GNP in the 1960s.[89] The decade that followed promised to be even uglier: between 1970 and 1973 real wages declined by 6 per cent. Strikes became routine in the Indian Railways, Central Reserve Police, Air India, public-sector steel plants, insurance companies, and banks. These necessitated a response. For her part Mrs Gandhi, her professed left-wing politics notwithstanding, took a dim view of the deteriorating industrial relations. She endeavoured to cripple the unions and create a "disciplined" and "committed" workforce that would cease being a hindrance to her macroeconomic objectives of maintaining low wages, boosting government savings, and increasing capital investment.[90] Her preference was the "pay commission model" in which

---

[84] Rudolph and Rudolph, *The Modernity of Tradition*, pp. 24–6.

[85] Gough, "Indian Peasant Uprisings", pp. 1391, 1405.

[86] Shetty, "Structural Retrogression in the Indian Economy", p. 211.

[87] Frankel, *India's Political Economy*, p. 498.

[88] Idem, "Compulsion and Social Change", p. 221.

[89] Blair, "Mrs Gandhi's Emergency", p. 254. Nehru and his daughter presided over a period in which the share of wages in GVA declined from 63.4 per cent in 1950–1 to 53.2 per cent in 1972–3. In other words, surplus value in the same period had grown from 36.6 to 46.8 per cent of GVA. See Table 12 in Selbourne, *An Eye to India*, p. 430.

[90] Her view, in essence, mirrored those of M.K. Gandhi's, who desired a paternalistic state—or, even better, a set of paternalistic private-sector industrialists—that would steward worker interests.

wages were settled not by bargaining but by fiat. Her cabinet was openly hostile to organised labour as well. Planning Minister D.P. Dhar, for instance, complained in 1974 that when workers "went on asking for more wages and bonus [*sic*], they snatched morsel [*sic*] from hungry mouths ... It became a vicious circle—wages chasing the prices and prices following the wages."[91] For such figures it certainly helped that industrial relations in India were built on a Congress superstructure. The largest national labour federation, the INTUC, was affiliated to the Congress and followed, on the whole, party diktat. Of this union Myron Weiner wryly observed once, "their loyalties are to the Congress Party, then to the present government, to the nation, and last of all to the workers."[92] In the early 1970s the ascendant S.A. Dange faction of the Communist trade union, AITUC, too, supported the incumbents, whom it saw as progressive. When the two unions formally entered into an agreement in February 1972 to form the National Council of Trade Unions, it only made overt what was already well known: that together INTUC and AITUC were essentially a trade-union cartel sustained by state patronage, and that they had virtually crowded out independent labour politics.[93] Furthermore, the RBI's decision to hike interest rates through 1974 had the effect of reducing the bargaining power of unions to push up wages in line with inflation.[94] There being little point in taking matters to the negotiating table, organised labour resorted to more strikes and demonstrations. The failure of Mrs Gandhi's industrial relations policy was palpable: in 1964, 7.7 million workdays were lost to strikes and lockouts; by 1974 the figure had shot up to 40.3 million.[95]

All in all, then, despite the Congress' corporatism, organised labour remained an important actor in the landscape of disaffection. The high point of working-class power was the railwaymen's strike of 1974, which showed not only the extent to which citizens could be mobilised for a cause in which demands were defined in material terms—here was a lesson for Jayaprakash Narayan—but also the limits of such struggles in the absence of external support, for the JP Movement stood aloof from it.

[91] *Congress Marches Ahead—VIII*, p. 166.

[92] Weiner, *The Politics of Scarcity*, p. 78.

[93] Punekar, "Trade Union Unity", p. 1071.

[94] *The Reserve Bank of India: Volume 3*, pp. 378–80. For similar developments in the advanced capitalist countries in the late 1970s and 1980s, see Tooze, *Crashed*, p. 44ff.

[95] Rudolph and Rudolph, *In Pursuit of Lakshmi*, p. 227.

Nearly two-thirds of the employees of the Indian Railways, which employed 1.8 million and was responsible directly or indirectly for the livelihood of one out of fifty Indians, participated in the strike of May 1974, which was brutally put down amidst dismissals and detentions. Because of the sheer scale of this state enterprise, the Indian Railways had always maintained a special place in the life of the republic. Each year, until as late as 2016, a separate budget was presented to parliament a few days before the union budget that covered everything else. Strong parliamentary control had typically meant that railwaymen got a raw deal. Their wages were settled by central government pay commissions that left them with little room for manoeuvre. Indeed, between 1947 and 1974 the three commissions that had deliberated on the subject had each systematically undervalued the dearness allowance that was supposed to factor in inflation. Worse, in this period a third of railwaymen—600,000—had had their contracts casualised: no job security, sick leave, or any kind of social protection, then, for these lives lived under the protective shadow of Nehruvian socialism. Unsurprisingly, discontent had been building up for years. In 1973 it reached a tipping point with the nationwide drought and inflationary spiral. It was only a matter of time before a radical trade-union organiser such as George Fernandes emerged on the scene, pushing for a confrontation with the state.[96]

Fernandes had lived a peripatetic life, running away from home aged sixteen to become a Catholic priest, before deciding three years later that the ecclesiastical world was a far from equal one: the rectors, he noted, had a high table for themselves and ate better food than the seminarians. He then left Bangalore to join the growing trade-union movement in Bombay. Rising through the ranks, he became in 1973 the leader of the socialist All-India Railwaymen's Federation (AIRF), one of the two major railway unions, the other being the Congress-controlled National Federation of Indian Railwaymen (NFIR). When Fernandes took over the AIRF—incidentally, one of his predecessors was Jayaprakash Narayan—it was a pale ghost of its former self. Large sections of it had switched to the Congress union— once described as a "professional strike-breaking unit"—to which workers went when they wanted a promotion or a transfer.[97] All that was left of the AIRF were a handful of socialists and Royists, followers of the CPI founder M.N. Roy and his doctrine of "radical humanism". At first, as AIRF presi-

---

[96] Sherlock, "Workers and Their Unions", pp. 2311–13.
[97] Ibid., p. 2311.

dent, Fernandes wanted to buy time, build an organisation of note before launching a strike. But it soon transpired that the conditions of workers were much worse, and for collective action much better, than he had imagined. In March 1974 he convened the National Coordination Committee for Railwaymen's Struggle, demanding immediate parity in wages with other public-sector undertakings; industrial-worker status, as stipulated by the 1919 ILO Convention, for all casually employed workers; an eight-hour work day; and a living wage. Within less than a month of the committee's existence he had consolidated enough support among the rail unions—by then the NFIR–AIRF distinction had ceased to matter—to threaten Delhi's rulers with a "Bharat *bandh*", a nationwide strike. "Realise the strength you possess", he said to a union crowd in March, "a seven days' strike of the Indian Railways, every thermal station in the country would close down. A ten days' strike … every steel mill in the country would close down … A fifteen days' strike … the country will starve."[98] Even P.N. Dhar, one of his harshest critics, was forced to concede that Fernandes was a "forceful personality, an indefatigable organiser."[99]

Leaving aside the threatening tone for a moment, Fernandes' demands, which in essence meant bringing wages and contracts of railway employees in line with other state-owned enterprises, would have struck anyone other than the Congress leadership as moderate. But as Mrs Gandhi's administration saw it, his demands entailed increasing government outlays by Rs 1350 crores. This crossed the soft state's red line for expenditure.[100] When the nationwide strike began on 8 May, the reaction of her government was, true to form, all fire and fury. First, the DIR was invoked to declare the strike illegal. Soon after, 60,000 were arrested under MISA. To prove the dispensability of the strikers, key passenger and freight services were kept running with the help of security forces. Railway fair-price

---

[98] *Why Emergency?*, p. 14; Selbourne, *An Eye to India*, pp. 14–18.

[99] The rest was less charitable, and more in line with Mrs Gandhi's assessment: "a demagogue who could inflame audiences with his fist-in-the-air oratory, and a political adventurer in need of a constituency": Dhar, *Indira Gandhi, the "Emergency", and Indian Democracy*, pp. 240–1.

[100] It was a strange time for the Indian Railways to worry about rising outlays: freight traffic, its main source of revenue, was set to grow by 75 per cent by the end of the Fifth Plan in 1979. Coupled with foreign aid and a nearly 4 per cent annual increase in passenger traffic meant that the fate of its coffers dictated against austerity. See the note on the "Freight Traffic Target for the Fifth Five Year Plan", 21 May 1973, Planning Commission Papers, File T&C/7(9)/73 vol. I.

shops were boarded up and the water and electricity supply to workers' quarters cut. "Red scare" tactics were used to discredit strikers in the eyes of the republic's *bien pensants*. The traitorous Fernandes, it was alleged, had written Mao a letter criticising the "ruthless repression" of the strike.[101] Then, left-wing leaders, among them the president of the republic V.V. Giri—who like Narayan had been one of Fernandes' predecessors as AIRF president—and the CPI trade-union leader S.A. Dange, were dispatched to inveigle the railwaymen into calling off the disruption to service.[102] In the event, under heavy repression by the army, the navy in Cochin, and the CRPF, the strike was called off on 28 May. In the purge that ensued, over 25,000 railway workers lost benefits and seniority, were evicted from their homes, and dismissed.

While the railwaymen's strike was the largest of its kind, it was far from being the only one. The strikes of Air India, Indian Airlines, and Life Insurance Corporation employees in 1972 and 1973 too had been put down in similar fashion, using a combination of police power and the threat or execution of layoffs and lockouts that the state had at its disposal.

New to the landscape of unrest was student radicalism.[103] This was no accident. The bulk of students enrolled in universities at the time belonged to a unique demographic cohort: coming of age in the 1960s, they were often first-generation literates, migrants from rural hinterlands aspiring to white-collar jobs. Inevitably, alienation, lack of cultural capital, the poor quality of education, and near-zero job prospects in a moribund economy fuelled protests.[104] In a 1967 documentary called "I Am 20", filmmaker S.N.S. Sastry questioned a number of twenty-year-olds born in 1947 about their thoughts on the nation that they were coeval with. The responses captured the disillusionment of the young in the same manner that some of the angsty films of the early and mid-1970s, *Sholay* and *Ankur* included, would later do. "I think of India when I think of long queues. People wait-

---

[101] *Why Emergency?*, p. 15.

[102] Giri had been one of the founders of the AIRF in 1924: transcript of interview with V.V. Giri, Acc. No. 379, NMML Oral History Project, p. 43; Lockwood, *The Communist Party*, p. 85.

[103] A few precedents existed: students had played important roles in Kerala when the Communist government was overthrown in 1959; in Tamil Nadu over the anti-Hindi protests of 1965; and in Andhra Pradesh during the call for a Telangana state in the late 1960s and early 1970s. See Jones and Jones, "Urban Upheaval in India", p. 1032.

[104] Naik, *Policy and Performance*, pp. 13–17.

ing patiently for buses, for rations", said a woman languidly. All that the postcolonial state had achieved was the "freedom to starve, to go naked, to die of hunger, and to go uneducated", an engineering student bitterly reflected.[105] Part of the problem was structural: in 1960–1 just over a million students were registered in colleges. A decade later there were three and a half times as many.[106] The apathy of the political classes compounded it. For Mrs Gandhi, education was not really a state concern. She assumed it was better handled by the private sector, which needed to encourage vocational learning to reduce the burden on colleges. Thinkers at India's premier research councils agreed. For the ICSSR's J.P. Naik, it would be in everyone's best interests "to reduce the spiralling demand for higher education." It was small wonder, then, that in 1974, India had "the dubious distinction of harbouring more than half the illiterate population of the world."[107] Nor was life exponentially better for the literates, the young amongst whom were entering the job market in hard times. A survey early in the Emergency revealed that 24 per cent of educated youths aged eighteen to twenty-four were out of work.[108] Accordingly, Mrs Gandhi's education policy was in a shambles: incidents of "student indiscipline" rose from 172 in 1960 to 3861 in 1970 and 11,540 in 1974.[109] In the latter year, enraged young Indians displayed a vanguardism in Gujarat and across the North that, as we have seen, led to protests that snowballed into the JP Movement, precipitating the Emergency.

In the final analysis, "total revolution" and its attendant *andolans*, *bandhs*, *dharnas*, *gheraos*, *hartals*, and *morchas* made perfect sense to the malcontent in Indian society.

The Limits of Promissory Politics

The economy aside, the magnitude of social discontent resulted also from the expectations that Mrs Gandhi had aroused by adopting a populist style from the 1967 election campaign onwards: she promised a lot but rarely delivered. For almost ten years she had held out hopes of meaningful

---

[105] Subramanian, "Midnight's Grown-ups". The film itself can be found on YouTube.

[106] Rudolph and Rudolph, *In Pursuit of Lakshmi*, p. 295.

[107] Naik, *Policy and Performance*, pp. 31, 6. For the view that the Nehruvian state shirked its education duties, see Sherman, "Education in Early Postcolonial India", pp. 504–20. This was "DIY socialism", she mordantly comments.

[108] Hart, "Explanations", p. 283.

[109] Rudolph and Rudolph, *In Pursuit of Lakshmi*, p. 300.

redistribution and a rise in living standards. As early as May 1967, after her electoral setback, she had the Congress Working Committee adopt a Ten-Point Programme, a wish list of socialist desiderata. During the time of the party split of 1969, election campaigns of 1971–2, and her opposition to the JP Movement in the years that followed, Mrs Gandhi continued to project the party as an agent of progress. But poverty did not go away and none of the promises were fulfilled. In 1971, Mrs Gandhi's party had declared in its manifesto that, if given another term, it would lower the land ceiling to 10 to 54 acres per family, depending on the quality of land and number of crop cycles per year. Laws to this effect were passed but the resistance put up by party leaders and state governments saw to it that they were poorly implemented.[110]

At the time of the Emergency, then, 57 per cent of rural households were either landless or held less than 2.5 acres—all together, they held just 7 per cent of the republic's arable lands. On the opposite end of the social scale, 12 per cent of households owned 60 per cent of country's cultivable acreage.[111] In a word, the republic's 584,000 villages, where four-fifths of the country resided, were growing restive. Despite the circumstances, however, a revolutionary overthrow of the state failed to occur in India. In part, this was because of the fragmented nature of the peasantry— divided as it was into a plethora of faiths, castes, and *jatis*, all cross-cutting one another—as well as the coercive role of the state. In a sense, the two amounted to the same thing: the religious sanction of caste was of the same coercive order as state violence. Moreover, the two worked in tandem. For fealty to the smaller gentry stemmed in no small part from caste solidarity. More rebellious peasants, for their part, had to contend with rural bosses who had come to acquire muscle power of their own: pistols and rifles proliferated in the countryside, as landlords trained private militias to protect hoarded grain and land from local guerrillas. As for the state's police and paramilitary power, it can be discerned in the common fate that befell all major agrarian uprisings: Telangana between 1946 and 1951; Thanjavur, Kilvenmani, Tanjore, and Srikakulam between 1967 and 1969; and the Naxalite movement that followed in their wake. All were either stamped out or made to suffer ignominiously. But this was not

---

[110] P.S. Appu, who had been appointed Land Reforms Commissioner in 1970, bore testimony to this "lack of political will." Appu, *Land Reforms in India*, pp. 158–73. For more on land reforms, see Jaffrelot, *India's Silent Revolution*, pp. 134–5.
[111] Frankel, "Compulsion and Social Change", pp. 226–7.

surprising. For the police were virtually in the employ of the bullock capitalists, especially since 1967, when many of them had first ridden to power in the assemblies.

Still, even if the discontented did not overthrow the state, their patience with the Congress' promissory politics was wearing thin. After her new-found leftism, then, for Mrs Gandhi the land question should have taken on a renewed urgency. If she had followed through with her socialist rhetoric, the Congress would have not only kept dissent under check but consolidated for itself a voting bloc *nonpareil.* In numerical terms, no single caste was as big as the class that stood to gain from a reorganisation of tenure. To be sure, the grand old party would have alienated the gentry, but this, as we have seen, it had already accomplished, not least with the Congress split and the ascendancy of socialists in her party. When the balance sheet is drawn, the damage done to the party's networks and coffers by expropriation would have been offset many times over by the benefits of collective farming: *inter alia,* less privation and a growing identification with the leaders of the republic *sans* intermediaries. Given the poor land-population ratios in the Indian countryside, which left, on average, each citizen with 0.71 acres, and the high cost of adopting irrigation technologies of the green revolution—roughly \$400–\$1,000 in mid-seventies prices—collectivisation was the only way in which India's Malthusian problem of productivity could be addressed without widening inequality.[112]

This, however, was a road not taken. Mrs Gandhi was happy to work within the confines of a system where rural landlordism went unchallenged. There was, of course, no absence of discussion on the matter. In July 1972, for instance, the CWC passed an ambitious resolution on land reform that laid out the blueprint for its implementation.[113] Unlike the previous top-down efforts in which the political classes waited for their policies to trickle down from state assemblies to districts, villages, and eventually, farms, the CWC's new "mass movement approach" called upon district-

---

[112] Ibid., pp. 226, 230. At an exchange rate of Rs 8 to a dollar, spending Rs 8000 would have been twenty-two times the average annual income of Rs 366—simply put, unaffordable. These expenditures were necessary because India's canal irrigation systems were never designed for the "introduction of scientific agriculture." Unable to provide enough water—the peckish high-yielding varieties demanded a lot more—India's canals also lacked master drainages, cross-regulators for the "controlled rotation of watering," and the ability to tap underground water. Ibid., p. 229.

[113] *Congress Marches Ahead—VI,* pp. 177–81.

level cadres to "educate" farmers and aid in expropriation.[114] But little effort was made to convert these pieties into anything substantial. And less than two years after coasting to victory on a platform of "Garibi Hatao" [get rid of poverty], Mrs Gandhi announced a *volte-face*: "if anybody tries to say that poverty can go in my lifetime or during my tenure as prime minister, it just cannot. It has very deep roots."[115] During the Emergency, recantations continued unabated: "you should realise that removing poverty or uplifting the villages is not the responsibility of the government alone but is everyone's responsibility," she declared.[116]

What explains this chasm between words and performance? At least three reasons could be put forward by way of explanation: the Congress' past record, the position of the smaller gentry in the early seventies, and the imperfect transformation of the grand old party.

First, the very ethos of land reform, as it were, ran counter to the Congress ideology. As early as the 1930s, M.K. Gandhi had made it more than clear whose side the Congress was on in the countryside. "Congressmen cannot, we do not, seek to injure the zamindars," he said in 1931, warning tenants against non-payment of rent, "we aim not at the destruction of property. We aim only at its lawful use." The next year, he inveigled his party into passing a resolution titled "Reassurance to Zamindars". On paper, it seemed at the time that Nehru was an early critic of Gandhi's. But as prime minister, he sought a "moderate land policy" that merely encouraged cooperative farming and land ceilings—with no timetable or fixed targets.[117] Moreover, while *zamindari* was abolished by a number of states in the early fifties, little changed on the ground. The intermediaries now became "personal cultivators", with old tenants rechristened "hired labourers", now worse off than before, having lost the few vestiges of tenancy rights that had existed prior to abolition, such as the "permanent right of occupancy to the land". Some of these ex-*zamindar* "personal cultivators" remained in practice absentee landlords, owning in excess of 5000 acres, even as late as 1975. Ceilings, too, were subject to nomenclatural manoeuvre. To begin with, they applied only to individual holdings, prompting landlords to resort to *benami* (nominal) transfers of

---

[114] In the tiered system, the ceiling ranged from 10 acres of most fertile to 54 acres of least fertile land for every family. Ibid., pp. 177–8.

[115] *TOI*, 12 April 1973, p. 12.

[116] *Statesman Weekly*, 9 August 1975, p. 6.

[117] Frankel, *Political Economy*, pp. 51–52, 101.

land to kith and kin. In this they were abetted by repeated delays in implementation caused in part by run-ins with the judiciary, and in part by the unwillingness of parliamentarians—a significant number of them landowners—who would mandate reform in state legislatures, only to return to their rural constituencies and frustrate them. Moreover, this Swiss cheese model of legislation came with loopholes built into them: landowners could exceed the ceiling if their homesteads fell in their landholdings or if their acreage was licensed as a sugarcane farm, pledged as Bhoodan, or used to produce fodder.[118]

Second, the green revolution of the late 1960s had further strengthened the hands of rural elites, making the task of expropriation considerably harder. What this period of agricultural involution had achieved was for *zamindars* nothing short of the "imperial dream":

> Within a year or two of the programme's [the green revolution] inception, virtually every district could field a fine crop of demonstration ex-zamindars— the *rai sahibs* with their 30-, 40-, 50-, 100-acre holdings, their multiplication farms of the latest Mexican wheat and Philippines paddy, their tube-wells gushing out 16,000 gallons an hour, much of it on highly profitable hire, their tractors, their godowns stacked with fertiliser, their cold-stores ... their brothers and sons in the civil service and industry, the army, and the police, sending regular remittances to swell the family accounts in pre-Mutiny fashion ... in short, a tenth of the zamindari, but ten times the income.[119]

And third, the failure to reform the party during Mrs Gandhi's tenure. While the Congress split and the centralisation of the disbursement of election tickets had virtually released the party from the clutches of the rearguard between 1969 and 1972, the years that followed witnessed a swift counterrevolution that quickly undid the work of the Congress Left: large swathes of the old-guard gentry surreptitiously crept back from the Congress (Organisation) into Mrs Gandhi's party, the Congress (Requisitionist), which, to P.N. Dhar, writing in 1973, was "fast becoming a dung-heap of defectors."[120] A CWC deliberation of November 1971 had sought to prevent precisely this kind of cross-pollination between the two Congresses. But events in Andhra Pradesh in 1972, when 200 Reddy Congressmen rebelled against reforms that threatened their monopoly over land, proved too much for the prime minister. To prevent a repeat, Mrs

---

[118] Jannuzi, "India's Rural Poor", p. 186.
[119] Whitcombe, "What Happened to the Zamindars?", p. 179.
[120] Lockwood, *The Communist Party*, p. 57.

Gandhi opened wide the party doors. Returning to the fold in largest numbers were Congressmen in Gujarat, Punjab, Bihar, and West Bengal, the rest not far behind.[121] Similarly, the Congress Right came to be tolerated at the highest levels of the party—even figures such as Y.B. Chavan and Jagjivan Ram, who never missed an opportunity to rail against "left adventurism".[122] The upshot was that the Congress (R) "degenerated into an unaudited company for winning elections": the logic of raising money, distributing seats, and funding campaigns trumped all political concerns.[123] This, in short, was the triumph of the gentry. It was only to be expected, then, that these men would bury land reform at any cost.

Defeats for the Left followed in short order. In 1973, a frustrated K.D. Malaviya quit the party's Political Training and Cadre Building Department—which had been tasked with introducing land reform on ground—that he headed.[124] But as discontent grew, and violence erupted in Gujarat and Bihar, a panic-stricken Mrs Gandhi decided to reopen the question of land reform. In May 1974, the CWC announced the creation of a new category of party workers, "active members", who would receive tutoring in land reform implementation.[125] In November, the first of the training camps was set up at Narora, a small town in the district of Bulandshahr, Uttar Pradesh. Inaugurating it, party president Barooah declared that it would be possible to see "about 50,000 to 100,000 cadres" roving about the countryside in good time.[126] In February the next year, a second camp sprung up in Shillong, this time headlined by AICC general secretaries Purabi Mukherjee and P.V. Narasimha Rao. Here, the grand old party was already in retreat: questions of tenure were barely touched upon. Instead, Congressmen focussed their energies hurling invectives against the JP Movement and the "communal and obscurantist elements behind it."[127] The camps came to nothing. In the event, between 1972 and 1975,

---

[121] Kochanek, "Mrs Gandhi's Pyramid", pp. 106–7.

[122] *Congress Marches Ahead—III*, p. 58; *Congress Marches Ahead—IV*, p. 42.

[123] Khilnani, *The Idea of India*, p. 45.

[124] *Congress Marches Ahead—VI*, p. 203.

[125] "Active members" were Congressmen in government—MPs, MLAs, town councillors, *zila* and *panchayat* officials—who "subscribed" to the "principles of secularism, socialism, and democracy," believed in temperance and a casteless "integrated society," and were "habitual wearers of *khadi*." *Congress Marches Ahead—IX*, pp. 50–1.

[126] *Congress Marches Ahead—X*, p. 297.

[127] Ibid., pp. 303–9.

years in which thirteen of the republic's twenty-two states passed ceiling legislation, only 62,000 acres were redistributed.[128]

Instead of attempting genuine land reform, Mrs Gandhi appeared to be more interested in floating cack-handed ideas of rural renewal. What of the problems posed by low labour productivity? What was needed was a "youth against famine" programme in which students would be mobilised as they were in "other countries". "In China", she noted, they improved productivity by mobilising "school children to catch flies", and "in Holland ... school children are mobilised today to go and catch the beetles which attack the potatoes. In England also there is some such programme".[129] Water and electricity shortages? These were the result of the Indian "attitude of waste". Unlike in "more advanced countries, Europe particularly", in India, apparently, citizens consumed too much. Fertiliser shortages? Ever since "the other fertiliser—the chemical—has come", farmers have forgotten the art of "using every bit of organic fertiliser."[130] Small harvests? "Kitchen gardening should be encouraged as a mass movement."[131] The few pragmatic solutions that could have brought about meaningful alterations in the cadastral geography—*inter alia* making appeals to land reforms above challenge in the courts, moving to the centre the competencies of states to deliberate on agrarian matters, changing the referent in ceiling bills from "individual" to "family" landholding—were never attempted.

Inaction in the countryside was partially compensated for in other realms. Here, results were mixed. The nationalisation of 400 banks and businesses between 1971 and 1974, for instance, was well received by the press.[132] The government was praised for protecting people's savings from the hands of the corrupt life-insurance industry, saving sick industrial units

---

[128] This included most of the large ones—Uttar Pradesh, Rajasthan, Madhya Pradesh, Bihar, Orissa, Andhra Pradesh, Karnataka, Assam, Haryana, Himachal Pradesh, Punjab, Gujarat, and Tripura: *Congress Marches Ahead—XI*, p. 81; Frankel, *Political Economy*, pp. 476, 506–7.

[129] *Congress Marches Ahead—IX*, p. 140.

[130] Ibid., pp. 144–5.

[131] *Congress Marches Ahead—X*, p. 13.

[132] This included firms in the coking coal, steel, gold, copper, railway construction, and general insurance industries. This, along with the Monopolies and Restricted Trade Practices Act (MRTPA), was to help bring capital under state control. The MRTPA, however, proved ineffectual: expected to investigate some 1200 companies, it discovered only five monopolies in the first two years of its existence. See Kochanek, "Briefcase Politics in India", pp. 1278–1301.

from collapse, and reallocating resources to reflect planning priorities.[133] Less successful, however, was the stab at state trading in wheat in 1973, which resulted in an acute shortage and the abandonment of the idea a year later.[134] Other progressive reforms came unstuck as well. For instance, the Raj Committee's report of 1972, which called for taxes on agricultural property, was quickly buried. The same fate met the Hathi Committee that in 1974 recommended the nationalisation of drug companies. The accrual of state power, in short, had failed to translate into a reordering of society, Indira Gandhi's "socialism" having produced more benefits to Delhi's rulers by way of purges and reshuffles than to the country's citizens.

In essence, Mrs Gandhi had boxed herself into the pursuit of two policies that were impossible to reconcile: economic growth by stimulating capital formation in the private sector and redistribution by incremental legislation. The first at the expense of the second was hardly a sound strategy for the building of a modern populist democratic party like the one the Congress Left—on whose backs she was temporarily riding—had in mind. The second, even if pursued resolutely, was hardly an adequate response to problems of great proportions: drought, wage stagnation, and growing inequality. In the event, all that Mrs Gandhi had offered the people, then, were mere promises—and the frustrations stemming from unfulfilled commitments went a long way in explaining the magnitude of the popular protests of the mid-1970s.

Indira Gandhi's War on the Judiciary and the Judges' Response

The twin defeats of the Gujarat election and the Allahabad judgment reached Mrs Gandhi's desk within hours of each other on 12 June 1975. They were both, in a sense, outcomes of the same process: her centralisation of power.[135] Again, some contextualisation is needed to make sense of the way the judiciary used Mrs Gandhi's crimes against her.

The "peccadillo" that the judiciary settled upon to chastise her was evidence not of its legal pedantry but the desire to exact revenge on her for endlessly stepping on its toes since 1967. To be sure, the war over compe-

---

[133] For instance, nationalisation helped channel more credit to the petite bourgeoisie and rural India: Torri, "Factional Politics and Economic Policy", p. 1096.

[134] Out of the annual output of 25 million tons, the government procured only 5.5 million, Punjab accounting for over half that figure: Ladejinsky, "Wheat Procurement in India", p. 93; B.M., "All Eggs in the Food Basket", p. 462.

[135] See the Introduction.

tencies between the executive and judiciary had raged *sans* interruption since the constitutional settlement of 1950. But there was a difference in degree between what went on before Mrs Gandhi's accession and after. As D.P. Mishra saw it, Nehru's "dictatorial tendencies" had left only "the husk of democracy" during his rule, but Mrs Gandhi, on this account, went the whole hog and threw even the husk out of the window.[136]

In the battle between Mrs Gandhi's government and the courts the opening salvo was *Golak Nath v. State of Punjab*. In that 1967 ruling the Supreme Court showed its mettle by acting as a major stumbling block to Congress land-reform ambitions when it sided with a gentry family over the state. When Henry Golak Nath, a Presbyterian minister, died in 1962 leaving some 500 acres of land in Punjab to his two offspring, Inder and Indira, and their four children, Jullundur's collectors decided that the six coparceners were entitled to thirty acres each. The surplus land, 320 acres, was set aside for redistribution. Protesting against the disbursement of their demesnes, the Naths took their cause to a number of collectors and judges, each of whom ruled more or less in favour of redistribution. But when the matter reached the apex court, it not only reversed the older rulings but went on to suggest that certain parts of the constitution were unamendable. In its reading, fundamental rights, of which the right to property was one, could not be altered by parliament.

Since at least 1951 tensions had existed between on the one hand the right to property, which was fervidly defended by justices, and on the other the welfarist desiderata listed in the non-justiciable "directive principles" of the constitution, championed in the main by socialists and communists. In 1967 it was *déjà vu* all over again. On one side was Mohan Kumaramangalam, panjandrum of the Congress Left: "the directive principles cannot be implemented without taking away at least some of the fundamental rights."[137] On the other was Chief Justice Koka Subba Rao: the constitution needs "to be worked, and not to be destroyed."[138] His was the "basic structure doctrine" that placed parts of the constitution beyond the reach of parliament: which parts were considered basic was never made clear, but it was evident that the Supreme Court meant to include all fundamental rights.[139]

[136] Mishra, *The Nehru Epoch*, pp. 346–7.

[137] Austin, *Working a Democratic Constitution*, pp. 205–6. At the time he was advocate general of Madras.

[138] Ibid., p. 200.

[139] This reversed the precedents set by the Shankari Prasad and Sajjan Singh cases

At this juncture Mrs Gandhi was hardly seeking land reform. But the conservatism of the courts made the judiciary a convenient scapegoat for the failings of her regime. For their part the judges did little to disabuse people of this notion. In fact just weeks after *Golak Nath*, Chief Justice Rao resigned to make—with the Swatantra's support, tellingly—a bid for the presidency.[140] Not that Mrs Gandhi's attacks on the judiciary counted for much at this point in time. She had an ally, Socialist MP Nath Pai, move a bill to reverse the ruling, but when parliamentarians tried and failed to pass this piece of legislation over the next two years she did nothing to remedy the situation.[141] The dissident Congressmen who refused to obey the party whip on the bill, after all, had their uses. That she was fighting battles both within the party and without helped her garner popular sympathy and justify the glacial pace of reform. All this was to change. The *casus belli* were two judgments that made quick work of her latest policy initiatives, both involving far greater stakes than anything she had mooted before.

First was the question of bank nationalisation. Proposed for the first time in 1934, then more forcefully in 1948 when Nehru supported it, and yet again in 1953 when Narayan did, the idea enjoyed support across the political spectrum: on the Left, Principal Secretary P.N. Haksar had long wanted to clip the wings of "rapacious and buccaneering" bankers; on the Right, Morarji Desai had played an important role in the passage of a 1968 act that extended, albeit piecemeal, the "social control of all banks".[142] In the event, when the president signed an ordinance in 1969 allowing for the takeover of fourteen banks that held 85 per cent of the country's deposits, Rustom Cowasjee Cooper, a shareholder in one of them, filed a petition with the Supreme Court challenging the decision. The Swatantra's Minoo Masani and the Jana Sangh's Balraj Madhok followed suit, using the same line of

---

in 1952 and 1965, respectively, which upheld the unconstrained ability of parliament to amend the constitution. Ibid., pp. 200–1. Austin speculates that the nationalisation of a metal-packaging company, and the consigning of over a hundred land laws into the constitution's Ninth Schedule—which immunises laws from judicial review—prompted the Supreme Court's "basic structure" reading.

[140] He lost to Zakir Husain, the Congress candidate.

[141] Pai was not even supported by his own party: Rammanohar Lohia, who received his PhD in 1933 from Berlin University, declared the Pai bill akin to the Enabling Act of the same year. Ibid., pp. 203–4.

[142] Austin, *Working a Democratic Constitution*, p. 209ff. For both quotes, see p. 213.

argument as Cooper: that the ordinance violated Articles 19 and 31 of the constitution, that is, the right to private property and adequate compensation for expropriation, respectively. As was to be expected, the apex court was sympathetic. With near-unanimity an eleven-judge bench struck down the nationalisations.[143] It was only by watering down a new ordinance, and then the ensuing act, that Mrs Gandhi managed to implement her programme without judicial interference.

The second policy initiative related to the abolition of the princes' privileges, their privy purses having been the result of an outlandish pact between the union and the princely states, a scattering of over 500 kingdoms that had coexisted on the subcontinent with the Raj. The ruling princes had accepted London's "paramountcy" whilst retaining, at least on paper, their titles and territories. After independence, the "purses" given to them were state allowances to the tune of 8 per cent of the revenue from the territories they once controlled, "free of income tax and in perpetuity." These were doled out annually to the former potentates.[144] By the early 1960s V.S. Naipaul's *précis* of the princes' predicament—that theirs was a "bogus, extinguishable glamour"—resonated not just with the socialists in Nehru's administration but also with Syndicate bosses such as K. Kamaraj and Atulya Ghosh.[145] It was argued that a country as poor, hungry, and illiterate as India could ill afford draining its exchequer on former maharajas and nawabs. Nehru, in theory, concurred, but on reflection suggested that seeking to redistribute wealth by breaking a constitutional covenant was not the right way to go about it. He opted for a more stolid approach, writing letters to the princes. "Dear Friend", they began, and went on to entreat them to voluntarily reinvest a portion of their fortunes in social programmes. The replies he received were, of course, few and far from forthcoming.[146]

His daughter, in contrast, showed greater fortitude when she took up the baton. In 1970 the Twenty-fourth Amendment Bill sailed through parliament with the requisite two-thirds majority, allowing the state to strip the princes of their titles and allowances, much to the dismay of the Consultation of Rulers for India [*sic*], their lobbying outfit.[147] The upper

---

[143] It was not the ordinance the judiciary struck down, but an act that lawmakers had passed to replace it in the interim. The lone dissenter, A.N. Ray, would later be appointed as chief justice over the heads of three judges.

[144] Austin, *Working a Democratic Constitution*, p. 221.

[145] Naipaul, *India: A Wounded Civilization*, p. 27.

[146] Austin, *Working a Democratic Constitution*, p. 222ff.

[147] Ibid., p. 225. The amendment had, so to speak, overtaken Mrs Gandhi's position

house, however, failed to pass the amendment by a single vote—149 voted in favour, 75 against. "You have saved us", an elated Maharajah of Bikaner taunted Mrs Gandhi after the vote. "We will execute you", came the curt reply.[148] Acting quickly, she had the president "derecognise" the princes and their allowances the same night, 15 August. Then followed a repeat of what had transpired with the nationalisations. The Cooper of this case was a young Madhavrao Scindia, then a Jana Sangh MP like his mother.[149] He petitioned the Supreme Court to strike down the presidential order as unconstitutional, a violation of Articles 19 and 31. The government's defence, that it could do as it pleased with the paramountcy it inherited from the Raj, failed to impress. The ruling went in the plaintiff's favour.[150]

In short, the picture that emerged from *Golak Nath* (1967), *Rustom Cowasjee Cooper* (1970), and *Madhavrao Scindia* (1971) looked bleak to a government bent on executive supremacy. A confrontation between the two branches of government was inevitable. But by 1971 the Congress was hardly alone in its dissatisfaction with the judiciary: the sentiment was common across the board. Among the country's ten largest parties, eight called for a recasting of the constitution in their election manifestoes, most wanting to strengthen either or both the executive and the legislature at the expense of the judiciary. For the CPI(M), the 1950 settlement had "to go lock, stock and barrel."[151] In similar fashion, three of Mrs Gandhi's closest advisers, Gokhale, Kumaramangalam, and Ray—termed the "three musketeers" by the press—sought to "restore" parliamentary supremacy.[152] Belief in the directive principles being "more fundamental than the fundamental rights", then, was par for the course.[153]

---

on the privy purses—at the time of its passage she initially sought to delay it because she was working on a secret deal with the princes: Krishnan, *Chavan*, p. 172.

[148] Austin, *Working a Democratic Constitution*, p. 228. Lest this appear as class-war rhetoric, it must be noted that Mrs Gandhi's own view of the princes was far more ambivalent. Of the thirty-seven of them who contested the 1972 state elections, twenty-four were on Congress tickets—all with Mrs Gandhi's complicity: Narain and Sharma, "The Fifth State Assembly Elections in India", p. 325.

[149] Scindia joined the Congress a decade later.

[150] Justices Ray and Mitter were the two dissenters who sided with the government.

[151] Austin, *Working a Democratic Constitution*, p. 235.

[152] Ibid., pp. 236–7, 287.

[153] Attorney general Niren De, cited in ibid., p. 241.

After the grand old party received a renewed and augmented mandate in 1971, amendments to liberate parliament from the vice-like grip of conservative justices followed in short order. The first was the Twenty-fourth Amendment, whose passage in August 1971 gave parliament the green light to amend fundamental rights and made it obligatory for the president of the republic to assent to all amendment bills placed before him. Then, on 1 December, the Congress steamrollered through parliament the Twenty-fifth Amendment, which rewrote the property law—Article 31—with an additional clause. This forbade the courts from challenging legislation that "subserved the common good" and reduced the "concentration of wealth".[154] A day later came the Twenty-sixth Amendment, which finally did away with the privileges and privy purses that had inflated the egos and fortunes of princes for almost a quarter of a century. The next day— 3 December—India and Pakistan were at war. The president, in response, declared a national emergency, curtailing a number of fundamental rights, further tilting the balance in favour of directive principles.

Having already forfeited power to the executive, the Supreme Court in 1973 finally made a last-ditch effort to defend itself from Mrs Gandhi's onslaught. Its opportunity arose when Swami Kesavananda Bharati challenged the Kerala government's attempts to take over his *muth* (temple) as part of its land-redistribution effort. On the advice of jurist Nani Palkhivala, the ascetic argued that the Twenty-fourth and Twenty-fifth Amendments had, in essence, altered the "basic structure" of the constitution. The government's lawyer, H.M. Seervai, countered the charge by making the rather facile case that "unlimited amending power should not be understood as an abuse of power."[155] Walking a fine line, the apex court's judgment was an unlikely legal achievement in that it acknowledged executive ascendancy without completely undermining the judiciary's *raison d'être*.

In the run-up to the ruling, Mrs Gandhi's aides had left no stone unturned: it was suggested that the case be delayed beyond Chief Justice Sikri's retirement;[156] one judge was informed that his promotion to chief justice was

---

[154] Ibid., pp. 240, 244. The amendment also replaced the word "compensation" with the more discretionary "amount", pre-empting the courts from questioning the adequacy of the compensation received by the expropriated owners.

[155] Ibid., pp. 261–2. Seervai was the advocate general of Maharashtra. He was called in because Attorney General Niren De was away at the Commonwealth Lawyer's Conference.

[156] In the end, the judgment was delivered on 24 April 1973. Sikri retired the next day.

contingent on a favourable verdict;[157] another lunched with S.S. Ray, who tried to sway him.[158] The judges, possibly because they feared future reprisals, struck a bargain: they upheld the constitutionality of the Twenty-fourth and Twenty-fifth Amendments—barring a single clause in the latter—thereby overturning *Golak Nath* and, in effect, declaring open season on fundamental rights.[159] At the same time the Supreme Court suggested that while parliament could freely amend the constitution—even the right to property—abrogating its "essential features" was off limits: there existed a "basic structure doctrine". By this argument some aspects of the constitution—*inter alia*, democratic governance and federalism—constituted an indestructible bedrock which no amendment could alter. For Mrs Gandhi it was the latter part of the judgment that counted for more.[160] Unsurprisingly, then, the upshot was her strengthened resolve to curb the judiciary.

On 25 April, just a day after *Kesavananda Bharati*, Mrs Gandhi struck yet another blow against judicial independence by passing over three judges to appoint A.N. Ray—the only dissenter in both the nationalisation and privy-purse rulings—as chief justice. As for the superseded judges, namely Shelat, Hegde, and Grover, they had proven their worthlessness in joining three other dissenters in the Kesavananda case and suggesting that fundamental rights, too, belonged in the constitution's basket of unamendable "essential features".[161] The government was unabashed in its defence of the

---

[157] Justice Chandrachud.

[158] Justice Mukherjea.

[159] This was the clause in Article 31C that disallowed a law from being challenged in court if it was in compliance with Article 39 (b) and (c)—on the "common good" and "concentration of wealth", as seen earlier. In the event, the apex court had managed to uphold its power of judicial review. The other part of the Twenty-fifth Amendment, which disallowed the courts from challenging the compulsory acquisition of property on account of the compensation paid, was accepted by the justices.

[160] A sense of defeat was compounded by the mistaken belief that they had packed the Supreme Court with loyalist judges. Justices Mathew, Palekar, Chandrachud, Beg, and Mukherjea were all ostensibly the Congress' point men, having been picked for the job by Kumaramangalam (he picked the first justice), Gokhale (the next two), and S.S. Ray (the last two). As it happened, three of them—Palekar, Mukherjea, and Chandrachud—joined the majority in striking down the clause in Article 31C because they felt it altered the basic structure.

[161] The appointment of chief justices is dictated by seniority. But this was mere convention, with no legal sanction, Mrs Gandhi's aides argued. On this episode, see Nayar, *Supersession of Judges, passim.*

supersession of judges. For Kumaramangalam, Hegde was a "brilliant judge though of a different philosophy"; Grover "a lesser person"; and Shelat of little interest because he, in any case, was set to retire in two months.[162] "A judge's basic outlook", he averred, had to mirror the government's. Kumaramangalam was seconded by Haksar, who argued that judges must be "committed" to the philosophy of the incumbents.[163] For Mrs Gandhi, personal reasons dovetailed with political ones. As Gokhale and N.K. Seshan, her private secretary, later surmised, it was Hegde's decision to uphold Raj Narain's appeal and introduce new evidence in the Allahabad case that had made him *persona non grata*.[164]

The legal community was outraged by the supersession: 10,000 lawyers in Bombay and Madras boycotted the courts; the Supreme Court Bar Association called for a new appointment process; the superseded judges resigned and, along with the outgoing chief justice, S.M. Sikri, boycotted Ray's swearing in. Collectively, it all portended a final act of revolt that was to follow. Indeed, the 12 June 1975 ruling was less the result of Mrs Gandhi's electoral misdemeanours than the culminating point of this long-standing rancour between the two branches of government.

In sum, the policies pursued by Mrs Gandhi and their attendant blowback brought to the fore a formidable set of opponents. Some were pounding the gavel in court, others the doors of her besieged residence. Five days after the twin shocks and eight days before the Emergency, Charan Singh remarked that Mrs Gandhi, armed with an army chief and president of the republic "of her own choice", could dispense with the Lok Sabha and Supreme Court "with just one stroke of the pen."[165] Reflecting her authoritarian preferences as well as her penchant for inflating threats to ensure her political survival—temporary resignation in June 1975 and electoral defeat in March 1976 were the worst-case scenarios, both nugatory in the rough and tumble of democratic politics—her manoeuvres on the night of 25 June 1975 confirmed that he was not far off the mark.

* * *

[162] Austin, *Working a Democratic Constitution*, p. 282. For a fuller statement of Kumaramangalam's views on the judiciary, see Kumaramangalam, *Judicial Appointments.*

[163] Haksar, *Premonitions*, pp. 200–8.

[164] Austin, *Working a Democratic Constitution*, p. 282.

[165] *TOI*, 17 June 1975, p. 5.

While the JP Movement and the Allahabad judgment were the immediate causes of the Emergency, the way they unfolded can only be understood by broadening the lens.

The JP Movement then appears as only the tip of a formidable iceberg. First, it had endowed legitimacy and respectability to its shadow army, the Sangh Parivar, which to Indira Gandhi and some others in the grand old party was a fascist organisation. To these Congressmen, the Hindu nationalists were not adversaries, they were enemies. It was a straightforward case of either them or us.

Second, the JP Movement was an expression of discontent that was not only connected to economic crises—inflation, joblessness, and rising inequalities—but also exacerbated by frustrations. For Indira Gandhi's populist rhetoric had aroused expectations that were belied. The persistence of the protests and its pervasiveness showed Mrs Gandhi the difficulty of wooing Indian voters by repeating old promises. The middle class, industrialists, and the ruling elite were meanwhile convinced that strong decisions were needed to contain labour agitations and to restore law and order. Years of discontent and demonstrations were not directly responsible for the imposition of the Emergency, but they made it more acceptable to sections of society eager for a return to "normalcy".

Third, the Allahabad judgment cannot be seen in isolation, for it was in part the result of years of open conflict between the judiciary and parliament. Because of Mrs Gandhi's populist style, again, her claim was that legislative—and by implication executive—power should, as the voice of the people, prevail over the third estate. Judges were bound to resist such an assault, even if only out of self-preservation.

Her populist style also resulted in the personalisation of conflict and acute political polarisation. Instead of looking for consensus and compromise, Mrs Gandhi appeared relentlessly on the offensive.

The breakdown of law and order not only convinced the Indian bourgeoisie and establishment that strong measures were needed, Mrs Gandhi herself came to the same conclusion in the wake of the murder of one of her ministers in 1975. On 2 January the railways minister, Lalit Narayan Mishra, was in Samastipur, Bihar inaugurating a new broad-gauge line that would connect that small town on the Burhi Gandak River to New Delhi. That morning, when he walked over to the dais, a colossal explosion threw him off his feet; he succumbed to his injuries the next day, becoming the first cabinet minister to be assassinated in independent India. It would take forty years for investigators to collar the assassins—four Anand Margis who wanted to see the "big sinner" eliminated for facilitating a pact between the Communists and the Congress.[166] Mrs Gandhi, on the one hand, concluded that the JP Movement and its "cult of violence" had created an atmosphere that licensed political assassination: killing Mishra was only "a dress rehearsal" to kill her.[167] On the other, figures in the opposition, including Narayan, wondered if Mishra's murder was an inside job to shut up the minister—permanently—who as the Congress' bagman, had presided over an empire of graft. For it soon emerged that the minister's office at the railway headquarters, Rail Bhavan, had been sealed, apparently to conceal the malfeasances of Sanjay, who, it appears, had some dodgy papers relating to Maruti stashed there.[168]

But even during those heady days, it was not at all clear that Mrs Gandhi would resort to authoritarianism. In fact, in the run-up to the Emergency, it was another "ism" that she deployed in her bid to draw attention away from the strikes, protests, and judicial procedures targeting her: nationalism. On 18 May 1974, ten days into the railway strike, came the explosion of a nuclear device at Pokhran. The euphoria, however, was short-lived. After a small uptick that month, her favourability ratings reached an all-time low in September that year.[169] In the early months of 1975 Mrs Gandhi sought to defuse tensions in the Kashmir valley. The region had been in the throes of violent conflict since an episode in the summer of 1973, when students of Anantnag College chanced upon a "blasphemous" drawing of Muhammad in an old encyclopaedia for children. To this end the Kashmir Accord was signed on 24 February 1975.[170] By its terms Sheikh Abdullah was released from house arrest and made chief minister.[171] In return he acknowledged India's sovereignty

---

[166] Frank, *Indira*, p. 368; *India Today*, 9 June 1997; *Business Standard*, 19 December 2014; *Indian Express*, 9 December 2014; Saran Singh, Chief Secretary, Bihar, to S.L. Khurana, Secretary, MHA, 13 September 1975, MHAP, File 228/1/75–AVD–II; Bakshi and Chaturvedi, *Bihar Through the Ages*, pp. 194–5.

[167] Bhattacharjea, *Unfinished Revolution*, p. 225.

[168] A.S., *Who Killed L. N. Mishra?*, pp. 9, 31.

[169] Perkovich, *India's Nuclear Bomb*, pp. 187–8.

[170] See Mrs Gandhi's statement on the accords: 24 February 1975, MHAP, File 10/4/75–RP.

[171] After serving as the state's prime minister between 1948 and 1953, Sheikh Abdullah had been incarcerated by Nehru for having the temerity to suggest a plebiscite on Kashmir's accession to the republic, as promised by Delhi's rulers in 1947.

over Kashmir.[172] Six weeks later, on 8 April, the Indian Armed Forces moved into the kingdom of Sikkim, a "protectorate" of India's bordering its north east. In recent years the country's potentates, Chogyal P.T. Namgyal, the hereditary ruler, and his wife Hope Cooke—who had left her "WASP girlhood" and "New York socialite" years behind—had been pushing for more autonomy in their national affairs, in the process discomfiting Delhi, whose apparatchiks were sticklers for the standstill agreement of 1948. Sikkim's sovereignty had extended only over domestic matters; foreign and defence issues were handled by India.[173] The arrival of Indian troops under the garb of a military exercise left the Chogyal frantically broadcasting the invasion on radio. A few hams picked up signals in England, Sweden, and Japan, but none responded. Namgyal was placed under house arrest, and six days later a dubious referendum was held, "integrating" Sikkim into India and ending 333 years of Chogyal rule.[174]

Pokhran, Srinagar, and Gangtok notwithstanding, Mrs Gandhi failed to deflect attention from protests and the number of court cases that the first family was fighting. Samastipur, Allahabad, and Ahmedabad pointed to the fact that she was running out of options. Pressing the "panic button", she felt, was the only way out of the impasse.

All the same, it would be remiss to suggest that the Emergency was merely Mrs Gandhi's response to the popular and juridical threats to her rule. Two more dimensions—one psychological, the other institutional—remain to be explored. Here again we will see that she alienated important figures, and made life-long enemies and, more importantly, destroyed the checks and balances that could have prevented her from turning the country over to dictatorship.

---

[172] Sheikh Abdullah to Mrs Gandhi, 11 February 1975, MHAP, File 10/4/75–RP.

[173] Gray, "The Fairy Tale That Turned to Nightmare", p. 3. See also Cooke, *Time Change*.

[174] The hustings lasted a mere seventy-two hours. Congressmen campaigned backed by CRPs, who even beat up voters outside booths when polling began; indeed, the "votes" on many an occasion were cast by paramilitary proxies. Over 97 per cent voted in favour of integration: Datta-Ray, *Smash and Grab*.

7

MRS GANDHI'S PERSONALISATION OF POWER, 1966–1975

If the JP Movement and the Allahabad High Court ruling featured prominently in Mrs Gandhi's decision to impose the Emergency, so too did her authoritarian impulses. In fact, this aspect of her character has not gone unnoticed by commentators.[1]

But the fact that she was an "authoritarian personality", an analytical category at the intersection of psychology and the social sciences, is not in itself a sufficient explanation for the Emergency. Again, one needs to go beyond immediate causes. Here we identify the conditions which made the expression of such a personality possible: why was Mrs Gandhi able to impose her will so decisively?

In answering this question we focus on the power structure of the Congress. Its evolution, under the aegis of Mrs Gandhi, was a key variable because her personality would not have mattered much had a system of checks and balances continued to prevail in party and government. But after the Congress split of 1969 she reshaped both the organisation and the state in such a forceful way that these safeguards ceased to exist.

Indira Gandhi: Predisposed to Tyranny or Working Towards Survival?

The psychological analyses that affirm Mrs Gandhi's predisposition to authoritarianism typically hinge on two defects in her person: a lonely

[1] See P.B. Mayer's review of the tropes in Emergency literature: Mayer, "Congress (I), Emergency (I)", pp. 130–2.

childhood and a lack of intellect. In the estimation of Vijaya Lakshmi Pandit, Nehru's sister, for example, Indira was a "lonely person", an "only child", as well as a "clever girl" who did "not devote herself to her studies". Both created a "strain of obstinacy" that was to define her behaviour on the eve of and during the Emergency.[2] Henry C. Hart shows an equal interest in Mrs Gandhi's "psychological predispositions" in his study of the causes of the Emergency. Drawing on Harold Lasswell's *Psychopathology and Politics*, he notes the frequency of the adjective "insecure" in her oeuvre—collected volumes of speeches and a slim autobiography—concluding that her "divided and vulnerable sense of herself", in full display during the Emergency, owed to her childhood.[3] W.H. Morris-Jones concurs. While asserting that "not everything needs to be traced back to the curious childhood" of the prime minister, he sees in the "painfully shy and introverted schoolgirl [who] dreamt of leading her people like Joan of Arc" the seeds of a paranoid personality that shaped the events of June 1975.[4] In these accounts Indira Gandhi's sense of insecurity accompanies a growing penchant for ruthlessness. Hart, in particular, sees it in quasi-Darwinian terms: "at the core of Indira Gandhi's mature identity [was] the determination to dominate, lest she be dominated."[5]

Indira Gandhi's feelings of vulnerability seem traceable to her growing up in a nationalist household during the twilight years of the Raj: "The whole house was always in such a state of tension that nobody had a normal life. There were police raids, arrests, and so on", Mrs Gandhi remembered; "it seemed my parents were always in jail."[6] To this could be added Nehru's immersion in politics and neglect of his wife Kamala, who, afflicted with tuberculosis and in desperation availing herself of the services of the Ramakrishna Mission, apparently turned Mrs Gandhi against her family's vocation. Kamala died when Indira was eighteen.

For Vijaya Lakshmi Pandit's daughter Nayantara Sahgal, Indira Gandhi's insecurity owed to her relationship with her father, a towering figure who made her full of complexes and doubtful of her "own capacities".[7] To be

---

[2] Pandit, *The Scope of Happiness*, pp. 21–2.

[3] Hart, "Indira Gandhi", p. 243.

[4] Morris-Jones, "Whose Emergency", p. 458.

[5] Hart, "Indira Gandhi", p. 266.

[6] Ibid., pp. 243, 246.

[7] Sahgal, *Indira Gandhi*, p. 13. Of course, while Nehru, who unlike his daughter loved talking ideology and morality, in practice such encumbrances eluded him: Frankel, *India's Political Economy*, *passim*.

sure, unlike her father, she was not very well read at all. Her formal schooling was limited, not only because of the years spent in Tagore's Santiniketan, where experimental art and poetry came in lieu of conventional classroom learning, but also because when sent to Oxford she failed to take her degree. It is unlikely that perusing her father's letters, which he sent her from the Raj's prisons, served as an adequate substitute for a good university education.[8]

Nevertheless, to suggest that loneliness and her intellectual limitations led her to press the panic button in 1975, as some writers do, is scarcely credible. To understand Mrs Gandhi's authoritarian personality, then, requires a more analytical approach to her years in power, especially the decade that preceded the Emergency.

Facets of an Authoritarian Personality

Here, a relevant starting point is none other than *The Authoritarian Personality*, the doorstopper that Theodor Adorno published in collaboration with three psychologists at the University of California, Berkeley. Adorno and his co-authors famously developed the "F-scale"—the "F" stood for "Fascist"—in which nine characteristics were identified to help foretell an authoritarian disposition.[9] Such potential could be discerned if an individual exhibited "conventionalism" ("rigid adherence to conventional, middle-class values"), "authoritarian submission" (a submissive attitude "toward idealised moral authorities"), "authoritarian aggression" (the rejection of those "who violate conventional values"), "anti-intraception" (an aversion to individual opinion and human emotion), "superstition and stereotypy" (the belief in "mystical determinants" of fate), "power and toughness" (an "exaggerated assertion" thereof), "destructiveness and cynicism" (specifically, the belief that a dog-eat-dog society necessitates aggression), "projectivity" (seeing "plots and conspiracies" in the outside world, which are, in fact, the work of one's imagination), and "sex" (the projection of transgressive sexual acts upon one's opponents).[10] The last variable is one we do not propose to deploy in relation to Mrs Gandhi—not because of *pudeur* on our part but because one finds few references to sexuality in the

---

[8] Jawaharlal Nehru's 196 letters written between 1930 and 1933 weigh in at 1192 pages. They are collected in Nehru, *Glimpses of World History*.

[9] Adorno, *The Authoritarian Personality*, pp. 222–4.

[10] Ibid., pp. 228–41.

world of Indian high politics. This, in part, owed to the heteronormative familism of the time, which required neither explanation nor challenge. Moreover, Mrs Gandhi most certainly did not demonstrate an "exaggerated concern" with the "sexual goings-on" of her colleagues and rivals, as Adorno's schema would have it.

Writing in McCarthy's America, which was too squeamish to point fingers at leaders in its own land, Adorno concerned himself instead with the susceptibility of voters to authoritarian propaganda. However, since Mrs Gandhi never ran on a platform to turn India over to dictatorship, it is fair to turn the tables on Adorno and put under the microscope Mrs Gandhi herself rather than the electorates which reconfirmed her in office in 1967 and 1971.

What of her conventionalism? She was undeniably hostile to ideologies of all stripes, a reflection of her shallow commitment to political values. She admitted as much in a 1963 interview with the NBC's Welles Hangen: "I don't really have a political philosophy. I can't say I believe in any -ism ... I wouldn't say I'm interested in socialism as socialism. For me it's just a tool."[11] Oddly enough, in her lexicon, being a tool was a term of approbation. During the Emergency she felt much the same about democracy—as earlier chapters have made clear. But, as so often happens with politicians, the disavowal of political ideology cloaks strong personal convictions that become apparent in political practice. In this respect Mrs Gandhi was no exception, though she did occasionally blurt out her positions.

In 1971, for example, she noted that the guiding tenets of her premiership were "Hindu philosophy and a deep commitment to India."[12] In other words, religiosity and nationalism, both characteristic of conventionalism. These she believed only her party had the right to defend, for a recurrent feature of her declamations was an attack on all the unhinged forces bent on destroying the Congress consensus: "Democracy, independence of the judiciary, and fundamental rights ... would be threatened if we were to allow our faith to be eclipsed by defeatism and if we help alliances of the extreme left and right", she said two years later.[13] On another occasion: "The Congress did not believe in class war ... It was dedicated to truth [sic]."[14] This radical defence of the exnominated status quo evidently did

---

[11] Hangen, *After Nehru, Who?*, p. 181.
[12] Jayakar, *Indira Gandhi*, p. 230.
[13] Nayar, *Supersession of Judges*, p. 74.
[14] *Congress Marches Ahead—VIII*, pp. 195–6.

not require her to labour too much on practical matters. What of inequality? "Socialism" was no "magic wand", she argued, and the only way to "wipe out poverty" was "by hard work". She compared "the people" unfavourably to "our *jawans*", who not only had a demonstrably better work ethic than civilians but also engaged in the more difficult task of "guarding the frontiers".[15] Her reasons for wanting to eradicate poverty are particularly telling: "when we say we want to remove poverty, it is not simply because poverty is bad—it is bad. It is evil and ugly, and is a very big human problem—but also because it will create trouble for the country. If poverty and richness co-exist there will be social tension."[16] Education? "I don't know how important literacy is. What has it done for the West? Are people happier or more alive to problems? On the contrary, I think they have become far more superficial."[17] Redistribution? Determined individuals, she believed, and not nation-states, were the best agents of social change—the resolve of the republic's brightest could set everything to rights. To reverse inflation "we have to make sacrifices. We should restrict our purchases of consumer goods." To ensure high levels of industrial production, capitalists must "develop a spirit of sacrifice" in order to curb "indiscipline among workers". To achieve autarky, citizens would have to demonstrate "sacrifice and hardship" by going hungry; after all, she herself had given up wheat and rice towards this end.[18] The upshot of Mrs Gandhi's "conventionalism", then, was a strong preference for order—political as well as social—the relentless pursuit of which made her, in the words of Ashis Nandy, a practitioner of "pure politics": politics, for her, was a zero-sum game of hegemony.[19]

Authoritarian submission—in her case, submission to traditional, spiritual authorities—can be seen in the prime minister's dealings with Dhirendra Brahmachari and the "queues of astrologers" she consulted "at her Delhi bungalow".[20] Her spiritual masters came from all corners of the country, including Bihar, Uttar Pradesh, Pondicherry, West Bengal, and Maharashtra. The most important among these was Brahmachari, whom

---

[15] *TOI*, 30 September 1967, p. 9; *TOI*, 12 January 1968, p. 9.

[16] Gandhi, *My Truth*, p. 172.

[17] Carras, *Indira Gandhi*, p. 237.

[18] *SSWIG*, vol. 1, pp. 31, 53, 343; Jayakar, *Indira*, p. 145.

[19] "Sanctified by the amoral dispassionate politics preached in the *Arthashastra* and reflected in the political idiom and strategies of some of the characters in the *Mahabharata*, the Brahmanical concept of politics has always been a zero-sum game." Nandy, *At the Edge of Psychology*, p. 114.

[20] *Economist*, 29 May 1976, p. 11.

we encountered in Chapter 1: "tall and attractive" with a "superb phy-sique, enhanced by the fact that he wore few clothes even in cold weather", this yoga instructor also doubled up as an important, if informal, policy adviser.[21] Another figure who Mrs Gandhi held in high regard was Kamalapati Tripathi, Uttar Pradesh chief minister and amateur astrologer. In 1973, faced with protests and rising prices, Mrs Gandhi turned in des-peration to "the Mother", a Pondicherry mystic at the Aurobindo Ashram who purported to battle the dark forces of drought and stagflation; later that year the prime minister "received her benediction" from the Mother.[22] During the Emergency, completely isolated, Mrs Gandhi was known to visit Bengali mystic Anandamayi in Dehra Dun, and to consult "sage-philosopher" J. Krishnamurti.

Given to superstition and "stereotypy"? Just after independence, she had notoriously annoyed her father, who was famously a product of early-twentieth-century scientific rationalism, when she delayed her move to Teen Murti by hearkening to fortune-tellers. When the Allahabad judgment arrived in 1975 she wavered over the date on which to file her appeal: astrologers had to be consulted first.[23] Later that year, in November, she took counsel from tantrics before firing H.N. Bahuguna, chief minister of Uttar Pradesh. The business of auspicious dates was to return in 1980, when she filed her nomination papers at 12:30 p.m. on 6 October, again on the advice of astrologers; after she won, she refused to be sworn in as prime minister before 14 January, the holiest of days in the Hindu calendar: the winter solstice. Her behaviour was to grow even more erratic with time. When a solar eclipse occurred in February that year she scuttled indoors, to the surprise of all those around her, and shuttered herself in her room alone until it had passed. In short, the sheer profusion of otherworldly counsellors had the effect of shifting the focus of political authority in Mrs Gandhi's *Weltanschauung*—more important than popular approval was divine sanction.

Power and toughness? Even early on in her career, her exaggerated sense of self-worth was evident. She described herself as the *de facto* ruler during Nehru's late years: "people do not realise how much *papu* depended on me."[24] Informally, she had played an important role at Teen Murti, where

---

[21] Frank, *Indira*, p. 245.
[22] Masani, *Indira*, p. 278.
[23] Tandon, *PMO Diary I*, p. 386.
[24] Jayakar, *Indira*, p. 399.

she lived with her father, and during his seventeen years as premier he had grown increasingly reliant on his daughter, who began to take some of the most controversial political decisions of the 1950s on his behalf. In 1959, after assuming the Congress presidency, becoming the third Nehru to do so, she set herself to the task of toppling Kerala's elected Communist government. When the CPI took office in 1957, Mrs Gandhi reportedly told her father that "the Congress can't just stand by." Now, with her at the party helm, it no longer had to. She did not bother sweet-talking the press: "I intend to fight them and throw them out", she said to the *Hindu*.[25] Insinuating that the Communists were authoritarians, she campaigned alongside Hindu nationalists and the Muslim League against the state government's Education Bill, which sought to curb the monopoly on schools enjoyed by the Christian Church, the League, and the Nair Service Society. In the event, she convinced her father to throw out the Communists and declare President's Rule.

Four years later, not long after India's military defeat by the Chinese, Mrs Gandhi conspired with Nehru to announce the "Kamaraj Plan", named after the chief minister of Tamil Nadu who, India's astonished public was asked to believe, had scripted his own purge. Apparently, under the slogan of "party before post", he had proposed that six chief ministers and six cabinet ministers resign to help revive the party's grassroots.[26] After her father's death, as information and broadcasting minister Mrs Gandhi felt comfortable enough to step on the toes of Nehru's successor, Lal Bahadur Shastri, arriving in Madras when riots broke out and assuring local elites that, contrary to the past record of the centre, the union government had no plans to foist Hindi on the South. When a nettled Shastri confronted her, she declared that she did not see herself as a "mere minister of information and broadcasting" but as "one of the leaders of the country." With the press she was even more smug: "Do you think this government can survive if I resign today? I am telling you it won't. Yes, I have jumped over the prime minister's head and I would do it again whenever the need arises."[27] Nevertheless, the test of her indispensability never came to pass, for two months later, Shastri was dead. But before his passing, she had already begun mounting a coup: the prime minister had "swerved from the right

[25] Vasudev, *Indira Gandhi*, pp. 274–6.
[26] Kamaraj himself resigned as well and was elected president of the Congress, a post he held for four years.
[27] Malhotra, *Indira Gandhi*, p. 84.

path", she said in an interview, trying to dampen the khaki enthusiasm that had gripped the country after the 1965 war.[28] But militarism suddenly acquired a new utility the next time the two countries went to war. By then, of course, Mrs Gandhi had succeeded Shastri.

When in December 1971 the Pakistani air force bombed a handful of Indian air bases, her immediate reaction was: "Thank god, they've attacked us." Here was the opportunity to demonstrate power and toughness at its finest: a war. After brief skirmishes and a victory, she became "very very arrogant. She loved being called Durga", one of her aides later observed.[29] By the end of her first term Mrs Gandhi could barely conceal her contempt for parliamentary democracy: "Sometimes I feel that even our parliamentary system is moribund. Everything is debated and nothing gets done", she said to the *New Yorker*.[30] In her second term her appearances in parliament became infrequent. Better than debates were more linear forms of communication: radio and television; informal interviews with *Blitz*, a lifestyle magazine; and communiqués made during visits abroad. A combination of indispensability and infallibility, in short, prepared the ground for dictatorship. As Ashis Nandy observes, "Mrs Gandhi, long before she imposed her Emergency rule, had managed to affirm convincingly that she was the sole depository of power in the country."[31]

Destructiveness and cynicism? Its earliest manifestation, as seen above, was the purge of 1963 when twelve significant Congress ministers were "Kamaraj'd". Later, evidence of the same tendencies included deinstitutionalisation of the party, the splitting of the Congress, the purging of the very groupings on whose backs she rode to power: the Syndicate, CFSA, and Urs faction were all sidelined at various points in the 1970s.[32]

Projectivity? Here, her remarks on the Nehruvian years were revealing: "My father was a saint who strayed into politics ... He did allow everybody to grow. Even those whom we considered weeds. He did allow them to grow even though they were constantly threatening him."[33] Time and again she warned him against such figures who would "drag you down with their own rottenness." And in Nehru's penultimate year in power she was convinced that the would-be saboteurs had shifted their attention to her. When

---

[28] Masani, *Indira*, p. 134.

[29] Bass, *The Blood Telegram*, p. 337.

[30] Mehta, *Portrait of India*, p. 501.

[31] Nandy, *At the Edge of Psychology*, p. 120.

[32] More on this below.

[33] Hart, "Indira Gandhi", p. 257.

asked if she wanted to succeed Nehru, she said the question did not arise because "they'll kill me off."[34] Who "they" were, she did not care to elaborate. In any case, it mattered little. Rivalry and intrigue were never the stuff of ordinary politics for her; they were questions of life and death. Her competitors never just wanted her office, they wanted to wipe her off the face of the earth. "You do not know the plots against me", she said to the press, "Jayaprakash and Morarji*bhai* have always hated me. They were determined to see that I was destroyed."[35] But the adversaries of the day were not the only peril. In fact, especially during the 1970s, virtually every threat appeared to emanate from the CIA. The *ne plus ultra* of floating signifiers, the American spy agency appeared to be behind absolutely everything: the JP Movement, the Allahabad High Court ruling, workers demanding higher wages, communal riots, vote rigging, citizens protesting against rising prices, and assassination plots against her.

Such views quickly translated into authoritarian aggression. Her autobiographical writings and speeches are replete with paranoid worries over those espousing distasteful views—the "traitors", "anti-nationalists", "agitators", and "rumourmongers"—all who needed to be purged by supersessions, shuffles, and sackings.[36] Likewise, trade unions, student movements, and peasant uprisings had either to be crushed or rendered impotent.

What, finally, of her anti-intraception, her unemotive character? On this front, much has been made of her reserve. The adjectives used by her colleagues and biographers to describe her personality are typically "aloof", "cold", "secretive", "withdrawn", "reserved", and, more disturbingly for a career politician, "silent". Indeed, a number of figures reported "meetings" with her in which the dialogue was entirely one-way: often, when figures briefed her on events, voiced their opinions, and asked for her comments, it transpired that they were in essence talking to a wall: "she continued to keep silent."[37] Cabinet ministers too complained that "her studied silence"

---

[34] Mrs Gandhi to Nehru, 1 May 1958, cited in Gandhi, *Two Alone, Two Together*, p. 562.

[35] Jayakar, *Indira*, p. 286.

[36] Gandhi, *My Truth*, p. 162 *et passim*; *TOI*, 25 January 1973, p. 9; *TOI*, 9 March 1975, p. 7.

[37] This happened to many figures, including Malcolm Macdonald (the British high commissioner to India), Pupul Jayakar, Jayaprakash Narayan, J. Krishnamurti, Morarji Desai, the Chogyal of Sikkim, British Prime Minister James Callaghan, and Vijayalakshmi Pandit: Jayakar, *Indira*, pp. 204, 146, 226, 310, 376; Dhar, *Indira Gandhi, the "Emergency", and Indian Democracy*, p. 292; Malhotra, *Indira*, p. 283; Sahgal, *Indira*, p. 9.

frequently left them wondering if she was for or against a certain policy.[38] In parliament as well, she habitually "lapsed into silences", though these grew less frequent as time wore on.

What of friendships? Here again we see the same reserve. Her biographer observes that "at the age of fifty-one, she had only three intimate friends: Dorothy Norman, Marie Seton (both of whom she rarely saw)", and Pupul Jayakar, a friendship that was practically professional; days before her death, Mrs Gandhi commissioned Jayakar to write her official biography.[39]

To sum up: Nandy, who was the first to point to Adorno's relevance in the Indian setting, analyses Mrs Gandhi's "pure politics" as a set of positions that was "de-ideologized, amoral and uninformed by any compassion." Tellingly, he sees in her traces of Chanakya, the Indian Machiavelli.

This reading of Mrs Gandhi's political personality is well illustrated by her reactions to some of the biggest political events not long after her assumption of the Congress presidency in 1959: revulsion at the Communist victory in Kerala; dismay at Shastri's decision to return territories to Pakistan after the 1965 war; disdain towards the concerns of peripheral populations—less than a month into office she ordered the carpet-bombing of the Mizo Hills.

In brief, she showed affinities with the rightist values fortifying the F-scale: nationalism, militarism, a notion of welfare in which the poor must pull themselves up by their bootstraps, albeit with some chivvying from the political classes about national renewal. This in essence was paternalistic authoritarianism. "I feel that India is like a baby", she said on 25 June 1975, hours before declaring the Emergency, "and just as one should sometimes take a child and shake it, I feel we have to shake India."[40]

The Uncertain Making of a Dynast Born to Rule

An "authoritarian personality", then, Mrs Gandhi certainly had, and her quest for power reflected this. Competitors were, she thought, depriving her of her destiny. "Quite honestly, I was the only natural choice for the job", she later recalled.[41] The stakes for her were particularly high on 11 January 1966, when Prime Minister Lal Bahadur Shastri died, prompting

---

[38] Sahgal, *Indira*, p. 42.

[39] Frank, *Indira*, p. 310.

[40] Jayakar, *Indira*, p. 207.

[41] Mehta, *Portrait of India*, p. 500.

the Syndicate—a loose grouping of regional party bosses who constituted the Congress establishment—to go through the motions in search of a replacement, just as they had twenty months earlier, after Nehru's death. On that occasion, Mrs Gandhi had felt cheated out of a job she considered hers by right. This time round she was adamant. Indeed, on the night of Shastri's passing in Tashkent she all but threw her hat in the ring: "no one can be prime minister without my support", she asserted.[42] In the meanwhile the Syndicate set to work. Defence Minister Y.B. Chavan was found unacceptable by fellow Bombay leader S.K. Patil. Kamaraj, who had little knowledge of either Hindi or English, preferred manoeuvring behind the scenes. Morarji Desai, an old nemesis of this cartel, was certain to contest its choice. The Syndicate's task was therefore clear: to find a candidate who could defeat him if it came to a showdown in the Congress Parliamentary Party.

In the event, the bosses settled on Indira Gandhi, the woman of the moment.[43] Scion of the Congress' first family, she had held high positions in party and government and was widely identified, both within the Congress and without, as Nehru redivivus. This was doubly useful: a Nehru at the helm ensured dynastic continuity and popular legitimacy in the 1967 elections and, *a fortiori*, prevented Desai from becoming the cynosure of Indian political life. Besides, she came with experience. As the incumbent minister of information and broadcasting she was, unusually, designated the fourth-ranking minister in the cabinet and had been made a member of the Emergency Committee which dealt with issues of national security.[44] Having served as Nehru's aide at the prime minister's home during his seventeen years in office, she was familiar with the corridors of power and figures of the establishment.[45] During that long internship she had, despite being "nobody in the government", access to "every secret affairs [*sic*], every secret agreement, every secret correspondence, every important let-

---

[42] Jayakar, *Indira*, p. 177.

[43] For a detailed narrative of the machinations behind Indira Gandhi's selection, see Brecher, *Succession in India*, pp. 190–225.

[44] This was a compromise. She coveted the foreign ministry: transcript of interview with I.K. Gujral, Acc. No. 797, NMML Oral History Project, p. 119.

[45] Whenever a political leader, bureaucrat, or foreign dignitary visited Teen Murti, the prime minister's residence, Nehru made it a point to introduce Indira Gandhi to them: transcript of interview with Janak Raj Jai, Acc. No. 751, NMML Oral History Project, p. 217. Jai was a civil servant who worked under both Nehru and Mrs Gandhi between 1948 and 1969 in the PMS and at Teen Murti.

ter, inside the country [and] outside."[46] She had also served as a member of the Congress Working Committee and the Central Election Committee, giving her, in effect, a hand in both policy-making and the disbursement of tickets. Moreover, she never had any truck with ideology, either her father's "socialism" or Desai's free-marketeering. And finally, she maintained a low profile, was predisposed to compliance, and had the fewest enemies within Congress ranks, all qualities admired by the Syndicate and its lead king-maker, Kamaraj, who did most of the canvassing.[47] On the eve of the CPP meeting that was to decide Shastri's successor, she was sure of its outcome, even writing a letter to her son Rajiv, quoting Robert Frost: "How hard it is to keep from being king, when it is in you and the situation."[48] In the poll, Indira Gandhi coasted to victory with 355 votes to Desai's 169.

Even so, right from the start the Syndicate saw her as another stopgap prime minister who would not long outlast her usefulness. Indeed, many of them held her in contempt: for all practical purposes she was a mari-onette. To Desai she was "Indira-*ben*" (sister Indira), or just a "*chhokri*" (a slip of a girl).[49] Proving herself and consolidating power was going to be an uphill struggle. If she was born to be king, then, her king-makers felt otherwise. Purges, clashes, policy somersaults, and a thorough reordering of state–society, executive–judiciary, and party–government relations ensued.[50] Her paranoid style of politics, in brief, was deepened in no small measure by the need to break out of the Syndicate straitjacket. As a strategy it certainly worked. It left Kamaraj fuming: "a great man's daughter, a little man's great mistake", he muttered pathetically to a friend, and went on to keep Mrs Gandhi firmly ensconced in office for over a decade.[51]

Thus, if Mrs Gandhi's fiery personality predisposed her to authoritarian-ism, Congress bosses played no small part in fanning the flames. Obliquely, then, the Syndicate made the Emergency possible, because it was in reac-tion to the threats posed by it that she split the party and transformed it

[46] Ibid., p. 220.

[47] "Mrs Gandhi emerged from a process of elimination": Brecher, *Succession in India*, p. 236. In fact, she rarely spoke in parliament, using a proxy, Pattabhiraman, a minister of state, to ask questions on her behalf: transcript of interview with I.K. Gujral, Acc. No. 797, NMML Oral History Project, p. 99.

[48] Jayakar, *Indira*, p. 179.

[49] Hart, "Indira Gandhi", p. 258.

[50] This is the subject of the next section.

[51] Jayakar, *Indira*, p. 145.

into her creature.[52] So it is both her constitution and the circumstances she found herself in that explain her obsession with loyalty. As a figure who observed her at close quarters noted in his diary in December 1975:

> Mrs G's principal concern is her own personal position. She wants 200 percent loyalty—not hundred percent—from everybody and has surrounded herself with men of straw like Bansi Lal, P.C. Sethi. Everybody, whether a politician, civil servant, businessman or industrialist will be judged by personal loyalty to herself.[53]

But what of Sanjay, the other authoritarian personality at the centre of this drama?[54] Why did Mrs Gandhi let him implement his radical policies? Vinod Mehta, his biographer, speculates that she suffered from an acute guilt complex *vis-à-vis* her younger son. She came to regret "paying too much attention to her father and too little to her sons" through the 1950s. Sanjay—"the product of a broken home"—then was "mummy's boy, but mummy was seldom around."[55] As a result Mrs Gandhi sought in her later years to overcompensate for her lack of maternal care earlier, even to the point of breaking with her closest advisers. P.N. Haksar, for instance, probably the most powerful apparatchik in Delhi, was sacked in 1973 for suggesting that Sanjay's powers be kept in abeyance and Maruti wound up.[56] Notably, this happened after Haksar had spent six years at the helm of the PMS, years spent tirelessly in the service of the family, helping "get Sanjay out of several youthful scrapes involving drinks, cars, and women."[57]

---

[52] As discussed in the next section of this chapter.

[53] Subimal Dutt, Haksar's former boss, cited in Ramesh, *Intertwined Lives*, p. 365.

[54] Mrs Gandhi's physician had the following to say about Sanjay's personality: "He was methodical in everything he did. For instance, when he had breakfast, he always took everything in a fixed quantity and this never changed"; and about his aversion for dissent: "He had a short fuse where discussions and arguments were concerned. If you did not agree with him, his face would turn red and he would get up and walk out. He did not like to be contradicted." Mathur, *The Unseen Indira Gandhi*, pp. 92, 101.

[55] Mehta, *The Sanjay Story*, pp. 30, 35–6, 235.

[56] Tandon, *PMO Diary I* (entry of 4 January 1975), p. 132; Vasudev, *Two Faces of Indira Gandhi*, p. 33.

[57] Lukas, "India is as Indira Does", p. 86. Haksar and Mrs Gandhi maintained ties after the Emergency was declared, despite his criticism of the new dispensation. Ironically, "there is very strong evidence to suggest that Indira Gandhi's 20–point programme had been derived in large part from a note of Haksar that had been sent to her a day *before* her announcement." Ramesh, *Intertwined Lives*, p. 362.

Moreover, during the Emergency Sanjay's unrestrained attacks on Haksar and the Congress' Communist allies received barely a censure from his mother.[58]

For Ashis Nandy, Mrs Gandhi found in Sanjay what she could not in her advisers: loyalty. "It was not so much Indira Gandhi's search for an heir-apparent as her search for total loyalty which produced the political phenomenon called Sanjay Gandhi."[59] Such a temperament also dictated against the plurality of opinions: "gradually she was being left with only those who could present no political threat to her: her family and their hangers-on, a handful of unscrupulous bureaucrats and small-time politicians ..."[60]

Such conservative *ad hominem* analyses are of course risible. Not all products of broken homes go on to become dictators. Nor do all lonely children. Nor for that matter does a politician's search for loyalty inevitably lead to authoritarian rule. Whatever the reason for Mrs Gandhi never saying "no" to her second son, the question remains: why did she have her way all the time? At this point one needs to understand how she centralised power at the expense of institutions, including the Congress, from the late 1960s.

The Deinstitutionalisation of the Congress and the Centralisation of Power

To trace the genealogy of the Emergency, one could begin with the 1967 polls. On the eve of that election, pollster E.P.W. da Costa, the man who "brought Gallup to India", noted that the Congress "enters the political arena, for the first time, as a political loser, not as a guaranteed victor."[61] In that election the Indian National Congress, the party in control of the levers of power since independence in 1947, was in for a rude awakening. But its electoral humbling was not the only reason for the centralisation and deinstitutionalisation of the party that followed. The way Congress bosses tried to control Mrs Gandhi in the wake of their setback was

---

[58] In making a similar case in their accounts of the Emergency, both Vinod Mehta and Janardan Thakur cite a *Guardian* dispatch, probably an apocryphal story: over sumptuous fare with friends, the son apparently slapped his mother across the face six times as she sat motionless. Invariably, in this retelling, some kind of *kompromat* is hinted at, of which we will never know. See, *inter alia*, Mehta, *The Sanjay Story*; Thakur, *All the Prime Minister's Men*.

[59] Nandy, "Indira Gandhi and the Culture of Indian Politics", in idem, *At the Edge of Psychology*, p. 126.

[60] Ibid., p. 115.

[61] Guha, "An Indian's Verdict".

another. After all, for authority to concentrate in the hands of the few figures that belonged to Mrs Gandhi's cabal, it required the crippling of those men who had jobbed her into power: the Syndicate.

The Consequences of 1967

In a sense, the principal casualty of the fourth quinquennial poll was not simply the Congress but political authority itself. On the campaign trail hecklers pelted stones at Mrs Gandhi, breaking her nose. Nor were her opponents spared: Madhu Limaye of the SSP was waylaid and roughed up, and CPI(M) leader Jyoti Basu hit on the head. Meanwhile, inside the grand old party, against the backdrop of large-scale defections severely weakening it, the last months of 1966 witnessed a bitter struggle over constituency nominations between Mrs Gandhi and Morarji Desai, then the party's Number Two.[62] As it turned out, the bargaining efforts came to naught: losing 95 seats, the Congress barely scraped a majority with 283 MPs in the 516-strong Lok Sabha. All the major Syndicate figures—S.K. Patil in Bombay, Atulya Ghosh in Bengal, Biju Patnaik in Orissa, and K. Kamaraj in Madras—went down in defeat. The same fate befell five cabinet members, three ministers of state, six deputy ministers, and four chief ministers. In the concurrent state elections the party lost power to coalitions led by the Communists in Kerala, the right-wing Swatantra Party in Orissa, and cross-spectrum alliances in five other states.[63]

But in the electoral debacle and popular protests, Indira Gandhi saw creative destruction. The Syndicate barons, having lost their seats in parliament, were finally rendered impotent. A window of change had presented

---

[62] He wanted to make a bid for the leadership of the Congress Parliamentary Party, but in the aftermath of the 1967 elections was convinced against it: he was instead made deputy prime minister, an office only irregularly occupied, thus, a demonstration of Desai's influence within the Congress. See Brecher, "Succession in India 1967", pp. 425–6. Indeed, the landscape of defections was pan-Indian: Rajmata Scindia of the Gwalior palace left with her entire faction the D.P. Mishra–dominated Madhya Pradesh Congress; defections from the Bihar Congress resulted in the formation of the Jan Kranti Dal by a former PCC president; in Orissa a former chief minister formed the Jana Congress; and the incumbent president of the West Bengal PCC created the Bangla Congress after having briefly supported the communist opposition against his own party: Frankel, *India's Political Economy*, pp. 344–5.

[63] Kothari, "The Political Change of 1967", pp. 231–2; Hewitt, *Political Mobilisation and Democracy in India*, p. 79.

itself. In what followed, Indira Gandhi was to destroy what her father had achieved with the Congress. For Nehru had pooled the competencies of the state with regional leaders and party notables, seeing in the devolution of power his best chance of political survival. Seen instrumentally, the relationship between the premier and his party in early postcolonial India was one where the balance tilted to the latter: Nehru at the apex depended heavily on the state bosses for votes, policy implementation, and party funds; all the latter needed was that the ruler time and again look the other way. In essence Nehru was, in James Manor's formulation, "less the leader of the Congress than its prisoner."[64] This style of rule not only ensured his own longevity, it institutionalised the Congress and provided it local roots. It was precisely this arrangement that Mrs Gandhi upended while trying to emancipate herself from the party bosses—the Syndicate—who in 1967, luckily for her, had lost their seats in large numbers.

Crucial to her consolidation of power in the party was the CWC session of 12 May 1967, where, ironically, Mrs Gandhi was more spectator than participant. Still, as we will see, it was at this meeting that the dividing line was drawn; this session, then, was central to her political formation. Here, the party adopted a new Ten-Point Programme, hoping to stem its decline with a popular set of redistributive policies. Its contents were the usual socialist desiderata, which included the nationalisation of banks and general insurance, state control over foodgrains, curbs on monopolies, fair-price shops, living wages, and land ceilings. But the proponents of this wish list were not among nature's socialists. In fact the Congress leaders behind this programme included old-guard grandees such as the Syndicate's Atulya Ghosh and former finance minister C.D. Deshmukh.[65] In their minds the party's survival was uppermost.[66] But the Ten Points would have failed to come to fruition had it not been for the backing of the then-ascendant Congress Forum for Socialist Action (CFSA). This was a rebooted version of the Congress Socialist Forum which, during the middle Nehru years, had espoused land reform, the co-operativisation of agriculture, and an alliance with the Praja Socialist Party (PSP). The CFSA was

---

[64] Manor, "Indira and After", p. 317. See also Kothari, "The Congress 'System'", pp. 1161–73.

[65] Transcript of interview with Madhu Dandavate, Acc. No. 778, NMML Oral History Project, p. 83.

[66] Other Syndicate members concurred that socialist policies were necessary to revive the Congress: Kamaraj, "Why Congress Debacle?", pp. 9–10.

revived in 1962 with essentially the same programme and even the same leaders—Gulzarilal Nanda, Chaudhary Brahm Prakash, K.D. Malaviya, and Subhadra Joshi. After the 1967 polls, new life was injected into this forum by a group of entryist PSP men, the "Young Turks", figures such as Krishan Kant, Chandra Shekhar, Mohan Dharia, and Ram Dhan, all encountered earlier. Initially, Mrs Gandhi disliked the radicalism of this ginger group. To begin with, she was livid when the call to abolish privy purses was at the eleventh hour snuck into the Ten Points as an amendment by Mohan Dharia, general secretary of the Maharashtra PCC.[67]

The Leftist Card

However, Mrs Gandhi soon realised that though she was not a socialist, she could rely on the Congress Left to fight the Syndicate and Morarji Desai, her main, more conservative competitors. By 1969 she had effected a leftist mutation for a new truth had dawned upon her: "The whole mood of the country is Centre Left", she declared in an interview.[68] A timely weather-cock, she now firmly positioned herself with the CFSA, which at the time enjoyed the support of some 170 Congress MPs. She then proceeded to lay into the Congress Right at the Faridabad session of the AICC in April.[69] Emboldened, CFSA members rebuked party president Nijalingappa when he pleaded for a more capital-friendly regime. Privately he confided to his diary that the socialist insurgents were "scamps" and prepared for a final face-off. Publicly, too reticent to make his real views known, he defended himself by declaring that he was, in fact, a "socialist to the core".[70]

Three months later Mrs Gandhi took up the cudgels for socialism more forcefully in what came to be known as the Stray Thoughts Memorandum, a "hurriedly dictated" set of policies drafted by her principal secretary and confidant P.N. Haksar. This was read out on her behalf by cabinet minister Fakhruddin Ali Ahmed at a CWC meeting. Its substance was merely a rehearsal, at times almost verbatim, of the Ten Points and previous CFSA documents, but, this time round, crucially, it came with her imprimatur.[71]

---

[67] Krishnan, *Chavan and the Troubled Decade*, p. 164; Dharia, *Fumes and the Fire*, p. 4.

[68] Jayakar, *Indira*, p. 207.

[69] Dharia, *Fumes and the Fire*, p. 5.

[70] Mishra, *The Post-Nehru Era*, pp. 78–9; Nayar, *India After Nehru*, p. 143.

[71] That Mrs Gandhi's turn to the left remained at best Laodicean was clear in her speeches. For instance, at the Bangalore session of the AICC in July 1969 she said

Passed unanimously by the CWC, the memo even received the support of Desai, whose submission bore testament to the decimation of the Congress Right. A week later, blaming him for being a conservative burr under the progressive saddle, Mrs Gandhi stripped him of his finance portfolio, soon after which he resigned as deputy prime minister as well.[72] Meanwhile, the ranks of the Congress Left swelled as centrists of old stampeded in the direction of the new bandwagon.

In May the same year the rump Syndicate and the premier locked horns on yet another issue. Zakir Hussain's death had left the national presidency vacant, and convention dictated that the republic's vice president V.V. Giri, former union leader and darling of the Congress Left, assume the mantle.[73] The Syndicate, however, wanted as head of state their point man, Neelam Sanjiva Reddy. A vote in the Congress Parliamentary Board was taken which settled the question in their favour.[74] In the meantime Mrs Gandhi, then touring Japan, was tipped off by "personal allies" that Sanjiva Reddy's appointment was just the first step in an effort to pull the plug on her premiership. Once sworn in, he would remove her from office, she was told, and then call upon the Syndicate to demonstrate their numbers in parliament.[75] Upon hearing this she panicked. Now framing the nomination as if

---

that nationalising banks "might or might not be a good idea", "but it had become a slogan of radicalism"—"it is not right to cling to slogans": Austin, *Working a Democratic Constitution*, p. 178.

[72] The political landscape was altering rapidly: the "stray thoughts" were delivered on 9 July; Desai was fired as finance minister on 16 July. Despite the ideological colouring given to the decision, he was ousted primarily for his decision to back the Syndicate's candidate for president.

[73] Giri was once part of a radical collective that founded an "anarchical society" in Dublin in the 1910s. He later served as AITUC president in 1926 and 1942 and as general secretary of the All India Railwaymen's Federation from 1929 to 1936. See the transcript of interview with V.V. Giri, Acc. No. 379, NMML Oral History Project, p. 11.

[74] Giri received two votes: Mrs Gandhi's and Fakhruddin Ali Ahmed's. The latter would go on to become president himself. The abstentions included Indira Gandhi's ally Jagjivan Ram and the Syndicate member S. Nijalingappa. Reddy polled four votes: Kamaraj and S.K. Patil of the Syndicate; Morarji Desai, who was fired four days later; and, surprisingly, Home Minister Y.B. Chavan, who was from the prime minister's faction. Despite his dissent, Chavan was not axed because of his strong electoral base in Maharashtra: Austin, *Working a Democratic Constitution*, pp. 178–9.

[75] Frankel, *India's Political Economy*, p. 415.

it were a referendum on the Congress' place on the ideological spectrum, she had Giri, in his role as acting president, promulgate an ordinance nationalising fourteen private-sector banks.[76] She then let it be known that the upcoming presidential election was a "vote of conscience": the official Congress candidate was Reddy—backed by the Syndicate, and possibly the Jana Sangh and Swatantra party as well—but Giri, now contesting as an independent, was her preferred choice. When the results streamed in on 20 August, it turned out that her man had, with the backing of the Communist parties, the DMK, and the Akali Dal, narrowly won.

Inevitably, then, the Congress was split down the middle on the question of leadership. Led by Nijalingappa, the Syndicate expelled Mrs Gandhi from the party on 12 November. Anticipating the move, she quickly rustled up a new party and coalition within days: the Congress (Requisitionist),[77] with its 222 seats and external support from the CPI and DMK, was now in essence a government without a party.[78] Its obverse was the Syndicate-backed Desai-led faction, the Congress (Organisation), with 61 seats: a large party apparatus that in failing to dismantle Mrs Gandhi's parliamentary majority had wound up on the opposition benches. In short, the Nehruvian Congress system had finally been laid to rest.[79]

The Making of an All-Powerful Executive

With the Syndicate sitting on the other side of the fence, Indira Gandhi was free to pack her party's upper echelons with loyalists. They were drawn in the main from two pools: Congress veterans such as Fakhruddin Ali Ahmed, Y.B. Chavan, Jagjivan Ram, and Uma Shankar Dikshit comprised

---

[76] This was done on the same day, 19 July, as Desai's resignation as deputy prime minister.

[77] The odd party name comes from the early November entreaty of 441 of the AICC's 750 members, backed by Mrs Gandhi, to "requisition" an AICC meeting to replace Nijalingappa with a party president more to her liking.

[78] The CPI were less guided by ideology than by the fear of having to fight elections again if the assembly was dissolved: transcript of interview with Bhogendra Jha, Acc. No. 766, NMML Oral History Project, p. 37.

[79] "The crisis of 1969 was already pregnant with that of 1975", wrote Max Zins, drawing a connection between the legitimacy of the Congress leadership and the centralisation and authoritarianism that followed. See Zins, "Hegemony and Dominance", cited in Mayer, "Congress (I), Emergency (I)", p. 138. Mrs Gandhi had a similar reading: the "crisis had been brewing since 1969", she said during the Emergency: *SW*, 23 August 1975, p. 5.

one, and the Left that coalesced around the CFSA the other. The latter group had in this period received fresh stimulus by way of the "Kumaramangalam Thesis". Its Communist architect Mohan Kumaramangalam reasoned that it was unlikely that the Left could beat the Congress in an electoral system rigged against smaller parties lacking grassroots reach and pecuniary power.[80] Hence, more was to be achieved by pushing the Congress towards reform from outside the Communist Party than from within it. Better still, Communists could infiltrate the Congress *en masse* and steer its direction from within the grand old party itself.[81] To this end, Kumaramangalam decided in favour of entryism into the Forum. In this endeavour he was joined by other CPI members and sympathisers, including Chandrajit Yadav, Nandini Satpathy, D.P. Dhar, I.K. Gujral, K.R. Ganesh, Nurul Hasan, Rajni Patel, and K.V. Raghunatha Reddy, many of whom were handed cabinet positions by Mrs Gandhi in her bid to undercut Syndicate figures.

Within the broad Requisitionist coalition, four men stood out for their proximity to the prime minister. There was, first, P.N. Haksar, Mrs Gandhi's principal secretary from 1967 to 1973, who believed in making the bureaucracy "committed" to both the political leadership and a new economic programme inspired by "Marxian dialectics".[82] Second, Kumaramangalam.

[80] Kumaramangalam, *Communists in Congress*, p. 81ff. The "thesis" was privately circulated within the CPI in 1964, when the Forum was hostile to Communists, and kept hidden from public eyes until 1973, by which time the CFSA had readily taken in CPI members. Kumaramangalam, the son of a leading Tamil Congressman, was educated at the LSE and Oxford, where he befriended and became a confidant of Mrs Gandhi's. He left the CPI in 1966 to join the Congress five years later. Between 1971 and 1973, until his death in a plane crash on 31 May, he served first as minister of steel and heavy engineering, and then minister of steel and mines. Many Congressmen saw him as a mole.

[81] This had been attempted previously in the 1930s and 1950s, when the CPI attempted to infiltrate and steer from within the Congress Socialist Party on the one hand, and convince its more left-wing elements to split and join the CPI on the other. The twin strategies yielded no results in the former decade, and slight success in the latter, when the "Left Socialists", a grouping within the CSP, crossed over to join the Communists: transcript of interview with Madhu Limaye, Acc. No. 733, NMML Oral History Project, pp. 69–72, 76–80.

[82] Haksar, like Mrs Gandhi a Kashmiri from Allahabad, had studied in England and joined the foreign service on Nehru's advice after obtaining a degree from the LSE. His six years as an all-powerful principal secretary ended abruptly in 1973 when he was fired for being too critical of Sanjay's car enterprise. For his views,

Third, S.S. Ray, minister for education and later chief minister of West Bengal, whose friendship with Mrs Gandhi was built on adolescent association and epistolary empathy.[83] This morphed into an even closer professional relationship in later years when he rid his state of Naxalite insurgencies with paramilitary heavy-handedness and envisioned the Emergency's legal architecture. And fourth, H.R. Gokhale, former trade-union lawyer and Bombay High Court judge who was to become law minister, spearheading a number of constitutional amendments in parliament during the Emergency. In the popular press this quartet, along with the prime minister and half a dozen others, were called the "kitchen cabinet" and believed to be behind virtually every executive decision. But in truth, at this point in time these men commanded far less power than they did a hazy blueprint for the country's future.[84]

This changed after the 1971 general election. Prior to Mrs Gandhi's decision to go to the polls that year, not long after the Supreme Court overturned bank nationalisation and invalidated the abolition of privy purses, state and national elections had been a concurrent affair. By abbreviating the incumbent Lok Sabha's term to four years, Mrs Gandhi was, in effect, injecting a fresh populist tenor to the vote. Moreover, in forcing parties to fight general and state elections separately, this move significantly increased the costs of campaigning. Inevitably, the biggest beneficiary was the country's richest party.[85] Furthermore, gone were the local issues so important to local polls. In its place came Mrs Gandhi's person: "I am the issue", she said to *Newsweek*. The opposition parties picked on the theme: "Indira Hatao" (Get Rid of Indira), they chanted at rallies. Mrs Gandhi's response was both a riff and a deflection: "Garibi Hatao" (Get Rid of Poverty). It was rather easy, then, for Mrs Gandhi to paint her opposition as a bunch of reactionary outfits. In contrast to the motley crew of indus-

---

see Haksar, *Premonitions*; for his life, see Ramesh, *Intertwined Lives*. See also the *festschrift* for him: Sarkar, P.N. Haksar.

[83] See, for instance, a flirtatious 1974 sample from Ray to Mrs Gandhi after she suffered a minor horse-riding accident: "How did you manage to fall on your finger when there were so many other comfortable 'places' to fall on?" Jayakar, Indira, p. 257.

[84] The key people were never the same. At various times, Asoka Mehta, C. Subramaniam, Dinesh Singh, D.P. Mishra, F.A. Ahmed, I.K. Gujral, Nandini Satpathy, and Uma Shankar Dikshit were all members of it.

[85] Morris-Jones, "India Elects for Change", pp. 719–41.

trial and landed elites running against her, she showed a willingness to talk about, and to a very limited extent empathise with, rural resentment. Starved of funds and taken by surprise, the opposition fared badly in the snap election.[86] In contrast, the Congress (R) was an election machine, wealthy and organised. In no previous election had the prime minister and the Congress' Central Election Committee played such a decisive role in distributing tickets. Mrs Gandhi, it was felt, was personally invested in every MP's election. Technology worked in her favour: unlike her father, who had to rely on party workers mapping out elaborate routes by road for the campaign trail, Mrs Gandhi made extensive use of airplanes, clocking 30,000 miles in the skies, addressing 13 million people directly in 252 "big public meetings" over 41 days.[87] And building a cult of personality helped as well: thousands of posters and breastpins with Mrs Gandhi's face emblazoned on them were distributed wherever she went. As a Jana Sangh leader in Delhi rhetorically quipped, "The issue is performance versus an image—and how do you fight an image?"[88]

The handsome payoff for the Congress, which won 350 of the 520 seats, now offered Mrs Gandhi the mandate to start tweaking laws, which she did with a zest that precipitated a constitutional crisis, as we have seen. Ministries were staffed with loyalists: Kumaramangalam, Ray, Chavan, Ahmed, Gujral, Satpathy, and Gokhale were allotted portfolios. Three-quarters of PCC general secretaries, half the CWC, a third of the ministers, and a fifth of Congress MPs were CFSA members or supporters.[89] In a sense it could be said that it was this ginger group that in fact held the levers of power. In the sixteen state elections of March 1972 Mrs Gandhi's Congress, aided by an unprecedented war chest of Rs 200 million, once again emerged successful, netting 1926 of the 2727 seats it contested.[90] Despite being state

---

[86] Many parties relied on the patronage of the princes, whose funds had diminished since the abolition of their privy purses. Moreover, in 1969 Mrs Gandhi had also banned corporate donations to political parties. In practice, the policy was selectively implemented to the detriment of the opposition. Adding to the plebiscitary dimension of the poll was her decision to have the counting of votes moved from local offices to district towns, in effect reducing the influence of local elites, who were given to intimidating voters before elections and victimising them after.

[87] *Congress Marches Ahead—III*, p. 103.

[88] Palmer, "Elections and the Political System in India", p. 542.

[89] Austin, *Working a Democratic Constitution*, p. 187.

[90] Nayar, *India After Nehru*, p. 213.

elections, the polls, as in 1971, assumed plebiscitary dimensions, this time because India's recent victory in a war against Pakistan was largely seen as the work of the prime minister and her strong rapport with the generals.

With the snap and khaki elections of 1971 and 1972, respectively, Mrs Gandhi had established complete control at the centre and in the states. The new legislators were in the main younger and weaker: two-fifths of the MLAs elected in 1972 were neophytes lacking in the kind of patronage networks that had made their predecessors formidable political actors.[91] Similarly, the incumbent chief ministers were top-down appointments with no power base, doing the bidding of "consultative committees" deputed to the states by the high command.[92] As for the less-than-servile chief ministers, they were shown the door: for instance, Mohanlal Sukhadia, K. Brahmananda Reddy, Mohinder Mohan Chaudhury, and S.C. Shukla before the 1972 elections;[93] P.V. Narasimha Rao in 1973;[94] Chimanbhai Patel in 1974;[95] and Vasantrao Naik in 1975.[96] The more craven were on the other hand rewarded with longer tenures as well as pork barrel funds for capital-intensive projects—Ghanshyam Oza, P.C. Sethi, S.S. Ray, and Devraj Urs.[97]

Proximity to the prime minister, in any case, remained a supple notion: no one, not even members of her inner circle, was irreplaceable. Among those kicked out by the revolving door of the kitchen cabinet were even ur-loyalists such as D.P. Mishra and Dinesh Singh. The former, a familiar face at 1 Safdarjung Road between 1967 and 1972, was turfed out after he opposed her new favourites, Kumaramangalam and Bansi Lal;[98] the latter,

---

[91] Roy, "India 1972", p. 235.

[92] Narain and Sharma, "The Fifth State Assembly Elections in India", pp. 323–4.

[93] They were the chief ministers of Rajasthan, Andhra Pradesh, Assam, and Madhya Pradesh, respectively.

[94] Rao was made chief minister in 1971 primarily because he was weak—a "puppet" of the centre. But as he began consolidating power he upset both the old upper-caste elites he had displaced as well as the centre. Mrs Gandhi had him dismissed and imposed President's Rule in Andhra Pradesh: Sitapati, *Half-Lion*, pp. 39–41.

[95] After protests had led to the dissolution of the Gujarat assembly, Patel was in favour of new elections whereas Mrs Gandhi preferred President's Rule. She had her way, and he was suspended from the Congress for six years.

[96] Naik had been chief minister of Maharashtra for twelve years but was dismissed because "he was too independent and had a political following of his own, both of which were anathema" to the prime minister. For an eyewitness account of the firing, see Venkatasan, *Institutionalising Panchayat Raj in India*, p. 126.

[97] Of Gujarat, Madhya Pradesh, West Bengal, and Karnataka, respectively.

[98] Mishra was chief minister of Madhya Pradesh from 1963 to 1967. After becoming

minister of industrial development and internal trade, was dropped for harbouring "conspiratorial ambitions".[99] Shuffles at the level of the union were mirrored by kindred changes lower down: municipal power in the major metropolises of Bombay, Calcutta, Delhi, Hyderabad, Madras, and Bangalore, for instance, moved into the hands of functionaries hand-picked by Congressmen.[100]

As with the government, so with the party. The steady diminution of the Congress presidency could be traced by the nature of its occupants: in the early years of Mrs Gandhi's premiership the post was held first by Kamaraj and then Nijalingappa, both Syndicate members. After the Congress split it fell to Jagjivan Ram, a loyalist, albeit one who commanded a power base of his own among the Dalits of Bihar and the rest of the Hindi belt. He was made to resign shortly after the 1971 elections. Next in line was D. Sanjivayya, a loyalist with no independent source of power. A young Dalit from Andhra Pradesh, he was chosen only because Delhi's rulers wanted someone to rival the real powerhouse in his state, Chief Minister K. Brahmananda Reddy.[101] His untimely death in May 1972 cut short these plans. Shankar Dayal Sharma, his successor, served out the rest of the term and two more.[102] Put into his job only for his faithfulness to the prime minister during the party split, he announced early on in his presidency that he would play his "humble part" by taking cues from Mrs Gandhi's "wise and enlightened leadership" and fighting the opposition, who were at the heart of a "deep-seated conspiracy" to "weaken national unity".[103] From October 1974 until the end of the Emergency the president was the invertebrate D.K. Barooah, who owed his meteoric rise to his friendship with Feroze Gandhi, Mrs Gandhi's deceased husband. "People have faith in the Congress and in the leadership of Smt. Indira Gandhi", he would proclaim with forelock-tugging deference, "both are one and the same thing."[104]

---

embroiled in a corruption scandal in 1969, he was disqualified from contesting elections for six years. He remained a power broker in Delhi's corridors until around August 1972: Ankit, "A Regional Satrap", pp. 36, 46.

[99] Dinesh Singh's family—ex-royals from Kalakankar, Uttar Pradesh—had always been close to Mrs Gandhi, making the fall more dramatic to contemporary observers.

[100] Weiner, "India's New Political Institutions", p. 899.

[101] *Congress Marches Ahead—III*, p. 40.

[102] *Congress Marches Ahead—V*, p. 125.

[103] *Congress Marches Ahead—VI*, p. 40; *Congress Marches Ahead—VIII*, p. 205.

[104] *Congress Marches Ahead—XIII*, p. 25.

Publicly, the prime minister would try to brush aside such sycophancy with meek protestations: this was "perhaps a form of oriental excess, to which I pay no attention", she once said.[105]

A pliant party president gave Mrs Gandhi considerable leverage. This office-bearer, after all, elected half the score of members of the Congress Working Committee.[106] Moreover, she saw to it that CWC members also held ministries at the centre, the overlapping membership serving as prophylaxis against the kind of party–government disputes that had precipitated the split of 1969. Control of the Committee, in turn, translated into mastery over the Pradesh Congress Committees (PCCs), some of which were dissolved forthwith and reconstituted with the right kind of Congressmen. This, predictably, had a cascading effect, for PCC chiefs were responsible for making appointments to the District Congress Committees (DCCs). What is more, an amendment spearheaded by Mrs Gandhi to the party constitution enabled Congress presidents to go over the heads of the PCCs and appoint two members to all DCCs.[107]

In similar fashion Mrs Gandhi took control of the other two power centres of the party, the eight-member Congress Parliamentary Board (CPB) that supervised the parliamentary parties of the states, and the fifteen-member Central Election Committee (CEC)—the same octet plus an additional seven—which selected candidates for the general and state elections.[108] Through the 1950s and 1960s the main business of both had been to mediate between party factions. But in the new dispensation, topped up with additional powers, the CEC and CPB acquired the additional competencies of appointing and dismissing chief ministers and state-level ministers.[109]

Another virtual coup was the party election of December 1972, the first and only poll of its kind during Mrs Gandhi's tenure.[110] That it was a sham

---

[105] In an interview with David Selbourne. See Selbourne, *An Eye to India*, p. 96.

[106] The other half were selected by the All-India Congress Committee, the party's executive council made up of representatives from the provincial and district committees.

[107] Kochanek, "Mrs Gandhi's Pyramid", pp. 97–8.

[108] The CEC and CPB were subsets of the CWC. So, seen as concentric circles, the CPB, the smallest, was the inner one; CEC the middle; and CWC, the largest, the outer.

[109] The bodies were particularly successful in displacing the old guard in Uttar Pradesh, Punjab, Haryana, and Jammu and Kashmir—states where factionalism was high and easy to override.

[110] The next internal Congress elections, which were due in December 1975, were

became quickly apparent: three-fifths of the ten million voters were bogus; a number of candidates won without contest amidst corruption and intimidation. As always, loyalists prevailed over locals.[111] The outrage was nevertheless too much even for Congressmen. In the event, the debates were used as a pretext to return to a system more to Mrs Gandhi's liking, the top-down appointments of "*ad hoc* committees" and "consensus" candidates. Party democracy there would be none.[112]

The next office to be touched by the long arm of the prime minister was the presidency of the republic. No longer interested in keeping Giri on for a second term, she had him replaced in 1974 by a septuagenarian Assamese familiar, Fakhruddin Ali Ahmed, who would prove his worth on the night of the Emergency, when he agreed to turn the country over to authoritarianism.[113]

By the time Ahmed assumed office, the Congress Left—the last redoubt of a politics premised on policy rather than just power—had for all practical purposes ceased to exist. Suggesting that the CFSA had outlived its usefulness now that social reform had entered the political mainstream, Mrs Gandhi sought to have the forum dissolved. Two developments cleared the way for this eventuality. First, Kumaramangalam's death in a plane crash in May 1973 offered the prime minister more latitude in a party that already had a dearth of competing luminaries at the top.[114] And second, fissures emerged between the CFSA's anti-communist Young Turks and its former Communist figures such as K.R. Ganesh, K.D. Malaviya, and Chandrajit Yadav. Nevertheless, as it turned out, the more important factor, for Mrs Gandhi at least, was loyalty. There were some in the CFSA crowd that she approved of, conventional figures such as the chief ministers of Orissa and Punjab, Nandini Satpathy and Zail Singh, respectively; and some of whom

---

cancelled because many Congressmen feared they would be a sham. This apparatus for intra-party democracy would only be restored in 1996.

[111] Jeffrey, "The Prime Minister and the Ruling Party", p. 176. Even Congressman Shashi Bhushan laid into "irregularities" committed in the election: *Indian Express*, 2 January 1973, p. 4.

[112] Frankel, *India's Political Economy*, pp. 482–3.

[113] Privately, Ahmed would suggest to F.H. Mohsin, deputy minister of home affairs, that he was "unhappy" with the violence of the gentrification and sterilisation drives. Publicly, he did little to make this known: Brass, *An Indian Political Life*, p. 176.

[114] By comparison, Nehru was faced with panjandrums galore: Vallabhbhai Patel, B.R. Ambedkar, and Purushottamdas Tandon, to name a few.

she did not, fringe members such as Shashi Bhushan, a parliamentarian who in 1973 had famously called for "the creation of a limited dictatorship in India."[115] The radicalism of some of the CFSA's other leading lights had begun ringing alarm bells, too, especially amongst establishment figures who had returned *en bloc* to Mrs Gandhi's Congress in the wake of the 1971–2 polls: Krishan Kant, for instance, wanted all Congress MPs and MLAs to "sacrifice" a tenth of their lands and redistribute them among the landless.[116] Mohan Dharia, for his part, recommended ceilings on urban property: anyone owning houses worth over Rs 500,000 would have their excess acreages expropriated.[117] Moreover, in seminars on the "forces of right reaction", the CFSA also routinely denounced the old guard—Jagjivan Ram, Y.B. Chavan, T.A. Pai, and others—calling for a "purge" of such "undesirable elements". Once, they even crossed a red line: the CPI's Hiren Mukherjee, an attendee at one of the forum's meetings, called for the nationalisation of Sanjay's Maruti.[118] To eliminate such voices, Indira Gandhi hatched a plot. First, she asked Uma Shankar Dikshit, Congress Right minister and Aunt Sally of the CFSA, to launch the Nehru Forum in August 1972. Next, she encouraged the two organisations to engage in increasingly bitter conflicts that winter. Finally, suggesting that such vicious infighting was counterproductive, she had both fora dissolved in April 1973.[119] With their passing, then, what was left of the Congress was not a party but a personal fiefdom.

"Where is the Congress party that I should reorganise?" Mrs Gandhi once asked, "why do I need the party? I can depend on the administrative machinery for managing the affairs of the country."[120] Certainly, she controlled more levers of government than either of her predecessors and most of her successors. The cabinet and prime minister's secretariats, in particular, had turned into lodestones of power. The former was handed oversight of the domestic security agency, the CBI, along with sixty of the Home Ministry's hundred administrative divisions.[121] When the CBI, which

[115] Kochanek, "Mrs Gandhi's Pyramid", p. 104.

[116] *Congress Marches Ahead—VI*, p. 87.

[117] *Congress Marches Ahead—VIII*, p. 72.

[118] Lockwood, *The Communist Party of India*, p. 73.

[119] "Suitable action" needed to be taken against "those party members who indulge in mudslinging against each other and thus tarnish" the Congress' image: *Congress Marches Ahead—VIII*, p. 36.

[120] Vanaik, "The Rajiv Congress in Search of Stability", p. 71.

[121] Ganguly, "The Prime Minister and Foreign and Defence Policies", p. 152.

reported to the Home Ministry, was divested of its external intelligence operations by creating the RAW, the new body was made responsible to the Cabinet Secretariat. For its part, the PMS, once used chiefly for drafting the titular leader's speeches, came to acquire the Finance Ministry's Revenue Intelligence and the Directorate of Enforcement as well as the Home Ministry's competencies over civil-service appointments.[122] As the PMS' staff doubled to 242 employees—many of them not civil servants but independent advisers well disposed to Mrs Gandhi—and its expansive mandate began encroaching on parliamentary and ministerial territory, the protests against it grew strident. Starting in 1973, three no-confidence motions in as many years called out the PMS for stepping on parliament's toes. Opposition MPs also laid into Mrs Gandhi's misuse of the PMS' newly appropriated intelligence units to "spy on them".[123]

In the final analysis, the logic of deinstitutionalisation had resulted in a Catch-22. At the heart of it lay the dismantling of the old guard and the replacement of state bosses by sycophants. But with fewer patrons the party's influence on the ground diminished. Advisers repeatedly exhorted Mrs Gandhi to restore the party and put it to good use, implement reforms, and build momentum. As Y.B. Chavan rightly noted at a conference of DCC chiefs, the republic's Lilliputian bureaucracy was hardly the tool to bring about redistributive change: in the hands of functionaries, programmes were "bound to degenerate".[124] Similarly, at a May 1972 party conference, state leaders and cabinet ministers were united on "the need for involving party workers in the socialist programme of the Congress. There is no doubt that the party has got to develop a cadre to act as watchdog in the interest of the common man."[125] An AICC resolution five months later concurred: the party ought "to be cast in a new mould to create and to energise a myriad of points of contact, at all levels of the party with the people on the one hand, and with the instruments of governance on the other."[126] But for Mrs Gandhi, therein lay the rub. If the party grew more powerful, it would become less dependent on her. In the short run she tried squaring the circle by making tall promises of reform.

---

[122] It is disputed whether the PMS' control over the two agencies was *de facto* or *de jure*: Austin, *Working a Democratic Constitution*, p. 191.

[123] Hewitt, "The Prime Minister and the Parliament", p. 57.

[124] *Congress Marches Ahead—IV*, pp. 129–30.

[125] Zaidi, *The Annual Register of Indian Political Parties, vol. 1*, p. 85.

[126] Ibid., pp. 194–5.

Unfortunately for her it was not long before citizens became fully convinced that, in fact, none were forthcoming.

To sum up: the role that Mrs Gandhi's personality played in the establishment of an authoritarian regime cannot be underestimated. But this psychological factor needs to be seen in combination with others. First, she cultivated a hawkish attitude because she felt insecure, and she felt insecure primarily because her party leaders saw her as a cipher. Second, merely the fact that she had authoritarian tendencies did not make the Emergency inevitable. It was her transformation of the Congress party and the state machinery from the late 1960s onwards that made it impossible for party and government to resist her "constitutional dictatorship" in 1975. It can be surmised, then, that many democratically elected heads of state elsewhere in the world too would have acted as she did, had they not been constrained by robust institutions.

To conclude this chapter, we will return to our examination of populism and authoritarianism, and the reasons why Mrs Gandhi was able to prevail in 1975.

An Authoritarian Personality under Threat

From Populism to Authoritarianism

The political trajectory of India from the late 1960s to the mid-1970s offers a good illustration of the relation between populism and authoritarianism.

The new dispensation that Mrs Gandhi introduced in the late 1960s and even more clearly in the early 1970s clearly fulfilled the criteria of populism. Populist leaders assume and claim that they represent the people, that they *are* the people. This was encapsulated in D.K. Barooah's slogan "Indira is India and India is Indira". Mrs Gandhi was very likely convinced of the truth of this infamous aphorism because of her lineage. She could therefore develop a populist repertoire based on her direct relationship with the populace, as evident during the 1971 election campaign and in her radio broadcasts. Her populism was conducive to authoritarianism because it implied personalisation, a formidable concentration of power which made pluralism redundant.

This development was spurred, as we have noted, by two additional factors: first, her sense of insecurity; and second, the never-ending threat of rivals who exacerbated it. The consequence of these was the systematic political witch hunts described above. These purges were achieved in the name of the nation that she believed she embodied. As Ashis Nandy puts it, "those who criticized her, by definition, became attackers of the institution of the prime minister and those who opposed her became irresponsible or frustrated conspirators operating outside the boundaries of legitimate politics."[127] In this sense, then, since the prime minister embodied the nation, to oppose her was to oppose the nation.

To relate to the people and to eliminate her rivals, Indira Gandhi kept both party and government on a tight leash. This was in contrast to her father's élan. Indeed, for most of his premiership, Nehru was merely *primus inter pares* among a gaggle of state bosses. The oligarchy, for one, succeeded in derailing all of Nehru's land reform and nationalisation efforts. As a result, the socialist resolutions that he had steamrollered through the Congress' Nagpur and Avadi sessions of 1955 and 1959 foundered. On becoming food and agriculture minister in 1959, Bombay's S.K. Patil set himself to the task of dismantling wholesale the government trade in foodgrain. The same year, Neelam Sanjiva Reddy, Andhra Pradesh *satrap*, assumed the Congress presidency; thereafter, he was succeeded by fellow-Syndicate member and Madras party chief, Kamaraj. Soon after the military defeat visited by the Chinese in 1962, this cabal pressured Nehru into expelling his two economic *consiglieri*, Minister of Mines and Fuel K.D. Malaviya and Defence Minister V.K. Krishna Menon.

For yet others, the loaves and fishes were not to be found in office, but through the pursuit of private wealth. This demanded that the premier turn a blind eye to their transgressions. Nehru obliged. Thus, nothing transpired after the revelation that the Punjab chief minister, Pratap Singh Kairon, was running a gold and currency smuggling racket, or that his Oriya counterpart, Biju Patnaik, had added Rs 100 million to his fortunes, his business and political careers following analogous trajectories. Figures close to Nehru got off equally lightly, in no small part because of their generous contributions to party coffers and the role they played in oiling the Congress electoral machine: his secretary, M.O. Mathai, quietly disappeared from public office after it was revealed that he was in the pay of Indian businessmen and the CIA; similarly, no prison sentence or even a sustained inquiry followed after it transpired that Finance Minister T.T. Krishnamachari was behind the move to have a state-owned enterprise channel vast sums of money into the businesses of a top Congress donor.

---

[127] Nandy, *At the Edge of Psychology*, p. 122.

Paradoxically, therein lay the success of the "Congress system": the masses were kept in check—even violently so, as India's revolting peasants, secessionists, and peripheral populations were to discover—but the party *satraps* given a free hand. Both served the same purpose, namely the consolidation of Congress rule. But for myriad reasons Mrs Gandhi found this system wanting and set about making necessary changes. The upshot was the deinstitutionalisation of the Congress party as an instrument of change and an ever-increasing reliance on the bureaucracy.

In the early 1970s Mrs Gandhi had not only morphed into a convincing populist, in symbiosis with "her" people, but had also come to exert near-absolute power over the ruling party. It was this double concentration of power over populace and party that made the Emergency possible. The fact that she continued to feel insecure *vis-à-vis* her rivals, even if for good reason, only made matters worse, both for her and the country.

Mrs Gandhi's Calculus in 1975

In the immediate run-up to 25 June 1975, and in the following months especially, Mrs Gandhi's insecurities were to play a major historical role, precipitating the declaration of the Emergency and justifying its extension.

In June 1975, while protests on the streets calling for her resignation were gaining momentum in the wake of the Allahabad Court's judgment, it must be remembered that the greater and more immediate threat to Mrs Gandhi's rule emanated from within her party.[128] She was quick to grasp the new dynamic: the longer it took the executive to get its house in order, the faster the growth of the constituency demanding the party be saved from her sullied hands. In fact, contingency measures for a replacement were already in the pipeline. Over a hundred Congress MPs were ready to oust her. According to Nayar, even her arch-sycophant Barooah contemplated jumping ship, presiding at a meeting in the residence of Chandrajit Yadav, a prominent figure of the Congress Left. The cabinet ministers in attendance were divided over whether to replace Mrs Gandhi with Jagjivan Ram, the "seniormost member of the cabinet", or Swaran Singh, the "safe and pliable" cabinet minister since 1952.[129] Another contender, it briefly transpired, was S.S. Ray who, while no longer a minister at the centre, remained a fixture on the Delhi scene, making semi-weekly trips there from

---

[128] See the Introduction to this volume.
[129] Nayar, *The Judgement*, p. 15.

Calcutta, where he served as chief minister. But Ray, a childhood friend of Mrs Gandhi's, was far too loyal to her to join the clique of conspirators.

Meanwhile, around the same time Barooah and Yadav were plotting stealthily at night, some of the Young Turks—such as Chandra Shekhar, Krishan Kant, and Mohan Dharia—were likewise gunning for Mrs Gandhi in broad daylight, in full view of press and public: the preservation of the party took precedence over the career of the prime minister, they argued. The Congress could ill afford to go to the polls in February 1976 with a leader under investigation. Moreover, as Krishan Kant saw it, Mrs Gandhi's defenestration was in any case a given: the unrest was bound to "snowball into a revolution", bringing her down and with her the party too.[130] In the midst of this mayhem the Turks were being pulled in two very different directions. On the one hand Ram was liaising with UP chief minister H.N. Bahuguna and with Kant, both of whom endorsed his coup. On the other the loyalist Y.B. Chavan was busy pleading with Dharia to maintain unity in the parliamentary party. Between 12 and 18 June it appeared that Ram's stock was rising quickly: CPI trade unionist S.A. Dange and Congress' K.D. Malaviya began canvassing support for him while Ram himself commenced on a tour of Delhi's establishment, meeting party bosses and opening back-channels. To the veteran pressman Nikhil Chakravartty, all this infighting suggested that Mrs Gandhi had to be "more worried about [her] allies than [her] enemies."[131] But the latter, growing more strident by the day, could not have been too far from the prime minister's sights. Right outside her window was the *gherao* around her residence, and in the papers were Morarji Desai's plans, unequivocally stated: "We intend to force her to resign. For good ... I, thanks to Mrs Gandhi, have discovered that a woman is unsuited to head a government or rule a country ... The lady won't survive this movement of ours."[132]

The contest would sooner rather than later have moved to its resolution had only the best interests of the party been the issue. But this was no mere battle of ideas: the political survival of its protagonists was at stake. The Young Turks had very personal reasons to fight Mrs Gandhi. Dharia, for one, had been dismissed from the council of ministers by her in March for suggesting that the Congress open dialogue with Narayan's movement.

---

[130] *SCR*, vol. 1, p. 21.

[131] Chakravartty in Atma Jayaram to P.N. Dhar, 18 June 1975, SCP, Subject File 1, p. 28.

[132] Fallaci, "Mrs Gandhi's Opposition", p. 17.

Shekhar, for another, had had himself elected to the CWC in 1972 over her objections. For his part, Ram was no shrinking violet. All that his advice for Mrs Gandhi—that she best wait out the judicial process, for the Supreme Court was sure to give her a qualified stay—amounted to was the false assurance of a man who coveted her job. It was no secret that between Ram and Mrs Gandhi there was a history of bad blood. In the late 1960s it had been revealed that Ram had "forgotten" to file his taxes for well over a decade.[133] A scandal had ensued and she had contemplated firing him. But she had desisted, because he was a force to reckon with: not only had he been an establishment insider for more than three decades, he was also *the* Dalit face of Congress. After the 1971 elections it was estimated that he enjoyed the backing of some eighty MPs in the Lok Sabha. Besides, he had proven his loyalty to her in the past. While Desai and he had been part of the dozen "Kamaraj'd" by her in 1963, he had sided with her and not with Desai at the time of the Congress split. Still, she had grown to resent him, especially after his successful bids for the party presidency in 1969 and the defence portfolio the next year, riding simultaneously as it were two large horses, both charging towards the prime minister.[134]

The six days that followed Allahabad were probably the most precarious. She learnt from the Intelligence Bureau that she enjoyed the support of only 191 of the 350 Congressmen in parliament.[135] Factions commanded by party *satraps* accounted for the rest: the Turks and their allies, 24 MPs; sectional interest groups, in the main industrialists and the gentry, 21; alumni of the defunct Congress Forum for Socialist Action, 17; Y.B. Chavan, 15; Jagjivan Ram, 13; K. Brahmananda Reddy, 11; Kamalapati Tripathi, 8; H.N. Bahuguna, 5; D.P. Mishra, 4; and S.C. Shukla, 3. Another fifteen were opposed to "her for personal, political, and other reasons"; the remaining twenty-three were fence-sitters.[136] The threat, then, was twofold. First, she did not have the numbers in parliament to ram through ad personam constitutional amendments that could inoculate her against the courts. Such a move required a two-thirds majority. Second, and more worryingly, if the figure of 191 fell below 175—not an unlikely scenario given the long-standing predilection of parliamentarians for horse trading—the majority of

---

[133] For a running commentary on the scandal, see *TOI*, September and October 1969, *passim*.

[134] This is a paraphrase of D.P. Mishra's interpretation in Vasudev, *Two Faces of Indira Gandhi*, p. 36.

[135] The IB's bosses, in agreeing to spy for the prime minister, were way out of line.

[136] Jayaram to Dhar, 18 June 1975, SCP, Subject File 1, pp. 25–6.

Congress MPs could well supplant her by uniting behind some vacuous, albeit more scrupulous, non-entity with the moral authority to embattle JP's men at the polls in March, and, as a result, be better placed to ensure the re-election of Congress incumbents.

Even so, on 18 June it became clear that the tide had turned in her favour. By then both Swaran Singh and Y.B. Chavan, who had been hedging their bets, came out in her support, at least temporarily. Her legal *consiglieri*, S.S. Ray and H.R. Gokhale, lined up behind her as well. Ram decided to call off his revolt, perhaps realising the Herculean task he had set himself.[137] He was up against not only the long line of contenders who had yet to throw their hats in the ring, but also Mrs Gandhi, who, while weakened in Delhi, continued to command at her disposal the formidable apparatuses of party and state. In surmounting them Ram was sure to provoke a severe crisis, maybe even another party split, for which he had little appetite. As he said wearily some days later to an ally, Delhi councillor P.N. Singh, "the democracy we have fought for is finished. The responsibility is on you young people now."[138] When it became clear that Ram was on board, Mrs Gandhi had S.S. Ray and V.B. Raju, Rajya Sabha MP from Andhra Pradesh, arrange a parliamentary party meeting to affirm faith in her leadership. Haksar, now in the Planning Commission as deputy chairman after having fallen from grace for criticising Sanjay, was tasked with preparing this pledge. Ram, in the meanwhile, had gone the whole nine yards: he convinced five of the Young Turks, including its two Dalit panjandrums Dhan and Dharia, to steer clear of the meeting.

In the event, when 516 members of the parliamentary party—shorn of the Turks and their sympathisers—met on 18 June, they unanimously passed a resolution declaring that Mrs Gandhi's "dynamic leadership" was "indispensable" to the nation.[139] It was the turning point. Hereafter, criticism of Mrs Gandhi there was none. It no longer mattered whether the Supreme Court would offer an absolute or qualified stay. She would remain in office at all costs. The Turks, whose favoured candidate for the premiership—if they were to ever settle upon one—was estimated to have the support of seventy MPs on 12 June, were twelve days later to be found burning up

[137] It appears that Ram changed his mind between 16 June, when he met a number of senior Congress politicians still weighing the odds of challenging Mrs Gandhi, and 18 June when he broke his silence on the issue: Jayaram to Dhar, 18 June 1975, SCP, Subject File 1, pp. 27–9.

[138] Vasudev, *Two Faces of Indira Gandhi*, p. 39.

[139] Nayar, *The Judgement*, p. 16.

faster than a shooting star: the slim attendance at the banquet that Chandra Shekhar hosted for Narayan included but "twenty to twenty-five" Congress MPs.[140] Similarly, Nandini Satpathy, chief minister of Orissa, who arrived in Delhi late on the evening of the 18th, ended her vacillations and made sure that the next morning's papers carried her name alongside the other CPP signatories. In the days that followed, cabinet ministers, ministers of state, and chief ministers were busy lining up at Mrs Gandhi's residence to secure a place in her good books, and with luck a re-election ticket or a cabinet berth as well. The general elections, after all, were due in March 1976.

The attitude of Congress leaders in June 1975 and the way Mrs Gandhi speculated about their tactics show that, in spite of the deinstitutionalisation of the party that she had orchestrated, she felt herself vulnerable *vis-à-vis* faction leaders and individual rivals. This made the declaration of the Emergency even more necessary.

While Mrs Gandhi's sense of insecurity was fostered by disloyal Congressmen before the Emergency, it was reactivated during it, quite soon after it had been declared. The consensus among her biographers, it appears, is that by early August 1975 she was ready to see the back of Emergency rule. It was a fitting time for such contemplation: the rains had been generous, inflation and unemployment had fallen, the opposition weakened, and, if the logic of quinquennial polls still held any traction, elections were round the corner. The annual prime minister's address on 15 August, Independence Day, at the Red Fort would have been a fitting occasion to withdraw the Emergency, her advisers argued. But then something happened in Bangladesh that changed India's political equation.

Late at night on 14 August, the army took power in Dacca. The military coup, it was later revealed, had been years in the making.[141] Bangladesh's recent history had mirrored India's on many counts: high inflation in 1973, violent unrest and the coalescing of opposition parties soon after. In December 1974 Prime Minister Mujibur Rahman's response was to declare a state of emergency and a switch to presidentialism the next month, in the same breath effecting for himself a change in job title to suit the new dispensation. All newspapers, barring four that were heavily controlled, were banned, and all parties excepting Rahman's own, plus a few that merged with it, similarly outlawed. The *coup d'état* of the early hours of 15 August,

---

[140] *Blitz*, 10 December 1977, p. 21; *TOI*, 25 June 1975, p. 1.

[141] Lifschultz and Bird, "Bangladesh" (8 December 1979), pp. 1999–2014; idem, "Bangladesh" (15 December 1979), pp. 2059–68.

then, was the handiwork of sectional interests that had been denied the spoils of the new arrangement: in the main, the discontented right wing of the incumbent Awami League, and senior members of the Bangladesh Armed Forces. Together they plotted Rahman's downfall with the assistance of the CIA. On that fateful night, tanks encircling his house, the president was handed by Major Huda a pre-written resignation letter that he refused to sign. During the contretemps his sons emerged in the room. A scuffle ensued and Rahman was mown down by machine-guns. In the hunt that followed, all but two of the forty members of Rahman's family were shot dead.[142]

The next morning at Mrs Gandhi's residence the news from Dacca came as a bombshell.[143] "Whom can I trust?" she asked her friend Pupul Jayakar before leaving for the Red Fort, where she was, possibly, to announce the termination of the Emergency. For Indira Gandhi the assassinations in Bangladesh could hardly have failed to trigger thoughts of her own vulnerability. "Rahul [Gandhi, her grandson] is about the same age as Mujib's son", she wondered aloud,[144] leaving unspoken other parallels. Then came the impression of having found the perfect alibi. Making Mujibur Rahman a metaphor was not without its uses. In the letters to opposition figures that she penned in the days that followed, she made sure to mention the incident to extrapolate from it a simple prescriptive lesson: that at a time when threats to her person were imminent, the Emergency could not but continue.[145]

Her speech at the Red Fort eschewed any reference to the restoration of democracy. Indeed, what was to be a momentous oration turned out to be just another ordinary Indira Gandhi address: "Freedom is in danger", she

---

[142] The two survivors were his daughters, residents of Bonn at the time. Lifschultz and Bird, "Bangladesh" (15 December 1979), p. 2067; Franda, *Bangladesh*, p. 232. See also Ahamed, "The Coup of 1975", pp. 63–80; Maniruzzaman, "An Unfinished Revolution?", pp. 891–911.

[143] Granville Austin cites without naming an "impeccable source" who suggested that this could not have been true, for Mrs Gandhi heard about the coup only *after* delivering her address. See Austin, *Working a Democratic Constitution*, p. 313, n57.

[144] Jayakar, *Indira*, p. 220.

[145] See, *inter alia*, Indira Gandhi to N.G. Goray, 19 August 1975 in "Documentation of Emergency Period in India", Madhu Limaye Papers, microfilm copy, reel 13. She could not know how "the other members of the opposition view the Bangladesh developments", she noted, before speculating that they perhaps drew inspiration from it.

said, "I hear all kinds of things but I cannot hear everything ... The way is full of thorns but we are making history."[146]

This was not the first time Mrs Gandhi felt her life was in danger. Just a week before Rahman's killing, a former army captain, Dhaja Ram Sangwan, was caught with a telescopic rifle. In its crosshairs, it was said, was the prime minister, who was to meet her end *à la The Day of the Jackal.*[147] Another attempt was made on her life at a prayer meeting at Raj Ghat, M.K. Gandhi's cenotaph, on 2 October. During the commemorations a man with a knife had stealthily made his way past the security perimeter, only to be stopped by Shafi Qureshi, the minister of state for railways. On 18 March the same year, three months before the Emergency, another would-be assassin was thwarted, this time a lone gunman bearing a loaded twelve-bore shotgun. He was apprehended outside the Allahabad High Court where she was giving testimony. The motives of these men were never clear, but in the narratives of both pressmen and Congressmen—there being scarcely a difference at the time—blame was routinely placed on larger and more "sinister"—one of Mrs Gandhi's favourite words—forces: the Anand Marg, the JP Movement, the CIA. The last, in particular, was a convenient bugbear. But despite the innumerable times she accusingly referred to the spy agency before and during the Emergency, no CIA agents were ever named or expelled. Still, while the CIA of course had no role in turning India's working classes, peasants, and bourgeoisie against their rulers, her paranoia cannot be entirely dismissed. Coeval with these events were the Church Committee proceedings in the United States, then an ongoing investigation into the CIA's role in assassination attempts on, *inter alios*, Castro, Schneider, Allende, and Lumumba.[148] That these developments mattered to Mrs Gandhi is well known. After the coup in Chile, for instance, she declared that she "did not believe it for a moment that [Allende] had committed suicide ... he was killed."[149] The steady barrage of evidence uncovering the CIA's role in the years that followed proved that she was right in thinking so. Her Communist allies, too, warned her of foreign plots. Just a week before the Emergency was imposed, Pyotr Kutsobin, who ran the India desk at the Central Committee of the

---

[146] Jayakar, *Indira*, p. 219.

[147] Nayar, *The Judgement*, p. 83.

[148] Church Committee, *Alleged Assassination Plots*, pp. 261–4.

[149] *Congress Marches Ahead—IX*, p. 104. Some months later, on 9 April 1974, Mrs Gandhi dined with Hortensia Bussi, Allende's widow, in Delhi: *Socialist India*, 13 April 1974, p. 31.

Communist Party of the Soviet Union, landed in Delhi with a "long letter"—just one copy, "to be read and destroyed"—which warned of a "ramified conspiracy" that had already "been set in motion". Apparently, "all the leaders of the Subcontinent who were responsible for the establishment of Bangladesh" were to be assassinated. Naturally, the CPI was quick to tip off the prime minister with this latest piece of intelligence.[150]

* * *

The authoritarian turn in India, in short, owed in no small part to the élan of its premier. Indeed, the Emergency was foremost a *personal* response to a set of challenges to Mrs Gandhi's authority, including factionalism in the Congress, quite apart from the Allahabad judgment and the JP Movement. But conspiring to make the Emergency possible was a clutch of other actors, in the main members of her inner coterie, as well. For together they not only triggered a decade-long crisis through their relentless pursuit of power, but also produced the enabling conditions of authoritarian rule. After a fashion, then, the Emergency was also the upshot of the centralisation of power and the deinstitutionalisation of party and government.

[150] Sen, *A Traveller and the Road*, p. 344. Incidentally, three leaders involved in the 1971 war *were* killed: Mujibur Rahman in 1975, as seen above; Zulfiqar Ali Bhutto in 1979; and Mrs Gandhi in 1984, albeit in very different circumstances, none of which had anything to do with the creation of Bangladesh.

8

AN INCONGRUOUS COALITION

If most of the political parties opposed the Emergency, the regime was nevertheless supported by some of them, including the CPI, the Shiv Sena and some of the RPIs. The CPI extolled the Twenty-Point Programme, the Shiv Sena "an era of discipline", and the RPI public housing for Dalits and commitment to land redistribution. This heteroclite assemblage reflects the absence of a clear ideology behind Mrs Gandhi's government.

Similarly, Mrs Gandhi's appeal extended to myriad sections of society. Big business appreciated the productivist *zeitgeist*. Bullock capitalists hailed the new commitment to high procurement prices and the—*de facto*—recantation of land reform, the middle classes the end of tax-and-spend and the prospect of national renewal.

Levels of support, of course, varied from one stratum to another. For capitalists and the bourgeoisie the support was more organic. For others, such as the Communists and the bureaucracy, it involved some expediency, calculations that required weighty balance-sheet considerations. For yet others there was fear, opportunism, condescension towards the masses, and a convergence of interests with the regime in equal measure—the group that best exemplified this being the intelligentsia.

This incongruous coalition was partly overdetermined by the quest for order—political as well as social—that was felt in many different milieux. It was no accident that it was in the fertile grounds of mid-1970s politics— strikes, protests, and overall instability—that authoritarianism registered the high levels of support that it did. But specific circumstances aside, the extent of support that the Emergency regime received across society needs to be investigated as it tells us something about the political culture of India, and in particular about its relation to democracy.

The Initial Phase: For the Emergency or Against the JP Movement?

When the Emergency was declared, many united behind the new regime in opposition to the JP Movement. This sizeable population, tired of agitations and strikes, viewed Narayan's shock troops as an illegitimate and undemocratic force. For them an authoritarian fortress defending them against the forces of anarchy was a benign development. The views of Khushwant Singh, editor of the mass-circulation *Illustrated Weekly of India* and substantial property owner, are illustrative. For him, dissent was legitimate so long as there was no "coercion or violence":

> If there is any, it is the duty of the government to suppress it by force, if necessary … With my own eyes I saw slogan-chanting processions go down Bombay thoroughfares smashing cars parked on the roadsides and breaking shop-windows as they went along … Leaders of opposition parties watched the country sliding into chaos as bemused spectators …

"… or worse, abetters", Singh might have added. He even wrote Jayaprakash Narayan a disapproving letter, saying that "what he was advocating was wrong and undemocratic."[1] After the virtual siege of Ahmedabad and Patna, the railwaymen's strike, and the agrarian unrest, it was with a sigh of relief that the moneyed classes Khushwant Singh represented saw in the Emergency the route to restoring social order: at long last, they had their own Mussolini who would make the trains run on time.

The reason that Mrs Gandhi's Emergency appeared as necessary for the rule of law and even democracy in the eyes of Singh and his ilk was that her opponents were violent in their protests, sceptical of institutions, hostile towards "Western-style" democracy, and eager to supplant personality for programme.[2] Almost as if to confirm this, Morarji Desai gave a frank interview to the Italian journalist Oriana Fallaci on 25 June 1975, just hours before the Emergency was imposed, in which he made his not-so-democratic *modus operandi* clear. She asked: "But if yours is a democratic opposition, why didn't you wait till Mrs Gandhi's electoral mandate expired?

---

[1] Singh, "Why I Supported Emergency", pp. 60–1.
[2] For this view, see Kaviraj, "Indira Gandhi and Indian Politics", pp. 1697–1708; and Puri, "A Fuller View of the Emergency", pp. 1736–44.

Why didn't you attack her in the course of the normal election campaign due six months from now?" To which he replied: "One must strike the iron while it is hot, and it's becoming increasingly difficult to defeat her in a general election." Minutes later, he took the argument further: he was not prepared to wait for the verdict of the Supreme Court. "If, during the appeal trial, the Supreme Court should reverse the Allahabad verdict, that shouldn't surprise us." Asked, "So, what do you intend to do now?" Desai responded: "We intend to overthrow her, to force her to resign. For good."[3]

This may have appeared to the opposition leadership to be a sound, perhaps the only, strategy that they had before them. But it was also a deeply alienating one. Mrs Gandhi, deft operator that she was, was quick to portray her party and its allies as a coalition of anti-fascists safeguarding democracy by sacrificing a tiny part of it, the Emergency being the necessary amputation to arrest the gangrenous spread of fascism across the body politic. It was hardly surprising, then, that she reserved the bulk of her firepower to attack the Hindu nationalists of the Sangh Parivar, which at the time was too marginal and too extreme a force to mount a coup against her, or even gain a meaningful following. But threat inflation had its uses. Mrs Gandhi, in speech after speech both before and during the Emergency, read extracts from Golwalkar's 1939 Hindu manifesto, *We, or Our Nationhood Defined*: "the Germans drove out of their country the Jews only in order to maintain their racial and cultural purity … This is a lesson which India could learn and profit by." Mrs Gandhi also cited his *Bunch of Thoughts* of 1966: M.K. Gandhi's "leadership came as a bitter climax of the despicable tribe of so many of our ancestors who during the past 1,200 years sold their national honour and freedom to foreigners." Mrs Gandhi also mentioned government reports and judicial inquiries into communal riots that implicated the Parivar.[4] In her speech at the Congress plenary session in Chandigarh in December 1975 she declared that "if the Jana Sangh comes to power, it will not need [*sic*] Emergency. It will chop off heads. Heads were chopped off in Bangladesh and Chile. Persons there were not just detained. They were murdered."[5] Understandably, this discourse attracted many supporters from different

---

[3] Fallaci, "Mrs Gandhi's Opposition", p. 17.

[4] *Lok Sabha Debates*, vol. 53, no. 2 (22 July 1975), cols 48–9. For the original quotes, slightly more prolix but of the same essence, see Golwalkar, *We, or Our Nationhood Defined*, p. 43, and idem, *Bunch of Thoughts*, p. 153.

[5] Zaidi, *The Annual Register of Indian Political Parties—vol. 23*, p. 391.

quarters. But there were other reasons why the regime's apologists approved of the new dispensation, too.

Communists and the Congress: A Contingent Alliance

If any group did not require convincing that Mrs Gandhi's party was the bulwark against "fascist" forces, it was the CPI. It was in fact persuaded of this long before the JP Movement took hold of the national imagination, and the support it lent the Emergency regime was the culmination of a spasmodic rapprochement between the two parties that had been under way since the late 1960s.

The 1969 Congress split had come as an epiphany for the CPI leadership: shorn of its conservative elements and in need of support to muster enough numbers in parliament to amend the constitution, the party that Mrs Gandhi led appeared to be one that the Communists could do business with. Moreover, they were won over by her programme—the nationalisation of banks and insurance companies as well as the promise of land reform.[6] Besides, there were many communists and socialists among Mrs Gandhi's advisers, including P.N. Haksar and P.N. Dhar. Nor was it lost on the CPI leadership that the Congress Left was then stronger than at any time in postcolonial history. Within its own ranks the CPI had internal factions: a go-it-alone Left, itself divided between the insurrectionally and electorally inclined, and a Right more amenable to alliance and entryism. Typically, in periods when the CPI Right and the Congress Left held the upper hand, the two parties tended to warm towards each other. This was the case briefly in 1947, for the most part between 1956 and 1964, and after 1969.[7] Citing the influence of the "historic compromise" in Italy, where its counterpart the PCI decided to embrace the Christian Democrats, the CPI declared in one of its 1970s resolutions that "the old concept of anti-Congressism" was "barren and reactionary".[8] Earlier it had already moved in

---

[6] Lockwood, *The Communist Party of India*, pp. 77–8.

[7] Under the leadership of P.C. Joshi, Ajoy Ghosh (until his death in 1962), and E.M.S. Namboodiripad, respectively. The intermittent periods—1948–50, 1950–1, 1951–6, 1964–9—witnessed a hardened anti-Congress politics under B.T. Ranadive, C. Rajeswara Rao, Ajoy Ghosh, and Rao again (he held the position until 1990), respectively. In 1964 the bulk of the CPI Left under the leadership of P. Sundarayya and E.M.S. Namboodiripad split from the party to form the CPM. The periodisation, is, in the main, Lockwood's. See his *The Communist Party of India*, pp. 1–36.

[8] Sen, *A Traveller and the Road*, p. 342. The Christian Democrats of Italy had, like

that direction, forming a coalition with the Congress in Kerala, ruling the state under a CPI chief minister from September 1970 on. Seat-sharing deals had followed in West Bengal and Punjab in 1972, and in Uttar Pradesh, Orissa, and Manipur in 1974. Nevertheless, the Communists knew better than to wholeheartedly embrace the rulers in Delhi. Indeed, the CPI tried keeping the Congress at arm's length when it became increasingly apparent that Mrs Gandhi's "socialism" detracted from more than added to the communist cause. While she made the occasional progressive decision, her leftist bona fides foundered on land reform and the railwaymen's strike which she violently suppressed. On both, the CPI found itself on the opposite side of the fence.[9]

Even so, the CPI continued backing the Congress, driven in part by Moscow's diktat,[10] and in part by its appraisal of the JP Movement: a "reactionary" and "communal" outfit riding on the coat-tails of the RSS and aiming for a *coup d'état*.[11] When the JP Movement gained momentum and took Bihar by storm, the first to fight its supporters on the streets were the Communists, one of the few cadre-based parties in the republic. The large turnout of some 100,000 counter-protestors in Patna on 3 June 1974 was far from unusual.[12]

Impressed by its ability to mobilise, Mrs Gandhi and Lalit Narayan Mishra pushed for improving ties with the CPI, prevailing over Jagjivan Ram, the other big Congress leader in Bihar. Early in 1974 it appeared that relations between the two parties were going through a rough patch, with the CPI withdrawing from the governing coalition in West Bengal and deploying its cadres to campaign against the Congress in Gujarat and Andhra Pradesh. But by October that year fences had been mended:

---

the Congress in India, held power uninterruptedly since the birth of the Italian republic in 1946.

[9] The Communists also fought hard in parliament to prevent the passage of MISA in May 1971. See Lockwood, *The Communist Party of India*, p. 81.

[10] An "agreement" worked out between the CPI and the Soviet Union's CPSU in 1960 "allowed" the former to ally with "progressive" parties—even the dominant "party of the bourgeoisie". See Sen Gupta, "Communism Further Divided", pp. 162–6.

[11] As CPI MP Bhogendra Jha saw it, the JP Movement probably had the hand of the CIA in it, and India may well have ended up like Chile, with an assassinated prime minister and a puppet regime: transcript of interview with Bhogendra Jha, Acc. No. 766, NMML Oral History Project, p. 37.

[12] Lockwood, *The Communist Party of India*, p. 86.

Congress president D.K. Barooah was among the prominent participants at the World Anti-Fascist Conference in Patna, sharing podia with its organisers, the leaders of the Communist Party of India.[13]

When the Emergency was declared the CPI endorsed it along with the Twenty-Point Programme in its Central Executive Committee meeting of 2 July. It committed itself to oppose the "right reactionary parties" and their "foreign imperialist" backers plotting the downfall of Mrs Gandhi's "progressive" government. Yet, in that statement the Communists let it be known that it remained wary of "monopolists and other anti-social exploiters", who were certain to try to turn the "emergency powers" to good account. They resolved to oppose such forces, thus rationalising their presence in the governing coalition. More importantly, the CPI saw the Emergency as an opportunity to push forward some of its desiderata: nationalising "some" industries, taking "stern action" against the CIA, and extending the franchise to eighteen-year-olds.[14]

The vigilance, however, was confined to party documentation. In the real world the CPI was quick to call off all strikes that it supported at the time, tame the All-India Bank Employees' Association, and withdraw from land-reform agitations in Assam and Bihar.[15] Not long after, the National Federation of Indian Women, the party's 300,000-strong affiliate, too, announced that it would "fully support the Twenty-Point economic programme", organise *padayatras* (marches on foot), and take stock of landholding patterns and moneylending activities in the *mofussil* to aid the regime in its redistribution efforts.[16] Likewise, Indrajit Gupta, the CPI spokesperson in parliament, threw his weight behind the regime in the session that ratified president Ahmed's use of Article 352 to declare a state of emergency. It was on predictable lines, then, that Gupta's speech invoked Mrs Gandhi's favourite bugbear:

We know, the Sangharsh Samiti announced on the 25th on the Ramlila Grounds was to have as its secretary and main organiser [the Jana Sangh's] Shri Nanaji Deshmukh, who has disappeared and has evaded arrest and probably has gone underground, as far as I know ... I am sure and our party is sure

---

[13] Tiwari, *Democracy and Dissent*, pp. 218, 100; Sen Gupta, "Communism Further Divided", p. 173.

[14] Sen Gupta, "Communism Further Divided", pp. 168–9. Only in 1988 was the voting age lowered from twenty-one to eighteen.

[15] Lockwood, *The Communist Party of India*, p. 124; *SW*, 5 July 1975, p. 3.

[16] Scott, "Emerging from the Emergency", p. 118.

that if this matter [the Emergency] had been delayed by another 8–10 days, something else would have happened. This we consider to be a catastrophe.[17]

In August the CPI rehearsed these arguments in a pamphlet, *Fascism and the Politics of Power*, again with the liberal use of counterfactuals: in the coming months, under the umbrella of the JP Movement, "the RSS and similar stormtroopers were to become the spearhead of action"; the "conspiracy to capture power was drawn up in meticulous detail."[18] CPI MP Srinivas Sardesai took the argument to its logical conclusion, an apologia for authoritarianism: the threat emanating from the opposition made "a mechanical conception of civil liberties based on an abstract theory of individual freedom" indefensible.[19] On the question of censorship, too, then, the CPI and the Congress concurred. In parliament Gupta brazenly lashed out against the press. If pressmen, who were in the pockets of "big capitalists", were:

> ... allowed to function normally freely today, by now, within twenty or twenty-five days, they would have created havoc in the country. Every day, all kinds of imaginary and cooked up stories would have been pedalled out [*sic*]. One day they would have said that Indira Gandhi is making a secret trip, overnight dash to Moscow, to get her orders from there and rush back ... They would also have said that the Soviet army is massing on the border and that they may march in any time.[20]

Because the CPI's was a position arrived at ideologically and not conveniently, as was the case with the Congress, it came, to Delhi's rulers at least, with greater doctrinaire encumbrances. It made the CPI's leaders uneasy, for example, at the flurry of incentives that Mrs Gandhi was handing out to industrialists like K.K. Birla. Indrajit Gupta went as far as to suggest that Birla's newspaper, the *Hindustan Times*, ought to be censored more effectively. More generally, he recommended tightening the leash on all captains of industry: "I am not saying that they should be arrested tomorrow, but at least a proper watch should be kept on them."[21] Rather disingenuously, the CPI had failed to realise that Indira Gandhi did not consider Indian capitalists her enemies.

---

17 *Lok Sabha Debates*, vol. 53, no. 1 (21 July 1975), cols 118, 121.

18 Mukherjee, *Fascism and the Politics of Power*, pp. 34–5.

19 Lockwood, *The Communist Party of India*, pp. 123–4.

20 *Lok Sabha Debates*, vol. 53, no. 1 (21 July 1975), col. 126. Indeed, the underground press of the resistance pedalled such stories: see Chapter 9.

21 *Lok Sabha Debates*, vol. 53, no. 5 (25 July 1975), col. 93.

And with time the cracks only grew wider. In February 1976, when the Congress reduced the legally required minimum bonus to which workers were entitled, the gulf between them found voice in parliament. Gupta was at his sardonic best: in 1971 "a new decision was taken to raise the minimum bonus from 4 per cent to 8.33 per cent", he noted almost plainly: "that was done precisely for populist considerations." Mrs Gandhi interjected: "That is wrong", but Indrajit Gupta continued over her: "That was done in 1971 on the eve of general elections, and it was done as a populist slogan to get the votes of the working class … When it suits you, you take to populist slogans; when it is not necessary, you talk against populism." When the bill was passed 183 to 38, CPI MP Ranen Sen declared "4th February 1976 the blackest day for the working classes in India."[22] Scarcely a month had passed since Gupta had locked horns with Mrs Gandhi over Congress efforts to beef up MISA. On that occasion he had flayed the prime minister for the "kind of misuse" to which she was opening up MISA, making possible the re-arrest of a citizen even after detention orders had been revoked.[23] The National Federation of Indian Women had grouses of its own. When, at the time of the Forty-second Amendment, it recommended the revision of the right to property to designate women equal property holders after marriage, its calls went unheeded.[24] In December another exchange between a Communist parliamentarian, Bhogendra Jha, and the prime minister highlighted the mutual misperceptions. When Jha voiced his disapproval at the firing of Nandini Satpathy, "who ran one of the better state governments", Mrs Gandhi's reaction was thunderous: "this means that the CPI is flouting my rule."[25] It was a revealing comment. To Mrs Gandhi the CPI needed to behave less as an independent party than a loyalist faction of the Congress from which no dissent could be brooked.

What rankled the CPI further was that, despite the alliance, they had effectively been outhoused by Mrs Gandhi's ministries. The "implementation committees" established for executing the Twenty-Point Programme also kept the CPI at bay, and the party remained but a junior partner in all states except Kerala, where relations between the CPI chief minister and

---

[22] Mavalankar, *"No, Sir"*, pp. 96, 98.

[23] *Lok Sabha Debates*, vol. 56, no. 12 (22 July 1976), col. 206.

[24] Scott, "Emerging from the Emergency", p. 121.

[25] Transcript of interview with Bhogendra Jha, Acc. No. 766, NMML Oral History Project, p. 92. My translation from the Hindi.

the Congress leadership was anything but amicable. In the West Bengal "implementation committee" the CPI held only four seats out of fifty-one. In December 1975 the West Bengal Youth Congress went as far as to sever links with the Communists, belatedly realising that their "ideologies and programmes are different."[26] Shut out from the grand old party's campaigns and with no independent media to rely on, the CPI decided to gather news from the bottom up, sending its cadres on *padayatras* across the republic in early 1976. Covering "44,000 villages across 270 districts", what emerged from this fact-finding mission became a major bone of contention between the two parties: witnessing at first hand the coercive sterilisations and the growing precedence accorded to Sanjay's Five-Point Programme over the Twenty Points it had endorsed, the CPI's attacks on the young Gandhi grew increasingly strident.[27]

The lack of empathy cut both ways. In the eyes of Congressmen the CPI's *Link*, though not quite a party publication, was becoming an embarrassment, as were the CPI cadres, some of whom were even incarcerated for protesting against the ham-fisted sterilisation drive in Uttar Pradesh. For his part Sanjay, in a March 1976 visit to Calcutta, averred that "never again will the red flag fly in Bengal."[28] Three months later, in an interview with *Surge*, there came a fuller statement of his contempt: "the Communists may have a small cadre that actually works but if you take all the people in the Communist Party, the big wigs—even the not-so-big wigs—I don't think you'd find a richer or more corrupt people anywhere."[29] His other comments were of the same order: the economy was better handled by the private sector, socialism was *passé*, tax cuts were necessary. His mother's reaction to this press outing was fairly tepid. She believed only that her son had "made an exceedingly stupid statement about the Communists" but had, even in his denseness, stumbled upon a hidden truth: the CPI did not support her enough; had they been more sympathetic he would probably never have made the remark.[30] Still, Sanjay was forced to recant because

---

[26] Sen Gupta, "Communism Further Divided", p. 173.

[27] Lockwood, *The Communist Party of India*, pp. 131, 128; *SCR*, vol. 3, p. 115.

[28] Selbourne, *Through the Indian Looking-Glass*, p. 18.

[29] Vasudev, *Two Faces of Indira Gandhi*, pp. 206–7. Dhar had the interview retracted in late August: Dhar, *Indira Gandhi, the "Emergency", and Indian Democracy*, p. 324.

[30] See the handwritten note on Sanjay's interview that Mrs Gandhi sent to Dhar, reproduced in the latter's memoir: *Indira Gandhi, the "Emergency", and Indian Democracy*, p. 326.

Mrs Gandhi hit the nail on the head when she told him: "[if the Communists wish] to stay with us on our terms, what do we lose?"[31]

By the autumn of 1976 even the CPI had tired of playing Polonius to the authoritarian regime, mostly because Mrs Gandhi had by this time overplayed her hand. On 4 October she had written a stern letter to Chandra Rajeswara Rao, CPI general secretary, about his party's "opposition to our family programme. This is now reaching limits which cannot coexist with cooperation with us."[32] Some days later, on the 27th, the CPI's Central Executive Committee passed a resolution on the "Misuses of the Emergency". Around the same time the Communist union, AITUC, began clamouring for the restoration of workers' rights and the bonus. In January 1977 the party launched a national campaign protesting the growing gap between wages and inflation—the result of Mrs Gandhi's industrial policy. Hundreds were arrested under MISA.[33] During these months Gupta kept up the pressure in parliament, laying into the "misuse" of MISA by corrupt police officers, the humbling of the "progressive press", the crippling of the working classes, and Mrs Gandhi's torpor in handling hoarders and landlords. At the state level, too, it grew clear to CPI bosses that the alliance benefited them little. Even the most powerful of them, Kerala's chief minister, Achutha Menon, was well aware that backed by police power, a burgeoning union presence, and control over the airwaves, the Congress could effortlessly pull the plug on the coalition in the only state where it played second fiddle; sooner rather than later, K. Karunakaran, leader of the state Congress, would make his chief ministerial ambitions plain.[34]

These tensions notwithstanding, it must be remembered that the CPI never broke with the Congress to join hands with the opposition. At least three reasons explain this. First, ideologically the logic of the Kumaramangalam Thesis continued to influence the residual Communist leadership: if the possibility of social change was negligible from within the combine, it was impossible outside it. Moreover, by moving from compromise to compromise the Left had fallen out of step with the *zeitgeist*, descending from the peak years of the Congress Forum for Socialist Action to the last months of the Emergency. The levers of state power, whether by proxy or alliance, then, appeared to be its best shot at retaining relevance.

---

[31] Nayar, *The Judgement*, p. 89.

[32] Dhar, *Indira Gandhi, the "Emergency", and Indian Democracy*, p. 324.

[33] Lockwood, *The Communist Party of India*, p. 159.

[34] Ibid., pp. 143–70.

Second, unfortunately for the Communists their movement had little place in a resistance which flourished with Red Scare rhetoric. For instance, in his letters to the prime minister that were duly circulated underground, Jayaprakash Narayan accused Mrs Gandhi of surrendering the republic to "Russian overlordship", which he believed had been engineered with help from CPI myrmidons.[35] Joining JP's men underground, then, was never on the cards. More importantly, going into hiding would have seriously affected the Communist chain of command: its top leaders certainly would have wound up in prison and its cadres decimated, hurting the party's prospects were a snap election to be called.

And third, the CPI's leadership had slowly but surely succumbed to the temptations of the Congress' Garden of Eden. For their alliance with Mrs Gandhi's party had ushered in an entirely novel lifestyle for the Communist leadership. In December 1975, for example, the CPI celebrated its fiftieth anniversary with aristocratic sumptuousness, congratulating itself with "albums, an official brief history", memoirs, and special issues on having turfed out its competitors, the CPI(M) in Andhra Pradesh and Kerala. "The party was in high spirits and growing", a Central Executive Committee member later wrote in his memoir, recalling the rollicking final months of authoritarianism. His tales of the Emergency feature tours of Prague, Berlin, and Moscow: proximity to power had put him on the international lecture circuit. Another perk was meeting the Tamil film star M.G. Ramachandran. Later, after an accident while touring Assam, even his convalescence was a pleasant spell in Delhi's expensive Willingdon Hospital, where he was "given VIP treatment" after senior Congressmen came to inquire about his condition.[36] In short, the highlights were interactions with celebrities, foreign travel, and an induction into polite society. Once in its midst, it was hard for the apparatchiks to turn their backs on it.

Maharashtrian Partners: The Shiv Sena and the RPIs

Sujata Anandan points out that Bal Thackeray, the head of the Shiv Sena, "began by opposing the Emergency" but changed his mind under pressure.[37]

---

[35] Narayan to Mrs Gandhi, 21 July 1975, Jayaprakash Narayan Papers, Instalment III, Subject File 328.

[36] Sen, *A Traveller and the Road*, pp. 353, 355–9.

[37] Anandan, *Hindu Hriday Samrat*, p. 37.

Congress Chief Minister S.B. Chavan "gave him two options: either prepare for arrest like other leaders of the opposition parties or don his Sunday best to be driven to the local Doordarshan studios and issue a statement supporting the Emergency."[38] Thackeray, who "had no desire to relive the nightmare of the three months in prison in 1969", preferred to shower both Mrs Gandhi and the Emergency regime with encomia, not only on Doordarshan but also in the pages of *Marmik*, the Sena's weekly. His shock troops, the 100,000 members of its *shakhas* and 30,000 unionists of the Bharatiya Kamgar Sena, were pressed into the service of the authoritarian regime.[39] Thackeray endorsed virtually every programme of the Congress, both local and national. In Bombay the Shiv Sena assented to the crackdown on beggars and other gentrification measures that it had long championed.[40]

Even as they fielded candidates against one another, the two parties had since at least the late 1960s enjoyed a symbiotic relationship, sharing common enemies in the Communists, whose unions dominated the city's mills,[41] and the Dalit Panthers, a militant group that drew on Buddhist and Marxist writings and railed against that "motherfucker God of the Brahmans for laughing shamelessly in the face of Untouchable despair."[42] In 1973 the Shiv Sena and the Congress (R) had joined hands in the Bombay municipal elections against the communists.[43] A year later they had struck an electoral alliance in a failed bid to defeat the CPI's Roza Deshpande, daughter of the Communist trade unionist S.A. Dange. Certainly, the grand old party that routinely laid into Hindu nationalism had no compunctions striking this devil's pact even after sixteen Shiv Sainiks had been sentenced for the murder of a Communist MLA in 1970, a killing that had prompted the bye-election in which the Sena had its first parliamentarian elected.[44] It can be surmised from these developments that the closeness of the Bombay Congress to the Sena, and Thackeray's cheering on of the Emergency regime, were probably the reasons why the

---

[38] Ibid., p. 38.

[39] Gupta, *Nativism in a Metropolis*, p. vii; Heuzé-Brigant, "Populism and the Workers Movement", p. 122.

[40] Selbourne, *An Eye to India*, p. 268.

[41] On the Shiv Sena's anti-communism, see Gogate, *The Emergence of Regionalism in Mumbai*, p. 58.

[42] Contursi, "Political Theology", pp. 320, 326.

[43] Gupta, *Nativism in a Metropolis*, p. 165.

[44] Ibid., pp. 134, 148–9; Palshikar, "Shiv Sena", p. 1497.

party survived the months of authoritarian rule without a ban. In the 1977 election the Shiv Sena refused to field a single candidate. Instead its cadres campaigned *en masse* for the Congress, even as many in its ranks resigned; still, in 1978 Bal Thackeray decided to support the Janata Party, pragmatically, for the state elections.

The RPI was the other Maharashtrian party supporting the Emergency. More precisely, five of the factions resulting from previous splits of the party that B.R. Ambedkar had conceived in 1956 backed the regime. Again, this strategy was of a piece with previous arrangements: the Gaekwad group had already entered into an alliance with Indira Gandhi's Congress in 1971. And in 1975, four other factions—all named after their leaders: the Kamble, Gawai, Khopragade, and Bhaiyyasaheb Ambedkar (B.R. Ambedkar's son) groups—too, came to support the Emergency. At the polls in 1977, though, while the Gawai faction remained an ally of the Congress, Khopragade shifted to the Janata party.[45]

Businessmen and the Congress: A Convergence of Interests

Capitalists, Mrs Gandhi declared on various occasions during the Emergency, were a "vociferous minority", "powerful forces" attempting to derail the socialist state. Yet as the months of authoritarianism wore on it transpired that such statements were one thing, policy another. Indeed, her relations with some captains of industry were the inverse of her association with the CPI; the latter she tolerated on sufferance, but with the former the connection was more organic. Here, historical reasons can be adduced: big capital was the major beneficiary of the Nehru years, cornering the benefits of import-substituting industrialisation, selective licensing, and cheap labour. In contrast, Mrs Gandhi's corporatism was less concerned with the first two elements of this set—over her early years in power, import duties were reduced, the rupee devalued, and forty-two industries delicensed— and more with the third dimension: she continued pushing wages down in real terms.

Generally speaking, during the Emergency she doubled down both on Nehru's socialist asseverations, which with "Garibi Hatao" had grown even shriller, as well as his capital-friendly policies. Both periods, Nehru's and Mrs Gandhi's, had as the centrepiece of industrial policy the disbursement of public funds for the financial and technical assistance of a handful of

---

[45] Gokhale, *From Concessions to Confrontation*, p. 253.

private empires.[46] In Nehru's years they had survived the postcolonial settlement unscathed despite the sustained threats of anti-trust legislation and nationalisation (as Howard Erdman put it, "Nehru's bark was far worse than his bite"); during Mrs Gandhi's first decade in power the total assets of the twenty largest industrial houses increased by 150 per cent, a period in which the national output grew at an annual clip of 3 to 3.5 per cent.[47]

When the Emergency was declared Mrs Gandhi offered capitalists significant concessions: top tax rates were cut, exemptions for business entertainment expenses introduced, capital gains and corporation taxes slashed, nationalisation put on the back burner, dividend ceilings removed, excise duties lowered, investment allowances increased, strikes banned, unions crippled, and licensing selectively liberalised.[48] Many of these policies were, of course, the product of direct liaisons between state and capital. At least two of the Twenty Points—streamlining licensing and chastening labour—had their roots in the Tata Memorandum of 1972, in which the eponymous industrialist called for a complete reassessment of industrial policy, tailoring it to suit the major players who were, after all, "the most resourceful and experienced" enterprises in business.[49] What of the allocation of licences? "Less emphasis [should] be laid on concentration of economic power *per se* and more on the use made of it and on performance and merit", Tata suggested. What of union activity? Here he said it was time the "government ... now take a firmer stand", for it can ill-afford "the heavy loss of production and the gross public inconvenience repeatedly inflicted on it by labour unrest."[50]

During the Emergency, over 300 export items that did not require foreign exchange or government capital were delicensed and twenty-nine indus-

---

[46] This was done in the name of import substitution. See Chibber, *Locked in Place*, pp. 127–48 *et passim*.

[47] Erdman, "The Industrialists", p. 173.

[48] *Economic Survey, 1976–1977*, pp. 26–9; *India 1977–78*, pp. 285–6; Toye, "Economic Trends and Policies", p. 311; Blair, "Mrs Gandhi's Emergency", p. 257.

[49] J.R.D. Tata, "Suggestions for Accelerating Industrial Growth"—more popularly the "Tata Memorandum" (hereafter referred to as such), 17 May 1972, P.N. Haksar Papers, Instalment III, Subject File 225. "The government will fully consider the suggestions you have made", Mrs Gandhi pledged in her reply on 17 July 1972. On 23 August, Tata wrote back to her saying that he was "distressed" to find that the contents of the "confidential" memorandum had been leaked to "the Leftist Press". No better evidence of their camaraderie is needed than a perusal of their common lexicon. See PMSP, File 38/87/1972 PMS.

[50] Tata, "Tata Memorandum", pp. 309, 283.

tries were allowed the "utilisation of installed capacity beyond licensing capacity."[51] Additionally, prevailing over the heads of the CPI and the Congress Left, industrial interests succeeded in having promoted as minister for industry and supplies T.A. Pai, who had long favoured sweeping privatisation and the creation of a "national sector"—where public-sector units would be "opened up to private investors".[52] On the other hand some left-wing ministers were dropped, including Minister of State for Petroleum and Chemicals K.R. Ganesh, who drew support from trade unions, and Minister of State for Civil Supplies R.K. Khadilkar, an advocate for more nationalisation. Others on the Left had their portfolios pruned, as was the case with Minister of Petroleum and Chemicals K.D. Malaviya, whose ambit was bifurcated, petroleum remaining in his hands while the chemicals and fertilisers bit was given to Prakash Chand Sethi. The reason for this is not hard to discern: Malaviya had laid out a plan that would, to the horror of private pharmaceutical companies, ensure by 1979 that the market share of the two public-sector giants, the IDPL and HAL, increase from 33 to 60 per cent. Moreover, his past as a nationalising oil minister had made him suspect. By contrast Sethi, as chair of the Souvenir Committee and manager of the Congress war chest, enjoyed a special rapport with capitalists.[53]

Some analysts were quick to recognise the convergence of interests between the Congress and capitalists during the Emergency. In a perceptive piece written in September 1975 the journalist Arun Shourie saw this class as the biggest beneficiary of the regime, describing the transition to authoritarianism as a virtual coup by industrialists and landlords.[54]

Indeed, underlying the corporatist dispensation was the conviviality between business houses and the grand old party. Some of these connections went back generations, a legacy of the coupling of Indian capital and Indian nationalism. The Birla family is a case in point: Ghanshyam Das

---

[51] *SW*, 9 August 1975, p. 1; Note by the Ministry of Industry and Civil Supplies on the "liberalisation of licensing", 17 October 1975, PMSP, File 37/633/14/1975 PMS.

[52] Erdman, "The Industrialists", p. 141.

[53] See the Ministry of Petroleum and Chemicals' note "on the Hathi Committee's Report on Drugs", which does not even mention nationalisation: 24 September 1975, PMSP, File 17/1315/1975 PMS. More on the Souvenir Committee below.

[54] See Shourie, *Symptoms of Fascism*, p. 31. A similar argument is made in Gupta, "The Political Economy of Fascism", pp. 991–2. However, capitalists neither instigated the Emergency nor became its *raison d'être*; they merely welcomed and supported it because they benefited from it.

Birla had lived "in the shadow of the Mahatma".[55] For the last five months of his life Gandhi had in fact put up at the industrialist's bungalow on Albuquerque Road in Delhi, where he was assassinated. Birla's son Krishna Kumar remained on good terms with Nehru in the 1950s, even befriending his daughter. For their part the first family quite unabashedly cosseted the Birla empire: in 1959 they handed the Birlas the entire power grid generated by the costly Rihand Dam Project for throwaway prices, and in 1970 a controversial licence to build a fertiliser factory in Goa even as Congress socialists demanded an investigation into Birla concerns.[56] With pecuniary power came a growing interest in politics proper, elections taking the place of backroom lobbying. More than his father, it was K.K. Birla who developed this penchant for politics; it was his "hobby", as he put it in his *Reminiscences* of Mrs Gandhi.[57] With Ghanshyam Das Birla's blessings he backed her against Desai during the Congress split, despite his unmistakable sympathies for the Swatantra party. Nevertheless, in the 1971 general election he contested and lost the Jhunjhunu seat in Rajasthan on the latter's ticket, an act which Mrs Gandhi readily forgave after he agreed to help Sanjay kickstart his automobile venture. The two scions got along, meeting "every four to six weeks" to discuss cars and capital.

It was not long after Birla's 1971 defeat that Mrs Gandhi, to alleviate the bitterness of this failed politician, appointed him to the Planning Commission.[58] "Overwhelmed by the kindness and affection of Indiraji for this gesture", he returned the favour in April 1975 by inviting her to inaugurate the annual session of FICCI.[59] In his address on the occasion he recalled the growing number of "man-days lost to strikes and lockouts" in the 1970s and enquired whether the prime minister would make good on something she had "suggested some time back": that "there should be a moratorium on strikes and lockouts for at least five years." Continuing to curry her favour in the aftermath of the Allahabad verdict, Birla decided "to organize a procession of businessmen to demonstrate our solidarity with her."[60] Flanked by 500 capitalist comrades, he marched to her residence

---

[55] Birla, *In the Shadow of the Mahatma*.

[56] Brass, *An Indian Political Life*, p. 78; Awana, *Pressure Politics in Congress Party*, p. 318.

[57] Birla, *Indira Gandhi*, p. 1.

[58] At the time, K.K. Birla was not only running the family firm but also serving as vice president of FICCI, the apex business forum in the country.

[59] Birla, *Indira Gandhi*, p. 45.

[60] Ibid., pp. 195, 50.

where she thanked him for his support. When the Emergency was declared, Birla announced in a speech laced with antiphrasis that:

> I have never been an admirer of the Emergency ... However, immediately after the declaration of Emergency peace and calm returned in [*sic*] public life, law and order were fully restored, discipline in every walk of life became noticeable, strikes and lockouts were greatly reduced, punctuality in the running of trains vastly improved, government servants—particularly railway employees—became very courteous to the public. If only all that could have been achieved without resort [*sic*] to a declaration of Emergency![61]

When Birla expressed his unfulfilled "desire to enter the Rajya Sabha", Sanjay resourcefully suggested that he contest from Uttar Pradesh. He did in November 1975 but lost again, this time because of the opposition of Chief Minister H.N. Bahuguna who, according to Sanjay, "had betrayed the trust reposed in him by his mother" by hiring four tantrics to pray for the annihilation of the ruling family.[62] Confessions from the tantrics were extorted and Bahuguna was forced to resign despite his loyalty as a foot-soldier. Over the first five months of Emergency rule Bahuguna had seen to it that his state accounted for 90 per cent of arrests made in the republic. He had also raised funds for the party from the sugar lobby and through kickbacks in the construction industry on "the occasion of [Mrs Gandhi's] birthday."[63] K.K. Birla was eventually elected to the Rajya Sabha on a Congress ticket in 1984.

J.R.D. Tata chorused K.K. Birla's sentiment when the Emergency was declared: "Things had gone too far. You can't imagine what we have been through here—strikes, boycotts, demonstrations. Why, there were days I couldn't walk out of my office onto the street." Barely two months into the Emergency he expressed his gratitude in the pages of *Commerce*: "government have [*sic*] in the recent past shown encouraging signs of being willing to reconsider some of their economic policies in the interest of stimulating production."[64] On other occasions he waxed lyrical about "Sanjay's pragmatism", "overflowing with praise for the young man" and concurring with his assessment that "the parliamentary system is not suited to our needs."[65]

---

[61] Ibid., p. 53.

[62] Ibid., pp. 40, 44.

[63] Shibban Lal Saksena, MP, to Morarji Desai, Prime Minister, 16 January 1978, Morarji Desai Papers, Subject File 13.

[64] Erdman, "The Industrialists", p. 126.

[65] Dhar, *Indira Gandhi the "Emergency", and Indian Democracy*, p. 313.

Beyond writing memoranda and columns, Tata also made his influence felt in the growing interpenetration between the public and private sectors. Wadud Khan, managing director of the government's Steel Authority of India Limited, "on deputation from Tata Iron and Steel" during the Emergency, was a case in point.[66]

One member of another family conglomerate, the Oberois, also publicly supported the regime. The Emergency, he said, is "just wonderful ... we used to have terrible problems with the unions. Now when they give us any troubles [*sic*], the government just puts them in jail."[67]

There is no doubt that Mrs Gandhi's class war resulted in far fewer "man-days lost" to strikes: from 33.6 million in 1974 to 2.8 million in 1976; the number of strikers fell from 2.71 million to 550,447.[68] And while the working class was "disciplined", no corresponding policies targeted their bosses, who grew even more stentorian than in the past: in the same period, man-days lost to lockouts *rose* from 6.6 to 9.9 million. In July 1976, for instance, 96 per cent of the man-days lost were to lockouts.[69] More so than before, the rights of industrialists trumped those of workers.

On the few occasions when Mrs Gandhi did express concern over the sharp spike in layoffs and lockouts, governors and chief ministers alike hastened to reassure her that such fears were ill-founded.[70] Meanwhile, many Maharashtrian firms—Globe Auto Electricals, Apar, Voltas, Mahindra & Mahindra, and Goa Shipyard—had each laid off at least a tenth of their workforce. Events at the last were particularly acute: when all its 1300 workers went on strike, their INTUC leader along with eleven others in the Congress union were thrown in prison under MISA. The situation in West Bengal was worse. At least nine companies laid off at least 1000 workers each. Industries in and around Kanpur fared no better: as a result of the sustained lockouts, the 2000 workers at J.K. Rayon were "reported to be starving".[71] In sum,

---

[66] Lukas, "India is as Indira Does", p. 93; Erdman, "The Industrialists", p. 150, n53.

[67] Lukas, "India is as Indira Does", pp. 92–3.

[68] Rajagopal, "The Emergency as Prehistory", p. 1039.

[69] *EPW* Editorial, "Locked Out", p. 1709.

[70] See the letters from Indira Gandhi to S.B. Chavan, S.S. Ray, and Chenna Reddy, Governor of Uttar Pradesh, as well as their replies, 13, 16, 17, and 23 December 1975, PMSP, File 37/633/15–A/1975 PMS.

[71] "Table on layoffs, retrenchments, and lockouts in the Bombay region", "Table on layoffs, retrenchments, and lockouts in the Calcutta region", and "Some cases of recent closures/alleged large scale layoffs, lockouts", all in PMSP, File 37/633/15–A/1975 PMS.

nearly 500,000 workers were laid off in the first six months of the Emergency. As a result in February 1976 an amendment to the Industrial Disputes Act was hastily passed in the Lok Sabha, making it mandatory for all "establishments with more than 300 workers" to secure government approval before layoffs.[72]

Outside the halls of Parliament House, however, Congressmen sang a different tune. Addressing a joint convention of the Youth Congress, National Students Union of India, and AITUC, Sanjay announced that one of the aims of the new regime was "the stopping of wage increases".[73] A few months later, making a case for the slashing of bonuses, he asked rhetorically, "what was more important: bonus or the survival of industries providing jobs to a large number of people?" He then proceeded to blame the "working class" for shrinking from "some of the decisions" made by INTUC, the only union that placed the national interest "above other considerations".[74]

Some years before the Emergency, Sanjay had morphed into a one-man lobby for industrial interests. His failed stab at the people's car had made him empathise with entrepreneurs and understand their frustrations, he once noted painfully to *Surge*, even as he rhapsodised rather incongruously over "the efficiency of the private sector" in the same breath: "The expertise and the hard work that they have, you'll never get in a public sector."[75]

Capital was appreciative of this benevolence. Birla, for one, continued patronising the Congress by financing prohibitively expensive advertisements in the *Souvenirs*, a series of volumes ostensibly commemorating policy decisions and major events in the life of the Congress, even though many of its issues never even saw the light of day.[76] Other industrialists were no slouches in his footsteps. In a list that read "like a *Fortune* list of top firms", P.C. Sethi, the Congressman in charge of the party's "Souvenir Committee", received as "advertisement money" a total of over Rs 200 million, which included Rs 5,350,000 from the Tatas, Rs 1,160,000 the Birlas, and Rs 500,000 the Times Group.[77]

The investing classes which, here as elsewhere, served as a barometer of upper-middle-class dispositions, too reflected no discontent with authori-

---

72 Toye, "Economic Trends and Policies", p. 310.

73 Lockwood, *The Communist Party of India*, p. 118.

74 *TOI*, 31 October 1976, p. 1.

75 Vasudev, *Two Faces of Indira Gandhi*, p. 202.

76 Birla, *Indira Gandhi*, pp. 57, 205–8, 101. The ads often cost Rs 10,000 to Rs 20,000 per page.

77 *India Today*, 15 March 1979.

tarianism. Regime stability led stock markets to rally by over 10 per cent in the first six months of the Emergency; by comparison the victory of the democratic but unstable Janata two years later resulted in a 20 per cent slump in the corresponding period.[78]

Rural elites came hard on the heels of the beaming industrialists and the upper bourgeoisie. This owed to Mrs Gandhi's decision to inflate grain prices through high procurement prices in order to offset the effects of the good monsoon of 1975. While market prices for wheat had fallen by around 25 per cent to Rs 90–95 a quintal, procurement prices were pushed upwards to a record level of Rs 105.[79] In fact, the grain "surplus" widely advertised in contemporary papers was not just the result of increased supply but also of decreased demand. Simply put, on account of higher prices, India's rural poor were cutting back on foodgrain consumption.[80] Boosting the profits and prospects of the smaller gentry were also lower fertiliser prices and the state's poor performance when it came to expropriating land and abolishing debt bondage. Furthermore, mindful that the unpredictable rain gods would not be as generous year after year, in 1976 Delhi's rulers bumped up the budgetary allocation for irrigation by 45 per cent.[81]

Mrs Gandhi's policies had, however, unwittingly created a problem for both industrialists and the rural elite: frozen wages—caused by the suppression of unions and executive despotism—were pushing down demand. In other words this was the dilemma of "over-production and under-consumption". Here too Mrs Gandhi had an answer, as the "Brazilian model" was made a priority in Delhi's policy-making circles: the "excess" industrial output of the public sector as well as government food stockpiles were dumped on export markets to make it easier for rural elites and private-sector industrialists to find a domestic market for their goods.[82]

---

[78] See the Janata party's "Statement on Economic Policy", 23 November 1977, PMSP, File 37/692/1977 PMS.

[79] Toye, "Economic Trends and Policies", p. 304.

[80] "A buffer stock of 17 million tonnes has been created": B.M., "Food Surplus for Export!", pp. 1449–50; *NYT*, 15 January 1977, p. 15.

[81] Blair, "Mrs Gandhi's Emergency", p. 257; Toye, "Economic Trends and Policies", pp. 305, 314; Ministry of Finance, *Budget for 1976–77*, pp. 3–4.

[82] Selbourne, *An Eye to India*, p. 229; Blair, "Mrs Gandhi's Emergency", p. 258. In essence, by sustaining losses in cheap sales on the international markets, the government was ensuring that the private sector would not have to do the same: the latter could then access domestic markets virtually unencumbered by public-sector competition.

In the event, the 1976 budget, which for the first time included detailed and systematic pre-budget discussions between industrialists and the administration, sought to give capitalists more incentives than ever before: taxes on profits, capital gains, and wealth were reduced, ostensibly to deter evasion. So fixated was Mrs Gandhi on making her "generosity to the rich" known that she began making choices that seemed inexplicable for an authoritarian ruler: budgetary allocations for the bureaucracy, police, and prisons were scaled back and some of their personnel fired.[83] "Populism is out, profit-making is in", enthused the *Economist* after the budget. Its Asian equivalent, the *Far Eastern Economic Review*, was equally unequivocal: "India's economy got down to business in 1976", it reassured its readers, quoting approvingly the Emergency slogan "work more, talk less". The budget heralded a "shift from fiscal theology to fiscal rationalism", said the delighted conservative jurist Nani Palkhivala.[84] Two months later, on 12 May 1976, Mrs Gandhi believed the budget had not done enough for capitalists; further excise and tax reliefs were announced.[85]

This mollycoddling led B.M. Birla (K.K.'s uncle) to exclaim that India was finally ready for a "big leap forward" now that the "political leadership has shown itself to be strong and imaginative" and "labour has ... realised its responsibilities to the nation."[86] Meanwhile, Finance Minister C. Subramaniam argued that with increased investment and production the republic was "poised for [a] great leap forward"; Congress MPs extolled the "imaginative, meaningful, and growth-oriented budget". Mrs Gandhi suggested that workers "put their heart and soul into increasing production without asking for any rewards at the present moment."[87] In short, state and capital spoke with the same voice.

The Discreet Charm of the Bourgeoisie

What of the middle class? Its upper segments either kept a low profile, politically speaking, or supported the Emergency. A memoir by Tavleen

---

83 Toye, "Economic Trends and Policies", p. 312.

84 *Economist*, 20 March 1976, p. 91; *1977 Yearbook*, p. 177; *SW*, 27 March 1976, p. 3.

85 *SW*, 15 May 1976, p. 7.

86 He failed to register the irony that his assertion echoed a Chinese Communist Party campaign slogan. The three B.M. Birla quotes come from *TOI*, 12 May 1976, p. 7; *TOI*, 5 May 1976, p. 1; Selbourne, *An Eye to India*, p. 246.

87 *SW*, 8 November 1975, p. 5; *TOI*, 16 March 1976, p. 1; Selbourne, *An Eye to India*, p. 246.

Singh, socialite and fashionable society's foremost sociologist, documents the ennui of this class, whose long dinners of "European *hors d'oeuvres*", capons, and "spicy Goan prawn curry" had during the Emergency condemned them to postprandial torpor in their natural habitat: "landscaped gardens", swimming pools, farmhouses that were "modernistic glass palaces" filled with "beautiful things".[88] "Most people" of this stratum were "supporters of the Emergency", she notes in *Durbar*. As for the rest, herself included, they did not believe in making their opposition known outside their gated communities, within which they remained largely confined: "During the Emergency, my social life seemed to become an endless series of dinner parties", she writes.[89]

Ashis Nandy explains the way the middle class supported the Emergency by its "deepseated fear of chaos and disorder", which had become even more acute because of the JP Movement:

> Alienated from a society which has lived for centuries in a near-anarchic state, they project into their political leaders the search for a more cohesive, well-defined, "hard" and purposeful politics. They choose to ignore the possibility that in a heterogenous fragmented polity, the search for order may easily degenerate into a search for a leader who would freeze the society and impose on it a stability which would destroy the spirit of the civilization.[90]

Two beliefs, one theoretical and the other substantial, both widely shared by the Indian middle class, aided in hastening approval of the new regime. The first was the shibboleth of regime difference: that liberal democracies are incapable of economic acceleration owing ostensibly to the trade-off between freedom and growth. The second, a consequence of the first, was that the Emergency had helped bring down prices, ending a three-year spell in which the rupee had lost half its buying power and inflation had spiralled out of control. That China was "growing faster" in the 1950s and 1960s was widely attributed to its authoritarian regime: ergo, the belief that "discipline" was pushing the growth button.[91] Similar ideas were held by

---

[88] Singh, *Durbar*, pp. 35, 42.

[89] Ibid., p. 22.

[90] Nandy, "Indira Gandhi and Indian Politics", pp. 115–16.

[91] Echoes of these beliefs had trickled up into the chambers of Delhi's ruling elites. See, for instance, Jagjivan Ram's remarks on "discipline" and "political stability" as a "pre-requisite for economic development": Zaidi, *The Annual Register of Indian Political Parties—vol. 24*, p. 120. Mrs Gandhi similarly suggested that democracies were incapable of "reach[ing] out to the poorest in the land": Palmer, "India in 1975", p. 110.

democrats-turned-authoritarians in other countries, notably South Korea and the Philippines, even as the reverse proved true in both cases: growth rates had halved in the former since the authoritarian turn; market fluctuations in the latter confirmed that autocrats are rarely the high modernisers they claim they are.[92]

The middle classes were all the more on board, both ideologically and materially, with the Emergency regime's transgressions, mostly because they suffered the least in the new dispensation. They escaped the worst of the sterilisations: the rural middle class, given their wealth and affinity with power networks, had in effect proofed themselves against the scalpel; in any case the green revolution had already seen to it that this class were better disposed in favour of smaller families than the rural poor.[93] "Motivating" and dealing with *dalals* achieved the same for their urban counterparts, as we noted early on in the book.

In the event, large sections of the middle classes saw the violence that accompanied sterilisations as a necessary evil, serving the greater good even.[94] The sterilisation drive in Chandigarh, for instance, benefited from the efforts of the Rotary Club and local industrialists, who gave an "extra incentive of Rs 50" to those willing to be operated.[95] For some there was also money to be made from the programme. In Delhi, middle-class citizens set up their own for-profit private family planning camps in Paharganj, Trans-Yamuna, and Chandni Chowk to "help" local authorities meet targets.[96]

The middle classes were also the beneficiaries of Sanjay's gentrification programme. This was, incontrovertibly, on account of its *raison d'être*: removing the poor from inner cities in order to make space for the moneyed classes. But their concern was not always housing. In Hissar, Haryana, for example, a government library was flattened to "improve the traffic

---

92 Gupta, "A Season of Caesars", p. 330.

93 Ibid., p. 380. For empirical proof on lower fertility rates among those with higher incomes than the poor, see Anker, "The Effect of Group Level Variables", pp. 63–76.

94 Opinion pieces and letters in newspapers serve as a useful weathervane for middle-class opinion: see, *inter alia*, *TOI*, 24 February 1976, p. 8; *TOI*, 24 April 1976, p. 7; *TOI*, 15 April 1977, p. 8.

95 *SCR*, vol. 3, p. 199.

96 They were all shut down because the administration was less than enthusiastic about operations being conducted in "places other than proper institutions": "Organisation of Motivational Camps and Alleged Excesses Relation to Family Planning Programme in Delhi", no date, SCP, Subject File 6, p. 7.

flow", and in Karnataka hovels were razed to pave the way for "shopping and business centres". In Uttar Pradesh "the beautification of the route from airport to secretariat" was made a policy priority to give the bourgeoisie, "both foreign and Indian", a good "impression of the capital city", leaving a slew of demolitions in its wake.[97] Unsurprisingly, then, cars bearing bumper stickers screaming the propaganda slogans of the regime were a regular sight across the country: "She stood between order and chaos", "she saved the republic", "courage and clarity of vision, thy name is Indira Gandhi", "don't indulge in rumour and loose talks [*sic*]."[98]

The regime also secured the co-operation of this class with sweeteners. The March 1976 budget reduced duties on television sets, refrigerators, water coolers, cars, stainless steel blades, and pedestal fans.[99] Already by June the press was reporting a significant increase in purchases of these coveted appliances, bespeaking middle-class consumption and satisfaction. With cheaper goods came better services: bureaucratic absenteeism "dropped so sharply" that "seats and desks" proved inadequate for what had become a "superfluous workforce".[100] It helped to see that trains "ran on time".[101] In short, the sum total of a consumerist society's concerns—in the language of economists "goods and services"—was taken care of by the authoritarian state. If living the good life meant ceding rights, so be it.

The Janus-like Intelligentsia

While Indian academics were divided over the authoritarian regime, it is still fair to describe the Emergency as a time of *trahison des clercs*. Sections of the Delhi University Teachers' Association, for instance, welcomed the Emergency on 26 July 1975, even as some of their colleagues wasted away in Mrs Gandhi's carceral complex. The Delhi University vice chancellor even agreed to the state administration's Kafkaesque request to hold examinations *in situ* for jailed students. To this end the university also volunteered to set up a "special centre for such students" at the Ram Lal Anand

---

[97] *SCR*, vol. 3, pp. 212–13, 217.

[98] Thapar, *All These Years*, p. 413.

[99] *SW*, 20 March 1976, p. 1.

[100] *Times*, 17 July 1975, p. 4.

[101] This was a particular boast of Shafi Qureshi, railways minister, who, perhaps unconsciously, was channelling the fascist dictum that "Mussolini made the trains run on time": *SW*, 23 August 1975, p. 7.

College, "just a mile from Tihar Jail."[102] Nevertheless, compliance was one thing, apologia another. On the latter side of the spectrum were the vice chancellors of, respectively, Benares Hindu and Madras universities, K.L. Shrimali and Malcolm Adiseshiah, both awarded the Padma Vibhushan in April 1976 for their efforts. This duo, while more prominent than their peers on account of their conferments, were not exceptions. Lauding the regime or turning a blind eye to its depredations were the vice chancellors and some professors in the universities of Rajasthan, Kerala, Mysore, Calcutta, Santiniketan, and the JNU.[103]

Several university administrations gave the police *carte blanche* to act against dissenting students.[104] Typically, the police intervened on campuses with the connivance of the vice chancellors, who often either welcomed the opportunity to put their universities "in order", or accepted state interference without protest.[105] On 25 September 1975 an Ambassador teeming with policemen in plain clothes, with DIG P.S. Bhinder at the wheel, drew up at the JNU, kidnapped a doctoral researcher, and hauled him off to prison. His crime? He was mistaken for a student who had been seen protesting before Maneka, Sanjay Gandhi's eighteen-year-old wife, who read German at the university. He was kept in custody, the mistaken identity notwithstanding, for it transpired that he "allegedly" belonged to the Students' Federation of India, the union of the CPI(M).[106] As the months passed, the police presence on campuses grew, both overtly and covertly, with inspectors enrolling themselves as students.[107]

The capitulation of universities was mirrored by the acquiescence of public intellectuals. Fali S. Nariman, an additional solicitor general who resigned in protest when the Emergency was declared, remembers the Australian high commissioner mentioning to him an encounter with Mrs Gandhi at the time, which ended with her remarking on the pusillanimity of the intelligentsia. Even the autocrat herself expected more opprobrium

---

[102] *SCR*, vol. 2, p. 43.

[103] Selbourne, *An Eye to India*, pp. 309–10; idem, *Through the Indian Looking-Glass*, pp. 27, 74–5; Puri, "A Fuller View", p. 1737.

[104] Raj Thapar remembers in her memoir that "mounted police roamed the campuses for a while" and that "students [were] picked up from their hostel beds" and sent packing to Tihar. Thapar, *All These Years*, p. 415.

[105] *SCR*, vol. 2, p. 56; Prakash, *Emergency Chronicles*, p. 29ff; Pattnaik, *Student Politics and Voting Behaviour*, p. 205ff.

[106] *SCR*, vol. 2, pp. 56–8.

[107] Scott, "Emerging from the Emergency", p. 124.

to come her way from this bastion of the Indian Left.[108] Why, then, did it not? Fear, certainly, played its part. But remarks, both stray and sustained, suggest that other variables have to be factored in.

Christian centres of learning in Bombay, such as the Agnel Junior Technical College and the Father Agnel Ashram, gave the Emergency their ecclesiastical approval in the name of social and political order: "the present strategical plan saved in time the country which was drifting away."[109] Satish Chandra, medievalist and chairman of the University Grants Commission (UGC), commended the regime for allowing "peace" to "return to universities", adding, in a curious turn of phrase, that before the Emergency "teachers' associations" tended to behave like "trade unions".[110] Many academics appreciated the leftist and secular dimensions of Mrs Gandhi's rhetoric, which was accepted at face value.[111]

The views of Bipan Chandra, a Marxist historian at the JNU, can serve as illustration of the thought-world of academics at the time. His book on the Emergency, *In the Name of Democracy* (2003), shows that he shared many assumptions with Mrs Gandhi. In it he suggests that because the regime's main targets were "anti-social elements", "the far-left Naxalites", and "banned organisations" such as the RSS, the intelligentsia in the main supported the regime change.[112] He chides the Emergency's critics, including constitutional historian Granville Austin, for being "unfamiliar with the real ideology" of the RSS and its "authoritarian potential". Yet, on the other hand, Chandra prefers to soft-pedal the sheer institutional violence of the Emergency in his account. What of the infiltration of universities by disguised policemen? "There was very little effort to interfere with research or teaching in the universities". The casualties of the sterilisation programme? Here, the accent lies not on the fates of sterilised, but on those searching for volunteers, who had to engage in the "particularly unedify-

---

[108] Nariman, *Before Memory Fades*, p. 188.

[109] Father C. Rodrigues to Haksar, 19 July and 30 September 1975, P.N. Haksar Papers, Instalment III, Subject Files 352 and 355, respectively. In an assessment of church–state relations during the Emergency, Saral K. Chatterji, the director of the Christian Institute for the Study of Religion and Society, lamented the "full support" that "churches, groups and individuals within the Christian community" gave the authoritarian government: see Chatterji, "Church–State Relation [*sic*]", p. 74.

[110] *TOI*, 4 March 1976, p. 4.

[111] *TOI*, 15 January 1976, p. 11.

[112] Chandra, *In the Name of Democracy*, p. 172.

ing" task of motivating. What of the working classes? Their living standards "had not been affected"; "greater social discipline" benefited, and the "excesses" eluded, them. The "rich peasants?" "I may point out, parenthetically", that the attempt to "implement land ceiling laws and virtually destroy the rich peasantry was basically foolhardy". The upshot of such a view is that Chandra finds it "inexplicable" why "someone as sensitive, imaginative and politically-shrewd [*sic*] as Mrs Gandhi failed" to "provide a healing touch". And how could this have been provided? Not by doing away with the "sterilisation and slum clearance programmes", but merely by "one major radio address explaining the[ir] rationale". No bigger proof is needed to demonstrate the betrayal by the intellectual classes of their social function than to cast an eye over the arguments Chandra mobilises by way of extenuation. In his view the "indictment of the [behaviour of] Indian intellectuals during the Emergency" is "not entirely warranted" because they did in fact "express their anger", except they did so only "in private", awaiting "the right moment to voice it in public."[113]

Bipan Chandra was not alone in defending the silence of the intelligentsia. Rasheeduddin Khan, an academic and Rajya Sabha MP, readily voted for the Fortieth Amendment curtailing judicial review. "I couldn't sleep last night ... My conscience hurt", he told his friends the next day; yet Khan went on to serve another term after the Congress nominated him a second time in 1976.[114]

There is no doubt that fear motivated many intellectuals to support the regime. It did not help that Delhi's rulers had declared open season on them. Mrs Gandhi routinely laid into the "cynicism of our intelligentsia", dubbing its members "one of the greatest obstacles" in the smooth governing of her police state.[115] When Romila Thapar, historian at the JNU, became one of the few who refused to sign a panegyric on the regime authored by Chalapati Rau of the *National Herald*, she had her income-tax assessments for the previous decade reopened for questioning. For protesting against the forced sterilisation drive, Vaid Guru Dutt, octogenarian Hindi novelist, suffered two weeks in the lock-up.[116] Durga

---

[113] Ibid., pp. 143, 155, 183, 191, 330, 227–8, 229, 204, 210, 230, 233.

[114] Thapar, *All These Years*, p. 415.

[115] Hart, "Introduction", p. 29; *SSWIG*, vol. 2, p. 84.

[116] Because that was not seen as adequate grounds for arrest, the authorities suggested that it was in response to his "seditious" 1973 novel *Madhu*—which contained "derogatory references [*sic*]" to Mrs Gandhi's 1971 election campaign—that he had been taken into custody: statement of Jagmohan, deputy sec-

Bhagwat, a Marathi woman of letters and winner of the Sahitya Akademi, met the same fate for having the gall to suggest that "the Emergency harmed creative writing."[117] The Hindi novelist and memoirist Phanishwar Nath Renu and the Kannada writer K. Shivarama Karanth lodged their dissent by returning their Padma Shri and Padma Bhushan, respectively. Unable to express his opinions in the hostile environment of Emergency India, Renu became an émigré in Nepal; Karanth left the town of Puttur to compose ballets with "lilting music" in the Karnataka countryside.[118]

The *khadi*-clad leftist regulars at the Indian Coffee House in Delhi's Connaught Place who had once liaised with opposition party figures and dissenters of every stripe were soon deprived of this bustling site of protest. Once Sanjay got wind of the existence of these cafe communists, he ordered a couple of bulldozers and had the Coffee House flattened in January 1976 and the land underneath it handed over to property developers.[119]

In the world of higher education Miranda House, a women's college affiliated to Delhi University, emerged as one of the few centres of active resistance, preventing Sanjay from visiting its premises and blocking the takeover of the teachers' union by a nominated council led by the principal. Still, their opposition remained confined within the college's walls because of a massive surveillance programme launched by the police in the neighbourhood. The students then were reduced to staging symbolic signs of protests, such as shaving their heads and developing a sense of silent camaraderie.[120] But Miranda House was an anomaly in the college landscape. More common were the numbers seen in demonstrations at the Ruia, Ruparel, Patkar, Parle, and Bhavan's Colleges in Bombay, whose ranks rarely included more than a handful of professors and a few dozen students.[121]

Towards the end of the Emergency, sections of the intelligentsia rediscovered their mettle. On 25 October 1976, for instance, a number of public

---

retary to the lieutenant governor of Delhi [not to be confused with Jagmohan of the DDA], 15 February 1978, SCP, Subject File 7, p. 154.

[117] Mulk Raj Anand to Mrs Gandhi, no date, perhaps September 1976, in MLP, reel 8; Haldar, "Emergency Prey", p. 22.

[118] Narain, "A Sociological Analysis of Phanishwar Nath Renu's Novels", p. 5.

[119] Plys, "Political Deliberation and Democratic Reversal", pp. 117–42.

[120] Scott, "Emerging from the Emergency", pp. 199–201.

[121] See the report on these protests in MLP, reel 13.

figures, including eminent historians, economists, sociologists, journalists, novelists, and filmmakers, signed a letter protesting against the Forty-second Amendment Bill and demanding that the grand old party go to the polls, work the bill into its campaign platform, and engage in public debate over it before ramming it through an impotent parliament.[122]

The Bureaucracy: The Primacy of Institutional Survival

Not for nothing was the metaphor most commonly used for the bureaucracy the "steel frame". With the coming of the Emergency, the civil service successfully negotiated its second regime change, the first being the handover of power from imperial British to Congress hands. *A fortiori*, whilst it had lost some of its competencies to the executive in 1947, it picked up a few by way of recompense in the early and mid-1970s. As Delhi's rulers had come to realise, the bureaucracy remained dependable as ever in the face of uncertainty.[123]

Why was this so? Principally, this owed to their distance from the general public, which since the days of the Raj had left administrators living above society, even while ruling it from within its midst. Prestige and privileges were preserved in the postcolonial period. Government housing, special access to land lots in the capital's newest suburbs, generous pensions, and a system of assured promotions based on seniority were grist to the mill for those in the civil services' middle and upper echelons. As for those in the IAS, who were right at the top, affluence had removed them from the realities of ordinary life. In 1973 their salaries hovered between Rs 12,000 and Rs 36,000, thirty to a hundred times the mean wage and far higher than the incomes of professionals in their early careers. IAS officers were not infrequently to be seen driving imported cars and living among "landlords and businessmen"; their chief interaction with the working class was "with the *bhangis* in their houses", that is, their Dalit cleaners from the ordure-collecting caste.[124] Their gentlefolk origins and competitive careerism had

---

[122] They included, *inter alia*, Sarvepalli Gopal, Romila Thapar, Susobhan Sarkar, Raj Krishna, Mrinal Datta-Chaudhuri, Vinayak Mahadev Dandekar, Krishna Bharadwaj, André Béteille, Triloki Nath Madan, Nikhil Chakravartty, Romesh Thapar, George Verghese, Vijay Tendulkar, Mulk Raj Anand, and Mrinal Sen: Chandra, *In the Name of Democracy*, p. 169.

[123] Rudolph and Rudolph, *In Pursuit of Lakshmi*, pp. 75–7.

[124] *TOI*, 27 July 1976, p. 6; *TOI*, 11 November 1973, p. 6.

largely insulated them from the people they governed, making them a class apart from society.[125]

Successive governments had also proofed them against rebellion. Insulating them from taking matters in their own hands was the slick "professionalisation" of the services, which, in the present context meant a sharp divergence between policy-making and policy implementation. Furthermore, the emphasis on "department norms" and "standard operating procedures", too, reduced their agency to question orders from above.[126]

To the civil services the Emergency came as a shot in the arm. In mid-August 1975 in an interview with Mrs Gandhi, the *Blitz*'s R.K. Karanjia wondered who would implement the Twenty-Point Programme, a valid concern in a time of deinstitutionalisation. Her reply was "the entire central government, the state governments, the bureaucracy, as well as every agency which the government has."[127] Her own party escaped mention. But this was hardly surprising: Congress cadres barely had a functional presence in the *mofussil*. Even sixteen months into the Emergency, the CWC was still trying unsuccessfully to collect lists of "active members" to "activise" the DCCs and implement the Twenty Points.[128]

With boosted powers, then, it was only to be expected that the bureaucracy welcomed the new dispensation. On the whole, no resistance was shown, few resignations tendered. The broad reaction of officers was "generally one of approval and even enthusiasm."[129] In its taxonomy of bureaucratic sins the Shah Commission pointed to the existence of three kinds of public servants in Emergency India: some "simply acted in compliance", others carried out orders "a little [more] zealously than others", and yet others "exceeded or misused or abused their powers."[130] While the commission made it its business to reprimand only those who fell in the last category, the attention here is on all three, for the complicity—varying degrees of it notwithstanding—of the "steel frame" in its entirety played no small part in greasing the wheels of the Emergency regime.

---

[125] Jain, "The Role of Bureaucracy", pp. 24–5.

[126] Encarnation, "The Indian Bureaucracy", pp. 1137–44.

[127] For a transcript, see Gandhi, *Era of Discipline*, p. 148.

[128] Frankel, *India's Political Economy*, p. 549. It is not unusual for societies moving towards authoritarianism to shift the locus of power from the political to the administrative: Misra, *Government and Bureaucracy in India*, pp. 374–5.

[129] Heginbotham, "The Civil Service", p. 69.

[130] *SCR*, vol. 2, p. 146.

If getting the bureaucracy on board was an urgent priority for Mrs Gandhi, it proved rather easy on account of the executive's hold over it.[131] On 26 June, hours after the declaration of the Emergency, Mrs Gandhi convened an unprecedented conference of top civil servants. "This was the first time ever that all secretaries had been called for a meeting with the prime minister", P.N. Dhar later recalled: she "exhorted them to tone up the administrative machinery, cut delays in decision-making, and produce tangible results." In short, they were now the vanguard of the authoritarian regime.[132]

At the top of the new chain of command were the 229 experts, consultants, and bureaucrats of the Prime Minister's Secretariat. Effectively a parallel government, the PMS was responsible not just for quotidian policy-making but also authoritarian *démarches* against some of the bureaucrats themselves, in effect getting those lower down the pecking order to fall in line.

Those lacking "integrity" and "efficiency"—euphemisms for those disapproving of, or ambivalent about, the new dispensation—were forced into early retirement, and in a few cases incarcerated. The first victims in this landscape of transfers, demotions, suspensions, and dismissals were, in fact, made apparent a few days before Mrs Gandhi pushed the authoritarian button. On 22 June the home secretary Nirmal Mukherjee, who was thought "too legalistic", was replaced by the Rajasthan chief secretary Sardari Lal Khurana, who was "considered more pliable".[133] Three days later it was announced that the IB chief Atma Jayaram, who had "failed" Mrs Gandhi in failing to foretell the Allahabad judgment, was going to be replaced by Surinder Nath Mathur, inspector general of police of Punjab.[134] With the coming of the Emergency, such interference grew more routine. On 10 July 1975, for instance, the union government circulated instructions to the ministries to flush out every quarter "government servants who had outlived their utility and who were of doubtful integrity."[135] The next year, the drive had not let up. A "conference of

---

[131] The Shah Commission would later observe that it was the absence of a "*droit administratif*" on Indian soil that had made it politically far easier for the republic's rulers to muscle in on the bureaucracy without judicial challenge than it would have elsewhere: *SCR*, vol. 3, p. 231.

[132] Dhar, *Indira Gandhi the "Emergency", and Indian Democracy*, p. 304.

[133] Nayar, *The Judgement*, p. 31.

[134] *TOI*, 25 June 1975, p. 5.

[135] The next day, a similar letter went out to the state governments. *SCR*, vol. 3, p. 34.

chief secretaries" was convened on 7 May 1976 where the attendees were counselled to "retire in public interest" any officer with a "stained record or reputation or efficiency [*sic*]."[136] The lieutenant governor of Delhi was of the same mind: he "would not hesitate to put even senior IAS officers behind the [*sic*] bars under MISA."[137]

In sum, 25,962 public servants were "prematurely retired" during the Emergency.[138] While a majority were Class III employees, a number of IAS officers were ousted as well, indicating that high office was no guarantee of job security.[139] A slew of constitutional amendments ensured that their fates remained in the hands of officials who arbitrarily presided over kangaroo tribunals; appeals against sackings were futile. That so many were purged suggests that the bureaucrats did not support the Emergency *en masse*, but also that the regime was ahead of them. For Delhi's rulers had a rather straightforward strategy for dealing with the bureaucracy: instil fear in the many by hounding a few.

At all events the plan worked, confounding the expectations of many who had hoped that "the chief proponents of modernisation" would also be "among the chief defenders of democratic processes." Only a very few major officials resigned and made their contempt of the Emergency regime publicly known. It needs a microscope, in fact, to find them, for only three figures show up in the literature: an additional solicitor general, a federal Reserve Bank employee, and a joint secretary in the Home Ministry.[140] Most of those contemplating resignation quickly dispatched with the notion: "I thought of it, but who would know? Only my wife and children—and they would find out because there wouldn't be any food on the table", said a government official to the *New York Times* in April 1976.[141] The threat of imminent arrest was a big worry. For Delhi municipal commissioner B.R. Tamta the choice was simple: "Resignation is not an

---

[136] Ibid.

[137] *SCR*, vol. 2, p. 34.

[138] Four states accounted for 55 per cent of them: Andhra Pradesh, Madhya Pradesh, Maharashtra, and Rajasthan. A sixth of the total figure ostensibly belonged to the twenty-six banned organisations: *SCR*, vol. 3, pp. 34–6.

[139] See, *inter alia*, K.L. Pasricha, Chief Secretary, Madhya Pradesh to P.R. Rajgopal, Secretary, Shah Commission of Inquiry, 21 January 1978, Shah Commission of Inquiry Files, File SCI/206/MP/77AA–T3.

[140] Heginbotham, "The Civil Service", p. 71; Kuldip Nayar, "Black Days of Emergency", p. 3.

[141] Lukas, "India is as Indira Does", p. 89.

answer. Either I have to go to jail or work here."[142] Equally dreaded was the prospect of administrative reform, for every functionary knew its implication well: heads would roll, a spectre Mrs Gandhi gleefully raised time and again. March 1976, for example, witnessed the publication of the Kothari Commission Report, which sought to introduce a new examination system that would "eliminate a large number of candidates having less potential for success." It came to naught. The next month, similar accidie followed the prime minister's endorsement of a fourteen-page note prepared by two retired bureaucrats, L.P. Singh and L.K. Jha, on "improving efficiency in administration".[143]

The upshot of this regime of fear was a tamed bureaucracy. Public employees began to "show up on time and to work their full day", giving up on their old ways of late arrivals, "casual routines", and "extended breaks".[144] Raids were regularly carried out on government offices, sending tardy *babus* and their blasé managers packing.[145]

The propinquity of leading bureaucrats to political bosses in the states ensured that the pressures faced by weak state leaders were shared by top mandarins. When S.B. Chavan, chief minister of Maharashtra, was given a dressing down by Sanjay Gandhi for the dismal arrest figures in his state, he had his private secretary Madhav Godbole look into the matter. In true procedural fashion the functionary saw this as an issue of poor "performance" and set to work to improve it. He procured "comparative data" from other states, pushed orders down the bureaucratic hierarchy, and made "arrangements" for the "periodical review" of the numbers in "officers' meetings".[146] Done in such clinical fashion, it is hardly surprising that the question of disobeying orders never arose. That the logic of targets had so completely desensitised bureaucrats is borne out by the remarks of Bihar family-planning officials who could describe the death toll of eighty in the state's sterilisation programme as "modest".[147]

Unfortunately for the civil servants, their participation in the numbers game resulted in their being hoist with their own petard once Sanjay's family-planning drive intensified. Government departments, as noted ear-

---

[142] Statement of Tamta, 5 August 1977, SCP, Subject File 2, p. 184.

[143] Dwivedi, Jain, and Dua, "Imperial Legacy, Bureaucracy, and Administrative Changes", p. 261.

[144] Heginbotham, "The Civil Service", p. 69.

[145] *Times*, 17 July 1975, p. 4.

[146] Godbole, *Unfinished Innings*, p. 106.

[147] *SCR*, vol. 3, p. 175.

lier, were handed out absurdly high targets. For instance, in Karnataka, the 26,000 officials of the revenue department alone had to produce 90,000 sterilisation certificates from within their ranks. Nevertheless, because many of the "disincentives"—the bureaucracy's euphemism for penalties—were rolled out by state governments only towards the end of 1976, or were planned to commence mid-1977 or later that year, the abrupt decision to call off the Emergency saved the majority of bureaucrats from having to suffer the consequences.[148]

For all that, both bureaucratic fears and resistance need to be put into perspective. As the Shah Commission, whose familiarity with functionaries was first-hand, noted, "the public servants have not infrequently unduly [*sic*] exaggerated the fear under which they were functioning ... in a number of cases, officials were almost anticipating the wishes of those in authority, however illegal, immoral, and incongruous."[149]

This stands in marked contrast to the tendency to pin the blame of all the Emergency's transgressions on "higher-ups", the first family and its cronies.[150] Another clue presents itself in the figures: as we have seen, only 25,962 of the country's 13.4 million public-sector employees were purged during the Emergency—a mere 0.19 per cent.[151] The idea was never to cast off the steel frame but to intimidate it into submission.

From this an inductive principle emerges: authoritarian transitions see to it that bureaucrats in modern societies rarely resign on principle. Rather, they cut their losses through compliance, wilfully throwing themselves into the programmes of their political bosses who, sooner or later, realise their indispensability. In early March 1977, when the tide appeared to be turning, the bureaucracy once again sided with the politicians it believed were likely to become its future masters: the All India State Government Employees Federation, for example, distanced itself from the "excesses" of family planning, blaming them in their entirety on the Congress leadership.[152] Within a few months more than half of the functionaries fired by the grand old party had been reinstated by the Janata. Yet another transfer of power had been safely negotiated by the circumspect civil servants of the Indian bureaucracy.

* * *

[148] Ibid., pp. 170–206.
[149] Ibid., vol. 3, p. 229.
[150] See, *inter alia, SCR*, vol. 1, p. 67.
[151] Eapen, "Trends in Public Sector Employment", p. 8.
[152] Weiner, *India at the Polls*, p. 38.

The *Indian Express'* Kuldip Nayar remembers that when he was asked by a British journalist, just four days before the declaration of the Emergency, "how people would react if Mrs Gandhi were to take over" and mount an auto-coup, he had ruled out such a move:

> India would never accept dictatorship. If someone tried to impose it, there would be a revolt. The people who had gone through the fire of freedom struggle would have the strength and courage to fight totalitarianism. The Congress had raised the standard of revolt against the mighty British Raj; it would do so even more vigorously if anyone tried to subvert Indian democracy from within.

But just six days later, and two into the dictatorship, when the same newspaperman came to see him again, Nayar was forced to admit that he "had been too smug about the dedication of my country and my countrymen to democracy."[153] The Cassandras had trumped the Panglossians. Nayar was especially disenchanted with the popular response, or lack of it: "Here were the best intellectuals [*sic*]—educationists, jurists, civil servants, doctors, lawyers and so on—but most of them preferred to keep quiet."[154]

The question then arises why so few within the Indian elite fought for democracy. Two kinds of explanation, in addition to the general climate of fear, are evident.

First, as discussed earlier, India's dominant political culture is only very tentatively based on the core values of democracy: liberty, equality, fraternity. One of us has argued elsewhere that India did not become a democracy on account of its elites having internalised these values, despite their traction in the thought-worlds of key figures such as Nehru and Ambedkar, both before and after 1947. Instead, democracy dovetailed with India's needs insofar as it seemed best suited to accommodating the country's social, cultural, and political diversity. Its specific manifestation here was a pragmatic arrangement between elite groups, namely the ruling class of Congress leaders and the bureaucracy, the capitalist milieu, the dominant peasantry, and the remnants of the aristocracy. Each of these groupings was so strong in its own right that none could rule over the others. Democracy in India was thus a compromise, a trade-off between these groups which had forced them into an unspoken alliance. Certainly, the political class was in the driver's seat as it controlled the state, but its most important formation, the Congress, needed capitalist and peasant support

---

[153] Nayar, *In Jail*, p. 11.
[154] Idem, *The Judgement*, p. 65.

to win elections.[155] This reading of Indian democracy, which draws inspiration from the work of Dankwart Rustow and Mancur Olson,[156] goes a long way in explaining the role of cultural diversity in the Indian polity: democracy here offered a solution to elite groups potentially locked in rivalry. In the event, they settled on a convenient collaborative arrangement, the Congress rulers drawing on both the funds of capitalists and vote banks of landlords in order to win elections. Democracy not only offered the three power centres the right framework for bargaining, but also the right system for ruling a highly stratified, multilingual, multi-religious, and ethnically diverse society which could only be represented by myriad spokespersons. Thus, if democracy took root in the 1950s and 1960s, it was not on account of the commitment to the values of liberty, equality, and fraternity on the part of a small segment of the "dominant proprietary classes"—to use Pranab Bardhan's term for the aggregate of India's capitalists, bourgeoisie, and gentry—but because of pragmatic calculations.[157] Unsurprisingly, with the changing of the guard that witnessed the rise of authoritarian personalities such as Mrs Gandhi and Sanjay, those who were still prepared to carry on the fight for democratic values were few and far between—not least because they were a marginal presence in the country to begin with.

This interpretation suggests that democracy in Emergency India was a collateral casualty of the resilience of long-standing social and cultural values and attitudes, including a deep-rooted sense of hierarchy and respect for authority. Emblematic here is the explanation put forward by Nirad C. Chaudhuri, who sees the roots of Indian docility during the Emergency in the caste system: "submission to authority is natural to the Hindus; they actually prefer an authoritarian regime."[158] We will revisit this interpretation below.

The second reason why there were so few defenders of democracy among the Indian elite has already been documented in this chapter: many sectional interests shared in the objectives of the Emergency. The CPI and a smattering of intellectuals appreciated its socialist overtones despite the apparent lack of substance behind the rhetoric. Indian capitalists found that

---

[155] Jaffrelot, *La démocratie en Inde*.

[156] Rustow, "Transitions to Democracy: Toward a Dynamic Model", pp. 337–63; Olson, "Dictatorship, Democracy and Development".

[157] Bardhan, *The Political Economy of Development in India*.

[158] Chaudhuri, "How and Why Mrs Gandhi Ruled", p. 17. For variants of this trope, see Drieberg and Mohan, *Emergency in India*, pp. 104–5.

aspects of economic liberalisation worked in their favour, the suppression of worker unrest in particular. The middle class for its part hailed this as an "era of discipline" after years of protests in the street. And bureaucrats were not in the least against acquiring even more power in the regime's weaponisation of the executive.

Conclusion to Part II

"Why Emergency" was a question India's rulers themselves asked in 1975. The explanations advanced by Mrs Gandhi have been mentioned in Part I.[159] We have explored others in this part of the book. When a concatenation of events in June 1975 exposed the extent of dissatisfaction with her government, Mrs Gandhi's instinct was to double down. Here, these immediate causes have been put in perspective in order to illustrate their profound impact, taking into account both the origin of Mrs Gandhi's confrontation with the judiciary, which harked back to the late 1960s, and the deep socio-economic roots of the JP Movement, which Marxist political economists have often underestimated. In many such critiques economic turmoil and the extra-parliamentary opposition of the early 1970s meant that the "interests of big industrial capital" had to strike back.[160] In such an environment the Congress, a political front of the captains of industry, needed to clamp down on the opposition with greater vigour than ever before. The result was the Emergency, under which mass-scale suppression was aimed at shoring up "Indian and foreign monopoly capital", all without requiring solutions to "any of the structural problems of the Indian economy."[161] This is, of course, a caricature of the regime, since capitalists neither instigated the Emergency nor were they its *raison d'être*—in truth, they merely welcomed, supported, and benefited from the regime. To account for India's authoritarian turn, then, we need to go one step further and make sense of the JP Movement from a larger sociological perspective:

---

[159] *Why Emergency?*

[160] Frank, "Emergence of Permanent Emergency in India", p. 463.

[161] Ibid. For similar analyses, see Vanaik, *The Painful Transition*, p. 93ff; Chatterjee, *A Possible India*, pp. 12–66; Zins, *Strains on Indian Democracy's*. But cf. Gupta, whose "A Season of Caesars", pp. 315–49, sees the Emergency as a "political crisis" independent of any "social crisis". Ayesha Jalal concurs: India's authoritarian turn demonstrated more "the salience of the power of non-elective institutions" than the concerted action of "class power". See Jalal, *Democracy and Authoritarianism in South Asia*, p. 156 *et passim*.

beyond the prestige of its leader, the movement can only be understood as the upshot of a deep social crisis. Indeed, as we have seen, it was not all down to a state-capital nexus aimed at curbing the opposition parties. There was disaffection across the board: the smaller gentry, students, peasants, and working class—all had grouses aplenty.

Here, Mrs Gandhi's authoritarian personality, another overdetermined variable in the literature, too, has been placed in a broader context. We have argued that Mrs Gandhi could only prevail and impose the Emergency because of a transformation of the Congress party in the late 1960s and early 1970s into an over-centralised and personalised political machine. And finally, moving beyond deinstitutionalisation, we believe the Emergency was also made possible because of the support it received from a very heterogeneous coalition of communists, Shiv Sainiks, RPI cadres, industrialists, trade unionists, bureaucrats, and sections of the intelligentsia. This baroque assemblage primarily reflected the political culture of the bourgeoisie, the class most supportive of the Emergency.

Beyond the political culture of this class, the future of India's elite groups was at stake. Their scant resistance to the Emergency suggests that their commitment to democracy was rather shallow. What seems to have mattered most to them was access to positions of power; fundamentally, self-interest rather than belief in the values of liberty and freedom of expression dictated their responses.

We have also highlighted the culture of deference within which Indian society operates. One of the sources of this tradition, the caste-related habit of mind, was remarked upon in the context of the Emergency by Nirad C. Chaudhuri. Another commonplace attitude in the Indian setting is the traditional relationship between master and disciple, variously known as *guru–shishya parampara* or the culture of *ustaad–shagird*. These valorise submission; a critical temperament has no place in a society that places a premium on obedience. Within a political context, this translates into a general approval of strongmen. B.R. Ambedkar in his closing speech to the Constituent Assembly in 1949 made a similar observation:

> There is nothing wrong in being grateful to great men who have rendered life-long services to the country. But there are limits to gratefulness. As has been well said by the Irish Patriot Daniel O'Connel [*sic*], "no man can be grateful at the cost of his honour, no woman can be grateful at the cost of her chastity and no nation can be grateful at the cost of its liberty." This caution is far more necessary in the case of India than in the case of any other country, for in India, Bhakti or what may be called the path of devotion or hero-wor-

ship, plays a part in its politics unequalled in magnitude by the part it plays in the politics of any other country in the world. Bhakti in religion may be a road to the salvation of the soul. But in politics, Bhakti or hero-worship is a sure road to degradation and to eventual dictatorship.[162]

A quarter of a century later, "hero-worship" dovetailed well with populist authoritarianism. For her part Mrs Gandhi was ready for the part she was destined to play. She saw herself as the embodiment of the people as well as the nation, a leader born to rule. In November 1975 she declared she had given the republic a "bitter dose" for good reason: "however dear a child may be, if the doctor has prescribed bitter pills for him, they have to be administered for his cure. The child may sometimes cry and we may have to say, 'take the medicine, otherwise you will not be cured.'"[163]

And finally, it is our view that the authoritarian rule of Mother and Son became possible not only because the dominant political culture of India relied heavily on illiberal norms, but because Mrs Gandhi's transformation of the Congress made it possible. If democracy was established in 1947 not on the basis of values but as a compromise between elite groups, such a pluralist system survived simply because no single sectional interest was strong enough to turf out all its competitors. Nehru's India, then, was quite dissimilar to Mrs Gandhi's.

Of course, both the first premier and his daughter presided over extremely violent, trigger-happy state apparatuses that made frequent use of arbitrary power. But the difference was that, barring in the republic's peripheries, Nehru pooled the competencies of the state with regional leaders and party notables, seeing in the devolution of power his best bet for political survival. Mrs Gandhi on the other hand, with her constant cabinet shuffles, her elevation and demotion of state bosses, and her institutional "reforms", transformed the party organisation into an instrument of her "kitchen cabinet"—her group of loyalists, who too, ironically, were subject to the capricious kicks she bestowed on her revolving-door. The upshot was that while Nehru could use brutal suppression to put peasants, the working classes, "secessionists", "chauvinists" and other opponents in their place, he was canny enough to always retain the backing of a large section of the elite who, as time worn, enjoyed ever larger slices of the political pie. In essence, it was this balance of co-opting elites and suppressing dissent that ensured the longevity and relative success of Nehru's political career, his

---

[162] Cited in Jaffrelot and Kumar, *Dr Ambedkar and Democracy*, p. 196
[163] *SSWIG*, vol. 3, p. 228.

party, and even the postcolonial Indian state. Nehru's premiership was one in which the Congress' negotiated centrism had been the regnant ideology: secularism was espoused, but confessional politics given a place in both party and society; a "mixed economy", *à la* Roosevelt's New Deal, held in high regard by Nehru, sought to attract private-sector industrialists (by way of state patronage) as well as self-professed socialists (through redistribution and planning); and a non-aligned foreign policy, where Nehru endeavoured at once to distance the postcolonial state from security dependency and economic liberalisation and avoid isolationism. In short, the "Nehruvian consensus" was less a product of the leader's fiat than the negotiated outcome of a power-sharing arrangement between India's heterogeneous elites.[164]

This was the arrangement that Mrs Gandhi upended. The centralisation of competencies and deinstitutionalisation of the state alienated the very elites that had been instrumental in keeping her coevals and predecessors so firmly ensconced in power. True, she fought them because the Syndicate wanted to control her, and unlike Nehru she did not fancy being a "prisoner" of her party. But in alienating the powerful, Mrs Gandhi haemorrhaged support in all directions.

This in itself was not problematic. A progressive politics could have certainly allowed Mrs Gandhi to bypass the elites—and in the short run this is exactly what the promissory rhetoric of Garibi Hatao, building cadres, and lording over the airwaves helped her achieve in the early 1970s. Nevertheless, as we have seen, such efforts quickly foundered. A Left populism failed to take root. The result was the JP Movement, Ahmedabad, Allahabad, and finally the Emergency.

That her authoritarian regime was met with a weak or spineless opposition, however, needs to be qualified by taking into account those who fought for democracy in 1975–7 and took huge risks by doing so.

---

[164] Frankel's *India's Political Economy* remains the *locus classicus* of Nehru's paradoxical ambitions of ushering in economic growth and radical social transformation within the confines of an accommodating centrist politics. Of course, "'socialism" remained Nehru's preferred watchword, despite the strong currents of communitarian liberalism chipping away at it: Bayly, "The Ends of Liberalism", pp. 605–26. See also Kothari, "Political Consensus in India", pp. 1635–44; Kochanek, *The Congress Party of India.*

PART III

RESISTANCE AND ENDGAME

9

AN UNEVEN RESISTANCE

To the country's progressive democrats there was no bigger surprise than the fact that most Indians coolly accepted the republic's sudden slide into dictatorship. C.G.K. Reddy, a veteran Lohiaite,[1] was one of them:

> I could hardly believe my eyes when I saw not a sign of any protest, not even groups of people gathered in street corners agitating and discussing the calamity that had overtaken the country ... I told myself that, as the day advanced, at least a few of the *lakhs* of people, who had gathered only the previous evening to hear JP ... would organize themselves to resist what was virtually a dictatorship. My expectations and hopes were belied.[2]

In fact JP himself felt helpless: "if we believe in democracy, we must play the game right ... We need at least five thousand volunteers to man each constituency—and we don't have even the semblance of an organisation."[3]

Still, resistance to the Emergency was not entirely absent. Sections of the press, judiciary, political class, and civil society opposed the regime, even if only in circumspect fashion. Socialists, Hindu nationalists, Akali Dal and CPI(M) cadres, and some revolutionaries were among the many

---

[1] An epigone of Rammanohar Lohia (1910–67), the self-ascribed "socialist" whose positions were in fact closer to M.K. Gandhi's, especially his allergy to expropriation and industrialisation. In Lohia's world an idyllic communitarianism trumped state ownership; villages, cities; moral politics, the political economy; and religious tolerance, secularism.

[2] Reddy, *Baroda Dynamite Conspiracy Case*, p. 17.

[3] Cited in Thapar, *All These Years*, p. 434.

who went underground and fought the new dispensation. But only by stripping away their lore, hawked in volume after volume since the Emergency, can one accurately gauge the significance of their protests during the months of authoritarianism.[4] Seen in this light, the resistance appears uneven and unimpressive. A number of malaises stand out: factionalism, tokenist gestures, and worse, a proclivity to cavort with Delhi's rulers in order to one-up their comrades in prison and underground. Our assessment therefore only confirms the received image of Congress autocrats bringing the country effortlessly to heel. In a word, then, the Emergency was dictatorship by consent. Resistance never came anywhere near toppling the regime. Democracy was restored at a time of Mrs Gandhi's, and not her critics', choosing.

The Media: A Landscape of Contrasts

Generalising about the role of the media during the Emergency proves a daunting task, for some papers mounted a semblance of a critique even whilst complying with the censors, others unhesitatingly fell in line, and yet others turned coat and succumbed to Delhi's rulers. For all that, it can still be said with certitude that a minority of the fourth estate resisted dictatorship.

Pressmen Ajoy Bose and John Dayal confirm that their ranks were guilty as charged: "Of all the victims of the Emergency state, the Indian press had been the most willing—a willing slave that enthusiastically accepted its fate."[5] Instances of invertebrate reportage are easy to come by. There is, for example, the cover story of a new fortnightly that was virtually a mouthpiece of the regime, *India Today*: its puff piece on Sanjay described him as an "idealist, but ... no ideologue", a man who "shuns power" but nevertheless has as his "paramount passion" the desire "to mould and lead the youth of India". Why? Because he is "energetic" and "self-driven"; political leadership "comes naturally to him". These attributes "dovetailed to [*sic*] other essentials: talent, competence, and diligence."[6] In kindred

---

[4] The latest of these are Kapoor, *The Emergency*; Prakash, *The Emergency*.

[5] Dayal and Bose, *The Shah Commission Begins*, p. 176.

[6] Rajagopal, "Sanjay Gandhi". Under Uma Vasudev's direction, *India Today* toed the government line. It was only after her ouster by the paper's proprietors that the magazine grew somewhat independent, prompting a furious Mohammad Yunus, Mrs Gandhi's press czar, to issue threat after threat. As it turned out, there was no retribution, probably owing to the tiny and mostly foreign readership of the magazine: Aroon Purie, 19 December 2017, interviewed by Kai Friese, Oral Histories in the Long Emergency Collection.

spirit, R.K. Karanjia praised in the pages of *Blitz* Mrs Gandhi's "highly evolved renaissance mind" of "vast dimensions". He went on to describe an "unknown fact" about the prime minister that perhaps he alone knew: "possessed of a dormant serpent-power coiled in sleep at the base of her spine," she was "carried into a higher dimension of consciousness, blossoming into genius, whereby the knower transcends the known."[7] For *Illustrated Weekly of India* editor Khushwant Singh, another panegyrist of the first family, Sanjay was "Indian of the Year"—the cover story complete with encomia in acrostic that spelt out his name.[8] "More power to Sanjay!", Singh had enthused in an editorial a few months earlier.[9]

Piare Lal Sharma, unanointed Congress court historian, was not far behind. After making his name with 1972's *World's Greatest Woman*, Sharma fixed his eyes on the titular character's son. The result was *World's Wisest Wizard: A Psychography of Sanjay Gandhi's Cosmic Mind*. Infatuated with his 29-year-old subject, Sharma describes the size of Sanjay's chest—"about 36 inches when empty; when full it takes a very good expansion"—and his "facial features"—"extremely sweet" face, eyes like "shining petals", ears "like pearl shells".[10]

There were occasional exceptions in this milquetoast media landscape. On 29 June 1975 a hundred journalists assembled at the Press Club to pass a strongly worded resolution: "We the journalists assembled here deplore the imposition of censorship and urge upon the government to remove it immediately. We also demand the release of journalists already detained."[11] Still, when Kuldip Nayar, who had organised this effort, sent the resolution to Mrs Gandhi and Information and Broadcasting Minister V.C. Shukla, it was decided to anonymise the signatories. The journalists rightly believed that were their names revealed, reprisals would have followed. Shukla pressed Nayar to divulge the names, but in vain. The limits of such petitioning were apparent because, soon after, when Nayar had a similar resolution passed by the Press Council, he found his peers had grown reluctant; and

---

[7] *Blitz*, 10 January 1976, cited in the *Guardian*, 19 February 1976, p. 12. He was quick in updating his opinions a year later. When the Janata was in power, Karanjia dubbed Mrs Gandhi a "ruthless dictator" and the "Sanjay caucus" an Indian "parallel to the Hitler gang": *Blitz*, 27 May 1978, p. 1.

[8] *Illustrated Weekly of India*, 23 January 1977, p. 5.

[9] *Illustrated Weekly of India*, 14 October 1976, p. 43.

[10] Mehta, *The Sanjay Story*, p. 171.

[11] Nayar, *In Jail*, p. 6. The *Hind Samachar*'s Jagat Narain and the *Motherland*'s K.R. Malkani were among those apprehended in the first wave of arrests.

moreover its chairman, Justice Iyengar—to quote his letter to V.C. Shukla, with whom he was, revealingly, in touch—"was able to convince them that this is not necessary or desirable."[12]

The truth is that dissent was difficult. Editors who failed to defer to Delhi were threatened with arrest. Even printing blank spaces in lieu of editorials—an accepted form of protest since the late years of the Raj—was not permitted.[13] Criticism of the United States, Idi Amin, and Augusto Pinochet was banned: the first to promote good ties and the latter two to prevent readers from drawing unmistakable parallels between the Indian regime and the Ugandan and Chilean juntas. Even quotations from M.K. Gandhi, Tagore, and the prime minister's father were censored.[14] The *National Herald*, a Congress organ, went a step further by deciding unilaterally to remove the motto it printed below its masthead: "Freedom is in peril, defend it with all your might", a quote wrongly attributed to Nehru, the newspaper's founding editor.[15]

But the press was itself complicit in its capitulation. As Prithvis Chakravarty, secretary general of the National Union of Journalists, rather disingenuously suggested, "It is not for us to question the government's sincerity. We must accept the prime minister's word." When questioned about his responsibility to protect the fourth estate, he continued artlessly: "So what shall I do: jump from the Qutab Minar? Go to the Himalayas? Stop shaving?"[16] While in some states, such as West Bengal and Punjab, the large presence of censors ensured everything went through them, in others, as well as in the capital, the onus of deciding whether material had to be put before functionaries or not was put on editors. Indeed, for the most part it was on their own initiative that pressmen chose not to print "objectionable" matter rather than put material before censors, or publish it freely and face the consequences later. Fear was certainly a factor, but so was time: if an article was sent for blue pencilling, the story was in effect put on a "conveyer belt at [one] end of a tunnel", and there was no knowing how long the wait would be before it "came out [at] the other end".

---

[12] Ibid., p. 9.

[13] *SCR*, vol. 1, p. 34.

[14] Peiris, "India's Media", p. 33; Niranjan Haldar, "Emergency Prey: Rabindranath", in *The Pen in Revolt*, p. 20.

[15] Historian Mushirul Hasan notes that Indira Gandhi spotted the slogan on a Second World War propaganda poster in Brentford in November 1939 and sent it to her father: *Hindu*, 16 May 2012.

[16] Lukas, "India is as Indira Does", p. 92.

Sometimes it never did, and on other occasions it often took a day or two, by which time the news had already been overtaken by events.[17] The result was that for all practical purposes pre-censorship had been "replaced by self-censorship".[18]

Tellingly, some of the greatest tales of press resistance in Emergency India were about literary inventiveness, prior restraint having foreclosed other avenues of lettered dissent, such as the obloquy, or even the ironic rundown. The Bombay edition of the *Times of India*, for instance, three days into the regime carried the obituary of "D'Ocracy—D.E.M., beloved husband of T. Ruth, loving father of L.I. Bertie, brother of Faith, Hope, Justice, expired on 26th June."[19] Likewise, there was room for allegory to flourish. Mrinal Datta-Chaudhuri's essay on fascism in Europe was one such. The parallels, left unsaid, were unambiguous for readers of *Seminar*: the tale told was of a strong leader buttressed by a youth movement with a cultish following, who attempts to overcome national backwardness with development, but on failing to do so resorts to propaganda, nationalism, and rhetoric about discipline, pushing the country and its institutions off the precipice.[20] In the spirit of the New Left, the May issue of the same journal celebrated leftist formations that "dissented within a dogma" and broke from "orthodox communism". It carried pieces by Svetozar Stojanovic, a Serbian philosopher who rejected "the statist myth of socialism"; and by Eurocommunist figures Georges Marchais, Santiago Carrillo, and Enrico Berlinguer—general secretaries of the main communist parties in France, Spain, and Italy, respectively—all of whom embraced parliamentary democracy and railed against "centralisation, authoritarianism, and bureaucratisation".[21] Still, Delhi's rulers had little appetite for veiled criticism. The journal was forced to close the next month.

Yet all kinds of publicists continued to attack the Emergency indirectly. Early on in the new dispensation, Behram Contractor lampooned the Twenty-Point Programme in his satirical column in *Femina* by creating fatuous lists of his own: a Six-Point Programme to change the diet of South

---

[17] Lukas, "Press Censorship in India", pp. 3–4.

[18] This was an observation made in a diplomatic cable from the American embassy in New Delhi to the State Department: Anderson and Clibbens, "'Smugglers of Truth'", p. 21.

[19] *TOI*, 28 June 1975, p. 2.

[20] See Datta-Chaudhuri, "Fascism", pp. 29–32.

[21] *Seminar*, vol. 201, no. 1 (May 1976), pp. 9, 10, 14, 22.

Indians, a Thirty-Point Programme on the import of Czechoslovakian films.[22] But this soon ended and he contented himself with writing about cricket and mangoes, "the only subjects considered safe during the era of censorship."[23] *Indian Express* cartoonist Abu Abraham lamented in *Seminar* the intolerance towards humour in authoritarian societies across the world; one of few which he did not name was the one that had censored his work dozens of times.[24] K. Shankar Pillai, his mentor, had a pithier take: "Dictatorships cannot afford laughter."[25] Just a month into the regime, he felt compelled to shut down *Shankar's Weekly.*[26]

Two English dailies that stood up to the regime were the *Indian Express* and the *Statesman.* The former's owner, Ramnath Goenka, especially, had long been a thorn in the prime minister's flesh.[27] Mrs Gandhi had initiated a number of spurious legal enquiries against him since his much-publicised meetings with Jayaprakash Narayan in 1974.[28] During the Emergency the paper was asked to submit "for scrutiny by the censor" any column authored by Kuldip Nayar.[29] Later, Goenka "was asked to sell his publishing empire" of thirty-five newspapers and magazines.[30] But this, it transpired, would have been "too costly" for state purchase. Thereafter, the government sought to achieve the same result with a change of tack. K.K. Birla was sworn in as the new chairman of the *Express* board, and along with him were inducted five Congressmen and sympathisers as members.[31] With over half the board's strength of eleven being regime supporters, the grand old party finally had the majority it needed to call the shots. The retooled board's first order of business was to "retire compulsorily" the paper's refractory editor-in-chief S. Mulgaokar.[32] Despite the change of guard the

[22] Scott, "Emerging from the Emergency", p. 218.

[23] *Tehelka,* 16 April 2001.

[24] See Abraham, "The State of Humour", pp. 74–5.

[25] Basu, *Underground Literature,* p. 65.

[26] Pillai, "Farewell", 27 July 1975, in MLP, reel 4.

[27] Coomi Kapoor dedicates a chapter to Ramnath Goenka in her book, *The Emergency,* pp. 125–62.

[28] Goenka to Mrs Gandhi, 17 and 22 July 1974, SCP, Subject File 16, pp. 94–8.

[29] Nayar, *In Jail,* p. 8.

[30] Idem, *The Judgement,* p. 111. This included, *inter alia,* the *Financial Express, Loksatta, Screen,* and myriad Tamil, Telugu, and Kannada journals.

[31] They were Kamal Nath, A.K. Antony, G.D. Kothari, P.R. Ramakrishnan, and Vinay K. Shah: "Affidavit of Ramnath Goenka", September 1977, SCP, Subject File 16, p. 46.

[32] Nayar, *The Judgement,* p. 111.

Express continued to toe an independent line, publishing blank editorials, Abu Abraham's satirical cartoons,[33] and tangentially critical essays.[34] Moreover, Goenka blocked moves to axe two senior journalists, Kuldip Nayar and Ajit Bhattacharjea, and finally in November 1976 dismissed the board members that Delhi's rulers had foisted on his paper. The same month he also won a court case that halted the state's efforts to auction off the *Express'* air-conditioning and water-cooling plants for 3 per cent of their market value.[35] This, crucially, helped keep the paper afloat, since V.C. Shukla had long since stopped all government advertisements to it, depriving the *Express* of a regular income stream of "nearly Rs 1.5 million every month."[36]

The *Statesman*, in contrast, was an unlikely champion of democracy. This role it could assume only once the expiry of his term on 30 September 1975 displaced its editor and Emergency enthusiast N.J. Nanporia. An upset Shukla tried in vain to have him reinstated before concluding that the only method to bend the paper to his will lay in authoritarian diktat. Its Delhi edition was regularly subjected to prior restraint, and efforts were made to pack the board of its Calcutta counterpart with government directors after the paper was accused of "mismanagement"—printing extra copies at a time of newsprint shortages. When that failed, Shukla and company essayed a hostile takeover.[37] In the opening salvo K.K. Shah, the son of the Tamil Nadu governor, approached the paper's shareholders, trying to convince them to let Bombay PCC President Rajni Patel act as their proxy in company meetings. When this failed, Cushrow Irani, the journal's managing director, who had refused to restore Nanporia to the editorship, had his passport impounded. Shortly after, a number of lawsuits were filed against him for illegally acquiring a subsidiary company in 1971. Nevertheless, the

---

[33] One of them depicted strident Congressmen at the December session of the party. "From Komagatu Maru Nagar [where the conference was held] we now take unanimity to the masses", read the speech bubble: reproduced in *Seminar*, vol. 200, no. 1 (April 1976), p. 43.

[34] For instance, a review of a book on the history of Buddhism was titled "When India Was Indu": *Indian Express*, 16 May 1976, p. 8, reproduced in Paul, "'When India Was Indira'", pp. 205–7. See also "Nehru: A Study in Isolation", a review of a Nehru biography, which all too evidently contrasts his style of rule with hers: *Indian Express*, 8 February 1976, p. 1.

[35] *Economist*, 6 November 1976, p. 79.

[36] Nayar, *The Judgement*, p. 111.

[37] Henderson, *Experiment with Untruth*, pp. 95–8.

paper stood its ground, refusing to let the party in power dictate its editorials or take over its board.[38]

In the event, while the editors of the *Express* and *Statesman*, V.K. Narasimhan and S. Nihal Singh, respectively, fought tooth and nail to protect their papers from the hands of censors and Congressmen, it must be remembered that both locked horns with the regime in but a few instances. A perusal of their daily reportage reveals, in the main, a matter-of-fact affirmation of the Emergency and its policies. Their front pages, in particular, read like government press releases, the latest declamations of ministers and routine denunciations of the regime's enemies—domestic and foreign, real and imagined—duly reported without outrage or even comment. Perhaps it was precisely this kind of hedging that allowed them to last out the Emergency.[39]

Provincial papers, which accounted for thirteen of the eighteen banned during the Emergency, were better positioned than their English equivalents to resist the prior restraint regime.[40] This they did. On the whole they were smaller, more defiant, and owned by minor industrialists who had less to lose by ruffling Delhi's feathers. Because they operated largely under the radar, it was harder to control them.[41]

Towards the end of the Emergency, pressmen plucked up more courage. In the last quarter of 1976, especially, it appears that reports of arrests, forced sterilisations, and abuses of power more commonly made it to the front pages of some newspapers. Column inches railing against the mismanagement of the economy likewise grew longer. In an unprecedented move, in October 1976, 222 "professional journalists" from across the country—Delhi, Calcutta, Madras, Poona, Bombay, Surat, and beyond—signed a petition condemning the regime of prior restraint and posted it to the prime minister.[42]

The Judiciary: Ambivalent to the Core

As mentioned above and as evident from the habeas corpus case, the apex court appeared to be rather pusillanimous. This case, which kept a five-judge bench busy for thirty-seven working days between December 1975

---

[38] Rawla and Mudgal, *All the Prime Minister's Men*, pp. 71–3.

[39] See the *Statesman* and the *Indian Express, passim,* between 1975 and 1977.

[40] *White Paper on Misuse of Mass Media*, p. 72.

[41] Dayal and Bose, *The Shah Commission Begins*, p. 177.

[42] See the letter dated 19 October 1976 in "Documentation of Emergency Period in India", MLP, microfilm copy, reel 3.

and February 1976, was probably the most important to be heard during the Emergency. The Supreme Court had to decide whether personal liberties needed to be upheld in the face of the executive in the context of the Emergency. All the judges wrote separate judgments, but the result was that the court upheld the executive's power to detain people, thereby denying citizens the right to move a habeas corpus petition in a high court under Article 226 during Emergency rule. The advocates who argued the case, including Shanti Bhushan, Soli Sorabjee, and V.M. Tarkunde, found the verdict "appalling". Their assessment is clearly supported by the manner in which judges justified their decision. Chief Justice Ray went as far as to suggest that during a state of emergency the courts "have nothing before them to enforce." This was not unusual, he hastened to add, for "the rule of law must differ in shades of meaning and emphasis from time to time and country to country."[43] Justice Beg went much further when he said that the "care and concern bestowed by the state authorities upon the welfare of detenus who are well-housed, well-fed and well-treated is almost maternal", akin to that of a parent who can justly take "preventive action against those children" who "threaten to burn down the house they live in."[44] The positions of Justices Chandrachud and Bhagwati were more ambivalent but closer to Ray's. The only dissenting judge, Justice Khanna, argued that "even in the absence of Article 21 [which guaranteed the right to life and personal liberty] in the Constitution, the state has no power to deprive a person of his life or liberty without the authority of law."[45]

The majority ruling was less vivid than Beg's position, but equally unequivocal: "no person has any *locus standi* to move any writ petition under Article 226 before a high court for habeas corpus or any other writ or order or direction to challenge the legality of an order of detention."[46] The detainees, then, remained in jail. For his part, Justice Chandrachud conveniently came to show remorse later. Two months after he was controversially appointed chief justice by the Janata—amid protests from large sections of the judiciary over his habeas corpus ruling—in a speech to FICCI on 22 April 1978, he said: "I regret that I did not have the courage to lay down my office [*sic*] and tell the people: well, this is the law."[47]

---

[43] *ADM Jabalpur v. S.S. Shukla, Supreme Court Reporter* (1976), p. 329.

[44] Ibid., p. 371.

[45] Ibid., p. 210.

[46] Ibid., p. 477.

[47] In the same breath, Chandrachud went on to defend his habeas corpus decision: *Opinion*, 9 May 1978, p. 1. See also Austin, *Working a Democratic Constitution*, p. 438.

Legal guilds, whose members were in a sense best positioned to understand the implications of the constitutional tweaking brought on by the state of emergency, in contrast, were at the forefront of the protests. The Maharashtra High Court Bar Association issued a condemnation of the regime, and its Delhi counterpart elected Pran Nath Lekhi, a lawyer serving time in Tihar, over a candidate backed by Sanjay, D.D. Chawla. The Congress retaliated in predictable fashion: the chambers of district- and sessions-court lawyers were razed to the ground in demolitions, and over a hundred attorneys were incarcerated.[48] All the same, some lawyers continued to speak their mind. The former chairman of India's Bar Council, Ram Jethmalani, compared the country's leaders to Mussolini and Hitler.[49] Fali S. Nariman, an additional solicitor general who in May 1975 had had his term extended for three more years, resigned on 27 June to protest the change in dispensation.[50] A number of lawyers spoke at a convention in Ahmedabad on 12 October 1976 organised by the Citizens for Democracy.[51] Among the speakers calling for the restoration of fundamental rights were Minoo Masani and two former chief justices, J.C. Shah, who went on to head the eponymous commission, and M.C. Chagla. When the Congress attempted to shore up legal support for its constitutional dictatorship, the response it received was underwhelming. Just 600 of the 1800 invited lawyers showed up for the government-sponsored Karnataka State Lawyers Conference on 8 November. In the resolution that was to unanimously laud Mrs Gandhi's successful appeal to the Supreme Court that tossed out the charges of electoral malversation, only ten votes were cast in her favour.[52]

Still more important was the role of high courts, which in Emergency India became redoubts of the *Rechtsstaat*. In Allahabad, for example, the chief justice questioned gratuitous arrests. His Bombay peer spoke out against the ill treatment of prisoners and the police attempts to break up

---

[48] Nayar, *The Judgement*, pp. 96–7.

[49] Henderson, *Experiment with Untruth*, p. 121. Jethmalani, who was granted political asylum in the United States, continued the occasional criticism of the regime from his teaching position at Wayne State University, Detroit: *Newsweek*, 4 October 1976.

[50] Nariman, "Memories of June 1975".

[51] This was an organisation that the Bombay lawyer V.M. Tarkunde had founded along with Jayaprakash Narayan in 1974 in response to the circulation in high political circles of an "anonymous paper" calling for the trimming of juridical powers and the adoption of presidentialism.

[52] Nayar, *The Judgement*, p. 95.

private meetings of lawyers. The Bombay High Court also ruled against censors who were trying to suppress the publication of *Freedom First*, a magazine run by lawyer and politician Minoo Masani. It struck down the Bombay police commissioner's order prohibiting meetings of more than five people if their "intention" was to broach the topic of the Emergency.[53] The Delhi High Court, too, took up the cudgels for press freedom, preventing the municipal corporation from winding up the *Statesman* and the *Indian Express*, allegedly for tax evasion.[54] Its Gujarat equivalent did the same to prevent the shuttering of *Bhoomiputra*, a Gujarati daily that had published a speech on the importance of civil liberties by Mohammedali Currim Chagla, former foreign minister and Bombay chief justice.[55]

The case of Murlidhar Dalmia, chief advisor at the Technological Institute of Textiles (TIT), Bhiwani, confirms that the courts were the most powerful institution to confront the regime head-on. Early on during the Emergency he had run afoul of the chief minister of Haryana, Bansi Lal, who was trying to pack Kurukshetra University—to which the Bhiwani Institute belonged— with loyalists by firing some of its senior management. Dalmia, because of his tardiness in getting the TIT principal sacked, was falsely detained for "inciting" labourers at the institute and for being a "staunch follower of the RSS."[56] His family entreated K.K. Birla—Dalmia knew the tycoon through the latter's position as chairman of the Cotton Spinning and Weaving Mills— who then spoke to Lal to have him released; Birla's aides also beseeched union ministers Gokhale, Reddy, Chavan, Ram, and Pant to do the same; and finally, Dalmia's wife obtained an "interview" with Mrs Gandhi, who through their meeting uttered not a word to the despairing woman. The courts, then, were her last resort. By pointing to "technical infirmities" in the MISA order that had in effect prevented Dalmia from exercising the writ of habeas corpus, the Delhi High Court came to his rescue twice, in November 1975 and February 1976, both times allowing him to evade arrest.[57] Police attempts to

[53] Divan, "Courts and the Emergency", p. 225. In the former case, Justices Madon and Kania asserted in their 21 February 1976 judgment that it was "not the function of the censor to make all newspapers speak in chorus"—the "censor is appointed the nursemaid of democracy and not its grave-digger."

[54] *Guardian*, 2 November 1976, p. 4.

[55] *SCR*, vol. 1, p. 35. For the judgment, Justice S.H. Sheth was transferred to Hyderabad.

[56] "Detention under MISA of Shri Murlidhar Dalmia", no date, SCP, Subject File 11, p. 4.

[57] *SCR*, vol. 3, p. 14.

arrest Dalmia from the steps of the court itself, too, failed, amidst much protest and drama. Nevertheless, with the Supreme Court's 28 April 1976 habeas corpus ruling, Dalmia, along with many like him across the country, lost the right to battle the republic's rulers with writs. He was arrested five days later.

Meanwhile, Delhi's autocrats redoubled their efforts to do away with the legal resistance plaguing their regime. In the capital the minister of state for home affairs, Om Mehta, started transferring unamenable judges to the country's peripheries. In early 1976 Mrs Gandhi refused to extend U.R. Lalit's term and to elevate Additional Judge R.N. Aggarwal, who was due for promotion as a permanent judge, at the Bombay and Delhi high courts, respectively; the latter's sin, evidently, was that he had been part of the two-member MISA bench that released Kuldip Nayar.[58] The director of the Intelligence Bureau, S.N. Mathur, had thereafter outed him as an RSS sympathiser, soon after which Mrs Gandhi decided not to approve his promotion.[59] As for Justice S. Rangarajan, the other half of the duo on that bench, he was transferred to Assam.[60] All in all the prime minister was personally behind the transfer of at least sixteen judges in May and June 1976.[61] Naturally, the threat of professional exile had its desired effect. Moreover, an escalation of violence remained on the cards, if only tacitly: a judge's wife, for instance, recalls fearing that her husband would be "accidently run over" while on his morning stroll.[62] Others dreaded the ostracism that Fali Nariman endured after his resignation: "no one except sincere and genuine well-wishers wanted to drop in (or to be seen dropping in) on us", he later remembered.[63] Yet others would have chosen to censor

---

[58] Statement of S.L. Khurana, Home Secretary, MHAP, File VI/11034/56(132)/80/ISDVI.

[59] Statement of S.N. Mathur, MHAP, File VI/11034/56(132)/80/ISDVI. The former, Lalit, whose term was up for extension, met a similar fate. Despite securing the recommendations of the Bombay chief justice, governor, and Maharashtra chief minister, he ceased to function as additional judge, for Mrs Gandhi refused to sign off on it. After cross-examining witnesses, the Shah Commission concluded that it could not adduce the reasons for her "arbitrary decision": "Case summary relating to the refusal to re-appoint Shri Justice U.R. Lalit as Additional Judge of the Bombay High Court", MHAP, File VI/11034/56(132)/80/ISDVI.

[60] Statement of S.L. Khurana, Home Secretary, MHAP, File VI/11034/56(132)/80/ISDVI.

[61] *SCR*, vol. 1, pp. 49–52.

[62] Austin, *Working a Democratic Constitution*, p. 345, n58.

[63] Nariman, "Memories of June 1975".

themselves after recalling the fate that befell P.M. Mukhi, Bombay High Court judge, who suffered a heart attack on hearing that he was to be transferred to Calcutta. Even as his friend, Law Minister H.R. Gokhale, an alumnus of the same court, tried to repair the damage by having the order rescinded a few day later, Mukhi went into cardiac arrest at his residence once again, this time fatally.[64]

Still, some in the legal community put up a tough fight against the transfers regime. For instance, S.H. Sheth, Gujarat High Court judge, challenged his transfer to Hyderabad and filed a writ petition against the government, which his High Court upheld, demanding the government quash the order. What can be surmised as political pressures impelled Sheth to later comply with the transfer order, but his case became a useful precedent for the courts: high courts across the country managed to prevent the transfers of forty-four judges in its wake.[65] In short, excluding the handful of supine justices of the Supreme Court, judges and lawyers alike at the middle and lower levels of the judicial pyramid staved off with a modest degree of success the trespassing hand of the executive.

The RSS and the LSS: Between Resistance and Compromise

In contrast, the resistance shown by the Hindu nationalist organisations around the Rashtriya Swayamsevak Sangh that formed the Sangh Parivar, as well as of parties of the Lok Sangharsh Samiti (LSS), proved more ambiguous.

Looking back from a distance of over four decades, and from a time of Hindu nationalist prepotency, perhaps the development of greatest importance during the Emergency was the legitimacy that the regime accorded Hindu nationalism, a process that the JP Movement had already initiated. Indeed, poured into the crucible of authoritarianism, the political settlement that emerged was a singularly altered one. The Sangh Parivar (literally the RSS "family"), via the Jana Sangh, was one element in the motley collection of the LSS that, in the twenty-one months of dictatorship, came to overpower the rest, largely because of the well-oiled organisation of the RSS. Andersen and Damle point out that "the grass roots structure of the LSS included many RSS workers, which presented the RSS cadre with an unprecedented opportunity to gain political

---

[64] *TOI*, 7 September 1976, p. 6.
[65] Nayar, *The Judgement*, p. 151.

experience and to establish a working relationship with political lead-ers."[66] These efforts rendered it the bona fides that had been denied it since the early years of the republic, when its political "untouchability", as some of its leaders used to quip, had been plain to see.[67] But as we will see, even as the Sangh Parivar opposed the Emergency regime, it also tried to win friends across the aisle in prison and without, and even attempted to negotiate for clemency with Delhi's rulers.

Sangh Parivar leaders took part in an important underground meeting on 26 June 1975 at Kashmere Gate in Delhi, just a day into the Emergency. Preponderant among the participants were Delhi Jana Sangh figures, Congress (O) members being a distant second. The accent of the protests, it was decided, would lie on the organisation of *satyagrahas* (literally "truth-force"; civil disobedience) in different parts of Delhi and beyond.[68] The metaphor took inspiration from the anticolonial struggle, another period of scattered protests which grew in number and determination as national consciousness spread, at times being brutally suppressed, at others thriving on account of temporary deals hammered out with the rulers. On the question of tactics, too, the Emergency-era *satyagraha* drew on the playbook of its inter-war precursor: the use of underground papers and rumours to offset censorship, the courting of arrests, and appeals to the troika of nationalism, democracy, and the rule of law.[69]

This reliance on an outmoded grammar of dissent reflected the deep-seated anxieties of the Hindu nationalists. Long excoriated in the Nehruvian period for their ambivalence towards colonial rule, this epigonic "second freedom struggle" was to be one of their own.[70] By emulating the Gandhian techniques of the first freedom struggle, then, the RSS hoped to make up for lost time by quickly appropriating the nationalist repertoire from which it had until then been excluded. The most obvious attempt was a proposed restaging of the Dandi March of 1930, in which M.K. Gandhi

---

[66] Andersen and Damle, *The Brotherhood in Saffron*, p. 212.

[67] This, of course, was a pun all the more distasteful given its overwhelmingly Brahmanical make-up and ideology. "Untouchables" in any other sense they certainly were not.

[68] Sinha, *Operation Emergency*, pp. 49–50, 57.

[69] A Congressman in 1942: government suppression has "made the whole country a sort of whispering gallery." Vinod Mehta on the same during the Emergency: the grapevine in Delhi was thick with rumours." See Frykenberg, "The Last Emergency of the Raj", p. 52; Mehta, *The Sanjay Story*, p. 70.

[70] Sahasrabuddhe and Vajpayee, *The People versus Emergency*, p. 6.

and his followers had walked a 240-mile stretch between Ahmedabad and the coastal town of Dandi to protest the salt laws of the Raj. In the newer version masterminded by the local RSS, former Gujarat chief minister Babubhai Patel was to play Gandhi's role in a mimetic journey on India's Independence Day. However, on 9 August 1976, six days before the event, Patel was arrested along with dozens of *satyagrahis* littered across the villages through which their cortège was to pass.[71]

Even in the first few weeks of the *satyagrahas*, it was clear that the RSS was the dominant force. To a great extent this owed to its size. According to its general secretary, the RSS had some 8500 *shakhas* in 1975, each with around 50–100 participants. The total strength of the RSS, therefore, was between 425,000 and 850,000. Then there was the rest of the Sangh Parivar: the BMS, a labour union of 1.2 million in 1977; the ABVP, a student union of 170,000.[72] There were other affiliates, too. All in all, the Parivar probably counted around 2 to 3 million members.

The deep connections of the RSS to the JP Movement helped as well: when the key protagonists of Narayan's insurgent forces came together to form the Lok Sangharsh Samiti the evening before the Emergency was declared, the Parivar was well positioned to absorb a number of central positions in the new outfit, which then grew into the nerve centre of the underground. The Jana Sangh's Nanaji Deshmukh was made its secretary. A large number of those detained during the Emergency—4 per cent according to the government, 33 per cent to the Sangh—came from the RSS and its affiliates.[73] This greatly influenced its makeover from a fringe force in the Indian political imagination to one that could have its own man sworn in as prime minister in two decades' time. The RSS bosses were quick to realise that the Emergency was in fact a windfall. "What could not have been achieved in twenty years will be possible in two" was the message they sent out to their cadres.[74] This was going to be *their* struggle.

In good time, even the Socialists were to be found acknowledging the Sangh's indispensability underground. "The grassroot level organisation of the RSS alone is intact. Go to them. They will help you", Achyut Patwardhan, co-founder of the Socialist party and once a scourge of the

---

[71] *Lok Sangharsh Samiti*, 20 September 1976, pp. 2–3, in MLP reel 1.

[72] Andersen and Damle, *The Brotherhood in Saffron*, p. 215.

[73] Sahasrabuddhe and Vajpayee, *The People versus Emergency*, pp. 212–17; Jaffrelot, *The Hindu Nationalist Movement*, p. 276.

[74] Kelkar, *Lost Years of the RSS*, p. 133.

Hindu nationalists, said to his party rank and file.[75] "That attitude of 'who is not with me must be my enemy' that has dogged the opposition for the last thirty years finally came to end, all thanks to the quandaries we faced together because of the Emergency", Narendra Modi, then a young *pracharak,* later observed.[76] Modi, who spent this period disguised as a Sikh with the *nom de guerre* Prakash, not only distributed grey literature and liaised with Sanghis abroad, but escorted political fugitives, including Socialists like George Fernandes, to safe houses as well.[77] It was small wonder, then, that the Socialists came to appreciate the accommodating RSS more than they did the grand old party, its left-wing *in extremis* and authoritarian Right ascendant. "We emerged from jail not as a coalition of parties but as a single party", noted Chakradhar, a former Rajya Sabha Socialist who spent fourteen months incarcerated in Hyderabad with a number of Sangh and RSS activists.[78] The turnabout in the Socialist position could not have been starker. Led by Limaye in the early 1970s, the party had rejected the "anti-Congressism" of its old guard and endorsed the grand old party's newfound progressivism;[79] it took the propinquities forged in Mrs Gandhi's prisons for the party to return to its Lohiaite origins.[80]

For their part, elements within the Sangh not otherwise keen on merger quickly reconciled to building bridges with the rest of the opposition when news began to emerge of Sangh defections to the Congress.[81] Sure enough, many in the RSS who were imprisoned under MISA returned home as changed men, becoming "active supporters of the Congress, if not its active workers." The Jana Sangh in Uttar Pradesh, for instance, pledged its "full support" to the government on 25 June 1976, promising not to engage in "any activity which disturbs the peace and security of the state"; thirty-four Jana Sangh MLAs in Madhya Pradesh and Uttar Pradesh crossed over to join the ruling party.[82]

---

[75] Ibid., p. 135. See Mehta and Patwardhan, *The Communal Triangle in India,* pp. 154–92.

[76] Modi, *Aapatkaal mein Gujarat,* p. 200. Our translation from the Hindi.

[77] For his efforts, Modi was promoted to *sambhaag pracharak* (regional organiser) in 1978. See Mukhopadhyay, *Narendra Modi,* pp. 120–1.

[78] Weiner, *India at the Polls,* pp. 28–9.

[79] Interview with Madhu Limaye, New Delhi.

[80] Brass, *An Indian Political Life,* p. 157.

[81] Limaye, *Janata Party Experiment,* vol. 1, p. 117.

[82] Selbourne, *An Eye to India,* p. 336. The AICC happily accepted them into the party fold: *Congress Marches Ahead—XIII,* p. 18.

These defections were not the only sign of the Sangh Parivar's ambivalence to the regime. Indeed, its *satyagrahas* and *sangathan* (mobilisation) represented just one half of a two-pronged strategy. Immediately after the declaration of Emergency, on 27 June Balasaheb Deoras, the *sarsanghchalak* (chief) of the RSS, wrote "a letter of guidance" to the organisation's workers: they "should continue Sangh work in accordance with directions of those appointed for the purpose by *sar-karyavaha* [general secretary] Shri Madhavrao Muley."[83] In essence, a new division of labour had emerged: Muley was to lead the resistance underground while Deoras himself, who was arrested on 30 June, adopted a conciliatory attitude, penning missives to the prime minister from his cell in Yerawada Central Jail, Poona. On 22 August Mrs Gandhi received the first instalment of his epistolary courtship: "From the jail I listened with rapt attention to your broadcast message relayed from AIR and addressed to the nation on August 15, 1975. Your speech was suitable for the occasion and well balanced."[84] After the plaudits Deoras moved on to more substantial matters, regretting the ban on the RSS and the arrest of "approximately 23,000 [RSS] workers":

> What could possibly be the right cause of banning the Sangh is difficult to assess and to attribute through the ordinance. The RSS has never done anything as [*sic*] might hamper the smooth running of the government, the internal security and peace of the country. The aim of the Sangh is to unite the All-India Hindu community, to organise and emulate [*sic*] the same. The organisation tries to discipline our society ... the organisation has never advocated the cause of violence, neither it has [*sic*] initiated anyone to such acts ... Though the field of the Sangh is limited only to the Hindu community, yet nothing is taught here against any non-Hindu society [*sic*] ... This is my humble prayer to you that you shall kindly keep the above in view and shall lift the ban on [*sic*] RSS. If you think it proper, my meeting with you will be a source of pleasure to me.
>
> Yours faithfully,
> Madhukar Dattareya Deoras.[85]

No reply was forthcoming. Despite the rebuff, Deoras wrote her a second letter on 10 November, traversing the same terrain but this time laying it on thick. "Let me congratulate you as five judges of the Supreme Court have declared the validity of your election", he crooned, before proposing

---

[83] Sahasrabuddhe and Vajpayee, *The People versus Emergency*, p. 96.

[84] The letter is reproduced in BLD leader Brahm Dutt's account of the Janata party, *Five Headed Monster*, p. 138.

[85] Ibid., pp. 139–41.

to put the Sangh's cadres at her service: "Set free thousands of RSS workers and remove the restrictions on the Sangh. If done so [*sic*], power of selfless work on the part of *lakhs* of RSS volunteers will be utilized for the national upliftment (government as well as non-government) and as we all wish, our country will be prosperous."[86]

When she failed to respond yet again, Deoras sought to recruit as his emissary Vinoba Bhave, whose *ashram* he had visited in 1973 shortly after becoming *sarsanghchalak*. "The Sangh has neither been violent nor encouraged acts of violence. The main function of the Sangh is to rectify man. The RSS volunteers are asked to observe control and discipline, hence it can have no place for violence", he wrote on 12 January 1976. Deoras was ignored by Bhave as well. A presumably dejected Deoras then sent him yet another letter when he heard that Mrs Gandhi was scheduled to visit Paunar on 24 February.

> It is my prayer to you that you kindly try to remove the wrong notion of the prime minister about the Sangh, and as a result of which [*sic*] the RSS volunteers will be set free, the ban on the Sangh will be lifted and such a condition will prevail as to enable the volunteers of the Sangh to participate in the planned programme of action relating to country's progress and prosperity under the leadership of the prime minister.[87]

Bhave, who was not in the least interested in picking up the cudgels on behalf of any opposition group, whether of the Left or the Right, disappointed many of his hangers-on who had hitched their wagons to the resistance. Instead, he counselled conciliation: he was not going to allow his religious preferences get in the way of friendships of old, especially not those that had yielded him material benefit. In 1960 Mrs Gandhi had lobbied the Mysore government to grant him a piece of land in Bangalore.[88] During the Emergency the closest he came to criticising the regime was when he laid into its callousness on the issue of cow slaughter: nothing short of a nationwide ban would satisfy the Acharya.[89] To this end he threatened to start a fast on 11 September 1976, but on 8 September Mrs Gandhi pre-empted him by announcing that precisely such legislation was

---

[86] Ibid., pp. 141, 144.

[87] Ibid., pp. 146, 148.

[88] Mahadevi Tai of Vinoba Niwas to Mrs Gandhi, 1 August 1967, PMSP, File 38/100/1967 PMS.

[89] Amiya Rao and B.G. Rao, "Underground Literature During the Emergency: A View from Delhi", in *The Pen in Revolt*, p. 3.

in the offing. Bhave called off the fast with adroit flattery: "The problem of [*sic*] ban on cow slaughter in India is, by and large, solved. The credit goes to 1. the [*sic*] God; 2. Mother Rukmini [Bhave's mother]; 3. Gandhiji; 4. Indiraji. The first three are in heaven. Indiraji is on earth. Thanks to Indiraji! Ram Hari."[90] Not everyone in the Sarvodaya Movement was as lily-livered: in what was one of the most hair-raising episodes of the Emergency, Prabhakar Sharma, 65-year-old Sarvodayite, immolated himself after writing an angry letter to the prime minister.[91]

The spectrum spanned by the RSS was smaller—no Vinoba Bhaves or Prabhakar Sharmas—but not by much. Constructive ambiguity had its uses. On the one hand, Deoras hoped he could have the ban on his organisation lifted by turning the Sangh's cadres into the shock troops of the regime, the entryism remaking the Congress, perhaps even the nation, in its image. On the other, Muley's *satyagrahas* had indisputable propaganda value. It is no accident that the official history of the RSS in Emergency India, *The People versus Emergency: A Saga of Struggle*, glosses over the Deoras letters; only a version of the first is reproduced, not in full, and almost *en passant* at the very end of the book.[92]

Deoras was not alone. Hans Raj Gupta, former Delhi mayor and "provincial RSS *sanghchalak* [organiser] for Jammu and Kashmir, Punjab, Chandigarh, Haryana, and Delhi", too, wrote Mrs Gandhi a similar letter from Tihar, promising in exchange for lifting the ban the beginning of a "new era of co-operation" between the Parivar and the Congress, the former assisting the latter in its "nation-building activities".[93] According to the Jana Sangh MP Subramanian Swamy, "Atal Bihari Vajpayee also wrote apology letters to Indira Gandhi, and she had obliged him. In fact for most of the 20-month Emergency, Mr Vajpayee was out on parole after having given a written assurance that he would not participate in any programme against the government."[94] In November 1976 Swamy, who was abroad trying to stir up the diaspora, was told by Muley that "the RSS had finalised the document of surrender to be signed" at the end of January 1977. "On Mr. Vajpayee's insistence", Swamy was to be the sacrificial lamb "to

---

90 Chandra, *In the Name of Democracy*, pp. 223–4.

91 "Self-Immolation as a Protest Against the Dictatorship", 30 October 1976, in MLP, reel 1; Ostergaard, *Nonviolent Revolution in India*, p. 262.

92 Sahasrabuddhe and Vajpayee, *The People versus Emergency*, pp. 592–3.

93 Gupta to Indira Gandhi, 16 February 1976, in MLP, reel 13.

94 On the role of Swamy during the Emergency, see Chapter 6 in Kapoor, *The Emergency*, pp. 127–52; and Swamy, *Evolving with Subramaniam Swamy*.

appease an irate Indira and a fulminating Sanjay whose names I had successfully blackened abroad by my campaign."[95] In the event, no surrender took place, hence no oblation either, for Mrs Gandhi announced a snap election on 18 January 1977.[96]

What were the Sangh Parivar's activities underground? After Deoras' arrest the bulk of the RSS leadership quickly went into hiding.[97] *Swayamsevaks*, the Sangh's foot soldiers, were instructed to continue showing up at the *shakhas*, but in plain clothes instead of in their identifiable white shirts and khaki skirts.[98] On 4 July 1975 Muley invited the surviving chiefs of the Sangh—among others Bhaurao Deoras (brother of the *sarsanghchalak*), Rajendra Singh, Sunder Singh Bhandari, Dattopant Thengadi, Nanaji Deshmukh, and Moropant Pingle—to his residence to take stock of the situation. It transpired that virtually the entire RSS machinery was intact. It had certainly helped that on 25 June 1975 itself, some of the RSS leaders had "come to know of what was coming", as the Jana Sangh's Deshmukh later admitted.[99] Only one *prant pracharak* (provincial organiser) and 189 of the RSS' 1356 *pracharaks* (full-time organisers) had wound up in prison.[100] The rest were safe underground, occasionally resurfacing at the numerous "summer camps" that the organisation held as part of its routine activities.[101] Indeed, the chain of command was uninterrupted: directives flowed from Nagpur, the Sangh's headquarters, to the *prant pracharaks*, who passed them on to the *vibhag pracharaks* below them, who in turn relayed them further down to the district and *tehsil* levels—all in the span of a few days.[102]

[95] Swamy, "Unlearnt lessons of the Emergency", *Hindu*, 13 June 2000 (http://www.thehindu.com/2000/06/13/stories/05132524.htm), accessed on 1 September 2018.

[96] Rajagopal, "Sangh's role in the Emergency", p. 2798.

[97] For a personal testimony, see Kelkar, *Lost Years of the RSS*.

[98] "Daily summary of information of CID (Special Branch), Delhi", 26–27 June 1975, MHAP, File VI/11034/56/80(29)ISDVI.

[99] How he came across this piece of information is anybody's guess. Government informants? See Deshmukh, *RSS*, p. 75.

[100] The *prant pracharak* was Sudarshan. Sahasrabuddhe and Vajpayee, *The People versus Emergency*, pp. 30, 305–7.

[101] For instance, the locations of the "summer camps" organised in May 1976 only aimed to impress the geographic breadth that the RSS could traverse: Delhi in the north, Kanyakumari in the south, Bombay in the west, and Calcutta and Dibrugarh in the east: Ram Singh, Commissioner for Home Affairs and Secretary to the Government to all district magistrates and superintendents of police, 15 May 1976, MHAP, File VI/11034/80/56(299)/ISDVI.

[102] Sahasrabuddhe and Vajpayee, *The People versus Emergency*, p. 309,

Despite the strength of its clandestine networks, the RSS preferred not to fight the Emergency on its own. At an August 1975 meeting that brought its tactical positions into sharper relief, its leaders reasoned that while "the RSS had the capacity to save democracy by itself", going it alone risked a post-Emergency settlement that was a democracy only in a formal sense: a hegemonic Congress confronting a gaggle of opposition parties on the verge of extinction. How, then, were the "defunct political parties [to] be revitalized?" In the main by the RSS. "Thus the Sangh had to work on two fronts. On the one hand it had to revitalize opposition parties and on the other organise a strong public opinion for the re-establishment of democracy. Hence the decision of the RSS to conduct all activity in the name of the Lok Sangharsh Samiti."[103] But democratic rule was not an end in itself. The Sangh's commitment to representative government, as Thengadi inadvertently argued in his preface to the Sangh's official history, was only skin-deep:

> It is accepted on all hands that the present democratic process in India is not a growth of the soil and it is neither adequate nor favourable nor capable [*sic*] from the point of view of conditions in and requirements of the country. But its protection can save the country from dictatorship. It can afford scope for the thinking and action necessary for a new system that accords with the tradition, nature and circumstances of the country. In a dictatorship this is not possible. So opposing the dictatorship of the Emergency became a natural duty of the Sangh.[104]

---

[103] Ibid., p. 308.

[104] Thengadi, "Preface: Lamp at the Threshold", in ibid., p. 29. A few pages below, Thengadi adds that given the Indian "situation of extreme illiteracy and poverty the British model cannot but lead to great corruption ... Only the model derived from the temperament and tradition here can give the expected results. Still it is necessary that while considering such a system *the makers of a new constitution* should make a comprehensive and careful study of the constitutions of all countries in the world as well as of the special features of the post-second industrial revolution period. Shri Guruji [Golwalkar] had indicated this direction, in clear terms at the conference in Thane ...": ibid., p. 45. Emphasis added. The reference here is probably to the 1971 camp that Golwalkar attended in Thane, which might have been his last interaction with RSS workers on account of his ailing health. There he "discussed in depth other ideologies and did a comparative study of other belief systems and elaborately explained how the Hindu philosophy alone is capable of ensuring highest standard of welfare for the [*sic*] humanity and yield [*sic*] permanent happiness." See "Nation Remembers Social Reformer, Second Chief of RSS Guruji Golwalkar On His 109th Jayanti", *Samvada*, 15 February 2015 (http://samvada.org/2015/news/guruji–109–jayanti/).

In the event, the question was settled in favour of coalition politics. The LSS' secretary was Deshmukh—until his arrest in August 1975—and the better part of its cadres were Sanghis. So it was decided by RSS leaders and *pracharaks* in Delhi that the LSS was the perfect barque for capture. Liaising with the Samiti was bound to bring it into contact with a large spectrum of opposition politicians—just as the Parivar's involvement in the JP Movement had in the run-up to the Emergency. In the Samiti high command the Parivar was represented by Jana Sanghis—Madan Lal Khurana, Sunder Singh Bhandari, and Subramanian Swamy—and D.P. Thengadi of its workers' union, the Bharatiya Mazdoor Sangh; on the other side were the Socialist Party's Surendra Mohan, the Congress (O)'s Ravindra Verma, and Jayaprakash Narayan's secretary Radhakrishna. "On the insistence of the Sangh and the Jana Sangh", Verma was appointed chief of the LSS, dressing up the organisation with a fig-leaf of consensus.[105] When he was arrested in early 1976, another middle-of-the-road figure, this time the Congress (O)'s Digvijay Narayan Singh, was handed the reins. Unsurprisingly, then, the LSS was about as ambivalent about resisting the regime as the RSS, in no small measure because it relied so heavily on the latter.

The work of the LSS was, in the main, to orchestrate *satyagrahas* and distribute clandestine literature. The accent on civil disobedience owed as much to its inter-war Congress precedent as it did the contemporary communist one. The first of the Emergency's large demonstrations was led by the CPI(M)'s E.M.S. Namboodiripad in Trivandrum on 7 July 1975. The RSS' Kerala branch decided to follow suit. Over the next few days nearly 2000 of its workers were arrested in protests. Impressed by the results, the LSS deliberated in favour of a nationwide *satyagraha*. But three elements were needed for the making of such a movement: "a widespread communication network, an organised underground infrastructure, and popular support"— and they were all found wanting.[106] As a result "the Samiti took the decision for a token *satyagraha* from 15 to 25 July 1975." Its objectives, the Sangh's official history notes, were threefold, each for a specific audience: the state, Sanghis in prison, and Sanghis without. First, "to assess the government's intentions and its preparedness and to warn it that if it did not retrace its dictatorial steps it would meet with countrywide opposition." Second, "to keep up the morale of those in jail by assuring them that those on the outside were not sitting idle." And third, "to shore up the people's

---

[105] Sahasrabuddhe and Vajpayee, *The People versus Emergency*, p. 95.
[106] Ibid., p. 94.

sagging morale, to mentally prepare them for extending moral support to a future large-scale struggle."[107]

All the same, organising *satyagrahas* was one thing, a sincere commitment to them another. As Nanaji Deshmukh put it in a "letter of guidance" that he circulated to Sanghis across the country: "This is an individual *satyagraha* and only those workers will participate in it who have a warrant against them and who are not in a position to carry on [*sic*] underground activities."[108] His effort to dissuade organisers from taking part in the protests has to be analysed *pari passu* with another decision of the RSS: "political leaders would lead these *satyagrahas* and the Sangh should not throw all its might into them."[109] In other words it was preparing itself for the long haul. By steering clear of *satyagrahas* and the risk of imprisonment, Sanghis would outlast their competitors and become the hegemonic opposition to the regime.

The LSS mobilisation, then, was to be modest, the priority being lifting the ban on the RSS, and the restoration of democracy a means to that end. In November 1975, during the second round of *satyagrahas*, Rajendra Singh, a senior RSS figure, exhorted *swayamsevaks* in a widely distributed circular to remember their calling: "those who are out to destroy our divine mission have come to the conclusion even after full use of bestial power that this force cannot be put down. On the other hand, in spite of suffering and terror, every one of our workers is fully confident that the final victory will be ours, that justice and *dharma* will triumph."[110] Muley spoke in the same voice: "I appeal to all brothers to participate in this *dharma yuddha* [holy war] with all their might but with the usual discipline and peacefully for the protection of truth, justice and national values and for the removal of obstacles in the way of our divine mission."[111] In both formulations, democracy escapes mention. Both, however, refer to a religious crusade as part of the Sangh's "divine mission".

With such rhetoric in full view, it was no accident that the prodromes of the "RSS question"—its preponderance in the opposition, both ideologically and numerically—which was to blow up in 1979, lay in the underground debates of the LSS during the Emergency. For instance, when Ravindra

[107] Ibid.
[108] Ibid., p. 96.
[109] Ibid., p. 97.
[110] Ibid., p. 206.
[111] Ibid., p. 119.

Verma, before launching the July *satyagraha*, suggested that a charter of demands be presented to Mrs Gandhi first, and that the LSS take to the streets only if she rejected it, he unintentionally opened up a Pandora's box of competing objectives. For the Sanghis, lifting the ban on the RSS was paramount; for the rest, such a demand was not only unreasonable but was sure to warrant a rebuff. Why did *their* organisation always have to climb down from their demands, the Sanghis retorted. In the event it was one of them, Bapurao Moghe, who relented: admitting that the Sangh leadership was torn between fighting against the ban or for democracy, he accepted on behalf of his organisation the position of the Socialists on sufferance. The demand to eliminate the ban was removed from the charter. What transpired in the days that followed is not known, but in his letter to Mrs Gandhi on 6 November, Verma *did* ask for the ban to be withdrawn. Just four days later came Deoras' second letter to the prime minister, making the same request. This, in short, was a silent coup for the Sangh. It was clearly in control of the Samiti.[112]

Mrs Gandhi, of course, ignored Verma's ultimatum, given that one of his requests was revocation of the Emergency. In response, on 14 November the LSS launched a ten-week *satyagraha* to make good on its threat.[113] But their zeal apart, in numerical terms it became increasingly clear that the LSS *satyagrahas* were a fairly circumspect affair. Hans Raj Gupta, former mayor of Delhi, was among the few Jana Sangh leaders to participate in the July 1975 protests and go to jail for it. As for the states where civil disobedience worked best, Punjab and Gujarat, this was for extraneous reasons: on account of support from the Akali Dal in the former, and the permissible environment fostered by the incumbent Janata government in the latter. Elsewhere, especially in the Hindi heartland, the Sangh's baili-wick, the protests were a dismal failure; in fact, the Sangh did better in the South than in its North Indian redoubt. In the November round of protests the Karnataka contingent was the largest, with 15,000 *satyagrahis*, mostly from Mangalore, an RSS stronghold; and Kerala, Ground Zero of civil disobedience, a not-so-close second with 9000. By comparison Bihar and Uttar Pradesh each produced 8000; and Delhi 5000, most of whom came along not for a Sangh event, but one headed by Maniben Patel, Congress

---

[112] Ibid., pp. 123, 126.

[113] Ibid., p. 188. The date, 14 November, was chosen for the launch because it was the birth anniversary of Mrs Gandhi's father. "Listen, tormented soul of Pt. Nehru!", began one of its leaflets.

(O) MP and daughter of Vallabhbhai Patel, who led a women's *satyagraha* in Chandni Chowk.[114]

These figures of course can hardly be trusted, given their provenance. Still, remarkable is how small they are despite their obvious inflation. In spite of being a very large organisation of 425,0000 to 850,000, the RSS by its own admission only managed to convince 155,000 of its members to join in the *satyagrahas*, not all of whom were Sanghis in the first place.[115] Of these 45,000 were detained, slightly more than four-fifths (36,500) of whom, the Sangh contends, belonged to its ranks. The government figures are less than an eighth of the Parivar's: its carceral complex recorded the presence of only 2794 RSS and 1358 Jana Sangh members.[116]

Table 9.1: State-wise Satyagrahis of the Sangh Parivar, November 1975–January 1976

State	Number of satyagrahis	Number of arrests (under MISA and DIR)	Number of Sangh Parivar members arrested (under MISA and DIR)
Jammu and Kashmir	800	422 (356)	327 (127)
Punjab	7000	5457 (2899)	3276 (2306)
Himachal Pradesh	300	108 (111)	89 (76)
Haryana	1000	393 (620)	364 (424)
Western UP	8000	1927 (1862)	1402 (1219)
Eastern UP	10,000	2585 (1809)	2235 (1424)
Bihar	15,000	1910 (2876)	1370 (726)
West Bengal	2000	1129 (108)	795 (51)
Assam	300	160 (207)	128 (144)
Orissa	1000	302 (271)	202 (57)
Andhra Pradesh	5000	1655 (703)	1630 (672)
Tamil Nadu	2000	779 (64)	592 (61)
Kerala	8000	4645 (1273)	3051 (362)
Karnataka	26,240	8740 (1548)	8117 (1478)
Maharashtra	10,000	7048 (1833)	6066 (1619)
Vidarbha-Nagpur	5220	2000 (609)	2040 (592)
Mahakoshal	1000	270 (1326)	269 (1160)
Madhya Bharat	2000	506 (3550)	487 (3166)

[114] Interview with Jagdish Shettigar, 11 February 1994, New Delhi; *Economist*, 24 January 1976, p. 32; Sahasrabuddhe and Vajpayee, *The People versus Emergency, passim*.

[115] *Organiser*, 4 June 1977, p. 11.

[116] Jaffrelot, *The Hindu Nationalist Movement*, p. 276.

Gujarat	10,000	3165 (141)	2373 (113)
Rajasthan	5000	1682 (849)	1592 (596)
Total	154,860	44,965	36,405

Source: Sahasrabuddhe and Vajpayee, *The People versus Emergency*, pp. 212–17.
Note: The credibility of this data is suspect. There is a clear discrepancy between the number of arrests on the one hand, and those made under MISA and the DIR on the other—in some cases, the latter, by definition a subset of the former, is even the larger of the two numbers. The absence of Delhi is noteworthy, too. Mahakoshal and Madhya Bharat refer to the south-eastern and north-western tracts of Madhya Pradesh, respectively; Vidarbha-Nagpur, the eastern districts of Maharashtra. Nonetheless, such data has its uses, especially because the official figures do not distinguish between political arrests, and those for black marketing, petty crime, and tax evasion. Moreover, that the number of *satyagrahis* was in the hundreds of thousands, and not in, say, the millions or tens of millions, is in itself noteworthy.

Apart from its role in protests, the Parivar made its presence felt in two other spheres of public life: welfare and the underground media—not to mention the diaspora, to which we will return in the next chapter. The first of these, in particular, helped the Hindu nationalists improve their image and acquire for themselves a reputation for magnanimity. The Parivar was badly affected by imprisonment, harassment, and even death: eighty-seven Sanghis died in prison, mostly in Uttar Pradesh and Madhya Pradesh. More than a handful were tortured and 50,000 had their houses searched, if the RSS' official account, *The People versus Emergency*, is to be believed. In this context the Parivar took care of its members and their kin.[117] By mid-1976 it was helping at least 3000 families of its rank and file who had either died or were operating clandestinely for the cause. It got them by with monthly disbursements of Rs 150 to Rs 500, money raised by a thousand members of the Sangh's upper echelons who apportioned a part of their salaries to this end.[118] These sums went a long way: as the "prisoner data questionnaires" from the jails show, most of the RSS men were farmers or social workers with seven to ten dependents each.[119] It was perhaps to counter this parallel welfare state that the government in some states, such as Rajasthan, initiated in December 1975 a stipend for the families of detainees that were the "sole bread winners" of a household: an "*ex gratia*

---

[117] Sahasrabuddhe and Vajpayee, *The People versus Emergency*, pp. 245–97, 612; *Organiser*, 28 May 1977, p. 5.

[118] Puri, *Bharatiya Jana Sangh*, pp. 238–9; Sinha, *Operation Emergency*, pp. 117, 119.

[119] MLP, reels 9 and 10.

payment" of a third of the detainee's income, floored and capped at Rs 50 and Rs 100, respectively.[120]

The Sangh was not the only welfarist outfit of the resistance. On a smaller scale the Socialist Party was as well. Bombay Socialist leader P.V. Mandlik, for instance, organised relief funds, books, and parole. He kept the families of incarcerated Socialists abreast of prison activities, providing news on the health and lives of the detainees.[121] Readers of the party daily, the *Janata*, were asked in its pages to contribute to the "Political Prisoner's Family Relief Fund" run from Pune.[122] The Socialists also had their own version of the *satyagraha*, the Jan-Jagruti Yatra, in which senior party figures went from town to town attending conferences and preparing people for the eventual election that they were certain would be called.[123]

News circulated underground too. Three bulletins published out of Delhi dominated this landscape: the Jana Sangh organ *Janavani*, a six-page weekly, boasted the best sales, usually between 5000 and 25,000. It also had the largest reach, circulating not just in the neighbouring states but sometimes even in Bombay and Calcutta. The other two were the *Delhi News Bulletin* and the *Delhi Samachar*.[124] Other small and short-lived publications were *Resistance*, a Delhi-based English journal run by a young Socialist, Lalit Mohan Gautam, which printed only two issues; the widely distributed *Crusader*, three issues of which saw the light of day; and *Pratirodh* and *Yuva Sangharsh*, run by BLD youth leaders Rajendra Choudhari and Rama Shanker, respectively, both of which were quickly discontinued.

---

[120] Notification by the Commission for Home Affairs and Secretary to the Government, 18 December 1975, MHAP, File VI/11034/80/56(299)/ISDVI. A total of Rs 147,000 was allocated for this purpose to twenty-six districts in Rajasthan: see the note from G.R. Yadav, Deputy Secretary to the Government, Home Department, Rajasthan: 15 November 1975, MHAP, File VI/11034/80/56(299)/ISDVI.

[121] See the many Marathi letters and postcards he sent to fellow Socialists in MLP, reels 5 and 6.

[122] *Janata*, 16 May 1976, p. 9, in MLP, reel 14. See the party's report on its "Special National Convention", 28 November 1976, Jayaprakash Narayan Papers, Instalment III, Subject File 338.

[123] See, *inter alia*, Prabhabhai Sanghavi to Dandavate, 19 November 1975, in MLP, reel 7.

[124] The latter was in Hindi, and the former two in English and Hindi at first, and then only in Hindi when its Anglophone readership began to drop. See also Sinha, *Operation Emergency*, p. 128.

There was naturally little co-ordination in this brief burst of literary resistance. Some of it was provided by Radhakrishnan, JP's secretary, and Nanaji Deshmukh, but their arrests brought it to an end. The few attempts made to create a single journal that would bring together the Sangh, Socialist, and BLD organs came to naught.[125] The closest the opposition parties came to creating an ecumenical voice for the resistance was the LSS' *Satya Samachar*, the name a dig at Hindustan Samachar and Samachar Bharati, the state-owned news agencies. This effort kicked off in June 1976 with the publication of 2000 cyclostyled copies of its 21-page issue. After a promising start, the arrest a few months later of its promoters P.K. Chandla and Shanti Desai, who were caught carrying 500 copies, ensured that *Satya Samachar* too became unreliable and infrequent.[126] Nevertheless, sporadic publication with a regular format—detention figures on the front page; a précis of *satyagrahas* conducted across the country and a catalogue of transgressions in press and politics in the next few; an *intermezzo* of "news flashes"; graphic accounts of torture; and, as closure, didactic advice and a round-up of past and upcoming resistance activities—helped foster an imagined community within the resistance, a sense of belonging, even if it was not shared beyond its own narrow circles.[127]

Regional journals such as the *Lok Sangram*, brought out by three leading figures of the RSS in Lucknow, circulated underground too. This Parivar paper stayed under the radar for a while. In some places it was delivered by hand to avoid a postal trail. When discovered, its publishers kept the local police on their toes for a couple of months. Finally, they were subjected to "vigorous interrogation" by the police who had been led to their dissenting lair by informants.[128]

The diaspora had its own *samizdat* literature: *Swaraj*, printed in London, *India Abroad* in New York, *Satyavani* in both, all of which managed to slip into the republic through resistance networks.[129] These news digests compiled reports from foreign outlets, mostly the *Economist* and the London

---

[125] Amiya Rao and B.G. Rao, "Underground Literature During the Emergency", in *The Pen in Revolt*, p. 2.

[126] Sinha, *Operation Emergency*, p. 131.

[127] A number of issues of *Satya Samachar* can be found in the Jayaprakash Narayan Papers, Instalment III, Subject File 320 and in MLP, reel 1.

[128] Report of J.M. Jain, IGP, Intelligence Department Police, 12 September 1975, MHAP, File II–14011/35/75–S&P(D–IV) KW 20.

[129] *Satyavani* was a monthly affiliated with the FISI, edited by Makarand Desai, a Gujarat MLA who had emigrated to London after the assembly was suspended.

Times, but also the *Guardian*, *New York Times*, *Financial Times*, and the *Washington Post*.

Seen together, these circulating notes from the underground were of dubious quality, not unlike the Congress propaganda found on the airwaves, making it all the harder to ascertain the role of the resistance. Sunil Khilnani puts the problem in a nutshell: "Anyone who has tried to write about the Emergency knows that it is a Hall of Mirrors, where accusation and counter-accusation, information and disinformation, trip over one another's heels"; from this one cannot help but "emerge bruised".[130] All the same, assessing which side of fact or fiction the majority of the underground literature tilts is much simpler. For instance, in some of this material one encounters Russian generals calling the shots in Delhi—apparently they were part of a Soviet conspiracy to "keep India as a destitute nation."[131] In one insider's assessment, because these papers were so prone to "exaggeration" and "keen on puffing up" the parties that were behind them even as they were hamstrung by dismal budgets, they quickly lost credibility in the eyes of their readerships.[132] Regional outfits suffered similar problems. Of the RSS' Kannada organ *Kahale* an observer noted, "quality-wise, one may not go into raptures. That it [existed] is the main point. It kept flickering hope alive."[133]

This reflexive humility was all but lost in the aftermath of the Emergency, when dissenters began boasting of their *samizdat* and *satyagrahas* having led to the end of authoritarianism.[134] One of the writers in *Voices of Emergency*, an anthology of resistance poems, wryly points out that not all the compositions in it had been authored during the Emergency: he had been surprised to find one of his adolescent ramblings, written long before 1975, reproduced in the volume.[135] In truth the lettered resistance was an

[130] Khilnani, "States of Emergency", *New Republic*, 17 December 2001, p. 45.

[131] Nayar, *The Judgement*, p. 63. Much of the Moscow-baiting came from George Fernandes, who, perhaps in an attempt to appeal to his Socialist International interviewers, argued that the USSR, in cahoots with the "dictator from Kashmir"—Mrs Gandhi—was "taking the country towards balcanisation [*sic*]": "Exclusive Interview with George Fernandes", *Socialist Affairs*, vol. 26, no. 1 (January–February 1976), p. 61.

[132] Amiya Rao and B.G. Rao, "Underground Literature During the Emergency", in *The Pen in Revolt*, p. 2.

[133] C.H. Prahlada Rao, "The Kannada Scene", in *The Pen in Revolt*, p. 19.

[134] Sahasrabuddhe and Vajpayee, *The People versus Emergency*, *passim*.

[135] Bhagat, *The Contemporary Conservative*.

obscure concern, boasting at its peak only 600 centres where bulletins were printed and purchased.[136] Many of these were routinely disrupted by police raids, dispelling the energies expended on covertly distributing material, counterfeiting government seals, and procuring "respectable looking envelopes" to make the literature appear official and pass undetected in the postal system.[137] The fledging resistance was, in short, of far less import than is made out.

The CPI(M): Underground and in Parliament

Like the Sangh Parivar, the CPI(M) had some of its members underground and others in parliament. In another sense, its predicament was not dissimilar to that of the CPI, albeit in its mirror image. For both communist parties had decided to lay with "opposing bourgeois bedfellows": the CPI(M), for its part, had to adjust to working in a coalition that included its confessional and neoliberal enemies.[138] Essentially a regional party, its support lay only in a handful of enclaves: trade unions in West Bengal and to a lesser degree in and around Madras and Delhi, parts of the Bengali countryside, and among dedicated party cadres in West Bengal and Kerala.[139] In 1969 and 1970 it lost control of the latter two states—the only ones it ever held power in (as part of a coalition in Calcutta, and independently in Trivandrum). Both governments, which rode to power thanks to inter-communist co-operation, collapsed as a result of rivalry between them: they were replaced after a brief period of President's Rule by a Congress–CPI combine in Kerala when the latter turned coat, and a Bangla Congress-backed coalition in West Bengal. In a sense the CPI(M) had been underground ever since. Pushed out of democratic politics, many of its

---

[136] "Life Line of Information During the Emergency", no date, Jayaprakash Narayan Papers, Instalment III, Subject File 320.

[137] Amiya Rao and B.G. Rao, "Underground Literature During the Emergency", in *The Pen in Revolt*, p. 2.

[138] Sen Gupta, "Communism Further Divided", pp. 153, 165. Both the CPI and the CPM negotiated the hostile milieu of the Indian political system by reversing their previous positions: for instance, in 1974 the CPI backed the DMK in Tamil Nadu but opposed it in Pondicherry, eventually approving of the Congress decision to impose President's Rule in Tamil Nadu in 1976. The CPM's policies were the exact opposite: opposing the DMK from 1972 to 1975, then supporting it during the Emergency.

[139] Ibid., pp. 157–8.

cadres joined the Naxalites. The coming of the Emergency, then, made little difference to the party's fortunes.[140] By June 1975 all CPI(M) MLAs in Tripura were already in prison because the Congress, on the verge of collapsing in the state and fearing a party split, had simply decided to lock up its opponents. Soon after, two of its MPs (Jyotirmoy Basu and Nurul Huda), two members of its Central Committee (A.K. Gopalan and E.M.S. Namboodiripad), twenty MLAs, and large swathes of its cadres in West Bengal, Kerala, Tamil Nadu, and Maharashtra joined them in jail. Some of its press organs, the Malayalam *Deshabimani* and the *People's Democracy* in English, were censored.[141] Its strength in the union movement was whittled down. As a party document noted, the INTUC and AITUC had virtually been rendered "the espionage corps of the government" during the Emergency, preventing workers in other unions, including the CPI(M)'s CITU, from building solidarities or opposing Congress corporatism.[142]

Still, the CPI(M) put up a spirited resistance, especially in parliament, where Gopalan, who was released from a week-long prison stint on account of his hunger strike, and Somnath Chatterjee, whose bid to flee abroad was thwarted when government officials impounded his passport, flayed the grand old party in fiery speeches in defence of democracy.[143]

At first blush, as at the time of the JP Movement, the CPI(M) decided to keep at arm's length from the LSS. But reality, both before and during the Emergency, was more complex. In September 1974 Puchalapalli Sundarayya, the party's general secretary for ten years, curtly informed Jayaprakash Narayan that his party would not join any grouping that contained Hindu nationalist and right-wing elements.[144] Yet, as mentioned, the CPI(M) in West Bengal *did* allow the JP Movement and its head to make use of its cadres in the run-up to the Emergency.

Authoritarian rule and suppression made the CPI(M) more relenting than ever before. On 3 September 1975 it clamoured for the creation of a "united

[140] See, for instance, the 30 March 1975 editorial in *People's Democracy*, a CPM weekly, decrying the (external) "Emergency", under which "several thousand" communists had been "jailed, tortured, maimed for life": *Documents of the Communist Movement in India*, vol. 17, pp. 26–7.

[141] P. Sundarayya, General Secretary of the CPM, to Mrs Gandhi, 9 April 1976, Jayaprakash Narayan Papers, Instalment III, Subject File 319.

[142] Politburo resolution, 3 September 1975 in *Documents of the Communist Movement in India*, vol. 17 p. 74.

[143] For excerpts, see Chatterjee, *Keeping the Faith*, pp. 48–55, 259–72.

[144] Ankit, "Janata Party (1947–77)", p. 42.

front" encompassing the Left and Right of all hues, a call it renewed on 25 October: it was time for all "democratic parties" to work together.[145] A few months later, recognising that the future appeared bleak—"one by one, the pillars of the bourgeois parliamentary system are being removed, and a totalitarian framework emphasising the dictatorship of the Congress is being prepared"—its Central Committee agreed that "compelling factors" had ensured that, were it invited to join the cross-party talks under way, it "should have no hesitation in having joint actions with any party that supports our position except the Jana Sangh, *unless avoidable.*"[146] In other words—the amphibology is broken down in the paragraphs that follow—it wanted no truck with the Sangh, but if forced it would reconcile itself to an alliance with Hindu nationalists.

This decision split the party right down the middle and even made P. Sundarayya hand in his notice. In his apoplectic letter of resignation, later published as a 174-page volume, he decried his party members for even considering an alliance with the "pro-imperialist" Jana Sangh and "para-military fascist" RSS, lamenting the CPI(M)'s inability to mobilise trade unions and peasant fronts to oppose the regime.[147]

After Sundarayya's exit the party's centrists led by Jyoti Basu—a known admirer of Narayan's who had in the 1940s served under him as vice president of the AIRF—decided to double down. On 20 July 1976 the party called for an end to "adventuristic" tactics and the need to build bridges with democratic parties, ostensibly to secure the support of the agrarian and industrial working classes.[148] Basu, who was spearheading these moves, had over the past months been in touch with the Socialist Party's George Fernandes, who was trying to woo him into joining forces with the LSS. Their joint effort would help battle the "fascist" tendencies within it and also, more realistically, warm the Marxists to the coalition in the making.[149]

As it turned out, while the CPI(M) did not join the LSS and the other parties underground, its theoretical acceptance of a *volte-face* paved the way for the seat adjustments it would make with the Janata Party—which included the Jana Sangh—in 1977. On 7 November 1976 the Politburo

---

[145] *Documents of the Communist Movement in India*, vol. 17, pp. 71, 106.

[146] Notes from the CPM Central Committee meeting in Madras, 22–28 January 1976, Jayaprakash Narayan Papers, Instalment III, Subject File 319.

[147] Sundarayya, *My Resignation*, p. 1.

[148] *Documents of the Communist Movement in India*, vol. 17, p. 260.

[149] See, for instance, Fernandes to Basu, 2 May 1976, in MLP, reel 5.

declared that while it "held discussions with the Socialist and other Left Parties for evolving a minimum common programme", it would stop short of an outright merger with elements that included the far right. It was decided that subscribing to the "formation of a single party by the amalgamation of disparate parties ... is neither principled nor will it be enduring ... At best it is an election manoeuvre that would bring no good to the people." But, not long after elections were announced on 6 February 1977, the CPI(M) agreed to tactically put up candidates to "prevent the division of opposition parties' votes", even as it recognised that "the parties that comprise the Janata Party" contained within it "an extreme Rightist point of view, essentially representing the same vested interests which the ruling Congress party represents."[150] When choosing between the coalition and the ruling incumbents, in short, it appeared to the CPI(M) that the former was the lesser evil.

Between the RSS and the CPI(M), at extremes of the political spectrum, were the mainstream opposition parties: the Congress (O), the BLD, and the Socialist party. How did they respond to the Emergency?

Mainstream Politicians, Fence-sitters and the Making of the Janata Party

As with the Left and Right, so with centrist politicians. They too continued to take part in Lok Sabha and Rajya Sabha sessions, thus giving credence to Mrs Gandhi's democratic pretensions. But not all of them did. Socialist MPs Madhu Limaye and Sharad Yadav, for instance, writing from their prison cells tried to reason with their non-Congress peers in August 1976: parliamentarians, they correctly noted, no longer held the "popular mandate and justification ... for continuing in a house whose term [had] expired." Both had resigned on 18 March and now asked those on the opposition benches to avail themselves of their "last honourable chance of getting out."[151] But barring a few walk-outs sporadically staged, opposition lawmakers clung to their seats in parliament.

Certainly, the lack of fortitude amongst the political class was striking. Mohan Dharia, especially, proved rather adept at tying himself in knots: in a fascinating speech he condemned "at the outset ... this monstrous operation", the Emergency, even as he professed to be an "ardent admirer" of its

---

[150] *Documents of the Communist Movement in India*, vol. 17, pp. 377–8, 386–7.

[151] Limaye and Yadav to lawmakers in the opposition, 10 August 1976, cited in Ankit, "Janata Party (1947–77)", p. 46.

policies: "I am here to welcome those programmes", he enthused, before cataloguing Congress' achievements of the past few years.[152] For the majority of parliamentarians, complicating the calculations was the prospect of prison, where languished three score of their colleagues. Most MPs, in fact, were in denial. They sought refuge in routine.

> [They] regularly visited the Parliament House, signed the register of daily attendance, sat chitchatting in the central hall, peeped in the library, probably attended the committees, and so on. With all this, they drew the usual salaries and allowances, but they were increasingly getting indifferent towards what happened in the House.[153]

Still, their common adversity notwithstanding, the opposition remained a house divided. While in January 1976 the *Economist* was already reporting the existence "in formal terms" of an "alliance" comprising the largest "four opposition parties"—Congress (O), Socialist Party, Jana Sangh, and Bharatiya Lok Dal—on the ground, events were moving at a much slower pace.[154] Hopes of a combine only became real in March, when the quartet constituted a steering committee for the purpose.[155] It was only in late September and early October that the working committees of each party deliberated independently on the merger.

Its driving force, it became apparent early on, was the possibility that Indira Gandhi might "order ... a snap election at a time and on terms of her choosing." So the ranks of the opposition needed to have "a common symbol [and] a common platform" if they were to fight the Congress effectively.[156] Symbols were hard to come by. Democracy, as an idea, was deemed nebulous; religious imagery, as in the late colonial years, too divisive; and emblems of the resistance, virtually non-existent. Those detained were scattered across the country and knowledge of their whereabouts was

---

[152] *Lok Sabha Debates*, vol. 53, no. 2 (22 July 1975), cols 257, 259.

[153] Mavalankar, "*No, Sir*", p. 176.

[154] *Economist*, 24 January 1976, p. 32.

[155] The meeting was held in Bombay on 20 and 21 March 1976. Apart from the four major parties, its attendees included members of the DMK, Revolutionary Socialist Party, independents, and "Sarvodaya workers". The programme of the coalition was to be hammered out in discussions between Socialist N.G. Goray, the BLD's H.M. Patel, the Congress (O)'s Shanti Bhushan, and the Jana Sangh's O.P. Tyagi. For their statement to the press, see the Jayaprakash Narayan Papers, Instalment III, Subject File 328.

[156] George Fernandes to Narayan, 27 January 1976, cited in Ankit, "Janata Party (1947–77)", p. 45.

far too dependent on hearsay to be of use. There was, in short, "no Bastille, no Yerawada", and no common programme.[157] This, it was hoped, would not prove a stumbling block, and politicians would simply set aside their differences. As the Socialist leader Madhu Dandavate argued, "when there was a danger of fascism in the world", and when in the opposition "some were communists, others were capitalists, and rest were liberal democrats", it was thought best at least temporarily to forget about sectional interests.[158] As it turned out, things were different in 1970s India. The opposition leaders did not know what ideas they could rally around, a confirmation of what we have suggested about the dominant political culture of India: that democracy had little conceptual purchase. The JP Movement's "total revolution" had become a dead letter. Jayaprakash Narayan himself, the glue holding the parties together thus far, was no longer interested in resistance. Ailing from a kidney infection, he was released from prison on 12 November 1975.[159] In the weeks that followed he engaged only in limited activism, mostly from the Gandhi Peace Foundation where he was put up, occasionally speaking to foreign correspondents. On 4 December his parole was revoked and he was placed under stricter watch. The building of bridges, then, was the responsibility of the party bosses themselves. No arbiter facilitated the task.

Some opponents were prompt to make deals with Indira Gandhi who was, as ever, keen to divide her enemies. She made it clear that she was prepared to spare all those who subscribed to the Twenty-Point Programme and decided to renounce politics. Politicians from all quarters rushed to join the queue. In many cases parole was granted when detainees "voluntarily" gave up membership of their parties, indicating that the real burr under the Congress saddle was not violent extra-parliamentary action, but the existence of a plurality of parties—that is to say, the very nature of democratic politics. Coomi Kapoor mentions three members of the Sangh Parivar—Prabhu Chawla, Balbir Punj, and Shriram Khanna—who "signed the Twenty-Point Programme" in order to be set free.[160] Mulayam Singh Yadav, a young socialist leader at the time, also remem-

---

[157] Hart, "Introduction", p. 13.

[158] Transcript of interview with Madhu Dandavate, Acc. No. 778, NMML Oral History Project, p. 105.

[159] Narayan suggested to the BBC that he was probably poisoned in prison, and that his health deteriorated due to "unnatural causes": Henderson, *Experiment with Untruth*, p. 37.

[160] Kapoor, *The Emergency*, p. 35.

bers that "two Sanghis" who shared his cell got out of jail the same way.[161] Indeed, this was a nationwide trend, confirmed by both the grounds for arrest and release: for example, two Gujarati cousins who had been arrested in Goa for having "supported the Janta Morcha in Gujarat 1972 elections [sic]", two Socialists in Manipur, and a Jana Sanghi from Punjab were among the many released from prison only after they resigned from their parties.[162]

Mrs Gandhi submitted some of her opponents to strict conditions in jail to make them give in. This technique was particularly effective with aristocrats whose cushioned existence was a world removed from the prison cells they were thrown in. Gayatri Devi, after suffering the hardships of Tihar jail, wrote a letter to Mrs Gandhi in which she declared: "I support your 20-point programme. I may be released. I will not participate in politics. If you like, you may impose any other condition as well."[163] For the young Madhav Rao Scindia, a Jana Sangh MP who had fled to Nepal, even the threat of prison was enough: he returned home only after expressing his support for the regime and disavowing politics in a letter to Mrs Gandhi.

The most interesting case was Charan Singh, who was released from prison before most figures of his standing on 7 March 1976. While Desai and others were held until January 1977, those on the outside wondered whether the BLD chief had struck a deal with the government.[164] This was perhaps Mrs Gandhi's intention.[165] It also helped that Singh's ability to turn coat was never doubted by his peers. It was widely believed that he had offered to crush the JP Movement during its peak, demanding in return that he be made home minister.[166] This leader of rural proprietors, who was indeed in dialogue with the prime minister to probe the possibilities of a merger, did little to dispel such rumours. Mrs Gandhi, knowing that he could be brought over, had initiated talks with one of his lieutenants, Satpal Malik, who was transferred to Tihar jail in order to start negotiations with his leader in January 1976.[167] Singh was released two months later, along with a few others—Radhakrishna,

---

[161] Interview with Mulayam Singh Yadav, 18 January 2018, in Lucknow.

[162] *SCR*, vol. 3, pp. 93, 103, 128.

[163] Cited in Kapoor, *The Emergency*, p. 257.

[164] Fernandes to Singh, April 1976, in MLP, reel 1.

[165] Brass, *An Indian Political Life*, pp. 192, 207.

[166] Jaffrelot, *India's Silent Revolution*, p. 308.

[167] Interview with Satpal Malik, 25 October 1998, New Delhi.

Asoka Mehta, Biju Patnaik, and Piloo Mody—in an effort to make the move look less suspicious.[168]

For his part Patnaik was prepared to compromise and even mediate between Singh and Mrs Gandhi. In March 1976 he wrote to the former singing the praises of the prime minister's son: "I must say that I am enjoying young Sanjay's exhortations to his party workers." Perhaps, he argued, the scion ought to be commended for suggesting that parties "stop political quibblings" and join the Congress in getting "on with the task of nation-building at the grassroots level."[169] On other occasions Patnaik, who also owned the Kalinga conglomerate, had plainly told Yunus he had "no desire to be in politics" for he had more pressing matters to attend to—such as making sure "his own business", in reality a considerable industrial empire, remained a going concern.[170]

In the ensuing months Charan Singh undermined the making of a united opposition even as his peers were in favour of a merger of their parties. Working towards a single party without a common programme was to put "the cart before the horse", he said, his lack of enthusiasm being then interpreted by many as evidence of his dalliance with the enemy; around the same time he was also trying to convince Narayan to open a dialogue with Mrs Gandhi.[171] Elaborating on the rural proverb, he added that a single party would give the Jana Sangh and RSS, with their large cadres, an undue advantage; it would leave the BLD, which had thus far always punched above its weight—cloaking its Uttar Pradesh small-gentry interests as national rural ones—a "second grade member" of the amalgam. The May 1976 "policy and programme" document drafted by Narayan, which implicitly called for exchanging the parliamentary for a presidential system, added to his reservations, as did its ambiguous calls for a "total revolution". To Singh the plans "smack[ed] of totalitarianism".[172] In other aspects, though, the programme smacked of Congress-style schizophrenia, a por-

---

[168] On this episode, see Kapoor, *The Emergency*, pp. 266–7.

[169] Limaye, *Janata Party Experiment*, pp. 120–1, 193. The letter was leaked to the Socialists by Krishan Kant, who probably got hold of it from his old Congress contacts.

[170] Yunus, *Persons, Passions, and Politics*, p. 254.

[171] Singh to Narayan, 1 June 1976, cited in Ankit, "Janata Party (1947–77)", p. 45.

[172] Ruparelia, *Divided We Govern*, p. 74. Note the role of an all-powerful ombudsman and the vague description of "total revolution" in the "Policy and Programme of the New Party", 23 May 1976, Jayaprakash Narayan Papers, Instalment III, Subject File 337.

tent of the dissensions to come under Janata rule: its authors wanted to give land to the tiller, yet at the same time pack off all the landless to cottage industries, away from farms. The document called for more planning and better labour relations, even as it suggested, perplexingly, that planning would have to be done from the "bottom up", with less of a role for the state, and that better labour relations would only be possible with the accommodation of a bigger and freer private sector.[173] In his letter Singh also brought up the question of "dual membership"—should Jana Sanghis be allowed to retain their RSS membership when they joined the new party? Certainly not, for that would result in a Hindu nationalist appropriation of the new party, he contended. The Jana Sangh's leaders lashed out against Singh's criticisms, reminding him of his previous endorsements of the RSS.[174]

By the time Singh came around to the merger, it was the Sanghis and Socialists who had second thoughts about being pushed along to the altar. In part this was because their upper echelons were jailed, slowing down decision-making, and in part because of their own widely divergent ambitions and readings of the Emergency. Madhu Dandavate, the leader of the Socialists, for instance, was in November 1975 convinced for some reason that a letter written by retired British Labour MP Fenner Brockway to Mrs Gandhi advising her to seek Narayan's co-operation to "restore normalcy in the country" was the "key to the revival of the reconciliation process", for, after all, the prime minister was "keen to end the Emergency at the earliest."[175] The passage of time helped correct such misapprehensions. Still, the party was torn over any alliance that included Sanghis.

For George Fernandes, party chairman, building solidarities with other parties, "even if you do not agree with the words and deeds of some of them", was very much a part of the rough and tumble of politics.[176] N.G. Goray, whom he was trying to convince, thought otherwise. The latter, who was playing a complex and dangerous game, was at this point also engaged in talks with Mrs Gandhi, who, therefore, knew all about the "secret conclave of the Socialist Party in Gujarat" where the leadership had

---

[173] "Resolution passed by leaders of various opposition parties and the members of the Steering Committee who met in Bombay on 22nd and 23rd May 1976", in MLP, reel 1.

[174] Tyagi to Singh, 21 August 1976, cited in Ankit, "Janata Party (1947–77)", p. 47.

[175] Transcript of interview with Madhu Dandavate, Acc. No. 778, NMML Oral History Project, pp. 124–5.

[176] Fernandes to Goray, 26 May 1976, in MLP, reel 1.

collided over whether to join hands with opposition parties or the Congress.[177] Ultimately, Fernandes prevailed over Goray. Socialist scepticism over the question of dual membership was overcome around February 1976. This did not mean that Fernandes had cemented his position in the party. As late as November Surendra Mohan, general secretary, was still plotting a coup against him.[178] All the same, by the end of May all parties had succeeded, at long last, in getting even those in prison to sign off on the proposed merger.[179]

But the path forward remained unclear. The Socialists wanted six weeks to consider the matter, Narayan to head the new party, and parity between its four constituents in the new working committee, despite its cadres being the smallest of the quartet. Meanwhile, a party—Singh suspected it was the Jana Sangh—was behind a smear campaign against the BLD chief: he had been released from prison because his party was on the verge of folding into the Congress, that being the word on the street.[180]

As for the Congress (O), it had a rather pragmatic reason to oppose the merger: it received Rs 100,000 in rents every month from all the properties held under the party name, the Indian National Congress, which it had retained since the split of 1969. Were it to abandon that name, its estates would fall into the hands of Mrs Gandhi's Congress. Knowing exactly what its leaders were hinting at, Bhanu Pratap Singh of the BLD caustically remarked to the Congress (O)'s Asoka Mehta that the merger was most assuredly not going to be "the extension of your own party."[181] Mehta's party had other troubles too. While its central leadership came around to the merger, its state chapters in Tamil Nadu, West Bengal, and Gujarat continued expressing reservations about it.

An ailing Jayaprakash Narayan strapped to a dialysis machine was then brought in to arbitrate disputes between the four parties, whose leaders had been writing letter after letter to him cavilling at each other's behaviour.[182] This he duly did in the last three months of 1976. His efforts culmi-

---

[177] Fernandes was firmly against dealings of any kind with Mrs Gandhi: Rajeswar, *India*, pp. 90–1.

[178] Madhu Limaye, *Janata Party Experiment*, vol. 1, pp. 165–6, 194.

[179] The signatories included Samar Guha, Surendra Mohan, Piloo Mody, Bhairon Singh Shekhawat, and K.R. Malkani: "Pledge", 26 May 1976, in MLP, reel 4.

[180] Ankit, "Janata Party (1947–77)", pp. 47–8.

[181] Bhanu Pratap Singh to Asoka Mehta, 2 November 1976, cited in ibid., p. 48.

[182] In mid-June 1976 Mrs Gandhi offered to purchase him a "dialyser machine" worth Rs 90,000, but he refused the sum: see their letters in MLP, reel 13.

nated in a conference attended by the leaders of the Jana Sangh, Socialists, and the Congress (O)—the BLD chose not to attend—on 11 November, when the troika passed a unanimous resolution to form a single party. Later the same month the BLD, which by then appeared to be on board with the others, proposed a broad division of power within the new party: it would have a BLD president; two general secretaries, one each from the Jana Sangh and the old Congress (the latter was also given the party vice presidency); Socialists were to be satisfied with a new party name, the "Indian Socialist Congress", instead of an older one that had been proposed, the "National Democratic Congress"; as for the state- and district-level general secretaries and working committees, they were to be elected, in essence handed to the outfit that could mobilise the largest cadres, the Jana Sangh, which could rely on the full might of the Sangh Parivar.[183] The Socialists, surprisingly, were amenable to this arrangement, passing a resolution for the merger with near-unanimity. The Jana Sangh too voted in favour of it. But the Congress (O) shot it down, finding unacceptable Singh's desire to be party president.[184]

By the end of December, most of these agreements of early November had unravelled. Quite bizarrely, Singh made ending resistance to Mrs Gandhi's regime a precondition of the merger. He was also in favour of an agrarian party symbol—"a *kisan* driving a pair of bullocks yoked to a plough"—that the old Congress objected to.[185] The Socialists soon discovered that they were only going to be at the margins of the new party, which was led by "diabolical" forces.[186] Mehta, in the meantime, opened a channel to Mrs Gandhi, who proposed, perhaps only to frustrate the efforts of the mutually suspicious quartet, a merger of the Congresses. Similar talks were in the works between Delhi's rulers and Harekrushna Mahtab, leader of the Jana Congress, an Oriya party. And in Tamil Nadu the DMK's Karunanidhi had agreed to "co-operate" with the Emergency regime.[187] On 16 December Mrs Gandhi scored yet another victory when opposition leaders from the big four parties, and many others, sent her a letter accepting

---

[183] Bhanu Pratap Singh to Asoka Mehta, 29 September 1976, in MLP, reel 3.

[184] Surendra Mohan to Narayan, 10 December 1976, Jayaprakash Narayan Papers, Instalment III, Subject File 338.

[185] N.G. Goray to Narayan, 1 December 1976, cited in Ankit, "Janata Party (1947–77)", p. 50.

[186] Narayan to Limaye and Fernandes, December 1976, cited in ibid., p. 51.

[187] Limaye, *Janata Party Experiment*, p. 200.

"reasonable restraints" on democracy and agreeing to work on social programmes alongside the Congress.[188]

The profound ambivalence of some of the key figures of the opposition is evident from the meeting which took place at Biju Patnaik's place on 4 December 1976. Singh and Patnaik conferred on this occasion with Om Mehta and Mohammed Yunus, and agreed on a compromise: the government would lift the Emergency—restoring democracy and liberating political prisoners—and the opposition would abstain from any agitation.[189] On 1 January 1977 Patnaik followed up with the minister of state for home affairs by suggesting that there was a "large area of agreement" between "the government and the opposition".[190] While nothing concrete emerged from this dialogue, what it revealed was that opposition leaders even during the final weeks of the Emergency never stopped trying to strike a deal with Mrs Gandhi.

Socialists Madhu Limaye (in prison), George Fernandes (underground), and S.M. Joshi (leading the campaign on the streets), it appears, were probably the only high-ranking opposition figures to condemn *tout court* all efforts to negotiate with the Congress, seeing in such parleys only the legitimation of authoritarian rule.[191] The others would take longer to arrive at this conclusion. It was as late as 16 January 1977, two days before Mrs Gandhi announced a snap election, that Singh realised the futility of talks with the prime minister. On that day he wrote to Narayan suggesting rather presciently that an election was imminent. With her foes divided, her victory was a foregone conclusion for Singh, who noted that the opposition would do best by not contesting "in the farce".[192] In the event it did, forming in the face of adversity and exactly a week after his letter, the polycephalous Janata Party, which coasted to victory.

---

[188] The figures included the Socialist leaders Goray and Samar Guha; Jana Sanghis Vajpayee and O.P. Tyagi; the BLD's H.M. Patel, Piloo Mody, and Charan Singh; the DMK's Karunanidhi and Era Sezhiyan; the old Congress' Asoka Mehta; and independent Krishan Kant. New Delhi Embassy to the Bureau of Near Eastern and South Asian Affairs, 17 December 1976, (https://search.wikileaks.org/plusd/cables/1976NEWDE18242_b.html), accessed on 11 February 2018.

[189] Kapoor, *The Emergency*, p. 271.

[190] Patnaik to Mehta, 1 January 1977, in MLP, reel 3.

[191] Limaye, who was arrested on the first day of the Emergency, remained in prison until 7 February 1977. Fernandes was arrested on 10 June 1976 and released on 21 March 1977, after the elections.

[192] Singh to Narayan, 16 January 1977, cited in Ankit, "Janata Party (1947–77)", p. 52.

Direct Action Underground: The Limits of Limited Violence

The mass incarceration of political leaders and guileful co-option of some of their comrades assured Indira Gandhi of the stability of her rule. But it did not deter a set of utopians from taking a shot at revolution. Those of them who escaped arrest found their way into one of two broad underground clusters: one led by George Fernandes, Socialist leader and face of the railwaymen's strike of 1974, and the other by the Jana Sangh's Nanaji Deshmukh and Subramaniam Swamy. Only the former group had revolutionary ambitions of some kind; Deshmukh's and Swamy's Hindu networks, as seen above, contented themselves with *satyagrahas*, literary activism, and protests abroad.

Fernandes had, according to his lieutenant C.G.K. Reddy, "a one-point programme: remove that woman."[193] *Satyagrahas* were not going to cut it for him. As for efforts to reason and negotiate with the prime minister, they were "embarrassments to the underground movement." And the "reasonable restraints" letter seen above was "a pure and simple surrender document admitting indirectly that the Opposition was guilty of all that Mrs Gandhi had accused them of."[194] As Reddy put it in his assessment: "the act of going to jail helped only marginally in building morale, and failed totally in keeping the government off balance."[195] Throwing the regime out of kilter necessitated a dose of violence—of the "non-killing and non-injuring type"—Fernandes' band of militants decided.[196] Targeted killings, the usual *modus operandi* of such activity, were ruled out: assassinating Mrs Gandhi "could hardly solve the problem. It may remove the person but not change the system which made it possible." Instead, the accent was placed on sabotage to "remove the fear that had been successfully injected into the minds

---

[193] Indeed, Mrs Gandhi's gender had been a thorn in Fernandes' flesh. When he was later imprisoned, he fulminated against the wardens "following the orders of this woman." Analogously, of his trial he later wrote that "I and my comrades behaved like MEN": Reddy, *Baroda Dynamite*, p. 164. Capitals in the original. Such sexism was not unusual. J.B. Kripalani, eighty-eight, once the Mahatma's right-hand man, was deprived of imprisonment—for him, a badge of honour—during the Emergency, probably owing to his senescence, prompting him to observe: "When a witch goes through a street destroying everything, she leaves one house untouched": Henderson, *Experiment with Untruth*, p. 27.

[194] Reddy, *Baroda Dynamite*, pp. 75–6.

[195] Ibid., p. 25.

[196] Rajeswar, *India*, p. 82.

of the people and had paralysed them."[197] Such ideas—the preference for limited violence, a preoccupation with national esteem—drew on a repertoire of early-twentieth-century revolutionary thought in the subcontinent.[198] The ideological debt was acknowledged by Reddy, who reasoned that the Quit India Movement of 1942, "principally a violent one", had succeeded on account of its violence "in not only keeping the British government off balance but also electrif[ying] the people."[199]

As early as July 1975 Fernandes settled on dynamite as his weapon of choice. The targets were to be bridges, railway lines, and drainage systems. That month his group got in touch with quarry owners who supplied them with explosives in Baroda, Gujarat, where the reach of the Emergency had been halted by the incumbent non-Congress government. The leaders of the two enclaves of the opposition, however, were far from forthcoming. The Gujarat government "in the name of non-violence and constitutionalism" was "on the defensive". The rulers of Tamil Nadu were more encouraging. Reddy, who worked for the *Hindu* in Madras, in fact met the DMK leadership virtually every month. Era Sezhiyan, one of its MPs, "almost thought like us", he concluded, and Fernandes began to build a rapport with Karunanidhi. Still, the Tamil government preferred to maintain a low profile, believing it could enjoy a majority in the Madras assembly only so long as it "outmanoeuvre[d] Mrs Gandhi".[200] In Gujarat, especially, Fernandes tried hard to win recruits but the Socialist base that he drew on was rather weak there. So he then sought conservative allies, befriending Viren J. Shah, a businessman and former Swatantra MP who in his youth had been attracted to communism.[201] More figures lent support to the endeavour, their professions covering a spectrum only seen in caper films:

---

[197] Reddy, *Baroda Dynamite*, pp. 26–7.

[198] Jaffrelot, "The Making of Indian Revolutionaries (1885–1931)", pp. 119–72.

[199] Reddy, *Baroda Dynamite*, p. 27.

[200] Ibid., pp. 78–9.

[201] Shah ran Mukand Steel and Iron Works. He had served as a Swatantra MP in the late 1960s, an independent in the Rajya Sabha in the mid-1970s, and a BJP MP in the 1990s. Interestingly, he had been one of the six trustees of the International Youth Centre—encountered in Chapter 1—along with Mrs Gandhi. On Shah's account, the eponymous owners of Mukand's holding company, Bajaj, were "victims" of massive and politically motivated tax raids. On a single day, apparently, 1100 officials searched 114 premises owned by the company; no improprieties were found. See the brochure of the IYC, no date, SCP, Subject File 23, p. 30; deposition of Rahul Bajaj, SCP, Subject File 19, p. 45; interview with Suketu V. Shah, the son of Viren Shah, in Paris on 8 August 2017.

business consultant to the *Hindu* C.G.K. Reddy, actress Snehalata Reddy, mill worker Motilal Kanojia, lawyer Prabhudas Patwari,[202] Indian Airlines Captain R.P. Huilgol, and his surgeon daughter Dr Girija Huilgol. Fernandes' gang was soon ready to spring into action. They purchased 924 sticks of dynamite at a cost of Rs 4620 on 8 March 1976.[203]

The first target was a railroad network and the Arrah Telephone Exchange in Bihar, a state where the frequency with which railway lines were blown up made such acts a part of the local idiom of dissent. Soon Fernandes sought more stimulating targets, those that attracted government attention. His people blew up railway tracks in Bangalore and then set off explosions in three of Bombay's busiest railways stations—one each on 10 December 1975, Christmas Eve that year, and on the first anniversary of the Emergency the following year.[204] A few attacks down the line most of the gang, who by then had lost their Gujarati and Tamil safe havens, had wound up in prison. The CBI took in the brother of Huilgol *fille* and tortured him, hoping he would give up his family members.[205] When this failed they resorted to another strategy. They had Bharat Patel, a Gujarati businessman with activities in Dubai, stitch them up. Posing as a partisan sympathetic to the cause, Patel offered to arrange for equipment to develop a clandestine radio station. When a few of Fernandes' men arrived in Baroda on 9 March 1976 to pick up the contraptions, they were met by officers waiting for them.[206] Other arrests followed: on 28 March Reddy and Captain Huilgol were captured in Delhi; on 7 April and 1 May

---

[202] Patwari was also a prominent Congress (O) leader in Gujarat and a trustee of M.K. Gandhi's Sabarmati Ashram.

[203] The Gujarat state government's report on the Baroda Dynamite Conspiracy, 11 August 1976, MHAP, File 228/4/76–AVD–II.

[204] Reddy, *Baroda Dynamite,* p. 95; CBI note on the "Baroda Dynamite case", 17 July 1976, MHAP, File 228/4/76–AVD–II; M.S. Kasbekar, Joint Secretary, Home Department, Bombay, to R. L. Mishra, Joint Secretary to the Government of India, 29 July 1976, MHAP, File 228/4/76–AVD–II; "Alleged Wrongful Confinement and Torture of Shri Lawrence Fernandes by the Police and Maltreatment in Jail", no date, SCP, Subject File 10, pp. 9–10.

[205] See Girija Huilgol's affidavit in MLP, reel 5.

[206] In another version of the story, Bharat Patel ratted on what, in fact, were his comrades after speaking to Chimanbhai Patel, who hoped to regain Mrs Gandhi's trust by helping her defeat the resistance. In yet another, Bharat was successfully blackmailed by the CBI, who were threatening to arrest his businessman nephew, Sharad Patel, "over misuse of licenses". See Reddy, *Baroda Dynamite,* p. 83; Nayar, *The Judgement,* p. 146.

more of their ranks in Delhi, Madras, and Bangalore. Finally Fernandes, who had once narrowly escaped the clutches of the police by disguising himself as a Sikh, was arrested in a Calcutta church on 10 June. By the end of July nearly the entire gang was in prison: eleven were picked up in Bombay, six in Baroda, five in Delhi, and one each in Patna and Calcutta. The list of those in custody reveals that many of the "conspirators" were journalists: K. Vikram Rao, a student leader from Uttar Pradesh, was the *Times of India* correspondent in Baroda; Kirit Bhatt, the *Indian Express'* in the same town; Dr G.G. Parikh edited the socialist daily *Janata*, and Kamlesh Shukla another socialist publication, the weekly *Pratipaksha*.[207] Another cluster included Bombay trade unionists probably pressed into service by Fernandes.[208]

On the first day of the trial a handcuffed Fernandes tried to convert the courtroom into a site of protest with his statement: "We, and the chains we bear before you today, are symbols of the entire nation which has been chained and fettered by a dictatorship which has established itself in our country."[209] So he was vindicated, in the end, in his criticism of the LSS: it was pointless to protest non-violently in an age of censorship. Barring the *Statesman*, no Indian paper reported on his arrest.

How, then, does the balance sheet appear: did the Baroda bombers, with their poor organisation, unsustained violence, and insufficiently articulated politics, fare any better than the Samiti? Among its "achievements" was a front-page protest advertisement it placed in the London *Times*; pamphlets read out and meetings attended by C.G.K. Reddy in London and Brussels; a line derailed here and a bomb set off there. Its most ambitious project, an attempt to set up a Radio Free Europe-style broadcasting outlet, failed when contacts in the Greek resistance protesting against the junta and Japanese trade unions both proved unable to help.[210]

The Akalis engaged in direct action, too, mostly in Punjab. On 30 June 1975 the Shiromani Akali Dal, in a special executive meeting held at the

---

[207] Shukla had taken over the journal after Fernandes, its former editor, was arrested.

[208] For their names, see Reddy, *Baroda Dynamite*, pp. 139–140.

[209] Ibid., p. 102. The trial was a short one. The government was unable to prove anything immediately, and Fernandes was granted bail. Shortly after, he was re-arrested under MISA. The case against him was officially withdrawn on 26 March 1977, four days after he was released on bail. That day, 22 March, he had, after "campaigning" from his prison cell, won the Muzaffarnagar seat on a Janata ticket in the general election.

[210] Rajeswar, *India*, p. 82.

Golden Temple in Amritsar resolved to oppose "the fascist tendency of the Congress."[211] A week later, on 7 July, the Akalis launched a "Save Democracy Morcha", courting arrest *en masse*. Prakash Singh Badal, one of the party's leaders who spent the whole period of the Emergency behind bars, remembers:

> The very first day that the Emergency was imposed, we held a meeting at Amritsar to discuss the situation. A messenger from Indira Gandhi brought the offer of perpetual "rule" with no interference from the Congress government at the Centre, if we did not oppose the Emergency. We, however, were not bothered about ruling Punjab. We had to consider what role to play, given our history and heritage. We decided to launch a *morcha* against the Emergency. We were the only political party to launch a series of protests against the Emergency [*sic*]. Akali Dal workers have never sought to reduce their sentence by tendering an apology. There were people who did not seek any relaxation even to attend the funeral of their sons.[212]

What accounts for such forthrightness? To Pritam Singh, the Akalis were simply eager to defend democracy and protect minority rights, theirs included.[213] J.S. Grover, however, offers a more pragmatic explanation: the Akalis opposed the Emergency because "they were unhappy with the Congress over the delay in starting work on the Thein Dam, discrimination in the allocation of heavy industry, and unremunerative prices for farm produce."[214] Throughout the Emergency the Akali protest was organised from the precincts of the Golden Temple. Their agitation resulted in the arrest of 40,000 Akalis. Decimated, they spent the latter months of the regime under the radar, cautiously liaising with the LSS.[215]

* * *

This chapter is in a sense the obverse of the one preceding it in that Chapter 8 concerns the rule—those classes and parties that supported the Emergency—and this chapter the anomaly—the regime's opponents, who were very few and far between. As we have seen, tilting the balance in

---

[211] Harinder Singh, "The Emergency & The Sikhs" (https://www.sikhri.org/the_emergency_the_sikhs).

[212] "We were offered 'rule' if we didn't oppose", *The Tribune*, 25 June 2015 (https://www.tribuneindia.com/news/comment/-we-were-offered-rule-if-we-didn-t-oppose/98155.html).

[213] Singh, "Class, Nation & Religion", pp. 55–77.

[214] Grover, *The Sikhs of the Punjab*, p. 214.

[215] S. M. Joshi to Harchand Singh, August 1976, in MLP, reel 8.

favour of supporters to the detriment of dissenters was a generalised sense of fear, and, more structurally, the shallowness of Indian democracy. Fear probably played a more significant role as far as journalists and lawyers were concerned, though the political class, too, hardly comes out looking anything but timorous. Still, as in Soviet Russia and Vichy France, the Emergency threw up some courageous figures—such as Ramnath Goenka and Fali Nariman—who opposed the country's autocratic rulers even from within the ranks of the establishment.

The shallowness of India's democratic culture was particularly obvious in relation to the RSS and its subsidiaries. True, some of them fought the Emergency underground, but their fight was not so much for democracy as for having the ban on them lifted. Their chief negotiated with the regime with the same aim in mind, committing himself to support the new dispensation if the RSS could work freely again.

Many other political parties turned out to be almost equally unimpressive. Almost all of them had leaders who tried to strike a deal with Mrs Gandhi. This attitude was consistent with the decision of most parties to let their MPs participate in parliament. This only provided the regime the façade of respectability it craved while also undermining the credibility of the opposition. Few revolutionaries articulated their resistance to the regime in terms of democratic values. In the event, their courage notwithstanding, it was not because of them that Mrs Gandhi decided to lift the Emergency in January 1977.

If she faced such a feeble opposition, the question arises: why did she call off the Emergency?

10

LIFTING THE EMERGENCY

WHAT RETURN TO DEMOCRACY?

When Indira Gandhi announced a snap election on 18 January 1977, her decision seemed inexplicable to many observers. The reason she gave, evidently hoping to win with a strong mandate, was to have "an opportunity to cleanse public life of confusion."[1] The communiqué caught virtually every political commentator, domestic and foreign, unawares. Emblematic of the consensus on this matter was the judgment of Andre Gunder Frank, German-American economic historian of the *longue durée*, who had proclaimed on the eve of Mrs Gandhi's announcement that India was heading towards a "permanent Emergency".[2]

A first explanation for Mrs Gandhi's *volte-face* lies in the recesses of the logic of the Indian polity, under whose constraints the Emergency regime—as a "constitutional dictatorship"—operated. By dint of repetition, the quinquennial polls had acquired the weight of tradition. There was no other way for Indian elites to legitimise their rule.[3] To be sure, the liberal aspects

---

[1] *Financial Times*, 19 January 1977, p. 1.

[2] By the time this was published, not only had elections been called but Mrs Gandhi was a fortnight away from defeat and ejection. See Frank, "Emergence of Permanent Emergency in India", p. 463.

[3] Incidentally, Pakistan partially shared in this legacy, as evident from the need for military rulers to abandon the uniform and go to the polls sometime after their coups. See Jaffrelot, *The Pakistan Paradox*, Chapter 6.

of democracy—liberty, equality, fraternity—were of little moment in the Indian setting; still, its demotic dimension prevailed on account of the pervasiveness of populism at the national and regional levels.[4] Popular consent, in a word, mattered. As the historian D.A. Low points out, this peculiar aspect of the Indian polity harked back to the late colonial period. Moreover, he notes that the events of 1975 followed 1932 to the letter. The latter year was when the British imposed what a Raj staffer ironically described as "civil martial law": without resorting to direct military rule but making ample use of the colossal emergency powers vested in the Government of India Act, the British arrested their political opponents without trial, and, with the help of an amenable police force, brought the colony to heel. This style of rule was eventually ended and elections were held in 1937. Writing in late 1975, Low perceptively suggested that Mrs Gandhi would do the same, holding and losing an election in due course.[5]

While she may not have consciously emulated the precedent, the limits of the Indian political repertoire were no doubt hardwired into Mrs Gandhi's thinking.[6] Throughout the Emergency she was at pains to stress its impermanence: "we, however, are committed to elections", was a common refrain; polls were par for the course in the world's largest democracy, she insisted in interviews to *Socialist India, Blitz, Saturday Review,* and *Bild am Sonntag*.[7] P.N. Dhar spoke of the thrill his boss felt on the hustings: "She longed to hear again the applause of the multitudes."[8] The idiom of electoral politics had been internalised by Congressmen, even if they wanted nothing more than to dispense with its attendant inconveniences, *inter alia*, the opposition, dissimilitude.

Her party members felt the same. In December 1976 alone, P.N. Dhar, P.N. Haksar, B.K. Nehru, Om Mehta, and D.P. Chattopadhyaya were among

---

[4] Jaffrelot and Tillin, "Populism in India".

[5] Low, *Eclipse of Empire*, pp. 161–3.

[6] Lest it appear that the faith in constitutionalism on the part of Delhi's rulers is overdetermined in such an interpretation, it should be noted that, even from the gloom of incarceration, opposition figures continued to think in constitutional terms. Jayaprakash Narayan, for instance, was certain in September 1975 that the Emergency was to end soon, for the parliamentary elections were "drawing near". Adding that while she did possess the power to extend the Emergency, he suggested that she would not exercise it, for she knew how "flimsy that pretext would be": *The Pangs of Conscience*, p. 10.

[7] *SW*, 16 August 1975, p. 1. See also Morris-Jones, "Whose Emergency—India's or Indira's?", pp. 460–1.

[8] Dhar, *Indira Gandhi, the "Emergency", and Indian Democracy*, p. 344.

the many figures who tried to sway her into scheduling fresh elections at some point in the new year.[9]

Whilst elections had been suspended at the national and state levels, local ones continued unabated during the Emergency. Jabalpur, Madhya Pradesh elected a mayor in August 1975.[10] In December polls were held in over 1700 district and *taluka panchayats* in Gujarat.[11] The next month a Janata Front mayor was re-elected in Ahmedabad after the party swept the municipal corporation elections.[12] In March 1976 the biennial indirect elections to the Rajya Sabha elections, too, proceeded as before the Emergency: the Jana Sangh's L.K. Advani was returned despite being in prison.[13] Thirty-nine municipalities in Rajasthan held elections in July.[14] In short, democracy, however disfigured, remained central to the way in which Delhi's authoritarian rulers understood political legitimacy.

If elections *had* to take place, the question then is: why did Mrs Gandhi consider them necessary in early 1977? The decision-making process leading up to the election is unlikely to have been a planned affair. As late as 5 November 1976 the Lok Sabha had extended the Emergency by another year: elections were thus intended for 18 March 1978. On 18 December 1976 the president of the republic signed off on the Forty-second Amendment, fortifying the powers of the executive and consolidating the Emergency regime. And yet exactly a month later Mrs Gandhi announced elections.

This inconsistency is typical of sultanic regimes, where an atmosphere of arbitrariness permits leaders to indulge themselves. There is no getting away from the fact that Mrs Gandhi's character counted for a lot in the run-up to the decision to lift the Emergency. But there are of course other explanations that need to be assessed.

---

[9] Ibid., pp. 348–9. Haksar, who was opposed to the Emergency, could well have been misleading the premier when he wrote to her in early January suggesting that the "general situation in the country" was "favourable" for holding an election: Lockwood, *The Communist Party of India*, p. 132. B.K. Nehru had advocated a turn to presidentialism in the early months of the Emergency. A year down the line, he had come to the conclusion that "what was being done under the Emergency was not quite as rosy as, sitting in faraway London, I had assumed it was": Nehru, *Nice Guys Finish Second*, p. 559.

[10] *SW*, 16 August 1975, p. 3.

[11] *SW*, 20 December 1975, p. 1.

[12] *SW*, 17 January 1976, p. 14.

[13] *SW*, 3 February 1976, p. 4.

[14] Secretary of Government and Director of Elections, Rajasthan to the Inspector General of Police, Rajasthan, 13 July 1976, MHAP, File VI/11034/80/56(299)/ISDVI.

Elections as an Antidote to Escalation: A Return to Normal Political Life?

The first explanation on offer emphasises Mrs Gandhi's realisation that the Emergency was not sustainable if she was to legitimise her rule; and that elections were the best way to clip Sanjay's wings since she did not have it in her to say no to him.

Mary Carras and Pupul Jayakar, for instance, argue in their separate analyses that Mrs Gandhi saw the poll as the only way to stop Sanjay, who had got out of hand.[15] Senior Congressmen P.N. Dhar, C. Subramaniam, and Vasant Sathe suggested versions of this at the time.[16] On most accounts, this theory is supported by two kinds of evidence.

First, that Mrs Gandhi could not ignore the excesses of the sterilisation programme. Revulsion at the programme had gained momentum in the course of 1976. The hostility was fostered by rumours which, in the absence of press freedom, took on a life of their own. One of the most persistent of these was that sterilisation sapped the virility of men.[17] In fact, in popular discourse the operation was referred to as *khassi* (castration). Tellingly again, a Delhi neighbourhood bordering Uttar Pradesh, many of whose residents had wound up there by way of the scalpel, came to be known as "Castration Colony".[18] Women were reported to complain that they had been turned into *bewas* (widows) by the state, because with sterilisation "our men are no longer men."[19]

In one rumour that led to a stampede in Uttar Pradesh, the idea was spread that vaccines administered to children in schools were in effect surreptitiously sterilising them.[20] The same scare was doing the rounds in Rajasthan, where citizens turned against the immunisation programme, preferring to risk contracting tuberculosis, smallpox, diphtheria, whooping cough, typhoid, and cholera than wind up unknowingly sterilised.[21] In effect

---

[15] Jayakar, *Indira Gandhi*, p. 312; Carras, *Indira*, pp. 244, 247ff.

[16] Dhar, *Indira Gandhi, the "Emergency", and Indian Democracy*, pp. 348–51; Vasudev, *Two Faces of Indira Gandhi*, pp. 176, 188.

[17] See, for instance, the letter that Arun Bhatia, Collector of Satara, and M.R. Kher, Chief Executive Officer, Satara Zilla Parishad, sent out to village bureaucrats exhorting them to dispel these myths: 5 February 1977, SCIF, Subject File 1120.

[18] Tarlo, *Unsettling Memories*, p. 173.

[19] Mehta, *The Sanjay Story*, p. 164.

[20] *Lok Sangharsh Samiti*, 23 November 1976, p. 2, in MLP, reel 1.

[21] A.V. Nag, Deputy Secretary to the Government, Medical and Public Health Department, Government of Rajasthan, to all chief and deputy chief medical and health officers, 28 February 1977, MHAP, File VI/11034/80/56(298)/ISDVI.

the programme fuelled a growing distrust of the state as citizens began keeping away from healthcare. As news spread of citizens dying on sterilisation tables, the association of *nasbandi* in the popular imagination shifted from impotency to incapacity. A survey revealed that a third of couples perceived the operation as associated with "death or long-term illness."[22]

It was in the context of the family-planning programme that some 240 violent incidents were recorded by the police. The first major occurrence was in Narkadih, a village in the Sultanpur district of Uttar Pradesh, where rural folk chased away officials, including the divisional commissioner, who had come to "motivate" them. After having been forced to turn tail they then returned with a handful of policemen who fired on the villagers, killing thirteen.[23] In Bihar the police shot at protestors in Dhanbad, Patna, and Purnea, incidents in which at least one citizen died. In Gurgaon and Sonepat, both in Haryana, four were felled by police bullets for failing to submit to the operation. In Uttar Pradesh twelve bit the dust in three districts and 1544 were arrested across the state. In Maharashtra clashes between citizens and the police had become so frequent that the administrators of sterilisation camps were instructed in October 1976 to completely dispense with the use of police officers. The next month similar orders prohibited the association of policemen with camp officials in Gujarat and Uttar Pradesh.[24]

In October the district of Muzaffarnagar in Uttar Pradesh became a flashpoint of resistance. Here, as elsewhere, people were picked up at railway stations and bus stands, threatened with arrest under the DIR or MISA, and then forcibly sterilised. When eighteen Muslim youths were incarcerated for refusing sterilisation, the community opted for collective action. They marched to the authorities, pelting stones and demanding the release of those who had been jailed. The police replied with tear gas and bullets, killing thirty-three. During the curfew that was imposed shortly after, another four were shot dead. Meanwhile, fifty kilometres west of Muzaffarnagar, Muslim protests picked up in Kairana. The police pursued people into a nearby mosque where they had sought refuge, killing three in the altercation.[25] Similar incidents littered other parts of Uttar Pradesh that autumn. A

---

[22] Misra, Simmons, Ashraf, and Simmons, "Reflections on the Future of Family Planning", p. 1585.

[23] Nayar, *The Judgement*, p. 135.

[24] *SCR*, vol. 3, pp. 174, 178, 195, 175, 185.

[25] Nayar, *The Judgement*, p. 135.

[26] *SCR*, vol. 3, pp. 163, 169, 202.

block development officer in Basti who was updating family-planning registers was confronted by bitter villagers who hacked him to pieces. In the spiral of violence that followed they in turn were killed wholesale by vengeful policemen.

Keeping a lid on such events was getting less and less easy as time passed. The regime tried maintaining full control over the sterilisation narrative on its radio and television monopolies, in newspapers and propaganda films, and through prior restraint. Yet few believed the Home Ministry when it tried to dismiss the yellow press by pinning the blame on "obscurantist and communal" government officials, whose "sense of hostility" apparently hinged on "their failure to undergo sterilisations themselves."[26]

When news of the resistance to family planning reached Mrs Gandhi, she first turned a deaf ear to it, insisting that such reports were exaggerated. But shortly after the Muzaffarnagar episode, a minister of state at the centre, Shahnawaz Khan, and Khurshed Alam Khan, Rajya Sabha MP, showed her a report cataloguing instances of police violence in the district. P.N. Dhar tried to warn her as well, bringing to her notice an eighteen-page report on family-planning "excesses" that the communists had prepared.[27] The IB also regularly updated her on the growing unpopularity of the programme. These were all dismissed as "anti-Sanjay propaganda".[28] Nevertheless, in October 1976 Mrs Gandhi did grudgingly confirm that "some deaths have taken place due to firing", only to snap back with an unsurprising *tu quoque*: "on the other hand, several policemen and other citizens were killed by violent groups." This was not a retreat, she hastened to add, "for we do believe" the "programme of sterilisation" to be "important and most urgent". In other words the loss of a few lives was not going to cut any ice with her.[29]

Her rhetoric apart, the violence did needle her into second thoughts. Many states, and eventually Mrs Gandhi as well, had come to the conclusion that the intensification of the programme was proving counterproductive. In November 1976 the chief secretary of Rajasthan decided that "in view of the *rabi* season and the need for consolidation of public opinion" it was time for moderation: from here on the focus would be on "genuine volunteers" only. This in effect allowed farmers to sow their crops that month without fearing sterilisation and the attendant loss in productivity,

<hr>

[27] Dhar, *Indira Gandhi, the "Emergency", and Indian Democracy*, pp. 324–5.

[28] Rajeswar, *India*, p. 77.

[29] *NYT*, 28 October 1976, p. 14.

for it usually took a couple of weeks to recuperate.[30] The reluctance of the union in allowing the passage of Maharashtra's sterilisation bill of August 1976 showed that it shared the reservations of that functionary. While the bill was in line with the *zeitgeist* on most counts, one of its provisions achieved notoriety: it called for the "compulsory medical termination of pregnancy" if it was found that a couple already had three children.[31] On 8 December, when the bill was supposed to come up on the cabinet agenda, it never did, probably because it was deemed excessive and shot down either by one of the ministries or the PMS. On 18 February 1977, when the bill was sent to the president of the republic for his approval, Mrs Gandhi suggested inaction: such draconian legislation had the potential to damage Congress prospects in the upcoming elections. Already in November 1976 Mrs Gandhi was beginning to wonder about the merits of the sterilisation regime, describing the decision of the Himachal Pradesh government to jack up by 600 per cent the rents of those in government housing who refused to get sterilised as "rather harsh".[32]

The second reason why she called off the Emergency that several of her biographers point to relates to her psychological distress. Pupul Jayakar's life of Mrs Gandhi is a case in point. In August 1976 Jayakar, who was also an old friend of the premier's, suggested to her that she meet J. Krishnamurti, "a sage" she consulted. Mrs Gandhi met Krishnamurti on two occasions at Jayakar's place, once on 24 October and then in November. During the second meeting Krishnamurti told Jayakar he "was deeply touched by her [Mrs Gandhi's] ability to listen, and by *her refusal to defend her actions.*"[33] She herself later spoke about this meeting to Jayakar, who reported it thus: "She had described to Krishnamurti the events in India *over the last year.* 'I am riding on the back of a tiger [like Durga, incidentally]', she had told him. 'I do not mind the tiger killing me, but I do not know how to get off its back.'"[34] Parliament had extended the term of the Emergency by another year three weeks before, on 5 November, but for Jayakar Mrs Gandhi's encounter with Krishnamurti, and what she told him, showed that Mrs Gandhi was desperately looking for a return to normal life. Jayakar believes this is when she started to think an election was the

[30] *SCR*, vol. 3, pp. 191–2.
[31] Ibid., p. 162.
[32] Ibid., p. 159.
[33] Jayakar, *Indira Gandhi*, p. 310. Emphasis added.
[34] Ibid., p. 312. Emphasis added.

solution. Mrs Gandhi's quest for a way out was spurred by her realisation that under Sanjay's influence the Emergency was getting out of hand. Her son of course was not at all pleased with his mother's decision to go to the polls. "I couldn't help it", Sanjay later said; he had tried stopping her but "she was too much influenced by the communists."[35] But this narrative, as it were, cutting off the umbilical cord a second time to spite her face, seems insufficient.

A second explanation for the timing of the termination of the Emergency concerns external factors.

What International Pressures?

It would be a bit of a stretch to attribute the lifting of the Emergency to diplomatic pressure. For foreign governments on both sides of the Iron Curtain had come to coolly accept the Emergency in 1975, confirming the non-ideological character of the new dispensation. The Soviets continued to fund the Congress party through L.N. Mishra and other channels, and Moscow continued to support Mrs Gandhi in exchange for trade concessions.[36] At the same time, the US embassy and Sanjay enjoyed a friendly rapport. Moreover, there was no Cold War interference by either superpower in the day-to-day running of India's affairs.[37] One of the reasons for the West's complacency, in spite of its notional commitment to liberal democracy, was that in the US and Europe the Emergency was well thought of by the business world. Foreign capital benefited in at least three ways under Congress rule, both before and during the Emergency.

First, because the 752 foreign enterprises present in the country at the time of the Emergency played a disproportionate role in Indian economic life, foreign capital was able to extract meaningful concessions from the Indian state. Accounting in 1974 for 30 per cent of the total value of assets in the country's private sector, these firms had the lobbying heft to ensure that, at least in a select few sectors, foreign enterprises were preferred over their Indian counterparts. For instance, Union Carbide, a multinational, was allowed to expand *sans* competitors its capacity for

---

[35] Mehta, *The Sanjay Story*, p. 136.

[36] Mitrokhin, *The World Was Going Our Way*, p. 317.

[37] Mayer, "Congress (I), Emergency (I)", p. 143; Dhar, *Indira Gandhi, the "Emergency", and Indian Democracy*, p. 329.

the manufacturing of carbaryl, even when nearly thirty Indian enterprises had the knowhow.[38]

Second, the Indian state, after its appetite had been whetted by growing remittances, had grown increasingly willing to export cheapened Indian labour to factories abroad. The implication of this shift in worldview was spelled out by the head of a West German trade mission whose candour none of his Anglo-American *confrères* could match: "as [India] entered into the free market economy ... with [its] vast material resources and low labour charges", it was "an ideal partner for joint structures and collaboration in third countries", he exclaimed in 1976.[39] The picture could not have been more vivid: Indian wage-labourers facilitated by Atlantic capital toiling in Middle Eastern tyrannies, each party more willing than the other to lower labour costs and standards.

And third, steady devaluation of protectionism and dilution of the Foreign Exchange Regulation Act had accelerated India's integration into the global economy. This of course allowed an increasing variety of foreign products to enter the Indian market.

During the Emergency these three trends intensified. On 2 April 1976 the Indian state struck a deal with foreign investors: in return for precious foreign exchange, overseas firms were permitted majority shareholding, and hence managerial autonomy, in joint ventures. This was achieved through an amendment to the Foreign Exchange Regulation Act: all that was required of foreign companies was evidence that they would export 60 per cent of what they produced on Indian soil. This was in no small part the panicked response to the blackmail of multinationals, which, led by the computer giant IBM, were threatening to pull out of the country unless regulations were eased. With the stick came the carrot: Japan announced a major commodity loan to India in light of the April decision.

Three days later came another law allowing profits from debased Indian labour to be siphoned off abroad: non-resident Indians (NRIs) were granted permission to invest in the country's "basic industries".[40] They could remit their profits tax-free and were exempt from wealth taxes. The protestations of the Planning Commission—which suggested that both Indian citizens as well as foreigners would be put at a disadvantage—were

[38] Selbourne, *An Eye to India*, p. 13; Madhu Limaye to Mrs Gandhi, 21 December 1973, PMSP, File 17/1532/1973 PMS.

[39] *Economic Times*, 11 March 1976, cited in Koshy, "Indian Emergency", p. 55.

[40] Selbourne, *An Eye to India*, p. 235.

quashed from above.[41] NRIs were also to enjoy higher interest rates on deposits and lower taxes on real-estate investments than their native counterparts.[42] Meanwhile, plans to nationalise foreign pharmaceutical firms and tea plantations were quickly disavowed. To this end the Hathi Committee Report of 1975, which called for nationalisation in response to India's growing dependence on foreign pharmaceuticals that had "amassed huge private wealth" in India, was buried.[43]

International support for the Emergency regime was secured by assurances to foreign governments and businessmen. For his part, William Saxbe, the US ambassador to India who had famously been Nixon's attorney general during Watergate, was able to "better appreciate ... Emergency rule" after India lent support to American interventionism in Africa and set out a policy to dispatch Indian labourers to construction projects in the Middle East run by Kellogg, Bechtel, Marcona, and Kaiser. In exchange, an American trade delegation promised to send India 500,000 tons of discounted rice and wheat as well as weapons-grade uranium. Paul Kreisberg, another embassy figure, later fondly reminisced that the twenty-one months of authoritarianism were "among the best in recent years for Indo-American relations."[44]

Similar deals were struck with Bahrain, Britain, Iran, the Netherlands, and the Soviet Union. In January 1976 Delhi promised to send Manama "an additional 15,000 workers" to drudge for construction companies in the kingdom.[45] Authoritarianism also offered the way out of an impasse in the relations between former colony and metropole. Britain's trade deficit with India had long been a thorn in London's flesh. Because of wage differentials, it was realised that getting Indians to buy more would be a hard sell. The world of defence contracting, a more opaque sector, offered a solution. The sale of Jaguar fighters was foisted on the Indian High Commission, and the two countries set up the Indo-British Economic Committee in January

---

[41] See the note by the Deputy Chairman of the Planning Commission, 12 September 1975, P.N. Haksar Papers, Instalment III, Subject File 354.

[42] Mukherjee, *The Dramatic Decade*, pp. 90–1.

[43] *Seminar*, vol. 190, no. 1 (June 1975), p. 29. MNCs produced 56 per cent of the "bulk drugs" consumed in the country.

[44] Selbourne, *An Eye to India*, p. 239; *Mainstream*, 25 June 1977, p. 25.

[45] P.M.S. Malik, Indian Ambassador to Bahrain, "Brief note on visit of Bahrain's Labour Minister to India", 11 January 1976, P.N. Haksar Papers, Instalments I and II, Subject File 85.

1976, holding trade talks in London in April. Private arms dealers rushed in, equally eager to do business with Emergency India.[46]

In this context the British support for the Indian regime was bipartisan, from Labour Left to Tory Right. Michael Foot suggested that it was a "monstrous lie" that Mrs Gandhi "wanted to be a dictator". Margaret Thatcher believed the Emergency served the Indians well in "tackling problems like world recession and inflation."[47] The FCO concurred: "an authoritarian regime is better equipped than a democracy to force through the reforms which are needed to make India less of a burden on the world."[48] Following this logic, in 1976 the Overseas Development Ministry increased its aid to India by over 30 per cent.[49]

The English press, while substantially hostile to the dictatorship, nevertheless opened their pages to contrarian voices. In the *Observer* Jennie Lee praised Mrs Gandhi for realising that the "Westminster model has demonstrably failed" and for "outwitt[ing] her tormentors and detractors." Amit Roy argued in the *Sunday Telegraph* that Mrs Gandhi had preserved the "nation's democratic framework" with "shock treatment". In the balance sheet drawn by Eldon Griffiths for the *Times*, "the gains of the [Emergency's first] year ... quite massively outweighed the losses."[50]

Britain was not the only European country doing business with India during the Emergency. France's Chirac, as mentioned, arrived on a visit, praising the regime and then meeting J.R.D. Tata at the Hôtel Matignon on his return.[51] And in exchange for the purchase of Dutch manufactures, which included drilling equipment, barges, and fertilisers to the tune of Fl. 450 million, India secured a Fl. 50 million increase in aid—a third more than the "normal commitment"—and a number of debt-relief measures from the Netherlands.[52]

---

[46] Nehru, *Nice Guys Finish Second*, pp. 551–2; *SW*, 17 April 1976, p. 6: Singh, *One Life is Not Enough*, p. 168.

[47] *Times*, 7 January 1977, p. 7. Both returned starry-eyed from their sojourns in Emergency India. Thatcher, then the leader of the opposition, had a good rapport with Mrs Gandhi, a fellow alumnus of Somerville College, Oxford.

[48] Chaudhuri, "Re-reading the Indian Emergency", p. 486.

[49] See the spreadsheet attached to this article: Claire Provost, "UK Aid: Where Does it Go to and How Has it Changed since 1960?", *Guardian*, 14 April 2011 (https://www.theguardian.com/news/datablog/2011/apr/14/uk–aid–spending–history#data), accessed on 1 September 2018.

[50] *Observer*, 25 April 1976; *Sunday Telegraph*, 25 April 1976; *Times*, 25 June 1976.

[51] J.R.D. Tata to Mrs Gandhi, 11 May 1976, PMSP, File 38/87/1976 PMS.

[52] See the "Brief for discussions with Drs. [*sic*] J.P. Pronk, Minister for Development

The communist world proved no different than the one of Atlantic capitalism. Trade in textiles, heavy water, alumina, wheat, satellite communications, colour-television sets, and computers, along with a tacit agreement to turn a blind eye to rouble–rupee exchange-rate manipulation, was reason enough for Moscow to give the Emergency its ringing endorsements in the pages of *Pravda* and *Izvestia*. At first there was some friction. In October 1975, the USSR refused to extend a line of credit worth 30 million roubles for the supply of spare parts for HAL aircrafts when India protested against the revision of the rupee-rouble ratio; the Soviets were no longer content with the old conversion rate of Rs 8.33 to a rouble. As it happened the deal went through in May 1976 when India acceded to Russian demands. The new rate, Rs 10 to a rouble, increased the costs of servicing debts owed to the USSR. The change of course had no direct impact on trade, since all of it was denominated in rupees. But because India effectively repaid its debts through exports, the country would have to ship far more manufactures to the Soviet Union on account of this deal. In exchange came political support. The KGB *rezidentura* in Delhi and the Soviet-funded World Peace Council received a fresh injection of money from Moscow to run a campaign against Mrs Gandhi's enemies, the foremost of which in its opinion was the CIA.[53]

Besides the USSR and the West, partners of the developing world, too, were sanguine. Tehran was offered a number of joint ventures put together by the newly set-up Indo-Iranian Business Committee, leading its visiting prime minister, Amir-Abbas Hoveyda, to remark "somewhat nostalgically" that "he "felt as if he was in his own country."[54] Back home, in conversation with Indian officials, the Shah of Iran promised investment in "several new industries", adding that the Emergency best suited the Indian economy:

Cooperation, Royal Netherlands Government", 27 December 1975, P.N. Haksar Papers, Instalments I and II, Subject File 85.

[53] See the "Report on the visit of Defence Secretary's Delegation to the USSR", May 1976, P.N. Haksar Papers, Instalment III, Subject File 300; "Brief record of meeting held on November 26, 1975 between Foreign Secretary and Mr. S.A. Skachkov, Chairman of the State Committee for Foreign Economic Relations", 4 December 1975, P.N. Haksar Papers, Instalments I and II, Subject File 218(i); Selbourne, *An Eye to India*, p. 241; Chaudhuri, "Re-reading the Indian Emergency", p. 481; Communist Party of India (Marxist) Resolution, 3 September 1975, p. 2, in "Documentation of Emergency Period in India", MLP, microfilm copy, reel 1.

[54] *SW*, 15 May 1976, p. 4; *SW*, 17 January 1976, p. 3.

"each country has to find its own system of government. No country should ape another system not suited to its conditions."[55]

The World Bank was impressed by Mrs Gandhi's handling of industrial relations. As a reward, in 1975–6 donor nations lavished the country with Rs 9.39 billion in aid; not since 1967–8 had India witnessed such levels of foreign assistance.[56] And in May 1976 the Aid-India Consortium made available $1.7 billion.[57] Given the large volumes of imports flowing into the country to keep food prices down—hence to maintain peace in the countryside—India could well have developed a balance-of-payments crisis. That this did not come to pass owed in the main to growing remittances and the deluge of aid flowing in. In 1976, the Fifth Five-Year Plan was revised to reflect that 15 per cent of outlays would come from external assistance, most of it from the World Bank, United States, Japan, and the other advanced capitalist nations, making them, as it were, complicit in the propping up of the Emergency regime.[58]

If the outside world mattered to Delhi's rulers, their enemies, perforce, took cognisance of it, too. Indeed, foreign governments and international organisations were approached by Mrs Gandhi's opponents as well, sometimes via the Indian diaspora. Here, the Rashtriya Swayamsevak Sangh's preponderance was plain to see, thanks in no small measure to the work of an itinerant *swayamsevak*, Chamanlal, who travelled around the world activating the Parivar machinery. He toured the length and breadth of the United States, meeting Sanghis in Los Angeles, Washington, Michigan, New York, and even Youngstown, a small industrial town in Ohio; he also liaised with RSS sympathisers in eighty-two countries. Another peregrinating activist was Subramaniam Swamy, Jana Sangh MP in the Rajya Sabha, professor at IIT Delhi, and former Harvard associate professor, who, along with his wife Roxna, escaped arrest by fleeing the country, spending the rest of the Emergency on the lecture circuit in Britain,

---

[55] Transcript of discussions between the "Shahanshah and Shri M.G. Kaul [Economic Secretary, Ministry of Finance] and Shri R.D. Sathe [Indian ambassador to Tehran]", 23 February 1976, P.N. Haksar Papers, Instalment III, Subject File 336.

[56] India received Rs 4250 million in aid on average during the three years before 1975–6: Toye, "Economic Trends and Policies in India", p. 308.

[57] *NYT*, 29 May 1976, p. 3.

[58] India's foreign-exchange reserves nearly doubled from Rs 9.69 billion in 1974–5 to Rs 18.69 billion in 1975–6. Aid in the latter year was Rs 9.39 billion: Toye, "Economic Trends and Policies in India", pp. 308–9.

Canada, and the US.[59] In August 1976 Swamy flew back to India disguised as a Sikh, walked into a Rajya Sabha session when a list of obituaries was being read out, shouted that one could add "democracy" to the list, and ran out. The RSS had planned his getaway, so he was soon en route to Nepal.[60] Three weeks later the upper house expelled him *in absentia* for his "foul innuendoes".[61]

Outside the Sangh were other prominent figures who made their presence felt overseas: Rajni Kothari, a political scientist at Columbia University; Leila Kabir Fernandes, wife of the imprisoned George Fernandes;[62] Ram Jethmalani, chairman of the Bar Council of India, who had been granted political asylum by the United States.[63] They were among the many dissidents who raised funds for the resistance and lobbied foreign governments, with little success, to exert diplomatic pressure on New Delhi.

The resistance in the homeland also benefited from the largesse of Indian *émigrés* in the West, in the main Gujaratis—figures such as Mukund Mody, a paediatrician-turned-activist in America, and myriad textile merchants in Leicester, Birmingham, Hong Kong, and Nairobi.[64] These networks belonged for the most part in the Sangh's nebula, harvests reaped by Hindu nationalists after decades of contact with affluent Hindu migrants in Britain, North America, and East Africa.[65] The RSS, then, was best placed to dominate the resistance abroad, especially in Britain. The Hindu Swayamsevak Sangh (HSS), its British chapter, organised protests and

---

[59] Sahasrabuddhe and Vajpayee, *The People versus Emergency*, pp. 516, 511, 527–30. For an account of their activities, see the memoir of Roxna's sister Coomi Kapoor, *The Emergency*.

[60] Anderson and Clibbens, "'Smugglers of Truth'", p. 14.

[61] *Rajya Sabha Debates*, vol. 97, no. 17 (2 September 1976), col. 11.

[62] She had emigrated to Washington, DC. In September 1976 she testified against Mrs Gandhi's regime before the Subcommittee on International Organizations of the Committee on International Relations. See her statement in MLP, reel 1.

[63] In 1971 his failed bid to the Lok Sabha as an independent for the Ulhasnagar constituency was backed by the Jana Sangh and the Shiv Sena. During the Emergency, he divided his time between Canada and the United States, protesting at rallies and on radio. In 1977 he was returned as a Janata Party MP, and later went on to serve as a BJP cabinet minister.

[64] Sahasrabuddhe and Vajpayee, *The People versus Emergency*, p. 517; the advertisements in a FISI pamphlet titled "The International Conference", 24 April 1976, in MLP, reel 6.

[65] For more, see Jaffrelot and Therwath, "The Sangh Parivar and the Hindu Diaspora", pp. 278–95.

meetings in all four corners of London—Wembley, Chalk Farm, Ilford, Croydon—as well as a march to the Indian High Commission. Along with the Bharatiya Swayamsevak Sangh, its African counterpart, the HSS helped set up the Friends of India Society International (FISI), an RSS cell in London.[66] Abroad, Sanghis spoke not in the language of Hindu nationalism but human rights and the Cold War to attract attention to their cause. For example, Subramaniam Swamy, who authored a pamphlet for FISI, blamed the Emergency on a left-wing conspiracy masterminded by Mohan Kumaramangalam—by then long dead—and the Soviets.[67] In a letter it sent Amnesty International, the FISI portrayed Balasaheb Deoras as a philosopher and social activist—as it were an Indian Solzhenitsyn—conveniently eschewing mention of the RSS.[68]

The activities of Mrs Gandhi's opponents abroad reinforced critical assessments of the Emergency. As time wore on the lashings from Western outlets grew in ferocity, in part because these presses, shorn of their foreign correspondents, had increasingly come to rely on RSS outposts in their countries to source news on India.[69] The BBC, for instance, once got hold of a news story when its broadcasters spotted it in the pages of a diaspora paper in London run by a Jana Sangh MLA, who, in turn, had received this particular piece of information from a certain Narendra Modi, a *pracharak* in Gujarat. Protests in the early months of the Emergency impressed upon the MEA the imbrications between the Western media and Indian diaspora. To this end all embassies were asked to prepare a "blacklist of undesirable Indians" against whom action could be taken—passports impounded and scholarships rescinded.[70] But it never quite dawned on the Indian leaders that the poor coverage was not uniquely the handiwork of conniving Sanghis, but rather their own doing. This they were to learn the hard way. When the Indian High Commission in London lobbied the Wilson and Callaghan administrations to rein in the British press, the best it could manage was to get a few journals of the diaspora that were critical of the Emergency, such as *Amar Deep* and *Gujarat Samachar*, to turn coat and start endorsing it.[71]

<hr>

66 Anderson and Clibbens, "'Smugglers of Truth'", pp. 10–12, 14.
67 See his *What Killed Democracy in India: An Analysis of Mrs Gandhi's India* (Friends of India Society, no date), in MLP, reel 6.
68 FISI to Amnesty International, 10 January 1977, in MLP, reel 6.
69 Sahasrabuddhe and Vajpayee, *The People versus Emergency*, pp. 514–18.
70 Anderson and Clibbens, "'Smugglers of Truth'", pp. 26, 35.
71 Sahasrabuddhe and Vajpayee, *The People versus Emergency*, p. 512.

International mobilisation against the Emergency gained momentum in 1976. In March, in the *New York Times*, eighty Americans, including Nobel laureates, historians, political scientists, newspapermen, and popular writers, excoriated Mrs Gandhi for suspending fundamental rights.[72] Across the Atlantic, with a dreary sense of *déjà vu*, the London *Times* on India's Independence Day, 15 August, carried a six-column petition deploring the Emergency, signed by a similar number of local MPs, academics, and literary personages.[73]

The regime also drew criticism from media freedom watchdogs like the International Press Institute, and from national federations of trade unions such as the AFL-CIO, and eventually even foreign governments. Charles Windsor cancelled a visit to India, as did US President Ford more vocally: "It is really very sad that 600 million people have lost what they have had since the mid-nineteen-forties", he said.[74] At a soirée in Buckingham Palace, Louis Mountbatten expressed his dismay to the Indian high commissioner: "You have locked up all my friends", he said of his royal peers in Indian prisons.[75]

Mrs Gandhi's attempts to clamp down on foreign criticism and the opprobrium itself formed something of a feedback loop. When the diaspora coalesced around the Indians for Democracy in Washington, for example, the MEA responded by impounding the passports of four of its members. That only heightened the uproar. The same ensued when the Indian leadership censured protestors in London who were campaigning to free Jayaprakash Narayan by tying themselves to a statue of M.K. Gandhi.[76] And when the Socialist International planned to send a delegation that included West German chancellor Willy Brandt and Irish Labour politician

---

[72] *NYT*, 5 March 1976, p. 6. The figures included Joan Baez, Noam Chomsky, Bernard Cohn, Francine Frankel, Allen Ginsberg, Lewis Mumford, Dorothy Norman, Arthur Schlesinger, Myron Weiner, and John Updike.

[73] *Times*, 15 August 1976, p. 3. They included Fenner Brockway, Nirad Chaudhuri, Daniel Ellsberg, Milovan Djilas, A.J.P. Taylor, Mirabehn, Spike Milligan, W.H. Morris-Jones, Philip Noel-Baker, E.F. Schumacher, and over five dozen British MPs.

[74] *NYT*, 19 September 1975, p. 8. Ford's criticism of authoritarianism, however, was not why Indo-American relations briefly soured. As Kissinger pointed out, what piqued the DC establishment was Mrs Gandhi's "continued allegations against the CIA": Chaudhuri, "Re-reading the Indian Emergency", p. 491.

[75] Singh, *One Life is Not Enough*, p. 162.

[76] BBC radio news bulletin on 4 October, 0730 hours. For the transcription, see the All India Radio Files of 1975, Subject File 2.

Conor Cruise O'Brien to see Narayan, Mrs Gandhi, to avoid the bad press, denied it permission.[77] The backlash to that decision was even worse for her. Soon after, criticism poured in from the Austrian Chancellor Bruno Kreisky and the Swedish Prime Minister Olof Palme as well.[78]

In short, Mrs Gandhi's counter-propaganda efforts to legitimise the Emergency came to nothing. At first the responsibility for this failure fell to the diaspora itself. "India should use these people in its publicity drive in the same manner as Israel uses the Jews", she wrote to the MEA.[79] When the Indian *hasbara* failed, the government freighted party heavy-weights to make the case for the regime. Y.B. Chavan, one of the first cabinet emissaries dispatched from Emergency India, was heckled in Chicago and booed when he insisted on answering only a select few written questions after his talk. Deputy I&B minister Dharam Vir Sinha's voyage to America went along the same lines. After realising that audiences were less interested in his anodyne talk on "Gandhiji and his Relevance" than in quizzing him on contemporary affairs, he "lost his temper", "left the hall", and "cancelled a press conference."[80] Triloki Nath Kaul, ambassador to the United States, tried pathetically to berate the American media rather than discuss the Emergency itself—theirs was a "knee jerk reaction of a very free and affluent press", he suggested in despair.[81] Similarly, other foreign outings ended up as evasive, low-key affairs: these included H.R. Gokhale's to Washington, DC, Om Mehta's to New York, Hitendra Desai's to London; and Congress general secretaries Purabi Mukherjee, P.V. Narasimha Rao, and Maragatham Chandrasekar's to Iraq, Tanzania, and Bulgaria, respectively.[82] All were quick to realise,

---

[77] The Indian government, on its part, concluded that the Germans were "erroneously drawing from their own prewar experiences": see the Ministry of External Affairs' "Background Note on the Federal Republic of Germany", 17 January 1976, P.N. Haksar Papers, Instalments I and II, Subject File 85. Despite the criticisms emanating from journalists and politicians of the FRG, its aid to India in 1976–7—DM 365 million—was of the same order as the previous year.

[78] International Press Institute, "Press Squeeze in India", Jayaprakash Narayan Papers, Instalment III, Subject File 320.

[79] Anderson and Clibbens, "'Smugglers of Truth'", p. 38.

[80] *Satya Samachar*, 10 November 1976, p. 2, in "Documentation of Emergency Period in India", MLP, microfilm copy, reel 1.

[81] Cited in Chaudhuri, "Re-reading the Indian Emergency", p. 484.

[82] *Satya Samachar*, 10 November 1976, pp. 2–3, in MLP, reel 1; Zaidi, *The Annual Register of Indian Political Parties—vol. 23*, p. 565.

in the words of London's deputy high commissioner, that "it was virtually impossible to sell the Emergency" abroad.[83]

This was quite a blow to Mrs Gandhi, who treasured international opinion. The truth of this is amply evident in her correspondence with Dorothy Norman, her New York photographer-friend. During the Emergency their back-and-forth came to an abrupt halt when the premier discovered that her girlfriend of many years had joined ranks with fellow high-society New Yorkers in demanding an end to authoritarianism in India. Sending her what were probably some trinkets as memorabilia, Indira wrote her an acid letter, "if you can bear to accept a gift from the Great Dictator, here is something which I had kept for you some years ago—it is from Bhutan."[84] It would take the death of Sanjay in 1980 for the two women to warm to each other once again. The vindictiveness on Mrs Gandhi's part, it is fair to conclude, stemmed from a sense of betrayal, that from the one foreign friend who was to have her back at all times.

The proud display in her house of accolades she had received from international organisations, both before and after the Emergency, too speak of her desire for adventitious approval. These included honorary doctorates from the University of Oxford and Sorbonne in 1971 and 1981, respectively, a Soviet commemorative stamp in the latter year, a plaque presented to her in 1982 by the Population Council, a certificate from the United Nations Population Award in 1983.[85] The last two were the products of spin during her third term, another indication that Mrs Gandhi craved Western validation. Ramachandra Guha is certainly on to something in his speculation that it was Bernard Levin's acerbic reporting in the *Times* in the last quarter of 1976 that convinced Mrs Gandhi to call off the Emergency.[86] The same could be said of the scathing quintet of reports that John Saar of the *Washington Post* filed in November after an undercover visit to the country as a businessman.[87]

Indira Gandhi was even more sensitive to the decline in India's image as Pakistan's improved. Just eleven days before she announced elections, the premier next door, Zulfiqar Ali Bhutto, had done the same in Pakistan. Mrs

---

[83] Singh, *One Life is Not Enough*, p. 165.

[84] Norman, *Indira Gandhi*, pp. 149–50.

[85] These can be seen in the flesh at the Indira Gandhi Memorial Museum in Delhi.

[86] Guha, *India After Gandhi's*, pp. 519–21. Apart from the *Daily Telegraph*—the only "paper which was not against us"—the entire gamut of the British press was critical of the Emergency: Nehru, *Nice Guys Finish Second*, p. 561.

[87] *Washington Post*, 7, 8, 9, 10, and 11 November 1976, all p. 1.

Gandhi, like any self-respecting nationalist, knew better than to be cast as a dictator while her South Asian nemesis was enjoying his moment in the sun: it certainly upset the natural order of the world, as if Alice had stepped through the looking-glass. "Could the image of India be that of a dictatorship while Pakistan became a democracy?", she wondered aloud.[88] "Even they are taunting us for not being a democracy! We must have an election", she said to one of her associates soon after.[89] In essence the perception of India abroad, more than international pressure *per se*—after all, there were no sanctions against India—explains in part why Mrs Gandhi decided to hold elections in 1977.

Fighting to Win—At Any Cost

A third and most obvious reason to hold elections in 1977 was that Mrs Gandhi felt she would win. Her party was accustomed to permanent incumbency, so the prospect of losing power would have indeed seemed slim. Inflation for the past two years had been lower than in the previous five. The generous monsoons of 1975 and 1976 had translated into bountiful harvests, maintaining peace in the countryside. Intelligence reports from December 1976 struck the right note: sure, disaffection was growing, but then again, only an election could halt it from creating "serious law and order problems."[90] The memos produced by the IB typically put the Congress figure at 220 to 270 seats, suggesting she was certain to retain power, either alone or in coalition.[91] Moreover, the Doubting Thomases who suggested that the grand old party no longer enjoyed the kind of popularity it once did had all been sidelined. This made it all the harder for Mrs Gandhi to keep up to date with public opinion, but also much simpler for her to just go along with the reports she received.

She also now believed she could rely on a new political force, the Youth Congress, at a time when the Congress seemed more and more unreliable. In October 1976 news had travelled of meetings held by disgruntled Congress MLAs in Uttar Pradesh, Punjab, Haryana, and Bihar, where parliamentarians had laid into the Forty-second Amendment. And in November, 150 Congress MPs had abstained from the vote that postponed

---

[88] Jayakar, *Indira Gandhi*, p. 308.
[89] Yunus, *Persons, Passions, and Politics*, p. 259.
[90] Rajeswar, *India*, p. 92.
[91] Hewitt, *Political Mobilisation and Democracy in India*, p. 147.

elections a second time. By then Mrs Gandhi was certain that her plans to transfer agrarian competencies from the states to the union would be stonewalled by the largely rural parliamentarians.[92] The Youth Congress, then, appeared a more loyal instrument.

Under Sanjay's leadership this outfit of 700,000 had grown by February 1977 to include over six million members.[93] It was as early as 30 September 1976 that the YC president Ambika Soni had called for elections and "relaxation" of the Emergency—the objective, of course, was to corner for the youth organisation as many tickets as possible. In the event, when the Congress got down to the business of fielding candidates in January 1977, around 150 to 200 of the total of 542 were picked by Sanjay, most of them "young, inexperienced, and unknown", and a few even with criminal records.[94] Mrs Gandhi, good *materfamilias*, was happy to encourage the strengthening of her son's hold over the parliamentary party, for Sanjay was not, in any real sense, a competitor; his gain was hers. Besides, her party could do with more "discipline".

In any case, what could possibly go wrong? The opposition leaders and their cadres, many of them just released from prison, had but eight weeks to campaign. And to file their nomination papers they had even less, precluding in effect the protracted negotiations that were necessary for the building of alliances. Some, such as George Fernandes, were kept incarcerated even over this period. Just a week before the country went to the polls, local organisers of the Janata were picked up and sent packing to prison—for no reason except to prevent them campaigning.[95] Furthermore, while the Home Ministry had instructed the states "to relax the rigour of emergency [*sic*]" on 20 January, authoritarian rule had, both *de facto* and *de jure*, remained in place.[96] A few regulations governing the press were lifted, but the Press Censorship Act continued. Journals were handed out a document by the Ministry of Information and Broadcasting—the "Code of Ethics"— which offered guidelines on how to cover the hustings.[97] The government's broadcasting monopolies, Doordarshan and AIR, were given a list of thirty "specific themes" to cover, the accent being on making Mrs Gandhi and the

---

92 Ibid., p. 10.
93 Its own leaders put the figure at ten million: Mendelsohn, "The Collapse of the Indian National Congress", p. 55.
94 Weiner, *India at the Polls*, p. 15.
95 *TOI*, 16 March 1977, p. 9.
96 *SCR*, vol. 3, p. 77.
97 *SCR*, vol. 1, p. 38.

Emergency "appeal easily to the people". L. Dayal, principal information officer, and Harry J. D'Penha, chief censor, made veiled threats to editors.[98] And the I&B minister V.C. Shukla made certain that nothing "which might undermine the aims of the Emergency" was published. He kept his word. For instance, he saw to it that an AIR correspondent in Raipur who covered a speech by Vijaya Lakshmi Pandit—Mrs Gandhi's aunt and, for the purposes of the poll, adversary—was fired.[99] When the opposition parties held their largest rally on 6 March in the capital, Doordarshan broadcast *Bobby*, a Bollywood tear-jerker, with the intention of keeping Delhi's middle classes indoors. The public-service broadcasters were pressed into the service of the party more directly as well, their personnel coerced into campaign work of all kinds, from translating Congress manifestos into regional languages to designing posters.[100] Two days before the country went to the polls Sanjay's jeep was ambushed by a gang in the Gandhi pocket borough of Amethi. Since he emerged unscathed from a volley of bullets and the matter was not investigated, it seems fair to surmise that the whole episode was a set-up to garner sympathy and inflate the threat to the incumbents.[101] Even if victory was inevitable for the ruling party, no stone was left unturned to obliterate the competition. For, as D.K. Barooah saw it, the Emergency was not only a time to consolidate Mrs Gandhi's rule but also an opportunity to ensure that there would be "no other party except [*sic*] Congress to go for the next election."[102]

With the stick, as always, came the carrot: the Congress government in Uttar Pradesh promised to halve land-revenue taxes; in Bihar, to offer free medical care to those who protested alongside Congressmen against the Raj; in West Bengal, "increase rent allowances and medical grants"; in Haryana, Himachal Pradesh, and Punjab, set aside "additional dearness allowances". In all, some $200 million in state funds was spent on eleventh-

---

[98] Ibid., pp. 47, 38–9. They were asked to publish opinion pieces by Congress panegyrists such as Rasheeduddin Khan and to suppress news of sterilisations.

[99] An influential figure, Vijaya Lakshmi Pandit had served under her brother, Jawaharlal Nehru, as ambassador to Moscow, Washington, Mexico, London, and Dublin; head of the Indian delegation to the UN; and governor of Maharashtra. After Nehru's death she inherited his Lok Sabha seat. See Pandit, *The Scope of Happiness*, pp. 13–23. See also *SCR*, vol. 1, pp. 45–6.

[100] "Misuse of Media", no date, SCP, Subject File 17, pp. 16, 90; "Das Committee of Inquiry: Translation of Congress Manifesto", 9 June 1977, ibid, p. 28.

[101] *TOI*, 16 March 1977, pp. 1, 9.

[102] Selbourne, *An Eye to India*, p. 198.

hour pork-barrel programmes.[103] Alliances struck in opposite ends of the country—with the AIADMK in Tamil Nadu and the National Conference in Jammu and Kashmir—were to compound the distorting benefits of first past the post.[104] Reports later emerged of large wads of cash being carried in "tin boxes" to the constituencies of Sanjay and his cronies.[105] On the whole the asymmetrical campaign, as well as the congeries that passed for her opposition, were enough to convince Mrs Gandhi and virtually every observer of the Indian political scene that victory in the polls for the Congress behemoth was a foregone conclusion.

The 1977 Polls

After she announced the snap election, Mrs Gandhi's adversaries dealt her two deft blows that completely altered the shape of the contest. First, on 23 January 1977, four days after the leading lights of the four largest parties in the opposition—Charan Singh of the BLD, Atal Bihari Vajpayee of the Jana Sangh, Asoka Mehta of the Congress (O), and Surendra Mohan of the Socialist Party—met at the residence of Mrs Gandhi's *bête noire* Morarji Desai, the merger of this quartet was announced. Arrangements for a new national executive were quickly hammered out: when it was convened for the first time, it comprised nine Congress (O) members, six Socialists, five each from the Sangh and the BLD, and two Congress rebels, the weightages being a broad reflection of the balance of power within the Janata.[106] Emboldened by this rapid consolidation, the DMK, CPI(M), and Akali Dal quickly entered into seat adjustments with it. The CPI turned coat as well, backing the new formation, even as it hedged its bets by allying with the grand old party in a handful of constituencies. Congress Young Turks Chandra Shekhar, Ram Dhan, and Krishan Kant, all figures expelled by Mrs Gandhi, joined the Janata, too.

However, it was the second blow, which came on 2 February, that did for her. That day Jagjivan Ram, along with H.N. Bahuguna and Nandini Satpathy, former chief ministers of Uttar Pradesh and Orissa, all of whom

---

[103] Weiner, *India at the Polls*, p. 48.

[104] This served the Congress well. The NC and AIADMK polled 30.6 and 35 per cent; in combination with the Congress' 22.3 and 15.2 per cent vote share in the two states, the Congress and its allies managed to bag 4 of the 5 seats in Jammu and Kashmir and 32 of the 39 in Tamil Nadu.

[105] Mukherjee, *The Dramatic Decade*, p. 113.

[106] Limaye, *Janata Party Experiment*, vol. 1, p. 215.

had been on the receiving end of Sanjay's machinations, decided to strike out on their own. Along with their resignations came two important announcements: the formation of a new party, the Congress for Democracy (CFD), and an electoral arrangement with the Janata.[107] The former defence minister continued to command impressive support among the Dalits of the Hindi belt; it was only to be expected, then, that he would refuse to countenance the de-selection of all his men, a process already under way. Surely, the decimation of his base was only a prelude to his eventual ejection from the cabinet, Ram reasoned.[108] The last straw, of course, was when he snuck a peek at the list of candidates drawn up by the Congress Parliamentary Board: virtually every ticket meant for his faction had been cornered by Sanjay's coterie.[109] Power and prestige for the Dalit leader, then, would have to be sought outside the grand old party. And here came crumbling down one important pillar in the Congress' "coalition of extremes"—upper castes at one pole, Dalits and Muslims at the other.

In the event the troika of Ram, Bahuguna, and Satpathy were joined by thirty-five Congress MPs, putting the CFD in the unique position where it enjoyed the advantages of both incumbency and insurgent appeal. To halt the growing exodus from the party, a panic-stricken Mrs Gandhi decided to clip Sanjay's wings. The number of Youth Congressmen given party nominations was slashed to twenty, a tenth of the previous figure, and the old guard was assiduously courted.[110] When the Congress released its manifesto on 8 February, it was clear to all that the party was on the defensive. In addition to the usual nostrums about secularism and socialism was a vehement defence of its "faith in democracy": "absolute, irrevocable, and unshakeable."[111]

What of the other traditional Congress base, the Muslims? It appeared that Mrs Gandhi was set to lose the qaum as well, in no small part because of Sanjay's palpably Islamophobic gentrification and sterilisation drives in Delhi and beyond. Convincing their co-religionists to turn their backs on the grand old party were two Abdullahs, both local leaders who, for the press of the time, were rightly seen as bellwethers of the community. The first, Syed Abdullah Bukhari, the Shahi Imam of Delhi's Jama

---

107 Ram said his party would "try to avoid triangular contests": *The Indian Express*, no date, cited in Lal, *Elections Extraordinary*, p. 49.

108 Roy, "Why Mrs Gandhi Lost", p. 165.

109 Hewitt, *Political Mobilisation and Democracy in India*, p. 147.

110 Weiner, *India at the Polls*, pp. 15–16.

111 Zaidi, *The Annual Register of Indian Political Parties—vol. 24*, p. 370.

Masjid, met Ram shortly after the formation of the CFD, expressing his support for the coalition and going as far as to suggest that the ban on the RSS be lifted, for, apparently, the Hindu nationalists were not behind communal violence; the Congress alone was.[112] Bukhari actively campaigned for the Janata in the capital, Bombay, Hyderabad, and in other Muslim enclaves across the country, winning local elites to his cause. The second, Sheikh Abdullah, chief minister of Jammu and Kashmir, was equally responsible for making the violent gentrification and family-planning programmes the *causes célèbres* of the Muslim community. His visit to the Turkman Gate in May 1976, especially, which was followed by his damning indictment of the living conditions of the capital's Muslims, brought home some ugly truths.[113] When it came to the election, however, Sheikh Abdullah's National Conference aligned itself with the Congress, as it had in 1975 when he was sworn in as chief minister. Still, his begrudging support aside, Bukhari's defection, and even more importantly the impact of Sanjay's policies in 1976, swayed a sizeable number of Muslims. As it turned out, the Congress would win only 16 of the 78 seats reserved for Scheduled Castes, and in just 20 of the 81 constituencies with large Muslim populations.[114]

The winner, the Janata Party, was as much of a "heteroclite cartel" as the Congress.[115] Bringing together the CFD, the Jana Sangh, the BLD, the Congress (O), and the Socialists, the glue holding the Janata was the bitterness of having been locked up in Mrs Gandhi's prisons. The entreaties of Jayaprakash Narayan, who from his ward at the Jaslok Hospital was pressing them all to set aside their differences, were of import as well.[116] At first Narayan was sceptical: the poll "would be a farce", he contended.[117] George Fernandes, who from his prison cell was soon to win by a lead of 330,000 votes—at the time among the largest margins in postcolonial Indian history—had concurred: "She will defeat [us] ... and legitimise the Emergency

[112] Wright, "Muslims and the 1977 Indian Elections", p. 1215.

[113] His statement is reproduced *in extenso* in *Satya Samachar*, 12 June 1976, p. 9, in MLP, reel 1.

[114] Weiner, "Congress Restored", p. 341.

[115] Ali, "The Fall of Congress in India", p. 45.

[116] This proved vital when it came to forming ministries, where each constituent party wanted their own men in power: Jayaprakash Narayan to Morarji Desai, 27 March, 4 and 5 April 1977, Morarji Desai Papers, Subject File 9.

[117] Transcript of interview with Madhu Dandavate, Acc. No. 778, NMML Oral History Project, p. 127.

and send us back to jail."[118] But then again both Narayan and Fernandes were well aware that spurning the democratic challenge after months of castigating authoritarianism would have been disingenuous. The election would have to be taken seriously. The merger helped tilt simple plurality voting in their favour.

Spurred by the momentum of constituencies flocking to it, the Janata components succeeded in fashioning a consensus despite their differences. The party presidency was handed to Chandra Shekhar, whose "secular and socialist" credentials, it was hoped, "would falisify [*sic*] the Congress Party's claim that the Janata Party is RSS dominated."[119] The party manifesto announced that "bread cannot be juxtaposed against liberty, [for] the two are inseparable." It promised to return Indian democracy to the very *status quo ante* the Janata men had once rebelled against—gone were the platitudes of "total revolution"—and to correct the "urban bias" of its political economy.[120] Still, this semblance of unity could not mask the contradictory pulls and pushes of its partisans: only it would take until after the polls for the macroeconomic nightmares to become manifest. Some in the party wanted higher taxes, others preferred not to crowd out private savings. A few called for higher government spending, while the rest either shuddered at the prospect of extending the tax base to the countryside, worried about inflation, or carped about the need for balanced budgets. Some wanted to lure Western capital, others to kick out the multinationals already present in the republic. The Left called for land reform, the Right in this coalition happened to be men who belonged to the small gentry, the dominant castes, and even the aristocracy. Some drew the support of industrialists, others of trade unions. But few at the time had the inclination to get their heads around these antinomies. The new party's "line of attack", both in the campaign and later in office, was simple enough: to highlight the "atrocities committed during the Emergency" and the malversations of the Congress' first family.[121]

---

[118] Ibid., p. 217.

[119] The Janata Party's "Notes of the Discussion on Publicity Strategy", 18 May 1977, PMSP, File 37/692/1977 PMS.

[120] Lal, *Elections Extraordinary*, p. 103. The manifesto can be found in its entirety in ibid., pp. 102–32. Academics and journalists Rajni Kothari, Raj Krishna, and George Verghese were involved in authoring the document: Verghese, *First Draft*, p. 237.

[121] Weiner, *India at the Polls*, p. 108ff.

That the elections were free and fair was an "achievement" many remarked upon, both during and after the poll. Arguably the press was freer and more ambivalent than ever before. The papers reflected a spectrum of opinion, with what were virtually state organs, such as the *Hindustan Times* and the *Hindu*, on the one hand; the fiercely independent *Indian Express*, whose circulation shot up threefold in the span of a few weeks, on the other; and the *Times of India*, the newspaper of record, somewhere in between.[122] A recent law had made elections in India, as it were, even "fairer": votes were no longer counted at every polling station; ballot boxes in every constituency were instead totalled together, making it harder for parties to tell with any degree of precision where votes were coming from, thus sparing voters from potential reprisals. This development was heavily advertised by the press and the Election Commission in the run-up to the election, no doubt deterring intimidators and freeing voter conscience.[123] The polling days, from 16 to 20 March, went by without controversy, the 383,000 polling stations being closely watched by 208 state and central armed battalions and 467,000 police officers.[124]

The results, which were announced on 22 March, make for difficult reading. Certainly, they were not the blanket repudiation of authoritarianism that much of the press touted at the time. Since 1980, especially, when Mrs Gandhi returned to power, this thesis—the collocation of regime type and party preference—has become more tenuous. How could the republic's citizens bring themselves to elect an autocrat again? To Malte Pehl, who uses Spearman's rank correlation coefficient to test a number of independent variables against the Congress seat and vote shares in 1977, the variable to have maximum impact on the election was the unity among non-Congress parties; voter association with regime type was of little moment. Next in significance was the thoroughness with which detentions and sterilisations were conducted in the state. The variable of least consequence was voter turnout, belying the received narrative of massive electoral participation—of forthright citizens marching to the polling stations in defence of democracy; at 60.4 per cent in

---

122 Ibid., p. 23.

123 This was first introduced in 1971, when Mrs Gandhi's Congress appeared to be at its weakest. The intention was to make it impossible for the better institutionalised Congress (O) to know with any certainty which neighbourhoods were voting against them.

124 "Note analysing the deployment of forces for the general elections to be held in March 1977", 27 January 1977, MHAP, File III.11039/2/77-G&Q, vol. I KW pps.

1977, it was only moderately higher than in 1971 (55.3 per cent), and marginally lower than in 1967 (61.3 per cent).[125]

The rout of the Congress, then, can be primarily attributed to the distorting effect of plurality voting, the very system that allowed the party to pile up huge majorities in previous elections. So while the Congress vote share fell from 44 to 35 per cent between 1971 and 1977, the decline in its seat share was much steeper: from 68 to 28 per cent.[126] The same logic worked to the Janata's advantage: polling about 20 per cent more votes than did the grand old party, it won nearly twice as many seats—298 to the Congress' 153.[127]

But the excesses of the Emergency still sealed the fate of the Congress, which proved to be resilient only in parts of the country that saw less of it. That the Hindi belt—which saw the worst of the regime—had it worse than the southern peninsular states was reflected in the voter turnout. While it grew by 9, 10.5, 12, 13.5, and 20 per cent in Haryana, Uttar Pradesh, Bihar, the Punjab, and Himachal Pradesh, respectively, the corresponding figures for the southern and western states of Maharashtra, Andhra Pradesh, Karnataka, and Kerala were 1, 3.3, 5.5, and 14.5 per cent—and in Tamil Nadu voter turnout *fell* by 3 per cent. The divergence, of course, was not entirely down to the greater incidence of "little Sanjays"—politicians, government officials, landlords, and local toughs—in the North, where the regime was better institutionalised.[128] In the South the authoritarian–democrat dyad was complicated by the presence of the Jana Sangh, BLD, and Socialists in the Janata, all parties that, in their bid to refashion the peripheries in the image of the heartland, wanted to supplant the local Dravidian languages of these lands with Hindi.[129]

---

[125] See Pehl, "Democratic Backlash?", pp. 319–20. Blair suggests otherwise: that if Kerala and Gujarat are omitted from the analysis, voter turnout assumes greater significance. Mayer counters, suggesting the meaningless of excluding certain states over others: if instead West Bengal and Tamil Nadu are excluded, voter turnout shows a strong *negative* correlation with the anti-Congress vote. See Blair, "Mrs Gandhi's Emergency", pp. 259–60, and Mayer, "Congress (I), Emergency (I)", p. 149, n70. While the effects of voter turnout on the fortunes of individual parties may be contested, what is certain, as we will see below, is that the sharp rise in turnout in the North as compared with the South is an indication that citizens of the former felt a much larger incentive to vote after the Emergency than did their southern counterparts.

[126] 1971: 355 seats; 1977: 153 seats.

[127] The Janata clinched 54 per cent of the seats with 41 per cent of the vote.

[128] Weiner, "The 1977 Parliamentary Elections in India", p. 625.

[129] Narain, "India 1977", p. 110. For more on the North–South divide, see Chapter 5.

All in all, there can be no doubt that the Congress' dramatic fall in vote share in the North—in Bihar from 40 to 23 per cent; Haryana 53 to 18; Uttar Pradesh 48 to 25; Delhi 65 to 30—was the result of the popular repudiation of Emergency rule. The Congress took just 5 seats of the 290 in the eight major states of the North, a steep decline from its showing of 192 in the previous Parliament.[130] And there was no greater rebuke to the incumbents than Mrs Gandhi's and Sanjay's humiliating upsets in their own constituencies, Rae Bareilly and Amethi. The prime minister lost to Raj Narain, her old foe, and her son to Ravindra Pratap Singh, a local bruiser who had spent the last eighteen months in prison. With them their cronies—Bansi Lal, H.R. Gokhale, Pranab Mukherjee, Swaran Singh, V.C. Shukla—all went down in defeat.

Would the Congress happily transfer power to the Janata? It was not immediately clear. Mrs Gandhi made much of the fact that she would "abide" by the results: having to state what in any democratic society was plainly obvious hinted otherwise. Just before the poll she had had Mani Misra, who was in charge of military intelligence, replaced by a friendly Kashmiri face, Hardyal Kaul, brother of T.N. Kaul, the ambassador to the United States. It was about the same time that the capital witnessed a most unusual bustle: the military top brass was to be seen liaising with the political leadership at a number of conferences.[131] And soon after the election Mrs Gandhi and her son invited T.N. Raina, chief of army staff (COAS), for a chat. "There are about 300 districts in the country. One infantry platoon is sufficient to control each district", Sanjay told the COAS, "Thus we can control India by deploying 300 platoons or about 25 infantry battalions; a mere three or four divisions. The party [the Congress], supported by paramilitary forces and the police, can deal with other administrative details." Mrs Gandhi's presence in the room confirmed her acquiescence to the suggestion. Raina, who owed his job to her because she had superseded others to hand it over to him, however, refused to entertain this harebrained, albeit as he put it "mathematically correct", scheme.[132] As a result the planned coup died a quick death.

The first family was on its last legs. A few days after the upset, the inevitable question of leadership raised its head. Meeting at the residence of Chandrajit Yadav, 125 Congressmen put forth their demand to have party

---

[130] Blair, "Mrs Gandhi's Emergency", p. 260.

[131] Kuldip Nayar, *The Judgement*, p. 176.

[132] Wilkinson, *Army and Nation*, p. 147.

president D.K. Barooah removed and Sanjay's right-hand man Bansi Lal expelled. That achieved, Y.B. Chavan and K. Brahmananda Reddy, joined by the regime's old loyalists C. Subramanian and T.A. Pai, who by now had turned coat, levelled their sights on Mrs Gandhi. The criticisms were of course too little and too late, inviting the predictable *tu quoque*. A more sustained and decorous bid for power followed in May when the party presidency was put to a vote, but to no avail. Reddy, Mrs Gandhi's candidate (he was back on her side) beat S.S. Ray, the legal architect of the Emergency (who had by then switched sides), 317 to 160.[133] Intra-party peace, however, was short-lived. Only a few months later the former premier, true to character, prompted Reddy's defection to the old guard when she made a failed bid to take over the presidency herself. In January 1978 the Congress split over the issue. Chavan, then the head of the CPP, took with him the bulk of the party, leaving behind the Congress (Indira). Tellingly, unlike in 1969 no attempt was made to conceal the naked power struggle in an ideological casing.

The Unmaking of the Emergency—How to Punish the Culprits?

On 23 March 1977, Mrs Gandhi's penultimate day in office, she had B.D. Jatti, the acting president since Ahmed's death on 11 February, revoke the internal Emergency and MISA. Upon taking office the Janata lifted the ban on the twenty-six parties, withdrew the regime of prior restraint, and called off the external Emergency. At its outset the incumbents reversed many of the amendments that had concentrated power in the office of prime minister in particular and the executive in general. Over the coming months the ability of the courts to adjudicate on prime ministerial matters was restored, five-year terms reintroduced, the life of President's Rule capped at six months, and pressing the panic button made harder: only in cases of "armed rebellion", instead of "internal disturbance", could a state of emergency be declared with a two-thirds majority in Parliament; additionally, this legislative mandate required bi-annual renewal.[134] Later, in the Supreme Court, the question of parliamentary supremacy came back to the fore with the Minerva Mills case of 1980, the fears induced by Mrs Gandhi's

---

[133] The other two candidates, Karan Singh and Nek Ram Sharma, polled 16 and 3 votes: Zaidi, *The Annual Register of Indian Political Parties—vol. 24*, p. 220.

[134] Indira Gandhi, then briefly in parliament, was among the majority that passed the Forty-fourth Amendment.

return pushing the judiciary to assert itself by striking down the clauses of the Forty-second Amendment of 1976 that bestowed on Parliament unfettered amendment powers. This, in effect, was a return to the *status quo ante*: the basic structure doctrine, warts and all.

After the 1977 elections Morarji Desai, the seniormost figure in the coalition, was sworn in as prime minister.[135] The Janata's first order of business was to consolidate power. Less than a month into his term, Desai, citing the precedent of 1971, argued that Mrs Gandhi's party had lost the confidence of voters in the states and imposed President's Rule in nine of them, demanding fresh elections. In its efforts to bury the Congress, then, the Janata was already beginning to resemble the grand old party itself. The dismissal of the nine Congress state governments even received the Supreme Court's stamp of approval. B.D. Jatti, acting president, at first refused to dissolve the assemblies, proving his loyalty to the party that had installed him as vice president. But to make him comply with the executive the Janata rulers, ironically, invoked the dreaded Emergency-era Forty-second Amendment, which forced him to fall in line.[136] Snap elections were called, propelling the Janata to power in Rajasthan, Uttar Pradesh, Haryana, Himachal Pradesh, Madhya Pradesh, Bihar, and Orissa; the CPI(M) in West Bengal; and the AIADMK in Tamil Nadu, all of whom were firmly ensconced in office by June 1977.

Within two weeks of coming to power the Janata, egged on by Charan Singh, decided to "bring to book all those guilty of excesses." Desai, not to be outdone, suggested "maximum punishment" for Mrs Gandhi.[137] To this end eight commissions of inquiry headed by retired judges were set up to investigate Mrs Gandhi, her son, some Congress chief ministers, the maltreatment of Jayaprakash Narayan in prison during the Emergency, and the death of Rammanohar Lohia.[138] Soon after, the CBI had the former premier's phones tapped, her Mehrauli farm searched with metal detectors for buried treasures, and Sanjay's Cessna licence revoked.

---

[135] The Jana Sangh, which had nearly half as many MPs again as the Congress (O), coolly accepted this.

[136] Nayar, *The Judgement*, p. 191.

[137] *SW*, 5 December 1978.

[138] Lohia, who died in 1967, was a major Socialist figure and architect of the SVD governments of the 1960s that were the Janata's predecessor. Congress skulduggery, it was widely suspected in Janata circles, was to blame: Guha, *India After Gandhi*, p. 528.

The *pièce de resistance* was the constitution of the Shah Commission on 7 April 1977.[139] Culling from the 48,500 complaints it received, this commission decided to investigate 2342 of them, referring 35,487 to state governments and central ministries.[140] Working with a small staff of 324 that shuttled endlessly between the states, which were tasked with collecting information, and the capital, where it was pieced together, the commission initiated investigations in May, commenced hearings in September, and delivered three reports in March, April, and August 1978.[141] The pressures it worked under were immense, ministers urging it to make haste and Congressmen either dismissing it entirely or threatening its members anonymously.[142] Justice J.C. Shah, for instance, received letters allegedly sent with the consent of 500,000 Youth Congress workers who threatened to demolish his house, sterilise him, his wife, his "family members including all small children [*sic*]", and then execute him.[143] But Congress fears that Shah was a "motivated" partisan, even if genuine, were unfounded. In truth, this judge cut an ambivalent figure. During the Emergency the only instance when he had joined the ranks of the resistance was his attendance at a seminar discussing the perils of presidentialism. But for the better part of its course he was, in fact, a sympathiser of the regime, applauding its programmes alongside twenty-three other lawyers, academics, and social workers at a three-day "conference" organised by Vinoba Bhave in his village, where the two dozen savants signed a statement calling for the

---

[139] *SCR*, vol. 1, p. 2. This figure includes only complaints received before 31 July 1977, the Commission's cut-off date: ibid., p. 3.

[140] *SCR*, vol. 3, p. 218.

[141] *SCR*, vol. 1, p. 2; Department of Personnel & A.R. to the Director, CBI, 23 July 1977, MHAP, File 201/14/77/-AVD-II; "Important event of the week ending 12.8.77", and "Important event of the week ending 7.10.77", no dates, MHAP, File VI/11034/34/77/Com.Sec.

[142] While the Janata hoped to see Mrs Gandhi behind bars at the soonest, the convening of the Shah Commission was not a step in that direction. Indeed, as the Department of Legal Affairs noted, the commission and the criminal proceedings against Mrs Gandhi were completely independent processes. It was disingenuous of the Janata rulers to suggest that the commission's reports had any bearing on her prosecution. See the note written by P.H. Ramchandani, Joint Secretary & Legal Adviser, 5 July 1977, Shah Commission of Inquiry Files, File 815.

[143] "Five *lakhs* strong youth congress workers [*sic*]" to Justice J.C. Shah, 16 November 1977, SCIF, File 31016/4/77–Coord/SCI. Shah received dozens of similar letters: see the same file, *passim*.

opposition to adopt a "fresh" approach, assist Mrs Gandhi in "consolidation" of the Emergency's "gains", and ease the transition to democracy.[144]

Still, to Mrs Gandhi the commission was nothing more than "political vendetta", "a continuing process of political denigration and character assination [sic]."[145] When it emerged that Shah would not grant her permission to cross-examine the investigating officers as witnesses, she took her woes to the press.[146] She then snubbed two invitations to appear before the commission, ostensibly because the oath of secrecy she had sworn on taking office prevented her from disclosing any information about the Emergency.[147] She finally made the trip to Patiala House, where the case was being heard, on 9 January 1978, only after she received an official summons compelling her to do so.[148]

In those halls she displayed the same insolence: she refused at first to go through the courtly motions of entering the witness box and being sworn in for testimony. In her statement she was eager to emphasise the collective responsibility of the cabinet: "my colleagues enjoyed complete freedom of action within their allotted fields."[149] Yet, even as she denied knowledge of

[144] *TOI*, 17 and 19 January 1976, both p. 1. For the entire list of names, see the Hindi communiqué signed by all those who attended the *acharyas'* conference: MLP, reel 14.

[145] Mrs Gandhi to Shah, 21 November 1977, MHAP, File VI/11034/56(132)/80/ISDVI. Ironically, she invoked Article 21, which had been suspended during the Emergency, to suggest that the commission was to "irreparably damage" her reputation; and "reputation is a part of my personal liberty ... and I cannot be deprived of the same."

[146] *NYT*, 10 January 1978, p. 3; *SCR*, vol. 1, p. 3. Mrs Gandhi and Pranab Mukherjee led the effort to question the legality of the commission: Pranab Mukherjee to Justice Shah, no date, MHAP, File VI/11034/56/80(320)/ISDVI. As the commission pointed out, only in "adversarial" proceedings—that is, civil and criminal ones where the court is an impartial referee between the prosecution and the defence—can investigating officers be cross-examined; the present task was merely an "inquisitorial" one, where the court was interested solely in ascertaining facts: *SCR*, vol. 1, pp. 10–13. The ironic choice of words was not lost on V.U. Eradi, director of the commission: "when I say "inquisitorial", it must be shorn of all the sinister aura the expression ... has acquired ... in certain foreign countries where inquisitions were held": "Ruling Given by the Chairman in Mrs Gandhi's Case", 10 January 1978, MHAP, File VI/11034/56/80(320)/ISDVI.

[147] *SCR*, vol. 1, p. 15.

[148] Ibid. Counselling her on this matter was her lawyer, Frank Anthony, an Anglo-Indian nominated to every Lok Sabha between 1952 and 1977. His machinations are catalogued in "Ruling Given by the Chairman in Mrs Gandhi's Case", ibid.

[149] Mrs Gandhi to Shah, 21 November 1977, MHAP, File VI/11034/80/56(328)/ISDVI

the "excesses", Mrs Gandhi proceeded to rationalise them in their setting. "Circumstances" had forced her hand. In the hearings the accent, however, was never entirely on her actions, for she cleverly turned the stick in the reverse direction, accusing Shah of putting paid to her bank nationalisations in 1969 for a simple reason: he was a shareholder in some of them. Shah, remarkably, played along, defending his decision, allowing the commission to become an inquiry into the judge himself. For his part, Mrs Gandhi's son shared in her contempt for the law, behaving as if it was applicable but to mere mortals: he refused to give sworn testimony, inviting the commission to declare his actions a "clear violation" of the Indian Penal Code.

As it turned out the Janata's efforts to incarcerate Indira Gandhi proved Sisyphean. She was locked up for the first time on 3 October 1977 but let off the next day. In December 1978 the Janata took another stab at *lex talionis*, this time by setting up a parliamentary privilege committee to investigate the scuttling of an inquest into Maruti.[150] The breach of privilege earned her a week in prison, having been decided after a vote of 279 to 138 in Parliament. All Mrs Gandhi could muster in her defence was an indignant speech in which she declared, "I am not guilty", and accused the Janata of "convert[ing] the House into a sort of medieval star chamber."[151] This time round her feeble response—reminiscent of Nixon's plea of 1973: "I am not a crook"—was not enough to get her acquitted. After being expelled from the Lok Sabha she, along with her secretary R.K. Dhawan and CBI director Devendra Sen, served a week-long jail sentence that began on 19 December. In separate cases between August and October a number of other Congressmen were briefly placed behind bars as well.[152] Yet another attempt was made to arrest Mrs Gandhi in May 1979, when she was, along with R.K. Dhawan and deputy inspector general P.S. Bhinder, tried by a special court for the incarceration of Bhim Sen Sachar, octogenarian former chief minister of Punjab, during the Emergency. It was not long before charges were dropped because of insufficient evidence.[153]

* * *

[150] See Chapter 2.

[151] *TOI*, 14 December 1978, p. 1.

[152] CWC resolution condemning the arrests, 3 October 1977, reproduced *in toto* in Mukherjee, *The Dramatic Decade*, pp. 296–7; Limaye, *Janata Party Experiment*, vol. 1, p. 515.

[153] See the report by T.N. Mishra, Superintendent of Police, CBI Special Investigation Unit, 3 June 1979, MHAP, File 260/8/79-AVD-II.

The reasons why Mrs Gandhi lifted the Emergency can only be conjectured. The usual argument trotted out in a number of biographies is that she was fundamentally a "democrat", and, even if she was not, there were traces of her father within her.[154] But this is not to say much by way of explanation: we have to focus on several other factors which contributed to the decision. The abrogation of the Emergency was probably done summarily, as in a sultanic regime where the ruler's interest in arbitrariness as a strategy to display authority plays a major role.

At the outset we have to recognise the ambivalent character of the Emergency as a "constitutional dictatorship". We have shown that Mrs Gandhi was willing to stay in a zone of liminal legality within which elections remained the only source of political legitimacy. And yet this belief could have been kept in abeyance, with elections being postponed again and again. Therefore the question remains: why was the Emergency lifted in January 1977?

The timing we believe had something to do with three factors. First, despite the way her entourage of sycophants had insulated her from the realities of India, by the autumn of 1976 Mrs Gandhi had become aware of at least some of the regime's excesses. She could attribute to these the deterioration of India's image abroad. Course correction meant holding elections in order either to legitimise the Emergency's transgressions or put an end to it—and clip the wings of Sanjay to whom she could not easily say "no".

Second, her decision had to do with the international context. Mrs Gandhi was sensitive to critiques from abroad, and the fact that Pakistan decided to hold elections probably precipitated her own move in early 1977.

Third, and probably most important, she decided to contest elections because she was certain she would win. This confidence owed in part to the biased information she received from her entourage, and in part to the fact that the opposition was in a shambles.

She was wrong, but not that far off the mark if one goes by the electoral map of 1977: the Congress was routed in the Hindi belt because of Sanjay's excesses and the unity of the opposition, but it remained powerful every-where else. The Indian voter did not unanimously seize the opportunity to dislodge Delhi's dictators. In the three years that followed, even the victori-ous Janata Party proved incapable of prosecuting them for their crimes.

[154] See, *inter alia*, Malhotra, *Indira Gandhi*; Sahgal, *Indira Gandhi*; Frank, *Indira*; Carras, *Indira Gandhi*; Limaye, *Janata Party Experiment*, vols 1 and 2.

Voter behaviour and Janata incompetence raises questions about the nature of Indian democracy: do they together reflect the superficiality of India's democratic culture? And are they signs that the Emergency was not illegal enough, or not seen as sufficiently illegal, to warrant judicial prosecution? Indeed, we may need to conclude that a proper trial never took place for two reasons: first, that the Emergency regime remained constitutionally ambiguous, and second, that Indian democracy has for long been an analogously ambiguous affair. This was evident in how quickly, sensing the Janata Party's internecine struggles and inability to rule, voters forgot and forgave; Mrs Gandhi and Sanjay staged a comeback less than three years after their 1977 defeat.[155]

This assessment helps us to qualify the Emergency not only in the abstract as an ambivalent form of authoritarianism, but in a comparative perspective *vis-à-vis* the periods of democratic rule that bookended it.

---

[155] Tavleen Singh's 1980 interviews in Rae Bareilly, the constituency Mrs Gandhi contested and lost in 1977, showed how easily voters chose to "forgive" the prime minister for the Emergency: see Singh, *Durbar*, p. 116.

CONCLUSION

INTERPRETING THE EMERGENCY

At a time of Hindu majoritarian ascendancy and the rise of illiberal democracy in India, the Emergency continues to elicit interest in the contemporary press, the past informing the present. But as is often the case when history is mined to search for morals, straightforward and didactic interpretations crowd out complex ones.

In the dominant *imaginaire*, Indira Gandhi is often portrayed as an absolutist dictator who eliminated free speech, dissent, and liberty. This view, in writing off agency on the part of the rest of the nation, omits mention of the role that a motley coalition of classes and political parties on the one hand, and an ambivalent as well as divided opposition on the other, played in legitimising the Emergency.[1] Contemporary accounts also present a romantic view of the underground—here agency is overdetermined—overlooking its chaotic nature and marginal influence to weave the narrative of a successful democratic movement eventually displacing an autocratic premier in 1977.[2] A more revisionist repertoire, especially popular among

---

[1] See, *inter alia*, Nayar, *The Judgement*; Mehta, *The Sanjay Story*; Kapoor, *The Emergency*; Guha, *An Anthropologist Among the Marxists*, p. 186ff; Hart, "Indira Gandhi".

[2] See, *inter alia*, Sahasrabuddhe and Vajpayee, *The People versus Emergency*; Nayar, *The Judgement*; Kapoor, *The Emergency*; Mankekar and Mankekar, *Decline and Fall of Indira Gandhi*; Kelkar, *Lost Years of the RSS*; Advani, *A Prisoner's Scrap-Book*; Malkani, *The Midnight Knock*; Deshmukh, *RSS*. The Shah Commission reports, too, blame virtually every transgression of the regime on Sanjay: *SCR*, vol. 2, p. 119.

Mrs Gandhi's apologists, describes the Emergency as a social revolution that promoted progressive policies.[3]

The Emergency was in fact a far more complex phenomenon. Certainly, it was postcolonial India's first experiment with authoritarianism. But of what kind? And how may we explain its establishment as well as its place in India's history?

Here in the Conclusion we place the regime in a longer perspective. Was the Emergency an aberration, a parenthesis of twenty-one months after which the country returned to the *status quo ante*? Or was it on the contrary a turning point after which things were altered for ever? Or should it be seen as a moment in a larger history showing as many continuities as ruptures?

The What and Why of the Emergency

The first two parts of our book have offered an interpretation of this atypical variant of political authoritarianism. In Chapters 1 to 3 we characterised this regime as an autocracy that, though "sultanist" and arbitrary, chose the path of legitimacy rather than outright absolutism, which entailed operating at least seemingly within juridical and parliamentary restraints.

In the main these restraints were constitutional. Mrs Gandhi did not suppress or set aside the constitution. Eager to project the Emergency as a democratic endeavour, she instead chose to amend its provisions to recast Indian political life. Her constitutional dictatorship therefore retained features of parliamentary democracy, including the continuation of parliamentary sessions, and some mainstays of the rule of law, including the relative autonomy of the Supreme Court. That such sweeping changes occurred on the back of the same forces that governed the country before the Emergency— Congressmen, the judiciary, parliament, the bureaucracy, and the police— highlights the fact that Mrs Gandhi's power was not quite as absolute as much of the existing literature imagines. The courts, parliament, and the

---

[3] See, *inter alia*, Dhar, *Indira Gandhi, the "Emergency", and Indian Democracy*; Mukherjee, *The Dramatic Decade*; Drieberg and Mohan, *Emergency in India*. In a weaker version of the same argument, it is suggested that while Mrs Gandhi's government aided industrialists and undermined democracy—hence she was no champion of the democratic Left—she got trains to run on time, cracked down on smugglers, and brought peace to the republic after years of popular protest and union activity. For this view, see Chandra, *In the Name of Democracy*, and Mrs Gandhi's early biographers: Moraes, *Mrs Gandhi*; Sahgal, *Indira Gandhi*; Malhotra, *Indira Gandhi*.

institutions of the *Rechtsstaat* were interfered with but not abolished; and no serious efforts were made to implement the far-reaching changes that Mrs Gandhi and her counsellors sometimes spoke of: a new constituent assembly, a shift to presidentialism, and the consolidation of a single-party dictatorship. The announcement of a snap election in January 1977, abruptly ending the autocratic experiment, was another manifestation of the constitutional fetters the premier and her party had placed themselves in.

But because these fetters proved mostly ineffective, there is little doubt that this constitutionally permitted dictatorship did in its actual operation fulfil the criteria of authoritarianism. If parties and trade unions were not formally banned, the upshot was that many of their leaders were nonetheless imprisoned—and some even tortured. If parliament continued to function as before, the absence of jailed MPs and the hegemony of the ruling party saw to it that parliamentary debates were rendered meaningless—all the more so as the press was not free to express dissent. And if the regime never did for the corporate media, Mrs Gandhi nevertheless disciplined it through censorship, intimidation, and financial persecution.

The Emergency fulfilled two other criteria of authoritarianism: it promoted no ideology, and, relatedly, it tried to depoliticise society. The absence of ideology is evident from Mrs Gandhi's lack of doctrinal consistency. While her Twenty-Point Programme suggested her leftist inclinations, very few progressive reforms were in fact implemented. The parts of the programme that were followed through, the disciplining of labour and liberalisation of the economy, were the bits intended to please India's capitalists. In this respect the Emergency shows affinities with a peculiar type of social organisation: corporatism.

If the Emergency had no ideology, its leadership style centred around the personality of Mrs Gandhi, and populism was its main idiom. A depoliticised society could have only one good reason to be out in the streets: to support the supreme leader. Mrs Gandhi played on nationalist sentiments, cashing in on that relatively unideological "ism": patriotism. It was always local saboteurs, fifth columnists, and foreign powers that had it in for India.

The Emergency also calls to mind "sultanism", a variant of authoritarianism in Juan Linz's typology. This "ism", already obvious in 1975 through the arbitrariness and nepotism of Mrs Gandhi's regime, was further manifest in 1976 with the rise to power of Sanjay, whose sterilisation and gentrification drives pushed the Emergency in a more violent direction.

If the Emergency was not the same all the time, it was not the same everywhere either. The final chapter of Part I documented the contrast between North and South India, two meta-regions which we disaggregated to factor in other variables, including the character of the dominant party and the ruling chief ministers. This diverse geography of the Emergency further complicates an already complex version of authoritarianism.

The chasm between policy announcements and implementation involved another restraint on Mrs Gandhi: her regime was hijacked by sectional interests—Sanjay Gandhi and the Youth Congress, capitalists, the emerging Congress *satrapies* that were Mrs Gandhi's clients—that prevented her from delivering on her progressive promises. While the latter may have been suspect since she first espoused them (around the time of the Congress split of 1969), the handful of socialist policies that were adopted in the late sixties and early seventies—such as the nationalisation of a small number of banks and private enterprises, a commitment to break up monopolies, manoeuvres calculated to expedite expropriation, and the attempts to build grassroots cadres in the Congress to reduce the party's dependence on the gentry—were all abandoned one after another during the Emergency.

Finally, Mrs Gandhi was thwarted by circumstances. The initial "successes" of the Emergency—inflation under control, foreign exchange and food reserves dramatically improved—were the results not of authoritarian rule but the generous monsoon rains of 1974 and 1975, and a tightly run monetary policy.[4] Around June 1976, when inflation began climbing again, Mrs Gandhi's hold over the Emergency narrative started to crumble. The Emergency was, in short, an authoritarian regime operating in a space constrained by the constitution, clientelism, and circumstance.[5]

In our analysis we have distinguished the Emergency's immediate causes from the longer-term factors that made it possible. The JP Movement and the Allahabad judgment have therefore been contextualised: the former as the outcome of a deeper socio-economic crisis, and the latter in conflicts between the executive and the judiciary since the late 1960s.

---

[4] The PMS admitted as much: see its "20-Point Economic Programme Review of Implementation", 3 August 1975, PMSP, File 37/633/15-A/1975 PMS. Money supply had begun decelerating months before the Emergency. See Annexure 3 in *The Reserve Bank of India: Volume 3, 1967–1981*, p. 430.

[5] The thrust here has been on the latter two, if for no other reason than to escape the constitutional determinism that has dogged many contemporary interpretations of the Emergency, wherein not only are the prodromes of authoritarianism seen in the Constituent Assembly debates of 1946–9, but, for all intents and purposes, a causal link is drawn between the two set pieces three decades removed from one another. See, for instance, Prakash, *Emergency Chronicles*.

CONCLUSION

Yet another explanation for the Emergency was sought in an interrogation of the authoritarian personalities of its two protagonists. This too was put in perspective: the Emergency is in our account the culminating point of a process of personalisation and centralisation of power going back to the gradual replacement of old-guard Congressmen by new and loyal followers and the weakening of state institutions in the late 1960s.

The Emergency was also made possible because Mrs Gandhi could rely on a large coalition of supporters, ranging from the Communist Party of India to their capitalist arch-enemies. For the Left, the Emergency was a tool for redistribution and secularisation. For industrialists it heralded an era of discipline: lower wages and higher profits. For the middle class the Emergency meant the return of political and social order after years of unrest.[6]

The coalition of the supporters was so large, the hold of the regime over society so severe, the dissidents so few, and international pressure so weak that the Emergency would probably have continued had Mrs Gandhi not decided to go to the polls—for reasons we examined in Part III. Democracy, we suggest, fell apart so quickly in India in 1975 because its core values, including liberty, were poorly institutionalised in the Indian setting. This raises a larger question: if postcolonial India could turn its back so quickly on democracy, where does the Emergency fit in its history?

A Parenthesis? A Turning Point? Or More of the Same?

Scholars have read the Emergency variously. For some it was an aberration, an interregnum, a parenthesis of twenty-one months; for others it was a turning point after which nothing was the same. Yet others argue that between the authoritarian regime and democracy before and after, there was a difference of degree not nature. There is something to be said for each of these interpretations, the third in particular.

We could start our survey with the first interpretation. To the nationalist historian Bipan Chandra, the Emergency, along with the JP Movement, "proved to be mere passing interludes in the long march of Indian democracy ... India's 'political miracle' has continued."[7] His argument is a rather conventional one: the Emergency was declared on 26 June 1975 and with-

---

[6] On the relation between the Indian middle class and the Emergency, see the excellent article by Rajagopal, "The Emergency as Prehistory of the New Indian Middle Class".

[7] Chandra, *In the Name of Democracy*, pp. 283, 294.

drawn on 23 March 1977, at which point political prisoners were freed, censorship lifted, and power transferred. Fear vanished just as quickly as it had taken root, and institutions recovered the relative autonomy they had enjoyed before June 1975. Journalist Janardan Thakur echoes this view: "After I had finished writing *All the Prime Minister's Men* in July 1977, I had shoved all my notes and clippings on Mrs Gandhi into a large envelope, sealed it with sellotape and consigned it to the bottom of my filing cabinet, hoping it would never have to be brought out again, except to be thrown."[8] In this interpretation the Emergency is but a moment, a blink of the eye, which yields no lessons because nothing in it really applies to anything afterwards. This is roughly a call to amnesia.[9] It is possibly one of the reasons why there have been such few books on the Emergency.[10]

This interpretation, we believe, is both flawed and problematic. It is, for one, convincing only from a strictly legal point of view. True, the damage the Emergency did to Indian political institutions was to a large extent soon undone. But those who see the Emergency as a "turning point", as Gyan Prakash does in his *Emergency Chronicles*, rightly point out that such reductionism detracts more than it adds to our understanding of Indian democracy.

The Emergency, incontrovertibly, was a milestone. As Prakash notes, the Janata was quick to reinstate preventive detention and put to use the

---

[8] Cited in Tarlo, *Unsettling* Memories, p. 202.

[9] The very fact that no trial worth its name could ever take place, too, contributed to erasing the Emergency from India's collective memory. When Mrs Gandhi came back to power in 1980 she not only disbanded the L.P. Singh Committee that investigated the misuse of intelligence agencies during the Emergency and withdrew all the cases against her in the courts, she also destroyed all copies of the Shah Commission Report her government could lay its hands on. In 2010 Era Sezhiyan, realising that the Shah Commission report was no longer available, published extracts from it under the title *The Shah Commission: Lost and Regained.*

[10] A second reason, as Nandy puts it, is the "enormous political effort [that] has gone into wiping out the Emergency as a live memory" after the Congress returned to power. Nandy, "Emergency Remembered". A third is the guilt that much of the intelligentsia felt after 1977. In Emma Tarlo's judgment, regret was rife among the upper segments of society: many "journalists, government servants, politicians, writers or activists felt they could have done much more to oppose the Emergency." Tarlo, *Unsettling Memories*, p. 224. We have highlighted another factor above: the lack of commitment to democratic values among India's elite groups.

authoritarian regime's laws to serve its ends.[11] He also discerns in the Emergency the onset of another malaise: the growing power of money and muscle in Indian politics. On this account, traditional political intermediaries, that is, members of political parties, gave way to "influence peddlers" with criminal and corporate connections. After the Emergency, the regime changed, but these figures remained a fixture on the Indian political landscape. Today, "an army of fixers and middlemen operate at every level to distort and corrupt the everyday experience of democracy, turning it into 'a feast of vultures'."[12]

Indeed, there is no gainsaying the fact that the Emergency accentuated the criminalisation of politics. A case in point was Arjun Das, whose protection rackets pre-dated the Emergency by a year.[13] Many of the villains of 1975–7 long remained influential in the party apparatus; some of them stoked the 1984 anti-Sikh riots in Delhi.[14] Because of the impunity the architects of this authoritarian regime enjoyed after the Emergency was lifted, it soon became a truism that Indian politicians were above the law. In sum, the mould of the typical post-Emergency politician was forged in the crucible of the Emergency.

The Emergency also, as we noted, furthered the mainstreaming of Hindu nationalism that the JP Movement had initiated. The Sangh Parivar gained a new legitimacy in 1975–7 because of its role in the underground resistance. As L.K. Advani declared, the stigma of "untouchability" had gone.[15] The Bharatiya Janata Party, heir of the Jana Sangh, was created in March 1980 in the context of the Janata Party's disbandment, and included former Congress (O) leaders such as Sikander Bakht. But even before its founding, the rehabilitation of Hindu nationalism had begun. The number of RSS *shakhas* jumped from 8500 in 1975 to 11,000 in 1977. After the Emergency, it further increased to 13,000 in 1979, 17,000 by 1981, and 20,000 by 1982. In the early 1980s, the RSS had a million members according to an official

---

[11] Prakash, *Emergency Chronicles*, pp. 376, 379.

[12] Ibid., pp. 376–7.

[13] Thakur, *All the Prime Minister's Men*, p. 141.

[14] Coomi Kapoor notes that "many of the key players in the Congress in later years were his [Sanjay's] protégés. These include Pranab Mukherjee, Kamal Nath, Ambika Soni, Ghulam Nabi Azad, Ahmed Patel, R. Gundu Rao, Ashok Gehlot, Digvijay Singh, Jagdish Tytler, Vayalar Ravi, Kalpnath Rai, Anand Sharma, (Dumpy) Akbar Ahmed, Ram Chandra Rath and Gufra-e-Azam." Kapoor, *The Emergency*, p. 329.

[15] Interview with L.K. Advani, 11 February 1994, New Delhi.

report of the Government of India.[16] In parallel, BMS membership increased, too, from 1.2 million in 1977 to 1.8 million in 1980, and the ABVP's from 170,000 in 1977 to 250,000 in 1982.

The Emergency was, finally, a watershed moment for industrial relations. It threw an already skewed balance of forces out of kilter. In the years that followed, the last vestiges of working-class politics were imperiously wiped out from the republic. After a number of wage freezes and bonus slashes, the Essential Services Maintenance Act of 1981, which allowed for the banning of strikes and the arrest of obdurate workers who refused to work overtime, and institutionalised the use of the armed forces as blacklegs, was another nail in the workers' coffin. The swan song of the labour politics of old was the unsuccessful 1982 textile strike in Bombay, brutally put down by millowners and the Congress government, leaving 150,000 unemployed. In its wake, the bargaining power of labour rapidly diminished. Unions were denied recognition, leaders fired, and the workforce increasingly casualised—all with state complicity.

New neoliberal nostrums swept away what little appetite the Indian state had for controlling the commanding heights of the economy. A growing rejection of statism in the wake of the Emergency encouraged industrialists, wealthier and more determined than ever, to step in.[17] Dhirubhai Ambani, founder of the Reliance conglomerate, guilefully pointed out in the pages of *India Today* that capital markets had grown by 2500 per cent between 1980 and 1985, even as the state struggled to fund power projects, the railways, and public enterprises. "There is no money in the government, that is true, but there is money with the public. We can pump that money to a hundred Reliances and build a strong country", he enthused.[18] This was after growing his businesses in the shadow of Mrs Gandhi.[19]

In the 1980s "socialism" was no longer needed even as a rhetorical device. In her last term, Mrs Gandhi, as before, had no qualms in playing second fiddle to private capital: credit extended by public banks to pri-

---

[16] *Balasaheb Deoras with Delhi newsmen in the press club of India, March 12, 1979,* New Delhi: Suruchi Sahitya Publications, pp. 7 and 32, referred to in Jaffrelot, *The Hindu Nationalist Movement and Indian Politics,* p. 302, n. 102; Andersen and Damle, *The Brotherhood in Saffron,* p. 215.

[17] In this, the intellectual groundwork had already been laid by early postcolonial Indian socialists, all of whom placed a greater accent on "self-help" than on the state: Sherman, "A New Type of Revolution", pp. 485–504.

[18] Rajagopal, "The Emergency as Prehistory", p. 1007.

[19] See McDonald, *The Polyester Prince.*

vate industries doubled; licensing procedures were centralised and expedited; export credit agencies set up to pump capital into the private sector; taxes lowered; legislations aimed at weakening monopolies and restricting foreign-exchange transactions diluted; free-trade zones inaugurated; and state expenditures increasingly met by indirect taxation. After her passing, Mrs Gandhi's son Rajiv continued these policies until the voters kicked him out.[20]

While it is clear that "the Emergency enjoys an afterlife", it is also obvious that some of the developments that Gyan Prakash sees as the Emergency's legacies in fact pre-date the regime—by his own admission. The calibre of political personnel is a case in point. "After Nehru's death [in 1964], the political elite became consumed with scheming to maintain power in response to the rapid unravelling of state–society relations", he writes, before lamenting that "politics became only a chess game of power".[21] Likewise, much ink is spilled equating Narayan with Mrs Gandhi. On Prakash's account, the two titans had pushed Indian politics in a different direction long before the Emergency. In highlighting the similarities in their élan, Sudipta Kaviraj, too, makes the case that both Narayan and Mrs Gandhi—by resorting to populism, substituting personality for programme, welding Left rhetoric with conservative praxis—irredeemably changed the political landscape well before she pressed the panic button.[22]

If the turning point of Indian political history was marked by the rise of what Ashis Nandy calls "pure politicians", why, then, single out the Emergency for this development? For other watersheds are equally compelling: 1967, the first time Congress hegemony was seriously threatened; 1964, the year of Nehru's death; or even 1947, when Indian elites for the first time came to fully control what was soon to become the Indian republic. In the final section of the Conclusion, we will explore the continuities between the Emergency and the periods that bookended it.

Differences of Degree—and Nature

For all the high political changes of the mid-1970s, it must be remembered that for large swathes of society, the Emergency made no fundamental difference: neither for political prisoners and those who were tortured, nor for the Indian masses, and especially not for the poor.

---

[20] Maiorano, *Autumn of the Matriarch*, pp. 90–2, 94.
[21] Prakash, *Emergency Chronicles*, p. 378.
[22] Kaviraj, "Indira Gandhi and Indian Politics", p. 1703.

First, there is the fact of the state's weak penetration into the countryside, which somewhat insulated the *mofussil* from the authoritarian dispensation, more so the further one went from the regime's core—Delhi, Haryana, and western Uttar Pradesh. Beyond this perimeter, that the Emergency arrived tardy to the *mofussil* is evident from Lee Schlesinger's study of a village in the Satara district of Maharashtra. Private discussions of the *anibani*—the Emergency, literally "commotion", "fervour"—only began to take shape several months after its declaration.[23] In fact, it was only around September 1976 that the Emergency came home in this village: policemen from the state capital knocked on doors and scouted fields, extracting as much as they could in cash or kind and threatening those who resisted with MISA arrests. The violence, however, was minimal. Just thirteen men from this village of 400 families were sterilised.[24]

Here, local authority was in practical terms a function of caste and landlord power: people had no time for claptrap about democracy and liberty. Paradoxically, villagers had a marked preference for *hukumshahi* over *lokshahi* (authoritarianism over democracy) because a strong state meant work got done. In any case, the Emergency did not really belong there. The quip of a low-level administrator in the village illustrated how common it was in rural settings to make light of the regime change: he was "considering declaring a state of emergency in the village", he would joke to anyone who cared to listen.[25] Locking up the opposition, cracking down on black marketeers, and browbeating lethargic bureaucrats to turn up on time were seen as urban concerns; rural issues, on the other hand, related to poor land distribution, caste oppression, credit undersupply, mercurial landlords, corrupt policemen and administrators—and these as ever went unaddressed. As for the belated arrival of the Emergency in the few thousand villages where it seems to have been experienced, the regime in power hardly seemed an aberration. Certainly, there was some awareness of the greater barbarity that the Congress was perpetrating on the poor through its sterilisation drive. This owed to the fact that in the absence of a welfare state, the scalpel was robbing indigents of their only asset: the ability to produce children, who as adolescents would have laboured in the fields, and as adults provided for their aged parents. But still, every report of rural injustice on the front pages of the dailies of the 1960s and 1970s confirms that

---

[23] Schlesinger, "The Emergency in an Indian Village", p. 628.
[24] Ibid., pp. 632, 638, 641.
[25] Ibid., pp. 629–30.

the "excesses" of the Emergency were of the same coercive order as quotidian state–society and class relations experienced for years on end before the Emergency arrived. The 1977 election bears out the truth of this: while the Congress polled on average 40 per cent in urban constituencies, it registered 47 per cent of the vote in rural ones.[26]

In a sense, the same could be said of the urban setting, too. Here, in terms of quotidian policy-making the Emergency appears neither as a parenthesis nor as a turning point, but the intensification of an established style of rule.

Several of the draconian policies associated with the Emergency, in fact, predated it. It was in June 1974, for instance, that the Wage Freeze Act was rammed through Parliament, allowing for half of every citizen's dearness allowance to be withheld from them as "compulsory deposit". Likewise, gentrification and mass sterilisation were well under way before the Emergency.

The poor were the main targets of birth-control policies before the Emergency and remained so during it. In 1973, a survey of over half a million respondents who had been sterilised found that about 75 per cent earned less than Rs 100 a month. In most places, the "cash incentives" offered for these surgeries were worth at least a month's income, and in a few, such as Gorakhpur, over twice that. Moreover, some of the sterilisation drives were cynically timed during drought periods, when it was known that labour shortages would drive the unemployed straight into the operating theatre. Furthermore, the tyranny of numbers, both in terms of targets and incentives, dictated that the poor be kept in the dark about alternative contraceptive methods. A survey of rural India in 1972 showed that only 9.4 and 18.2 per cent were aware of the existence of the pill and prophylactics, respectively, whilst 70.5 per cent knew what a vasectomy entailed.[27] In the event over a million sterilisations took place every year in the late 1960s and 3.1 million in 1972–3, tellingly more than the 2.6 million figure for the first year of the Emergency.

As with the sterilisation programme, so with the gentrification of cities. In Delhi, Jagmohan, the chief architect of "beautification", was already in charge in 1975 and, as he put it, during the Emergency "the same scheme, the same policy, and the same procedures were continued; only the pace of work increased."[28] Indeed, while the two and a half years to June 1975 wit-

[26] Weiner, *India at the Polls*, p. 79.
[27] Vicziany, "Coercion in a Soft State—Part 2", pp. 563, 568.
[28] Jagmohan, *Island of Truth*, pp. 1, 45.

nessed the demolition of 1800 houses in the capital, the nineteen months that followed saw the destruction of 150,105.[29] It was in early 1975, a couple of months before the Emergency, that Jagmohan published his manifesto for urban renewal, *Rebuilding Shahjahanabad: The Walled City of Delhi*. By then he had already put some of his dreams of rebuilding Delhi into practice, having initiated slum-clearance operations as early as 1967.[30] The Emergency simply allowed him to see his dreams materialise more quickly.

Similarly, Mrs Gandhi's war on beggars had an older history. As early as 1954, the then Congress Bombay chief minister, Morarji Desai, had a bill shot down that was aimed at providing beggars with public housing. It would cost the state "a crore of rupees" to "convert the beggars into useful citizens", he protested; rather than "divert funds from development projects", a simpler solution was to have beggars "kept on the run by the police."[31] In 1967 a small town in Maharashtra piloted a programme whereby authorities arrested beggars and carted them off to work on bunding and railway projects without pay. "If the experiment is successful", this form of modern slavery would take root in other cities as well, *zila* officials enthused.[32] In 1972 the Lok Sabha's estimates committee proposed making "wilful begging by able-bodied persons" a penal offence.[33] The press shared in these values. In 1960, when 10,000 beggars unionised in Hyderabad demanding unemployment benefits, the *Times of India* opined that it would "absurd" for beggars to "be enabled" in this manner—"it is for the families themselves to try and provide for any member who, through infirmity, is unable to make a living for himself."[34] In a 1973 profile of Bombay's beggars, the *Times* alleged they were making "easy money", that the town was a "safe haven" for them, and that most were not even "genuine" beggars: in fact "hardly 20 to 25 per cent" of them worked, which was unfortunate, because they had a tendency to spend their "leisure hours" gambling.[35] Similarly, the regular supply of stories of "rich beggars" found with thousands of rupees as well as the aesthetic concern regularly voiced in opinion pieces that they were "spoiling" neighbourhoods—nowhere was the "sight of beggars" more "harrowing than in the

---

[29] Ibid., p. 78.

[30] Ibid., pp. 31–3.

[31] *TOI*, 4 April 1954, p. 10.

[32] *TOI*, 14 July 1967, p. 3.

[33] *TOI*, 18 November 1972, p. 6.

[34] *TOI*, 7 November 1960, p. 6.

[35] Not once in the profile was a solution proposed: *TOI*, 25 November 1973, p. 3.

capital, spruced and dolled up with fountains and gulmohurs"—and making it harder for "citizens" [that is propertied ones] to commute, were all part of the gentrification war waged against the lumpenproletariat by the state, the press, and the bourgeoisie.[36]

Emma Tarlo's remarkable historical ethnography of the Emergency's twin programme of gentrification and sterilisation, too, confirms the continuities between India under authoritarianism and the years preceding it. To her informants, Delhi's slum dwellers, the Emergency was the *nasbundi ka vakt* (the time of sterilisation).[37] But those twenty-one months were no better or worse than what came before or after. For this was neither the first nor the last time they were on the receiving end of state power. Resettlement was not a new phenomenon either; only "the scale of activities was different as was the speed of execution."[38] During the Emergency, as before and after, the poor were submitted to what Tarlo calls "forced choices": the inescapable and unchanging fact was that they could not escape the violence of the powerful, whether the state's or the local notable's.[39] In her judgment, Sanjay's sterilisation drive only brought into sharper relief the lived experience of India's working poor: "the commodification of the body was neither so exceptional nor so specific to the Emergency as such."[40] For one of her interviewees "it was one type of business which even today is still going on. If you go to Irwin Hospital then you will find people lined up on the pavement to give blood or to sell a kidney for money. What's the difference?"[41]

A brief survey of the Morarji Desai administration confirms that, to the average citizen, the years that followed the Emergency proved no better. A harbinger was the Janata Party's unforced embrace of the Twenty-Point Programme, which the new prime minister's secretariat endorsed *in toto*, describing it as "accepted national policy".[42] As with rhetoric, so with

---

[36] See, *inter alia*, *TOI*, 17 July 1961, p. 5; *TOI*, 12 February 1971, p. 3; *TOI*, 22 May 1971, p. 5; *TOI*, 25 July 1972, p. 4. The quote comes from Usha Rai, a journalist known for raising development and feminist issues. Female beggars "seem to be more persistent than men in asking for alms", she writes. Most beggars con passers-by with "usual tricks of the trade", but not all—"there are some genuine cases".

[37] Tarlo, *Unsettling Memories*, pp. 131, 173.

[38] Ibid., p. 140.

[39] Ibid., p. 177.

[40] Ibid., p. 200.

[41] Cited in ibid.

[42] Note on "Lok Sabha Starred Question No. 152", 1 April 1977, PMSP", File 37/633/Parl/Ques./1977.

action. By October 1977 Raj Narain, minister for health and family welfare, was threatening to cut off central funds to states that failed to render enough citizens infertile. The limited incentives on which the programme relied were producing less than stellar results, Narain averred.[43] In February 1979 his successor to the ministership was exhorting family-planning officials to apply "gentle pressure" on citizens baulking at the operation.[44] The main difference was that the pressure was now placed on women, for men had grown defiant since the Emergency.[45] Moreover, the Janata refused to offer recanalisation facilities to the bulk of the victims of the Emergency: ministrations were reserved only for the unattached and those with "less than two children".[46]

The gentrification of urban centres continued apace too. Old Delhi, one of the Emergency's most dreaded flashpoints, is as good an example as any. "In the master plan of Delhi there is a proposal for the removal of unauthorised fish markets from the Jama Masjid area ... is not anything being done in this behalf?" Morarji Desai enquired of the ministry of works and housing a few months into his term.[47] There was "no mention" of this in the city's master plan, he was informed; nevertheless,

---

[43] The incentives—"special increment in the form of personal pay", a more generous insurance policy, and lower interest rates to finance home construction—were introduced in December 1979. In the case of puerperal tubectomies, no special leave was granted because the existing maternity leave was deemed sufficient for recovery. See the memorandum on the "Grant of Special Leave to Government Servants for Undergoing Sterilisation Operation", 11 April 1977, MHAP, File 28016/3/78-Estt(A); memorandum of the Department of Personnel & A. R. on sterilisations, 9 January 1980, MHAP, File 11030/22/79-AIS-II.

[44] Vicziany, "Coercion in a Soft State—Part 1", pp. 386, 397.

[45] Thus, while three-quarters of sterilisations had been conducted on men in 1976–7, the next three years would witness a reversal: each year, women accounted for between 73 and 80 per cent of operations.

[46] Note on "Family Welfare Programme—facilities for recanalisation at government expense", 21 June 1977, MHAP, File 28016/4/77-Estt(A). The need to limit availability was in part guided by the fact that recanalisation necessitated forty-two days of hospitalisation, that is, twenty-one to recanalise each *vas deferens*: Ministry of Railways memorandum on recanalisation, 7 July 1978, MHAP, File 28016/4/77-Estt(A); Note by the Department of Personnel & A. R. on recanalisation, 14 October 1977, MHAP, File 28016/4/77-Estt(A).

[47] Special Private Secretary to the Prime Minister to the Secretary, Ministry of Works and Housing, 28 July 1977, Prime Minister's Secretariat Papers, File 7/419/1977 PMS.

the ministry began "look[ing] into ... the question of shifting", and within a month had accomplished the "removal of [the] unauthorised fish market."[48]

What of industrial relations? Here, Jayaprakash Narayan invoked both *laissez-faire* and *raison d'état*: "Some trade unionists ... are again pressing their sectional demands without heeding the national interest. They must remember that in doing so they are assaulting the open society."[49] Morarji Desai suggested with commensurate reactionary discomfiture that the "agitations ... instigated by members of Yuva Janata", the ruling party's youth wing, were doing "more harm than good to the cause of labour"; he felt it relevant to add begrudgingly that he had "no objection to their participation in trade union activities."[50] Likewise the Janata's economic policy statement was clear that strikes "could only be resorted to after the approval of the government", lest its fomenters face "penal and pecuniary action".[51] In other regards, too, the corporatism of the Janata years had clear affinities with the authoritarian regime that preceded it. Only a few months into his ministership, Labour Minister Ravindra Varma came out in favour of the National Apex Body that Mrs Gandhi had set up during the Emergency, whose sole objective was to curb the menace of collective bargaining by hammering out "conciliatory" settlements in boardrooms.[52] Despite the presence of many "socialists" in power, monopolies were left untouched: the Janata referred not a single case to the MRTP Commission in its first year in power; in its next two, it uncovered the presence of just two monopolies in the republic.[53]

That none of these trends was substantially altered, never mind reversed, when Mrs Gandhi returned to power in 1980 suggests that the

[48] K. Biswas, Director of the Ministry of Works and Housing to the Prime Minister's Office, 5 September 1977; R.M. Agrawal, Joint Secretary to S.M. Goyal, Commissioner, Municipal Corporation of Delhi, 5 September 1977; Deputy Secretary to the Government of India, Ministry of Works and Housing to the Prime Minister's Office, 2 October 1977. All Prime Minister's Secretariat Papers, File 7/419/1977 PMS.

[49] Narayan, *Towards Total Revolution*, vol. 4, p. 207.

[50] Desai to Chandra Shekhar, 24 February 1978, Morarji Desai Papers, Subject File 13.

[51] The Janata Party's "Statement on Economic Policy", 23 November 1977, Prime Minister's Secretariat Papers, File 37/692/1977 PMS.

[52] Rudolph and Rudolph, "To the Brink and Back", pp. 390–1.

[53] See the table in Beena, *Mergers and Acquisitions*, p. 33.

élan of Emergency rule had by then become a peculiarity of the Indian political repertoire.

* * *

Studying the Emergency helps us understand the nature of the Indian polity. For this period reveals both the vulnerabilities and limits of Indian democracy. It is fair to conclude, then, that in subjecting so many of its citizens to such inhumane treatment, the Emergency regime was merely intensifying recognisable trends from the past. In many domains, and for the poor especially, between Indian authoritarianism and Indian democracy there was only a difference in degree.

It is only such a bleak assessment that can account for the popularity that Mrs Gandhi and Sanjay continued to enjoy after the Emergency, even in places like Tarlo's Welcome Colony. Over thirty years after the lifting of the Emergency, Tarlo's interviewees, who had borne the heavy hand of the regime's sterilisation and gentrification drives, still believed that Mrs Gandhi had been "the greatest leader the country had ever had."[54] And that "you will not easily come across another man like Sanjay Gandhi ... the country needs a strong leader like Sanjay Gandhi."[55] While her informants did not approve of the atrocities of the Emergency, they simply did not attribute them to Mrs Gandhi and her son. For they believed the two "had been unaware of the sterilisation abuses being perpetuated in the name of family planning."[56]

The Emergency, in essence, helps us look at Indian history through different lenses. Seen from the perspective of subalterns and a citizenry almost continuously subordinated and oppressed by the state, this is the history of a constant struggle between the people on the one hand and the republic's rulers on the other. While the tribulations of ordinary Indians grew considerably during the Emergency, it is important to recognise that the difference was more a matter of degree than nature: the Emergency was, in essence, "more of the same".

Here, then, is a lesson for the present. If this reading of Indian political history is correct, there appears to have been no linear deepening of democracy in the country. But the past need not be prologue. Indeed, at a time when a Hindu nationalist authoritarian populism is accentuating, in

---

[54] Cited in Tarlo, *Unsettling Memories*, p. 205.
[55] Cited in ibid., p. 214
[56] Ibid., p. 212.

the manner that the Emergency did, the illiberal aspects of Indian democracy that have been present all along, all the while conforming to the shibboleths of democratic formalism, the task of putting Indian democracy to rights remains more pressing than ever.

SELECT BIBLIOGRAPHY

Official Records

National Archives of India, New Delhi

Ministry of Home Affairs Papers
Prime Minister's Secretariat Papers
Shah Commission of Inquiry Files
All India Radio Files

King's College London, UK

Shah Commission Papers

Bodleian Library, Oxford, UK

Lok Sabha Debates
Rajya Sabha Debates

Private Papers

Nehru Memorial Museum and Library, New Delhi

B.K. Nehru Papers
Jayaprakash Narayan Papers
P. N. Haksar Papers

National Archives of India, New Delhi

Morarji Desai Papers
Neelam Sanjiva Reddy Papers

Bodleian Library, Oxford, UK

Madhu Limaye Papers

Oral Histories

Oral History Transcripts, Nehru Memorial Museum and Library, New Delhi

Bhogendra Jha
Charan Singh

SELECT BIBLIOGRAPHY

I.K. Gujral
Janak Raj Jai
Jayaprakash Narayan
Jyoti Basu
Madhu Dandavate
Madhu Limaye
V.V. Giri

Oral Histories in the Long Emergency Collection, University of Göttingen, Germany

Ajoy Bose
Aroon Purie

Interviews

A (anonymous) in New Delhi on 9 April 2018
Bal Angre in New Delhi on 20 November 1989
Balraj Madhok in New Delhi on 10 November 1990
Jagdish Shettigar in New Delhi on 11 February 1994
Karan Singh in New Delhi on 9 February 1994 and 11 April 2018
K.N. Govindacharya in New Delhi on 19 November 1990
L.K. Advani in New Delhi on 11 February 1994
Madhavsingh Solanki in Gandhinagar on 21 April 2019
Mulayam Singh Yadav in Lucknow on 18 January 2018
Nanaji Deshmukh in New Delhi on 25 February 1994
Satpal Malik in New Delhi on 25 October 1998
Suketu V. Shah in Paris on 8 August 2017
Vijaya Raje Scindia in Shivpuri on 1 September 1987

Newspapers and Journals

Anand Bazar Patrika
Blitz
Economic and Political Weekly
Economic Times
Economist
Far Eastern Economic Review
Financial Times
Frontline
Guardian
Hindu
Hindustan Times
Illustrated Weekly of India
India Today
Indian Express
Lok Sangharsh Samiti
Mainstream
Newsweek

SELECT BIBLIOGRAPHY

New York Times
New York Times Magazine
Observer
Organiser
Outlook
Radiance
Samvada
Satyavani
Satya Samachar
Seminar
Socialist India
Statesman
Statesman Weekly
Sunday Telegraph
Tehelka
Telegraph
Times
Times of India
Tribune
Washington Post

Official Publications and Other Published Primary Sources

20-Point Economic Programme: A Review of Progress. New Delhi: Government of India Press, 1976.

1977 Yearbook. Hong Kong: Far Eastern Economic Review, 1977.

ADM Jabalpur v. S.S. Shukla, SCR, 1976.

Alam, Jawaid, ed. *Kashmir and Beyond: Select Correspondence Between Indira Gandhi and Karan Singh.* London: Viking, 2011.

Amnesty International Report: 1976. London: Amnesty International Publications, 1976.

Basu, Sajal. *Underground Literature During Indian Emergency.* Calcutta: Minerva, 1978.

Church Committee. *Alleged Assassination Plots Involving Foreign Leaders.* Washington, DC: United States Government Printing Office, 1975.

Congress Marches Ahead—III–XIII. New Delhi: AICC, 1971–6.

Documents of the Communist Movement in India, vol. 17. Calcutta: National Book Agency, 1998.

Economic Survey, 1975–1976. New Delhi: Government of India, 1976.

——, *1976–1977.* New Delhi: Government of India, 1977.

——, *1977–1978.* New Delhi: Government of India, 1978.

——, *2014–15.* New Delhi: Ministry of Finance, 2015.

Election Commission of India. *Statistical Report on General Election, 1977 to the Sixth Lok Sabha: Volume 1.* New Delhi: Election Commission of India, 1977.

——. *Statistical Report on General Election, 1977 to the Legislative Assembly of Kerala.* New Delhi: Election Commission of India, 1977.

SELECT BIBLIOGRAPHY

Emergency, The: Its Impact. New Delhi: Ministry of Home Affairs, 1977.

Gandhi, D.V., ed. *Era of Discipline: Documents on Contemporary Reality.* New Delhi: Samachar Bharati, 1976.

Gandhi, Sonia, ed. *Two Alone, Two Together: Letters Between Indira Gandhi and Jawaharlal Nehru, 1940–1964.* New Delhi: Penguin, 2004.

India 1977–78. New Delhi: Publications Division, 1978.

International Institute for Strategic Studies, *The Military Balance.* London: IISS, 1976.

International Press Institute, "Press Squeeze in India: Smaller Periodicals Are Also Feeling the Pinch", *IPI Report*, October 1976.

Kishore, Nawal. *Anand Marg: The Truth.* New Delhi: Directorate of Advertising and Visual Publicity, 1975.

——. *Soiling the Saffron Robe.* New Delhi: Directorate of Advertising and Visual Publicity, 1975.

Kumaramangalam, S. Mohan. *Communists in Congress: Kumaramangalam's Thesis.* Delhi: D.K. Publishing House, 1973.

Main Schemes of Non-Formal Education in the Fifth Five Year Plan. New Delhi: Ministry of Education and Social Welfare, April 1976.

Ministry of Finance, *Budget for 1976–77.* New Delhi: Government of India Press, 1977.

Mukherjee, S. *Fascism and the Politics of Power.* New Delhi: Communist Party Publications, 1975.

Narayan, Jayaprakash. *Towards Total Revolution*, vols 1–4. Bombay: Popular Prakashan, 1978.

Norman, Dorothy. *Indira Gandhi: Letters to an American Friend, 1950–1984.* London: Weidenfeld and Nicolson, 1985.

Pangs of Conscience, The: Letters from Prison by Jayaprakash Narayan to the Prime Minister and Sheikh Abdullah. Pune: Abhay Prakashan, 1976.

Pen in Revolt, The: Underground Literature Published During the Emergency. New Delhi: Press Institute of India, 1977.

Research and Policy Division. *Genesis of President's Rule in Gujarat.* New Delhi: Ministry of Home Affairs, October 1977.

Reserve Bank of India, The: Volume 3, 1967–1981. Mumbai: The Reserve Bank of India, 2005.

Selected Speeches and Writings of Indira Gandhi, vol. 1, January 1966—August 1969. New Delhi: Government of India, 1971.

Selected Speeches and Writings of Indira Gandhi, vol. 2, August 1969—August 1972. New Delhi: Government of India, 1975.

Selected Speeches and Writings of Indira Gandhi, vol. 3, September 1972—March 1977. New Delhi: Government of India, 1984.

Shah Commission of Inquiry: Interim Report 1. New Delhi: Government of India Press, 11 March 1978.

Shah Commission of Inquiry: Interim Report 2. New Delhi: Government of India Press, 26 April 1978.

Shah Commission of Inquiry: Third and Final Report. New Delhi: Government of India Press, 6 August 1978.

SELECT BIBLIOGRAPHY

Torture of Political Prisoners in India. Madras: Karunanidhi Printaids, 1977.

What Killed Democracy in India: An Analysis of Mrs Gandhi's India. No place: Friends of India Society, no date.

White Paper on Misuse of Mass Media During the Internal Emergency. New Delhi: Controller of Publications, 1977.

Why Emergency? New Delhi: Ministry of Home Affairs, 1975.

Zaidi, A. Moin, ed. *The Annual Register of Indian Political Parties: The Lengthening Shadows—vol. 23, 1974–1975.* New Delhi: S. Chand, 1984.

——. *The Annual Register of Indian Political Parties: Amid Encircling Gloom—vol. 24, 1976–1977.* New Delhi: S. Chand, 1984.

——. *Full Circle, 1972–1975: The Dynamics of a Social Revolution, The National Emergency.* New Delhi: Michiko and Panjathan, 1975.

Books and Journal Articles

Abraham, Abu. "The State of Humour". *Seminar*, vol. 197, no. 1, January 1976.

Adams, Gordon. *The Politics of Defense Contracting: The Iron Triangle.* London: Routledge, 1981.

Addy, Premen, and Ibne Azad. "Politics and Culture in Bengal". *New Left Review*, vol. 79, no. 1, May–June 1973.

Adorno, Theodor W., *et al. The Authoritarian Personality.* New York: Harper, 1950.

Advani, L.K. *A Prisoner's Scrap-Book.* New Delhi: Arnold-Heinemann, 1978.

——. *My Country, My Life.* New Delhi: Rupa, 2008.

Agwani, M.S. "God's Government: Jama'at-i-Islami of India". In Hussin Mutalib and Taj ul-Islam Hashmi, eds. *Islam, Muslims, and the Modern State: Case-Studies of Muslims in Thirteen Countries.* London: Macmillan, 1994.

Ahamed, Emajuddin. "The Coup of 1975 Against Sheikh Mujib of Bangladesh". *Journal of South Asian and Middle Eastern Studies*, vol. 13, no. 3, Spring 1990.

Ahmad, Irfan. *Islamism and Democracy in India: The Transformation of the Jamaat-e-Islami.* Princeton, NJ: Princeton University Press, 2009.

Ahmed, Farzand. "1978—Kissa Kursi Ka: Celluloid Chutzpah". *India Today*, 24 December 2009.

Ahmed, Hilal. *Muslim Political Discourse in Postcolonial India.* New Delhi: Routledge, 2014.

Ali, Tariq. "The Fall of Congress in India". *New Left Review*, vol. 103, no. 1, May–June 1977.

Anandan, Sujata. *Hindu Hriday Samrat: How the Shiv Sena Changed Mumbai Forever.* Delhi: HarperCollins, 2014.

Andersen, Walter K., and Shridhar D. Damle. *The Brotherhood in Saffron: The RSS and Hindu Revivalism.* Boulder, CO: Westview, 1987.

Anderson, Edward, and Patrick Clibbens. "'Smugglers of Truth': The Indian Diaspora, Hindu Nationalism, and the Emergency (1975–77)". *Modern Asian Studies*, vol. 52, no 5, 2018.

Anker, Richard. "The Effect of Group Level Variables on Fertility in a Rural Indian Sample". *Journal of Development Studies*, vol. 14, no. 1, 1977.

Ankit, Rakesh. "A Regional Satrap, a Hindu Nationalist and a Conservative

Congressman: Dwarka Prasad Mishra (1901–1988)". *Contemporary South Asia*, vol. 24, no. 1, 2016.

——. "Janata Party (1947–77): Creation of an All-India Opposition". *History and Sociology of South Asia*, vol. 11, no. 1, 2017.

Antulay, A.R. *Democracy, Parliamentary or Presidential.* Bombay: Government of Maharashtra, 1982.

Appu, P.S. *Land Reforms in India.* New Delhi: Vikas, 1996.

Arendt, Hannah. *The Origins of Totalitarianism.* London: Harcourt, Brace, and Company, 1976 [1948].

Austin, Granville. *The Indian Constitution: Cornerstone of a Nation.* New Delhi: Oxford University Press, 1999 [1966].

——. *Working a Democratic Constitution: The Indian Experience.* New Delhi: Oxford University Press, 1999.

Awana, Ram Singh. *Pressure Politics in Congress Party: A Study of the Congress for Socialist Action.* New Delhi: Northern Book Centre, 1988.

Bagchi, Amaresh. "Rethinking Federalism: Changing Power Relations Between the Centre and the States". *Publius: The Journal of Federalism*, vol. 33, no. 4, Autumn 2003.

Bakshi, S.R., and Ritu Chaturvedi. *Bihar Through the Ages: Volume Two, The New Awakening.* New Delhi: Sarup and Sons, 2007.

Baldev. *India from Indira to Morarji: Jan. 1966 to Sept. 1977.* New Delhi: International Reporter Publications, 1977.

Baloch, Bilal A. "Crisis, Credibility, and Corruption: How Ideas and Institutions Shape Government Behaviour in India". PhD thesis, University of Oxford, 2017.

Banerji, D. "Will Forcible Sterilisation Be Effective?" *Economic and Political Weekly*, vol. 11, no. 18, 1 May 1976.

Bardhan, Kalpana. "Rural Employment, Wages, and Labour Markets in India: A Survey of Research". *Economic and Political Weekly*, vol. 12, no. 27, 2 July 1978.

Bardhan, Pranab K. "On the Incidence of Poverty in Rural India of the Sixties". *Economic and Political Weekly*, vol. 8, no. 4/6, February 1973.

Bari, M. Ehteshamul. *States of Emergency and the Law: The Experience of Bangladesh.* London: Routledge, 2018.

Bass, Gary J. *The Blood Telegram: Nixon, Kissinger, and a Forgotten Genocide.* London: Hurst, 2014.

Basu, Alaka M. "Family Planning and the Emergency". *Economic and Political Weekly*, vol. 20, no. 10, 9 March 1985.

Bayly, C.A. "The Ends of Liberalism and the Political Thought of Nehru's India". *Modern Intellectual History*, vol. 13, no. 3, 2015.

Bechtoldt, Heinrich. "Indira's India: A Year under Emergency Rule". *German Foreign Affairs Review*, vol. 27, no. 3, 1976.

Beena, P.L. *Mergers and Acquisitions: India under Globalisation.* New Delhi: Routledge, 2014.

Benda, Julien. *The Treason of the Intellectuals.* New Brunswick and London: Transaction Publishers, 2009 [1927].

Bhagat, Dhiren. *The Contemporary Conservative: Selected Writings.* New Delhi: Viking, 1990.

SELECT BIBLIOGRAPHY

Bhattacharjea, Ajit. *Unfinished Revolution: A Political Biography of Jayaprakash Narayan.* Kolkata: Rupa, 2004.

Bhattacharyya, Amit Kumar. "Income Inequality and Fertility: A Comparative View". *Population Studies,* vol. 29, no. 1, 1979.

Bhushan, Prashant. *The Case that Shook India.* New Delhi: Vikas Publishing House, 1978.

Birla, G.D. *In the Shadow of the Mahatma: A Personal Memoir.* Bombay: Orient Longman, 1953.

Birla, Krishna Kumar. *Indira Gandhi: Reminiscences.* New Delhi: Vikas, 1987.

———. *Brushes with History: An Autobiography.* New Delhi: Penguin, 2007.

Blair, Harry W. "Mrs Gandhi's Emergency, the Indian Elections of 1977, Pluralism and Marxism: Problems with Paradigms". *Modern Asian Studies,* vol. 14, no. 2, 1980

Brass, Paul R. *An Indian Political Life: Charan Singh and Congress Politics, 1967 to 1987.* New Delhi: Sage, 2014.

Brecher, Michael. "Succession in India 1967: The Routinization of Political Change". *Asian Survey,* vol. 7, no. 7, July 1967.

———. *Succession in India: A Study in Decision-Making.* London: Oxford University Press, 1966.

Buckingham, Jane. *Leprosy in Colonial South India: Medicine and Confinement.* London: Palgrave, 2002.

Byres, Terence J. "Charan Singh, 1902–87: An Assessment". *Journal of Peasant Studies,* vol. 15, no. 2, 1988.

Carras, Mary. *Indira Gandhi: A Political Biography.* Boston: Beacon Press, 1979.

Carrasco, Daniel Kent. "Jayaprakash Narayan and *Lok Niti*: Socialism, Gandhism and Political Cultures of Protest in XX Century India". PhD thesis, King's College London, 2016.

Chandra, Bipan. *In the Name of Democracy: JP Movement and the Emergency.* New Delhi: Penguin Books, 2003.

Chatterjee, Partha. *A Possible India: Essays in Political Criticism.* Oxford: Oxford University Press, 1997.

Chatterjee, Somnath. *Keeping the Faith: Memoirs of a Parliamentarian.* New Delhi: HarperCollins, 2014.

Chatterji, Angana, Thomas Blom Hansen, and Christophe Jaffrelot (eds), *Majoritarian State: How Hindu Nationalism is Changing India.* London: Hurst, 2019.

Chatterji, Saral K. "Church–State Relation" [*sic*]. In Saral K. Chatterji, *The Meaning of the Indian Experience: The Emergency.* Madras: Christian Literature Society, 1978.

Chaudhuri, Kalyan. "Disturbed Industrial Situation". *Economic and Political Weekly,* vol. 11, no. 18, 1 May 1976.

Chaudhuri, Nirad C. "How and Why Mrs Gandhi Ruled". *Sunday Anand Bazar Patrika,* 17 April 1977.

Chaudhuri, Rudra. "Re-reading the Indian Emergency: Britain, the United States, and India's Constitutional Autocracy, 1975–1977". *Diplomacy & Statecraft,* vol. 29, no. 3, 2018.

SELECT BIBLIOGRAPHY

Chib, Sukhdev Singh. *Nineteen Fateful Months.* New Delhi: Light and Life, 1978.

Chibber, Vivek. *Locked in Place: State-Building and Late Industrialization in India.* Princeton, NJ: Princeton University Press, 2003.

Clibbens, Patrick. "'The Destiny of this City is to be the Spiritual Workshop of the Nation': Clearing Cities and Making Citizens during the Indian Emergency, 1975–1977". *Contemporary South Asia,* vol. 22, no. 1, 2014.

Contursi, Janet A. "Political Theology: Text and Practice in a Dalit Panther Community". *Journal of Asian Studies,* vol. 52, no. 2, May 1993.

Cooke, Hope. *Time Change: An Autobiography.* New York: Simon and Schuster, 1980.

Corbridge, Stuart, and John Harriss. *Reinventing India: Liberalisation, Hindu Nationalism, and Popular Democracy.* Cambridge: Polity, 2000.

Dam, Shubhankar. *Presidential Legislation in India: The Law and Practice of Ordinances.* Cambridge: Cambridge University Press, 2014.

Dandekar, K. "Family Planning Programme: What is Wrong with It?" *Economic and Political Weekly,* vol. 7, no. 43, 21 October 1972.

——, and Surekha Nikam. "What Did Fail?" *Economic and Political Weekly,* vol. 6, no. 48, 27 November 1971.

Dasgupta, Biplab. *The Naxalite Movement.* Bombay: Allied, 1975.

Datta-Chaudhuri, Mrinal. "Fascism". *Seminar,* vol. 197, no. 1, January 1976.

Datta-Ray, Sunanda K. *Smash and Grab: Annexation of Sikkim.* New Delhi: Vikas, 1984.

Dayal, John, and Ajoy Bose. *For Reasons of State: Delhi Under Emergency.* New Delhi: Ess Ess, 1977.

——. *The Shah Commission Begins.* Columbia, MO: South Asia Books, 1978.

Deleury, Guy. *India: The Rebel Continent.* New Delhi: Macmillan, 2015.

Derfler, Leslie. *The Fall and Rise of Political Leaders: Olof Palme, Olusegun Obasanjo, and Indira Gandhi.* New York: Palgrave Macmillan, 2011.

Deshmukh, Nana. *RSS: Victim of Slander.* New Delhi: Vision Books, 1979.

Deshpande, S.G. "Resettling a Squatter Resettlement". *Economic and Political Weekly,* vol. 11, no. 14, 3 April 1975.

Dhar, P.N. *Indira Gandhi, the 'Emergency', and Indian Democracy.* New Delhi: Oxford University Press, 2000.

Dharia, Mohan. *Fumes and the Fire.* New Delhi: S. Chand, 1975.

Diamond, Larry. *Developing Democracy: Toward Consolidation.* Baltimore, MA: Johns Hopkins University Press, 1999.

Divan, Anil B. "Courts and the Emergency under the Indian Constitution". In A.G. Noorani, *Public Law in India.* New Delhi: Vikas, 1982.

Dowbiggin, Ian. *The Sterilisation Movement and Global Fertility in the Twentieth Century.* Oxford: Oxford University Press, 2008.

Drieberg, Trevor, and Sarala Jag Mohan. *Emergency in India.* New Delhi: Manas, 1975.

Dutt, Brahm. *Five Headed Monster: A Factual Narrative of the Genesis of Janata Party.* New Delhi: Surge, 1978.

Dwivedi, O.P., R.B. Jain, and B.D. Dua, "Imperial Legacy, Bureaucracy, and Administrative Changes: India, 1947–1987". *Public Administration and Development,* vol. 9, no. 1, 1989.

SELECT BIBLIOGRAPHY

Eapen, Mridul. "Trends in Public Sector Employment and Earnings: Part One". *Social Scientist*, vol. 8, no. 8, March 1980.

Embree, Ainslee T. "The Emergency as a Signpost to India's Future". In Peter Lyon and James Manor, eds. *Transfer and Transformation: Political Institutions in the New Commonwealth.* Leicester: Leicester University Press, 1983.

Encarnation, Dennis J. "The Indian Bureaucracy: Responsive to Whom?" *Asian Survey*, vol. 19, no. 11, November 1979.

EPW Editorial. "Locked Out". *Economic and Political Weekly*, vol. 11, no. 44, 30 October 1976.

EPW Research Foundation. "Clippings". *Economic and Political Weekly*, vol. 10, no. 32, 9 August 1975.

——. "Effective Exchange Rate for the Rupee". *Economic and Political Weekly*, vol. 29, no. 3, 15 January 1994.

——. "Prices in Perspective". *Economic and Political Weekly*, vol. 11, no. 19, 8 May 1976.

Erdman, Howard L. "The Industrialists". In Henry C. Hart, ed. *Indira Gandhi's India: A Political System Reappraised.* Boulder, CO: Westview Press, 1976.

Falk, Bertil. *Feroze: The Forgotten Gandhi.* New Delhi: Roli, 2016.

Fallaci, Oriana. "Mrs Gandhi's Opposition: Morarji Desai". *New Republic*, 2 and 9 August 1975.

Fernandes, George. "Exclusive Interview with George Fernandes". *Socialist Affairs*, vol. 26, no. 1, January–February 1976.

Fox, Richard G. "Gandhian Socialism and Hindu Nationalism: Cultural Domination in the World System". *Journal of Commonwealth and Comparative Politics*, vol. 25, no. 3, 1987.

Franda, Marcus F. *Bangladesh: The First Decade.* New Delhi: South Asian Publishers, 1982.

Frank, Andre Gunder. "Emergence of Permanent Emergency in India". *Economic and Political Weekly*, vol. 12, no. 11, 12 March 1977.

Frank, Katherine. *Indira: The Life of Indira Nehru Gandhi.* New Delhi: HarperCollins, 2012 [2001].

Frankel, Francine R. *India's Green Revolution: Economic Gains and Political Costs.* Princeton, NJ: Princeton University Press, 1971.

——. "Compulsion and Social Change: Is Authoritarianism the Solution to India's Economic Development Problems?" *World Politics*, vol. 30, no. 2, January 1978.

——. *India's Political Economy: The Gradual Revolution, 1947–2004.* New Delhi: Oxford University Press, 2005.

Frykenberg, Robert Eric. "The Last Emergency of the Raj". In Henry C. Hart, ed. *Indira Gandhi's India: A Political System Reappraised.* Boulder, CO: Westview Press, 1976.

Gandhi, Indira. *My Truth.* New Delhi: Vision, 1980.

Ganguly, Sumit. "The Prime Minister and Foreign and Defence Policies". In James Manor, ed. *Nehru to the Nineties: The Changing Office of Prime Minister in India.* London: Hurst, 1994.

Germani, Gino. *Authoritarianism, Fascism and National Populism.* New Brunswick, NJ: Transactions Books, 1978.

Godbole, Madhav. *Unfinished Innings: Recollections and Reflections of a Civil Servant.* Hyderabad: Orient Longman, 1996.

Gogate, Sudha P. *The Emergence of Regionalism in Mumbai. History of the Shiv Sena.* Bombay: Popular Prakashan, 2014.

Gokhale, Jayashree. *From Concessions to Confrontation: The Politics of an Indian Untouchable Community.* Bombay: Popular Prakashan, 1993.

Golwalkar, M.S. *Bunch of Thoughts.* Bangalore: Vikrama Prakashan, 1968 [1966].

——. *We, or Our Nationhood Defined.* Nagpur: Bharat Prakashan, 1947 [1939].

Gore, Al. "The Politics of Fear". *Social Research*, vol. 71, no. 4, Winter 2004.

Gough, Kathleen. "Indian Peasant Uprisings". *Economic and Political Weekly*, vol. 9, no. 32/34, August 1974.

Gray, Francine Du Plessix. "The Fairy Tale that Turned to Nightmare". *New York Times Book Review*, 8 March 1981.

Grewal, J.S. *The New Cambridge History of India, vol. II.3: The Sikhs of the Punjab.* Cambridge: Cambridge University Press, 1990.

Guha, Ramachandra. "An Indian's Verdict". *Hindu*, 31 July 2005.

——. *An Anthropologist Among the Marxists, and Other Essays.* New Delhi: Permanent Black, 2009 [2001].

——. *India After Gandhi: The History of the World's Largest Democracy.* London: Macmillan, 2017.

Gujral, I.K. *Matters of Discretion: An Autobiography.* New Delhi: Hay House, 2011.

Gupta, Dipankar. "The Political Economy of Fascism". *Economic and Political Weekly*, vol. 12, no. 25, 18 June 1977.

——. *Nativism in a Metropolis: The Shiv Sena in Bombay.* New Delhi: Manohar, 1982.

Gupta, Jyotirindra Das. "A Season of Caesars: Emergency Regimes and Development Politics in Asia". *Asian Survey*, vol. 18, no. 4, April 1978.

Gwatkin, Davidson R. "Political Will and Family Planning: The Implications of India's Emergency Experience". *Population and Development Review*, vol. 5, no. 1, March 1979.

Haksar, P.N. *Premonitions.* Bombay: Interpress, 1979.

Hangen, Welles. *After Nehru, Who?* London: Rupert Hart-Davis, 1973.

Hardgrave, Jr., Robert L., and Kochanek, Stanley A. *India: Government and Politics in a Developing Nation.* Boston, MA: Thomson Wadsworth, 2008.

Harris, Ishwar C. "Sarvodaya in Crisis: The Gandhian Movement in India Today". *Asian Survey*, vol. 27, no. 9, September 1987.

Hart, Henry C. "Explanations". In Henry C. Hart, ed. *Indira Gandhi's India: A Political System Reappraised.* Boulder, CO: Westview Press, 1976.

——. "Introduction". In Henry C. Hart, ed. *Indira Gandhi's India: A Political System Reappraised.* Boulder, CO: Westview Press, 1976.

——. "Indira Gandhi—Determined Not to be Hurt". In Henry C. Hart, ed. *Indira Gandhi's India: A Political System Reappraised.* Boulder, CO: Westview Press, 1976.

Hasan, Mushirul. "Indian Muslims since Independence: In Search of Integration and Identity". *Third World Quarterly*, vol. 10, no. 2, 1988.

Heginbotham, Stanley J. *Cultures in Conflict: The Four Faces of Indian Bureaucracy.* New York: Columbia University Press, 1975.

——. "The Civil Service". In Henry C. Hart, ed. *Indira Gandhi's India: A Political System Reappraised*. Boulder, CO: Westview Press, 1976.

Henderson, Michael. *Experiment with Untruth: India Under Emergency*. Delhi: Macmillan, 1977.

Herring, Ronald J. *Land to the Tiller: The Political Economy of Agrarian Reform in South Asia*. New Haven, CT: Yale University Press, 1983.

Heuzé-Brigant, Gérard. "Populism and the Workers Movement: Shiv Sena and Labor in Mumbai". *South Asia: Journal of South Asian Studies*, vol. 22, no. 2, 1999.

Hewitt, Vernon. "The Prime Minister and the Parliament". In James Manor, ed. *Nehru to the Nineties: The Changing Office of Prime Minister in India*. London: Hurst, 1994.

——. *Political Mobilisation and Democracy in India: States of Emergency*. Abingdon: Routledge, 2008.

Hiro, Dilip. *Inside India Today*. London: Routledge and Kegan Paul, 1976.

Hirve, Siddhivinayak S. "Abortion Law, Policy and Services in India: A Critical Review". *Reproduction Health Matters*, vol. 12, no. 24, 2004.

Jaffrelot, Christophe. *The Hindu Nationalist Movement and Indian Politics, 1925 to the 1990s*. London: Hurst, 1996.

——. *India's Silent Revolution: The Rise of the Lower Castes in North India*. London: Hurst, 2003.

——. *La démocratie en Inde*. Paris: Fayard, 1998.

——. "The Making of Indian Revolutionaries (1885–1931)". In Hamit Bozarslan, Gilles Bataillon, and Christophe Jaffrelot, eds. *Revolutionary Passions: Latin America: Middle East, and India*. Abingdon: Routledge, 2018.

——. *The Pakistan Paradox: Instability and Resilience*. London: Hurst, 2015.

——, and N. Kumar, eds. *Dr Ambedkar and Democracy: An Anthology*. Delhi: Oxford University Press, 2018.

Jaffrelot, Christophe, and Ingrid Therwath. "The Sangh Parivar and the Hindu Diaspora in the West: What Kind of 'Long-Distance Nationalism'?" *International Political Sociology*, vol. 1, no. 3, 2007.

Jaffrelot, Christophe, and Louise Tillin. "Populism in India". In Cristóbal Rovira Kaltwasser, Paul A. Taggart, Paulina Ochoa Espejo, and Pierre Ostiguy, eds. *The Oxford Handbook of Populism*. Oxford: Oxford University Press, 2017.

Jagmohan. *Island of Truth*. New Delhi: Vikas, 1978.

——. *Rebuilding Shahjahanabad: The Walled City of Delhi*. New Delhi: Vikas, 1975.

——. *Soul and Structure of Governance in India*. New Delhi: Allied Publishers, 2005.

——. *Triumphs and Tragedies of Ninth Delhi*. New Delhi: Allied, 2015.

Jain, R.B. "The Role of Bureaucracy in Public Development and Implementation in India". *Southeast Asian Journal of Political Science*, vol. 15, no. 2, 1987.

Jalal, Ayesha. *Democracy and Authoritarianism in South Asia: A Comparative and Historical Perspective*. Cambridge: Cambridge University Press, 1995.

Jannuzi, F. Tomasson. "India's Rural Poor: What Will Mobilize Them Politically?" In Henry C Hart, ed. *Indira Gandhi's India: A Political System Reappraised*. Boulder, CO: Westview Press, 1976.

Jayakar, Pupul. *Indira Gandhi: A Biography*. New Delhi: Penguin, 1995 [1992].

Jeffery, Roger. "Allopathic Medicine in India: A Case of Deprofessionalisation?" *Economic and Political Weekly*, vol. 13, no. 3, 21 January 1978.

Jeffrey, Robin. "The Prime Minister and the Ruling Party". In James Manor, ed. *Nehru to the Nineties: The Changing Office of Prime Minister in India*. London: Hurst, 1994.

Jones, Dawn E., and Rodney W. Jones. "Urban Upheaval in India: The 1974 Nav Nirman Riots in Gujarat". *Asian Survey*, vol. 16, no. 11, November 1976.

Joshi, Ram, and Kirtidev Desai. "Towards a More Competitive Party System in India". *Asian Survey*, vol. 18, no. 11, November 1978.

Kamaraj, K. "Why Congress Debacle?" In Anjan Kumar Banerji, ed. *The Fourth General Election in India: An Analysis*. Calcutta: Benson's, 1967.

Kapoor, Coomi. *The Emergency: A Personal History*. New Delhi: Penguin, 2016.

Kapur, Devesh, John P. Lewis, and Richard Webb. *The World Bank: Its First Half Century*. Washington, DC: Brookings Institution Press, 1997.

Kapur, Jagga. *What Price Perjury? Facts of the Shah Commission*. New Delhi: Arnold-Heinemann, 1978.

Kaul, Triloki Nath. *My Years Through Raj to Swaraj*. New Delhi: Vikas, 1995.

Kaviraj, Sudipta. "Indira Gandhi and Indian Politics". *Economic and Political Weekly*, vol. 21, nos 38–9, 20–27 September 1986.

Kelkar, Sanjeev. *Lost Years of the RSS*. New Delhi: Sage, 2011.

Khilnani, Sunil. "States of Emergency". *New Republic*, 17 December 2001.

——. *The Idea of India*. London: Penguin, 1997.

Kidwai, Rasheed. *24 Akbar Road: A Short History of the People Behind the Fall and Rise of the Congress*. Gurgaon: Hachette, 2013.

Kochanek, Stanley. "Briefcase Politics in India: The Congress Party and the Business Elite". *Asian Survey*, vol. 27, no. 12, December 1987.

——. "Mrs Gandhi's Pyramid: The New Congress". In Henry C. Hart, ed. *Indira Gandhi's India: A Political System Reappraised*. Boulder, CO: Westview Press, 1976.

——. *The Congress Party of India: The Dynamics of One-Party Democracy*. Princeton, NJ: Princeton University Press, 1968.

Kogekar, S.V. "Constitution Amendment Bill". *Economic and Political Weekly*, vol. 11, no. 42, 16 October 1976.

Kohli, Atul. *Democracy and Discontent: India's Growing Crisis of Governability*. Cambridge: Cambridge University Press, 1990.

Koshy, Ninan. "Indian Emergency: International Reactions and Interpretations". In Saral K. Chatterji, *The Meaning of the Indian Experience: The Emergency*. Madras: Christian Literature Society, 1978.

Kothari, Rajni. "The Congress 'System' in India". *Asian Survey*, vol. 4, no. 12, December 1964.

——. "The Political Change of 1967". *Economic and Political Weekly*, vol. 6, no. 3/5, January 1971.

——. "Political Consensus in India: Decline and Reconstruction". *Economic and Political Weekly*, vol. 4, no. 41, 11 October 1969.

——. "Restoring the Political Process". *Seminar*, vol. 203, no. 1, July 1976

SELECT BIBLIOGRAPHY

Krishnan, T.N. "Demographic Transition in Kerala". *Economic and Political Weekly*, vol. 11, nos 31–3, August 1976.

Krishnan, T.V. Kunhi. *Chavan and the Troubled Decade*. New Delhi: Hind Pocket Books, 1973.

Kumaramangalam, Mohan. *Judicial Appointments: An Analysis of the Recent Controversy over the Appointment of the Chief Justice of India*. New Delhi: IBH, 1973.

Kumari, S. Shantha. "Permanent Sterilisation to Long-Acting Reversible Contraception: Is a Paradigm Shift Necessary?" *Journal of Obstetrics and Gynecology of India*, vol. 66, no. 3, 2016.

Laclau, Ernesto. *On Populist Reason*. London: Verso, 2010 [2005].

Ladejinsky, Wolf. "Land Ceilings and Land Reform". *Economic and Political Weekly*, vol. 7, no. 5/7, February 1972.

——. "Wheat Procurement in India in 1974 and Related Matters". *World Development*, vol. 3, nos 2–3, February–March 1975.

Lal, Kanwar. *Elections Extraordinary*. New Delhi: Jeet, 1977.

Lewis, Primila. *Reason Wounded: An Experience of India's Emergency*. London: George Allen & Unwin, 1979.

Lifschultz, Lawrence. "The Backlash of Emergency". *Far Eastern Economic Review*, 8 August 1975.

——, and Kai Bird. "Bangladesh: Anatomy of a Coup". *Economic and Political Weekly*, vol. 14, no. 49, 8 December 1979.

——. "Bangladesh: Anatomy of a Coup". *Economic and Political Weekly*, vol. 14, no. 50, 15 December 1979.

Limaye, Madhu. *Janata Party Experiment*, vol. 1. New Delhi: D.K. Publishers, 1985.

——. *Janata Party Experiment*, vol. 2. New Delhi: D.K. Publishers, 1994.

Linz, Juan J. *Totalitarian and Authoritarian Regimes*. Boulder, CO: Lynne Rienner, 2000.

Lockwood, David. *The Communist Party of India and the Indian Emergency*. New Delhi: Sage, 2016.

Low, D.A. *Eclipse of Empire*. Cambridge: Cambridge University Press, 1991.

Lukas, J. Anthony. "India is as Indira Does". *New York Times Magazine*, 4 April 1976.

M., B. "All Eggs in the Food Basket". *Economic and Political Weekly*, vol. 10, no. 11, 15 March 1975.

——. "Food Surplus for Export!" *Economic and Political Weekly*, vol. 11, no. 36, 4 September 1976.

Maddison, Angus. *Class Structure and Economic Growth: India and Pakistan since the Moghuls*. Abingdon: Routledge, 1971.

Maiorano, Diego. *Autumn of the Matriarch: Indira Gandhi's Final Term in Office*. London: Hurst, 2015.

Malhotra, Inder. *Indira Gandhi: A Personal and Political Biography*. London: Hodder and Stoughton, 1989.

Malik, Yogendra K., and Jesse F. Marquette. "Democracy and Alienation in North India". *Journal of Politics*, vol. 37, no. 1, February 1975.

Malkani, K.R. *The Midnight Knock*. New Delhi: Vikas, 1978.

Maniruzzaman, Talukder. "An Unfinished Revolution?" *Journal of Asian Studies*, vol. 34, no. 4, August 1975.

Mankekar, Dinkar Rao, and Kamla Mankekar. *Decline and Fall of Indira Gandhi*. New Delhi: Vision, 1977.

Manor, James. "Indira and After: The Decay of Party Organisation in India". *The Round Table*, vol. 68, no. 272, 1978.

——. "Party Decay and Political Crisis in India". *Washington Quarterly*, vol. 4, no. 3, 1981.

——. "Pragmatic Progressives in Regional Politics: The Case of Devaraj Urs", *Economic and Political Weekly*, vol. 15, nos 5/7, February 1980.

——. "Structural Changes in Karnataka Politics". *Economic and Political Weekly*, vol. 12, no. 44, 29 October 1977.

——. "Where Congress Survived: Five States in the Indian General Election of 1977". *Asian Survey*, vol. 18, no. 8, August 1978.

Masani, Minoo. *Is JP the Answer?* Delhi: Macmillan, 1975.

Masani, Zareer. *Indira Gandhi: A Biography*. London: Hamish Hamilton, 1975.

Mathur, K.P. *The Unseen Indira Gandhi: Through her Physician's Eyes*. New Delhi: Konark Publishers, 2016.

Mavalankar, P.G. *"No, Sir"*: *An Independent MP Speaks during the Emergency*. Ahmedabad: Sannistha Prakashan, 1979.

Maxwell, Neville. "Woman on a White Horse: India 1975". *The Round Table*, vol. 65, no. 260, 1975.

Mayer, P.B. "Congress (I), Emergency (I): Interpreting Indira Gandhi's India". *Journal of Commonwealth & Comparative Politics*, vol. 22, no. 2, 1984.

McCartney, Matthew and Roy, Indrajit. "A Consensus Unravels: NREGA and the Paradox of Rules-Based Welfare in India". *European Journal of Development Research*, vol. 28, no. 4, May 2015.

McDonald, Hamish. *The Polyester Prince: The Rise of Dhirubhai Ambani*. St Leonards: Allen & Unwin, 1998.

Mehta, Asoka, and Achyut Patwardhan. *The Communal Triangle in India*. Allahabad: Kitabistan, 1942.

Mehta, Ved. *Portrait of India*. New York: Farrar, Straus, and Giroux, 1970.

——. *The New India*. New York: Viking, 1978.

Mehta, Vinod. *The Sanjay Story*. New Delhi: HarperCollins, 2015 [1978].

Mendelsohn, Oliver. "The Collapse of the Indian National Congress". *Pacific Affairs*, vol. 51, no. 1, Spring 1978.

Mirchandani, G.G. *Subverting the Constitution in India*. Columbia, MO: South Asia Books, 1977.

Mishra, D.P. *The Nehru Epoch: From Democracy to Monocracy*. New Delhi: Har-Anand, 2001.

——. *The Post-Nehru Era: Political Memoirs*. New Delhi: Har-Anand Publications, 2001.

Misra, B.B. *Government and Bureaucracy in India, 1947–1976*. Oxford: Oxford University Press, 1986.

Misra, B.D., Ruth Simmons, Ali Ashraf, and George Simmons. "Reflections on the

Future of Family Planning". *Economic and Political Weekly*, vol. 12, no. 36, 3 September 1977.

Misri, Deepti. "Eve-Teasing". *South Asia: Journal of South Asian Studies*, vol. 40, no. 2, 2017.

Mitrokhin, Vasili. *The World Was Going Our Way: The KGB and the Battle for the Third World.* London: Basic Books, 2005.

Modi, Narendra. *Aapatkaal mein Gujarat.* New Delhi: Prabhat Prakashan, 2004 [1978].

Mohan, I. *The World of Walled Cities.* New Delhi: Mittal, 1992.

Mohanka, Payal Singh. "Religion and Conflict in India: A Sikh Perspective". *The Round Table*, vol. 94, no. 382, October 2005.

Moraes, Dom. *Mrs Gandhi.* New Delhi: Vikas, 1980.

Morris-Jones, W.H. "India Elects for Change—and Stability". *Asian Survey*, vol. 11, no. 8, August 1971.

——. "The Unhappy Utopia: J.P. in Wonderland". *Economic Weekly*, vol. 12, no. 26, 25 June 1960.

——. "Whose Emergency—India's or Indira's?" *World Today*, vol. 31, no. 11, November 1975.

Morrison, Barrie M. "Asian Drama, Act II: Development Prospects in South Asia". *Pacific Affairs*, vol. 48, no. 1, Spring 1975.

Mosher, William D. and Jo Jones. *Use of Contraception in the United States: 1982–2008.* Washington, DC: US Department of Health and Human Services, 2010.

Mudde, Cas. "Populism: An Ideational Approach". In Cristóbal Rovira Kaltwasser, Paul A. Taggart, Paulina Ochoa Espejo, and Pierre Ostiguy, eds. *The Oxford Handbook of Populism.* Oxford: Oxford University Press, 2017.

——, and Cristóbal Rovira Kaltwasser. *Populism: A Very Short Introduction.* New York: Oxford University Press, 2017.

Mukherjee, Pranab. *The Dramatic Decade: The Indira Gandhi Years.* New Delhi: Rupa, 2015.

Mukhopadhyay, Nilanjan. *Narendra Modi: The Man, the Times.* Chennai: Westland, 2013.

Müller, Jan-Werner. *What is Populism?* Philadelphia: University of Pennsylvania Press, 2017.

Mussells, Premila Menon. "Democracy and Emergency Rule in India: Political Change Under Mrs Gandhi". PhD thesis, University of Oklahoma, 1980.

Naik, J.P. *Policy and Performance in Indian Education, 1947–74.* Delhi: Orient Longman, 1975.

Naipaul, V.S. *India: A Wounded Civilization.* New Delhi: Vintage Books, 1976.

Nair, P.R. Gopinathan. "Decline in Birth Rate in Kerala". *Economic and Political Weekly*, vol. 9, nos 6–8, February 1974.

Nandy, Ashis. *At the Edge of Psychology: Essays in Politics and Culture.* Delhi: Oxford University Press, 1980.

——, "Emergency Remembered", *Times of India*, 22 June 1995.

Narain, Iqbal. "India 1977: From Promise to Disenchantment?" *Asian Survey*, vol. 18, no. 2, February 1978.

SELECT BIBLIOGRAPHY

——, and Mohan Lal Sharma. "The Fifth State Assembly Elections in India". *Asian Survey*, vol. 13, no. 3, March 1973.

Narain, Usha Kiran. "A Sociological Analysis of Phanishwar Nath Renu's Novels: A Study in Sociology of Literature". PhD thesis, University of Patna, 1989.

Narayan, Jayaprakash. *Prison Diary.* Seattle, WA: University of Washington Press, 1979.

Nargolkar, Vasant. *JP's Crusade for Revolution.* New Delhi: S. Chand, 1975.

Nariman, Fali S. "Memories of June 1975". *Hindustan Times*, 27 June 1998.

——. *Before Memory Fades: An Autobiography.* New Delhi: Hay House, 2010.

Nayar, Kuldip. "Black Days of Emergency". *Radiance*, 15 July 1995.

——. *In Jail.* New Delhi: Vikas, 1978.

——. *India After Nehru.* New Delhi: Vikas Publishing House, 1975.

——. *The Judgement: Inside Story of the Emergency in India.* New Delhi: Vikas, 1977.

——. *Supersession of Judges.* New Delhi: Indian Book Company, 1973.

Nayyar, Deepak. "India's Balance of Payments". *Economic and Political Weekly*, vol. 17, nos 14–16, April 1982.

Nehru, B.K. *Nice Guys Finish Second.* New Delhi: Viking, 1997.

Nehru, Jawaharlal. *Glimpses of World History.* New Delhi: Penguin Books, 2004 [1934].

Nimbkar, Krishnabai. *Trends in Tamil Nadu Politics During the Emergency.* Mumbai: Bharatiya Vidya Bhavan, 1996.

Nireekshak. "Willing to be Corrupted". *Economic and Political Weekly*, vol. 12, no. 17, 23 April 1977.

Noorani, A.G. *The Presidential System: The Indian Debate.* New Delhi: Sage, 1989.

Nossiter, T.J. "State-Level Politics in India, 1975–1977: The Emergency and its Aftermath in Kerala". *Journal of Commonwealth and Comparative Politics*, vol. 16, no. 1, 1978.

——. *Communism in Kerala: A Study in Political Adaptation.* Berkeley, CA: University of California Press, 1982.

Oldenburg, Veena Talwar. *Gurgaon: From Mythic Village to Millennium City.* New Delhi: HarperCollins, 2018.

Olson, Mancur. "Dictatorship, Democracy and Development". *American Political Science Review*, vol. 87, no. 3, September 1993.

Ostergaard, Geoffrey. *Nonviolent Revolution in India.* New Delhi: Gandhi Peace Foundation, 1985.

Ostiguy, Pierre. "Populism: A Socio-Cultural Approach". In Cristóbal Rovira Kaltwasser, Paul A. Taggart, Paulina Ochoa Espejo, and Pierre Ostiguy, eds. *The Oxford Handbook of Populism.* Oxford: Oxford University Press, 2017.

Pai, D.N. "Sterilisation as a Technique of Fertilisation Control". In *Aspects of Population Policy in India.* New Delhi: Council for Social Development, 1971.

Palmer, Norman D. "Elections and the Political System in India". *Pacific Affairs*, vol. 45, no. 4, Winter 1972.

——. "India in 1975: Democracy in Eclipse". *Asian Survey*, vol. 16, no. 2, February 1976.

Palshikar, Suhas. "Shiv Sena: A Tiger with Many Faces?". *Economic and Political Weekly*, vol. 39, nos 14/15, 3–16 April 2004.

Pandit, Vijayalakshmi. *The Scope of Happiness: A Personal Memoir*. London: Weidenfeld and Nicolson, 1979.

Pattnaik, Surendra Kumar. *Student Politics and Voting Behaviour: A Case Study of Jawaharlal Nehru University*. New Delhi: Concept, 1982.

Paul, Subin. "'When India Was Indira': *Indian Express*'s Coverage of the Emergency (1975–77)", *Journalism History*, vol. 42, no. 4, Winter 2017.

Pearson, Chris. "Stray Dogs and the Making of Modern Paris". *Past & Present*, vol. 234, no. 1, 2017.

Pehl, Malte. "Democratic Backlash? Revisiting Competing Explanations for the 1977 Post-Emergency Electoral Verdict in India". *Asian Journal of Political Science*, vol. 16, no. 3, December 2008.

Peiris, Denzil. "India's Media: Riding Out Censorship". *Far Eastern Economic Review*, 18 July 1975.

Pendakur, Manjunath. "Mass Media During the 1975 National Emergency in India". *Canadian Journal of Communication*, vol. 13, no. 4, 1988.

Perkovich, George. *India's Nuclear Bomb: The Impact on Global Proliferation*. Berkeley, CA: University of California Press, 2001.

Plys, Kristin. "Political Deliberation and Democratic Reversal in India: Indian Coffee House During the Emergency (1975–77) and the Third World 'Totalitarian Moment'". *Theory and Society*, vol. 46, no. 2, 2017.

Prakash, A. Surya. *The Emergency: Indian Democracy's Darkest Hour*. New Delhi: Meghnirghosh, 2017.

Prakash, Gyan. *Emergency Chronicles: Indira Gandhi and Democracy's Turning Point*. Princeton, NJ: Princeton University Press, 2019.

Prasad, Bimal. *Jayaprakash Narayan: Quest and Legacy*. New Delhi: Vikas Publishing House, 1992.

Punekar, S.D. "Trade Union Unity". *Economic and Political Weekly*, vol. 7, no. 22, 27 May 1972.

Puri, Balraj. "Era of Indira Gandhi". *Economic and Political Weekly*, vol. 20, no. 4, 26 January 1985.

——. "A Fuller View of the Emergency". *Economic and Political Weekly*, vol. 30, no. 28, 15 July 1995.

Puri, Geeta. *Bharatiya Jana Sangh: Organization and Ideology*. New Delhi: Sterling, 1980.

Rajagopal, Arvind. "The Emergency as Prehistory of the New Indian Middle Class". *Modern Asian Studies*, vol. 45, no. 5, 2011.

——. "Sangh's Role in the Emergency". *Economic and Political Weekly*, vol. 38, no. 27, 5 July 2003.

Rajagopal, D.R. "Sanjay Gandhi: A Driving Force". *India Today*, 15 September 1976.

Rajappa, Sam. "Kerala's Concentration Camps". *Seminar*, vol. 214, no. 1, June 1977.

Rajeswar, T.V. *India: The Crucial Years*. New Delhi: HarperCollins, 2015.

Raman, B. *The Kaoboys of R&AW: Down Memory Lane*. New Delhi: Lancer, 2013.

Ramaswamy, Sumathi. *The Goddess and the Nation: Mapping Mother India*. Durham: Duke University Press, 2010.

Ramesh, Jairam. *Intertwined Lives: P.N. Haksar and Indira Gandhi*. London: Simon & Schuster, 2018.

SELECT BIBLIOGRAPHY

Rangasami, Amritha. "Mizoram: Tragedy of Our Own Making". *Economic and Political Weekly*, vol. 13, no. 15, 15 April 1978.

Rao, Jr., Parsa Venkateshwar. *The Emergency: An Unpopular History*. New Delhi: Har-Anand, 2017.

Ratcliffe, John W. "Social Justice and the Demographic Transition: Lessons from India's Kerala State". *International Journal of Health Services*, vol. 8, no. 1, 1978.

Rawla, N.D. and R.K. Mudgal, *All the Prime Minister's Men*. New Delhi: Pankaj Books, 1977.

Reddy, C.G.K. *Baroda Dynamite Conspiracy Case: The Right to Rebel*. New Delhi: Vision Books, 1977.

Reddy, Snehalata. *A Prison Diary*. Bangalore: Human Rights Committee, 1977.

Rossiter, Clinton. *Constitutional Dictatorship: Crisis Government in the Modern Democracies*. Princeton, NJ: Princeton University Press, 1948.

Roy, Amit. "Why Mrs Gandhi Lost". *The Round Table*, vol. 67, no. 266, 1977.

Roy, Ramashray. "India 1972: Fissure in the Fortress". *Asian Survey*, vol. 13, no. 2, February 1973.

Rudolph, Lloyd I. and Susanne Hoeber Rudolph. *In Pursuit of Lakshmi: The Political Economy of the Indian State*. Chicago, IL: University of Chicago Press, 1987.

——. *The Modernity of Tradition: Political Development in India*. Chicago, IL: University of Chicago Press, 1967.

——. "To the Brink and Back: Representation and the State in India". *Asian Survey*, vol. 18, no. 4, April 1978.

Ruparelia, Sanjay. *Divided We Govern: Coalition Politics in Modern India*. Oxford: Oxford University Press, 2015.

——. "'Minimum Government, Maximum Governance': The Restructuring of Power in Modi's India". *South Asia: Journal of South Asian Studies*, vol. 38, no. 4, 2015.

Rustow, Dankwart. "Transitions to Democracy: Toward a Dynamic Model". *Comparative Politics*, vol. 2, no. 3, 1970.

S., A. *Who Killed L.N. Mishra? An Indian Express Investigation*. Bombay: Popular Prakashan, 1979.

Sahasrabuddhe, P.G. and M.C. Vajpayee, *The People versus Emergency: A Saga of Struggle*. New Delhi: Suruchi Prakashan, 1991.

Sahgal, Nayantara. *Indira Gandhi: Her Road to Power*. London: Macdonald, 1978.

Salter, Robert Graeme. "Swaraj and Sweepers: The JP Movement and the Future of Transformational Politics". PhD thesis, Victoria University of Technology, 2000.

Sarkar, Bidyut, ed. *P.N. Haksar: Our Times and the Man*. New Delhi: Allied, 1989.

Sartre, Jean-Paul. *Critique of Dialectical Reason*, vol. 1. London: Verso, 2004 [1960].

Sathe, S.P. "Forty-fourth Constitutional Amendment". *Economic and Political Weekly*, vol. 11, no. 43, 23 October 1976.

Sathe, Vasant. *Two Swords in One Scabbard: A Case for Presidential Form of Parliamentary Democracy*. New Delhi: NIB Publishers, 1989.

Sau, Ranjit. "Indian Political Economy, 1967–77: Marriage of Wheat and Whisky". *Economic and Political Weekly*, vol. 12, no. 15, 9 April 1977.

Scarfe, Allan, and Wendy Scarfe. *J.P.: His Biography*. Hyderabad: Orient Longman, 1997.

Schlesinger, Lee I. "The Emergency in an Indian Village". *Asian Survey*, vol. 17, no. 7, July 1977.

Schmitter, Philippe C. "Still the Century of Corporatism". *Review of Politics*, vol. 36, no. 1, January 1974.

Scindia, Vijaya Raje. *Princess: The Autobiography of the Dowager Maharani of Gwalior.* New Delhi: Time Books International, 1988.

Scott, Gemma. "Emerging from the Emergency: Women in Indira Gandhi's India, 1975–1977". PhD thesis, Keele University, 2018.

Seervai, H.M. *The Emergency, Future Safeguards, and the Habeas Corpus Case.* Bombay: N.M. Tripathi, 1978.

Selbourne, David. *An Eye to India: The Unmasking of a Tyranny.* Harmondsworth: Penguin, 1977.

———. *Through the Indian Looking-Glass: Selected Articles on India, 1976–1980.* London: Zed, 1980.

Sen, Mohit. *A Traveller and the Road: The Journey of an Indian Communist.* New Delhi: Rupa, 2003.

Sen Gupta, Bhabani. "Communism Further Divided". In Henry C. Hart, ed. *Indira Gandhi's India: A Political System Reappraised.* Boulder, CO: Westview Press, 1976.

Seshan, N.K. *With Three Prime Ministers: Nehru, Indira, and Rajiv.* New Delhi: Wiley, 1993.

Sezhiyan, Era. *The Shah Commission: Lost and Regained.* Chennai: Aazhi Publications, 2010.

Shah, Ghanshyam. "Ideology of Jayaprakash Narayan". *Economic and Political Weekly*, vol. 14, no. 9, 3 March 1979.

———. *Protest Movements in Two Indian States.* New Delhi: Ajanta Publications, 1977.

———. "The 1975 Gujarat Assembly Election in India". *Asian Survey*, vol. 16, no. 3, March 1976.

Sherlock, Stephen. "Workers and Their Unions: Origins of the 1974 Indian Railways Strike". *Economic and Political Weekly*, vol. 24, no. 41, 14 October 1989.

Sherman, Taylor C. "'A New Type of Revolution': Socialist Thought in India, 1940s–1960s". *Postcolonial Studies*, vol. 21, no. 4, 2018.

———. "Education in Early Postcolonial India: Expansion, Experimentation and Planned Self-help". *History of Education*, vol. 47, no. 4, 2018.

Shetty, S.L. "Structural Retrogression in the Indian Economy since the Mid-Sixties". *Economic and Political Weekly*, vol. 13, no. 6/7, February 1978.

Shils, Edward A. *The Torment of Secrecy: The Background and Consequences of American Security Policies.* Melbourne: Heinemann, 1956.

Shourie, Arun. *Symptoms of Fascism.* New Delhi: Vikas, 1978.

Singh, Charan. *India's Poverty and Its Solution.* Bombay: Asia Publishing House, 1964.

Singh, Harinder. "The Emergency & The Sikhs". *Sikhri.org.*

Singh, K. Natwar. *One Life is Not Enough: An Autobiography.* New Delhi: Rupa, 2014.

Singh, Karan. *Autobiography.* Bombay: Oxford University Press, 1994.

Singh, Khushwant. *Indira Gandhi Returns.* New Delhi: Vision, 1979.

——. "A New Wave from the Old India". *New York Times Magazine*, 30 March 1975.

——. "Why I Supported Emergency". *Outlook*, 3 July 2000.

Singh, Pritam. "Class, Nation & Religion: Changing Nature of Akai Dal Politics in Punjab". *Commonwealth and Comparative Politics*, vol. 52, 2014.

Singh, Tavleen. *Durbar*. Gurgaon: Hachette, 2012.

Sinha, Braj Mohan. *Operation Emergency*. Delhi: Hind Pocket Books, 1977.

Sitapati, Vinay. *Half-Lion: How P.V. Narasimha Rao Transformed India*. New Delhi: Penguin, 2017.

Sorabjee, Soli J. *The Emergency, Censorship, and the Press in India, 1975–77*. London: Writers & Scholars Education Trust.

Special Correspondent. "Landed and Landless in Surat District: Virtual Class War". *Economic and Political Weekly*, vol. 9, no. 25, 22 June 1974.

Srikhanth, H., and C.J. Thomas, "Naga Resistance Movement and the Peace Process in Northeast India". *Peace and Democracy in South Asia*, vol. 1, no. 2, 2005.

Srinivas, Lakshmi. "Land and Politics in India: Working of Urban Land Ceiling Act, 1976". *Economic and Political Weekly*, vol. 26, no. 43, 26 October 1991.

Srivastava, Ravi S. "Bonded Labor in India: Its Incidence and Pattern". *Cornell University ILR School Working Paper*, 2005.

Subramanian, Samanth. "Midnight's Grown-ups". *1843 Magazine*, May/June 2015 https://www.1843magazine.com/content/places/samanth–subramanian/mid-nights–grown–ups), accessed on 1 September 2017.

Sundarayya, Puchalapalli. *My Resignation*. New Delhi: India Publishers, 1991.

Swamy, Roxna. *Evolving with Subramanian Swamy: A Roller Coaster Ride*. New Delhi: Roxna Swamy, 2017.

Swamy, Subramanian. "Unlearnt Lessons of the Emergency". *Hindu*, 13 June 2000.

Tandon, B.N. *PMO Diary I: Prelude to the Emergency*. New Delhi: Konark, 2003.

Tarlo, Emma. "From Victim to Agent: Memories of Emergency from a Resettlement Colony in Delhi". *Economic and Political Weekly*, vol. 30, no. 46, 1995.

——. *Unsettling Memories: Narratives of the Emergency in Delhi*. London: Hurst, 2003.

Thakur, Janardan. *All the Prime Minister's Men*. New Delhi: Vikas, 1977.

Thapar, Raj. *All These Years: A Memoir*. New Delhi: Penguin, 1991.

——. "Just to Remember". *Seminar*, vol. 211, no. 1, February 1977.

Thapar, Romesh. "A 'Routine' Transfer". *Economic and Political Weekly*, vol. 6, no. 18, 1 May 1971.

Thengadi, Dattopant. "Preface: Lamp at the Threshold". In P.G. Sahasrabuddhe and M.C. Vajpayee, *The People versus Emergency: A Saga of Struggle*. New Delhi: Suruchi Prakashan, 1991.

Thomas, Raju G.C. *Indian Security Policy*. Princeton, NJ: Princeton University Press, 1986.

Tiwari, Lalan. *Democracy and Dissent: A Case Study of the Bihar Movement*. New Delhi: Mittal Publications, 1987.

Tooze, Adam. *Crashed: How a Decade of Financial Crises Changed the World*. London: Penguin, 2018.

Torri, Michelguglielmo. "Factional Politics and Economic Policy: The Case of India's Bank Nationalization". *Asian Survey*, vol. 15, no. 12, December 1975.

Toye, J.F.J. "Economic Trends and Policies in India during the Emergency". *World Development*, vol. 5, no. 4, 1977.

Tully, Mark, and Zareer Masani. *From Raj to Rajiv: 40 Years of Indian Independence*. New Delhi: BBC Books, 1988.

Tyler, Mary. *My Years in an Indian Prison*. Harmondsworth: Penguin, 1978.

Vaghul, Narayanan. *R.K. Talwar: Values in Leadership*. Navi Mumbai: Parksons Graphics, 2012.

Vanaik, Achin. *The Painful Transition: Bourgeois Democracy in India*. London: Verso, 1990.

——. "The Rajiv Congress in Search of Stability". *New Left Review*, vol. 154, no. 1, November–December 1985.

Varier, T.V. Eachara. *Memories of a Father*. Thrissur: Asian Human Rights Commission, 2004.

Vasudev, Uma. *Indira Gandhi: Revolution in Restraint*. New Delhi: Vikas, 1974.

——. *Two Faces of Indira Gandhi*. New Delhi: Vikas, 1977.

Venkatasan, Venkatachalam. *Institutionalising Panchayat Raj in India*. New Delhi: Concept Publishing Company, 2002.

Verghese, B.G. *First Draft: Witness to the Making of Modern India*. New Delhi: Tranquebar, 2010.

——. "Press Censorship Under Indira Gandhi". In Philip C. Horton, ed. *The Third World and Press Freedom*. New York: Praeger, 1978.

Vicziany, Marika. "Coercion in a Soft State: The Family-Planning Program of India— Part 1: The Myth of Voluntarism". *Pacific Affairs*, vol. 55, no. 3, Autumn 1982.

——. "Coercion in a Soft State: The Family-Planning Program of India—Part 2: The Sources of Coercion". *Pacific Affairs*, vol. 55, no. 4, Winter 1982–3.

Visaria, Pravin, and S.K. Sanyal, "Trends in Rural Unemployment in India: Two Comments". *Economic and Political Weekly*, vol. 12, no. 5, 29 January 1977.

Waghmore, Suryakant. *Civility against Caste. Dalit Politics and Citizenship in Western India*. New Delhi: Sage, 2013.

Warriner, Doreen. *Land Reform in Principle and Practice*. Oxford: Clarendon, 1969.

Weber, Max. *Economy and Society: An Outline of Interpretive Sociology*. Berkeley, CA: University of California Press, 1978 [1922].

Weiner, Myron. "Congress Restored: Continuities and Discontinuities in Indian Politics". *Asian Survey*, vol. 22, no. 4, April 1982.

——. *India at the Polls: The Parliamentary Elections of 1977*. Washington, DC: American Enterprise Institute, 1978.

——. "India's New Political Institutions". *Asian Survey*, vol. 16, no. 9, September 1976.

——. "The 1977 Parliamentary Elections in India". *Asian Survey*, vol. 17, no. 7, July 1977.

——. *The Politics of Scarcity*. Chicago, IL: University of Chicago Press, 1962.

Weisskopf, Thomas E. "The Persistence of Poverty in India: A Political Economic Analysis". *Bulletin of Concerned Asian Scholars*, vol. 9, no. 1, January–March 1977.

Weyland, Kurt. "Clarifying a Contested Concept: 'Populism' in the Study of Latin American Politics". *Comparative Politics*, vol. 34, no. 1, 2001.

SELECT BIBLIOGRAPHY

Whitcombe, Elizabeth. "What Happened to the Zamindars?". In Eric J. Hobsbawm et al., eds. *Peasants in History: Essays in Honour of Daniel Thorner*. Calcutta: Oxford University Press, 1980.

Whitney, Vincent Heath. "Population Planning in Asia in the 1970s". *Population Studies*, vol. 30, no. 2, 1976.

Wilkinson, Steven. *Army and Nation: The Military and Indian Democracy since Independence*. London: Harvard University Press, 2015.

Williams, Rebecca Jane. "Storming the Citadels of Poverty: Family Planning under the Emergency in India, 1975–1977". *Journal of Asian Studies*, vol. 73, no. 2, May 2014.

Wilson, Jon. "China and South Asia in the 1970s: Contrasting Trajectories". In Priscilla Roberts and Odd Arne Westad, eds. *China, Hong Kong, and the Long 1970s in Global Perspective*. London: Palgrave Macmillan, 2017.

Wood, John R. "Extra-Parliamentary Opposition in India: An Analysis of Populist Agitations in Gujarat and Bihar". *Pacific Affairs*, vol. 48, no. 3, Autumn 1975.

Wright, Jr., Theodore P. "Muslims and the 1977 Indian Elections: A Watershed?" *Asian Survey*, vol. 17, no. 12, December 1977.

Yergin, Daniel. *The Prize: The Epic Quest for Oil, Money, and Power*. New York: Simon & Schuster, 1991.

Yunus, Mohammad. *Persons, Passions, and Politics*. New Delhi: Vikas, 1980.

Zins, Max. "Hegemony and Dominance: The Congress 'System'". *Colloques Internationaux du Centre National de la Recherche Scientifique*, no 582, *Asie du Sud, Traditions et Changements*, Sévres, 1978.

——. *Strains on Indian Democracy: Reflections on India's Political and Institutional Crisis*. New Delhi: ABC, 1988.

INDEX

INDEX

INDEX

INDEX